S0-AFR-199

Man and His Changing Culture

By KENNETH D. WANN,

HENRY J. WARMAN, and JAMES K. CANFIELD

ALLYN AND BACON, INC. 1968

Boston Rockleigh, N.J. Atlanta Dallas Belmont, Calif.

LIVING IN OUR TIMES *Social Studies Series*

Man and His Changing Culture

Illustrations by Joseph Veno

Maps and Diagrams by Jeppesen & Co. • Richard F. Lufkin, Inc.

Library of Congress Catalog Number: 67-20778

CONTENTS

PART 1 — PEOPLE AND THEIR CULTURES 8

1. *Man and His Environment* 10
2. *Studying the World by Regions* 18
3. *Families and Communities* 36

PART 2 — EARLY CULTURES HAVE AFFECTED OUR WAYS OF LIVING 52

4. *Ancient Cultures in River Valleys* 54
5. *Cultural Gifts of the Ancient Greeks* 74
6. *Contributions of the Early Romans* 90
7. *Cultural Heritages from the Middle Ages* 108
8. *A Time of Change* 130

PART 3 — CULTURE REGIONS OF SOUTHWEST ASIA AND AFRICA 156

9. *The Dry World Culture Region* 158
10. *Africa South of the Sahara* 182

PART 4 — THE LANDS OF EASTERN ASIA 206

11. *Japan's Sun Is Rising Again* 208
12. *River and Mountain Peoples: China* 236
13. *South of the Great Himalayas* 264
14. *A Region of Merging Cultures* 288

PART 5 — EUROPE AND THE UNION OF SOVIET SOCIALIST REPUBLICS 314

15. The Soviet Union 316
16. The European World 346
17. Regions of Europe 374
18. Eastern Europe and The Mediterranean 410

PART 6 — THE PACIFIC WORLD 442

19. Melanesia, Micronesia, and Polynesia 444
20. Australia and New Zealand 466

PART 7 — COOPERATION BUILDS A BETTER WORLD 492

21. Our Changing Culture Regions 494
22. Our World Culture Region 512

APPENDIX 528

GLOSSARY 531

INDEX 534

MAPS

HISTORICAL

Four Early Culture Homes 55
Ancient Mesopotamia and Present-Day Countries 57
The Ancient Greek World 76
The Persian Wars 81
The Roman Empire 104
A Divided Roman Empire 105
Barbarian Invasions 109
Routes of the Crusaders 123
Trade Routes of the Middle Ages 126
Travels of the Norsemen 142
Travels of Marco Polo 143
Routes of the Explorers 144
Nations of Africa, 1955–1966 184
Japanese Expansion, World War II 225
China's Changing Boundaries 246
Gupta and Mongol Empires 277
British India in 1858 280
Indian Sub-continent Today 280
Routes of the Vikings 318
Expansion of Russia 322
Division of Poland 359
Napoleon's Empire 361
World War I 362
World War II 364
Explorations of the Pacific 471

NATURAL RELIEF, POLITICAL

Map of the World 12–13
Map Legend 16
North Africa and Southwest Asia 163
Israel 179
Africa 187
Japan 212
Eastern Asia 239
The Indian Sub-continent 268
Southeast Asia 290
U.S.S.R. 326–327
The European World 348
Physical Regions of Europe 355
Fennoscandia 380
The British Isles 389
Western Europe 397
Eastern Europe 411
Mediterranean Region 437
Global View of Pacific World 445
The Pacific World 453
Australia and New Zealand 485

CLIMATE, RAINFALL

Pressure Distribution, Monsoonal Winds in Eastern Hemisphere 30
Summer Rainfall, Eastern Asia 31
Winds, Rainfall, North Africa 161
Rainfall of Africa 188
Rainfall, Currents of Japan 211
Rainfall of China 250
Rainfall, Indian Sub-continent 267
Rainfall and Winds of Southeast Asia 292
Rainfall of Australia and New Zealand 478

LAND USE, RESOURCES

Oil of Dry World Region 176
Vegetation of Africa 188
Minerals of South Africa 199
Industrial Regions of Japan 233
Land Use in Southeast Asia 289
Natural Regions of U.S.S.R. 335
Minerals of U.S.S.R. 341
Land Use in Europe 353
Ocean Currents and Fishing of Fennoscandia 378
Minerals of United Kingdom 390
European Manufacturing Areas 399
Netherlands Delta Project 401
Potato Acreage in Europe 416
Minerals of Europe 418
Corn Acreage in Europe 422
Sheep in Europe 426
Hydroelectric Areas in Europe 427
Mediterranean Crops 433
Minerals of Australia 482

POPULATION

Eastern Asia 32
Southwest Asia and North Africa 165
Africa 193
Japan 232
World Population 237
India 285
U.S.S.R. 317
Europe 375
Australia and New Zealand 478

OTHER MAPS

Eastern Asian Lands 24
Lands of the Nomads 42
Lifeline of Egypt 63
Mediterranean Lands 91
Size Comparison of the Sahara to the United States 159
The Muslim World Today 172
Northern Polar Air Routes 209
Indo-European Language Families 350
European Common Market 371
European Railroads 398
World Time Zones 463

GRAPHS, CHARTS AND DIAGRAMS

High, Low, Middle Latitudes 28
Diurnal Wind Patterns 29
Greek, Roman Gods and Goddesses 101
The Four Seasons 185
Rice Production in Asia 291
World Rubber Production 298
World Tin Production 299
Culture Wheel 513

ACKNOWLEDGMENTS

PERMISSION TO USE THE PHOTOGRAPHS ON THE PAGES INDICATED WAS KINDLY GRANTED BY THE FOLLOWING:

Agency for International Development, 523 middle; **Allis-Chalmers,** 20; **American Spice and Trade Association,** 296; **Arabian American Oil Company,** 168 middle and bottom, 170, 501 left; **British Information Service,** 390, 391, 517 right; **Canadian Government Travel Bureau,** 349 top; **China Photo Service,** 254; **Chinese Information Service,** 248 bottom, 249; **Consulate General of Japan,** 215, 217, 218 right, 220, 227 left and right, 231 top, 232, 518; **Consulate General of Pakistan,** 273; **East African Travel Tourist Association,** 186 bottom; **FAO,** 168 top; **French Government Tourist Office,** 46 top left; **Government of Pakistan Archaeology Department,** 275; **Greece News Bureau,** 85; **Ava Hamilton,** 186 middle, 277; **Hong Kong Tourist Association,** 46 right; **Israel Information Service,** 500; **Japan National Tourist Association,** 222 top, 223, 228; **Japan Tourist Association,** 37 middle; **Kenya Information Service,** 201; **New York Port of Authority,** 416; **Pan American World Airways,** 349 middle; **Rhodesia Information Service,** 501 right; **Rhodesia National Tourist Board,** 200 right; **South Africa Information Service,** 200 left; **Standard Oil Company,** 169, 177, 293 top right, 294; **Swiss National Tourist Office,** 363; **Union Carbide Corporation,** 520 top; **United Nations,** 274, 308 top; **United States Department of Agriculture,** 43 top, 252; **WHO,** 26, 269, 272 bottom, 426, 446, 510 left, 515 bottom.

FOR THE PHOTOGRAPHS ON THE PAGES INDICATED, ACKNOWLEDGMENT IS MADE TO THE FOLLOWING:

Alpha Photos, 479 top and bottom; **Fratelli Alinari,** 79, 99 middle, 102, 135 top; **Bettmann Archive,** 100, 121, 139, 141; **Black Star,** 293 bottom right by Keating, 332 by Mayer, 336 top by Novosti Press, 412 by Schulke, 521 by Konig, 522 by Sullivan; 523 top by Moss; **Boston Museum of Science,** 66 top left and right; **Christian Science Monitor,** 198, 222 bottom, 515 top, 516, all by Converse; **Culver Pictures,** 133 right, 323; **Charles Phelps Cushing,** 135 middle, 174, 242 right, 376, 432; **Design Photographers International,** 11 bottom by Davis, 190 right by Kostich, 504 by Davis, 519 left by Frank; **A. Devaney, Inc.,** 244 left; **De Wys, Inc.,** 11 middle, 37 top, 199, 347, 356, 357 middle, 383 top, 384 bottom, 387, 392 right, 400 top right, 406, 421, 469 top and bottom right, 481 bottom, 486, 509 bottom; **Eastfoto,** 38, 257 left; **European Picture Service,** 458; **Free Lance Photographers Guild,** 171 bottom by Brown, 178, 448 second from bottom, 454 right by Konsiwo, 467 top right, 475; **Ewing Galloway,** 19, 41, 159, 164, 183 middle, 194, 255, 259, 306, 331, 333, 336 bottom, 338, 398, 403 right, 413, 422, 423 top, 473 bottom, 497; **Philip Gendreau,** 45, 64, 171 top, 281 left, 284 right, 297, 299, 303 bottom, 349 bottom, 357 bottom, 360, 367 left, 377 right, 383 top, 383 bottom, 384 top, 392 left, 396, 399, 400 top left and bottom left, 405, 407, 420 left, 423 bottom, 425, 433, 436, 449, 451 top and middle, 468, 473 top, 481 top, 484 top, 499 left, 503 right, 506, 508, 509 top, 519 right; **George Eastman House,** 150; **Gobelins Museum in Paris,** 111; **Historical Pictures,** 59, 84, 95, 99 top, 120, 125, 147 right, 148, 321, 325; **Weston Kemp,** 127, 317, 342 top, 381; **Christopher Knight,** 427, 507 bottom right; **Harold Lambert,** 242 left; **Life Magazine,** 28 by Jim Burke; **Talbot Lovering,** 11 top; **Metropolitan Museum of Art,** 70; **Monkmeyer Press Photo Service,** 33 by Maraini, 92 by Henle, 135 bottom by Henle, 183 top by Slater and bottom by Philcarol, 186 top by Fujihira, 447 by Fotenos, 448 bottom by Deller, 469 left; **New York Times,** 520 bottom; **Photo Researchers,** 40 by Acebes, 83 by Holton, 117 top by Henle, 166 by Holton, 167 by Frank, 175 by Holton, 190 left by Holton, 243 by Van Bucher, 251 left by Henle and right by Ayer, 257 right by Holton, 260 left by Holton and right by Charbonnier/Realites, 272 top by Daniell, 278 left by Wyatt and right by Van Bucher, 283 by Graham, 284 left by Holloway, 291 by Jules Bucher, 293 top left by Jules Bucher and bottom left by Rawson, 295 left by Riwkin and right by Van Bucher, 298 top by Schreiber and bottom by Drews, 301 by Ayer, 302 top by Doumie and bottom by Van Bucher, 305 top by Nat and Yanna Brandt, 309 by Van Bucher, 448 second from top by Ayer, 451 bottom by Fields, 454 left by Stage, 455 by Holton, 459 top by Brander and bottom by Lang, 462 by Fields, 473 middle by Werle, 474 by Drews, 477 by Ayer, 480 by Ayer, 482 by Brownlie, 483 top by Brownlie and bottom by Ayer, 487 by Werle, 499 right by Holton, 502 by Van Bucher, 523 bottom by Van Bucher; **Pip Photos,** 467 left by Carnemolla, 470 by Carnemolla, 484 bottom by Carnemolla, 505 by Carnemolla, 514 by Carnemolla; **Pix, Inc.,** 66 bottom by Reitz, 69 by Reitz, 71 by Reitz, 99 bottom by Lanks, 253 by Wollaston, 258 by Blau/Bedi, 261 by Darbos, 460 by Blau, 461 left by Hamilton and right by Wright; **Rand McNally & Co.,** 445; **Rapho Guillumette Pictures,** 357 top by Peterson, 368 by Johnson, 378 by Cash, 382 bottom by Cash, 393 by Goldman, 417 left by Pratt, 420 right by Taylor, 429 top by Goldman, 431 by Ciccione, 495 by Gullers, 507 left by Bryson and top right by Pelham; **G. R. Roberts,** 385, 404, 448 top, 467 bottom right, 479 middle, 496, 517 left; **H. Armstrong Roberts,** 37 bottom, 241, 244 right, 293 middle, 303 top, 307, 308 middle and bottom, 377 left, 394, 419, 429 bottom, 450, 474 left, 503 left; **Shepherd, William R.,** *HISTORICAL ATLAS*, Barnes and Noble, Inc., 112; **Shostal,** 213 by Tatch, 221 by Olson, 226 by Olson, 230 by Manley, 248 top by Colson and middle by Mattson, 265 by Bhansali, 279 by Manley, 282 top and middle by Nalawalla and bottom by Hufner, 305 bottom by Tsang; **Sovfoto,** 337; **United Press International,** 247; **Underwood Reserve Illustrators,** 365; **Wide World Photos,** 15, 43 bottom, 210, 216, 218 left, 219, 229, 240, 270, 271, 281 right, 319, 324, 328, 339, 341, 342 bottom, 352, 367 right, 371, 400 bottom right, 403 left, 414, 415, 417 right, 424, 428, 434, 435, 510 right; **Zentrale Farbbild Agentur,** 231 bottom, 305 middle.

PEOPLE AND THEIR CULTURES

PART 1

Certain ideas should be kept in mind as you read this book. These ideas are so important to your understanding of what you read that we call them basic ideas. These basic ideas will help you to understand people and the world in which they live.

The first idea to remember is that we live on a globe. We live on a globe that spins on an axis. Our globe whirls through space around the sun. This rotation and revolution of the globe results in the distribution of light and heat in varying amounts on the globe. For example, the idea of seconds, minutes, hours, and days is based on the fact that we live on a rotating globe. Our seasons, spring, fall, summer, and winter, are based on the fact that our spinning globe revolves around the sun. These facts affect most of the things we do in our lives.

The second basic idea to remember is that on our globe there are "standing places" for people. The "standing places" are those parts of the rock ball, or lithosphere, which emerge from the water ball, or hydrosphere, up into the air ball, or atmosphere. Some of the "standing places" are more favorable for living than others. These places are chosen because they have better combinations of land, water, and air. In the following chapters, you will read about land: fertile, desert, and mountain. You will read about water: springs, rivers, lakes, oceans, and rainfall. You will learn about the third element, air, when you read about monsoons, typhoons, tropical climates, dry climates, and tundra climates.

A third basic idea is that there are many differences and likenesses among the people on our globe and among the "standing places" on which they live. You will learn about the people of our

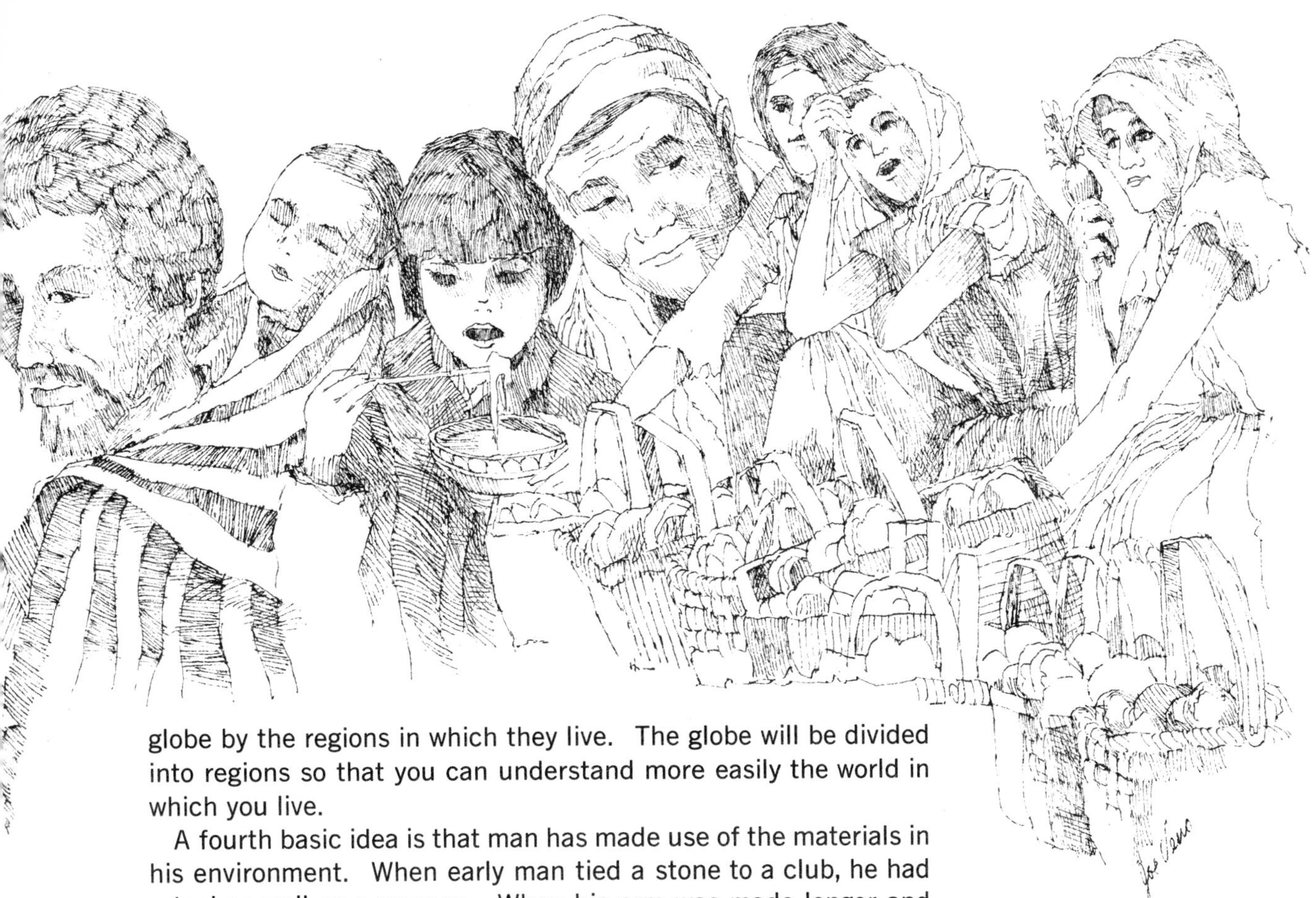

globe by the regions in which they live. The globe will be divided into regions so that you can understand more easily the world in which you live.

A fourth basic idea is that man has made use of the materials in his environment. When early man tied a stone to a club, he had a tool as well as a weapon. When his arm was made longer and stronger, he expanded the area over which he had control. Today people all over the world use modern transportation, the harnessed power of electricity, and even the atom as their tools and weapons. When man tamed and trained a dog, he made his hearing more acute and widened his protected area. Today radar does this for him world-wide. When man tamed and trained the donkey, camel, horse, and elephant, he made his legs longer and stronger. Today, the automobile, train, ocean liner, and astrojet make his travel shorter in time and more efficient.

The fifth basic idea to remember is that the geography of today is different from that of tomorrow. Wind, water, ice, organisms, and gravity are continually changing parts of the Earth's surface. Man also changes his standing places as he occupies them. Today's surface of the globe is but one slide in the long motion picture of the Earth's story.

As you read Part 1 of Man and His Changing Culture, you will learn how man's environment has helped shape the way in which man lives. You will learn how the world is divided into regions. You will learn about ways in which people live together. You will learn that the cultures of peoples vary because of the likenesses and differences in their physical and cultural environments.

CHAPTER 1

MAN AND HIS ENVIRONMENT

People on one part of the Earth differ from people on other parts of the Earth. There are great differences in the ways they live, in the work they do, and in the things they value. Even though there are great differences among the peoples of the Earth, there are many ways in which they are alike. As you study this book, you will learn much about man's differences and his similarities. You will come to understand how people have worked together to make a good life for themselves and for others.

MAN AND HIS SURROUNDINGS

To really understand people you must know about the **environment** in which they live. Environment is man's setting. Man is surrounded by people, objects, and natural conditions. These make up his environment, or what is around him. They help shape the way in which he lives. Let us see how the environment affects man.

Look at a globe which represents our world. You can see large masses of land rising out of the world's water covering. The seven largest of these land masses are called **continents.**

All of the continents of the world, except Antarctica, have had people living on them for many centuries. The three continents with the longest record of man's presence are Asia, Africa, and Europe. Scientists believe that the other continents, North America, South America, and Australia, have been occupied by people for a shorter period of time. There is reason to believe that man first came to North America only about twenty thousand years ago. Scientists believe that man has lived in Africa for nearly two million years.

The people on these continents have always struggled to make their living from the earth. On some of the continents the soils, the land surface, the dense vegetation, and the great extremes in temperature have caused man great difficulty. Other conditions, like too much snow or too little rain, have made it hard for man to develop a comfortable living in some

places. In other places, however, the land surface, soils, and climate have been favorable, and man has gained much for his efforts. Throughout the centuries man has attempted to improve his way of life by trying to make the earth yield a better living.

The Natural World

From the beginning man has adapted his ways of living to his **physical environment.** The term *physical environment* refers to the natural conditions around man. These natural conditions, such as the soils, land surfaces, climates, plants, and animals, differ on many parts of the Earth. For this reason, man has had to learn to use them in different ways. People in the warmer climates have ways of living which are different from those in colder climates. They build homes, wear clothing, and eat foods that are different from those in the colder climates. On parts of the Earth where the soil is deep and fertile and the climate favorable, man has obtained his living mainly by farming. In places where the surface of the Earth is rugged and the soil thin and infertile, man has turned to other means for earning his living.

Man has developed different ways of living in different environments.

As man's knowledge has increased, he has been better able to change the physical environment to suit his needs. Earliest man was the most dependent on his physical environ-

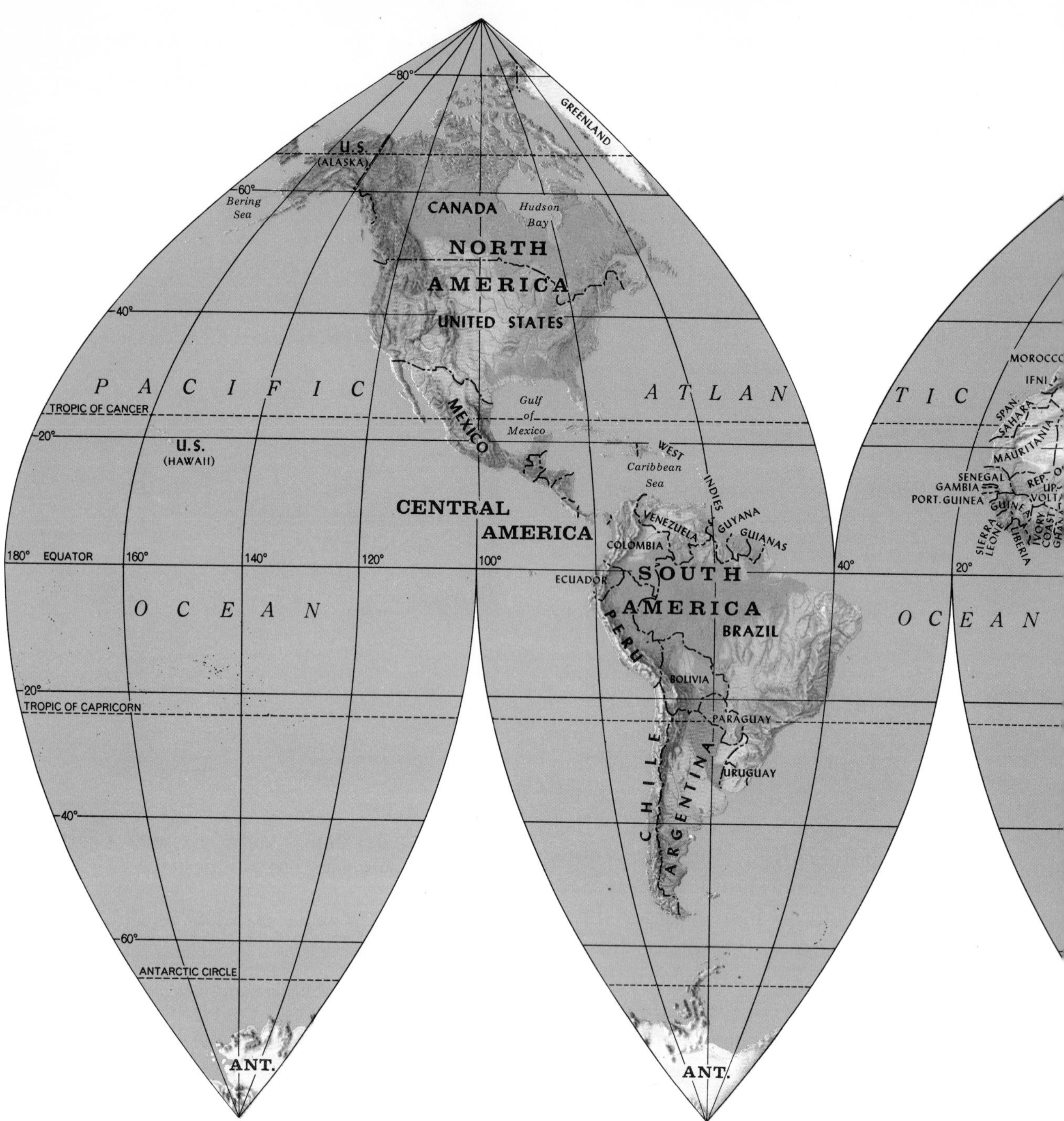

The best way to show the countries, islands, and oceans of the Earth is to show them on a globe. Because we must show the Earth on a flat piece of paper, we have taken a round globe and cut off pieces of it. Flattened out, the pieces which show the land areas look almost the same as they do on a globe. The ocean areas, though, have changed their shape. This type of map is called an equal-area projection map.

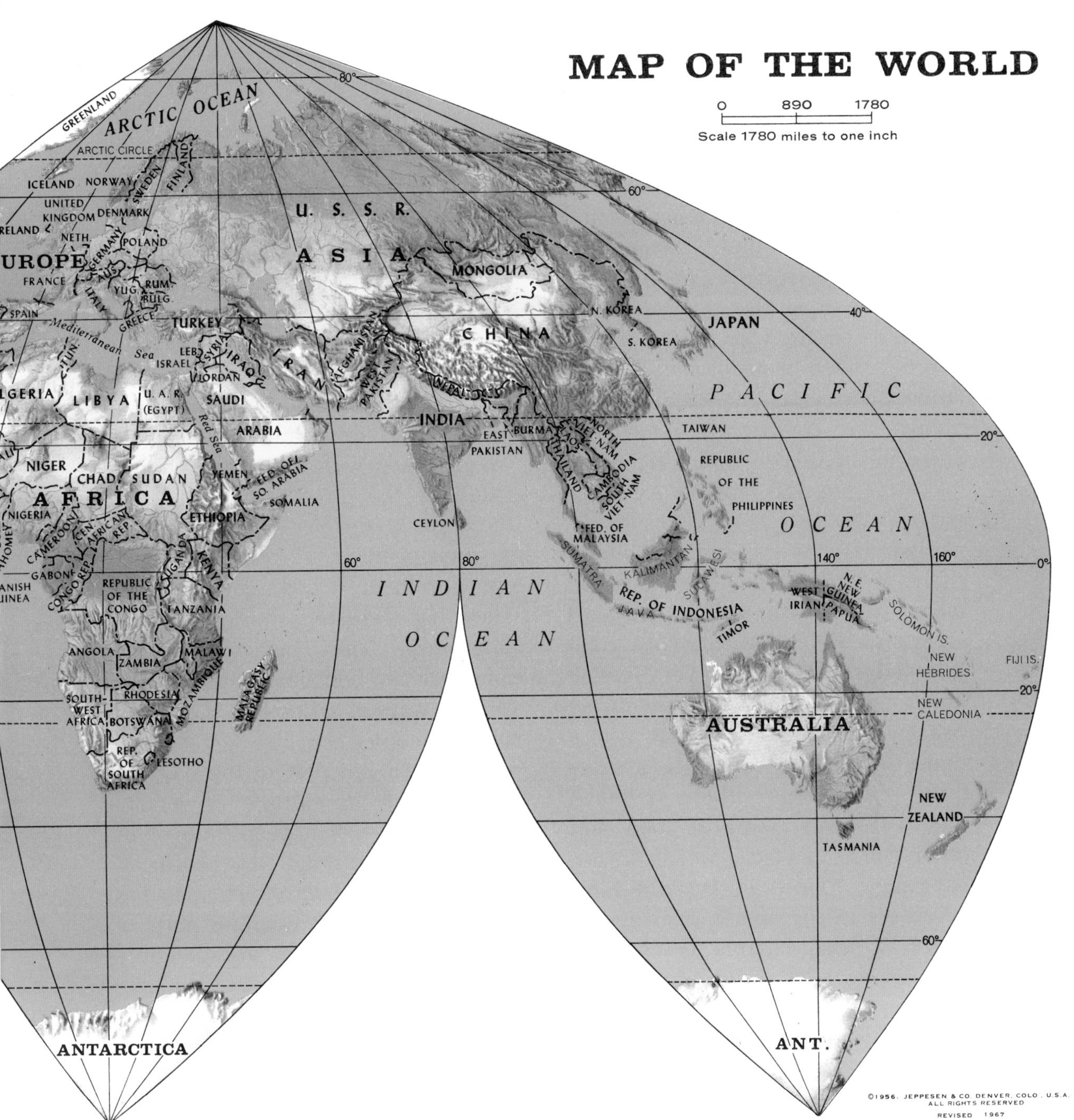

The map legend on page 16 will help explain to you what the different colors, shapes, and marks used on the maps in this book mean. The upper part tells how the sizes of cities are shown and what other special marks refer to. The lower part shows that the different bands of color indicate vegetation. It also shows how the different land features and geographical terms are illustrated on the maps in this book.

ment. He lived in trees and caves to protect himself from wild animals and from the climate. For food he ate the plants and animals he found growing around him. When the food was gone, he moved on to a place where the food was plentiful. He found other trees or caves for his home. When man learned how to farm, make simple tools, and build houses, he no longer needed to move about to get food. He could make the physical environment produce what he needed.

Man has always used his intelligence in order to develop more and more ways to control his physical environment. Today, man has great knowledge and ability with which he can change the environment to suit his needs. He can farm where there is little rain by bringing water from places where there is much rain. He can transport food and other goods to places which do not have them. He can adjust the temperatures in his homes and his factories to those suitable for comfortable living and productive work. Man has developed many ways of making his physical environment serve him. These ways have helped to make the differences in the ways people live.

The Man-Made World

The physical environment is important, but there is another important part of the environment which will help you understand the people of the world. This part, called the **cultural environment,** is man-made and must be learned. When studying the cultural environment of people, you look at the ideas and the objects that man has developed. The cultural environment also includes all the changes that man has made in his natural physical environment. As people have worked with the materials provided by the physical environment, they have developed habits and customs of living. They have developed religions and governments. They have created music, art, and languages. They have considered some ways of behaving as good. We call the ways of acting and the things which people consider good their **values.** All are part of the cultural environment, or **culture,** of people.

The culture of a people develops and changes through the centuries. The material things which man has developed are the **tangible** parts of the cultural environment. Tangible items are those which we can touch. We can locate them and study them. We can see how they differ from place to place.

The tangible parts of culture have been developed to meet the basic needs of people. The farms, factories, and homes, which man has built to supply his food, clothing, and shelter, can be easily seen and studied.

The ideas that man has developed are the **intangible** parts of the cultural environment. Intangible items

The performing arts, an important part of man's culture, can be seen and heard at Lincoln Center in New York.

cannot be touched, but their effects can be seen. The intangible parts of a culture are often the most important to the people.

The intangible parts of culture have been developed to meet man's need for an orderly way of life. Man has used his intelligence to create systems of religion, government, and education. The ideas of these systems differ from one culture to another, but they control the behavior of the people among whom they have been developed.

The intangible parts of culture are difficult to study. We can see church buildings, but it is difficult to measure the deep religious ideas and morals of a people. We can see capitol buildings and written laws, but how the government works and what effect it has on the people is difficult to evaluate. We can hear differences in languages, and we can see schools, libraries, and books. However, it is very difficult to judge how many people are well educated. In order to fully understand man's ways of living, all these parts of the cultural environment, or culture of a people, must be considered and studied.

THE HERITAGE OF THE PAST

All these parts of the culture have had their beginnings in the past. They are the result of what people

LEGEND

LONDON	over 2,000,000
Birmingham	500,000 to 2,000,000
Dover	under 500,000
National capitals	⊛
State or colony capitals	⊛
All other cities	•
Railroad	——+——+——
Point of interest	x
Undefined Boundary	— — — — —

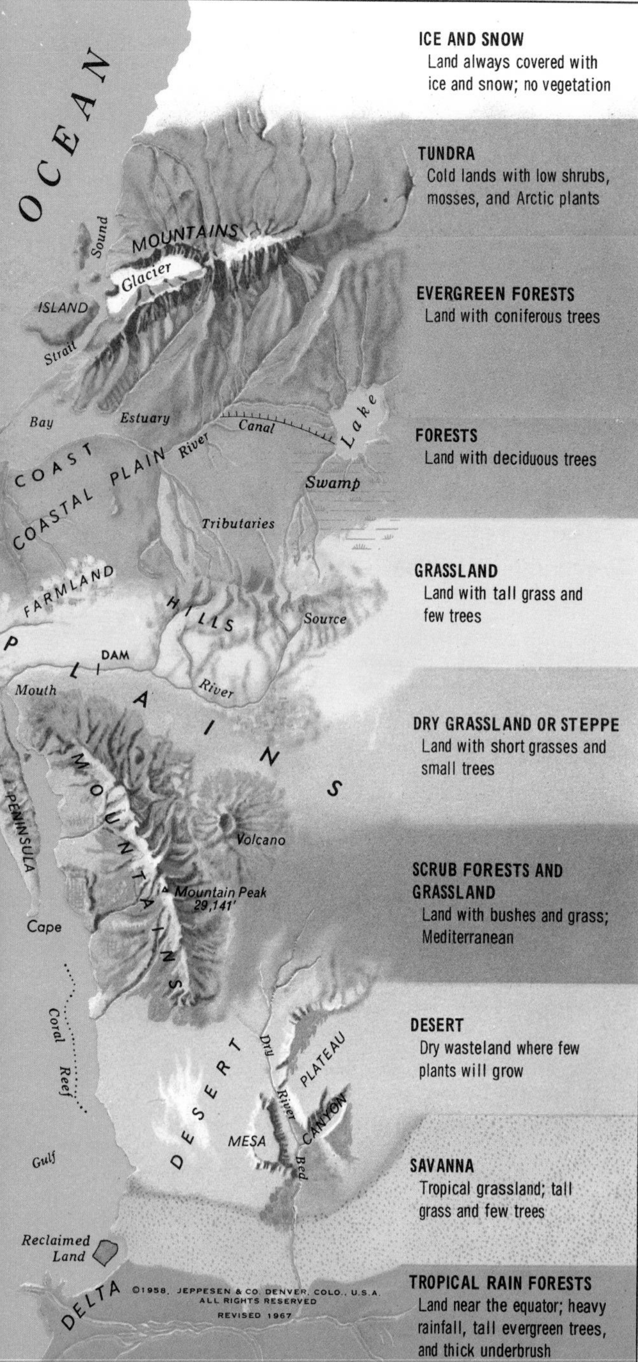

have developed through the centuries. We often call the culture, both tangible and intangible, the "heritage of the past." This is what our forefathers have handed down to us. Of course, this heritage has not been the same in all parts of the world or for all peoples. This is one reason why people differ in different parts of the world.

A few people live today exactly as their ancestors did. Some have made slight changes in their heritage over the years. Still others have made great progress and have contributed much to the generations which have come after them.

This "heritage of the past" does not end with the people of today. It goes on and on. Every day, changes are taking place as mankind lives in a combined physical and cultural environment. The heritage of people who live after us will be different from ours because we are contributing to their heritage.

Look again at the globe. You can see the continents of the world which have various combinations of physical and cultural environments. The peoples of these continents use their land differently, adapt to their weather conditions, and grow crops which they need. The man-made cultural items, such as dress, customs, art, language, and values, vary greatly from continent to continent. As you study this book, you will see how these differences in the physical and cultural environment affect man's ways of living on Earth.

Do You Know?

1. What is an environment?

2. What is a continent?

3. On which continents has man been living the longest time?

4. Which continent was the last to become inhabited?

5. What do we call the natural conditions which surround man?

6. What are four of these natural conditions?

7. Which power of man enables him to develop ways to control and change his surroundings?

8. What do we call the ideas, objects, and changes which man has developed around him?

9. What are the two major parts of the cultural environment called?

10. What do we call the cultural developments of our ancestors?

Learn By Doing

1. Make a chart comparing your parents' heritage, your heritage, and your children's possible heritage. Show the changes or progress which has been made in the following fields: Homes, Foods, Clothing, Communication, Education, Occupations, Machinery, Transportation, and Entertainment.

2. Place each item listed below under one of the following headings. Add other items to the list.

a. Physical Environment
b. Intangible Culture
c. Tangible Culture

farms	books	landforms
rain	customs	animals
homes	music	governments
values	planes	fertile soil
dress	religion	mountains

3. Find out how scientists determine the length of time man has inhabited various places on Earth.

Test Your Knowledge

1. Which continents do you think have the most favorable natural conditions? Explain why.

2. Over which natural condition does man have the least control? How has man learned to protect himself from this condition?

3. What are several ways man can change his physical environment to make it more suitable to his needs?

4. What do we mean by the cultural environment of man?

5. List some of the parts of the cultural environment of man.

6. Do cultural environment and culture mean the same thing? Explain.

7. How do the tangible and the intangible parts of culture differ?

8. Why have the tangible parts of culture been developed? Why have the intangible parts developed?

CHAPTER 2

STUDYING THE WORLD BY REGIONS

In social studies we try to understand man and the ways in which he lives. Specialists in the social sciences are continually seeking better ways of studying man and his environment so we can gain the needed understanding. The specialists have found one way of studying man that is very helpful. They divide the world into regions and study the ways man lives in each region. In this chapter you will learn how social scientists use the system of regional study. You will see how this system helps us to know better how to live and work with the people of the world.

DIFFERENT WAYS OF LIVING

As you study the people on the continents of the world, you will come to understand how and why people and their environments differ from place to place. Sometimes people in different areas of the same country live in different ways because the physical environment is different. Sometimes people in areas of different countries have a similar way of life because their physical and cultural environments are similar.

In order to study the cultures of people in many areas of the world, we will divide the world into "culture regions." In each culture region the people will have a similar way of life. They will live in a similar physical environment. They will have developed customs and ways of earning a living that are the same throughout the region. This means that they live in a region with a certain kind of culture. As you study the different culture regions of the world, you will come to understand how different cultural and physical environments cause differences in ways of living.

To illustrate how people and their cultures may be studied, we shall look briefly at two farmers in different regions of the world. One man lives on a farm in the state of Illinois. The other lives in a clearing in the Republic of the Congo. In studying these two farms we could look at the soil, the plants, the water supply, or even the sky. However, we shall contrast only the man-made things that have been devised to help these two men in their farming.

Farming in Different Regions

Early in the morning, Abdel, the Congolese farmer, leaves his thatched hut to work in his corn and yam field. Outside the hut he picks up a long-handled hoe with a worn, metal blade. Abdel's father had bartered for the hoe at the trading post several years before. His father had traded forty melons, two full baskets of yams, and three chickens for the hoe. The worn blade is now tied to its fourth handle. As Abdel walks along, he tightens the fiber threads which hold the blade to the handle.

Abdel's wife grinds meal for food outside her thatched-roof home.

On a similar morning in Illinois, John is having breakfast in the kitchen of his large, white farmhouse. He asks his wife to call the tractor salesman about the delivery of an attachment for his new tractor. He hopes that his new large tractor will last longer than his old one. The salesman guaranteed that his company would quickly replace any faulty parts.

John leaves the house, walks to the tractor shed, climbs onto the tractor seat, and starts the motor. He turns his new large tractor into the lane leading to the "south forty," the forty acres in the southern part of his 160-acre farm. He adjusts the big umbrella over the tractor seat, tilting it toward the east. He says to himself, "Going to be a hot one. I'd better turn on the sprinklers in the corn field, and open the valves to fill the waterholes for the cattle."

On the way to his clearing, Abdel pulls his wide, battered straw hat over his forehead. "Seems to get hotter every morning," he mutters. "On my way home, I'll take a few whacks at that mound of dirt blocking the stream, and make a path to let the water flow into my field."

When Abdel reaches his field, he begins to chop the weeds. Swish, swish, swish—the steady beat of his hoe soon becomes the rhythm of a song. Abdel hums and whistles while he works.

Modern machinery helps John farm.

John, after making sure that the cultivator on his tractor is lined up correctly over three rows of corn, starts the tractor down the long rows. At the end of the field he turns and comes back over three new rows. He travels row after row. A quick glance at his wristwatch reminds him that it is time for the news broadcast. He particularly wants to hear the long-range weather forecast. He turns on his transistor radio.

The broadcast reports the world, national, and local news. After the local news, current prices of corn, wheat, hogs, cattle, and hay are given. The weather reporter predicts that a two-day storm will move in the following night. John says to himself, "Guess I'll hold off on the sprinkler a day or so, and leave the drainage valve of the waterhole open a little bit." Then he thinks, "A two-day rain. Maybe Sara and the children would like to drive up to Chicago. It's only one hundred miles. I'm sure the children would like to stay overnight. I could fill the cattle bins with corn. The automatic feeders would take care of the chickens. I wouldn't have to worry about a thing. We could have a good time. There's lots to see."

Abdel stops humming and chopping, and listens. "Is that thunder I hear? Yes, and at this time of the day it means some very bad weather ahead." What would be done during the pelting rain? Abdel and his family would spend long hours in the thatched hut. Chickens would try to enter the hut through the open doorway. During the storm the food would be cooked inside the hut. No neighbors would drop by to visit. On sunny days what little news he got came from people passing by. Abdel, his wife, and his children might offer prayers to the gods to thank them for the rain and to plead for good crop yields.

These two contrasting farms and farmers show us how men in different places are alike and unlike. We could continue to list the different ways in which both families meet the same problems. However, the comparison given here shows you how a study of man by the region in which he lives helps us understand the people of the world.

REGIONS ARE UNITS OF STUDY

Suppose you were to start at Abdel's thatched hut and travel first in one direction and then in another. As you travel, you would find other farmers who grow corn and yams, raise chickens, live in thatched huts, and walk from one place to another. Their main farming tool would be the long-handled hoe. These ways of living, along with others, make up Abdel's culture. People who live in the same way as Abdel are members of the same culture. Since the cultural elements of the environment are similar, we think of the land area where they live as a culture region. We may even use one characteristic of this culture to serve as a symbol for the whole culture region. We could call this area of the Congo the "long-handled hoe region." We could draw lines around the "long-handled hoe region" on a map. The people in the "long-handled hoe region" have the same type of crops, domestic animals, and means of shelter and transportation. Do you see how boundaries or limits could be drawn around John's culture region?

The term *region* will be used throughout this book. It will be helpful to look deeper into its meaning at this point. We may do so by asking and answering two questions: "What is a region?" "Why do we look at the world and its people by culture regions?"

What Is a Region?

Very likely you already have a good idea of the meaning of region. You have heard of hill regions, mountain regions, plateau regions, and plains regions. Each of these regional types is a physical part of the world. Each is a type of landform on the Earth's surface. Each region differs from the others. The way each differs is given in its name.

You are also familiar with natural vegetation regions. You know about grassland regions, forest regions, desert shrub regions, and tundra regions. Each of these regional types is a physical part of the world. Each is a type of vegetation on the Earth's surface. Each of these regions differs from the other. Again, the way each differs is given in its name.

You also know that vegetation occurs on landforms. Therefore, we have plateau-desert regions, mountain-forest regions, and plateau-grassland regions. Once again, the way one region differs from another is given in its title.

If you traveled by car from New York to San Francisco, you would drive through many of these physical, geographic regions. There would be no man-made lines on the Earth's surface separating the mountain regions from the plains regions. The plateau-desert region might merge gradually into a mountain-forest region. Yet, you would know which one you were in.

A **region** is an area of the world in which a feature or a combination of features stands out. A **feature** is an important characteristic of the area. The world can be divided into regions on the basis of any one important feature. The feature may be part of the physical environment, part of the cultural environment, or a combination of both. For example, an area of the world where large forests are found may be called a forest region. In a forest region the lives of the people may be devoted to caring for the trees and cutting the trees for lumber.

What Is a Culture Region?

More often we mark off a region on the basis of several features which go together. We say they are inseparable. For example, we saw in the Republic of the Congo how several important features described the lives of the farmers. We noted the type of hoe, the corn and yam agriculture, and the thatched huts. An area of the world where several important features go together, like the "long-handled hoe region," is called a **culture region.**

We study the world by culture regions in order to help us better understand the peoples and the cultures of the world. Dividing the world into culture regions is a means of seeing the relationship of man to his own environment more clearly. It is a way of bringing out the important features of a region, such as climate, soil, crops, and customs. It is a way of showing features which are not present or not as important in nearby areas.

Studying culture regions of the world is like putting a part of a plant under a microscope. When magnified, you can look at that portion of the plant and better understand its parts. Just as the microscope gives us a clearer picture of the parts of the plant, studying a region gives us a clearer understanding of the ways man lives. It gives us a clearer picture of the various contributions of the different areas of the world to the world as a whole.

Marking Off Culture Regions

Man's ways of living may be used to describe a culture region. Sometimes the culture region of a people is described in terms of its agriculture. Learning about the cultural and physical environment of a people may be done through examining their farming. All people need food. We can look around to see how people secure their food. We can check to see if the agriculture is **diversified**—that is, if several crops are important. Many farms in the United States grow several kinds of crops. We can also note whether or not one or two crops dominate food production in a region. The wheat-growing regions of the central Canadian provinces are examples of one crop regions.

Another way of marking off regions is by the practices used in farming. The major farming tool used will tell us many things. We saw in the case of the Illinois farmer, John, an example of a highly mechanized farming culture. John used a tractor with a cultivator on his many acres of farmland. Abdel, the Congolese farmer, used a hoe on his small field. The statement that Abdel lived in a hoe culture tells us quite a bit about his way of farming.

If animals are the dominant food product, the region may be described by such terms as pastoral, ranching, herding, or simply as an animal economy. By **economy** we mean a way of making or earning a living. In some parts of the world where making or earning a living is difficult, or takes every waking hour, we may say that the economy is really the way of life of the people. The cattle drives you may watch on television are scenes from a region with an animal economy. The Plains Indians of the United States had a specialized animal economy. They depended on the buffalo, or American bison, for most of their food. People who depend mainly upon animals as the source of living are regarded as living in an **animal culture region.** The wealth of a man in an animal culture may be measured by the number of animals he owns. In the American West the number of cattle a man owned served as the measure of his wealth.

Some parts of the world have such heavy concentrations of industrial plants that they bear the title of industrial or manufacturing economies. They are manufacturing regions. The United Kindgom is an example of a manufacturing region. The United Kingdom depends heavily upon manufacturing as the main source of living. Most of her food is bought in other parts of the world. There is a constant flow of manufactured goods out of the United Kingdom, and a flow of raw materials and food into the country.

We also see large sections of the world where a language or a religion is an important cultural feature. The language or religion serves as a label with a broad meaning. Latin America refers to all countries in the Americas south of the United States. The major languages spoken there today are Spanish and Portuguese. Both come from Latin, the language of the ancient Romans, and are closely related in sound and in construction. Latin America, then, is a region where the major languages spoken are of Latin origin.

Sometimes we may mark off regions by religions. When the term *Muslim World* is used, it refers to the faith common to most of the people in a large part of the Eastern Hemisphere. The Muslim Region stretches from Morocco on the Atlantic Ocean eastward to the Philippines in the Pacific Ocean. The many people of the Muslim World vary greatly in racial backgrounds and ways of living. They share, however, the common belief in their religion.

This is not the only significant characteristic of the Muslim World. The main use of this label is its reminder that the countries of this region were

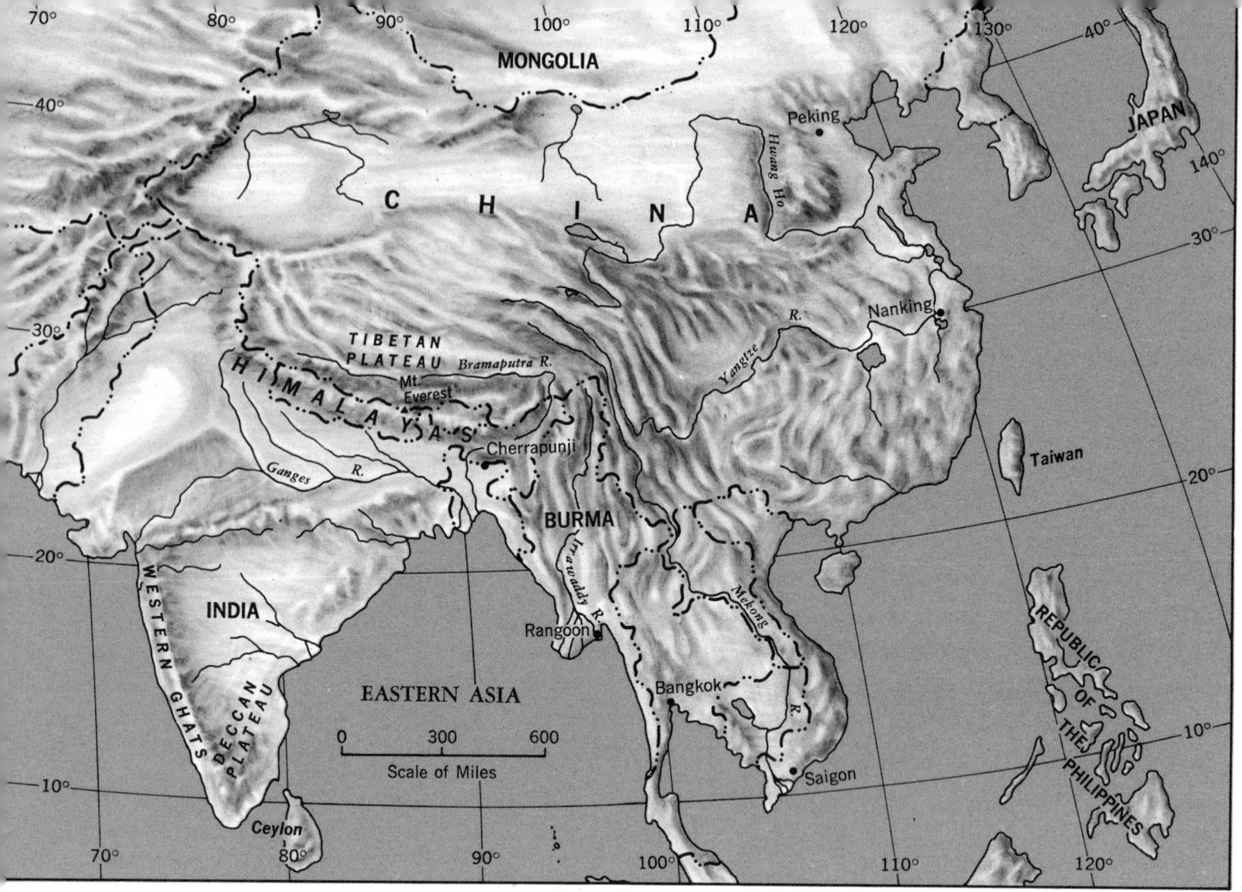

settled by the followers of Mohammed. To really understand this region, we must look further than its label. The Muslim World is a vast region. Its topography and natural resources are varied, but its climate and crops are similar. To understand how these factors affect man's ways of living, we will look closely at this large part of the Eastern Hemisphere later.

CULTURE AREAS OF EASTERN ASIA

Thus far, we have seen how a variety of different physical and cultural features may be used as a basis for describing regions. We have seen forest regions and plains regions. We have seen how crops, farming practices, animals, industry, language, or religion may be used as a basis for forming culture regions. Look at the map of Eastern Asia on this page. Locate the following nations: China, Burma, Thailand, India, and Ceylon. These divisions are political regions. Let us take this same land area of Asia and divide it into culture regions. These regions will be formed by examining the crops, climate, and landforms. We will point out a few inseparable features in each culture region. A more complete picture of this area will be given later in the book.

As we look at these three ways of describing regions, remember that each does not exist alone. Each has a relationship with the others. If you want to see the effect of a climate, you study the crops and the ways in which people live in the climate. If you want to understand the climate, you must examine the effect that landforms have upon the climate of a region. If you want to understand the people of these culture regions of Asia, you must understand the effect the natural and man-made features have on the way of life of the people. You should try also to learn about their values.

MAJOR CROP REGIONS

Some culture regions are named after the major crops grown in the regions. On the well-watered slopes and the wide flood plains of eastern and southern Asia, we have the rice region. The climate and soil in this area are excellent for rice growing. The dominant feature of the landscape is the rice field. Rice is the staple food of the people. The ways of living for millions of people are shaped by the farming of this all-important crop. The farmer's way of life is tied closely to rice production—its planting, growing, harvesting, and selling. Regions where rice is the main crop and the main food are called **rice cultures.**

On your map locate, in Southeast Asia, the two large cities of Rangoon in Burma and Bangkok, sometimes called Krung Thep, in Thailand. During peaceful times these cities serve as export centers for large quantities of rice. The rice is grown in large, warm, well-watered river valleys and on hillsides which extend inland from the cities. More rice is grown in these areas than is needed by the growers for their own food supply. The surplus rice is sold to other Asian countries which do not grow enough for their people. The Rangoon and Bangkok areas have surplus rice because these areas are not as densely populated as some of the other rice-producing regions of Asia.

Rice Has Several Growing Needs

Rice grows best in a **humid climate.** This is a climate in which the air contains much water vapor. In addition to a humid climate, rice needs very high temperatures in order to germinate and to grow. Temperatures over 70 degrees are required for the germination of the seeds. The seeds are placed in nursery beds. They are covered with straw and flooded with warm water. When they grow into six-inch shoots, they are planted in the fields. During the growing season the temperature should be much higher than 70 degrees.

Rice demands a great deal of water. Daily rains are needed during a large part of the growing season. A minimum growing requirement is an average annual rainfall of 50 inches. Five inches or more should fall each month of the four to six months growing season. If rains are not frequent enough, water must be brought to the **paddy,** or rice field, by means of irrigation ditches. Dikes must be built around the fields so that the paddies will be level for even flooding. Level paddies are easier to build on flood plains, valley floors, and deltas than on steep mountains.

There are places, however, where rice is grown on mountainsides. In Japan, Taiwan, China, Ceylon, and India man has, with great labor, forced the mountains to adapt to his growing needs. He has done this by terracing hill and mountain slopes. The picture of the rice terraces on this page shows how this has been done. Some rice terraces extend more than 1,500 feet up the slopes of a mountain. Terrace walls must be kept in repair. Stone retaining walls 20 to 50 feet high are sometimes used. Stream water is first directed into the highest terrace. The water then flows to lower terraces until each terrace has all the water it needs.

Another important need in the growing of rice is the layer of **hardpan** which forms about 6 to 12 inches below the surface of the soil. This is a layer of hard soil through which water seeps very slowly. The layer of hardpan helps to hold the water in

The rice terraces of Luzon, a province in the Philippines.

the paddy. You have seen how quickly water disappears into the sand at beaches. If the soil of the rice paddy was deep and sandy with no hardpan under the surface, the water would go right through it. The layer of hardpan helps, along with the paddy dike or the terrace wall, to keep a water-covering on the rice.

How Rice Is Grown

The task of growing rice is a difficult one. In early spring the soil of the paddy must be turned. Farmers use a primitive plow drawn by oxen or buffalo, or they spade the land by hand. Planted in these paddies are the small six-inch rice shoots which began as seeds planted in nursery beds. The shoots are set in wet soil about one foot apart. Then the fields are flooded. Sometimes the water flows on the fields by gravity. Sometimes farmers use water wheels to pump the water onto the paddies. Some even use hand buckets to carry the water to the fields.

During the growing season the paddies may be drained and cultivated two or three times. With the approach of the dry season, the water is drawn off and the fields are allowed to dry. Once the ground is dry and the rice is ripe, it is harvested. Then the rice is threshed, hulled, and stored. The farmer sorts the rice kernels carefully, and chooses kernels from the healthiest plants to save for planting the next crop.

Other Crops

Rice is not the only crop grown in the rice culture region. People in this area of Southeast Asia use the land in many ways. Hillsides not suited to irrigation and sandy soils that will not hold water are used to grow corn, sugar cane, vegetables, and fruits. During the dry season barley, wheat, and peas are grown on the rice lands. Flooded ricefields and permanent ponds are used for raising fish.

A Wheat Growing Region

We have looked at the warm, wet region of Southeast Asia. Let us turn to the cooler, dry region of northern China. While Thailand and Burma are rice regions, northern China is a wheat region. The rice-warm temperature region changes to a wheat-cool temperature region near Nanking, China. Locate this city on the map on page 24. In this northern region with its cooler, drier climate and easily worked soils, the farmers grow great quantities of wheat. In this region wheat has become the most important crop and the main food of the people. It is known as a **wheat culture region.**

Wheat requires a cool, dry climate. No rainfall during the last few weeks of growth and during the period of harvest is ideal. A period of dryness is needed so that the wheat stalks will stop growing and the heads on the

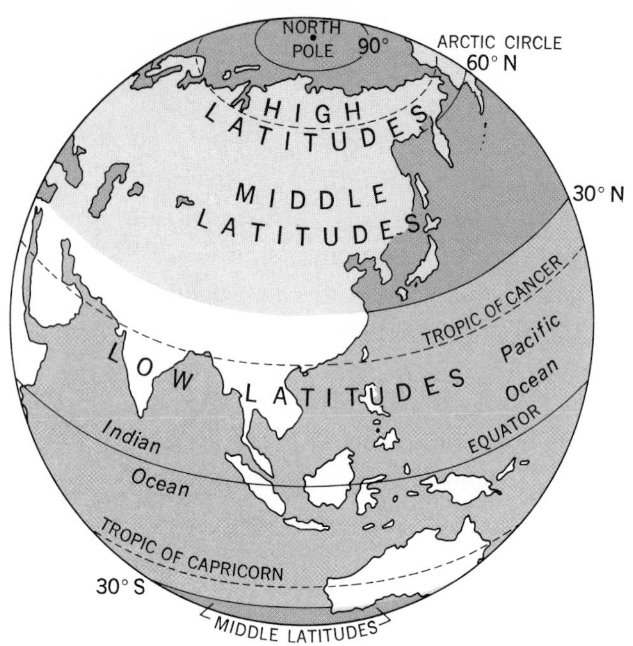

Lands in low latitudes receive the direct rays of the sun much of the year. These rays heat the surface of the Earth to a higher degree.

The dense vegetation in Eastern Asia results from the hot humid climate.

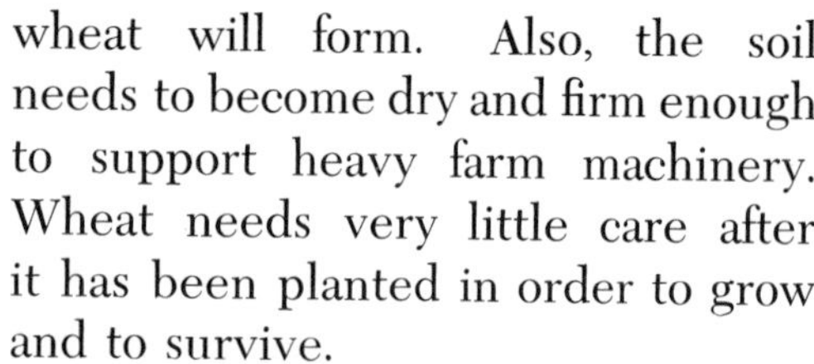

wheat will form. Also, the soil needs to become dry and firm enough to support heavy farm machinery. Wheat needs very little care after it has been planted in order to grow and to survive.

In northern China there are two wheat regions, the winter wheat region and the spring wheat region. Winter wheat is planted in the fall, grows during the winter, and is harvested in late spring. In order to grow and to survive, it requires a milder climate than spring wheat. Spring wheat is planted in the spring. It grows during the summer, and is harvested in the fall.

CLIMATE REGIONS

Regions are sometimes described in terms of climate. The huge land mass of Eastern Asia has a climate pattern which is the result of two great climate controls. The first control is its location in the low latitudes. Lands in low latitudes receive more direct rays of the sun. Rays that strike the Earth directly are concentrated. Those that strike at a slanting angle are spread out over a greater surface. Thus, the Earth's surface would be heated to a higher degree when the sun's rays strike the Earth directly. When the rays strike at a slanting angle, the Earth's surface is heated to a lesser degree. The land

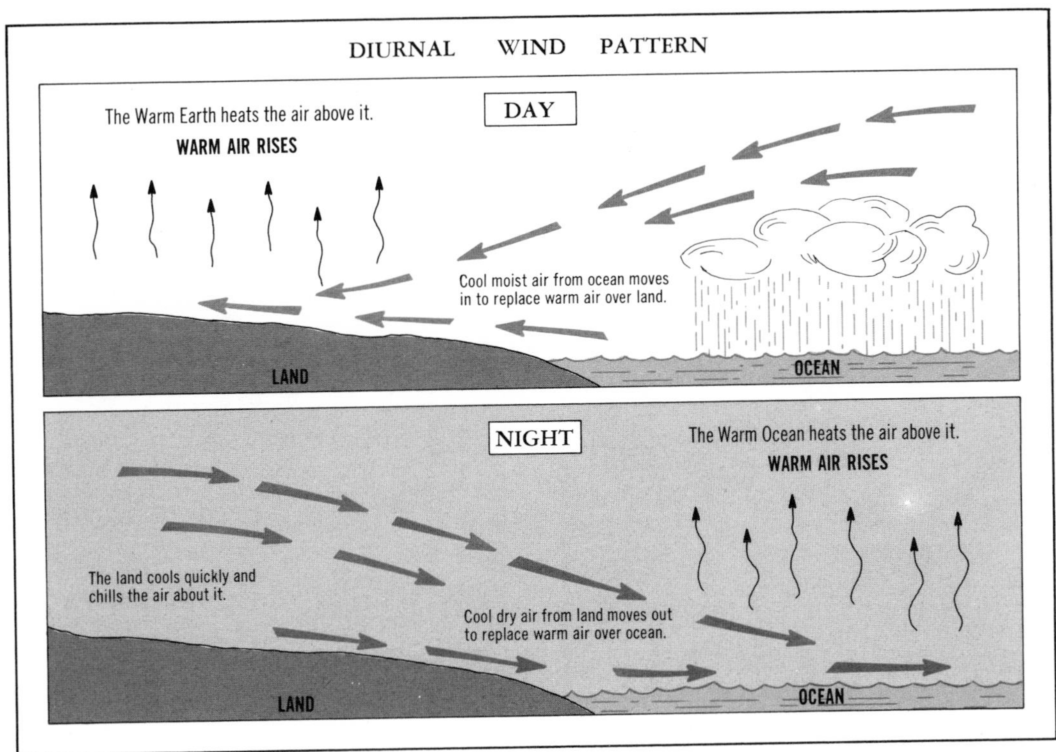

mass of Eastern Asia receives the direct concentrated rays of the sun much of the year.

The second major climate control lies in the nature of the surface struck by the sun's rays. Solid materials heat much faster and to a higher temperature than liquids. This may be seen in the case of water in a swimming pool and the cement pavement around the pool. On a very hot day the cement pavement may become very hot, while the temperature of the pool water may rise only slightly.

The reason for the difference in the temperature is that heat received by the two different surfaces is distributed differently. The heat in the cement pavement, or soil, or rock, is confined to an area near the surface. Heat received by water is spread down through the water. The greater the size of the body of water, the greater the area to absorb and spread the heat of the sun's rays. The landforms that heat the fastest are dry sand and rocks. For the same reason that land heats more readily than water, the land loses heat or cools off more readily. **Arid,** or very dry, regions are hot during the day but very cool at night.

Diurnal Wind Patterns

Let us turn to an example of how land and water bodies can affect a

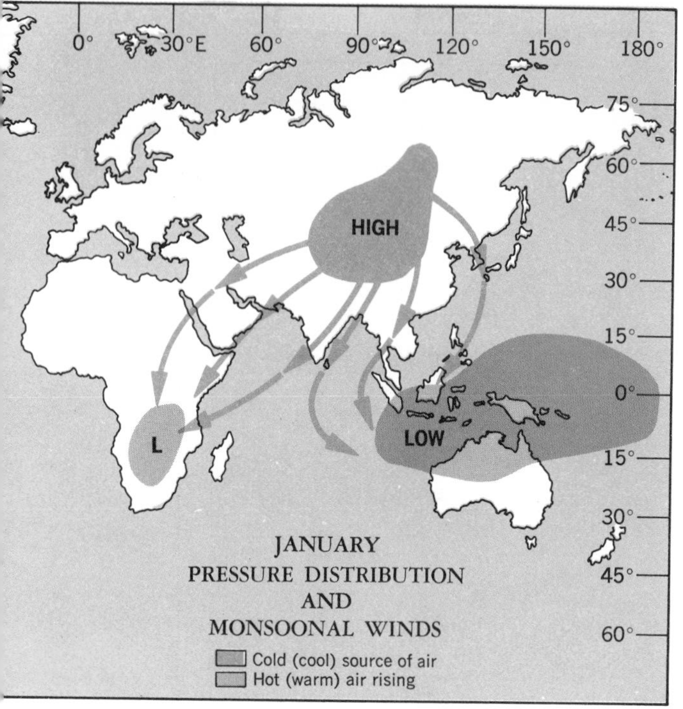

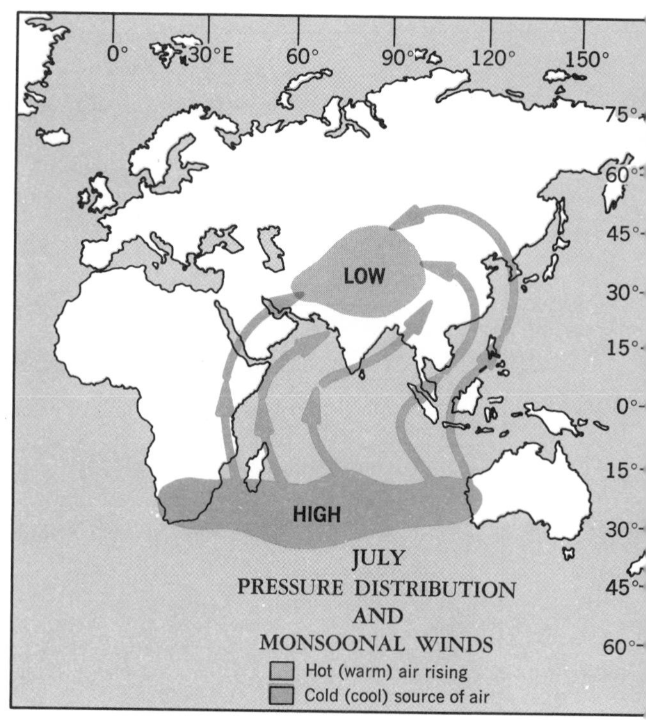

climate. Imagine you are at the seashore of the New Jersey coast at noon in the month of July. The sun is shining brightly. As the day passes, the sand becomes warmer and warmer. As the air above the beach is heated by the warm sand, it begins to rise. The rising warm air is replaced by the cooler air which is flowing in from the ocean. A sea breeze, or on-shore wind, starts to blow.

In the evening you notice that there has been a change in wind direction. The warmer air above the ocean water is rising and is being replaced by cooler air from the land. The breeze, now, is blowing from the land out over the ocean. This daily occurrence of sea-to-land, and then land-to-sea breezes in the summer months is called a **diurnal** wind pattern. The word *diurnal* means "daily."

Monsoon Wind Patterns

In southern Asia there is a **monsoon** wind pattern. During the months from April to September the land mass gets warmer and warmer. This is a result of the long, summer days with the rays of the sun striking the land mass more directly. The warm, humid air over the continent expands and rises. This area of light, warm air is called a **low pressure area.** The nearby oceans heat up less than the land. Cooler air from

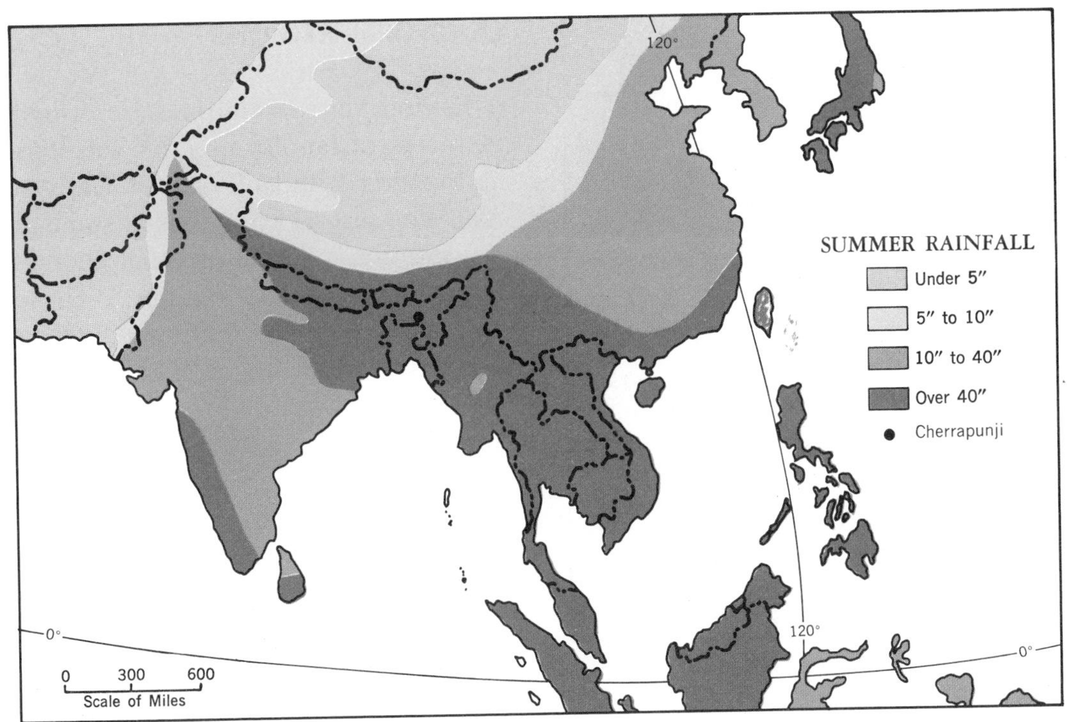

the oceans slowly moves into the low pressure areas—that is, from the Indian Ocean onto the Indian Peninsula. This steady on-shore wind is not diurnal. It continues to blow for four to six months.

While this seasonal wind is blowing onto the continent, it is the time of the **summer monsoon.** The cooler air coming off the ocean has much water vapor in it. Late in the afternoon when the temperature drops, the vapor reaches a saturation point and condenses into drenching rains.

One of the heaviest rainfall regions in the world is at Cherrapunji in India. Once 241 inches of rain fell there in one month. The yearly average at Cherrapunji is 458 inches of rain. The most surprising fact is that this amount of rain falls during the six months of the summer monsoon. The winter at Cherrapunji is almost rainless.

The wind pattern is reversed in the winter. During this season the low pressure areas are over the ocean because the air here is warmer than the air over the cooler land masses. The cooler, dry air from the land moves into the low pressure areas over the ocean, causing an off-shore wind. This off-shore wind is called a **winter monsoon.**

The crops and lives of the people of the monsoon regions depend greatly on the rainfall that comes with the summer monsoon. Crops, such as rice, cotton, corn, millet, and sugar cane, are sown at the beginning of the

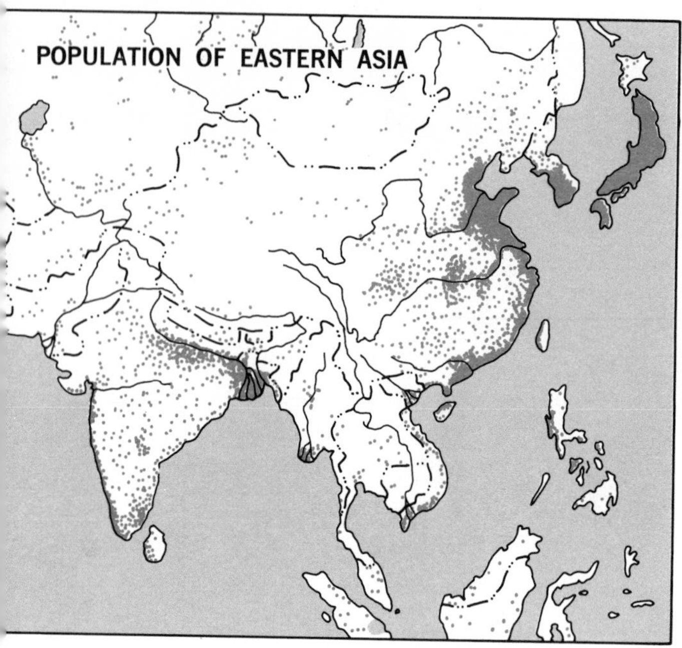

summer monsoon. If the rains start earlier than usual, planting may be late. If the rains are late, the plants may die in the fields. If the farmers do not correctly time the planting of the crops, disaster may occur. The result is that millions go hungry. Thousands may die.

People in the monsoon regions and in the wheat and rice regions of Asia face the problem of getting enough food. These regions contain over half of all the people in the world. Study the population map on this page. The total population of India, Pakistan, and Ceylon is over 600 million. The population of China is estimated to be over 700 million. The populations of these regions are continuously increasing. Providing two meals a day for all of these people is a difficult task.

LANDFORM REGIONS

Regions are sometimes described in terms of landforms. As you look at the crops and climate of Eastern Asia, you also need to look at some of the significant landforms that characterize some of the regions. These landforms have a definite effect on the crops and climate of the region.

RIVER VALLEYS

We have noted some of the flood plains and valleys in which rice is grown in Southeast Asia. China has similar landforms in her two great river valleys. Locate these areas on the map on page 24. One is drained by the long Hwang Ho, the other by the Yangtze River. The Yangtze is 3,000 miles long, which is about the distance from San Francisco to New York. At places, the rivers twist and turn and create great bends in the flat river valleys.

Millions of farmers live on the bends of these rivers. The valleys are subject to frequent flooding. As floodwaters recede, they leave mud and silt. The soil left by the floods is fertile and easy to prepare for planting. At times, the rivers cut new channels through the neck of the loops. The old river channel dries up as the river continues in its new bed. New irrigation canals have to be built to bring water to the farms once served by the waters that ran in the old riverbeds. People living in re-

Farming the cold dry lands of Tibet is difficult.

gions such as these can be said to be living in riverine cultures. Their way of life is closely related to the conditions of the rivers in their region.

Great Mountains and Plateaus

The most spectacular landform of the Asian continent is the great Himalaya Range that lies between China and India. This mountain range, the highest in the world, acts as a natural boundary between the two countries. It also serves as a barrier to the moisture-laden winds from the south. Much of the land north of the Himalayas is desert or near desert.

The world's highest mountain, Mount Everest (29,028 feet), is in the Himalaya Range on the Tibet-Nepal border. The southern slopes of the Himalayas descend sharply to the great river valleys of the Ganges and the Brahmaputra in India. The northern Himalayan slopes edge the Tibetan Plateau. This plateau has an average elevation of 10,000 to 15,000 feet, which is two to three miles above sea level. Because of the Himalayan rain barrier and the height of the plateau, Tibet has a high, dry, cold desert.

India also has a plateau area called the Deccan. It is, however, at a much lower elevation than the Tibetan Plateau. We have seen how the Himalayas have served as a rain barrier so that a high desert lies to the north. The Deccan Plateau, although not a desert, is also an area of little rainfall. The reason lies with the Western Ghats, a range of mountains bordering the western part of the Deccan Plateau. The highest faces, or ridges, of the Western Ghats are on the seaward side of the range. As winds cross the Ghats from west to east, they lose moisture on the ocean-facing slopes. As the winds rise higher on the slopes, they get cooler and are able to hold less water vapor. Upon descending the eastern side of the Western Ghats, they become warm, thirsty winds that seek to absorb moisture rather than drop it. The result is a dry climate for the Deccan Plateau.

A WORLD OF MANY REGIONS

As you have seen, there are countless ways to divide the world into regions. Each region has its own physical and cultural features. The people in each of these regions have developed their own way of life. By studying each culture region, you will be able to understand better the people of the world and the ways in which they live. People live together in many different ways.

Do You Know?

1. What part of the environment is the major cause of the differences in ways of living?

2. What name is given to an area of the world which has one important environmental feature? Give an example.

3. What name is given to an area of the world in which several features stand out? Give an example.

4. What is usually used to describe or mark off a culture region?

5. What does the term economy mean?

6. Do all regions have to include the same amount of land? Can one area be a part of two physical regions?

7. What is an animal economy? A rice economy?

8. What part of the world's population lives in Eastern Asia?

9. What are three types of landforms found in Eastern Asia?

Learn By Doing

1. Tell whether each statement is true or false.

a. The climate and crops of a region are affected by landforms.

b. Flood plains and river valleys are excellent areas to grow wheat.

c. Floods are always a hazard to the farmers of Southwest Asia.

d. The flood waters bring soil to the river valleys.

e. Severe floods often create new river valleys.

f. The soil left by the floods is very fertile.

g. The Himalayas act as a natural boundary between China and Burma.

h. The Himalayan Mountain Range serves as a barrier to the moisture-laden winds in the region.

i. Mount Everest, the third highest mountain in the world, is on the Tibet-Nepal border.

j. A range of mountains called the Western Ghats is the cause of the wet climate of the Deccan Plateau.

2. Select the correct answer to complete each sentence.

a. The climate pattern of Southeast Asia is caused by its location in the (high, middle, low) latitudes.

b. Lands in low latitudes receive (more, less) direct rays from the sun.

c. Rays which strike the Earth (directly, at an angle) spread out over a greater surface.

d. When the rays of the sun strike the Earth at a slanting angle, the Earth's surface is heated to a (greater, lesser) degree.

e. Southeast Asia (often, seldom) receives the direct, concentrated rays of the sun.

f. (Solid, liquid) materials heat much faster and to a higher temperature.

g. Heat received by two different surfaces is distributed (differently, the same).

h. Heat received by a (solid, liquid) surface is spread over a greater area.

i. The (greater, smaller) the size of a body of water, the (greater, smaller) the area to absorb and spread the heat of the sun's rays.

j. (Land, Water) holds its heat longer and cools off more (slowly, rapidly).

Test Your Knowledge

1. What do we call an area where there is a similar way of life because the physical and cultural environment is the same?

2. Abdel's culture region is called the "long-handled hoe region." Can you name John's culture region? Describe some of the physical and cultural elements of his region.

3. How can you tell one region from another? Is it easier to tell one physical region from another or one culture region from another? Explain.

4. What are some ways of marking the world off into physical regions? Into culture regions?

5. Why do we divide the world off into culture regions?

6. Describe an animal culture region. A rice culture region.

7. Compare the method of growing rice on a level flood plain with the method of growing rice on the mountain slopes of southeastern Asia.

8. How does a rice culture region differ from a wheat culture region? Discuss the climate, land, and nature of the work to be done.

9. What is the difference between a diurnal wind pattern and a monsoon wind pattern?

10. Divide Eastern Asia into as many culture regions as you can. Remember that a culture region can be based on any physical or cultural feature of the environment.

11. Describe the conditions of the summer monsoon and the winter monsoon in Eastern Asia.

12. Describe a continental region, a sea region, and a global region. Could you also have a moon and a planet region?

13. Using your hometown, name several different regions of which it is a part.

CHAPTER 3

FAMILIES AND COMMUNITIES

An important feature of the environment in which a man lives is the people with whom he lives and works and plays. These people influence what the man does and how he does it. They are a significant part of his cultural environment. Some of these people may be his family; others may be his friends and neighbors in the community in which he lives. They all are important to him. People living together in families and communities influence the ways each person lives.

WAYS OF LIVING TOGETHER

All people have some ways of living in common. As you study the ways in which people live together, you will come to understand man in his total environment, or mankind living in the world. There are many ways in which people can be grouped. Some groups are based on blood ties, while others are based on social ties.

In some parts of the world people live together in groups called **tribes** or **clans.** These people have blood ties because they are descendents of the same ancestors. You might even call them one "family." An Indian tribe has been called an Indian "family." Scottish clans have been called Scottish "families."

You and your relatives, your grandparents, aunts, uncles, and cousins, are a smaller family group. An even smaller group is the household, those who live as a family under one roof. This is an interesting word. Think! What does a house hold?

The parents and children of a family living in the same household are probably the most important cultural factors of the environment. This kind of family is the smallest and the most effective transmitter of culture. By this we mean the passing on to younger people the heritage of the past.

Human families are very different from families of other living creatures. Young animals are often separated from their mothers at an early age. Children, by staying in families a longer length of time, are prepared for adulthood. Parents give instruction in the most basic ways of living. Ideas, rules, and values are important cultural foundations of life which are transmitted to the young by families all over the world. These ideas, rules, and values may be different in each part of the world. Yet, every family teaches its young how to face the same basic problems of securing food, clothing, and shelter, and of providing for enjoyment in life.

You have seen how many blood groups can be formed. The blood relationships which exist between you and the members of your family are easy to recognize. People say that you look like your mother, or father, or some close relative, such as your grandfather. These physical inheritances are regarded as very strong bonds, or blood ties, that exist between members of the same family.

When studying a region, you will find that the family represents a very strong cultural factor. In order to understand a region, you will need to understand the effect family customs and practices have on the life of the people. Let us look closely at one example of the smallest unit of cultural environment, the family or household.

Families around the world transmit their customs and values. Younger members often combine modern and traditional cultural patterns.

A Chinese Family

Very strong blood ties are shown in the following story. It takes place in a town in the South China province of Changsha during the Chinese New Year, the "First Festival." The First Festival is as important to the Chinese as Christmas is to many peoples in Western countries.

People in the town prepare for the winter festival for a long time. They work very hard from early spring. If the fall rice harvest has been good, many farmers have extra money to spend on the festival. Many farmers buy new shoes and clothing for themselves and for their families. Farm families usually wear dark blue clothing, but for festivals they wear bright, colorful costumes. Mothers and daughters wear red and green to symbolize unusual joy.

During the First Festival the children do not have to go to school. It is a good time to visit relatives and bring them gifts of food and wine. All members of a family try to get together no matter how far away they live. Let us look in on the family gathering of the Wongs.

There are three sons in the Wong family. The oldest son, Lin-mei, is married. The next son is called Fa-pei, and the youngest son, Fe-nan. Each boy wears a long robe with a silk coat over it. The coats have embroidered designs on them.

The entire family has New Year's dinner together. Fa-pei and Fe-nan offer a drink to each of the older members of the family. They go first to their grandparents, next to their parents, and last to their brother, Lin-mei, and his wife. All members

Family ties and holiday celebrations continue to be important parts of the Chinese culture.

of the family toast each other and say good things to each other. It is a traditional Chinese custom, during the fifteen day New Year period, that only good things may be said to one another.

After the big dinner Fa-pei and Fe-nan play games with their grandparents and their parents. Most of the evening, however, the two boys play together. The light of large red candles and the flame of the fireplace shine brightly throughout the house.

Fa-pei and Fe-nan, wearing false faces, or masks, fight against each other with play swords. The false faces symbolize the faces of famous ancient warriors. The two boys stop their mock fighting when they hear the sound of a tremendous amount of firecrackers. Fa-pei and Fe-nan join the family in setting off their firecrackers.

After the firecrackers have been set off, the front door is closed and sealed for the rest of the evening. The ground floor of the house is then cleaned. The dust is swept toward the center of the house rather than outward so that the good fortune cannot leak out.

The entire Wong family stays up all night to see in the New Year. When light appears in the east, Fa-pei shouts, "The New Year is here." The Wongs again light candles. Fa-pei and Fe-nan pay their respects to their elders by kneeling before them and bowing their heads many times. Each member of the family says, "Long life" and "Good fortune" to each other. The front door is opened, and more firecrackers are set off to welcome the New Year.

On New Year's Day the neighbors visit each other offering good wishes and putting good fortune sheets on the front doors. When they meet friends on the street, they greet each other by folding their arms in front of them and saying, "Good fortune." The town is filled with joyful people.

Exciting plays about dragons and lions are given in the streets. The color red is everywhere. In China red symbolizes both good luck and good fortune. It also symbolizes the strong blood ties which exist among the Chinese people. Many parts of the First Festival are based on this belief in the importance of blood ties.

For many generations the Chinese people have believed that the family unit is very important. In some parts of China, however, the family is becoming less important. The belief that the family is more important than the government is discouraged by the rulers of China today.

Families Live Together in Communities

You have just studied one family in South China. In this region there are many families who live together because of their blood relationships. By understanding family life we are better able to understand community

The nomad is at home in the desert.

life. The word *community* refers to groups of families living together because of their social relationships. The term *community* may also be used to refer to the place where the group of people lives. A **community** consists of a group of persons living in the same area under similar conditions. The people who live in the same community follow the same customs and laws. They have common interests and privileges. They cooperate for the good of all.

COMMUNITIES DIFFER

You would not expect all communities to look alike, since their physical environments are not the same. Communities in different parts of the world have different weather and climate, different natural vegetation, and different soils. They are different not only in their physical environments, but also in the ways of living that make up their cultural environments. We shall see that certain basic needs are the same for all communities, but that these needs are met in different ways.

A Nomadic Community

Imagine that we spin a globe and let it come to a stop when we are looking at a hot, dry region of the world. One such area is the southern edge of the Sahara near Lake Chad in Africa. Let us look carefully at a community of herders who live on this flat desert. We shall see the close relationship between the cultural and the physical environments of the people in this community.

Our first look tells us that the dwellings are not permanent. They are tents. The tents are dark-colored and open on two or more sides. They protect the people from the hot sun. Openings in the tents allow air to move freely. The tents are light enough to be easily put up and taken down. These people frequently move from one place to another. We call people who regularly move from one place to another **nomads.**

Next we see the large number and the different kinds of animals. There are dogs, horses, donkeys, camels, sheep, and cattle. We do not see fields of grain or other crops. The nomads depend almost entirely upon their animals for food, clothing, and shelter. We say they have an animal economy. They get meat, cheese, butter, and milk from the animals. Rugs and clothing are made from animal wool. Animal skins supply leather which is made into shoes, riding gear, water bags, and tent coverings.

We also notice the dry appearance of the land about the community. In the dry climate in which these people live, water for drinking is very important and highly prized. In this land of little rainfall, streams do not flow all year round. Small ponds and hand-dug wells supply water when the streams are dry. The wells are often dug in dry stream beds. The use of water is carefully regulated. Water flows to each small garden through narrow ditches. When the supply gives out, the people are forced to move their tents and animals.

In this dry environment the heat of the sun's rays causes water in tubs, basins, or pails to evaporate quickly. The herders store drinking water in long-necked jugs and in bags made of animal skins. The jugs may be suspended from leather slings. Such jugs are easy to carry and allow little water to evaporate. Even when water vaporizes in the long, narrow-necked jugs or in the water skins, only a little of it passes into the open air.

Nomadic communities move often.

The nomads have no storehouses for food and supplies. They must be able to carry all their goods with them when they move. When the animals must be moved to a region with better resources of water and grass, the whole community, tents, household belongings, and people, must go along.

Since the nomadic herders move frequently, we do not see carefully marked lots or boundaries in their community. We do not see fences such as you may have around your home. In fact, fences are not wanted by the people of the communities in these dry regions. Do you see why?

The parts of the world where such nomadic peoples live may be seen on the map on page 42. The features

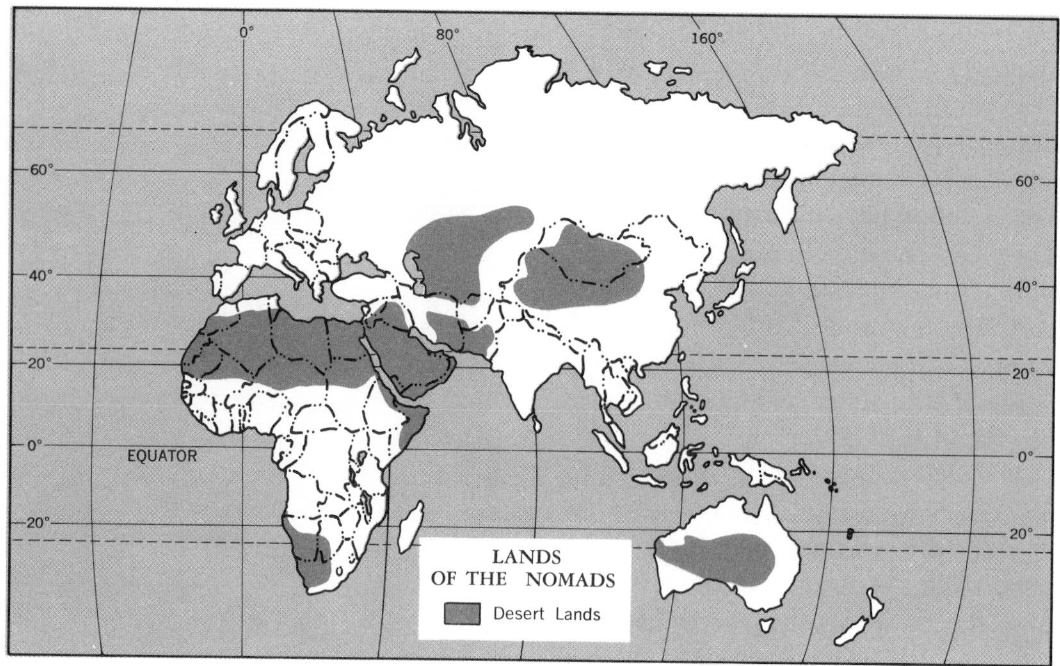

which characterize these regions are a dry climate, an animal economy, and small scattered communities of people who move about in search of water and feed for their herds. Do you see why the people in such regions of the world live this way?

A Farming Community

Let us select another community on the Earth. Turn the globe to northern Thailand in Southeast Asia. Here we have a community located on a gently sloping mountainside. There are very few animals in sight. The people are dressed in light clothing. Many of the men are bare from the waist up. What does this tell us about the climate?

The pattern of the farm plots is most interesting. As we look up the mountain, we see that the slope is checkered with small lots. Low ridges of earth separate the plots of farming ground. The tops of the ridges serve as footpaths by which farmers may walk from one farm plot to another.

When we ask about the ownership of these farm plots, we learn that they are owned by many different farmers. One farmer can own several lots, but they are scattered all over the mountain slope. If the average farmer were to have all his farm plots in one area, they would probably only amount to two or three acres.

The people who make up the farming community want boundary lines clearly marked. You remember that the nomadic herders of the Sahara wanted few, if any, boundaries. The two communities differ, then, in their need for clearly defined boundaries. However, the two communities are similar in their need for a fair distribution of water. The Thai community has much more water than the Sahara community. But because the Thai community is a permanent one and always uses the same source of water, it must also regulate the use of its water. The water must be carefully directed from one lot on the slope to another. The nomadic community's way of life is based upon animals; the Thai community's is based upon crops.

Rice paddies checker Eastern Asia.

An Urban Community

Let us spin the globe again and select an urban community in the eastern United States. How is this community similar to or different from those of the desert nomads or the crop-growers of the Thai mountain slope? Like the Thai community, nearly all of the land is blocked off into large and small lots. The major difference is that here houses, stores, and factories occupy most of the land. Large lots and tall buildings are owned by individuals or groups of individuals. People are able to point to their property and say, "This is mine."

Tall buildings occupy most of Boston.

Instead of growing crops or raising animals for food, the people of this urban community buy their food. They manufacture goods. For their work they are paid wages. With their wages they buy the food. It is brought into the city from the surrounding farm areas and from other parts of the country and the world. In the city animals are usually raised as pets. Plants are grown for pleasure, not because they are needed to feed the community.

Communities Have Different Languages

A cultural feature which makes a community different is its language. Languages have been developed to help people communicate their thoughts and ideas to others. By means of language, families pass on the cultural heritage of a community to the young. But language can also be a barrier to understanding others. So many different languages have been developed, that the people of one community may not be able to communicate with the people of another community except through an **interpreter.** An interpreter is a person who translates one language into another.

The boundary lines between nations not only show physical boundaries, but also often mark places where cultural changes in the spoken and written languages occur. In many of the nations on the European continent the people speak several languages.

Today a ferry makes it possible to cross from Dover in England to Calais in France. In crossing the Strait between the two nations a traveler has no language problems. The officials who check the people leaving England or entering France speak both English and French. In the major cities many Frenchmen speak both languages. But when a traveler decides to take a side trip to a village, he runs into difficulty. When he questions villagers in English about food, places to stay, or directions to other places, they cannot understand him. Looks of dismay, shakes of the head, shrugs of the shoulders, and open-handed gestures are all he gets. He has run into a real language barrier.

COMMUNITIES ARE ALIKE

We have seen some of the differences in communities throughout the world. Now let us see how they are alike. Let us examine ways of living which all communities have in common and which are necessary for their existence as communities.

Cooperation Is Important

When a community exists for a considerable length of time, the people in it tend to cooperate. An example of cooperation can be seen in the way a community handles the problem of its water supply. Let us look at an early settlement in our own country, and see how the settlers cooperated to supply water to all.

A small community of twenty families settled on a small plain. A fresh water stream flowed through the plain. The stream started in the mountains to the north. The people of the community did not take their water from the stream. Instead, each family dug its own well near home. A stone wall was built around the top of the well to prevent people from falling into the deep hole. The people had to lower an empty bucket down into the well. The bucket, attached to a rope, would fill up with water, and then be pulled to the surface. The people learned to use a roller to wind and unwind the rope. Later, pumps were used to get the water from a well.

For a time, this way of securing water worked well for each family. But soon, as more and more water was being used, the wells began to run dry. There were several reasons for this. There had been less rain. More crops were being watered. Also the growing number of people increased the demands for water. All families in the community faced the same water problem. What should be done to solve it?

The people hoped they would not have to carry water from the river to the town. A community meeting was held. Someone suggested going into the mountains and building a dam on the river to store water for the whole community. It was agreed that this was a good idea. The water behind the dam could then be carried through a system of pipes to the homes in the community.

This task was too big for one family to do alone. It could only be done if every family in the community cooperated. The regulation of the water flow had to be studied. The amount of water each family would receive had to be worked out carefully. Costs of building the dam and laying the pipes had to be met. Arrangements had to be made to collect

The public fountain in the square is still the main source of water in many communities around the world.

Whether in France or in Hong Kong, the policeman is the most obvious symbol of law and order in a community.

fees to pay for the maintenance of this water supply.

When you turn on a faucet to get a drink of water or to take a shower, you see the result of people's cooperation. The construction workers repairing city streets, men on trucks picking up rubbish, and policemen directing traffic are also results of cooperation among the people of your community.

Sometimes cooperation takes place among families living over a wide area of land. An example of such cooperation is the cattle roundup on our Great Plains. Ranchers who live far apart work together at round-up time. Cattle which have been grazing on the open range are herded together from miles around for branding and for shipping to market. Here the community's interest in raising and selling animals is strong and binds the people together.

Communities Have Standards and Rules

Every community has set up certain rules to protect the health of all and to promote the welfare of all. In Africa, forest dwellers either burn their refuse and waste or move away from them. Nomadic people move away from the waste that accumulates where they live. On the terraced slopes of Southeast Asia, people get drinking water from high up the slope. They throw waste water into lower streams that flow away from the village. City dwellers build sewer systems and sponsor "clean up" campaigns. They pay for rubbish collections.

Indians of the Iroquois nation also had rules and regulations about the use of water. A small stream flowing into the main river above an Indian village was used for drinking water and nothing else. As the water passed through the farming plots, each farmer used what he needed and then carefully directed the water to the farmer below. Swimming was permitted in the big river above the main camp. Washing of clothing was done on the riverbank right in front of the village. The refuse and waste from the camp were thrown downstream. By these regulations, care was taken to preserve and safeguard the health of this community.

Communities Need Law and Order

By having their marriage recorded, a couple meets some of the rules of their community. The methods of recording marriages differ from one community to another. In some communities a new design is added to a totem pole. In others, new threads are woven into a piece of cloth. In many communities a written account is entered in a set of books kept in a vault in a town or city hall.

Throughout their lives members of a community are acquainted with sources of authority. Authority may rest with a chieftain of a tribe as in parts of Africa. Authority may rest in a council of older persons as among some of the American Indians. Authority is sometimes placed with the oldest member of a family, as in parts of China. Authority may be turned over to officials elected by the people as in the community in which you live.

There are many kinds of **civil authorities.** The word *civil,* as used here, means "government." Civil authorities are those persons concerned with the government of a community. One kind of government official is the dictator whose word is law. A very different kind would be the official in a democracy elected by the people themselves. This official represents the people and is held responsible by them for his decisions. The form of government that a community sets up depends on its need for rules and regulations for keeping order.

Communities Need Codes of Conduct

In most communities there are written laws, but not all laws are written. Many are passed on by word of mouth in homes, schools, and churches. We often hear about **moral laws.** These have grown out of the **mores** of the people. Mores are unwritten laws of conduct and behavior which have been established in a community with the approval of the people.

Often the accepted ways of behaving toward one's fellow man come from religious teachings. People have always asked questions. "Where did I come from?" "Where am I going?" "What causes life?" "What happens after death?" People have sought answers to these questions in the teachings of the great religions. These religions have had a great effect upon human behavior and upon man's ways of living. For example, the sacred book of Islam, the Koran, contains teachings that are very exact about one's everyday behavior.

In all parts of the world man looks to a power beyond himself for order and control. In several of the culture regions studied later in this book, you will be introduced to other religious groups. You will see the role that religion plays in the lives of the people.

Communities Have Traditions

"But I've always done it this way." How many of us have heard this reply to a question we have raised about the way to bake a cake, sew on a button, plow a field, or clean a house? You have seen that each separate community, while doing many things the same way as its neighboring communities, may be quite different from other groups some distance away.

We read about some of the differences among a nomadic community in Africa, a Thai farming community, and an urban community in the United States. We saw that homes, ways of making a living, and dress may be different. We saw that communities form different kinds of government. All these different ways of living are called **traditions.** These traditions are the cultural heritages that through the years have proved to be "right" for the regions in which they have developed.

If these traditions are right for the regions in which they have developed, should we ever change any of them? One would have to turn to the past for an answer. Communities have undergone many changes in their ways of living before arriving at their present pattern of life.

All Communities Change

Some communities change very slowly and some quite rapidly. One might say that all communities have a force which works toward change. Even the communities that are seemingly unchanging to our eyes change over the years. They change so slowly and so gradually that the people within them do not always notice the changes. Other communities must learn to deal wisely with rapid changes. As changes take place, decisions must be made as to what is best for the community that is affected.

Change in man and his environment is continually taking place. Man does not live today like his ancestors lived. Yet, man's living today is influenced by the way his ancestors lived. To understand many of the customs and practices in families and communities today, we must understand the ways man has lived in the past. Man's cultural heritage has contributed to his present-day living. Social studies can help us understand present-day man by revealing the history of many of his customs.

Do You Know?

1. What are two ways of grouping people?

2. What is the meaning of the word *family*?

3. What is the most effective transmitter of culture? What is meant by this expression?

4. What are the basic needs of every man?

5. What are some of the cultural needs of every man?

6. What do we call the unwritten laws of conduct accepted by a community?

7. What is a nomad?

Learn By Doing

1. In this chapter communities were described on the Sahara, in Northern Thailand, and in Eastern United States. Tell which region is being described.

a. Dwellings are not permanent.

b. Water is carefully regulated because of the dry climate.

c. Many factories and stores line the streets.

d. The countryside is covered with many farm plots.

e. The entire community frequently moves.

f. Animals are important sources of food, clothing, and shelter.

g. Animals are raised as pets.

h. Water must be carefully regulated because the community depends on one source of water.

i. Boundary lines are clearly defined.

2. Communities are alike in many ways. Use your community to show examples of the following needs.

a. Cooperation is important.

b. Moral laws are necessary for order and control.

c. Traditions should be preserved.

d. Change is necessary and good in all communities.

Test Your Knowledge

1. The government of China has been trying to discourage the importance of family life. What changes do you think this will make in the lives of the Chinese?

2. Give two definitions of the word community. Do you live in a community? Are you part of a community?

3. Explain why family customs have an effect on the cultural life of the people of a region.

4. In what ways is community life similar to family life?

5. How does a wandering community differ from a stationary community? What are the basic needs of each group of people?

6. Can all people say, "This is mine?" If not, how are their lives affected?

7. How do languages divide people? How do they unite people?

8. Why is the work of an interpreter important in today's way of life?

9. What are traditions? Name some traditions that you think should be preserved.

10. Why do you think the democratic form of government has been the best for the United States?

11. Give some examples of cooperation which can be seen in your community.

12. What are some modern ways to protect the health of the people of a community?

13. What are some modern ways to promote the welfare of all people?

REVIEWING PART 1

A Special Project and Report

Study carefully the chart below before you begin the following project.

MAN IN A REGION
PHYSICAL IMPACTORS
CULTURAL IMPACTORS
MINERALS
ART
RELIGION
EDUCATION
COMMERCE
LAND USE
LAW, GOV'T.
SCIENCE
LANGUAGE
MAN THE FAMILY
SOILS
ANIMALS
VEGETATION
LANDFORMS
CLIMATE

Use your community or an important neighboring community to answer the following questions. Ask questions of people who can give you important information about the community. Use the library for research.

1. Define the word *community.*

a. What community have you selected?

b. Where is the community located?

c. What is the population of the community?

d. How large is the community?

e. Who are the people of your community? Are there large groups of people with a specific nationality or religion? Are there large numbers of men, women, or children? Are there large groups of students or large groups of elderly people?

f. What trends can be observed in the development of your community? Has the population increased or decreased greatly? Why?

2. What do we mean by the "physical elements" of a community?

a. What are the important features of the weather and climate of the region in which you live?

b. What are the important landforms of your region?

c. Describe the water system in your community.

d. Describe the soils of your community. Are they good for farming? Have fertilizers been added to improve the soils? Must special programs be planned to preserve the soils?

e. What types of vegetation are found in your community? Perhaps each student could select one element of vegetation for a special report.

f. What animals are found in your community? Are they mostly wild or domestic? How are the animals used? Have animals ever presented a problem?

g. Are minerals found within or near to the community? List the minerals and tell why they are important.

h. Have some physical elements influenced your community more than others?

3. What do we mean by the "cultural elements" of a community? What is meant by the word *tangible?*

a. How is the land of your community used? What parts of it are used for industry, for housing, and for entertainment?

b. What is the meaning of the word tenure? Do you know the exact boundaries of the property owned by your parents?

c. How have people helped to develop industry in your community through the use of science?

d. What elements of commerce, or trade, and transportation does your community have?

e. What visible items of communication are found in your community? Here you might describe the telephone system, post office, radio or television networks, and newspaper publications.

f. What role do buildings play in your community? Describe the physical appearance of your community. Is it old or new? Are the buildings tall? Are they placed close together? For what are they used?

4. What does the word *intangible* mean? There are many cultural elements that have been transmitted through the centuries. What does this mean?

a. Are there many different families in your community or are many of the families related?

b. How are the residents of the community cared for? Are the people of need given special care? Name some agencies which help the people of your community.

c. What is the major language of your community? Are other languages spoken?

d. What are the religions of the people of your community?

e. Describe in detail the government of your community. Who are the important leaders? List some laws by which your community is governed.

f. Describe the system of education in your community. Do most of the children attend public schools? Are there special schools? Are there colleges? In addition to schools, what means of education does the community have?

g. Are there museums in your community? Have you visited them? Is your community noted as the birthplace of a great writer, painter, musician, or scientist?

EARLY CULTURES HAVE AFFECTED OUR WAYS OF LIVING

PART 2

The culture man has today has been building up through the ages. One of the best ways to understand present-day cultures is to go back and look at some of the cultures of the past. We can see the beginning of many of the customs and practices that exist today by studying the cultures that existed thousands of years ago.

Two ancient and great civilizations were located in fertile river valleys. One of these early culture homes of man was in the Tigris-Euphrates Valley of modern Iraq. Another culture home of ancient peoples was in the Nile Valley of Egypt. Each year the rivers in these valleys overflowed their banks and flooded the land. In order to control and use the waters from the rivers, people living in these valleys had to unite and work together.

Later two great civilizations grew up on the northern shores of the Mediterranean Sea. They were the Greek and Roman civilizations. The heritage from the Greeks and Romans is intertwined in our lives today. For example, our present form of government owes much to the philosophy of the Greeks and Romans. Some of the old Roman roads and bridges are still in use in Europe.

We show our appreciation to the Greeks and Romans by drawing names for our space program from their myths. *Apollo* was one of the gods of the Greeks and Romans. The word *Gemini* comes from the Latin word for *twins*.

The period of time following the fall of the Roman Empire has been called the Middle Ages. The Middle Ages lasted for nearly a thousand years. It was a time when there was no strong central government like that of the Romans. In its place a feudal system of government gradually developed. The feudal system of kings, lords, knights, and serfs became widespread throughout Europe.

During the late Middle Ages, the Christian Church gave the people a purpose in life and did many things for them that the government had done before. In the twelfth century a series of wars was fought by Christian armies against Muslim armies over possession of the Holy Land. Soldiers who returned to Europe from these holy wars, or Crusades, brought back silk and cotton clothing, and sugar and spices. Merchants began to trade with people of the Near East for these goods. Trade between distant cities revived. Cities and towns began to grow in size. Cities took pride in building great cathedrals.

The period of time following the Middle Ages was a time of great change. Men began to rediscover the writings of ancient Greeks and Romans. They made new discoveries about the natural world around them. The New World was discovered and explored. Machines which gave men more power were invented. It was a period that marked the beginning of the Modern Age.

CHAPTER 4

ANCIENT CULTURES IN RIVER VALLEYS

What were early cultures like? Where were they located? Who gave us many of the things that are part of our culture today? Who invented writing? Who were the first law-makers? These questions are of interest to scholars who have wondered about the beginnings of our present-day civilizations. Scholars who study ancient people and civilizations have looked for answers to questions like these for a long time.

FOUR EARLY CIVILIZATIONS

Anthropologists and archaeologists have sought the answers to many of their questions about man's early cultures by digging in the remains of early civilizations. These scholars have discovered and uncovered four major culture homes. They have found that early homes of civilization were located:

1. *on the Hwang Ho (Yellow River) in China.*

2. *on the Indus River in West Pakistan.*

3. *on the Tigris and Euphrates Rivers in Iraq.*

4. *on the Nile River in the United Arab Republic (Egypt).*

The physical features of each of these four geographical sites seem to have been favorable for early permanent settlement. Each site had a regular, dependable supply of water and level land. We know little about the culture homes in China and West Pakistan because research has produced few findings. Archaeologists and anthropologists, however, have uncovered much information about the early civilizations in the Tigris-Euphrates and Nile River Valleys. We shall examine the physical features of these regions and read about the cultures that developed there.

The Tigris-Euphrates River Valley

The Tigris and Euphrates Rivers rise in high, rugged mountains to the north and northwest of present-day Iraq. The ancient name for Iraq was *Mesopotamia,* which means "land

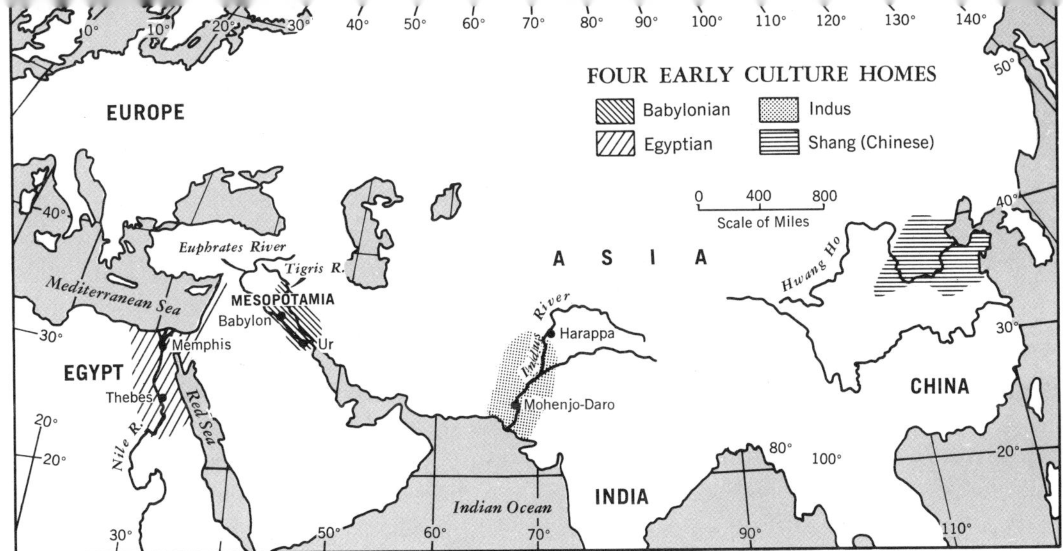

between the rivers." Locate this early riverine culture home on the map on page 57. In spring and early summer when snow melts in the mountains, the two rivers slowly fill, widen, and rise to flood stage. For thousands of years the rivers have flooded the land along their banks. As the flood waters move southward to the Persian Gulf, the **silt,** or loose soil, carried by the rivers is spread over the land. Through the years the rivers have built a vast flood plain of rich soil.

After the passing of the flood stage, lakes and snowfields that are high in the mountains continue to feed the rivers. Even in late summer and fall, water flows in the riverbeds. Before emptying into the Persian Gulf, the two rivers join and pass through a region of marshland.

The Tigris and Euphrates Rivers are **migrant streams.** This is a name given to rivers which begin outside of and flow through dry regions. Without these two rivers, the region of Mesopotamia would be almost completely dry. It has one of the world's driest climates. For example, the modern city of Bagdad has a yearly average rainfall of only six inches. Two inches fall during the summer growing season. The reason for this arid climate lies in the nature of the weather pattern in this part of the world.

In Chapter 2 you read about a huge low pressure center which forms over Asia in the summertime. Air flows toward this **low** from as far away as North Africa, another very dry area. The map on page 30 shows you the regions from which air flows into the summer low. As you can see, air that moves over North Africa and across the very dry Arabian Peninsula would not pick up moisture from the land. Thus, summer monsoon winds do not drop moisture in large quantities on the Tigris-Euphrates region.

In winter, the winds cross the Tigris-Euphrates River Valley from the opposite direction. You will remember from the map on page 30 that the winter monsoon brought cool, dry air to the people on the edges of the Asian continent. The

Mesopotamia region falls within this winter monsoon pattern. Thus the year-round climate is dry. Only the two rivers save this region from being completely arid.

Beginnings of Civilization

We do not know when animals were first trained or domesticated. Somehow man found that the keeping of domestic animals assured a supply of fresh meat and that cheese and butter could be made from milk. Man became a shepherd instead of a hunter. He drove his flocks from one grazing area to another. He could have only those possessions which he could carry with him. The size of his flocks and the number of people who could live off them were limited by the amount of available natural pastures. Early pastoral people probably lived together in small bands. A few families held together by blood ties would make up a band.

In early times the well-watered, fairly level land near the two great rivers served as a grazing ground for pastoral or shepherd people. Gradually these people discovered the art of agriculture. They settled in one spot and lived by farming as well as by raising animals. Not all of the people changed their way of life. Some pastoral people live in the "Land of the Two Rivers" today.

The Tigris-Euphrates River Valley was well suited to farming. Fertile soil, a warm climate, and a regular supply of water meant that two crops could be grown each year. The development of crude farm tools enabled man to cultivate larger fields. These factors, along with the grazing of domestic animals, made an abundance of food possible. The abundance of food enabled more people to live together. The communities which these people formed were the beginnings of a civilization.

THE SUMERIANS

The Sumerians were the earliest known group of people to settle in the "Land of the Two Rivers." They moved to the lower parts of the rivers between 5,000 and 6,000 years ago. They probably came from mountain lands to the northeast.

The Sumerians built canals to drain the swampy lands. These were also designed to prevent future flooding. Upstream, they diverted river water into irrigation ditches that carried the water into dry areas. Their systems of water control extended for hundreds of miles. The outline of their complex system of canals may be seen today from the air.

The drainage and irrigation systems of the Sumerians were not developed quickly or easily. It took many years to build the hundreds of miles of canals. Planning, building, maintaining, and protecting the canals required the work and cooperation of many people. Digging the ditches, carrying dirt from the ditches to fill

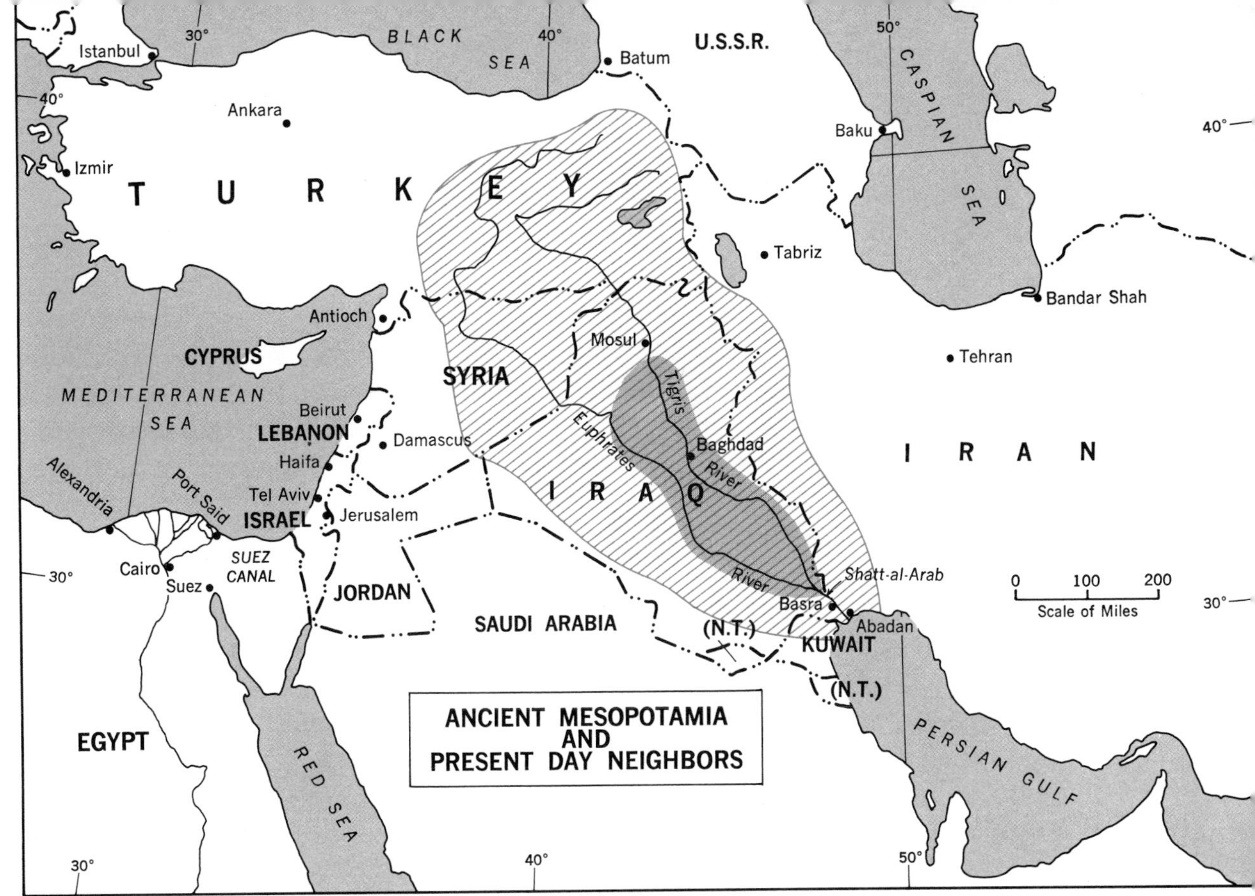

in the swampy fields, getting the fields ready for farming, and distributing the canal water fairly and regularly were difficult tasks. But without irrigation water the people could not grow the food they needed. Irrigation on a large scale was possible only through the cooperation of many people. The cooperation of the Sumerians, that resulted in changing swamps and desert into fertile land, was a remarkable step toward civilization.

The Growth of Cities

In time, several important Sumerian cities developed in favorable spots near the rivers. These cities were built in dry regions and on high ground in swampy areas. The permanent buildings of these cities were made of mud, the most common building material available. Mud was mixed with straw and made into bricks that were dried in the sun. But these sun-dried bricks would crumble and wash away when flood waters beat against them. Soon the Sumerians learned to bake the bricks with fire in order to make them moisture proof.

The Sumerians did remarkable things with bricks. Permanent temples and city walls were made from sun-dried bricks. The great mud walls protected a city from two enemies, the river during flood time and the nomadic invaders from neighboring areas. The baked bricks were used mainly to build the foundations of buildings. These sturdy foundations protected the buildings erected on them from floods. The baked bricks were also used on the outside of important buildings.

The Effects of a Surplus of Food

Fertile soil, good pastures for animals, and cooperative development of a system of drainage and irrigation canals resulted in more than enough food for all Sumerians. A surplus of food caused two remarkable things to happen. First, **specialization** developed because there was no longer a need for men and their families to devote all of their time to raising crops or tending their flock. It was possible for men to spend part of their time producing goods. Animal skins were no longer the only material used for clothing. The people learned how to weave cloth which was cooler and more comfortable in the hot climate of the river valleys. The Sumerians became famous for light woolen cloth. They also made pots and jars of clay for use in cooking. They learned how to use metal for many purposes. They put copper wheels on their wagons. They used metal tips on their spears and made helmets out of copper. They also made jewelry and figures of animals.

A few people became very skilled in weaving, in pottery making, and in metal working. Other people wanted the products they made. These skilled workers spent most of their time working at their trades. They did not have to farm. They traded their products for the food the farmers raised. In this way specialization began in the Sumerian communities. This means that men with skill in certain kinds of work would do only that work and not try to produce everything they needed.

The second result was that surplus food and cloth could be traded for the products not found in the Tigris-Euphrates River Valley. Grain, dates, woolen cloth, and leather goods were traded to other cities and regions for fine woods, precious stones, and metals, such as copper. These finer goods were wanted by the Sumerians.

Donkeys and boats were used to carry the heavy loads of goods both to and from other regions. Boats traveled along the hundreds of miles of irrigation canals. The large canals were used as the chief means of transportation by the people.

The exchange of goods between cities and peoples was an important result of surplus crops. But goods were not the only things carried by the traders. They also carried new ideas and new ways of doing things from one city to another.

The Gods of the Sumerians

The Sumerians had many gods and goddesses. Each Sumerian city worshiped its own god and had its own king. The Sumerians believed that each city belonged to a special god. They thought of him as having a human form and having human needs. He owned the city and the land. The people had to work to support the god. During the early Sumerian period, the king was the direct representative of the god and had great power over the people. As head priest, he pleaded with the god or gods for good crops. As ruler, he led his people into war against other cities, and directed farming, manufacturing, and trading.

The temple of the city god was the largest and most important building in each city. Rising from a huge dirt mound, the temple could be seen from all parts of the city and from the surrounding flat, marshy countryside. The shrine itself, the home of the god, rested upon the **ziggurat,** a four-sided, steep pyramid of bricks and earth. The Sumerians sometimes used this term, *ziggurat,* to refer to their temple.

Archaeologists have uncovered foundations and ruined sections of Sumerian temples. From these findings, they have gathered enough information to describe a temple as it was when it was first built. The shrine, or home of the city god, was at the top. Lower levels of the temple served as storehouses for wheat, barley, wool, and cloth. The lower rooms also served as offices for priests who made business deals and kept records of them. Near the base of the ziggurat stone cutters labored, smiths worked at their forges, and craftsmen wove cloth. The life of the community revolved around the temple.

The remains of a ziggurat-temple are in the ancient city of Ur in Iraq.

The priests acted as merchants and traders. They organized caravans to be sent to places that could supply materials not found in their country. They began to count or measure their wealth by the supply of precious items. Jewels, silver, and valuable or rare ornaments were measures of wealth. The priests made loans to the people of the city. They charged very high rates of interest. The Sumerians are known as the world's first bankers.

A Way of Writing Was Developed

Writing may have begun with the Sumerians and may have come about through their need to keep records. Such a need developed as the Sumerians began to have surplus food, to build systems of drainage and irrigation canals, and to trade with other peoples.

The Sumerians, unlike the early Egyptians and Chinese, did not use papyrus or ink pens. For writing materials they turned to the most common things in their environment, mud and the reeds which grew along the rivers. They wrote upon tablets of wet clay which formed lasting records when they were dried. The Sumerians found that wedge-shaped marks could be made easily by using the end of a reed. We call their way of writing, **cuneiform,** a word which means "wedge-shaped."

The earliest writing was a system of picture writing. A reed was used to draw a picture of an object on clay. If a record was to be made of the number of fish caught, pictures of fish would be drawn. This was a slow way to write. The Sumerians found ways to shortcut or abbreviate picture writing. The later markings did not look at all like the objects about which they were written. In order to write, the Sumerians had to learn over six hundred symbols that stood for objects, actions, and ideas.

The use of cuneiform writing stopped about two thousand years ago. The meaning of the cuneiform writing, found on clay tablets and rock carvings, troubled scholars during the eighteenth and nineteenth centuries. They could not read the messages. The clue to translating cuneiform writing proved to be an inscription on a cliff in present-day Iran. **Paleographers,** scientists who study ancient writings, found that the rock carvings were in three languages. They thought that each language described the same event. They reasoned that if they could translate one language, the others could be read. This proved to be true. The column written in Old Persian was translated first. Key words were used to help the scholars read the other two languages. One of these was written with cuneiform symbols. This translation helped scholars read other clay writings of the Sumerians.

The Sumerians Were Conquered

Sumerian cities were constantly forced to defend themselves from invaders. Sometimes one city quarreled with another city. The need of growing cities for more land may have caused the quarrels. The constant fighting between cities weakened the Sumerians. They were finally conquered by the Semites, a nomadic people, who moved southward into the "Land of the Two Rivers."

The Semites adopted most of the Sumerian culture, including their methods of agriculture, trading, working metal, business, and system of writing. Today we find it hard to tell just what parts of our "heritage of the past" come from the Sumerians and which from their conquerers, the Semites.

Of all the Semite cities, Babylon was the most famous. During the reign of the great king, Hammurabi, the Babylonians conquered many cities. In the Babylonian Empire, which is shown on the map on page 55, the government was no longer divided into many independent city-states as it had been with the Sumerians. Instead, the government became **centralized.** This means that all the cities were united under one strong government which gave all the orders. Hammurabi made all cities under his rule help pay the costs of running a central government by levying and collecting taxes in the form of wool or grain. The introduction of a centralized government was the first of two important cultural changes made by the Babylonians.

A second important cultural change, now a heritage of the past, was a set of laws known as the Code of Hammurabi. Hammurabi, regarded by the people as a ruler whom the gods had chosen, wanted to be fair and just. He drew up a set of laws and had them engraved upon hard stone. The written code made the laws of justice known to all.

Hammurabi's laws covered a great many matters. They provided regulations for land ownership, water distribution, marriage, and personal quarrels. They also included the punishments which were to be given to the guilty.

Some of the laws called for very cruel punishment. You may have heard the expression "an eye for an eye, a tooth for a tooth." Hammurabi's code actually followed this principle. If one man accidentally or purposefully put out the eye of another, his own eye was put out. If a son struck his father, the son's hand was cut off. The type of punishment was chosen to match the seriousness of the crime.

Thus far you have read about the beginning and early growth of civilization in the Tigris-Euphrates River Valley, one of four great culture homes of early times. Let us now turn westward to another great culture home, the Nile River Valley. Located in northeastern Africa, this culture home contributed greatly to the cultures of our modern world.

THE NILE FLOOD PLAIN OF EGYPT

Before studying in detail the early inhabitants of the Nile region, the ancient Egyptians, let us look at some of the physical features of this region. This early riverine culture region was located in the lower part of the Nile River Valley. It was called Egypt and is now a part of the United Arab Republic. Find this region on the map on page 63.

Very little rain falls in Egypt. The yearly average rainfall is under ten inches. Most of the rainfall is near the Mediterranean Sea. Slightly farther south, the city of Cairo has a yearly average rainfall of only one to two inches. Most of this falls in January. Still farther south in the Upper Nile Valley rain is even more scarce.

The Nile, like the Tigris and Euphrates Rivers, is a migrant river. Each year, until recently, it rose, overflowed its banks, and covered the land to the hills on either side. After the waters had returned to the river bed, a layer of fertile mud and silt remained on the land. These flooded flatlands, with their excellent soil for crops, were favorable for permanent settlements. The Egyptians depended solely on the Nile River to change the barren land into fertile soil for farming.

The Sources of the Nile

As you can see from the map on page 63, the sources of the Nile are in the wet tropical highlands of central Africa and Ethiopia. The Nile begins as two streams. One is called the White Nile and the other the Blue Nile. The White Nile flows from Lake Victoria in central Africa. One of the rivers that flows into Lake Victoria is the Kagera River, which is regarded as the true source of the Nile. The Blue Nile, the major tributary of the White Nile, contributes seventy per cent of the Nile's flood waters. It has its headwaters in the Abyssinian Highlands of Ethiopia.

The waters of the Blue Nile join those of the White Nile near Khartoum in the Sudan. The total length of the Nile from the head of the Kagera River to the Mediterranean Sea is 4,160 miles. It is the longest river in the world. It runs through dry lands for most of its length.

You will note that the waters of the Nile flow *northward.* The Nile flows *down* from the central African highlands *northward* to the Mediterranean Sea. Boatmen at Aswan on the Nile could say, "Let's go down *north* to Cairo." Can you locate these two cities? Between them is the main part of the Nile River Valley which was the culture home of ancient Egypt.

The Effects of the Climate

What are the features of the climate that cause the annual flooding of the Nile? From March 21 until September 21, the Northern Hemisphere is tipped more directly toward the sun than the Southern Hemisphere. At this time, vertical rays of the sun shine north of the equator. On June 21 the vertical rays of the sun fall on the parallel of $23\frac{1}{2}°$ North Latitude. This parallel, called the **Tropic of Cancer,** lies within the area of southern Egypt. As you recall, vertical rays of the sun provide more heat on the Earth than slanted rays. Great heat from the sun causes air near the Earth's surface to become warm and expand. The warm air rises and forms white, puffy clouds called **cumulus** clouds. The flat bases of these clouds are called the **level of condensation.** It represents the height at which the moisture in the air is condensed enough to appear as clouds.

As the heat increases and more water vapor condenses, the clouds accumulate, build upward, and are added to until they reach great heights. They appear to darken. At this stage they are called **cumulonimbus** clouds. When they have absorbed all the moisture they can hold, they have reached their **saturation point.** The rain pours down. The land underneath is soaked. Tiny rivulets run into streams; the streams flow into larger tributaries.

From March 21 to June 21, the vertical rays of the sun strike the Earth farther north each day. Heat accumulates and the rains increase. During this period, the rains are known as the "little rains." From June 21 to September 21 the vertical or direct rays of the sun progress each day back to the equator. This causes huge downpours known as the "big rains."

The increasing heat along with moisture-laden air from the Indian Ocean on the east and the Gulf of Guinea on the west cause torrential rains in the Abyssinian Highlands, the headwater areas of the Blue Nile.

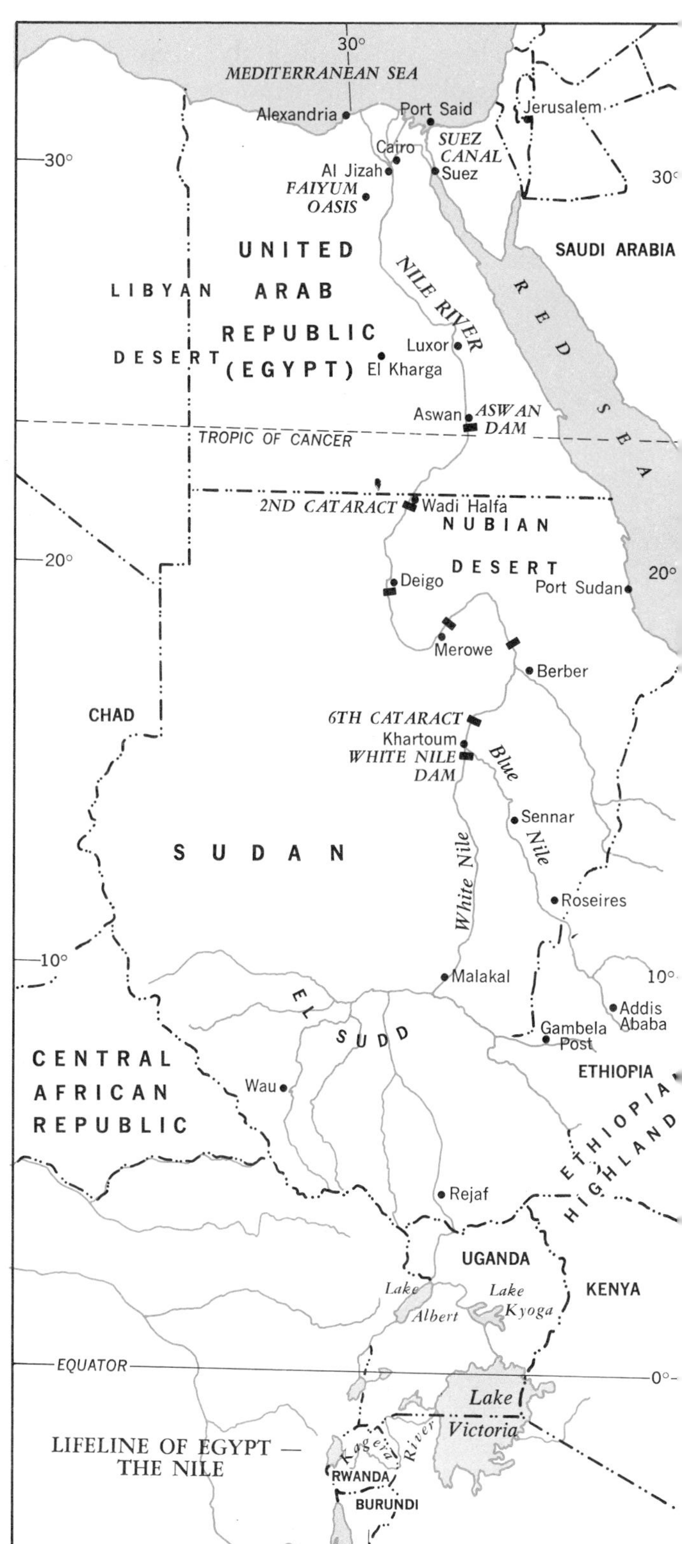

LIFELINE OF EGYPT — THE NILE

These rains cause the Blue Nile to swell. In late summer, as the flood waters from the Blue Nile flow northward, the waters of the Nile begin to rise. Water overflows the riverbanks and covers the flat valley lands between the ranges of barren, limestone hills on either side of the Nile Valley.

The White Nile loses tremendous amounts of water through evaporation as it finds passage through El Sudd, a huge swamp near its source. Nonetheless, the White Nile, fed by Lake Victoria, one of the world's largest lakes, provides a steady year-round source of water for the lower Nile.

In its descent to the Mediterranean Sea, the Nile tumbles over six **cataracts,** or waterfalls. The most northern cataract is at Aswan in Egypt. Today, at Aswan, a high dam has been built. Not only will the dam control the rise and fall of the Nile, but it will double electric power and store enough water to irrigate an additional 2,000,000 acres of land.

The Aswan Dam controls the Nile River.

We have seen how nature has provided a year-round source of water large enough to drive the Nile through the desert to the sea. We have also seen how the annual flood waters enrich the soil and make it possible to farm the dry land. Let us turn back to the time of the ancient Egyptians. They believed that the annual flooding of the Nile was caused by tears from the eyes of the goddess Isis. They believed she wept out of pity for the people of Egypt who had so little rain.

THE ANCIENT EGYPTIANS

We know more about the ancient Egyptian culture than about any other early culture home. There are several reasons for this. First, European scholars became interested in ancient Egypt at a time when the existence of the other early culture homes was unknown. Second, the Egyptians used stone and rock in addition to clay and mud bricks to construct buildings which have lasted through the centuries. The great pyramids were constructed with massive blocks of stone. The two great temples at Abu Simbel were cut out of a cliff near the Nile. Third, the climate is so arid that even the most delicate materials were preserved in tombs and in the desert sands.

The ancient Egyptians had the same favorable conditions for agriculture as the Sumerians. The climate was warm. The Nile supplied water and renewed the soil each year. These factors enabled the Egyptians to produce a great surplus of food. They produced such a great surplus that in later Roman times, Egypt was known as the "Granary of the Roman Empire."

Warm climate, fertile soil, and water do not in themselves insure the development of a civilization. Something more than a favorable physical environment is needed. This is human cooperation.

The ancient Egyptians united to build irrigation canals and to regulate the flow of water to their fields. They built dams to retain the flood waters. Mass labor was necessary for digging the canals and building the dams. By joining together to control the water for their fields, the Egyptians, like the Sumerians, were able to increase greatly the yield from their crops. The great quantity of food could feed specialized workers, potters, scribes, traders, and priests.

Scientific Gifts

The yearly flooding destroyed the boundary lines. After the flood waters receded, it was often difficult for one farmer to tell where his field ended and his neighbor's field began. The need for accuracy in drawing boundary lines led to the development of geometry as an aid in surveying and measuring land. The development of geometry also enabled the ancient Egyptians to plan the great pyramids, tombs, and temples.

The precise drawing of lots and the construction of the mighty pyramids were not guesswork. Skill and knowledge were necessary to estimate accurately the tremendous size, weight, and pressure of great blocks of stone piled one upon the other. The fact that some of the Egyptian buildings have stood for thousands of years is evidence of the skill of the ancient Egyptians.

The great pyramids of Egypt were built as tombs for the Pharoahs, or kings. Men have long wondered how the ancient Egyptians managed to get the great blocks of stone into place high up the sides of these buildings. The largest pyramid was 476 feet high and 764 feet on each side at the base. The stone blocks were quarried from the cliffs along the Nile River. The average weight of each stone was two and a half tons. How did the Egyptians lift these stones without heavy machinery?

Although no record has been found telling how the stones were put into place, scholars have put some information together. The pictures on page 66 show how they think that it was done. They believe that thousands of workers toiled for years to

The building of the pyramids is recreated in this scale model at the Boston Museum of Science. The model is so realistic that one forgets its tiny size until one sees a human hand next to it. Although worn and weathered by time, the pyramid of Cheops (also called Khufu) still stands after nearly five thousand years, together with the great Sphinx.

build each pyramid. They believe that each stone was dragged on rollers up sloping ramps of earth built around the sides of the pyramid. When the stone was pulled up to the right place, it was worked into position by levers. Timbers were laid along the ramps to reduce friction and make it easier to pull the heavy stones. When the pyramid was built up high enough, a stone called a capstone was placed on top. Then the workmen removed the ramps of earth.

The Egyptians also noted that certain positions of the stars coincided with the rise of the waters of the Nile. They kept records of the positions of the stars and of the heights of the flood waters each year. In this way they were able to forecast the time and the extent of the yearly flooding.

The Egyptians invented a calendar that divided the year into twelve months. Each month had thirty days, leaving five extra days at the end of the year. Our calendar is based upon this twelve month plan, but we have included the five extra days within our months, causing our months to differ in length.

Early Forms of Writing

About 3,000 B.C. writing appeared in Egypt. The earliest writing was in the form of **pictographs,** or pictures of things and actions. Later the Egyptians added written symbols for words, syllables, and sounds. Even after the development of letter symbols for most of the sounds in the Egyptian language, they continued to use pictographic writing. For three thousand years they continued to write with both pictographic and letter symbols. They would even write a word twice—once in pictographic form and once in letter symbols. Suppose you wrote the word *fish.* Wanting to be doubly sure that your reader understood what you wrote, you would also draw the picture of a fish above it. This system of writing was called **hieroglyphics.**

The ability to read hieroglyphics was lost for centuries. The discovery of the Rosetta Stone gave the clue to the deciphering of the Egyptian hieroglyphics. This stone was found during Napoleon's invasion of Egypt in A.D. 1799. It was discovered in the wall of an old Arab fort. One of the French soldiers noticed a stone with carvings on it that appeared to be in three languages.

The stone and its discovery attracted great interest. Napoleon had copies of the inscriptions made and sent to Europe. Scholars noted that one portion of the writing was in Greek. They translated it as an inscription commemorating Ptolemy V, a king of Egypt. The other writings were in two kinds of hieroglyphics. The translation of the Greek part of the stone enabled scholars to decipher the Egyptian portions of the inscription.

As you recall, the Sumerians wrote on damp clay. The material upon which the ancient Egyptians wrote was made from the **papyrus** plant, a reed that grew along the banks of the Nile. Our word "paper" comes from the Egyptian word *papyrus*. The Egyptians developed a process by which papyrus fibers were interwoven into a fine fabric on which they could use ink pens. The pens were fashioned from reeds which were sharpened to a point. Ink was made by mixing a vegetable gum with soot and water.

LIFE OF THE PEOPLE

The Egyptians were divided into four social classes. Royalty and the nobles were in the upper class. The class below this was made up of artisans, craftsmen, and merchants. The members of the third class were the unskilled workers. Slaves were in the lowest class. The Egyptians captured many slaves from the neighboring peoples. Slaves were used to do the difficult work in the construction of the great pyramids and buildings. They were used to row the ships or galleys. Sometimes they were used to fight in the wars.

The ancient Egyptians were dark-skinned with black hair. Usually they were short and slender. They were a family-loving people and had great love for children. Most of them were poor. They lived in simple houses made of sun-dried brick and mud. The houses, in the shape of squares or oblongs, were built around open courts. The floors were dirt, and the roofs were flat. An outside stairway led to the roof where the family often slept. There were few windows. Slits were cut high in the wall because larger windows would let in the hot, dry air.

The families lived very simply. They slept on mats thrown on the floor or the roof. They had stools, some boxes, and a few pottery jars and bowls. For food preparation they used a mortar in which grain was ground into flour and a stone slab in which dough was kneaded. Cooking was done in clay ovens or over open fires in the courtyards.

Bread, beer, fish, onions, and some other vegetables made up the regular diet of the common people. Many other foodstuffs were grown, however. In addition to grain, the Egyptians cultivated date-palms, pomegranates, figs, and grapes. They planted lettuce, beans and lentils, and gourds and melons. For meat they raised cattle, sheep, goats, pigs, geese, and ducks. Fish were caught in the Nile River.

The Wealthy Egyptians

The few wealthy Egyptians built large and beautiful houses of wood and brick. Windows were large and usually latticed. To keep the hot, dry winds out during the day, brightly colored drapes were hung over the windows. At night the drapes were drawn back to let the air circulate

Paintings on the walls of ancient tombs tell us much about the Egyptian way of life, their dress, and their writing.

through the house. These homes were furnished with beautiful rugs, ebony chests, and vessels of gold and copper.

Gardens and orchards usually surrounded the homes of the wealthy. Most gardens had a shallow pool. Lotus plants grew and bloomed here. The pool was also stocked with fish for the table of the wealthy noble.

The wealthy Egyptian nobles wore rich, beautiful clothing and decorated their bodies with fine jewelry. They wore long black wigs made of human hair or sheep's wool. These served as decoration, but they were also useful as a protection against the heat. The noble women blackened their eyebrows and used green paint to outline their eyes. They painted their lips red. They used henna to dye their fingernails orange or yellow. The Egyptian men and women wore elaborate head ornaments. The head ornaments signified the wearer's social class.

The Egyptians liked cats. Each family usually owned several. The cat was considered sacred. Therefore, the Egyptian family took very good care of their cats. Although many families also owned a greyhound, cats were more highly regarded.

The wheel was known to the Egyptians but they made little use of it for transportation. Chariots were only used by the nobility for hunting on the desert and by royal messengers. Travel by chariot was difficult in a land crisscrossed with canals and dikes. The nobility traveled primarily by boat or in litters.

Ways of Earning a Living

Most ancient Egyptians made their living by farming. Some were craftsmen who operated small shops. Others worked in mines or quarries. Some were traders.

The Egyptian farmer could grow two or three crops a year in the warm climate of the Nile Valley. Long-horned oxen were used to pull the plows. Wooden hoes were used to chop weeds. The farmer's work began each year as soon as the floodwaters of the Nile receded. He plowed and seeded the fertile fields and harvested his crops, until the waters began to rise again the next year.

Each village usually had a coppersmith, a potter, a weaver, and a jeweler. In the villages near the Nile there would usually be a shipbuilder. Boats were important to the Egyptians. They relied on water for transportation and trade.

Recovered Egyptian tools.

Egyptian ships sailed to many parts of the known world. They carried passengers and cargoes of copper, grain, linen cloth, papyrus, and precious stones. These they bartered or exchanged for wood, such as cedar and pine, and for gold, animal skins, ivory, and ostrich feathers.

Religion in the Ancient World

The Egyptians wondered about life and what happened after death. Great wealth and effort went into building and furnishing tombs for important people. The Egyptians believed that people who had led a good life would have another life in a place like Egypt. This place would be even more wonderful and enjoyable than Egypt had been. This meant that the bodies had to be preserved for this new life. The preserved body, which we call a **mummy,** was placed in a casket. In the case of royalty the casket was made of solid gold. Each casket was placed in a tomb. Tombs of the pharaohs blazed with gold. Gold was the leading precious metal found in Egypt. It was valued because it did not decay or rust and because its color was like that of the sun. Like the gods, it was eternal and did not die.

These tombs were filled with clothing, food, home furnishings, and jewelry. These were for use in the new world. The tombs were then

Pharoah Tut-ankh-Amon and his wife. The throne chair of gold and carved wood was found in 1922 in his tomb near Luxor, Egypt.

sealed. When archaeologists opened the tombs, they found that the articles had been preserved. Their study of these articles helps us to understand the lives of the ancient Egyptians.

The Egyptians believed in many gods. The names of at least 2,000 Egyptian gods have come down to us. The Egyptians did not have a single, unified religion. There were so many gods and so many beliefs that they became confusing even to the Egyptians. The fame of some of the gods rose and fell with the rise and fall of the city in which they were most popular. Ra was the god of the sun and was always shown in human form. Other gods were painted and sculptured in part human and part animal form. For example, Thoth, the inventor of language and writing, was usually shown as a man with the head of an **ibis,** a sacred bird. Osiris was ruler of the land of the dead. He was the judge of the dead who journeyed to his kingdom. His wife, Isis, later came to be worshiped throughout the Roman world.

The Egyptians Made Few Changes

This early Egyptian riverine culture lasted more than 2,500 years. Change was not valued by the Egyptians. The main inventions which form part of our own cultural heritage were introduced in the first 500 years of their known history.

The Egyptians left a rich cultural heritage. We can see in their past the beginnings of our mathematics, astronomy, architecture, written language, and calendar. They developed many ideas in both religion and medicine. They also left us a form of art which is so distinctive that it is easily recognized as Egyptian.

Do You Know?

1. What two groups of scientists have studied these culture homes? How do the studies of these scientists differ?

2. Where were the four major culture homes located? What important physical feature is found in each culture home?

3. Who were the first known inhabitants of the "Land of the Two Rivers?" By whom were they conquered?

4. In addition to goods, what was traded by the ancient peoples?

5. How did the writing materials of the Sumerians differ from those of the Egyptians?

6. What were the two important cultural contributions of the Babylonians? Explain each.

7. What is the ancient name and the present name for the region of the Tigris and Euphrates Rivers? Of the Nile River?

8. How did the Egyptians show that they believed in a life after death?

Learn By Doing

1. Tell whether each statement is true or false. Correct the boldface words in each of the false statements.

a. The Nile, **like** the Tigris-Euphrates, is a migrant river.

b. Flooded flatlands are **favorable** for permanent settlement.

c. The White Nile contributes **more** flood waters than the Blue Nile.

d. The Nile, **like** the Tigris-Euphrates, flows north.

e. The Upper Nile Valley has **more** rainfall than the Lower Nile Valley.

f. Lake Victoria is regarded as the true source of the Nile River.

g. From March 21 to September 21, the Northern Hemisphere is tipped more directly toward the sun than the Southern Hemisphere.

h. On June 21 the vertical rays of the sun shine directly on the **Tropic of Capricorn.**

i. From June 21 to September 21, the direct rays of the sun cause the **"big rains"** as they progress from the Tropic of Cancer to the equator.

j. Increasing heat causes moisture-laden clouds to reach their **saturation point** and pour down heavy rains.

k. Dams built at **cataracts** on the Nile will help to control the flooding of the Nile.

2. Tell which culture, the Sumerian, the Semite (Babylonian), or the Egyptian, was responsible for each feature or contribution listed below. Select two contributions and explain the effect they have on our culture today.

bankers	clay tablets
papyrus	geometry
ink pens	a ziggurat
pets	"makeup"
Babylon	hieroglyphics
calendar	baked brick

cuneiform writing
life after death
centralization
Code of Hammurabi
specialization
irrigation canals

3. Use the maps in this chapter to answer these questions:

a. In what country are the sources of the Tigris and Euphrates Rivers? Through what countries does each river flow?

b. Into what body of water do these two rivers flow? To what larger body of water does this connect?

c. Compare the combined length of the Tigris and Euphrates Rivers with the length of the Nile. Which is longer?

d. Does the Nile River or the combined Tigris-Euphrates Rivers have the most tributaries?

e. What river is formed when the Tigris and Euphrates Rivers meet? What is the nearest city?

f. What is the capital city of Iraq? Where is it located?

g. Compare the delta of the Tigris and Euphrates Rivers with the delta of the Nile. Which covers the largest area?

h. Locate the Lower Nile Valley. Are you close to or far from the Mediterranean Sea?

i. Note how the Nile River splits into distributaries north of Al Jizah. What term is given to a land area with such a river pattern? What type of soils would be found in this area?

j. Where are the sources of the Nile located? What lake is the source of the White Nile? The Blue Nile?

k. Where do the waters of the Blue Nile join those of the White Nile? In what country is this junction located?

l. In which direction do you travel when you go *down* the Nile River from Khartoum to Alexandria? By airplane, about how many miles would you travel?

m. Locate the Aswan Dam. In what country is the dam located? How many miles is Aswan from Cairo?

n. Note that the area around the Aswan Dam was the ancient culture home of the Egyptians. The waters of the Nile can now be controlled. What effect do you think the dam has had on the lives of the people in the region?

o. How many cataracts, or rapids, are located between Cairo and the White Nile Dam? What city is located at the White Nile Dam?

Test Your Knowledge

1. What do we mean when we say that the Nile and the Tigris-Euphrates Rivers are migrant streams? How is the word migrant related to the words migrate, emigrant, and immigrant?

2. What is meant by pastoral people? Explain how pastoral life developed.

3. What were the three conditions which made a surplus of food possible for the Sumerians? What were two results of a surplus of food? Explain your answer.

4. How does cuneiform writing differ from hieroglyphics? What is a pictograph?

5. What do we mean when we say that the areas of the Nile and the Tigris-Euphrates are riverine culture regions?

6. Give three reasons why we know more about ancient Egypt than any other culture home.

7. Cooperation is important in all communities. In what ways did both the Sumerians and the Egyptians show that they were willing to work together to develop their civilizations?

8. What products did the Egyptian ships carry to other ports? What types of cargo did they carry back?

9. How do we know that neither the Sumerians nor the Egyptians had a single, unified religion?

10. All communities change. Is this true of the Egyptian culture home? Explain.

CHAPTER 5

CULTURAL GIFTS OF THE ANCIENT GREEKS

Almost every part of our present culture reflects in some way the ancient cultures which developed around the Mediterranean Sea. The Egyptians gave us the calendar, the beginnings of mathematics, and a very distinctive form of art. Our religious heritage, including the concept of one God, came from the Hebrews. The Phoenecians were the world's first traders and explorers. Their alphabet became the basis of all Western alphabets. The great civilizations of the Greeks and the Romans also contributed much to our cultural heritage.

TWO GREAT CIVILIZATIONS

The Greek and Roman civilizations of long ago influenced our art, architecture, government, science, agriculture, and commerce. The Greeks and the Romans gave us great ideas about the living-together problems faced by many peoples. Of equal importance are the ideas of their great thinkers. The Greeks and the Romans thought a great deal about how each person should be regarded and treated. They gave us important ideas on man's existence, his attitudes toward life, his health, and his laws. The influence of the cultures of the ancient Greeks and Romans on the thinking and on the development of present civilization is wider than any other ancient culture. Let us turn first to the Greeks.

GREEK LANDS

The Balkan Peninsula extends from southeastern Europe into the eastern part of the Mediterranean Sea. At the southern end of the mountainous peninsula lies Greece. The map on page 91 shows you that the peninsula in this region has many prongs of land, or smaller peninsulas, jutting into the sea. Hundreds of islands are sprinkled in the sea not far from the mainland's jagged coastline. The land surface is rugged. Numerous small valleys are separated by mountain ridges and hills. The land itself is **eroded,** or worn away, in many places. It is estimated that only one-fourth of present-day Greece is **arable**—that is, capable of being cultivated. On this rugged land and along the jagged coastline, the Greek civilization flourished.

The expression, "Where Nature had done little, man did much," certainly applied to the early Greeks. There was much rocky ground which was unproductive. The thin layer of top soil had been removed by erosion in many places. Rains that fell or snows that melted were quickly soaked up by porous limestone or ran off the deforested slopes.

Nature, however, was not as severe as we might expect from the above description. The ancient Greeks were well satisfied with their land. The climate was bracing, but warm enough so that light clothing could be worn most of the year. The climate was and is something like that of Southern California. It has a pattern of winter rain and summer drought. Cereal crops must be planted in the fall and harvested in late spring or early summer.

The land was rich in marble and minerals. There were great quantities of marble in many beautiful shades. Marble is strong, long lasting, and easily worked. It was in great demand for buildings, statues, and reliefs.

Sources of Food

The staple foods of the people of ancient Greece came from grain. Wheat was made into bread. Barley flour mixed with water became porridge.

The long, dry summers provided an ideal growing climate for olives, figs, and pomegranates. The olive tree was widely planted. It served many purposes. The fruit was eaten. Oil pressed from the fruit was used as we use butter today. Olive oil was burned in lamps. It was also used as a body lotion.

The ancient Greeks used honey instead of sugar for sweetening. Tree crops, grain, and fish were the major sources of food. Fish were caught in the waters along the irregular, indented coast.

The Greeks began very early to look seaward for food. They obtained food not only from the sea, but also from trade with other cities, especially those in Asia Minor. The many gulfs offered calm, protected sailing waters and safe harbors.

Early sailors seldom went far from land. They had no compass and did not sail at night. Each evening the sailing vessel was drawn up on the beach. There the crew cooked its evening meal and spent the night. The many islands that dotted the Aegean Sea offered safe places for the night. The early Greeks soon established colonies on the nearby islands of the Aegean Sea and in Asia Minor. The Greek World, before it

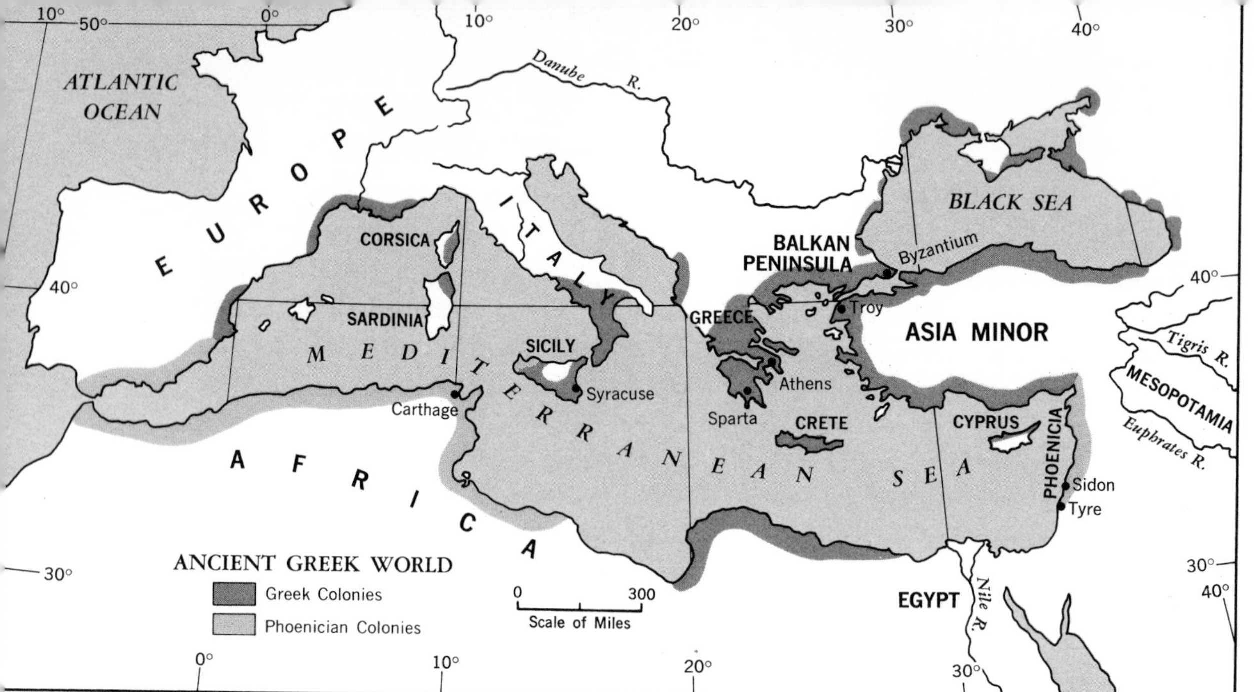

ended, had spread out over much of the Mediterranean. Notice on the map above that all of the colonies are located near the seas.

A SCATTERED NATION

Unlike the riverine cultures, the early Greek settlements were quite scattered. Travel across the rocky, mountainous landscape from one village to another was not easy. There was no river "highway" to touch and join together the whole of Greece as the Nile did in Egypt. Also, there was no need for the people to join together to control flood waters and build large canals.

Why did many **city-states** develop in Greece instead of one large nation? The answer may lie partly in the way these small city-states began. They developed in valleys that were separated from one another by the rugged landscape. Roads were very difficult to build through the rocky land. The people in one valley were isolated from the peoples in other valleys. They learned to cooperate with the people in their own valley, but not with the peoples in other valleys.

In the beginning the inhabitants of each valley came to regard themselves as a single, separate group or tribe. Each tribe was made up of several clans. These clans were family groups held together by strong blood ties. They traded goods and ideas with each other. They worshiped together and joined to resist outsiders. Their towns and cities were built around an **acropolis,** a fortification placed on a high spot overlooking the valley. The most famous hilltop fort is the Acropolis of Athens.

Each city-state watched to make sure that other cities did not become too powerful and take away its independence. As a result, none of the early city-states ever grew to a great size, either in population or in area. Ancient Greece never became united into one large nation, but the city-states of Greece did join together to resist the Persian invaders.

The small size of these early city-states had one great advantage. Each citizen was expected to perform the duties as well as enjoy the rights of citizenship. It should be remembered that citizenship was not limited to just those people who lived in the city. Citizens lived in the villages and on the farms surrounding each city.

The city-states had likenesses and differences. The major differences were in ways of living. These differences can be seen in the city-states of Sparta and Athens.

Sparta and Athens are located in southern Greece. Neither city is very far from the Sea. Athens, which is closer to the waters of the Mediterranean, has an outer port called Piraeus. Sparta is situated inland in the valley of the Eurotas River. This river empties into the Gulf of Laconia. These cities were the two largest and most powerful of the Greek city-states. The citizens of each city-state contributed in their own way to the greatness of ancient Greece.

Sparta

The population of Sparta was divided into three classes. A very small number were **Spartans,** or members of the ruling class. The **perioeci** were members of the middle class and carried on trade and manufacturing. The lowest class, the **helots,** were serfs or slaves who worked the land. They were owned by the state.

The helots were often unhappy in their slavery. They frequently revolted. The Spartans always had to be prepared to fight a war against rebellious helots. To retain their power over the helots, the rulers of the Spartans declared war on them once a year. During this time Spartan men could legally murder any helot thought to be dangerous to the state.

The Spartans, the ruling class of Sparta, were soldier citizens. The main task of the adult Spartan was to be a soldier. As a result, the education of the Spartan youths was almost entirely military in nature.

Both boys and girls learned body skills early in life in order to become strong and hardy. They ran, wrestled, and were taught to handle weapons. They learned to endure hardships as preparation for war. They sometimes endured severe whippings — just to prove they could "take it."

The Spartan emphasis upon physical fitness began with the birth of a child. In all other countries at that time, the father had the right to decide whether or not a baby should live. However, the Spartans took a newborn infant to the elders because the child belonged to the state. If the elders decided that an infant was weak or ill-shaped, the infant was abandoned in a chasm at the foot of Mount Taygetus.

At the age of seven, a Spartan boy was taken from the care of his mother. He lived with a company of 15 other boys and ate all his meals in a public dining hall. The bravest boy was made captain of his company.

After the age of twelve, boys were allowed to have but one garment to wear, a cloak. This had to last them for a year. They slept on **rushes,** or strawlike plants, which they gathered on the riverbank. They were not allowed to use a knife to cut the rushes. They had to break them off with their hands.

The Spartans were famous throughout Greece for loyalty to their laws. They were admired for their courage and willingness to lead this harsh life, but they were not imitated. The Spartans were afraid of new ideas. They were afraid of ideas that might upset their way of life. In order to keep their way of life unchanged, they discouraged trade with other cities. Strangers were not welcome to their city.

The Spartans dropped from their lives ways of living that might weaken them as soldiers. Gold and silver money were abolished. The only currency used was made of iron. They did not encourage the arts. They disapproved of painting, sculpture, and architecture. They allowed only choral speech and music. They learned only a limited amount of reading and writing.

Athens

Athenian boys, in contrast, were prepared for farming, business, the arts, and athletics. Nonetheless, the Athenians considered themselves just as well prepared and educated to defend and fight for Athens as the Spartans were for Sparta. The Athenians thought that the best preparation for war and citizenship was a general education. They wanted a citizen who was prepared to vote as well as to fight. A man had to be well educated to carry out his civic duty. He was expected to take part in choruses, both dramatic and musical, which were part of the festivals.

Not all people living in Athens were citizens. However, unlike Sparta, slaves made up only a small part of the population. Slaves were treated far better in Athens than they were in Sparta. Many slaves were able to buy their freedom.

The Athenian citizen lived simply. He was not afraid to use his hands, either for farming or for building. A citizen might even work alongside a slave, each receiving the same wage. The Athenian wanted a business or farm that was large enough to support himself and his family but which would also allow him to participate in the activities of the city. He wished to have time to prepare for festivals and to engage in civic re-

The famous Temple of Apollo, site of the oracle at Delphi, lies in ruins at the foot of the rugged Mount Parnassus.

sponsibilities. He wanted time to talk and argue with others in the market place about the purpose of life.

Solon, The Shaper of Democracy

At one time, in Athens, the small farmers and free laborers had a very hard life. Money was scarce. Farmers borrowed money on their farms at high rates of interest. Land holdings of a few rich men grew larger and larger as more and more small farmers lost their farms. Free laborers had no land to pledge in borrowing money. They had to forfeit their freedom if they could not repay a loan. Many became slaves.

The Athenians knew that these happenings might lead to serious trouble. They asked Solon to become the city's chief magistrate. Solon was a very rich merchant, who had traveled widely. He had learned much in his travels about the ways other people lived and was very popular with all the Athenians. He was elected chief magistrate so that he could help settle the troubles.

Neither the very rich nor the very poor were completely satisfied with the laws Solon passed. He made several **compromises.** This means that persons on each side of the dispute got something, but also had to give something. He passed a law that no Athenian was to be made a slave because of debt. All citizens who had been enslaved for debt were freed.

Some people wanted Solon to take land from the rich and divide it among the poor. Rather than this, he passed a law which limited the size of land holdings that one man could own. Under his laws, the borrower could no longer lose his citizenship if unable to pay a debt. Solon's laws wisely prevented serious trouble in Athens.

The reforms for which Solon is most famous were in another area. He made the Athenian ruling bodies, the Assembly and the Council, more democratic by opening membership in them to a wider range of people. He also passed a law that made it possible for any citizen, rich or poor, to become a member of the **Heliaea.** This was the court of justice to which a person could appeal a decision of the chief magistrate. It was also the court which tried rulers who had been accused of misconduct. This change meant that a ruler could be held responsible for his actions by all the people.

Members of the Heliaea were selected by lot from all the people. Thus, a Greek citizen who felt he had not been treated fairly could appeal to an impartial court made up of his fellow men. The democratic makeup of the Heliaea was the key to democracy which Solon gave to the Athenians. It was a gift to later governments that were based on the principle of **democracy,** or government by the people.

Throughout dangers and successes, Athenian ideas and ideals of democracy were kept alive and strengthened in practice. Many years after Solon's laws were introduced, a law was passed giving pay to men who served in the popular courts. This meant that poor men, along with rich men, could afford to give time and thought to participation in the government. Previously the poor, although permitted to serve, had been kept from serving by the necessity of earning a living.

THE PERSIAN INVASIONS

The Greeks valued their freedom above all else. Twice they were called upon to defend their freedom against a conquering people from the east, the Persians.

The Greek city-states in Asia Minor were conquered by the Persian warriors. Later, several of these Greek city-states in Asia Minor revolted against the Persians. They sent for help from some of the free city-states in Greece. Sparta refused to help the Asian Greeks throw off the Persian rule. Athens, however, sent help in the form of 20 ships. The Athenians and their allies burned the Persian city of Sardis, and retreated to the coast of Asia Minor. There, near Ephesus, they were defeated in battle by the Persians. The Athenians promptly returned home.

The Battle of Marathon in 490 B.C.

Darius, the Persian emperor, decided to punish Athens for burning Sardis and for daring to make war on him. He ordered the Persian army

to sail into the Bay of Marathon and land on the Greek mainland. The Athenians sent an urgent call for help to Sparta. The Spartans said they would help. But before they could arrive, the Athenians met the Persians on the Plain of Marathon. Ten thousand Athenians met three times their number. The Athenians won the battle at Marathon and halted, for a time, the Persian invasion of Greece.

The Athenians had shown the other Greek city-states that it was possible to withstand the mighty Persian Empire. They also set an example of a people who valued their freedom so greatly that they were willing to fight for it against impossible odds.

The Brave Defense at Thermopylae

Ten years after the Battle of Marathon, Darius's son, Xerxes, sat upon the Persian throne. Drawing upon all the resources of his mighty empire, he gathered a huge army with which to crush the small Greek city-states. Aware of the preparations of Xerxes, Athens and Sparta joined their military forces to withstand the coming danger. They called a meeting of all the Greek city-states to plan how they could best meet the invasion.

Xerxes and his army came by land and by sea. Foot soldiers crossed from Asia into Europe at Hellespont, a strait now called the Dardanelles.

They crossed the strait by means of a bridge of ships placed side by side. The Persian troops moved westward around the northern shores of the Aegean Sea. City by city, Greece was being overrun. The city-states of southern Greece decided to meet the Persians at Thermopylae. There the road to Athens ran between the sea and the swamps on one side and a steep cliff on the other. They sent an army under the command of the Spartan king, Leonidas, to meet Xerxes.

The Greek army withstood Xerxes' warriors well and held the pass. A Greek traitor told Xerxes of another mountain pass. Xerxes sent a secret force through this other pass in order to surprise the Greek army from behind. Deserters from the Persian army told Leonidas of Xerxes' plan for a surprise attack. Thereupon the main body of the Greek army fled to the south. Only a small group of soldiers, under the command of Leonidas, remained to defend the pass at Thermopylae. The defenders of Thermopylae fought bravely, but were overwhelmed by the mighty Persian army that attacked from both sides. The fame of the brave Greek warriors who stood and fought in the face of certain death has lasted to this day. An inscription to the Spartan dead was placed at Thermopylae. It read:

"Go, Stranger, to Sparta and tell
That here, obeying her command, we fell."

The Naval Battle of Salamis

The victorious Xerxes turned his army toward Athens. The Persian army easily entered Athens. Only a small band of soldiers remained to guard the Acropolis. After a short siege, the defenders were overcome. The buildings on the Acropolis were burned by the Persians.

The Athenians and their allies decided to make a stand with their fleet in the Bay of Salamis. The Greek fleet was under the command of Themistocles. His warship captains coaxed the Persian fleet to enter the small water passage between the island of Salamis and the mainland near Athens.

Xerxes sat on a high hill overlooking the sea. He sat there to watch his navy defeat the Greeks. Instead, he saw his own fleet defeated. What was left of Xerxes' crippled fleet returned to Asia. The Athenian victory at Salamis is one of the most famous in history.

The naval victory at Salamis, along with an army victory at Plataea, ended the Persian attempt to conquer Greece. These victories left the Greek city-states free to continue with their experiments in democracy and ideas. Athens was free to enter upon her "Golden Age."

THE GOLDEN AGE OF ATHENS

After the Persian Wars, Athens became the leading city-state of Greece.

Other city-states paid tribute to Athens to maintain a navy for their protection. Both warships and trading vessels were built. Trade with other city-states and with Italy, Sicily, and Asia Minor grew rapidly. The potters of Athens sent their black and red figured vases, dishes, and drinking bowls to Italy. Athens also exported wine and olive oil. Trading vessels returned to Athens with grain, copper, linen, and papyrus. Athens became the trading center of the Western World.

Joyful in their victory over the Persians, the Athenians, under the rule of Pericles, rebuilt the burned temples and the Acropolis. They wanted to build in a form that would reflect the greatness of the victory and do honor to the gods. They built a marble temple on the Acropolis in honor of Athena, the special goddess of Athens. Called the Parthenon, it was finished in 438 B.C. It has had a long history as a place of worship. It became a Christian church and later a Muslim mosque. Still beautiful, the ruined, time-worn temple overlooks Athens today. The Parthenon, shown on this page, represents the best example of Greek architecture.

The daily life of the Athenians was simple. While public buildings and monuments, such as the Parthenon, were made of marble and built with great care for proportion and beauty, private homes were plainly constructed and simply furnished. Rich and poor people alike wore simple garments. All walked barefoot or

wore sandals. A typical meal might have consisted of barley bread, onions, olives, and dried fish. Few men sought great wealth. They liked to have time to go to the **Agora,** the market place. Even if they did not plan to buy that day, they went to the market place. Conversation was a delight to the Athenian citizen. The Athenians regarded their way of living as the best in the world.

Greek Drama

Each year in March, the people of Athens gathered together to watch the best plays written during the year. The dramatic competition was part of the yearly festival in honor of the god Dionysus. A committee selected the best tragedies and comedies from the many submitted. Prizes were given to the winning plays.

The Theater of Dionysus at Athens.

Each of the authors of these plays was sponsored by a rich man who paid for the cost of presenting the play. The rich man also trained the chorus for the play. The chorus sang, danced, chanted, and spoke throughout the play. The committee assigned a few of the best actors in Athens to each of the plays. The rich man whose play won a prize was allowed to build a monument to his victory. One of these victory monuments is the monument of Lysicrates.

The plays given at the festival of Dionysus were performed in out-of-door theaters. These theaters, often placed on a hillside, were lined with stone seats. A drawing of the Theater of Dionysus at Athens is shown on this page. Notice that some of the words that label parts of the theater are familiar. The part labeled *orchestra* shows where the chorus performed.

Of the hundreds of plays written and acted in theaters such as this, only a few have survived. The major ones are *Antigone, Agamemnon,* and *Cyclops.* These three stand unmatched in greatness. They are one of our most precious heritages from the Greeks.

The Olympic Games

An important festival for all Greeks was the athletic contests at Olympia. They were held every four years in honor of the god Zeus. People from all over the Greek World came to the games at Olympia. The festival lasted for five days.

The first day began with sacrifices to the gods. Only athletes of Greek blood were allowed to compete. Each athlete vowed before the altar of Zeus that he would compete fairly.

On the second day, the four-horse chariot race was held. The chariot race was followed by the **pentathlon.** This event was made up of five parts. The word *pentathlon* comes from two

Greek words, *pente* meaning "five" and *athlon* meaning "exercise" or "skill." Wrestling, the javelin throw, the discus throw, the long jump, and foot races were the five **exercises,** or games of skill, included in the pentathlon.

On the morning of the third day, oxen were sacrificed to Zeus. In the afternoon, boys competed in wrestling, running, and boxing. The fourth day opened with foot races. These were followed in the afternoon by wrestling, boxing, and the **pancratium.** The pancratium was a mixture of boxing and wrestling.

On the final day of the Olympic festival the winners made their vows to Zeus. Winners of each event were crowned with wreathes of wild olive that came from a sacred grove at Olympia. A great banquet at the close of the fifth day ended the festival.

The period during which the Olympic Games were held was sacred. No city could make war during this period. Travelers to the games could pass through all of Greece unharmed.

The Olympic festival brought together athletes and visitors from all over the Greek World. The competitive spirit which existed among the athletes instilled a feeling of racial unity among the Greeks. It also served as a center for the exchange of ideas in the Greek World.

The festival at Olympia served as a model upon which the idea of our modern Olympic Games is based. The modern Olympics begin with a

An ancient rite opens the Olympics.

ceremony in which a flame is lit with a torch carried from the site of the ancient festival. We have added skiing, ice skating, and other events which were unknown to the early Greeks. We have dropped the brutal pancratium but have added the **decathlon,** a ten-event contest. In the ancient Olympics, the winner of the pentathlon was the all-round champion. Today, the world's greatest all-round athlete is the man who wins the decathlon.

An event held today, the **marathon,** was not a part of the ancient games. It is an endurance race, 26 miles and 385 yards in length. It was introduced into the modern games to commemorate a famous runner, Pheidippides. He ran 22 miles to Athens from the battlefield of Marathon to announce the victory of the Greeks over the Persians. Upon arriving in Athens he is supposed to have cried, "Rejoice! Victory is ours!" He then fell to the ground – dead.

GREEK THINKERS

A most significant contribution of Athens was the idea of individual freedom of thought and action. The citizens of Athens introduced something new to the world. They introduced a type of thinking in which there was a willingness to hear all points of view. Some men taught that "man should be free." They taught that man should be free to think as his intelligence and conscience led him to think. They insisted that man should not be told what to think by his ruler or by others. To be told what to think was a kind of slavery—a slavery of the mind. They argued that man would never know his rightful place in Nature if his mind was enslaved. This was a startling idea more than two thousand years ago. It is an idea still not fully realized.

Enslavement of body or mind could also prevent men from being able to reason out the answers to questions. "Why does this happen?" "What are the reasons for it?" These questions were in the minds of men in many of the Greek cities. For the first time in history, men had both the intellectual freedom and the leisure time in which to think about the answers.

Thales

Thales was a citizen of the Greek city of Miletus in Asia Minor. He visited Egypt where he learned geometry and astronomy from Egyptian priests. The Egyptians had learned simple geometry and astronomy through experience. They had not learned the reasons for the facts in these areas. They had not been curious enough to ask, "Why does this happen?"

Returning to Miletus, Thales used his ideas to prove several of the theorems which are taught in high school geometry classes today. He forecast an eclipse of the sun and amazed his fellow Greeks. The eclipse occurred on May 28, 585 B.C.

Thales recognized that change is everywhere. He tried to find some evidence of order or regularity in the changes. He sought the causes of the changes in nature rather than in stories of the gods. Thales thought that all things—men, stars, water, and trees—came from one substance and that, in the end, all things would change back to this one substance.

In looking to nature rather than to the gods for the answers to questions, Thales made the first step toward science and philosophy. This step marked one of the greatest changes in human thinking in the history of the world.

Socrates

The spirit of questioning that swept through the Greek World was well represented in the philosopher, Socrates. The ideas that Socrates taught are so much a part of our lives today that it is hard to realize they had a beginning so long ago.

Socrates believed that everyone should think for himself. Socrates was a lover of wisdom, a seeker of knowledge. He liked new ideas. He wanted all people to have the right to express new ideas, even though some people might not like the ideas.

Socrates was one of the greatest moral teachers who ever lived. He believed that knowledge is the greatest virtue and ignorance the greatest vice. He proposed that each man could find the truth through a "question and answer method" directed to himself. Socrates believed that any statement made by a person should not be "swallowed" without question. He taught that a statement should be thoroughly examined before it is accepted. By this criticism, the false part would be cut out. What was left would be true. Today we call the conversational method of questioning and answering as a means of teaching the truth, the "Socratic Method."

Some men in Athens did not agree with what Socrates was saying. They accused him of harming the thinking of the young and of introducing new gods into Athens. He was brought before the court of justice. This court was called the Council of Five Hundred and was made up of citizens who enforced the laws of Athens. As was the custom, the accused spoke in his own defense. By a narrow margin, the court voted him guilty of the charges. He was condemned to die.

His sons and followers tried to persuade him to escape. He reminded them that it was his obligation as a citizen to follow the laws of the city, no matter how unjust they might be. As his friends wept, he calmly drank a cup of hemlock poison. He then walked and chatted with his companions until he began to feel his limbs grow cold. Thereupon he lay down, covered his face with a cloth, and died.

The great Socrates, although an inspiring conversationalist and an able speaker, never set his thoughts down in writing. Most of what we know about Socrates comes from the books written by his greatest pupil, Plato. Plato's most famous work was called *The Republic.*

Plato

Like Socrates, Plato was a moral teacher. By this we mean he was concerned with helping people learn the right behavior. He spent most of his life teaching in the **Academy,** a school which he founded. He constantly urged human beings not only to know what is "good," but also to do "good." He said that man's mind is capable of creating a spiritual ideal of what man ought to be. Man should then try to achieve the ideal. Plato's thoughts and writings stress the ideal, or the highest good. Because of this, he is called an **idealist.** As an idealist, he believed that thoughts and ideas were more important than things.

Aristotle

Of all the students Plato taught, Aristotle stands out as the greatest. Aristotle was the master of logic, the founder of a "school of reason." He always wanted to know the "why" of everything. He studied and wrote much about languages, politics, science, and logic. He was an authority on many topics and fields of thought. Today, we still study many of his works.

The Importance of the Greeks

The cultural gifts of the Greeks to the world lay in their ways of living. The Greeks gave us the idea of democracy, the idea of the value of the individual, and the idea of the nature of man. They taught us to revere the right of man to have freedom of mind and behavior. Greek ideas of morals, ethics, and the good life brought a greater measure of dignity and worth to mankind.

Do You Know?

1. How and why did the settlements in Greece differ from the riverine culture regions?

2. What famous fortification protected the Greek settlements?

3. What group of people was the greatest threat to the freedom of the Greeks? How did the people of the city-states show that they valued freedom?

4. What is a compromise? Who made several changes in Athenian laws?

5. What city-state became the leading trading center of Greece? With whom did the people trade?

6. What goods were exported? What goods were imported?

7. What was the Agora? What two purposes did it serve?

8. To what did the word "orchestra" refer in ancient Greece? What are two present-day meanings of the word?

9. What idea, developed by the Greeks, is the basis of our democratic way of life?

10. What two fields of study were advanced by looking to nature for the answers to questions?

Learn By Doing

1. Tell whether the statements below describe the ways of living in the city-state of Athens or Sparta.

a. An all-round education was encouraged.

b. A child belonged to the state.

c. A citizen was prepared to vote as well as to fight.

d. Education was based on military training.

e. Physical fitness and body skills were emphasized.

f. Slaves made up a small part of the population and were often able to buy their freedom.

g. The men enjoyed conversation in the market place.

h. The father had the right to decide upon the fate of his child.

i. Painting, sculpture, and architecture were encouraged.

j. The population was divided into a ruling class, a middle class, and a lower class of slaves.

k. From the age of seven the male child led a harsh life and was loyal to the laws.

l. Iron was used for currency.

2. Using an encyclopedia, a dictionary, or a library book, identify the following:

Homer	lyre	Hippocrates
Doric	Sappho	Sophocles
Euclid	Herodotus	Phidias

3. Study the map on page 81 before you answer the following questions:

a. Why was it easy for the Persians to conquer the Greek colonies in Asia Minor?

b. Where was Darius defeated by the Athenians?

c. Where did Xerxes' army cross from Asia to Europe?

d. Where did Xerxes defeat the Athenians?

e. Where did the Greeks defeat the Persians?

f. At a later date Alexander the Great of Macedonia conquered the Greeks. Why was it easier for him than it was for the Persians?

Test Your Knowledge

1. Where is Greece located? Describe the land surface of this area. What advantages do the people have who live on the end of a peninsula?

2. What natural conditions made the Greeks satisfied with their location? How has the climate of the region influenced the way of life of the people?

3. Why did city-states develop in Greece instead of one nation? What are the advantages and disadvantages of a "broken" country?

4. Compare the amount and the treatment of the Spartan slaves to the slaves of Athens.

5. What was the Heliaea? How did it contribute to the development of democratic governments?

6. What is the best example of Greek architecture? Where is it located? In whose honor was it built? With what resource was it built? What is its main feature?

7. What was the major purpose of the festival of Dionysus? What is a patron of the arts?

8. The Greeks made many contributions to the development of sports.

a. In whose honor was the festival at Olympia held?

b. What is a Pentathlon, a Decathlon, and a Marathon?

c. The festival at Olympia is the basis for what modern event?

d. How does this event still serve as a center for the exchange of ideas?

9. What was the major contribution of Thales, of Socrates, of Plato, and of Aristotle?

10. Briefly explain the importance of these people and places to the history of Greece.

Asia Minor	Leonidas	Darius
Persians	Ephesus	Xerxes
Athenians	Sardis	Plataea

CHAPTER 6

CONTRIBUTIONS OF THE EARLY ROMANS

The brave and daring Roman soldiers conquered most of the known world. They built an empire which included the barbarians of northern Europe, the cultured Greeks, and people east and south of the Mediterranean Sea. The wise Roman governors held the great empire together in peace.

Rome became the great cultural center of the world. Into it poured people with different customs and languages. Into it came the varied products from the many conquered lands. Life in Rome was greatly enriched by these people and their customs, ideas, and products. From Rome these ideas and products were spread to all parts of the empire and, later, the world.

THE ITALIAN PENINSULA

Westward from Greece, across the Adriatic Sea, lies the boot-shaped Italian peninsula. On the map on page 91 notice that the Alps form a mountain barrier in the far north of Italy. Just south of the Alps is the very fertile, well-watered Po Valley. This flood plain is the only large plain in Italy. Today it is the leading agricultural and manufacturing region of Italy. It was also the leading agricultural region of Italy in the days of the Roman Empire. It was then and is now the center of the heaviest population. If you look on the map at the Po Valley region, you will see the names of the modern cities of Venice, Milan, Turin, Parma, Verona, Modena, and Bologna. Have you ever seen the words *Parma* or *Bologna* on items in a supermarket?

Starting in the Po River Valley, the Apennine Mountains extend through central Italy to Sicily in the south. This north-south chain of mountains is called the "backbone" of Italy. The Apennine chain of mountains is the most important landform feature of the Italian peninsula. At many places along the west coast of the peninsula,

the mountain ridges of the Apennine chain come close to the sea. The Apennines shelter some fine, warm, well-watered valleys. These valleys are very small, however, compared to the Po River Valley. The most important of these is the Tiber River Valley. This valley is the setting for the city of Rome. It is here that the ancient Roman civilization developed.

South of Rome lies the city of Naples. From Naples you have one of the world's grandest views. Here you can see the wide sweep of the Bay of Naples and the offshore Isle of Capri. Shown on page 92, the smoking cone-shaped volcano, Mt. Vesuvius, overlooks the Bay of Naples.

At the toe of the "boot" is the island of Sicily. On the eastern end of Sicily is Mount Etna. This great volcano rises over 10,000 feet and dominates the eastern end of the island. Like the Italian peninsula, Sicily is hilly and rugged. Travel between the cities of Sicily is almost easier by boat than by roads over the rugged land.

The climate of the Italian peninsula, south of the Po Valley, and of Sicily is very much like that of Greece. The winters are mild and rainy. The summers are hot, dry, and sunny. There are two plants, the olive tree and the grapevine, which do well in this type of climate. Their root systems and leaves are well adapted to a climate without summer rain. They were two of the staple foods of the ancient Romans.

THE EARLY HISTORY OF ROME

The history of Rome is a long one. Rome lasted as a ruling power for more than 1,000 years. Long before the Golden Age of Greece, several

Sleeping but active, Mt. Vesuvius overlooks the scenic Bay of Naples.

small villages grew up along the lower Tiber River. The villages were located on the top of small, steep hills near the river. The people banded together in these hilltop villages for protection against raiders from cities to the north and raiding herdsmen from the mountains. The small villages they founded on the hills near the Tiber River later became the city of Rome. In time Rome became the center of a mighty empire that stretched from the north of England to the Caspian Sea and the Persian Gulf. The following story is an interesting tale which later Romans invented about the founding of their city.

The Story of Romulus and Remus

In the town of Alba Longa lived a king named Numitor. Numitor was driven from his throne by his brother Amulius, who made himself king. Amulius wanted to be sure that none of Numitor's descendants would seek the throne. For this reason he killed Numitor's sons. He forced Numitor's only daughter Rhea Silvia to become a priestess. As a priestess, she was forbidden to marry. But the god Mars fell in love with Rhea Silvia, and she bore him twin sons, Romulus and Remus. Amulius ordered that the twin boys be drowned and Rhea Silvia be buried alive.

The twin boys were placed in a basket which was set in the river. Instead of sinking, the basket was carried downstream by the river waters. It came to rest in some rushes on the riverbank. A she-wolf heard the cries of the two infants. She carried them back to her den. There she cared for them.

Later a shepherd found the twins and took them home to his wife. The boys grew to manhood in the home of the shepherd. Numitor heard the shepherd describe how he had found the twin boys in the she-wolf's den. He recognized them as his grandsons. When Romulus and Remus learned of their true origin, they killed Amulius and restored their grandfather, Numitor, to the throne.

Romulus and Remus were determined to build their own city. With their grandfather's permission, they decided to build this city near the spot where the she-wolf had rescued them. Romulus thought that the new city should be built on the Palatine Hill. Remus thought it should be built on the Aventine Hill. They decided to let the gods settle the dispute. Each would stand one day from dawn to dusk on the hill of his choice and look for an omen from the gods.

At sunrise Remus saw a flight of six vultures. The news of his sighting was carried to Romulus. Romulus waited all day for a sign. None came. Finally, just before sunset he saw twelve vultures fly over the Palatine Hill. Remus claimed to have the only true omen. The brothers quarrelled. Their followers decided the argument in favor of Romulus.

The next day Romulus marked the boundary of his new city by plowing a deep furrow around the site. As Romulus and his men began to build a wall along the boundary line, the disappointed Remus made fun of the wall. To show how ineffective the new wall would be against invaders, he jumped over the few stones that had been laid. In anger over the scornful leap of Remus, Romulus struck his brother dead. He was immediately sorry. When the city was built, he placed an empty throne beside his own throne to show that Remus ruled Rome along with him. The city that was built within the boundary walls was named after Romulus.

ROMAN WAYS OF LIVING

In this chapter you will read about the Roman people and their ways of living. When we speak of the early Romans, we will be talking about Rome in the days when she was a republic. When we speak of the Roman Empire, we will be talking about Rome in the time of the emperors. This is the period when she ruled a large part of the known world.

The people of early Rome were farmers. The owners worked on their small farms side by side with their help. They cultivated their crops by hand. These early inhabitants of Rome had no work animals.

The three main crops of the Romans were olives, grapes, and wheat. Olive oil was as useful to the ancient Romans as it was to the ancient Greeks. It was used as we use butter today. Olive oil was also used in lamps. It was the main source for lighting. After bathing, people rubbed their bodies with olive oil. Grapes were eaten fresh or in the form of raisins. The juice of the grape was drunk fresh or in the form of wine. When wine was drunk, it was always mixed with water. Watered wine was a common drink. The Romans thought that plain water from wells, streams, and rivers was polluted and would make one sick.

The third main source of food for the ancient Romans came from winter wheat. Wheat was used in two ways. It was often pounded in a mortar and then mixed with water. In this form it was much like modern porridge. Wheat was also ground into flour and mixed with water, salt, and yeast. It was then kneaded, shaped, and baked into loaves of bread.

Clothing

In early Rome the most common garment was a **tunic** which reached just below the knee. The sleeves of the tunic were very short. The tunic was slipped on over the head. Tunics were made from natural white wool. A belt was tied around the waist. It was made from leather or woven from straw or reeds. Tunics were worn in the home and at work.

For more formal occasions a **toga** was worn over the tunic. The toga was the most characteristic Roman dress. You can see it on many of the ancient Roman statues. The toga was a heavy piece of white woolen cloth. It was draped around the body carefully so that it would fall in graceful folds. The deep folds of cloth that crossed the chest were used as pockets for small articles.

The toga was worn in the law courts, at public games, at religious ceremonies, and at marriages. Only Roman citizens could wear the toga. The toga could be made very white by treating it with chalk. This type of toga was called **toga candida.** It was worn by men running for public office. They wore the shining white toga to attract attention. These men were called **candidati** after the toga candida. Can you see how our word "candidate" came from the Roman word *candidati?*

Shelter

The very earliest Roman houses were small round huts made from twigs and reeds, and plastered together with mud. The roofs were thatched. For a long time, a hut like this stood on the Palatine Hill. It was kept in good repair, for it was thought to be the hut of Romulus.

In the days of the Republic, the rectangular-shaped house came into being. This one-room house in which all members of the farming family lived was called the **atrium.** Household activities such as cooking, weaving, eating, and sleeping took place in this one-room house. The walls were made of stone or sun-dried brick. A hole in the center of the roof was an important part of the house. It took the place of a chimney. Smoke from the fireplace escaped through the hole. There were no windows in the early Roman house. Natural light came into the interior through the hole in the roof. The Romans had a pool in the floor beneath the hole to catch rainwater. The roof was often slanted toward the roof opening so that rainwater would collect in the pool below the opening. This water was used for cooking and for drinking.

Later, in the days of the Roman Empire, Roman houses became

The atrium was the center of elaborate Roman homes. A central pool and family relics were used as decoration. Receiving a toga was an important event in a Roman boy's life.

elaborate with many more rooms. Nevertheless, the basic design of the one-room house remained a part of every temple and every many-roomed house. The name of the one-room house, the atrium, was kept for this room with the opening in the roof.

Family Life

In the Roman family the father was head of the household. When a child was born, it was placed before him. If the father wished, he could sell his child into slavery. He showed that he accepted the child by lifting it in his arms. The father owned the land, the slaves, the house and its furnishings, and his wife and children. A son who married remained a member of his father's household. A daughter, upon marriage, became a member of her husband's household.

The members of a family were very close and devoted to one another. Parents loved their children. The children loved and respected their parents. A mother's love has been shown in the story about Cornelia. Cornelia listened quietly to a woman who was boasting about the great quantity and beauty of the jewelry she wore. Then, the proud Roman mother placed her arms about her two sturdy sons and said, "These are my jewels."

Both parents taught their children to be obedient, but the father controlled and disciplined them. In learning to be obedient to their parents, the young were prepared to be loyal and obedient to the laws and government of Rome. The Roman pattern of strong family love and unity became the basis for the strong Roman Republic. In the home children learned patriotism, respect for authority, and reverence for religion.

Until the age of seven, boys and girls were taught in the home. Both parents taught their children manners, religion, and truthfulness. Children were told of the great deeds of their forefathers. The mother taught the children to read, write, and do simple arithmetic. Girls remained at home and learned the duties of a housewife. They were taught how to spin, weave, and sew.

Boys over seven were taught by teachers in schools. When not in school, boys learned the duties of a citizen from their fathers. They went with him to the law courts and to religious ceremonies. Fathers prepared their sons for the life of a soldier by teaching them boxing, wrestling, riding, and the use of weapons. If the family lived on a farm, boys helped their fathers plow, plant, and harvest.

Roman boys were given an education that prepared them to be excellent soldiers. They were taught at home to obey and respect authority. Stories of famous ancestors and their deeds developed pride in the family and in Rome.

Roman soldiers were accustomed to following orders. They received little pay. They lived on grain and vegetables and little or no meat. They looked forward to capturing a town to share in its plunder. In battle they tried to surpass the brave deeds of their ancestors. They were soldiers in the best army of their time and conquered country after country. Roman soldiers were encouraged to settle in these conquered countries.

CUSTOMS OF THE ROMANS

The earliest Romans had only one name. Later it became the custom to give a boy three names. The first name was his "given" name. The second was the name of the clan of which his family was a member. The third was his family name. The last two names were inherited. Let us look at the name of a famous Roman, Caius Julius Caesar. Caius is his given name. It is like your first name. The second name, Julius, tells us that he belongs to the Julian clan. This is a group of families that have common blood ties. They trace their ancestry back to one man whose name was Julius. Caesar was his family name.

Parents had only about eighteen boys' names from which they could choose. Girls were commonly given a feminine form of these names. Three Roman boys' names were Cornelius, Claudius, and Julius. Three Roman girls' names were Cornelia, Claudia, and Julia. Perhaps you know someone with one of these Roman first names.

Roman Feasts

At formal dinners, couches were placed around a table. The host and his guests lay on the couches. Slaves removed their sandals. Wives sat upright on the edge of a couch. Children sat on stools. The Romans did not use forks or knives for eating. They ate with their hands. They used spoons only for food that could not be lifted by the hand.

The slaves served a formal dinner in three parts. For the appetizer, guests could select from sliced eggs, onions, oysters, and pickled fish. For the main course, pork, duck, and lamb might have been served with several vegetables.

The number of different vegetables sold in the Roman market was almost as large as the number we can buy today. A Roman could select from celery, cucumbers, squash, lettuce, cabbage, beans, and peas. For dessert, the third course, fruit, nuts, and pastry might have been served. The following foods were unknown to the Romans: coffee, tea, butter, cocoa, tomatoes, potatoes, oranges, and sugar.

The simplest meal of the day was breakfast. It consisted of dry bread that was sometimes dipped in wine or sprinkled with salt. Olives, cheese, or raisins could also be eaten with the bread.

Wedding Traditions

After an engagement and before a marriage, the woman was given a gift of an iron ring. This ring was worn on the third finger of her left hand. It was placed on this finger because the Romans thought that a nerve in this finger ran straight to the heart. Have you ever noticed where married women wear their wedding rings today?

The month of June, named after Juno the goddess of marriage and motherhood, was chosen as a time for many marriages. Because of the many religious festivals in early June, the latter part of the month was more popular.

A wedding feast was held at the house of the bride's father after the marriage ceremony. Each guest received a piece of the wedding cake. The guests accompanied the new wife and husband as they walked through the streets to the house of the husband. In this procession the bride carried a torch made from a white thorn plant. The groom scattered nuts to the crowds of people who watched. This custom, although somewhat changed, is still with us. If you have tossed rice at a newly married couple, you have carried on an old Roman wedding custom.

When the wedding party reached the house, the husband carefully lifted his bride over the threshold. This was done to avoid the bad omen of having the bride slip the first time she entered the house. Inside her new home, the bride lit a fire on the hearth with the white thorn torch. Afterwards she tossed the white thorn torch to the guests. Each guest hoped to be the lucky one to catch it. Do you know of a similar custom practiced today?

Funeral Processions

Another custom of the Romans was the elaborate funeral. Funeral ceremonies for important Romans were very impressive sights. The funeral procession to the tomb was headed by a band of musicians. Next came a group of singers. The singers were followed by actors who wore wax masks and the dress of the dead man's ancestors. Then came the coffin carried on a high **bier.** A bier is a frame on which a coffin is placed. If the deceased had been a soldier, he was surrounded by the weapons and trophies of the enemies he had fought. The bier was followed by members of the family, relatives, friends, and freedmen, or former slaves.

If the dead man was of great importance, the funeral procession paused in the Roman **Forum** on the way to the tomb. The Forum was the center of the city containing government buildings and meeting places. The bier was placed in the Forum before the **rostrum.** The rostrum was a platform for public speaking. The men representing the dead man's famous ancestors sat on chairs around the bier. Crowds gathered to hear a son or relative give a funeral oration in honor of the deceased. The orator told the history of the great man's family. He also spoke of his virtues and deeds.

From the Forum the funeral procession went to the place of burial. There the grave, or tomb, was made sacred by the sacrifice of a pig. Tombs of wealthy Romans were very elaborate. Monuments to the dead lined the roads leading from Rome. Some of these tombs may be seen today.

SKILLS OF THE ROMANS

A network of Roman highways linked all parts of the empire to Rome. These roads were one of the Romans' finest engineering achievements. They were wide, smooth, and solidly built. Because these roads were made strong and watertight, some are still in existence.

The roads of the Romans served three purposes. They helped soldiers move quickly to the frontier to protect the vast empire. Supplies could be transported to the troops more easily. They also helped trade and the exchange of ideas increase among the people.

The great network of Roman roads led to the expression "All roads lead to Rome." Today we use this phrase when we want to say that there are many different ways to reach the same goal.

The engineering skill of the Romans showed itself in other ways. At least eleven great **aqueducts** carried 300 million gallons of water daily into the city of Rome. For a long time after the fall of the Roman Empire, these aqueducts were not used. Four of the aqueducts have been repaired and are used to supply water to Rome today. The earliest aqueducts were made entirely of fitted stone. Later they were made of stone, bricks, and cement. The Roman or Latin word for "water" is *aqua.* The Latin word *duco* means "I lead." Can you give the exact meaning of *aqueduct?*

The Use of the Arch

The Romans were also famous for their skill in building arched bridges. One of the most beautiful and impressive Roman bridges was built at Alcantara in Spain. The bridge is still in use and carries four lanes of traffic. It was built out of fitted granite blocks. The bridge is about 630 feet in length. It stands 170 feet above the riverbed.

Roman builders introduced the use of concrete. They made cement, the binding mixture in concrete, out of lime and volcanic ash. The use of concrete, "rock that can be poured," meant that buildings could be built more quickly than before. Can you explain why?

The Egyptians and Greeks had used only the beam to connect columns and walls. The distance that could be spanned by a **lintel,** or beam, was fairly short. If the distance was too great, a granite or marble beam would collapse from its own weight. The use of the arch allowed the Romans to span a much greater space.

One of the most famous buildings still standing in Rome is the Pantheon. The cement arch was used in making the roof of the Temple of the Gods. The 20-foot walls and the great 142-foot-wide dome were built out of concrete.

The bridge in Alcantara, the Pantheon in Rome, and an ancient road in Antioch are examples of Roman engineering skills which are in existence today.

Roman amphitheater at Arles, France.

The Amphitheater

Another type of building was the **amphitheater.** It was a round theater in which Roman games were held. The central part of the amphitheater was the **arena.** The word *arena* meant "sandy place." Sand covered the floor of the arena and was used to soak up and to cover up blood. The sports held in the amphitheater were very popular.

The most famous Roman amphitheater was the Colosseum. More than half of the Colosseum still stands. The Colosseum was built out of concrete and stone, and was faced with marble. It received its name from a huge 120-foot statue, or colossus, of the Emperor Nero which stood near the amphitheater.

Roman Games

Men who fought in the amphitheater were known as **gladiators.** Most of the men who became gladiators were forced to do so. Many were Christians who were sentenced to death because of their religious beliefs. Some were war prisoners; others were criminals who had been condemned to death. Still others were slaves who had tried to escape and had been caught. A few gladiators were professional fighters who chose to lead this dangerous life.

Gladiators fought with swords, spears, or daggers. Some wore armor and some fought without it. Some gladiators used nets to throw over their opponent. When an opponent became caught or entangled in the net, he was stabbed with a dagger.

Gladiators fought in pairs, in small groups, and sometimes in small armies. Often when two gladiators fought a duel, each used different weapons. A man who fought with net and dagger might be pitted against a man who fought with sword and shield. If an opponent was badly wounded, the victor turned to the audience for a sign as to whether the loser should live or die. The onlookers turned thumbs down if they wished the victor to kill his opponent. They turned their thumbs up or waved handkerchiefs if they wished the defeated man to live.

The Romans staged fights between elephants and tigers. Sometimes men were forced to fight lions. Animals were starved before the games. If the men were not able to kill the lions, they would be torn apart by the hungry animals. The Roman games continued until the Christian religion became influential enough to stop them.

GODS AND GODDESSES

The Roman Name		The Greek Name
Jupiter	King of the Gods	Zeus
Neptune	God of the Sea	Poseidon
Apollo	God of the Sun and Youth	Apollo
Mercury	Messenger of the Gods	Hermes
Mars	God of War	Ares
Cupid	God of Love	Eros
Juno	Queen of the Gods	Hera
Ceres	Goddess of Agriculture	Demeter
Vesta	Goddess of the Home	Hestia
Minerva	Goddess of Wisdom	Athena
Venus	Goddess of Love and Beauty	Aphrodite

ROMAN RELIGION

One of the factors that united the Romans in the Republic was their religion. The Romans thought of their gods as the protectors of the state. Thus, obedience to the state also meant loyalty to the gods who protected the state. The Romans kept the temples of the gods in good condition. The priests performed the religious ceremonies with great care. They thought that the gods in return would keep Rome safe and prosperous.

In form, the Roman religion was very much like that of the Greeks. The gods in both religions had similar duties. The Roman Jupiter and the Greek Zeus were gods of the sky. The Roman Minerva and the Greek Athena were goddesses of wisdom and protectors of craftsmen. The Roman Juno and the Greek Hera were goddesses of marriage and motherhood. The major Greek gods and their Roman equivalents are listed in the chart on this page.

The Greeks thought of the gods as beings that had human forms. These beings associated with humans and shared the same virtues and faults as humans. The Greek gods and goddesses quarrelled and fell in love. In contrast the Romans thought of the gods as spirits. There were thousands of spirits, each with its own task. A person could bargain for help from the gods or spirits by sacrificing and making promises to the appropriate god. For example, a farmer made sacrifice to Ceres, the goddess of the harvest, for a good crop. His wife made sacrifice to Proserpina, the goddess of flowers, for a beautiful garden.

In the Roman Senate, the orator Cicero speaks out against Catiline.

GROWTH OF THE ROMAN EMPIRE

Rome remained a ruling power for about 1,000 years. During that time the government of Rome went through several changes. Early Rome was ruled by a series of kings. Their power was limited by an **assembly** and a **senate.** The Assembly was made up of all citizens who were of military age. It did not have the power to make laws. It could only vote for or against matters brought before it by the king or the Senate. The Assembly nominated people for public office. It decided on war or peace and tried people accused of murder or treason.

The Senate was a group of about 300 citizens. A man who was elected a senator held the position for life. The Senate had the responsibility of looking carefully at all new laws which were proposed by the king. It was called upon to give advice to the king.

The Roman Republic

In 509 B.C. the cruel Etruscan king, Tarquin, was driven from his throne by the Senate. Rome became a **republic.** In place of the king, the Assembly elected two **consuls** to rule Rome. The two consuls shared the powers of a king. One consul could veto the other's proposed action. They were elected to office for one year. An ex-consul had to wait ten years before he could run for the office of consul again.

In the Roman Republic the Senate and the Assembly were retained. The **patricians,** the noble class, slowly gained control of the Senate and Assembly. The **plebeians,** the common people, revolted until they were allowed to have their own representatives in the Assembly. These representatives were called **tribunes.**

When the Etruscans and their king were driven out of Rome, they settled north of the Tiber River. Other hostile people lived in the Apennine Hills to the east and south of Rome. These enemies surrounded Rome. Cincinnatus was appointed a temporary dictator in Rome to help unite the patricians, the plebeians, and the neighboring cities in defeating these enemies.

Later the Gauls came from the north to invade Italy. They burned much of Rome and occupied it for seven months. They left after the Romans paid them a large ransom. As Rome grew in power, its neighboring cities became jealous and attacked. Rome conquered these cities and in 275 B.C. finally gained control of most of the Italian peninsula.

The Romans Look Beyond Italy

As soon as the Romans had united Italy, they began to look for colonies outside of Italy. Across the Mediterranean Sea on the northern coast of Africa was another powerful city. This was Carthage which had been established by the Phoenicians as a trading center. Carthage controlled the island of Sicily, which lies off the coast of Italy. Rome fought Carthage and won control of the island.

The people of Carthage did not forget their defeat in Sicily. Years later they sent a powerful army to attack Rome. The army was led by the great general, Hannibal. He used elephants in his army to do the heavy work, much as tanks are used in modern armies. Rome controlled the sea, so Hannibal marched his army across Spain and southern France. His greatest task was to get his elephants across the high Alps in northern Italy.

For many years Hannibal won victories in Italy and never suffered a defeat. But before he could completely defeat the Romans in Italy, he was called home to help defend Carthage. The Roman armies had made a surprise attack on the city. Hannibal was defeated, and the city was destroyed. After this defeat, Carthage gave up its colony of Spain to Rome.

Soon after the victory at Carthage, Rome turned to the Greek peninsula and defeated a powerful king, Philip V of Macedonia. Rome took over many of the Greek cities in Greece and in Asia Minor. By 146 B.C. Rome ruled most of the territory around the Mediterranean Sea. We can say that Rome dominated the Mediterranean World.

The conquered countries remained under the power of Rome partially because of the strength of the Roman armies and partially through the wise government of the Roman rulers. The Romans did many things to hold the territory they had conquered. They continued to build excellent roads so that it would be easy to travel between Rome and the conquered territory. They established colonies in the territory. They wanted faithful allies, as loyal as true Romans. They offered Roman citizenship to the important people. These colonies grew into peaceful towns where trade and business flourished. But peace around the Mediterranean was followed by trouble at home.

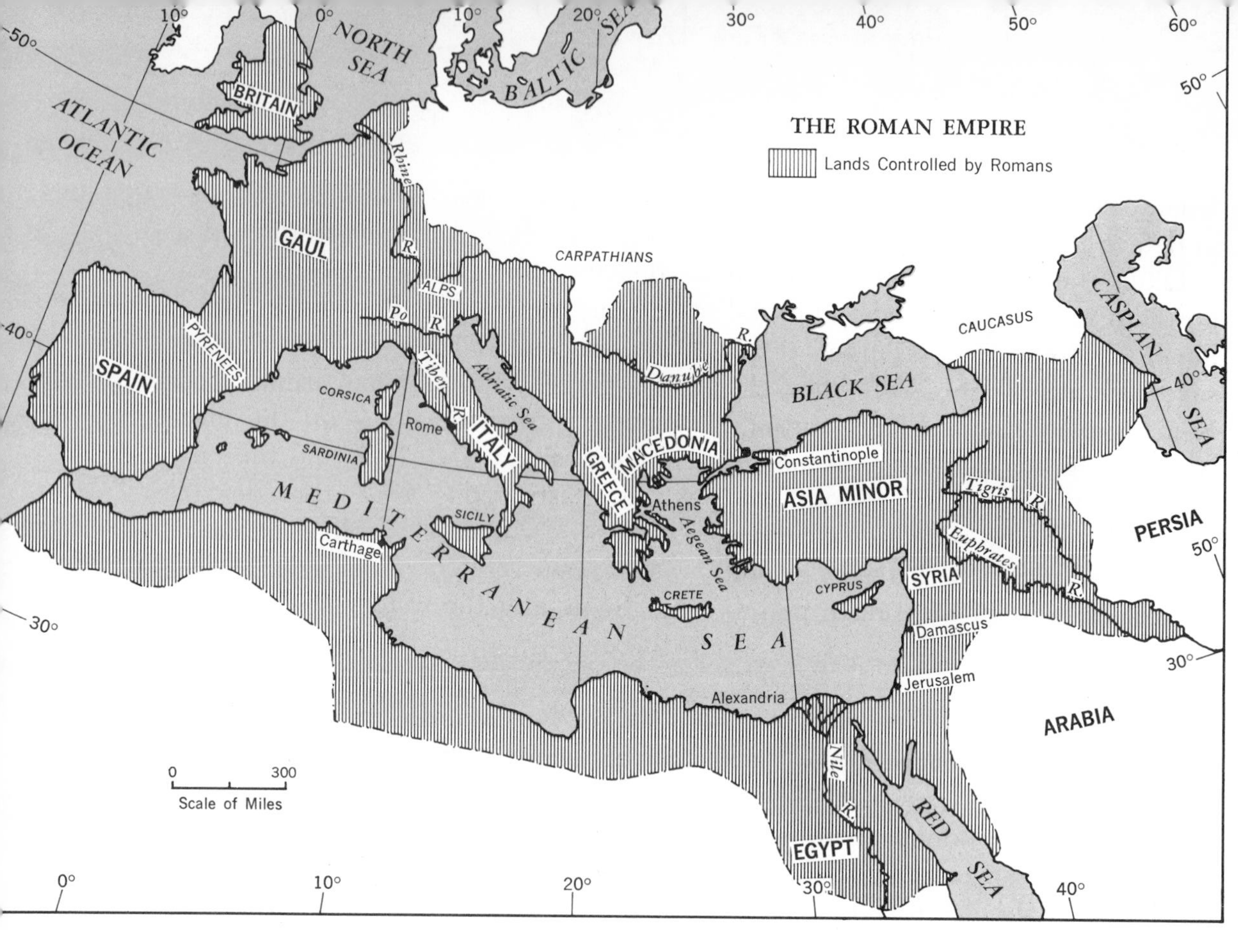

Internal Troubles

From 133 B.C. to 27 B.C. Rome was torn by internal troubles. The slaves of the conquered colonies revolted several times. Rome had to send an army to crush the revolt of slaves on the island of Sicily. Later great numbers of slaves on the Italian peninsula revolted. One leader of the slaves was the gladiator, Spartacus. About 100,000 slaves joined his army. He first tried to lead his army to the Roman frontier north of Italy. He hoped to settle his army of slaves in freedom beyond the Alps. The Roman armies blocked his way. He then turned south hoping to find ships in which he could take his army of slaves to safety in Africa. Rome gathered a huge army which met and finally defeated Spartacus and his army of slaves.

During this same period several bitter fights broke out between the landless farmers and the owners of great estates. The farmers wished to obtain some of the land owned by the wealthy landowners. They were not successful.

Another cause of internal trouble was that many of the conquered Italians on the peninsula wanted Roman citizenship. The Roman people were unwilling to grant it. A large group of Italians revolted against Rome and set up their own state. They raised a large army. Rome met this threat by granting them full Roman citizenship.

During this period of revolution Rome had many rulers. The only people who could gain power were army commanders. Some commanders were good rulers, but others ruled with cruelty and harshness. Finally, the government of Rome fell into the hands of Julius Caesar, a military leader who made himself dictator for life. Rome became a **dictatorship.** This one-man rule lasted for only five years. Some men, fearing the growing power of Caesar, murdered him in 44 B.C.

Augustus, Emperor of Rome

Julius Caesar's adopted son, Octavian, became the ruler in 27 B.C. after a struggle for many years with other men who wished to rule. Caesar's son took the name of Augustus and became the first emperor of Rome. As ruler of the **Roman Empire,** Augustus Caesar began many reforms in the government. He placed good governors in the provinces conquered by his father and other generals. The colonies lived together in peace. This period, known as the Roman Peace, lasted 200 years. No country was strong enough to wage a war on Rome. Trade flourished, and the people had great prosperity. The emperors who followed Augustus during the Pax Romana tried to carry out the reforms he had begun.

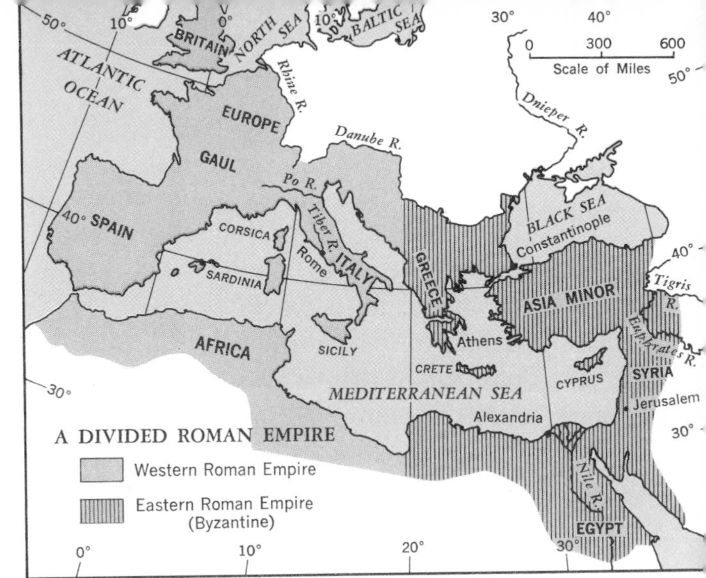

Life in the Roman Empire

Under the Roman Peace travel was possible and encouraged throughout the empire. This meant widespread free trade of ideas and goods throughout the empire. Huge supplies of all kinds of goods flowed into Rome from all parts of the empire. Gold and marble came from Greece. The Egyptians sent grain, glass, paper, and linen. Spain supplied silver, wheat, copper, mercury, and cork. The people of Asia Minor sent dried figs, pomegranates, perfumes, cedar wood, and spices. Goods came from countries outside the empire. Traders brought amber from Germany, silk from China, and diamonds, pepper, tigers, and elephants from India.

When the Roman Republic first had been established, the people had a voice in the government. As Rome grew larger and more and more territory came under its rule, the voice of the people was heard less and less in government matters.

After the Roman Republic became the Roman Empire, the people became used to having a succession of single, all-powerful rulers. They began to lose interest in the reforms passed by their one-ruler government. Many of the emperors who followed were weak rulers. Their lack of leadership and the people's lack of interest caused the power of the government of Rome to decline slowly.

While the **Western Roman Empire** passed through years of decline, lands farther east flourished. The Emperor Constantine, seeing the internal troubles of Rome and also the great wealth in the eastern half of the Roman Empire, moved the seat of the government from Rome to Constantinople in A.D. 330. The strong government established in Constantinople continued to enforce Roman law. Constantinople became a great trading center and the capital of the **Eastern Roman Empire.** The Eastern Empire lasted for nearly a thousand years after Rome itself had fallen to invaders. This shift of the government was one cause for the fall of the Western Roman Empire in A.D. 476.

Do You Know?

1. What are some of the important regions of Italy? Which is the leading region? Which is an island region?

2. What part of the Italian peninsula is labeled the "backbone?" Why?

3. Which early settlement on the Italian peninsula was located in the Tiber River Valley?

4. What are two important volcanoes in Italy? Where are they located?

5. What is a myth? What is a legend? How are they alike?

6. Is the story of Romulus and Remus a myth or a legend? Why?

7. What were the three staple foods of the ancient Romans? What was the common drink of the Romans?

8. What is the most characteristic dress of the Romans? What is the origin of our word "candidate?"

9. What important contributions of Roman engineers can be seen in the architecture of the Pantheon?

10. What was the amphitheater? What was the arena? Which was the most famous amphitheater? Where is it located?

11. What is the major difference between the gods of Greece and the gods of Rome?

12. What were the two classes of people in the Roman Republic? Who represented the common people in the Assembly?

13. What limited the ruling power of the King? Who limited the ruling power of the consul? Who limited the ruling power of the patricians?

Learn By Doing

1. Can you see relationships between the following lists? Match each item of column **B** with an item in column **A**.

	A	B
1.	King	Julius Caesar
2.	Republic	Pax Romana
3.	Assembly	Tarquin
4.	Dictator	Cincinnatus
5.	Revolution	Tribunes
6.	Emperor	A.D. 476
7.	Roman Empire	Constantinople
8.	Western Empire	Consul
9.	Eastern Empire	Spartacus
10.	Reformer	Augustus Caesar

2. Explain the importance of these dates and places to the expansion of Rome.

275 B.C.	Greece	Asia Minor
146 B.C.	Macedonia	Carthage

3. Explain the importance of these people or groups of people to the government of Rome.

Tarquin	Augustus Caesar
Cincinatus	Constantine
Spartacus	Julius Caesar

Test Your Knowledge

1. What was the atrium? Why was the hole in the center of the roof an important part of the house?

2. How did the education of the Roman youths help them become good soldiers?

3. What are some of the similarities between a Roman dinner and an American dinner?

4. Explain these terms: bier, Forum, rostrum, and orator. Why can we say that a rostrum is a symbol of free speech?

5. Why were roads carefully built throughout the empire? What do we mean when we say, "All roads lead to Rome?"

6. What is an aqueduct? Why was the aqueduct important to the Romans?

7. Who were the gladiators? What were the "games" that they played?

8. How long did the ruling power of Rome last? Give the dates.

9. How did the Romans treat the people they conquered? Why?

10. Why is Roman law especially important to us today? Explain the statement, "Man is innocent until proved guilty."

CHAPTER 7

CULTURAL HERITAGES FROM THE MIDDLE AGES

The Middle Ages was a period of about one thousand years following the fall of the Western Roman Empire. It was a time between the strong, well-governed Roman Empire and the strong governments which emerged in Western Europe. Some of the features of this period were the manor, the knight, the monastery, the guild, and the cathedral. Many changes and developments helped build a great new civilization in Western Europe. Many contributed to our present-day civilization.

THE DECLINE OF ROME

The fall of the Western Roman Empire did not happen suddenly. It took place over a long period of time. Just why Rome fell is not easy to explain. There was no single cause. Rome and its empire weakened for several reasons. **Plagues,** or very serious diseases, killed many people. Armies of people from the north overran much of the Roman Empire. The Roman rulers placed very high taxes on the people. Industry and trade slowly declined. Each of these played a part in the fall of the Roman Empire in the West.

During the second and third centuries A.D. two plagues swept through the Western Roman Empire. They left many parts of Italy without people. **Barbarians** from the north, named Teutons, invaded the Roman Empire time after time. These armies of people were warlike, wandering tribes. Some of the armies looted and burned towns and killed the Romans.

During this time trade and the manufacture of goods slowly declined. One reason may have been the decline in population. Another reason for the disappearance of trade was the lack of money. Because of the high taxes, the common people had very little money to exchange. Money gradually disappeared as a means of buying and selling.

Trade may have dropped off for another reason. Roads were not kept

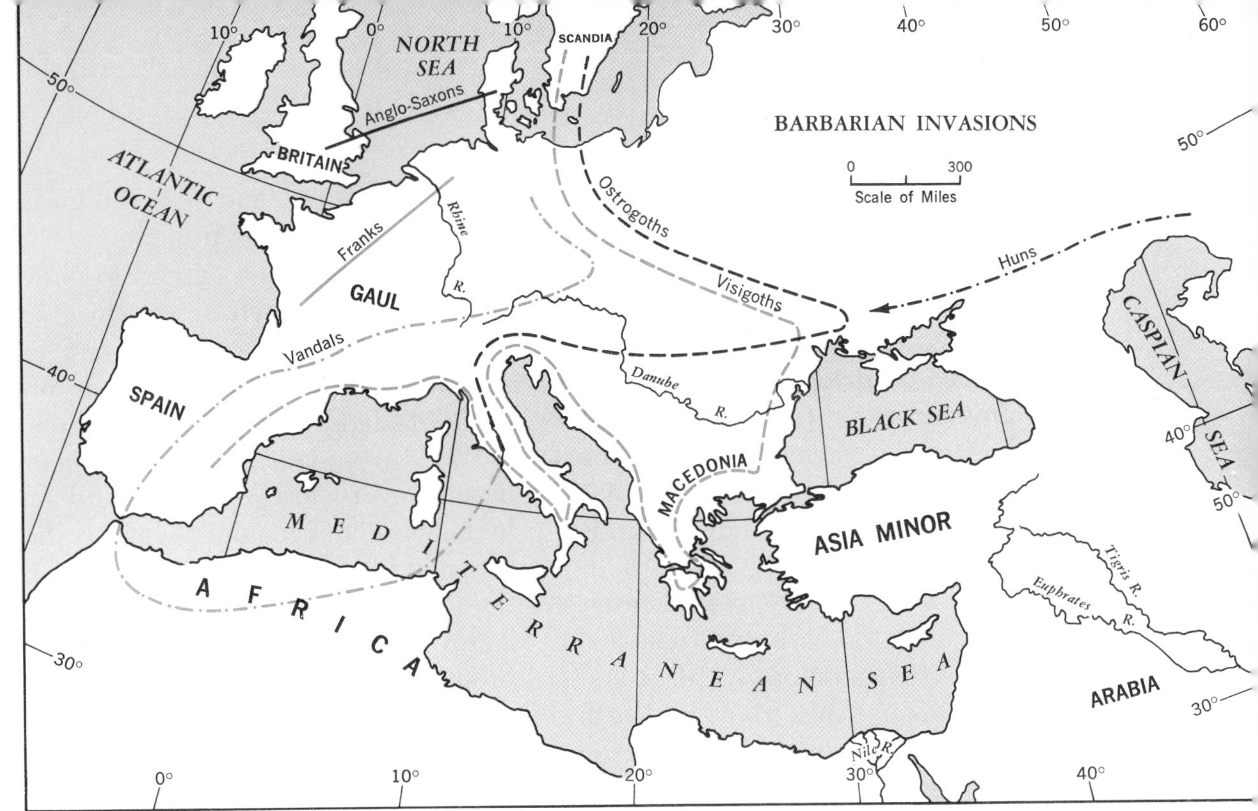

up. Some became impassable. Also, the rulers of Rome did not protect the travelers on the roads. Bandits made travel and trading dangerous. Traders who lost their goods to bandits no longer wanted to trade with people in other cities. Because of these conditions, goods could no longer be sent long distances. These last centuries of danger and poor living conditions in the Western Roman Empire are called the Dark Ages.

Ways of Living Change

The Roman government passed laws saying that every man had to do the same work as his father. This meant that a young man could not change jobs even if he could do another job better. Other laws tied the farmer to his farm. The government placed high taxes on the poor and middle class farmers. These farmers could not pay the high taxes. In order to meet their debts, they were forced to turn their farms over to rich and powerful noblemen. These lords paid the farmers' taxes and debts. The farmers rented their farms from the lords. These poor farmers were usually unable to regain their freedom. They became a kind of slave to the land and to the lord who owned the land.

Farmers were not the only ones whose lives were changed. A slaveowner could sell a slave as he sold a horse or a cow. With the decline in trade, many slaves were placed on the farms. They were used by the lords to grow food. They were also forced to serve as soldiers.

Some barbarian tribes entered Italy peacefully. They were invited by Roman rulers to settle on the lands that had been emptied of people by the plagues. These tribes were used to living by hunting and farming and war. Great numbers of the barbarians became soldiers in the Roman armies. In time, the Roman armies were made up almost entirely of barbarian soldiers.

Roman governors were not always wise in ruling the barbarians who had settled in their territories. More and more Teutonic tribes from the North pushed into the empire. One tribe of Teutons, the Visigoths, rose in revolt against the unjust rule of the Roman governors. In A.D. 410 they were powerful enough to march into Italy and capture Rome. They plundered the city which had stood unconquered for centuries. After looting and burning the city, they marched into Gaul, another part of the Roman Empire. Roman rule in the West came to an end when the Teutonic chiefs or kings seized control of the territories of the Roman Empire.

Men Seek Protection from the Lords

With the fall of the Roman Empire, people no longer could look to Rome for protection. Barbarian armies captured and killed the people or carried them off into slavery. The people were in constant fear for their lives and property. Many free men turned to the rich and powerful lords and their armies for protection. In return, the free men agreed to obey the lord. They also agreed to give the lord part of their crops and to spend part of their time working on the lord's land.

We have seen that many poor farmers were forced by law and by high taxes to become bound to the lord and his land. We have also seen that free men agreed to obey the lord and to work on his land in return for protection. We know that slaves worked for the lord. As the centuries passed, the differences in these three groups of people who worked for the lord became less and less. A person who was bound to the land and to the landowner was called a **serf.** In time the lords controlled many acres of land and many serfs. This system of granting protection in return for service lasted for several centuries. It is called the **manorial system.**

Were there any farmers who were not serfs in the Middle Ages? Yes. During the early Middle Ages many farmers kept their own lands. However, as the centuries passed, the number of these free farmers dropped greatly. Sometimes whole villages of free farmers were forced by powerful lords to become serfs. However, a few small farmers did manage to remain free. They lived mostly in mountainous regions or in marshlands. Their land was too poor or too difficult to farm to draw the interest of the great nobles.

Much can be learned about court life in the Middle Ages from the tapestries that brightened castle interiors.

The Middle Ages

In this chapter we will study the ways of living of the two great classes of people of the Middle Ages. We will first take a close look at how the serfs lived. We will then look at how the **nobility,** the class of people who owned the land farmed by the serfs, lived.

As you study the ways of living of these people during the Middle Ages, you should keep in mind these facts. The Dark Ages, or the last years of the Western Roman Empire, led into the Middle Ages. The Middle Ages lasted nearly a thousand years. It lasted from A.D. 500 to about A.D. 1500. During the early Middle Ages the people lived on farms or in small farming villages. It was a time when few people lived in the cities. The lords built high walls around their land for the protection of the people against barbarians. The system of feudalism resulted from the unsettled conditions and need for protection.

Many of the nobles or lords were leaders of the barbaric tribes who invaded the old Roman Empire. They settled in Gaul (France and Germany), in Spain, and in Britain. Western Europe was broken up into smaller areas controlled by the nobles. These nobles fought to gain power over more land. Some became kings of nations.

LIFE ON THE MANOR

A community in the Middle Ages was called a **manor.** The entire manor with its buildings, lands, and

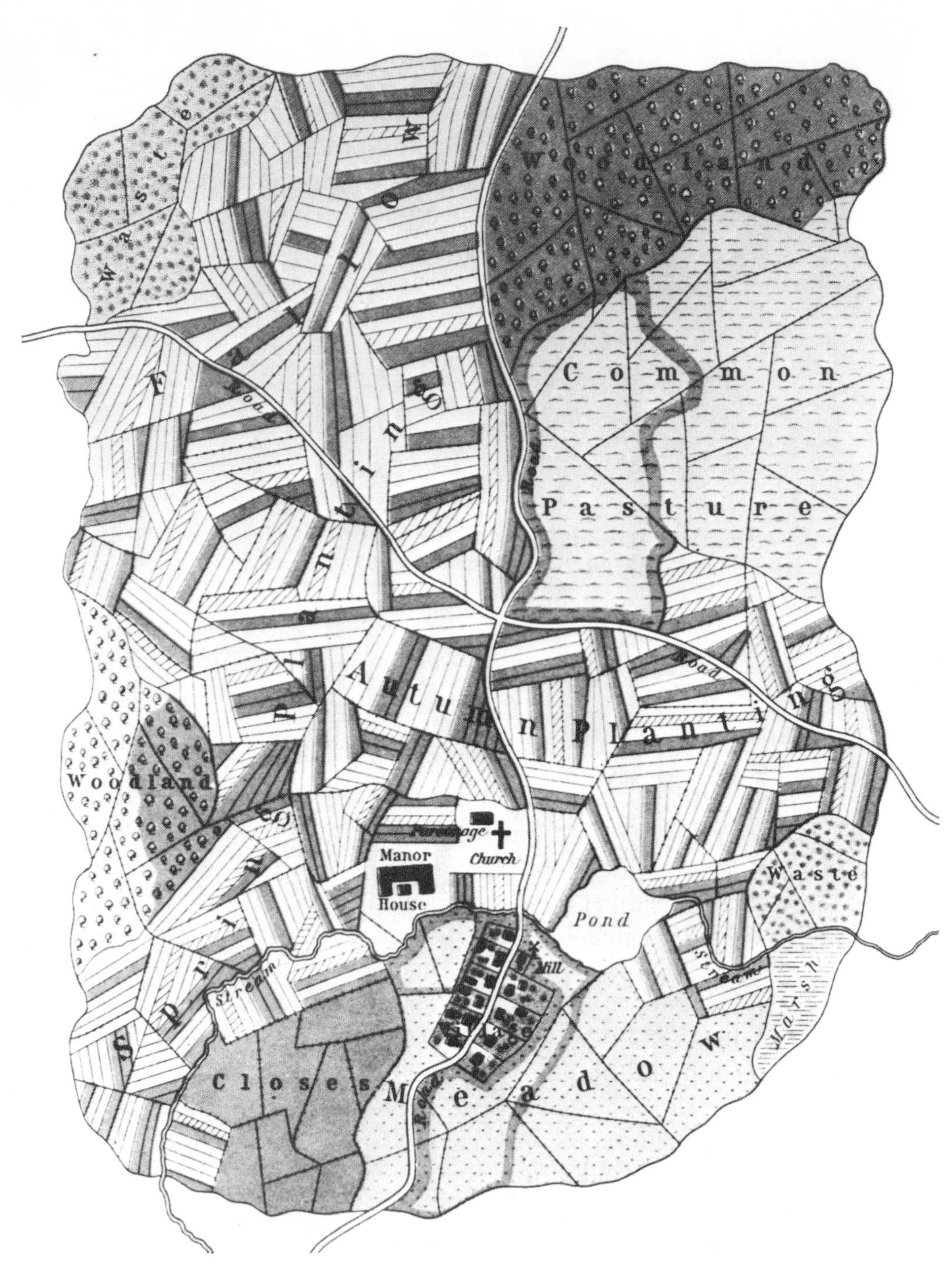

PLAN OF A MEDIEVAL MANOR

people belonged to a nobleman, or lord. It was made up of the manor house and land of the lord. The size of the manor house depended on the size of the manor. It also included a village in which the serfs of the manor lived. The land of the manor lord was divided into several fields which were farmed by the serfs. A typical manor also had some land which was used as a common pasture for all the animals of the manor. A small woodland or forest was often part of the manor.

The center of life on a manor was the village. The most important building in the village was the church. Near the church were the house and the fields of the priest. The rest of the village was made up of small huts in which the serfs lived. The number of huts in a village ranged between 10 and 50. Village huts were often huddled on a long, rough street or at crossroads.

The Homes of the Serfs

The serfs' huts were poorly built. Frames of the huts were made of wood. Walls were plastered with a mixture of clay, stone, and manure. Roofs were thatched with straw. Each hut had only one room. The floor was packed dirt or clay. Sometimes the dirt floor was covered with straw or rushes. If the rushes were not changed often, they began to rot. In the winter the floor became damp or wet.

Goats, pigs, and chickens wandered in and out of the huts. Chickens often laid their eggs in the huts. During the winter, some of the large farm animals were kept in the huts at night. Animal body heat was welcome on very cold nights. The animals were also safer in the serfs' huts. Hungry wolves were dangerous.

A fire, for cooking and for warmth during the winter, was built in a clay-lined pit in the floor. Smoke blackened the walls. Some of the smoke from the fire escaped through a hole in the roof. The rest of the smoke escaped through the door, through the window, or through cracks in the walls of the poorly built hut. In winter, the window was jammed with straw and rags. In spite of this, rain, snow, and cold winds found their way into the hut.

There was very little furniture in a hut. The family sat on three-legged stools or tree stumps. A plank of wood served as a table. Dishes and spoons were carved from wood. Serfs slept on straw or bags of dried plants.

A kitchen garden was planted behind the hut. Here the housewife grew vegetables and herbs for seasoning soup and meat. Among these herbs were parsley, sage, and garlic. Fruit trees also grew on the land behind the hut.

Farming by the Serfs

The three main fields which the serfs farmed stretched out from the village huts. Each field went through a three-year farming cycle. The first year a field was planted with wheat in the fall. The second year it was planted with barley in the spring. The third year it was left fallow, or unplanted. This was done so that the soil would have a chance to recover some of its natural fertility. Horses and cattle were turned into fallow farming land to feed on the grass. The droppings of the animals helped to fertilize the soil.

The fields that the serfs farmed were divided into long narrow strips. A typical strip of farmland was about 20 to 50 feet wide and several hundred feet long. The serfs liked to have each strip of farmland no larger than one day's plowing. If they had long strips of farmland rather than square plots of land, the oxen would not have to turn as often.

A serf might have several strips of farmland. Some of the strips would be near his hut. Others would be far away. The farmland was divided and scattered this way so that one farmer would not get all the land near the village or all the good farmland.

The hard work of farming was carried on with simple tools, such as the ax, hoe, and spade. The serf's plow was made of wood and tipped with iron. Since no one serf had enough tools and work animals to farm his own land, the serfs cooperated in farming. They shared the same oxen for plowing. They planted and harvested together.

Animals on the Manor

Oxen were used for breaking or plowing new land. Oxen are very powerful. In plowing they pull with a steady, strong, forward lean. Because horses move faster, they were more useful than oxen in fields that were clear of stones and easy to plow. Horses need a well-fitting collar, strong enough to withstand hard tugs. In the latter part of the Middle Ages when such sturdy collars were made, horses began to replace oxen in plowing all of the fields.

Most of the year sheep, oxen, and horses were left to search for their feed on the fallow farmland or in the forest. Hay was grown in meadows, but the animals were not allowed to graze in the meadows until after the hay had been cut and stored for winter feed. Even in good years natural hay was scarce, for the meadow land on which it grew was not as widespread as forest or farmland. In addition to the hay, tree leaves, small branches, and straw were stored for winter fodder. Often the stock of animal feed ran out before the winter was over. Most of the farm animals were killed for meat at the beginning of winter. Only breeding and plowing animals were spared.

Use of Forest Lands

In the early Middle Ages the land of Northern Europe was covered by great forests. As the population grew larger, more and more farmland was needed to support the people. Farmers moved into the northern land. They cleared great patches of forests and turned them into farming land. Forests gradually disappeared as more and more land was brought into use for crop production.

In the early Middle Ages the serfs were free to graze animals in the forest or woodland. They also gathered wood, branches, and twigs for fuel. Nuts and berries from the forest were used for food. In the late Middle Ages manor lords often enclosed the forest and kept it for hunting. In their leisure time hunting was their favorite sport. The manor lord appointed a forester to guard the forest land and its animals. If serfs were caught stealing fish, pigeons, or rabbits, they were cruelly punished.

Life of the Serfs

All members of the serf's family worked on the farm. They worked from sunup to sundown. They did not have time to learn to read and write. However, in the summer they rested during the midday heat. They had no means of protecting their crops against grasshoppers, caterpillars, and rats. These pests swarmed into the fields destroying the crops in a very short time.

The serf had to do many things for the lord of the manor. He had to pay for grinding his wheat into flour at

Aius, sanctus,
Cardia cardiani!
Mouse and she-mouse,
Hamster, mole,
Marmot, cony,
Young and old
Leave the land,
I command.
You are banned!
Up above and down below
From the fields get you hence,
Pestilence!
Go with you, where'er you go,
Afrias, aestrias, palamiasit!

(from Thompson, James Westfall. *Economic and Social History of the Middle Ages.* Volume II, p 760.)

A chant was used to drive away pests.

the mill. He could not kill the pigeons which fed on his grain. They were the property of the lord. If the serf wished to marry someone from outside the manor, he had to get his lord's permission and also pay a fee. He had to work a certain number of days on the land belonging to the manor lord. He had to repair the roads and bridges of the manor. He was also expected to give gifts to the lord of the manor. At certain seasons of the year, he was expected to give chickens and eggs to the lord. At Christmas, the gift might have been a fat goose.

Life on the manor had some advantages. The serf was protected by the lord. He could not be parted from his land. If the land was sold, he went along with it. Thus he could not lose his job. He did not have to fight in wars. The manor lord was bound to care for the serf in his old age. Although he worked very hard, he did not have to work on Sundays or on the many holidays.

Homes of the Nobility

In the early Middle Ages the home of the lord of a manor differed from the huts of the serfs in one major way. It was planned and built to withstand attack. The home was usually a tower made of wood. It was built on a large mound of earth which was surrounded by a ditch of water called a **moat.** Food and supplies were stored on the ground floor. The lord and his family lived on the main or upper floor of the tower. Sometimes this floor was just one large room.

In time, these **keeps,** or towers, were built of stone. The stone keeps were safer than the wooden ones. Even the stairs of the keep were made of stone to remove the danger of fire. Sometimes the builders left a gap in the stone stairs. The gap was covered with wooden steps. These could be removed at night or when the keep was under attack. At night, instead of stepping on the next stone riser, a surprise invader would fall through the gap.

By the late Middle Ages, the wealthiest lords had gradually enlarged these stone keeps into huge forts. High protective walls were built around the edges of the wide mound, and the moat was deepened. Castles with large halls were built within the walls. The lord also had gardens, stables, a blacksmith's shop, and a church for his own use inside the walls.

The huge castle of the lord had a large drawbridge across the moat. It had to be lowered in order to gain entrance into the castle grounds. It served as a protection along with the location on a mound, the walls, and the moat of the castle. If invaders managed to get inside the walls, the inhabitants of the manor retired to the stone keeps. There they could hold out as long as they had food and water.

The castles of the kings and the great nobles were very elaborate. The great hall was the center of activity in the castle. It was used for meetings and for meals. Dining was a grand affair with continuous entertainment. The castle had many bedrooms. The lord had his own private bedroom, while the guests shared the others.

Carpets and **tapestries** were used by the nobles. Carpets were used to protect the feet of the guests from the cold, damp floors. Tapestries were huge pieces of cloth woven by hand. They were hung on the castle walls. They usually had pictures woven into a beautiful design. The tapestries were used for decoration and for protection against drafts of cold air. For most of the nobility, tapestries were too costly to use in daily life. They were stored in wooden chests, and brought out and hung on the walls only when important guests came to the castle.

Castles had to be defended easily, so location was important. They were both homes and fortresses.

Homes of the Manor Lords

Many lords owned a great number of manors. Sometimes they sent an agent to oversee a smaller manor for them. These smaller manors did not have castles. The agent lived in a **manor house.** He was regarded as the lord of the manor by the serfs. The manor house of the agent, or manor lord, was only slightly larger than the huts of the serfs. The ground floor had two rooms, a large hall and a small bedroom. The upper floor had rooms for servants.

The manor house was more solidly built than the huts of the serfs. It was often built on a platform of stone. Thus, the floor of the manor house was less likely to be flooded than the floor of the serf's hut. Nevertheless, the manor house was drafty and damp in the winter. Cracks in the walls let in currents of cold air. Folding screens were used to protect people from the drafts.

The floor of the large hall was covered with rushes. As nobles and warriors ate, they tossed bones and scraps of meat to hunting dogs. Sometimes a dirty layer of rushes was covered with a fresh layer. The layer of rushes protected the feet of the manor house people from the cold, damp floors.

Furniture in the manor house was simple. People sat on benches or stools. The lord of the manor usually had a large chair with a carved back. Storage chests lined the hall. Tables were heavy, wooden planks set upon wooden frames which looked like our sawhorses.

Most of the people living in a manor house slept on the floor or on the dining tables in the hall. Sometimes they slept on small, flat mattresses filled with straw called **pallets.** These were stored in the chests during the daytime. The bed of the lord of the manor stood upon a raised platform. It was surrounded by curtains. These were closed at night to keep out the night air, which was thought to be dangerous.

Protecting the Manor

The job of protecting a manor and its serfs fell upon the lord of the manor. At first the lords trained slaves and serfs to fight. These people were soon replaced by professional warriors. Before the eleventh century, these warriors were little more than paid soldiers who lived in the manor houses of a great lord. The warriors could be called a military nobility for they were nobles who fought. Their main job was to protect the people on the manor at all times.

Many of these noble warriors earned the right to become knights. Each knight owed loyalty to a great lord, who was also a knight. The great lord in turn owed loyalty to a king. In peacetime each knight spent a part of each year working for his great lord. He helped guard the castle of his lord. In time of war the knight was expected to fight for the person to whom he owed loyalty.

After the eleventh century, many of the knights became manor owners. The great lord divided his land among a few knights as rewards for their outstanding service. The knights who became landowners did not own the land outright. The land was held as a grant from the great lord. In fact, the great lord held his land as a grant from his king or emperor.

The great lord and his landowning knights did not pay rent for the land. Instead, they had to give military service to the person above them, the knights to their lord, and the great lords to the king. In time of war each knight had to supply his great lord with horses, armor, and free men from his manor. The free men served as foot soldiers. Each great lord used the armies of his landowning knights in the service of his king. The king used the armies of his great lords to protect the people living in his kingdom and to expand his kingdom. The more great lords and manors a king had under his control, the more land he could conquer. This system of granting land in return for service was called the **feudal system.** The feudal system was a kind of government which was developed to protect the people.

Becoming a Knight

Knighthood had to be earned. It was not inherited or given as a gift. The path to knighthood was long and hard. It began when a lad of eight became a **page** to a great nobleman. During his time as a page, he was taught to read and write. He learned to fence with a blunt sword. His most important task was to learn the manners of his class. He had to learn the correct behavior for all occasions. He learned to wait gracefully and willingly upon others at the table and about the castle.

At the age of fourteen he was made a squire. A **squire** was an assistant to a knight. The squire took care of the knight's horses and polished his armor. He learned the serious tasks of dueling, riding, hawking, and handling a spear and a sword. He was tested on his manners, bravery, and especially on his loyalty. He was taught to protect the weak and to have a high regard for the women of nobility. He was taught to be considerate of other well-born people, to be brave, and to be generous.

When in battle, the squire rode with his master and cared for the knight's helmet, weapons, and horse. After years of practice and service to a knight, a squire was tested on his manners and his skills. His strength and courage were tested in combat with others before he could earn his right to knighthood.

A squire was made a **knight** by a king or a great nobleman in an impressive ceremony. Before the ceremony the squire kept watch beside his armor all night in a church. The next morning the knight he had served helped him put on his armor. He knelt before the nobleman who was knighting him. The nobleman gave him a tap with the side of a sword on the back of his neck. He said to the squire, "I dub thee knight." This ceremony was usually followed by a feast and a tournament.

The Armored Knight

In the early Middle Ages knights wore armor made of leather which had been heated and shaped. Leather armor was very hard. It looked like metal armor. In the eleventh century, a knight wore metal armor called a **coat of mail.** This was a covering of rings of metal sewn on cloth. Later coats of mail were made of interlinking rings of metal. The coat of mail gave some protection. It was worn over a layer of padded clothing. A coat of mail would protect the body unless the metal rings were broken. However, a blow from a heavy sword might seriously bruise a knight even though he wore padding.

Armor made from solid sheets of metal came into use in the thirteenth and fourteenth centuries. It was called **plate armor.** The knight who wore plate armor over padded clothing was better protected than the knight who wore chain mail.

A German knight of the 15th century.

The smooth, rounded plate armor made a sword glance off. It protected the wearer from arrows. But it did have a few drawbacks. Plate armor was very hot and stuffy for the wearer. It was also very heavy. A knight dressed in plate armor had to be hoisted by a pulley onto his horse. The knight's horse had to be strong enough to carry both knight and armor. Such a horse was called a **charger.** If a knight in armor was struck off his horse, he lay helpless on the ground. He was unable to rise or take off the armor without the help of his squire. The squire helped the knight to rise and manage his armor. However, when the knight was mounted and charging, he was a fearsome sight. He was the Middle Ages' equivalent of an armored tank.

Very few knights wearing plate armor were ever killed in battle. On horseback a knight was too well protected. Even when fallen, he was worth more alive than dead. If he were taken captive, ransom money would be paid for his return to his army.

With the invention of the closed helmet, the face of a knight was hidden. He could not be identified as friend or enemy. In order for his friends to know who he was, he wore a sign, sometimes a feather or a bright ribbon. The need to identify a knight started the use of designs on the knight's shield. The shield design, or **coat of arms,** told who the knight was. It belonged to the knight and his descendants.

Tournaments were combats among the knights. They provided valuable training for wars. Later they became sporting events at social gatherings. Great crowds of people gathered to watch. Ladies of the castle especially enjoyed the jousts. The **joust** was a combat between two knights on horseback in an enclosed field. Each knight carried a blunt weapon and tried to fell his opponent from his horse. The winning knight was given the handkerchief of a beautiful lady to wear on his helmet. Later, **tilting** became a favorite sport. In tilting, two knights on horseback charged toward each other. Each carried a long blunt lance and tried to knock the other off his horse. Tilting differed from jousting in that the knights were confined to the **lists,** long narrow lanes separated by railings, so that the horses could not meet.

THE CHURCH IN THE MIDDLE AGES

The Middle Ages was a period when there was no strong government. The Roman Empire with its strong government was gone. No new government had taken its place. There were no laws to protect the people. Many of the powers and duties of a government were assumed by the Catholic Church under the leadership of the Pope. Kings, nobles, and serfs were loyal to the same faith and to the same leader. Christianity was the one common bond of all the people of Western Europe during the Middle Ages.

The Christian religion began in Roman times. Its teachings influenced both the rich and the poor. Christians believed in a life after death. They taught that men and women, rich and poor, free and slave were equal in the sight of God. A person of any rank could join the Christian religion. It did not matter if he were a nobleman or a slave. During the Middle Ages, the church was the one place where a person could rise above the class in which he was born.

Early Christians sometimes suffered persecution. Some were burned at the stake, and others were thrown to wild beasts in the arena. These persecutions did not stop the spread of Christianity. If anything, they helped to make it stronger. By A.D. 400, Christianity had been recognized as the lawful religion of the Roman Empire.

The monasteries kept learning alive.

In the troubled times of the late Roman Empire and the early Middle Ages, Christianity gave people a purpose in life. The belief in the second coming of Christ helped people endure the hardships of their daily lives. The Christian religion appealed to the poor who had no hope of bettering their way of life. The Church did many things that the government had done before. It helped the poor. It gave protection to the people. It provided education for the young.

Life in the Monasteries

During the Middle Ages many men joined **monasteries.** These were communities of men who banded together to lead a simple, religious life. These men were called **monks.** They did not wish to live the life of fighting and evil which was all around them. They wanted to help the poor. The monks took a vow of poverty. They promised to own nothing and to work only to serve others. Their daily life was filled with prayer, religious services, and hard work. Monastery bells rang at daybreak to wake the monks from their sleep. The bells rang again when the monks filed into the church for the first religious service of the day. Bells rang for every time of prayer. They even rang for washing before a meal.

Monasteries were often given large areas of swamp or forest land by kings and great lords. The monks drained the swamps and cut down the trees of the forest. They turned the land into pasture and farms. Some monasteries were so highly regarded by nobles that they were granted manors. The monastery and its monks controlled the lives of the serfs of the manor just as the knight or great lord had done. Some monasteries gained so many manors, along with the land they had cleared, that they became very wealthy.

Work of the Monasteries

The monasteries of the Middle Ages were one of the chief means by which the ideas of the Greeks and Romans were preserved. The monasteries kept the arts of reading and writing alive. Some monks were given the task of copying ancient **manuscripts.** Some of these manuscripts were the writings of the Greeks and Romans. By this means some of the heritages from the Ancient World were saved.

Manuscripts were copied when an original manuscript became tattered and old. Others were copied when another monastery wanted to have a certain writing in its own library. The monks who copied manuscripts became highly skilled in copying and decorating the pages. Many of the beautiful manuscripts from the Middle Ages have been preserved in libraries and museums.

The monasteries had schools for the boys who wished to become priests or monks. Gradually the monks began to teach anyone who was interested in art, science, or literature. Village children were taught to read and write by the monks. In the late Middle Ages these schools of the monks became some of the first universities.

The monasteries also became places of shelter for travelers. The highway bandits and the barbarians made travel difficult. The monks fed and clothed many of the people. These people often helped the monks in return for protection. As a result, these manors of the monks became growing villages.

The Crusades

While the people of Europe were fighting among themselves, great

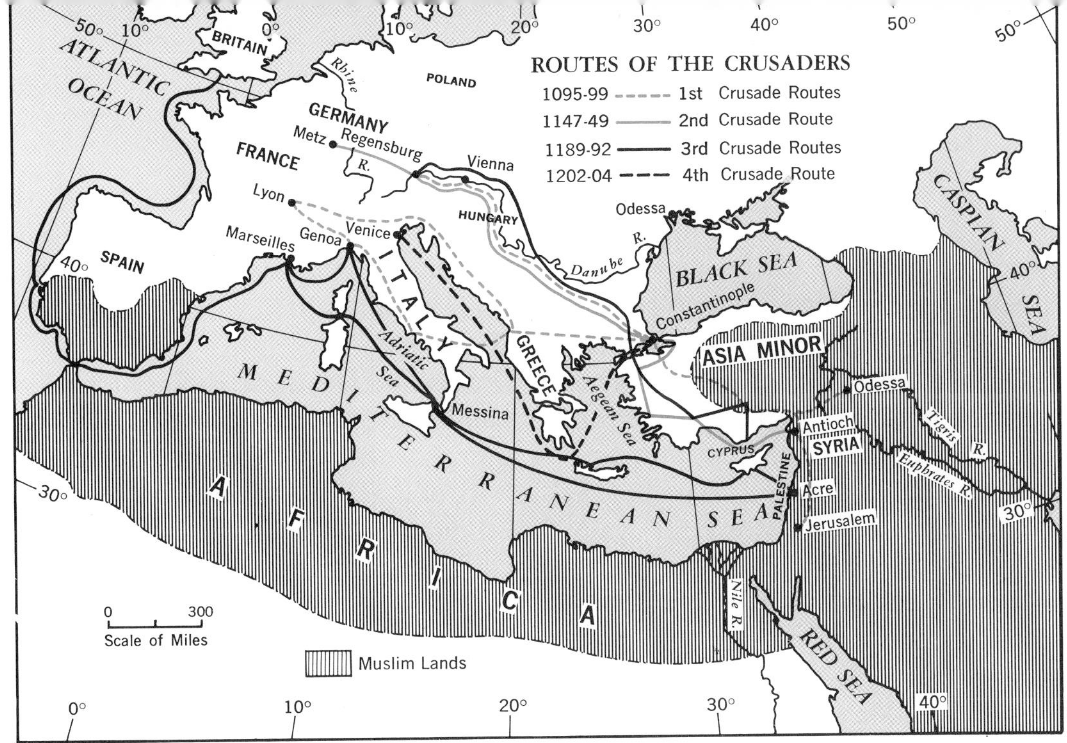

changes were taking place east of the Mediterranean Sea. In 632 A.D. a holy war began. This was a war between the Christians of the Eastern Roman Empire and the Arabs. The Arabs were followers of a new religion called the Muslim faith. You will learn more about this religion in a later chapter.

The Arabs conquered much of the land that had belonged to the Eastern Roman Empire. Palestine was one of the lands conquered by them. This is called the Holy Land because Christianity was started here. For many years the Arabs allowed Christians to visit the Holy Land. But in the eleventh century it became unsafe for Christians to go there. In 1095, Pope Urban, the head of the Roman Catholic Church, called upon the Christians of Europe to fight for the Holy Land. He asked the knights of Europe to forget their wars with each other and join in a war to capture Palestine from the Muslims. He called for them to join a war for the Cross, a **Crusade.**

Many knights and their foot soldiers joined the Crusades. They traveled by land and by sea to the eastern Mediterranean lands. They succeeded in capturing parts of the Holy Land, but they were not able to hold the land. The Muslims gained control of it again.

TRAVEL LEADS TO TRADE

Although the Crusades did not succeed in winning the Holy Land, they had a great effect on the people of Europe. Europeans learned about the riches of the Eastern lands. Crusaders saw beautiful cities. They saw people wearing silk and cotton clothing. They learned about the sugar and spices which came from China and India. When they returned to Europe, they told of the wonderful things they had seen. These stories made the people want all these goods.

During the Middle Ages most of the people lived in the villages on the manors. About the twelfth century, the population of Europe began to increase. Roads were built again and kept in repair. Trade between villages increased. Villages at crossroads and river crossings began to get more people. Soon they grew into towns. Do you see why villages at these locations would grow faster than others?

As a town grew larger, it needed more resources to supply its needs. One town might have lead mines. Another town might be close to deposits of iron ore. Still others, such as towns on the shore of the North Sea, had surplus supplies of dried fish to sell. Trade between towns increased. Towns became known for having special products, such as lead, iron, and dried fish, or even wool, lumber, and marble.

Men Learn Other Trades

Farming was no longer the only job open to men. Workers in the towns began to specialize in other jobs. Men could make a living by working at one job. Men made their living as bakers, butchers, or fish sellers. Weavers, tanners, tailors, and shoemakers became known for their craftsmanship. Men worked only at their special job. They used the money they earned from selling their products to buy the other things they needed.

Members of these different trades banded together for protection. These groups were called **guilds.** The members of a guild set fair prices on their products. No member of the guild could sell an article above or below the price agreed upon. It was thought a sin for a workman to sell an article for more than the cost of materials and labor. The guilds also wished to protect the quality of their products. A man who wanted to stay in a guild had to do excellent work. Members of a guild also helped each other in times of trouble.

Members of a guild lived and worked on the same street or in the same part of town. The names of the streets showed the craftsmen who worked there. For example, one street might be named Baker Street, another Tanner's Row. Still another might be called the Street of Silversmiths.

It was not easy to become a member of a guild. The guilds were run by master craftsmen. These masters took into their care one or more young boys who were called **apprentices.** During the period of apprenticeship, these boys lived in the master's home. In payment for their work, they received food and clothing. The period of apprenticeship lasted from two to seven years. The apprentice learned the trade of the master. He learned how to make shoes, or tan leather, or work gold. At the end of the apprenticeship, he became a **journeyman.** The journeyman was paid a little money for his work. The journeymen and apprentices carried on all the work of a shop under the direction of the master craftsman.

In time, a journeyman sought permission from the guild to become a **master.** He had to submit proof to the guild that he was worthy of membership. He brought before the guild a sample of his finest work, his **masterpiece.** If he was a weaver, he presented a fine piece of woven cloth. A silversmith might present a silver cup or bowl. If his work was accepted by the guild, the journeyman became a master and a full member of the guild. He could then set up his own shop and take in apprentices and journeymen.

The names of people today do not often tell the kind of work they do. In the Middle Ages they often did. What do you suppose the following men did for a living? To what guild did each of these men belong—Mason, Tanner, Potter, Wheelwright, and Smith? Can you guess where these names came from—Draper, Miller, Fuller, and Fletcher?

Trade within the Cities

As trade between the villages and towns increased, **market places** were established. These were places where

The master tailor's standards and prices were set by his guild.

craftsmen and farmers could set up stalls, and sell or exchange goods and food. They were set up in the towns which were easy for the people to reach. Because these market places competed with the local storekeepers, they were open only once a week.

As trade at these market places increased, the towns which had the best locations and the best products grew in size. They became the centers of trade for foreign goods as well as local goods. These towns held large **fairs** once a year. Merchants from far and near came to trade their goods. Local merchants competed with foreign merchants. Goods from all parts of Europe and Asia were bought and sold.

The fairs of the Middle Ages were similar in some ways to the county fairs of today. Merchants displayed their goods. Prizes were given for the best products. The fairs were

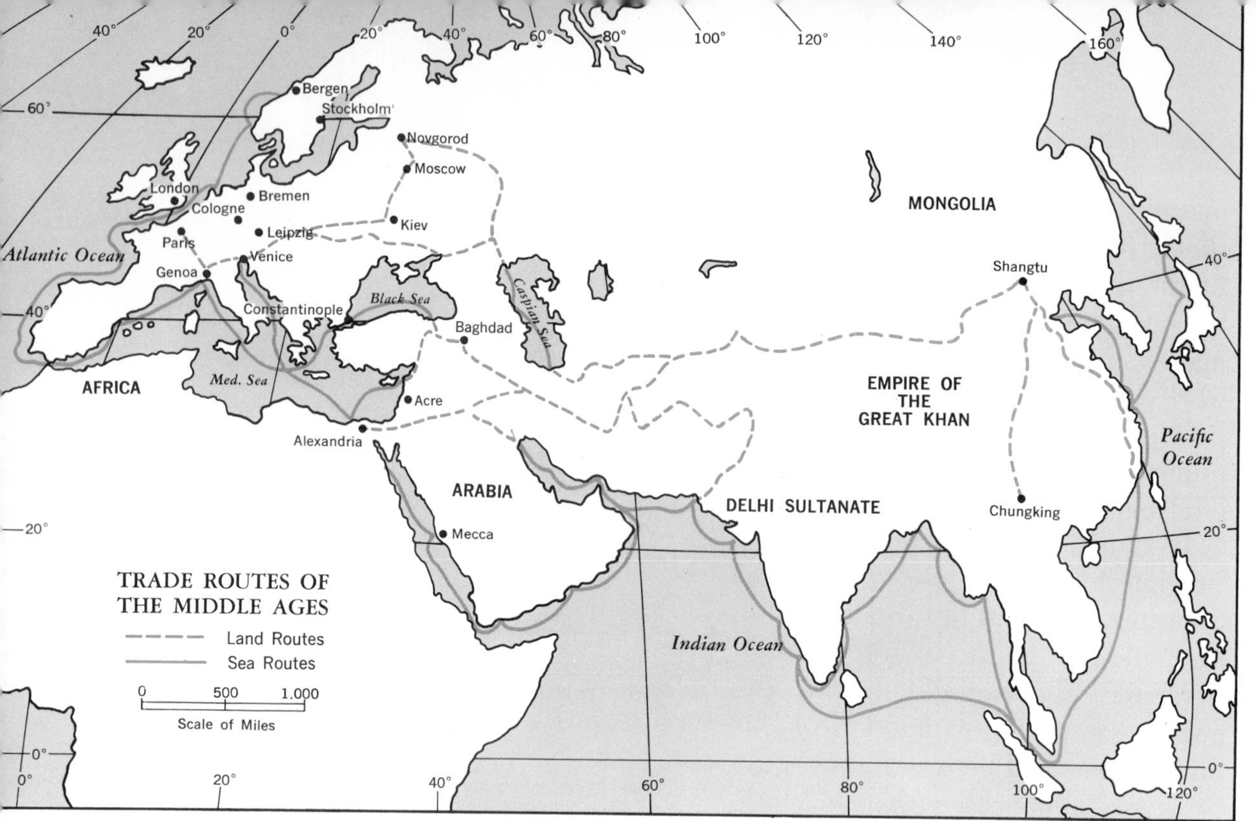

also places of entertainment. Singers, jugglers, and acts of all kinds amused the crowds that gathered. But the main purpose of the fairs of the Middle Ages was trade.

Goods were carried to the fairs by overland routes and by river and sea routes. Land routes connected such places as Paris, Bremen, Cologne, Frankfort, Leipzig, Prague, and Vienna. Many places in Italy became important trading centers. Ships carried goods from London, Acre, Constantinople, and Alexandria to the ports along the Mediterranean. Venice became the leading center in Italy for oversea trade. There were also important trading centers in Northern Europe, especially along the major rivers. Locate on the map these trading centers which later became the leading cities in Europe.

Great Cathedrals

In the late Middle Ages a great interest in building large churches arose in many cities in Europe. These large churches are called **cathedrals.** Most churches had been made of wood. Many of the great wooden churches of the Middle Ages had burned and been rebuilt several times. The new cathedrals were built of stone. The large blocks of stone for the cathedral had to be carefully shaped. Stones were lifted into place with great care. They were hoisted by rope and pulley. This was a difficult and dangerous task.

Each town tried to outdo the other towns in the size and magnificence of its cathedral. Sometimes great nobles joined guild members, women, monks, priests, and serfs in pulling carts of stone and wood for the cathedral. The carts of building material were hauled in silence to the site of the cathedral. When the people stopped to rest, they prayed and sang hymns. Although the priests and townspeople were anxious to finish a cathedral, it took many years to build. Some took as long as 20 or 30 years to complete.

The cathedral was the most magnificent building of the Middle Ages. It made all other buildings look very small indeed. The outside of the cathedral was richly decorated with statues and carvings. When built, it filled the viewer with awe and pleasure. In some cities the people were so proud of their cathedrals that they passed laws limiting the height of other buildings. They wanted the cathedral to soar above the roofs of all other buildings in the city.

The Cathedral at Rheims had more than 2,000 statues. Stained glass windows turned sunlight into beautiful colors. Some stained glass windows showed scenes from the Bible. Others showed craftsmen at work. Some of our information about the daily lives of the people who built the cathedrals comes from these scenes. We also learn about the clothing of the Middle Ages from these scenes. People of the Bible were dressed in the clothes of the Middle Ages, not in the clothing worn when the Bible was written. David might be shown in armor. Mary would wear the dress of a noblewoman of the Middle Ages.

Notre Dame, in Paris, is one of the most famous early Gothic cathedrals.

The great cathedrals of Europe are one of our tangible, cultural heritages from the Middle Ages. They also remind us of some of the better intangible heritages of these times. They recall for us the religious spirit of the people who built these great churches with so much love and devotion. They remind us of the time when cities began to grow again. Their beautiful marble, stained glass, and metal work remind us of the rebirth of trade. They tell us that travel had become safe enough to allow these precious materials to be brought from other cities.

The Development of Nations

We have seen that the Middle Ages was a time of transition. The way of life of the people in Europe was very difficult. With the strong government of the Roman Empire gone, the people had to find a new way of life which would protect them. They developed a system of land ownership in return for service called the Feudal System. It became a kind of government which provided for the protection of the land and people.

In the Middle Ages, Christianity was the one common bond of all the people in Western Europe. The leaders of the Church began to govern the actions of the people. The monasteries became the centers of education. The Crusades, although unsuccessful in their goal, helped expand the ideas and the trade of the Europeans.

The late Middle Ages saw a revival of trade and the regrowth of cities. Trade brought with it new jobs and new wealth. Men gained their freedom and began to lead a better life. Nations began to develop under the leadership of lords and kings.

Do You Know?

1. Who were the barbarians? Which group of barbarians settled on Roman land? Which tribe ransacked Rome?

2. What were three reasons for the decline of trade in the Roman Empire?

3. What caused free men to become bound to a lord during the Middle Ages?

4. Why did each of the three main farming fields go through a three-year cycle?

5. Why were fields divided into long strips?

6. What do we call a community of the Middle Ages?

7. What were tournaments? What were two types of tournaments? What were the lists?

8. What was the main purpose of the fairs? Where were they held?

9. What is a merchant?

Learn By Doing

1. Study the map on page 109. Then answer the following questions:

a. Which group of barbarians came from Eastern Asia?

b. From what part of Europe did the Ostrogoths come?

c. Trace the route of the Vandals. What were some of the territories through which they traveled?

d. What group came from present-day Denmark? Where did they settle?

e. From what area did the Franks come? Where did they settle?

f. Trace the route of the Visigoths. What parts of Europe did they conquer?

2. Follow these directions and draw a diagram of a manor.

a. Draw a line one inch long in the lower left hand corner of your paper. Mark it as shown. Use this line for your scale.

FEET
0 100 200

b. At the edge of your diagram place an arrow pointing to the directions north, south, east, and west.

N
W E
S

c. In the center of the paper draw a square, 50 feet on each side. This will represent the manor house, the home of the lord. West of the house, add a barn and a tool shed.

d. In the northwest corner of the page draw seven or eight manor huts. Mark each 30 feet long and 20 feet wide.

e. East of the manor house are three long fields: 1,200 feet long and 200 feet wide. One is for wheat, one for rye, and one for hay. Draw and label each field.

f. The remaining area is forested or fallow. Indicate the wooded sections and the grass areas by small figures as is shown:

g. Outline a church at the edge of the forest and place a cross on the building.

h. At the top of the diagram give the manor a name.

3. Select one of the following titles and write a descriptive composition.

The Cathedral of Notre Dame
A Knight in Shining Armor
A Medieval University
The Great Hall

Test Your Knowledge

1. What were some of the internal causes of the decline of the Roman Empire? What were the external causes? Which do you think had the greatest effect on the fall of Rome?

2. What was the manorial system? What was the feudal system? What service did the serf, the freeman, the knight, and the lord have to give to the person above him? What service did the king, the lord, and the knight give to the person below him?

3. What were the three steps to knighthood? What duties had to be performed at each stage?

4. In what ways did the Church unite the people of the Middle Ages?

5. In what ways did the monasteries serve the people?

6. What were the Crusades? Who fought in them? What was the major lasting result?

7. Can you give three reasons why manor villages developed into towns during the late Middle Ages?

8. What was a guild? What rules did they follow? What do we call the "guilds" of today? Do they follow the same rules?

9. How did one become a master craftsman? What were some of the crafts, or kinds of work, a young boy could learn?

10. Name two cathedrals built during the Middle Ages. Describe the Gothic style of architecture.

CHAPTER 8

A TIME OF CHANGE

The Middle Ages were followed by a period in history known today as the Renaissance. The re in Renaissance may be traced back to Latin, the language of ancient Rome. It means "again." The remainder of the word came from the Latin word nasci which means "to be born." Renaissance refers to the rebirth of learning which swept through the world as the Middle Ages gave way to modern times.

A TIME OF REDISCOVERY AND DISCOVERY

It is not easy to fix the time of change from the Middle Ages to the Modern World. First of all, the Renaissance did not begin at the same time in all countries of Europe. It began in Italy and spread later to other parts of Europe. Then too, many of the changes that affected life in the Renaissance began in the Middle Ages. For example, the Renaissance was a period of time when many universities were founded. Yet universities began in the Middle Ages.

Many of the ways of living of the people in the Middle Ages continued into this time. They did not suddenly change. For example, the system of serfdom came to a close in most European countries during the final years of the Middle Ages. Yet serfs were not freed in Russia until 1861. In general, however, the Renaissance in Western Europe lasted for about three hundred years. It lasted from about A.D. 1300 to about A.D. 1600.

The Renaissance, or rebirth of learning, which gradually developed and changed the world was caused by the growth of cities and towns in the late Middle Ages. As people freed themselves from feudalism, they had time to think about the past and to plan for the future. The cultures of the past helped them to build their own culture. The Renaissance was a time of rediscovery and discovery.

The Renaissance was a time when men rediscovered the ideas of the Greeks and Romans and other ancient peoples. It was a time when men became interested in the art and architecture of the Ancient World. It was a time when these valuable heritages of the past were rediscovered.

The Renaissance was a time when new ideas about the Earth and its place in the universe became known. New inventions were made that have had a great effect upon our ways of living.

New trade routes to the Far East were discovered. It was a time when trade was established directly with the Far East. It was also a time when new lands were discovered. Let us look at a few of the rediscoveries and discoveries that changed the world. These discoveries launched the Modern World.

The Writings of Ancient Peoples

The writings of the ancient Romans were not unknown during the Middle Ages. The monks of the Middle Ages read the writings of the ancient Romans with great interest. However, during the Middle Ages the **classics,** the writings of the Greeks and Romans, were not widely known. They were not often read outside the monasteries in which they were kept.

The Italian writer Petrarch (1304–1374) was the most famous poet of his day. He treasured the writings of classic times. He was one of the first men to collect ancient Latin manuscripts. Although Petrarch could not read them, he also collected Greek manuscripts. He realized that the Greek manuscripts held a rich world of ideas. His interest in the classics aroused the interest of other scholars in collecting ancient writings.

Rich merchants and nobles also became interested in collecting these writings of the past. They began to search eagerly for manuscripts of the great Roman and Greek writers. They hired men to search monasteries for rare manuscripts. They often had copies made of manuscripts they were unable to buy or to borrow.

Many of the Greek classics had been kept in Constantinople, the capital of the Eastern Roman Empire. By the fourteenth century, the Eastern Roman Empire had lost much of its land. Constantinople fell to the Turks in A.D. 1453. Fortunately, before the fall, many Greek scholars from Constantinople were invited by the wealthy to some of the cities of Italy. They brought with them manuscripts of Plato and Aristotle and other Greek writers. They taught Greek and read aloud the writings of the ancient Greeks. Italian scholars were delighted with the writings of the ancient Greeks and Romans that had been saved during the Middle Ages. Most of the writings of the Greeks and Romans that exist today were rediscovered between A.D. 1350 and A.D. 1500.

Ancient Manuscripts

Many manuscripts of the ancient writers had been neglected for nearly a thousand years. During those centuries some manuscripts were damaged or destroyed by fire, rot, and mildew. Perhaps the worst enemy of the manuscripts was man himself. In A.D. 1204 the armies of the Fourth Crusade captured Constantinople. The soldiers looted and burned. In the burning a great number of manuscripts containing the works of ancient Greek writers were lost. Our cultural heritage suffered a heavy blow from this act.

Three things helped to carry the manuscripts of ancient writers through a thousand years of neglect. First, as you recall, monasteries stored many writings. Second, monks of the ninth century made copies of worn manuscripts. Most of the manuscripts that men had after the Middle Ages were these copies made during the ninth century. Third, the manuscripts were written on **parchment.** Parchment is animal skin that has been stretched and rubbed. It is sturdy and durable. Until printing was invented, books were written on parchment.

Manuscripts were costly to make. They were written or copied by hand. A very long time was needed to make just one copy of a book. Parchment was expensive. Two or three hundred sheepskins might be used in making the parchment for just one book. The monks of the Middle Ages reused parchment when possible.

Sometimes the monks who copied manuscripts scraped the writing off old parchments and used the parchments again. Modern science has enabled us to read the first writing on a sheet of parchment. In this way some writings have been restored that would otherwise have been lost.

Some parchment manuscripts were written and decorated with great care. Some were so beautifully decorated that they are treasured as works of art. Manuscripts that were decorated with designs in brilliant colors are called **illuminated manuscripts.** An example is shown on page 133. One of the national treasures of Ireland is the *Book of Kells.* This illuminated manuscript was probably made in the eighth century.

The Invention of Printing

The invention of printing with **movable type** changed the slow, difficult process of bookmaking. Movable type was simply the letters of the alphabet carved on separate blocks of wood or stone. Printing had been invented in China, but the idea did not spread into Europe. The European inventor of printing is not known. However, Johann Gutenberg, a German bookmaker, has been given the honor. The first book printed in Europe with movable type was a Bible. It is thought to have been printed by Gutenberg in Germany in A.D. 1456.

The use of printing spread throughout most of Europe. Printing was introduced into Russia about one hundred years after its adoption in Western Europe.

The beautiful illumination of the Book of Kells shows the kind of handwork made obsolete by Gutenberg's press.

Books Helped Spread Ideas

The invention of the **printing press** made one of the greatest changes in our ways of living. Books printed on paper replaced the parchment manuscripts. They could be printed rapidly and in greater numbers. The ideas of the writers of ancient and modern times could now become known to great numbers of people. After the invention and widespread use of printing, the people of Europe entered a modern world, a world of print. They entered a world in which printed material gave man an easy and rapid way of communicating ideas.

Before the invention of printing, the ideas of the Ancient World were known only to a few people. They were known by pupils who listened to university scholars speak or read aloud the writings from scarce manuscripts. The invention of printing meant that anyone who could read could learn the ideas of ancient and modern writers. The written cultural heritage from the Greeks and Romans became widespread.

RENAISSANCE ART AND ARCHITECTURE

The Renaissance was a time when new advances in art and architecture were made. During the Middle Ages, the church helped painters. They were encouraged to decorate the churches with beautiful pictures. Naturally they painted pictures of characters from the Bible or other religious subjects. Following the Middle Ages, painters began to turn to nature for ideas. They painted landscapes and other objects they saw around them. Artists, such as Da Vinci, began to study the human body so that they could paint it more accurately. Painters began to learn how to give feelings of depth and space to a painting. Wealthy men began to help painters. Painters became important men who were recognized and honored for their talent.

Leonardo da Vinci (1452–1519)

Leonardo da Vinci was one of the greatest painters of the Renaissance. He left few paintings, but these are among the greatest paintings of all time. Perhaps the *Mona Lisa* is his most famous work. It is the picture of the wife of a merchant from the city of Florence. Originally, the colors of the painting were fresh and bright.

Another widely admired work of Da Vinci is *The Last Supper.* It was painted on the wall of a convent in Milan, Italy. The wall upon which he painted *The Last Supper* was damp. Soon after the work was finished, it began to crumble away. However, copies of the work and parts of the painting which are left show us the greatness of the work.

Michelangelo (1475–1564)

Michelangelo was the leading sculptor of the Renaissance. He carved powerful figures in marble. His statue of Moses is shown on page 135. Michelangelo was also a great painter. His paintings on newly spread wet plaster are well known. Paintings on wet plaster are called **frescoes.** His most famous frescoes were painted on the ceiling of the Sistine Chapel in Rome. Michelangelo worked on these frescoes for four and one-half years. In order to paint these frescoes on the ceiling, he had to lie on his back on a high, wooden scaffold.

Architecture

During the Renaissance, architects began to turn to Roman buildings and writings for ideas. They did not copy the architecture of the Romans. Rather, they took some of the ideas of classic times and used them in new ways. They borrowed the Greek column and the Roman arch. They took the Roman dome, such as the one we saw on the Pantheon. The Pantheon dome was the model for all the domes built during the Renaissance. The architects raised it upon a round building shaped like a **drum.** The drum gave added height to a dome. It made the dome look larger and more beautiful.

The most magnificently domed church of the Renaissance was St. Peter's in Rome. It was begun in 1506 and dedicated more than a century later. The church is decorated with the sculpture and paintings of the greatest artists of that time. You can see in the picture of

St. Peter's on this page the use of the arch, the column, the dome, and the drum. Notice how they have been changed into a style of architecture that is not a mere copy of Roman architecture.

At one time, while St. Peter's was being built, Michelangelo was in charge of construction. He wanted the dome to be the most important feature of the church. Later architects, however, carried the front of the church much farther away from the dome than Michelangelo had planned. For this reason, the splendor of the dome is not easy to see from the outside. Once inside, the beauty and size of the dome can still be appreciated.

The city and country homes of wealthy men also reflected the reborn interest in classic architecture. Country houses, such as the Villa Rotonda near Venice, set a new style. This style was widely followed in Italy and later in France and England. The Villa Rotonda, with its columns and arches, was designed by the architect, Andrea Palladio. Palladio had a powerful effect on Renaissance architecture. His name had been given to this style of architecture—**Palladian.**

Renaissance art and architecture were not limited to Italy. Other Western European countries produced artists who still rank among the best today. Velasquez in Spain and Van Dyck and Rembrandt in Holland were noted for their lifelike paintings.

Michelangelo's many talents can be seen in his fresco paintings, sculptured figures, and design of St. Peter's.

THE STUDY OF THE EARTH

People who have had time to think and reflect have wondered about the world about them. After the Middle Ages men had more time in which to think about the natural world. They tried to see if there were laws which were "Nature's laws." They began to experiment, test, and retest. They began to question many things. With the development of a greater emphasis on reason and direct observation, beliefs in magic and superstition dwindled. Science made rapid progress because of the growing practice of testing ideas by experiment.

Leonardo da Vinci Studied Nature

Leonardo da Vinci was as great a scientist as he was a painter. During the last years of his life, he devoted himself almost entirely to science. He was one of the first great thinkers of the Renaissance to wonder about nature. Da Vinci left notebooks of several thousand pages. In these he had jotted down his thoughts and made sketches of his ideas. These notebooks show us that Da Vinci's mind considered many things.

Da Vinci's main scientific method was one of careful observation of nature itself. He observed it closely. He was very interested in the flight of birds. He noted that the feathers on the front of a wing are stiff and firm. He noted that those on the back are soft and bend quite easily. He reasoned that the front feathers of a wing needed to be firm enough to meet the wind and air in flight. After studying the structure and flight of birds, he drew a sketch of a flying machine.

Da Vinci thought of many practical inventions. Here is his suggestion for a way of saving oneself in shipwreck at sea:

> *It is necessary to have a coat made of leather with a double hem over the breast of the width of a finger, and double also from the girdle to the knee, and let the leather of which it is made be quite air-tight. And when you are obliged to jump into the sea, blow out the lapels of the coat through the hems of the breast, and then jump into the sea. And let yourself be carried by the waves, if there is no shore near at hand and you do not know the sea. And always keep in your mouth the end of the tube through which the air passes into the garment; and if once or twice it should become necessary for you to take a breath when the foam prevents you, draw it through the mouth of the tube from the air within the coat.*

Ideas Change about the Universe

Up to the time of the Renaissance most men believed that the Earth was the center of our universe. They believed that the sun revolved around the Earth. True, the Greek astronomer Aristarchus believed otherwise. In the third century B.C. he wrote that the Earth and the other planets revolved around the sun. His theory was not accepted by later Greeks or by scholars of the Middle Ages. The idea that holds the sun as the center of the universe is known as the **helio-centric theory.** *Helio* means "sun" and *centric* means "center." You know that the word *geography* means "a study of the Earth." The idea that holds the Earth as the center of the universe is the **geocentric theory.**

Why did most men believe in the geocentric theory? Why did they think that the sun revolved around the Earth? Men believed this because of what they observed. You, too, see the sun appear to come up in the east. You see it appear to go down in the west. If you stand in one spot from sunup to sundown, which appears to move, the Earth or the sun? Note how our language holds on to the geocentric theory in the words *sunrise* and *sunset.*

Copernicus and Bruno

In 1543 Nicolaus Copernicus proposed that the Earth spins and circles the sun. This theory of rotation and revolution of the Earth startled the people. Copernicus was not the first man of the Renaissance to hold this theory. We find a statement in the notebooks of Da Vinci that speaks of the sun as the center of the universe. Copernicus, however, was the first to write a careful and thoughtful explanation of the heliocentric theory.

Copernicus thought of the heliocentric theory many years before he made it public. He developed it sometime in the years before 1515. Why did he wait so long to make his ideas known to the world? He may have feared the opposition of the Church. At that time the geocentric theory was a part of the Christian teachings. Whatever the reason, he waited many years before publishing his ideas. He died in 1543, the year his book was published.

Perhaps Copernicus had good reason to be cautious about making known his ideas. A few years after his book was printed, Giordano Bruno was burned at the stake for his beliefs. One of the charges brought against Bruno by the Church was that he taught the heliocentric theory. He said that there might be many suns and many planets with men upon them. Probably the most serious charge, upon which he was convicted and sent to the stake, was his teaching of a **heresy.** A heresy is an opinion on a religious doctrine that is opposite to the opinion held by the Church. Bruno taught that God is in each man. He taught that God is not a being apart and distant from man.

Kepler and Galileo

Copernicus and Bruno both believed that the Earth revolved around the sun. But this was not enough. Proof was needed that the heliocentric theory was true. The necessary proof was given by two men who lived a few years later. One man was Johannes Kepler (1571–1630). The other man was Galileo Galilei (1564–1642) who is best known by his first name, Galileo.

Kepler showed by mathematics that the Earth and the other planets move around the sun. Copernicus had believed that the planets moved in perfect circles about the sun. Kepler proved that the path of a planet about the sun is not a perfect circle but an ellipse. He also proved that each planet moves about the sun at a different rate of speed.

Galileo learned Greek and Latin as a boy. He later studied medicine. He discovered many natural laws that help us understand the things we see around us. In 1581 he watched the movement of a great chandelier in the cathedral of Pisa, Italy. He noticed the regular swing, back and forth, of the great chandelier. He used his own pulse to time the swing. He found that each swing of the chandelier took the same duration of time. Can you see why Galileo could use the pulse to time the swings of the chandelier? As a result of this observation, Galileo suggested that a swinging pendulum would be an excellent way to keep time.

The Studies of Galileo

Galileo also made studies of falling objects. He tried to time their fall. He used a water clock to measure the time of their fall. Galileo used the Leaning Tower of Pisa in Italy in his experiments with falling objects. He dropped two objects of different weight from the tower. Both objects reached the ground at the same time. This proved that they fell with the same speed.

Galileo attempted to measure the weight of air. His ideas resulted in the development of the **barometer,** an instrument which measures the pressure of air, and the **thermometer,** an instrument which measures the temperature. Today, these two instruments have helped scientists to measure heat and cold and to forecast the weather.

The Telescope

The **telescope** was invented in 1608 by Hans Lippershey. Lippershey lived in the Netherlands. He made his living by making glass lenses for reading. By chance, Lippershey found that different lenses put together in certain ways made objects appear larger or smaller.

Galileo read about this invention. He saw how useful this device would be in his studies of the stars. Galileo quickly made a telescope. He soon made other more powerful telescopes.

Galileo made many important discoveries with his telescopes. He discovered the moons of Jupiter. He discovered that there were great numbers of stars that could not be seen by the naked eye. He noted that Mercury and Venus had phases like those of the Earth's moon. He decided therefore that Mercury and Venus, like the Earth, revolved about the sun. Galileo published his findings in support of the heliocentric theory. His discoveries convinced many people that the theory of Copernicus was true.

Galileo Is Questioned

In 1616 church authorities called Galileo before them. They warned him that he would be punished if he continued to teach the heretical heliocentric theory. Galileo agreed to keep silent. He held his silence for sixteen years. In 1632 he published the famous *Dialogue on the Two Principal Systems of the Universe.* He had received permission from church authorities to publish the book. He had promised that the book would favor neither the geocentric theory nor the heliocentric theory. To an intelligent reader, however, the book clearly showed the heliocentric theory to be the right one.

Galileo was called to the church office in Rome that decided questions of heresy. Under threat of torture, Galileo publicly took back his belief in the heliocentric theory. He was probably wise to do so. He had already made his point. His writings were known throughout Western Europe. He denied the theory because he knew that time, rather than death, would prove him right.

There is a very interesting story about Galileo's denial. After denying upon his knees the truth of the heliocentric theory, he rose to his feet. As he rose, he is supposed to have spoken softly: "But the Earth *does* move!" Sentenced to prison, Galileo was allowed by the Church to return to his home in Florence. There he was allowed to spend the re-

Because the heliocentric theory was against Church teaching, Galileo was convicted of heresy by the Inquisition.

maining years of his life in a sort of house arrest.

We owe a great deal to Galileo. He gave us proof for the heliocentric theory. He gave us the laws of the pendulum and some ideas that led to the development of our modern thermometer and barometer. His discoveries were the beginnings of the natural sciences as they exist today. His ideas and experiments helped to change the world. Galileo is considered the father of modern science.

Isaac Newton

In the year of Galileo's death, 1642, Isaac Newton was born in England. This scientist proved beyond a doubt the truth of the heliocentric theory. Newton wondered why the planets did not "fall." Why did they stay in balance? He worked on this problem for over twenty years before he made his discoveries public. Newton had to wait until the exact size of the Earth was known. His proof depended on knowing the distance between the center of the Earth and the center of the moon. In 1670 Jean Picard, a French astronomer, correctly measured one degree of the Earth's surface.

With this information Newton proved his discovery of the **law of gravitation.** This is the law of nature that describes the force that makes all bodies in the universe attract one another. This law explained the motions of the planets. The force of gravity causes an apple or a leaf to fall to the earth. This same force pulls the moon toward the Earth and keeps it from flying off into space. It is the force that explains the heliocentric theory. Newton's law of gravitation applies to the entire universe as we know it.

The importance of Newton's efforts in uncovering nature's laws is shown in these two lines by Alexander Pope, an English poet.

Nature and Nature's laws lay hid in night:
God said, Let Newton be! and all was light.

Man Changes His Way of Thinking

Copernicus, Galileo, and Newton changed man's ways of thinking about the universe. No longer was the Earth the center of the universe. The shift to the heliocentric theory so strongly changed man's ways of thinking about the universe that it can be called the **Copernican Revolution.**

With the growth of science, men began to question old beliefs and superstitions, particularly those that dealt with witchcraft and the practice of magic. Demons and witches were burned for their magical practices. Many superstitious fears disappeared as facts were found by the scientists. The old fear of the effects from changes in the moon gradually disappeared, as men began to examine and to understand the nature of the surface of the moon.

NEW LANDS WERE DISCOVERED

The Renaissance was a time when new trade routes and new lands were discovered. Adventures during the Middle Ages set the stage for the discoveries of the Renaissance. Some very important discoveries were made during the Middle Ages by the Norsemen and by Marco Polo. However, except for Iceland, the settlements in the new lands made by the Norsemen were not lasting. Also, the trade route to the Far East, established by Marco Polo, was closed later to travelers. New routes to the Far East needed to be found. Before reading about the discoveries made during the Renaissance, let us turn to the stories of the Norsemen and of Marco Polo.

Discoveries of the Norsemen

We know that daring Norsemen sailed into the Atlantic Ocean in shallow open ships. They discovered Iceland and Greenland. They even discovered a land to the west of Greenland which they called Vineland. We know that Vineland was actually part of North America. The Norsemen settled in each of these new lands. These discoveries and settlements were made in the eighth, ninth, tenth, and eleventh centuries.

The settlement in Iceland was lasting. Some people who live in Iceland today are descendants of the Norse explorers of the Middle Ages.

Why were the settlements in Vineland and Greenland gradually abandoned? Perhaps the reason was a gradual change of climate. We know that about the twelfth century the climate in Vineland and Greenland became colder. A little ice age set in.

Few people outside of Northern Europe knew about the settlements in Vineland and Greenland. Even there, the knowledge of these lands gradually died out. The story of the Norse adventures in the New World might easily have been lost. Fortunately it was kept alive in a few manuscripts.

Travels of Marco Polo

In the thirteenth century travelers who found their way across Asia were welcomed by the rulers of China.

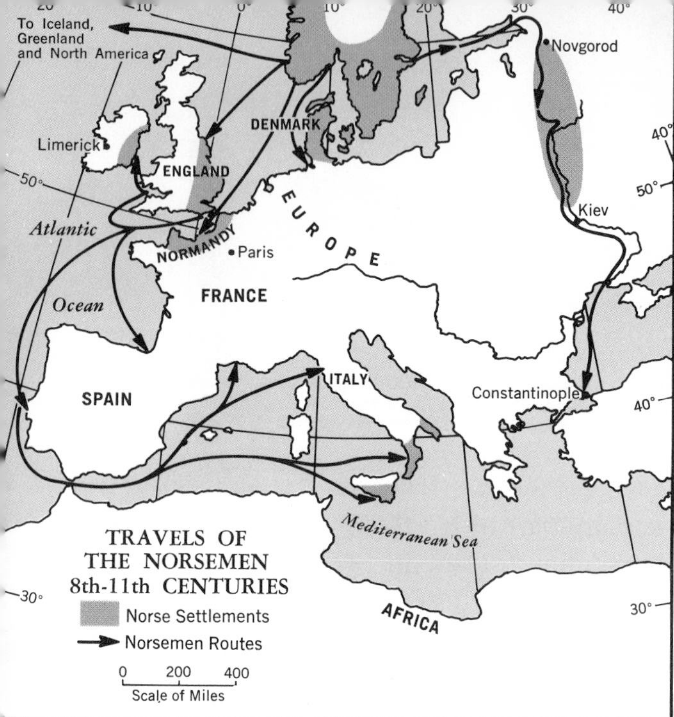

One of the first of these travelers was Marco Polo of Venice. Marco was about seventeen when he went with his father and uncle on the journey. They left Venice in 1271 and reached Cambaluc (modern Peking) in 1275.

China at that time was ruled by a group of people called the Mongols. The Mongol emperor was Kublai Khan. Marco's father had visited Kublai Khan's court on an earlier trip. The travelers were well received at the court of the great Mongol ruler. Marco became a favorite of Kublai Khan and traveled throughout China as his agent. Marco served Kublai Khan for seventeen years.

The Polos longed to return to their home in Venice. They sought permission from the emperor to leave China. He reluctantly granted it, and they reached Venice in 1295.

The Polos were not the only Europeans to reach China and return. But we know more about the Polos than the others because the story of Marco's travels was written down during a war between the city of Venice and the city of Genoa. Marco was captured by the Genoans and held prisoner. While in prison, Marco told the story of his travels to a fellow prisoner. This man wrote down Marco's story as Marco spoke. Marco told about the cities he had visited as an agent of Kublai Khan. He described the wealth, beauty, and customs of their peoples. This book became known throughout Europe.

Marco's travels interested the men of the early Renaissance. We know that his book was widely read, for many copies have survived from that time. His book was the chief source of information about life in the Far East for people of his time and for many years afterward. The story of Marco's travels through the Orient captured the interest of the people. They were more interested in the vast wealth he described than in the customs. Today we are interested in his descriptions of the Chinese ways of living at that time.

European contact with the Far East, which had begun in Marco's time, was soon broken. The people of China rebelled against their Mongol rulers and overthrew them. The new rulers closed China to foreigners. They were confident of the superiority of Chinese culture over that of other peoples. They decided that they did not need contact with other cultures.

New Routes to India Were Needed

In Marco's time, travel to India was more difficult than to China. Muslims held the lands between Europe and India. They controlled shipping on the Red Sea, the Persian Gulf, and the Arabian Sea. By 1500 Muslims controlled or ruled all lands touching the eastern Mediterranean. For this reason, Europeans could not trade directly with the people of India. Trade was possible only by going through the Muslims who acted as "middle men." Drugs, spices, pepper, silks, and jewels were carried by Muslims from India to ports on the Mediterranean. The two Italian ports, Venice and Genoa, controlled all European trade with India. Merchants of England, Spain, France, and Portugal had to trade with the Venetians or Genoans for goods from the Far East.

Merchants in Spain and Portugal wanted to find a new route to the Far East and India. They wanted to trade directly with the Indians for silk, pepper, spices, and jewels. They wanted to avoid paying the high prices demanded by the Italian merchants.

The Portuguese and Spanish knew that they would have to find a route not controlled by the Italians or the Muslims. Some Portuguese thought that if they sailed south along the western coast of Africa, they would eventually be able to turn north and reach India. Many attempts to find a direct trade route followed.

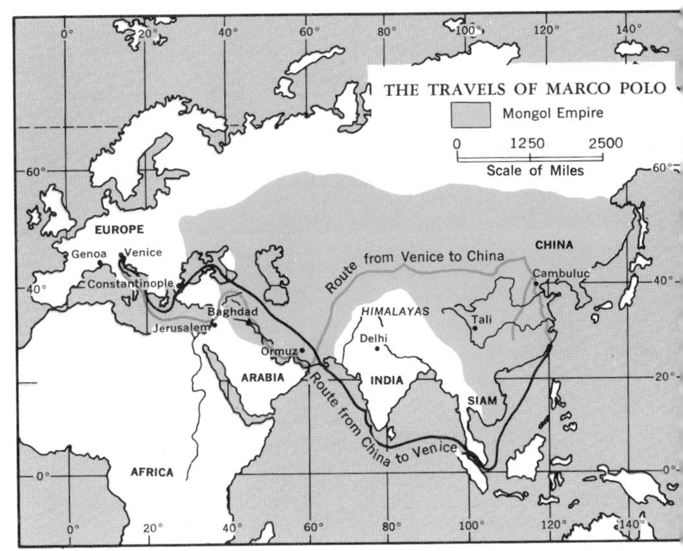

Prince Henry

One of the earliest leaders in Portuguese ocean exploration was Prince Henry the Navigator. Prince Henry built a center for the study of navigation, map-making, and astronomy in southern Portugal. He paid for the cost of the ships which sailed from his center on several trips to chart the coast of Africa. He was the prime mover in encouraging exploration of the South Atlantic along the coast of Africa.

The early Portuguese explorers found that the continent of Africa was much larger than anyone had imagined. Year by year, they slowly pushed their way south along the western coast of Africa.

Prince Henry died in 1460, but Portuguese exploration of the coast of Africa continued. In 1483 the Portuguese reached the mouth of the

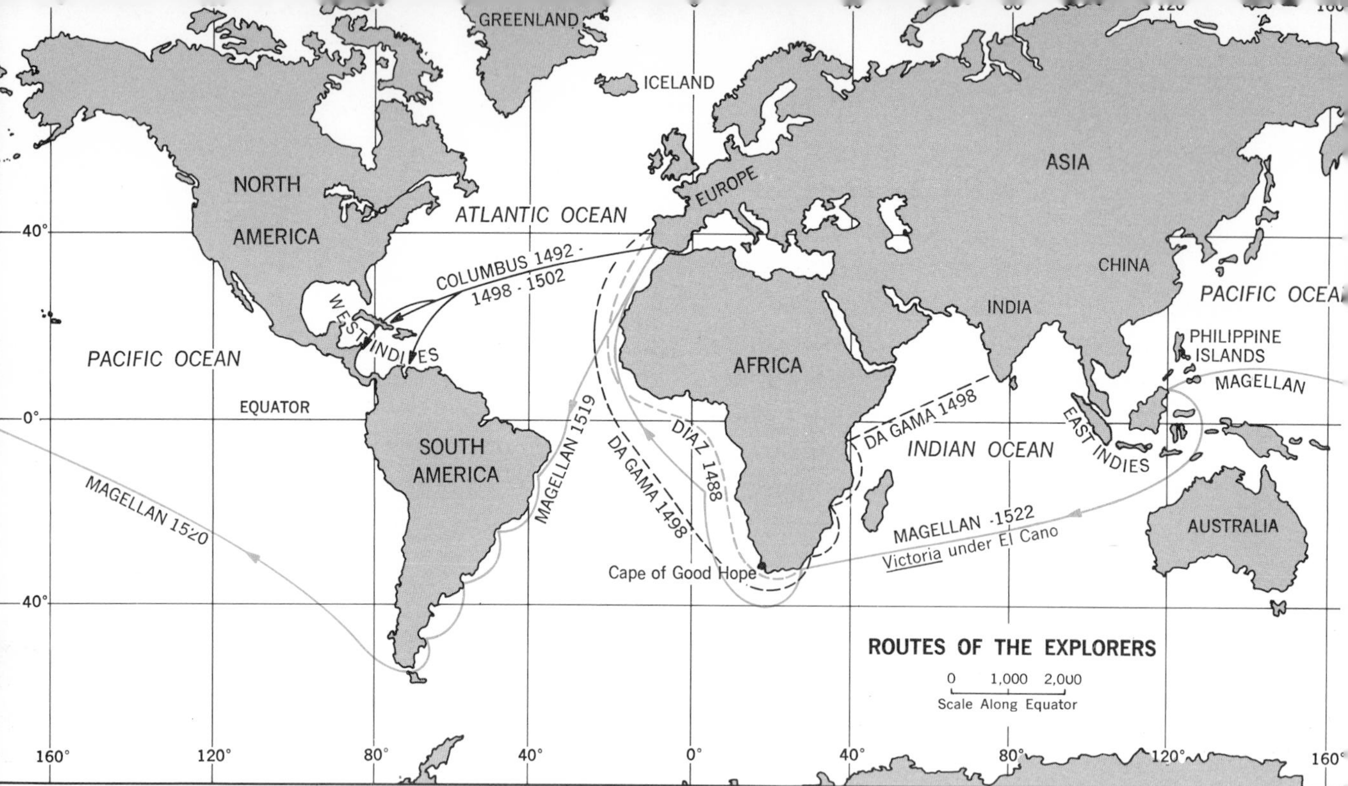

Congo River. In 1488 Bartholomew Diaz reached the southernmost point of Africa, the Cape of Good Hope. The Portuguese knew that the route to India and the riches of the East lay northward from that point.

Vasco da Gama Reaches India

In 1497, five years after Columbus discovered the New World, the Portuguese sent an expedition to sail round Africa to India. The leader of the four ships that set sail from Portugal was Vasco da Gama. After rounding the Cape of Good Hope, he picked up a Muslim navigator on the east coast of Africa. The Muslim navigator guided the Portuguese explorers across the Indian Ocean to the west coast of India.

Vasco da Gama returned to Portugal after having been away two and a half years. The trip had not been easy. He had lost two of his ships. Two-thirds of his men had died. He did return, however, with goods of great worth. He was the first man from Western Europe to reach India by sea around Africa. His trip completed the work and effort of 80 years of Portuguese exploration begun by Prince Henry.

The Portuguese did not want to share the knowledge of their African sea route with other countries. They spread frightening tales about the dangers of the South Atlantic. They also attacked any Muslim or Christian ship they met. By these means they kept themselves the masters of the African route to India for nearly one hundred years.

Other Men Seek a Route to India

In 1492, a few years before Vasco da Gama reached India by sailing round Africa, Columbus set sail for India. He tried to reach India by sailing westward. Educated men in the time of Columbus knew that the world is round. Columbus thought that Asia lay only 2,500 miles to the west of the Canary Islands.

You know the story of his voyage. You know that he thought he had reached some islands near India. He called the natives of the islands Indians. Other explorers soon realized that Columbus had not reached the East Indies but had discovered a new land. He had found a new continent that lay in the path of a westward route to India. In 1513 Spanish explorers found that another great ocean lay to the west of the newly discovered lands. A western sea passage to Asia was still to be found.

Ferdinand Magellan set out to find a passage to India in 1519. He sailed from Spain in command of five ships. He found a passage to the Pacific Ocean at the southernmost tip of South America. He crossed the Pacific to the Philippines. There, Magellan was killed in a battle with the natives of one of the islands. Of the five ships that had started the voyage, only one ship, the *Victoria*, returned to Spain in 1522. The *Victoria* had sailed round the world.

Magellan's voyage was of great importance. His ship, *Victoria*, was well named because his voyage was a great victory in man's search to understand the world. Magellan's voyage proved that Columbus had found a new world that was far from Asia. His voyage proved that the world is round. For the first time, man gained an idea of the relative sizes of the oceans and continents.

The English and French Seek New Lands

The English and French soon began to explore the North American continent. They hoped to find a northern sea passage which would be a short cut to Asia. They also hoped to find gold and riches in North America. In time, the English and French realized that there were riches other than silver and gold in the New World. North America was rich in fertile land, in great stands of timber, and in countless fur-bearing animals.

What was the effect of the explorations of the new lands? Trade between distant countries increased greatly. Man's geographical knowledge of the surface of the Earth became more accurate. All the great land masses of the world except Antarctica soon became known. Streams of people from Europe began to settle in North and South America.

The cultural heritage of the European settlers was very different from that of the North American Indians. The Europeans brought with them the metal plow and the harness for animals. The Indians had neither of these farming aids. The European settler could clear and plow far more land than an Indian farmer. The settler brought with him metal axes and saws. With these he could level trees easily and quickly. The Indian had to girdle a tree and then burn it. This process took much longer.

Many of the Indian tribes depended upon hunting along with some light farming for their food. When animal life in an area was used up, a tribe had to move to better hunting grounds. They needed tents that could be easily taken down and light enough to carry to a new camp. The European planned to settle in one place and make his living from farming. He did not want a temporary building. He used the trees he cut for timber and fuel. His house was solidly built for protection from the weather and from the Indians. The first homes which the Europeans built closely resembled European homes.

The Europeans brought with them weapons which were superior to those of the Indians. These weapons enabled the Europeans to conquer the Indians. These natives learned to use many of the new tools and new methods of farming brought by the settlers. But the Indians were not the only ones who benefited from the explorations. The Europeans were introduced to many new products, such as potatoes, tobacco, and furs. The "traders followed the flags of the explorers."

INVENTIONS CHANGE WAYS OF LIVING

The settlement of the new lands and the discovery of new products led to worldwide trade. Better goods of all kinds were needed. New methods of manufacturing were needed to keep pace with the demands. Scientists experimented with the forces in nature to find new ways to use them to aid mankind in his daily life. These experiments of the scientists during the Renaissance began to change ways of living. They paved the way for the inventions of the Modern Age.

New sources of power were uncovered and harnessed. Power-driven machinery took the place of hand-driven devices. Many workshops were enlarged into factories. Better goods were made in less time. The large cities changed in appearance. The selling of large quantities of goods led to wider and greater business interests.

The Development of the Steam Engine

We have seen how one idea, the heliocentric theory, caused a revolution in the way man thought about the Earth. We have also seen how one invention, the printing press, caused these thoughts to spread and to change the ways of living during the Renaissance. The beginning of the Modern Age saw the develop-

The Englishman James Watt's development of the steam engine in 1769 made it possible for the American Robert Fulton to build the first commercially successful steamboat, the *Clermont*.

ment of a revolutionary invention, the **steam engine.** The steam engine was "revolutionary" because it produced quick and quite complete changes in a rather short time.

Nearly 2,000 years ago Hero of Alexandria, a scientist of Egypt, experimented with the moving power of steam and made a revolving "toy." Little use seems to have been made of this interesting invention.

In the seventeenth century, the great Irish scientist, Robert Boyle, noticed that when water is heated, it turns into gas in the form of steam. Even more important, the steam expands and creates pressure.

The next development came from an idea of Thomas Newcomen, an English inventor. He made a steam engine in 1712 which pumped water out of coal mines. Coal taken from the mines was used to heat water. The heated water changed to steam. The expanding steam created pressure and pushed a plate in a big cylinder. The plate pushed air out causing a vacuum. The steam was released, and the pressure dropped. The plate moved back, and water was sucked up into the vacuum. Then the whole process began again. This steam engine needed a great deal of coal. It was too expensive to use except where coal was plentiful.

James Watt

The next great mind to turn to the steam engine belonged to James Watt, a skilled instrument maker.

A supervisor oversees the work in a steampowered factory.

Watt reasoned that costs could be cut if he could keep the cylinder hot all the time, and if a full "power stroke" could be designed. He realized that an engine which used less coal and more of the energy in the steam would be of great use. Watt worked for over thirty years to perfect his version of a steam engine.

Watt's most important addition to the steam engine was his use of the **piston,** the arm that went in and out or up and down within the cylinder of the engine. He attached the piston to a rod which was connected to a wheel. The wheel was designed to keep turning at an even pace. It could be used to turn machinery.

Watt had shown the world how to turn fire into a source of power. In a way, Watt made man's arms stronger and his legs longer. This modern machine opened wider the possibilities of a man-controlled world.

Uses of the Steam Engine

The steam engine changed several kinds of transportation. Robert Fulton used a steam engine to provide power for the first successful steamship in 1807. The ship was called the *Clermont.* By 1900, the steamship had replaced the sailing ship on the oceans' trade routes. In 1815 a train locomotive was invented that used steam as the source of power.

The steam engine changed several methods of manufacturing. It was used to turn machinery in factories. Its power could be used by many machines on different floors. A system of moving belts was used to accomplish this. A great advantage was that factories could be built away from water. Before the steam engine, factories that needed a source of power had to be built near streams or rivers for waterpower.

Although wood was a useful fuel for the steam engine, coal was found to be best. Deposits of coal became very important. Manufacturing cities grew up near great coal and iron beds.

The Textile Industry Changes

Inventions based on the steam engine had an enormous effect upon man's ways of living. In the chapter on the Middle Ages, you read about the work of certain craftsmen. In the Middle Ages and well into modern times, shoemakers made the complete shoe. Clothmakers in home shops, cleaned, dyed, combed, spun, wove, washed, and sold the completed cloth. All of these home or shop practices were changed in a very short time when steam power became available.

James Hargreaves invented a machine that could spin eight to eleven threads at once. He later improved the machine so that it could spin as many as 80 threads at the same time. This small machine was run by hand and could be used in the home. It was named a **spinning jenny** after his wife, Jenny. It increased the amount of thread spun in the home. Later, Edmund Cartwright invented a **power loom.** This loom could be run by waterpower, steam power, or even horsepower. When the piston engine was used to run these machines, several floors filled with many machines could turn out a great amount of thread and cloth.

THE INDUSTRIAL REVOLUTION

Work became specialized in the great new textile factories that were built. Attendants were needed to see that threads did not break. Workmen were trained to do one job quickly and well. The machines did not stop. The people had to keep up with them. The manufacture of metal spinning machines and looms led to an increase in the use of iron. The rise in the demand for iron called for an increase in the number of mines and an improvement in mining methods.

At the time of the rise in production of more and more manufactured goods, the population in Western Europe also rose. There were several reasons for this increase in population. The discovery of the New World brought new foods, such as the potato, into Europe. Improvements in living conditions and better foods helped to keep people healthier and free from disease.

England was the first to change from an agricultural nation to an industrial nation. It became a nation of factories and industrial towns. In time it came to depend upon other countries for its food supplies. It paid for these foods with its manufactured goods. This change in England has been called the **Industrial Revolution.** The use of machinery spread to other countries at different times. Its growth depended on the conditions and natural resources of the country.

Children often worked long hours.

Problems of the Industrial Revolution

There were many problems that came with the Industrial Revolution. The factory system of producing goods brought changes in the way men lived and worked. Skilled craftsmen, who had always made the entire product, often resented the factory which took away their customers. By making the same product faster, cheaper, and sometimes better, factories forced many craftsmen out of business.

The steps and tasks needed to make a finished product were divided among people working at different machines. Each man worked at his particular job for long hours. Supervisors and managers were appointed to watch and direct the men working at the different steps of the manufacturing process. The people in manfacturing towns came to be divided into workers and management.

In many early factories the working day was very long. Eight-, nine-, and ten-year-old children worked 12 to 15 hours a day, six days a week. Some workers walked to work in the dark and walked home again in the dark. Factory workers had no "coffee-breaks" as people today have.

In some factories the workers were no better off than serfs had been in the Middle Ages. Unskilled workers could be replaced quickly. In the country if work was cut down, a craftsman could turn to his farm for a living. In the city if a man or woman lost his job, he lost his only means of earning a living.

When a factory lost its **market**—that is, when it could not sell its products, it stopped production. Workers were laid off. If the market dropped for many factories the worker had great difficulty. Such periods of "lay-offs" are called **recessions** or **depressions.**

The factory towns often had a dense smoke cloud hanging over them. The coal used to make steam gave off much smoke. There were no laws as we have today to make factory owners control the smoke. This cloud cut down on the amount of sunlight. Polluted air and crowded conditions increased the possibility of sickness.

To combat some of the evils that came into being with the Industrial Revolution, workers began to group together. They realized that if they organized, they could present stronger demands. They saw that a show of strength would force the management to make life more pleasant and secure. Today groups of workers who join together to get better working conditions are called **unions.**

Workers and management tried to work out their problems. Sometimes they succeeded quickly. Often they took a long time. Once in a while their efforts ended in anger on both sides. The worker who is in a position to bargain with his employer is in a strong position. He is in a very different position from that of the slave of Rome or serf of the Middle Ages.

Farming Becomes More Scientific

The Industrial Revolution in England was accompanied by a change in farming practices. Cattle were carefully bred to produce animals that would give larger yields of beef. Larger sheep were bred. Farmers learned to apply new fertilizers to their fields. Crops increased in quality and yields in quantity. Farmers learned to plant clover. Clover increased the amount of nitrogen in the soil. When clover was plowed back into the earth, it improved the soil. Farmers no longer had to leave a field fallow every third year.

Some farmers found that by specializing in a certain product which they could grow well, they could make a better living. Farmers in one part of England began to specialize in growing grain. Farmers in another area began to raise vegetables to sell in the towns.

The Industrial Revolution made changes in men's work and living. It changed methods of farming and manufacturing. It improved man's ways of living because better goods and more money became available through trade. These discoveries and improvements helped men to move into better and happier ways of living.

THE INFLUENCE OF THE RENAISSANCE

The Renaissance was a time of great change in Europe. It was a time when men rediscovered the learning of the Ancient World that had almost been lost during the Middle Ages. It was a time when men made wonderful new discoveries about their natural world. There was a rebirth of interest in art and in architecture. Great painters and sculptors produced beautiful works of art for the fine new buildings.

The search for new trade routes led to the discovery of unknown lands. New sources of trade led to new and improved methods and machines for the manufacturing of goods. The Industrial Revolution caused great changes in ways of living and in places of living. There were greater concentrations of people. Dependence of the city on the farm and the farm on the city increased. Machines which gave men more power were invented. Cities grew as large factories were built and more people began to work in them.

But another "revolution" was taking place slowly. Some have called it the "Democratic Revolution." *Demos* means "people" in the Greek language. The people of the world were taking greater interest in themselves and in others. This personal concern is evident throughout the world today. In the remaining parts of this book you will learn about the great cultures which have developed in modern times.

Do You Know?

1. What is the meaning of the word *Renaissance?*

2. When was the Renaissance in Western Europe? What periods of history came before and after the Renaissance?

3. What valuable heritages of the past were rediscovered during the Renaissance?

4. What were four major discoveries of the Renaissance?

5. What are the classics? What Italian poet was noted for his collection of classics?

6. How did the subject of paintings change during the Renaissance?

7. Who discovered a route to China? What group of people discovered new lands during the Middle Ages? What were the results of these discoveries?

8. What is the heliocentric theory? Who first tried to explain this theory?

9. Who first proved the heliocentric theory? How did Newton prove the theory beyond a doubt?

10. Who was both a great painter and a great scientist? Give one example of his contributions to each field.

11. Why was *Victoria* a good name for Magellan's ship?

12. What were the results or the effects of the explorations during the Renaissance?

13. What two inventions of the Renaissance made the greatest changes in man's way of life?

14. What effects did the invention of the printing press have on the education of the people?

15. How did the working people of England try to get better conditions during the Industrial Revolution?

Learn By Doing

1. Select the correct words to complete the following sentences.

a. The use of the steam engine changed the methods of ____________ and of ____________.

b. The few Europeans were able to conquer the many Indians in North America because of their superior ________.

c. The ________ of Michelangelo can be seen on the ceiling of the ________ Chapel of Rome.

d. Two modern inventions, the ________ and the ____________, may have been based on the ideas of Da Vinci.

e. The experiments of Galileo led to the development of the ________ and the ____________.

f. Until printing was invented, books were written on __________.

2. Tell whether each man in column **A** was an inventor, a scientist, or an explorer. Then select his invention, field of study, or land discovery from column **B**.

A	B
1. Gutenberg	telescope
2. Kepler	printing press
3. Lippershey	power loom
4. Newton	steam engine
5. Prince Henry	spinning jenny
6. Da Gama	ellipse
7. Watt	Law of Gravity
8. Fulton	India
9. Hargreaves	navigation
10. Cartwright	steamboat

3. The word *manufacture* means to be made by hand. Show how the invention of the steam engine has changed the meaning of this word. Select the shoemaking or the clothmaking industry for your report.

4. Write a report on one of the following men. Use an encyclopedia or other reference books. Perhaps you can read a biography of the man.

Leonardo Da Vinci
Michelangelo Buonarroti
Galileo Galilei
Marco Polo
Robert Fulton

Test Your Knowledge

1. What were three ways that the manuscripts of the past were preserved by the monks?

2. How were the lives of the people changed by the rediscovery of the ancient manuscripts?

3. Describe the similarities and the differences between the ancient Roman architecture and the Renaissance architecture. Use the Pantheon and St. Peter's as examples.

4. What was the main scientific method of Da Vinci? Show how this method led men to believe in the geocentric theory.

5. What invention aided man in his observation of nature? Show how this invention helped to change man's ideas about the universe.

6. Explain why Spain and Portugal sought a new route to India.

7. What steps were taken by the Portuguese explorers to find the new route to India?

8. Describe the cultural differences between the Europeans and the Indians. How did each benefit from the explorations?

9. Describe the development of the steam engine.

10. Show how specialization in agriculture followed specialization in industry.

REVIEWING PART 2

Do You Remember?

1. What two major culture homes are located near the Mediterranean Sea? What is the present name of each region? Who were the ancient inhabitants of each region?

2. What is a paleographer? What does it mean to "break codes?"

3. What two important discoveries have helped us translate ancient writings?

4. How have the pyramids helped historians learn about the early Egyptian civilization?

5. What is the major difference between the Greek settlements and the Sumerian, Egyptian, and Roman settlements?

6. What were the two leading city-states of Greece? Which group of people believed in the democratic way of life?

7. Besides food, how were olives used by the Greeks and the Romans?

8. What examples of cooperation can be seen in the Greek and Roman civilizations?

9. What features of Greek and Roman architecture can be seen in the Renaissance style of St. Peter's? What additions were made?

10. What are some of the customs of the Greek and the Roman cultures which have come down to us?

11. What were the major causes of the fall of the Western Roman Empire?

12. What were the two major classes of people during the Middle Ages?

13. What were some of the changes brought by the Industrial Revolution to the people of England?

14. What were some of the problems brought by the Industrial Revolution?

Projects and Reports

1. Draw a time line that covers the years 1000 B.C. to A.D. 2000. Divide the line into sections of 500 years. Indicate on the time line when each of the following began and ended: the Greek World, Roman Republic, Roman Empire, Dark Ages, Middle Ages, Renaissance, and the Modern Age.

2. Identify each of the following. Tell why they were used and by whom they were used.

ziggurat	aqueduct	mummy
masterpiece	coat of arms	fresco
stained-glass	charger	keep

3. Imagine that you are a newspaper reporter during the Middle Ages. Write the headlines and a front page story about one of the important events of that time.

4. For each date given under **A**, select an important event given under **B.**

A

1.	3000 B.C.	7.	A.D. 1275
2.	27 B.C.	8.	A.D. 1456
3.	A.D. 330	9.	A.D. 1492
4.	A.D. 476	10.	A.D. 1608
5.	A.D. 570	11.	A.D. 1769
6.	A.D. 1095	12.	A.D. 1807

B

Marco Polo reaches Cambuluc
Eastern Roman Empire established
birth of Mohammed
invention of the telescope
writing appears in Egypt
Augustus Caesar made emperor
Columbus crosses the Atlantic
printing of the first book
the Crusades begin
Fall of Rome
Watt perfects the steam engine
Fulton invents first steamship

5. Select one of the following fields of study. Describe contributions made by the Greeks. Perhaps pictures and diagrams can be added.

Art	Commerce	Government
Sports	Science	Philosophy
Architecture	Agriculture	Education

Using Maps and Globes

1. Use the map of the Ancient Greek World on page 76 to answer these questions:

a. In what way did Greece's location at the end of the Balkan Peninsula help her to expand her power?

b. Along what two major bodies of water were the Greek colonies established?

c. Would it be easier to travel between Athens and Sparta by land or by sea? Why?

d. Was Rome a part of the Greek World?

e. What group of people settled in North Africa? In what city?

2. Study the map on page 104. Then answer the questions below.

a. How did Rome's location help her to expand her territory?

b. What are the present-day names for Persia, Gaul, and Asia Minor?

c. What large islands were part of the Roman Empire?

d. How far north did the Roman Empire extend? How far east?

3. Study the map on page 123 before you answer the following questions:

a. When was the First Crusade? Where were the Crusaders going? Who held the land which they sought? Did they travel by land or by sea? Through what major city did they travel?

b. From what areas did the men of the Third Crusade come? Did they travel by land or by sea? Through what areas did they travel?

4. Use the maps on pages 143 and 144 to answer the following questions:

a. How did Marco Polo's route to China differ from his returning route to Venice? Through what major city did he travel on his journey to China? On his returning trip? Was Marco Polo closer to India on his way to or from China?

b. What were the beginning and ending points of Vasco Da Gama's journey? What continents did he touch? What cape did he pass? Through what major bodies of water did he sail?

c. What name is given to the area discovered by Columbus? What ocean did he cross?

d. What continents did Magellan pass? Through what oceans did he travel? Where was Magellan killed? How long was the voyage of the *Victoria?*

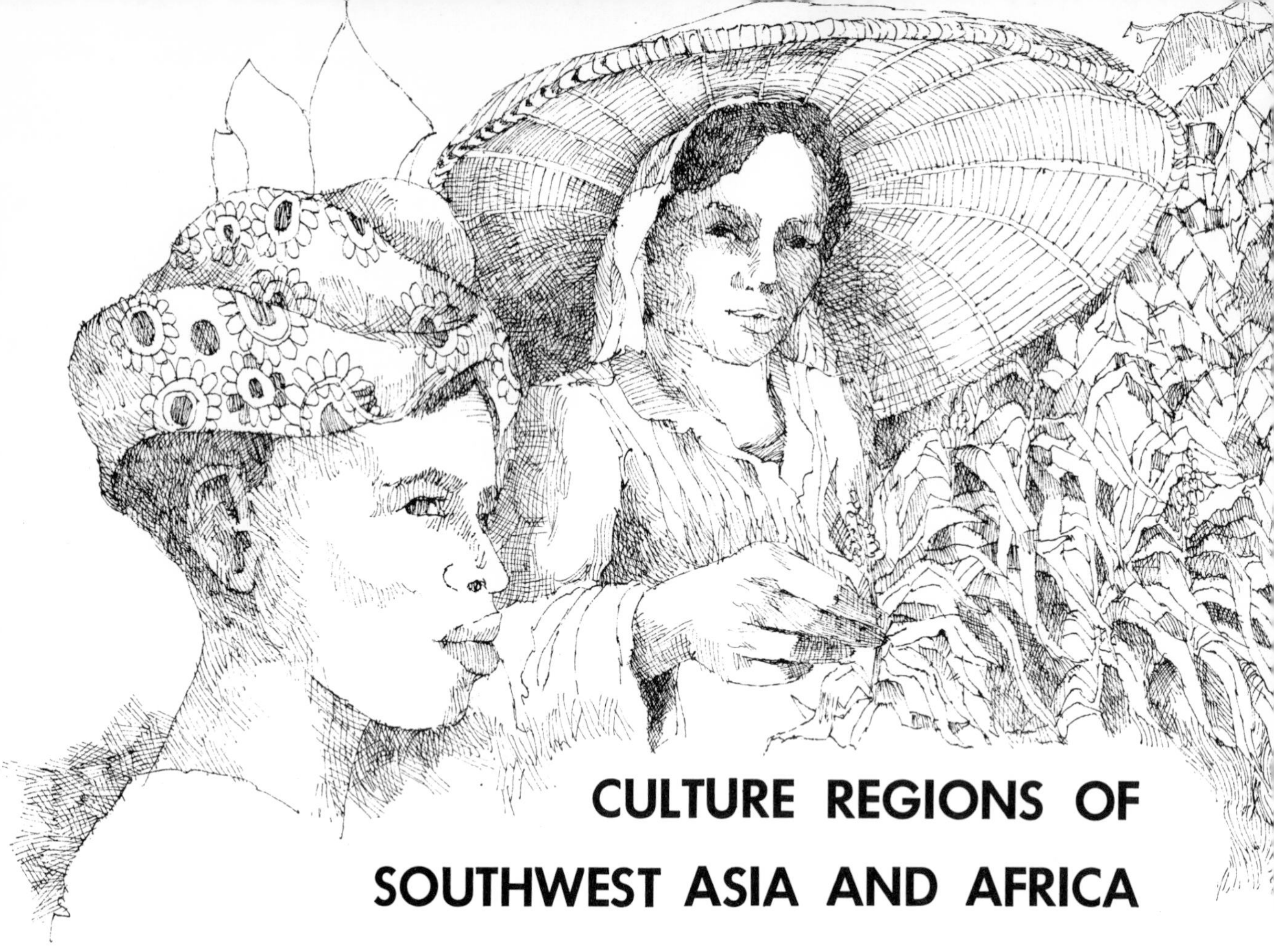

CULTURE REGIONS OF SOUTHWEST ASIA AND AFRICA

PART 3

A great region called the Dry World stretches across North Africa and Southwest Asia. There are two regionalizing features that are common throughout this part of the world. One is its dryness. The other is the religion of Islam, or Mohammedanism.

The scarcity of water has influenced life in the Dry World Region. Plants, animals, and people must adapt themselves to living in a region where rainfall is less than twenty inches a year.

Because of its scarcity, water is a carefully guarded resource. Ditches are sometimes covered to prevent evaporation of precious water. The parts of the Dry World that have the most water have the largest populations. For example, the valleys of the Nile River and the Tigris and Euphrates Rivers are able to support large populations. However, most areas are thinly populated.

Centuries ago, Islam began in Arabia and spread throughout the Dry World Region. Islam is the religion and Arabic is the language of most of the people of this region. Other religions are practiced and other languages are spoken in this region. Nonetheless, so widespread are the Arabic language and Islam that the boundaries of the Muslim World are almost the same as those of the Dry World Region.

Africa is a large continent that stretches far south in the Southern Hemisphere. Unlike the Dry Muslim World, there is no one climate or no one religion that can characterize or regionalize the rest of the African continent. Africa, south of the Sahara, is a very different region. It has many different climate regions. The people of Africa, south of the Sahara, are of many different colors, languages, heights, customs, and religions.

One regionalizing feature of Africa is that most of its countries have obtained their freedom only recently. Africa is a continent of young nations. The people of the newly independent nations of Africa are working rapidly to industrialize their countries. They are modernizing crop growing and cattle raising so that they can better support themselves.

Africa is thus a land of rapidly changing cultures. Until recently, many parts of Africa had been relatively untouched by the modern world. It is a land that is characterized by the meeting and conflict of modern industrial cultures and less advanced but age-old cultures. It is a land of contrast, where some people live in modern cities, and others continue to hunt and gather food near their small villages.

CHAPTER 9

THE DRY WORLD CULTURE REGION

People who live in desert regions have developed ways of living that make the best use of the limited resources. They find ways to use the limited amount of water to the best advantage. Many people regularly move from place to place. They raise animals that require little water and can live on the scant grass that grows in these regions.

The Dry World Region of North Africa and Southwest Asia has two large river valleys where large groups of people live. Only in these watered valleys can there be large-scale farming. In other parts of this region, scattered groups of people obtain their living from the dry land of the desert.

DESERT LANDS

Most of the region shown on the map on page 163 is desert land. This dry region extends east across North Africa into Southwest Asia. The map also shows that there are some mountain-plateau areas, but few rivers that start in and cross through the region. Only the Nile crosses the entire width of the desert lands. All these desert lands make up one large area called the Dry World Culture Region.

In North Africa there are eleven nations that lie wholly or partly in this dry region. Can you locate them? In Southwest Asia the dry lands stretch across the Arabian Peninsula and its neighboring countries. Notice that several nations of North Africa and Southwest Asia border on the Mediterranean. This coastal strip contains the centers of the heaviest population.

The Sahara

In North Africa the vast stretch of dry land, south of the population belt along the Mediterranean, is called the great **Sahara.** Sahara comes from the Arabic word *sahra* which means "desert." The Sahara is the largest desert in the world. In size, it is about 3,500,000 square miles. The Sahara stretches from the Atlantic Ocean to the Red Sea, a length of about 3,500 miles. Its average width is about 1,000 miles. The map on this page shows that the Sahara is almost as large as the United States. Notice that the distance from the western end eastward to the Red Sea is greater than the distance from San Francisco to New York.

Landforms of the Sahara

The Sahara has many kinds of landforms. Most of the desert is a fairly level plateau which ranges from 1,000 to 2,000 feet above sea level. There are scattered mountain ranges that rise from 6,000 to 10,000 feet above sea level. There are great low-lying basins. In the Sahara there are great stretches of barren sand and beds of gravel.

Two of the common types of desert surface in the Sahara are the **reg** and the **erg.** Reg is the level land with little or no vegetation that is covered with pebbles or gravel. Finer bits of sand have been blown away by strong desert winds. The erg is a large area of sand. It is the type of surface that we think of when we see the word *desert.* But the erg, or sea of sand, is only one type of land found in the Sahara. In fact less than one-fifth of the Sahara is sandy desert. The largest section of sandy desert can be found in southern Algeria. There is also a large section of sandy desert in western Egypt.

Underground streams run deep below the dry Sahara. Wells are used to tap this water for people and animals.

SIZE COMPARISON
OF SAHARA
TO UNITED STATES

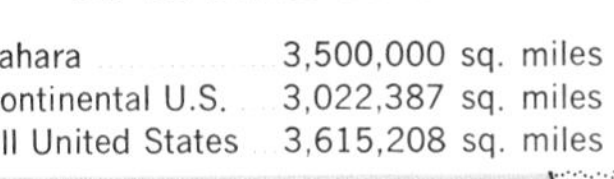

Sahara	3,500,000 sq. miles
Continental U.S.	3,022,387 sq. miles
All United States	3,615,208 sq. miles

Climate of the Sahara

Winds that cross the Sahara can be both ice-cold and scorching. The temperature on the desert may rise to 100 degrees during the day and plunge to below freezing at night. The world's highest recorded temperature of 136 degrees was taken in the Sahara.

Although landforms may differ, there is one feature common to all parts of the Sahara Region. That feature is dryness. There is so little rain that vegetation is scanty and in some places barely present. The Sahara is a region where less than 10 inches of rain falls each year. Even the little rain that falls does so irregularly. Some parts of the Sahara have gone three or four years without rain. There are times when rain falls but evaporates into the dry air before it reaches the ground. Let us see why this great stretch of land is so dry.

The Sahara, A Trade Wind Desert

In order to explain the dryness of the Sahara, we need to look at another region farther south, the part of Africa nearest the equator. This part of Africa extends from about 10° North Latitude to about 10° South Latitude. The highest temperatures and the greatest amount of rainfall in Africa are found in this zone. Here the sun shines directly overhead for most of the year. The sun's rays warm the earth. Reflected heat from the land warms the air. Heated air then rises. You can get an idea of how this occurs if you put your hand over a warm radiator.

All along the equator there is a wide zone of rising air. As warm air in this zone rises, cooler, heavier air flows in from the north and from the south to replace it. If you place your hand close to the floor near the radiator, you probably will feel cool air flowing to the bottom of the radiator. As the cooler air moves toward the equator, it becomes warmer and warmer. It takes moisture from the land surface. The warmer the air becomes, the more moisture it can hold. The heated winds cause surface water to evaporate. The lands these winds cross become very dry.

Just a short distance inland from the Mediterranean, cooler air starts to move across North Africa. It moves from the northeast to the southwest. The movement of air over the Sahara Region toward the equator is like warm wind blowing over a wet sidewalk. These Northeast winds cause the surface water on the land to evaporate. If the winds continue to blow for months and years as they do in the Sahara, a desert is created. When these regular winds were found to blow over large parts of the oceans, the sailors gave them a name. They called them **trade winds** because they could depend upon them to help drive their sailing ships on their trade routes.

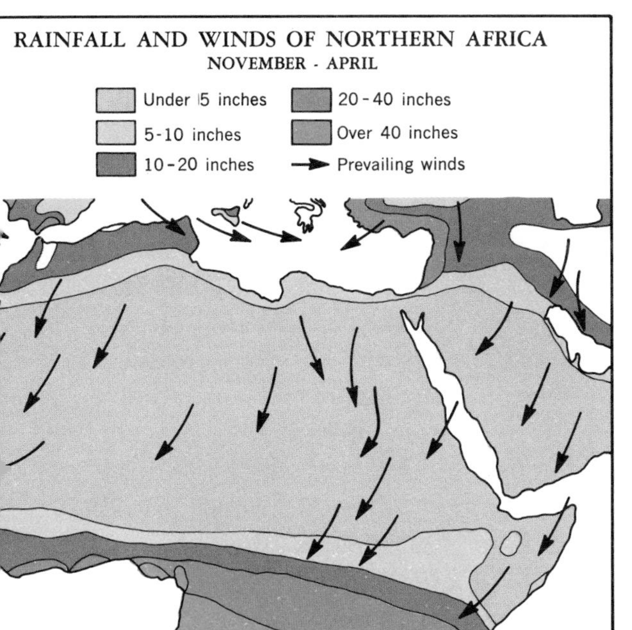

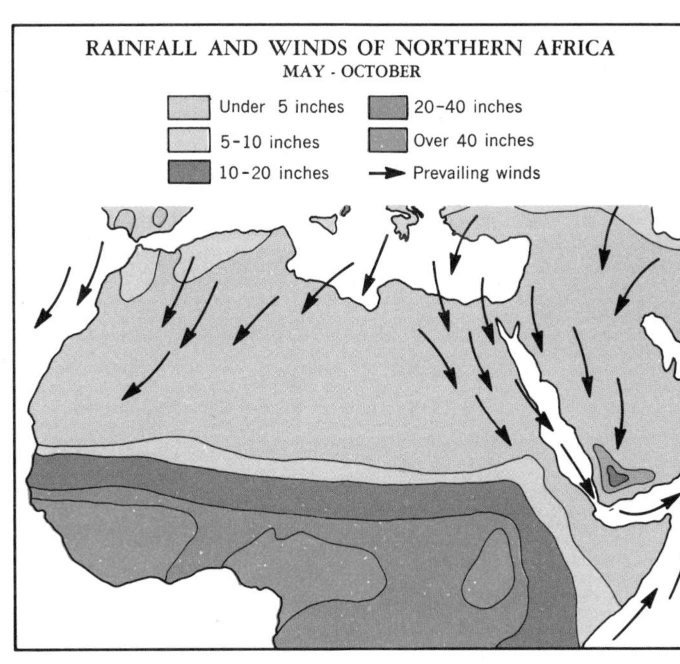

Dry Lands of Southwest Asia

The land of Southwest Asia inland from the population belt along the Mediterranean is also desert. See the map on page 163. The desert region covers the Arabian Peninsula and includes the northern countries of Jordan, Israel, Lebanon, and Syria. Farther east it includes Iraq, Iran, and West Pakistan. In this part of the Dry World Region the desert is called by different names. Two important deserts are the Rub' al Khali and the Syrian.

Throughout this region there are many kinds of landforms. You saw that ergs and regs and some plateaus and mountain ranges marked the Sahara. The Rub' al Khali and Syrian deserts on the Arabian Peninsula are sand-covered. Iran and West Pakistan, however, have high, dry plateaus and mountains. As you can see from the map, the Tigris and Euphrates Rivers in Iraq water the land between the two areas.

The Climate of Southwest Asia

The amount of rainfall and the temperature of a region depend on the altitude of the land and the existence of moisture-bearing winds. During the winter, the Northeast trade winds blow across these nations. These warm winds blow from sources with very little moisture. The little moisture which they do contain falls on the lands between the mountains and the seas. The altitude of the mountains and the plateaus of Iran, Iraq, and Turkey cause the rising winds to lose their moisture. These lands receive less than 20 inches of rainfall in a year's time.

As the Northeast trade winds move toward the equator, they become warmer and drier. This results in the desert lands of West Pakistan, Syria, and Arabia. Like the Sahara, these lands receive less than 10 inches of annual rainfall.

Look at the map on page 161. It shows the summer wind pattern of the Dry World Region. The summer winds blow from the southwest to the northeast. They come from the region near the equator and have no source from which to absorb moisture. These dry winds create the desert lands of the Dry World Region.

Plant Life in the Deserts

Plants that grow in these desert regions have adapted to the dry climate in several ways. All desert plants must be able to live on a small, irregular supply of water. The amount of water available is usually so limited that the areas of desert plants are widely spaced. The plants have large, spreading root systems. The wide network of roots spreads out to capture as much water as possible. The roots of some desert plants go very, very deep into the sand to reach, or tap, underground moisture.

The stems and leaves of desert plants are especially designed to conserve water. Some plants, such as the cactus, store water in fleshy stems or leaves over long periods of dryness. Some desert plants have developed thorns, or spines, that protect them from being eaten by animals. Still other plants are protected by their bitter taste.

There are a few watered spots in the desert world called **oases.** Here underground water has come to the surface in a spring. Trees and other plants will grow here. The desert soil is usually rich, and when water is present, crops will grow. Some oases have been enlarged by the drilling of wells which supply water for crops. Water for the oases usually flows in underground streams or seeps through the soil from nearby mountains where there is rain or snow.

FEATURES OF THE DRY WORLD

The peoples living in the Dry World Region have learned certain ways of living that are different from those in other regions. Throughout the Dry World Region there are similarities in the ways people earn a living, in the places where their settlements have grown, in the religions which they believe, in the customs they have developed, and in the progress they have made. As you read the remainder of this chapter, you will come to understand how the physical environment of these people has affected their way of life. You will see how they have made use of the resources of their region.

NORTH AFRICA AND SOUTHWEST ASIA

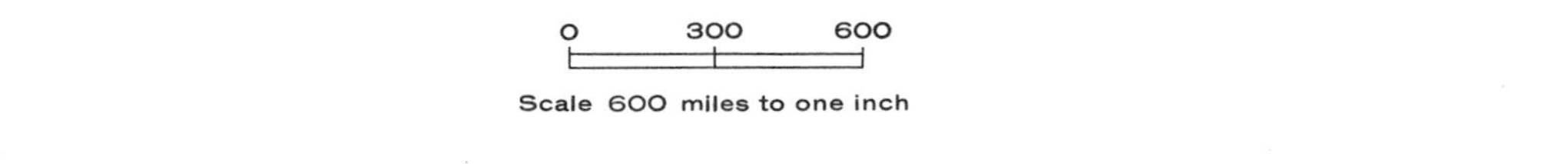

Cairo on the Nile dates from A.D. 969.

Population Centers

In Chapter 4 you read about two great early civilizations which developed in the Dry World Region. The Tigris-Euphrates and the Nile River Valley civilizations developed because they had large and regular supplies of water. The waters of these two rivers came from outside the Dry World Region. These areas were unlike the lands around them, which had very little water and no source from which to get it. Water, next to air, is basic to life. The ways people live in the Dry World Region are related to their water supply.

The population map on page 165 shows you the areas where the people live. These areas of the Dry World Region have enough water for drinking and for irrigation to support a large population. Notice that two of the places where great numbers of people live today are in the two riverine valleys. Only two cities in the Dry World Region have as many as 1,000,000 people living in them. One is Cairo, found on the Nile River in Egypt. The other is Tehran, located at the foot of the Elburz Mountains in Iran.

Except for the two riverine valleys and the coastal cities along the Mediterranean, the rest of the Dry World Region is marked by a pattern of scattered settlements. Some of these settlements are to be found on the desert oases. Although much larger in size than the continental United States, the Dry World Region has only a few more people living there.

Grazing Supports People

One of the regionalizing features of the Dry World Region is the lack of well watered lands. Without water for irrigation, farming is impossible in most areas.

There are, however, places where there is enough grass for animals to live. In these lands, grazing animals serve as the sole support of many people. The people are usually **nomads.** This means that they move from place to place in search of food for their animals. A population that depends solely upon grazing cannot be very large in a dry land. Grazing is limited to areas where grass can grow. These grasslands may be found at the bases of mountains or near the edge of a desert where rainfall is just enough for the grass to grow.

Nomadic peoples, moving from one spot to another in search of grass and water, need great areas of land. Where grass and water are plentiful, the nomads may camp for several weeks. Where grass is scanty, herdsmen must move often, sometimes every day. The movement of herds from one grassland to another may be easy. Most of the lands of the Dry World Region are fairly level.

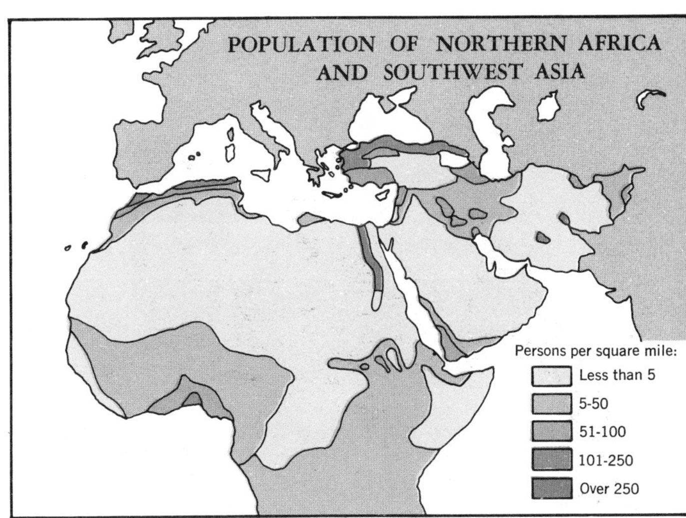

The Animal Economy

You remember that people who make their living entirely from animals are said to live in an animal economy. Those people who live off just one animal live in a **one-animal economy.** The peoples of the Dry World Region live in a **multi-animal economy**—that is, their living depends upon several kinds of animals. The domestic animals of the Dry World Region are well adapted to living in desert and near-desert lands. The animals that belong to nomadic tribesmen must be able to live off the scant desert grass and coarse, tough, and sometimes thorny desert shrubs.

The animals of the Dry World Region that are used by its people are camels, sheep, goats, and horses. Each of these animals is hardy. Each can stand **extremes of temperature**—that is, very hot and very cold temperatures. Each can live in areas of scanty feed. The camel is best suited to the area because it can go the longest without water and feed.

The Camel

Probably the best known and the most important animal of the Dry World Region is the camel. The presence and use of the camel in the Dry World Region is one of the culture features that mark it off from other regions. The camel is particularly suited for living in the desert. Because of its unusual features, it is able to live in the driest and sandiest parts of the desert. It can carry loads of goods weighing over 200 pounds. It is a very useful pack animal for people who have to travel the long distances between oases.

The camel's most striking feature, the hump, is the reason why he can travel such long distances. The camel's hump is formed by a deposit of stored fat and muscle. When the camel has to travel the long distances between water holes and grasslands, he draws upon this store of fat

The two-humped, or Bactrian, camel is native to Asia, and is shorter and thicker than the Arabian camel.

for energy. A camel which has drawn heavily upon this store of fat may have its hump almost disappear.

Before a long journey, a camel drinks as much as 30 gallons of water. This water is not stored in its hump. Rather, it is held in the tissues and cells of the camel's body. Man, in order to keep his body temperature at the same level on a hot day, must release large amounts of water through perspiration. The camel does not give off water from his body in such a manner. Its body temperature can rise without harmful effects. During the day, as the temperature of the air rises, the body temperature of the camel may rise as much as 11 degrees. This ability to tolerate a changing body temperature serves to keep water in the body. Because of this ability to conserve water in its tissues and cells and also in one of its three stomachs, the camel can travel for at least a week before needing more water. By eating desert plants that have moisture in them, he can travel for an even longer time.

A camel is an ugly, awkward-looking animal. Its long, shaggy hair ranges in color from dirty white to brown. It has long jaws with strong, sharp teeth. These teeth are useful in eating the thorny, tough desert vegetation. Its large, brown eyes are protected from the glaring sun and the blowing sand by heavy eyebrows. During a desert sandstorm, the camel will kneel, face away from the wind, and close its nostrils to slits in order to keep out the driving sand.

The camel's feet are well adapted to walking on the desert sands. Each foot is split into two, long, hoofed toes that are padded. These toes spread when weight is placed on them. These padded, hoofed feet support the camel on loose sand. A sharp-hoofed animal without such padded toes would sink into the sand. Because of these unique padded toes, the camel walks quickly and easily on the surface of the sand.

The camel is famous for its ill-temper. A camel being loaded for travel will fill the air with groans and cries of protest. As it is being harnessed or burdened, it may try to bite or kick its owner.

The Arabian camel, also known as the dromedary, is widely used throughout the Dry World as a draft animal as well as a carrier of people and goods.

Although not very friendly to man, it is very useful to man. An adult baggage camel may carry as much as 1,000 pounds. It may travel 25 miles a day. A caravan, or train, of twenty or more camels can carry large amounts of baggage. In ancient days, large caravans of 5,000 camels often brought goods from China and India to ports on the Mediterranean for shipment to Europe.

A mother camel will not travel without her baby. If the baby camel is too young to walk in the caravan, it must be carried on the back of a baggage camel. The mother camel cannot carry the baby camel on its back because she is not smart enough to know it is there. The baby must be carried by another camel, so that the mother camel will be able to see it and follow it.

The camel has been called the "ship of the desert." The most likely explanation for the title is the following. Through past centuries and even today, the camel has been used as the main carrier of goods across long stretches of desert. Until the invention of the airplane, the ship was the sole carrier of goods across long stretches of ocean. So the camel, being the sole carrier of goods across long stretches of desert, a sea of sand, came to be called the "ship of the desert."

In the Dry World Region, finding a source of water is of vital importance. The addax (top) gets its water from desert plants. Nomads (center) soon learn the location of water holes. Irrigation (bottom) makes agriculture possible.

Other Animals

The wild animals in the Dry World Region are also well adapted to living under the extreme weather conditions. One of these is the addax, a small horned antelope. The addax gets most of its water from desert plants. Another animal, the fennec, is a small desert fox. The fennec is a little animal with very large, long ears. It is fawn-colored so it blends in well with its desert surroundings. The fennec is **nocturnal**—that is, it hunts for food at night. The fennec can burrow into the sand quickly. It sleeps in a burrow during the day to avoid the high temperatures of the desert surface. A few inches below the surface the temperature of the ground is much cooler.

Life of the Nomads

The way of life of the nomad is based upon his animals—the goats, camels, sheep, and horses. The animals give him milk, cheese, butter, meat, and skins. Animal hair is made into clothing, and sometime into **felt.** Felt is pressed and matted wool or hair. Felt gives good protection against heat in summer and cold in winter. The tent of the desert nomad is often made of felt. In some parts of the Dry World Region, even the horse is used for hides, meat, and milk. Dried animal dung is burned for cooking and for warmth. Extra hides, meat, or cheese may be traded for dates, wheat, or for metal knives, cooking pots, or wood for tent frames.

Because the nomads are people who follow their herds, their permanent belongings are few and useful. The artistic expression of the nomads is turned to the useful products and things they need in everyday life. Beautiful clay articles are made. Narrow-necked jugs keep water from evaporating. Fine leather work may be seen on their saddles, belts, jackets, and boots. Some of their bowls are covered with leather, worked in beautiful designs.

An earthen or clay jug which is placed in a leather jacket has several advantages to the user. The jacket may be a solid piece of leather, or it may be made of leather strips. Each jacket would have leather thongs, or straps. The thongs can be used to tie the jug to a saddle or to sling the jug over the shoulder. The leather covering protects the jug. If a jug is accidentally dropped or bumped, the leather takes the blow.

The biggest advantage of a leather covering lies in its function of cooling water. A leather-covered jug is filled by dipping it into a pool or well. As it is dipped, the leather gets soaking wet. Leather dries very slowly. As moisture in the leather evaporates, the leather is cooled. As water evaporates from the leather, the jug and the water within it are made cooler. Repeated wettings and dryings make leather strips fit tighter. Sometimes the tight strips of leather make indentations on the clay surface of a jug.

A nomad and his family entertain friends. Both the tent and the clothing are well adapted to life in the desert.

The Sheik of the Nomadic Tribes

Another cultural feature of the Dry World Region is the pattern of authority in the family and the tribe. In the vast, thinly populated parts of much of the Dry World, authority is centered in the chief of a tribe called the **sheik.** He has the responsibility of looking after the welfare of his people. He decides when and where the tribe will move its tents and flocks. He settles disputes among members of his own tribe. He meets with chieftains from other tribes to settle matters of concern to the peoples of several tribes.

Oases Provide Desert Homes

Although oases are few in number, these scattered spots are important features of the Dry World Region. In contrast to the grazing lands of the nomads, the oases support permanent dwellings. The people of an oasis grow dates and small amounts of grain and vegetables for their own use. Some of the surplus dates are exported to other countries, or traded to desert nomads for animal skins, wool, and cheese. In this way, the oasis dweller gets the animal products he needs in exchange for the crops he grows.

The date palm tree is another Dry World feature which marks this region off from surrounding regions. To flourish, the date palm must have its roots near large amounts of water. Thus it will be found only on an oasis or in an irrigated grove. The date palm is a tall, graceful tree. It has a straight trunk and grows about 100 feet high. The clusters of fruit that grow on the date palm are one of the principal sources of food for the people of this region. The fruit of the tree is heavy with sugar and is delicious fresh or dried. The leaves of the tree can be woven into mats. Fiber from the trunk can be woven into rope.

In oasis settlements, mud huts and stone buildings take the place of nomadic tents. Oasis towns often serve as centers of trade for the Dry World, not only for the pastoral tribesmen of the region, but also for the people of the oasis in their trade with other settlements and the outside world. Rugs, lamps, pots and pans, dates, and other dried fruit are sold in the oasis market, which is held about once a week.

Some dangers face the people of the oasis. Water is still a problem. It must be used with great care. Shifting sand often threatens oasis gardens and date palm orchards. To prevent the land from being flooded with sand, trees and desert shrubs have been planted around the important gardens.

Life in Oasis Towns

Bazaars, or market places, can be found in the oasis towns and in the old sections of the cities. These bazaars have narrow streets lined with small shops. Merchants and craftsmen display their goods and skills. Many things are made by hand. Metal work and fine leather goods can be bought. Hand-woven woolen cloth and carpets are on display along with hundreds of other items. Carts, bicycles, donkeys, camels, and a few cars struggle to move through the crowded streets of the bazaars. This is a lively, colorful section of town.

Bargaining is an important part of shopping in the bazaars. A customer is invited to sit down and enjoy a cup of coffee while he bargains for the things he wishes to buy. No one pays the price the merchant first asks. The merchant does not expect him to do so. The customer then offers a very small sum of money. After much bargaining, the shopkeeper will reduce his price and the customer will pay more than he first offered. Everyone is then satisfied.

The smells of the bazaars are very interesting. Owners of small, eating places along the streets cook their food on charcoal fires. The smells of charcoal smoke and cooking food fill the air. The shops where spices are sold give off the fragrant odor of freshly ground pepper, curry powder, nutmeg, cloves, cinnamon, and other spices.

Agricultural products and manufactured goods are found side by side in the open markets of the towns.

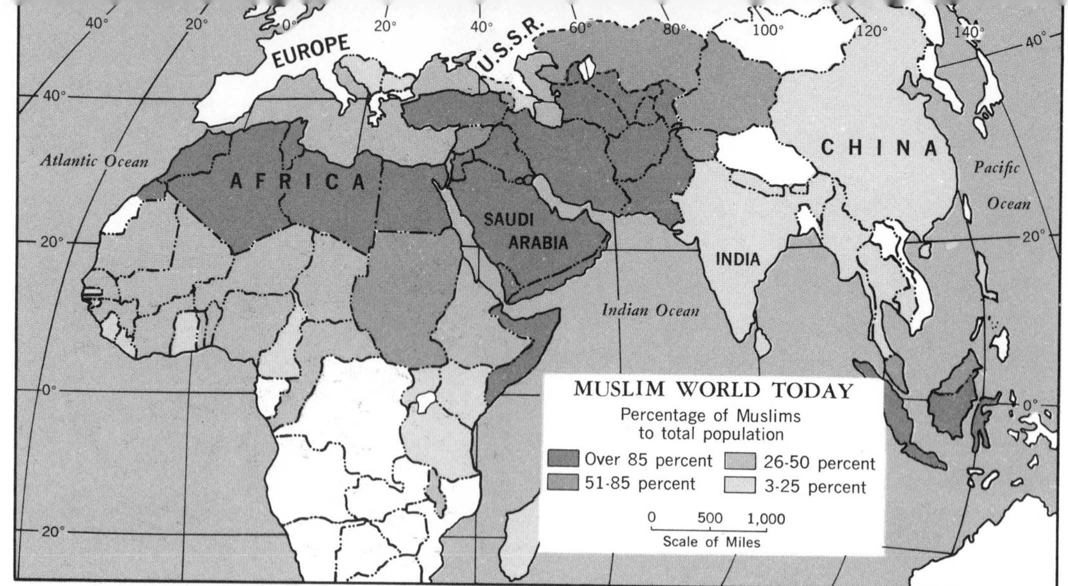

THE RELIGION OF ISLAM

Several great religions have had their origin in the Dry World Region. These religions have spread throughout the world. Judaism and Christianity both began in the Middle East. The religion of Islam began on the Arabian Peninsula. Islam is the dominant religion today throughout most of the Dry World Region. Islam is based upon the Koran, a sacred book in which the teachings of God, called Allah by the Muslims, were revealed to his prophet, Mohammed.

Mohammed was born at Mecca about A.D. 570. His father died before he was born. His mother died when he was six. He was next raised by his grandfather who died when Mohammed was nine. He spent the rest of his childhood in the home of an uncle. At the age of 25, Mohammed married Khadija, a rich widow 15 years older than he. Their marriage was very happy. Khadija was a source of comfort and help to Mohammed during much of his life.

Mohammed Becomes a Prophet

Mohammed thought deeply about good and evil. He often went to a cave in the desert near Mecca to think about life and the gods of his people. The Arabs of that time believed that the world was inhabited by a great number of demons. During his solitary reflections in the cave, Mohammed became convinced that there was but one God and Allah was his name. One night in the cave, Mohammed heard a voice from heaven commanding him to preach the word of God. From that moment on, he became a **prophet,** a man through whom God speaks.

During the first nine years that Mohammed preached the word of Allah, very few people listened to him or believed in him. Some of his followers lived in the city of Yathrib, 200 miles to the north of Mecca. The people of Yathrib had been fighting among themselves. They wanted a strong leader who had not been involved in their fights. The people of

Yathrib invited Mohammed to come to their city and rule them. Before accepting their invitation, he made them promise to obey him and to follow the teachings of Allah.

Mohammed's Flight

Enemies in Mecca wanted to prevent Mohammed from leaving their city. He secretly left the city and hid with a friend in a desert cave near the city. His enemies searched for him and passed very close to him without finding him. The story of this flight is an interesting one. In the cave, Mohammed's friend is supposed to have said with great fear, "We are but two." "No," replied Mohammed, "We are three, for God is with us." The enemies came to the mouth of the cave. They saw that a spider had spun its web over the entrance. They saw a pigeon sitting quietly on its nest. They believed no one had entered the cave for a long time.

Mohammed and his friend made their way by camel to Yathrib. There Mohammed was welcomed and was made the ruler of the city. Muslims call the flight of Mohammed from Mecca to Yathrib, the **Hegira.** One of the first things Mohammed did as ruler was to rename the city. He called it *Medina*, which means "City of the Prophet."

Mohammed proved to be an able ruler of the people of Medina. He settled their quarrels and stopped the fighting. Later, Mohammed returned to Mecca with an army and conquered the city. Soon nearly all the people in the city became Muslims.

The Spread of Islam

Before Mohammed died, nearly all of Arabia came under his rule. Within the next hundred years his followers conquered an empire that stretched from Spain to India. You recall that the Muslims conquered Constantinople and held the Holy Land for many years. During the Middle Ages, Arab traders carried the Muslim religion into the Far East. Today, the Muslim World forms a belt about 9,000 miles long that stretches from northern Africa into central Asia.

The Pillars of Islam

There are five rules that govern each Muslim in his relationship with Allah. These rules are called the **pillars** of Islam. The first pillar states that each Muslim must say aloud and believe wholeheartedly, "There is no god but Allah, and Mohammed is his prophet."

The second rule or pillar says that each Muslim must pray five times daily. He must say his prayers upon rising in the morning, at midday, in mid-afternoon, after sunset, and before retiring. As he says his prayers,

The Kaaba ("cube") in Mecca is the most sacred Muslim shrine. Pilgrims to Mecca walk seven times around it. Its black cloth cover, embroidered in gold, is replaced each year.

he faces in the direction of Mecca as a reminder of where his religion began. At noon on Friday, a Muslim must say his prayers in the **mosque,** the house of worship.

The third pillar of Islam calls for the Muslim to give alms—that is, to be generous to the poor. He must help the poorest people in their need.

The fourth pillar calls for the faithful Muslim to keep a fast during the month of **Ramadan.** During this month, he must not take any food or water between sunrise and sunset. Through fasting, going without food or water, a man is reminded of the feeling of hunger. Having felt hunger, he may be more ready to give food to someone in need. The fast of Ramadan also serves another purpose. It reminds the Muslim of two events in Mohammed's life. Mohammed first received the call from Allah to be a prophet during this month. The Hegira, or flight to Medina, happened during the month of Ramadan.

The fifth pillar says that each Muslim should make a pilgrimage at least once during his life to Mecca, the city where Islam began. Islam is one of the major cultural features of the Dry World Region. Its outward signs may be seen from one end of the Dry World to the other. The prayers that the faithful make five times a day remind one that this is the land of Islam. The mosques and the **minarets,** or small towers, from which the call to prayer is sounded are other signs.

MODERN LIVING IN THE DRY WORLD

Another cultural feature of the Dry Muslim World is its language. The Arabs who conquered North Africa and the Middle East, in the century following the death of Mohammed, brought with them their language. Not all people in the Dry World Region speak Arabic, but most of them do. The Arabic language serves as a common bond among the peoples in the different countries of this part of the world. People in the nations of the Dry World that speak Arabic and believe in the Islamic religion have a feeling of unity, of oneness.

Clothing of the People

The clothing that peoples of the Dry Muslim World wear is well suited to the climate. In the hot, dry climate of the Sahara you might think that the members of a caravan would be more comfortable in little or light clothing. Instead they are covered with long cloaks of loose, flowing cloth. Hands, face, and feet may be the only parts of the body exposed to the winds and the sun. They know that such dress is wise in the desert. It keeps them cool in the summer and warm in the winter.

A religious scholar wears a cap, or turban, and a garment that looks like a nightshirt. This marks him as a student of the Koran. In Arabia, the men wear a large kerchief over the head which is held in place by a thick, twisted cord.

A woman may wear a scarf over her head which can be drawn over her face in the presence of strangers. It has been a Muslim custom for many centuries that a woman always wears a veil to cover her face when away from home. But most women who live in the cities today have given up the veil. As the cities grow and more people travel to and from Western lands, many people own both native and Western style clothes. Both can be seen on the streets of the cities and at market places.

In Morocco, as in other parts of the Muslim world, many people continue to wear the traditional costume, while others adopt Western clothes.

Little Wood in the Dry World

One of the striking features of the Dry World Region is the scarcity of wood. In ancient times, forests grew over wide parts of the Dry World. Long ago, trees were cut faster than new trees could grow. Sheep and goats are very destructive in their grazing. They eat the seedlings that normally would grow and replace trees that have been cut. People also help keep the landscape barren of vegetation by gathering plants, twigs, and bushes for fuel.

The absence of large timber in many parts of the Dry World Region has left its imprint on the life of its people. Much of the furniture in your home is made from wood. But because of the scarcity of wood in the Dry World, there are few large pieces of furniture. The people sit on carpets rather than on chairs.

Natural Resources

The Dry World Region lacks wood, but makes up for the lack of this resource in another way. There are enormous reservoirs of oil under the sands of Iraq, Iran, Saudi Arabia, and Kuwait. These are the largest known reserves in the world. The nations of this region have shared much wealth from the development of these resources. Other countries of the Dry World Region also have stores of oil in the ground, but they have only recently been discovered. The wealth of the resources in the Sahara may some day equal that of the Middle East.

Centuries ago the people of these lands used surface petroleum and asphaltum for medicine and for binding building stones. It was also used to make boats waterproof. Today, the uses of petroleum are so widespread

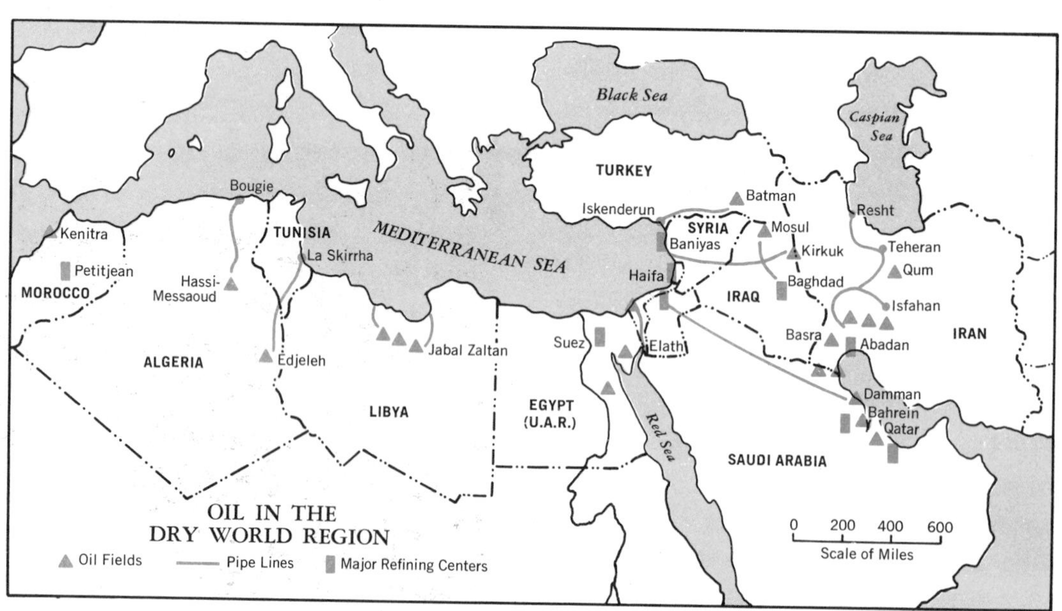

OIL IN THE DRY WORLD REGION

that it is hard to imagine living without them. For example, from petroleum we get gasoline, waxes, medicinal oils, lubricating oils, skywriting smoke, hair oils, and asphalt.

Petroleum is found in only a few places in the Earth's crust. It is so important that each nation is interested in finding new petroleum deposits and in safeguarding known ones. Many nations have come to the point of warfare in their attempts to control the use of oil in an oil-rich country.

Oil export is one of the main sources of revenue for the oil-rich nations of the Dry World. Money that comes from the sale of oil to other nations is used by governments to modernize the ways of living of their peoples. It is being used to build schools, hospitals, and roads. It also supports the costs of government.

Many people believe the Sahara can become a great industrial area. In addition to oil, other minerals have been discovered which could support industry. Uranium, iron ore, coal, copper, and beds of phosphate have been found in the rocky sections of the Sahara.

The oil pipeline is a symbol of the new wealth that has come to parts of the Dry World Region.

Progress in the Dry World Region

Life in the larger cities of the Dry World Region is much like life in European cities. Wide streets and avenues are gradually replacing the narrow, winding streets of the old sections of the city. Modern homes and large office buildings are being constructed. Electricity and telephones are fairly common. Much manufacturing is done by hand, but more and more modern factories are being built. There are large department stores where goods from many parts of the world can be bought.

The nations of the Dry Muslim World are making wider use of modern methods of transportation and communication. They are trying to give higher levels of education to greater numbers of people. They are using modern medicine and public health information to control disease and malnutrition. They are developing their own governments and are making progress in their independence. As they do, we shall see many changes in these lands. One country, Israel, is a remarkable example of progress.

Although the ancient city of Jerusalem is the capital of Israel, Tel Aviv (shown above) is the largest and most modern city. It is also the financial center of Israel.

MODERN ISRAEL

Israel is quite different from the nations, both large and small, which almost surround it. It is a new state, only about twenty years old. This is the Promised Land of the Jews. It is located in the ancient land of Palestine, the original homeland of the Jewish people. Its creation was recommended by the United Nations in 1947. In 1948 the land was proclaimed the State of Israel.

Many Jews from 74 different countries around the world are proud inhabitants of the new state. The returning "pioneers" make up a large percentage of the two and a quarter million population. These "pioneers" are not like those who settled North America. They are professional people: doctors, lawyers, teachers, and nurses. Scientists, engineers, and secretaries also went to help settle the nation. They had to leave behind many of their friends, ways of living, and personal goals. Many of them are now working in different occupations. Some are draining swamps, checking diseases, building reservoirs, and planting forests. Others are building homes, highways, and hospitals. Still others mine the quarries and practice scientific agriculture. All these people have cooperated in the building of a modern nation in the Dry World Region.

Nearly everything had to be provided to build this state. Most of the raw materials had to be imported because of the lack of resources in the arid land. Workers in all fields had to be given technical training. The agricultural experts had to develop the arable land. Cultivated land has been increased from about half a million acres in 1948 to over a million acres in 1961. Water has been channeled for irrigation and also harnessed for power.

More than one million immigrants entered the new state between 1948 and 1962. Close to 30 new towns have sprung up. Industries have grown. Textiles, leather, tobacco, chemical products, plastics, food products, diamond-cutting, automobiles, and electrical goods are being manufactured. There is a surplus of many of the above goods. They are sold abroad. In the short period of 14 years, exports increased in value from 30 to 240 million dollars. The progress of the new state is the result of what man can do with planning, capital, and determination. The cooperation of the Jewish people throughout the world has helped make Israel's goals come true.

One very remarkable goal has been reached. It is the re-use of the Hebrew language. It represents a rebirth of the language of the Bible. Israel, one of the world's newest states, uses one of the world's oldest languages as its official language.

The Jewish people face one major problem. Israel is located at the crossroads where many faiths were founded. The Jewish, the Christian, and the Muslim religions all began here. Many disputes have arisen because of the religious significance of some of the places located here. Jerusalem is a divided city, half in Jewish Israel and half in Muslim Jordan. The use of the water in the Jordan

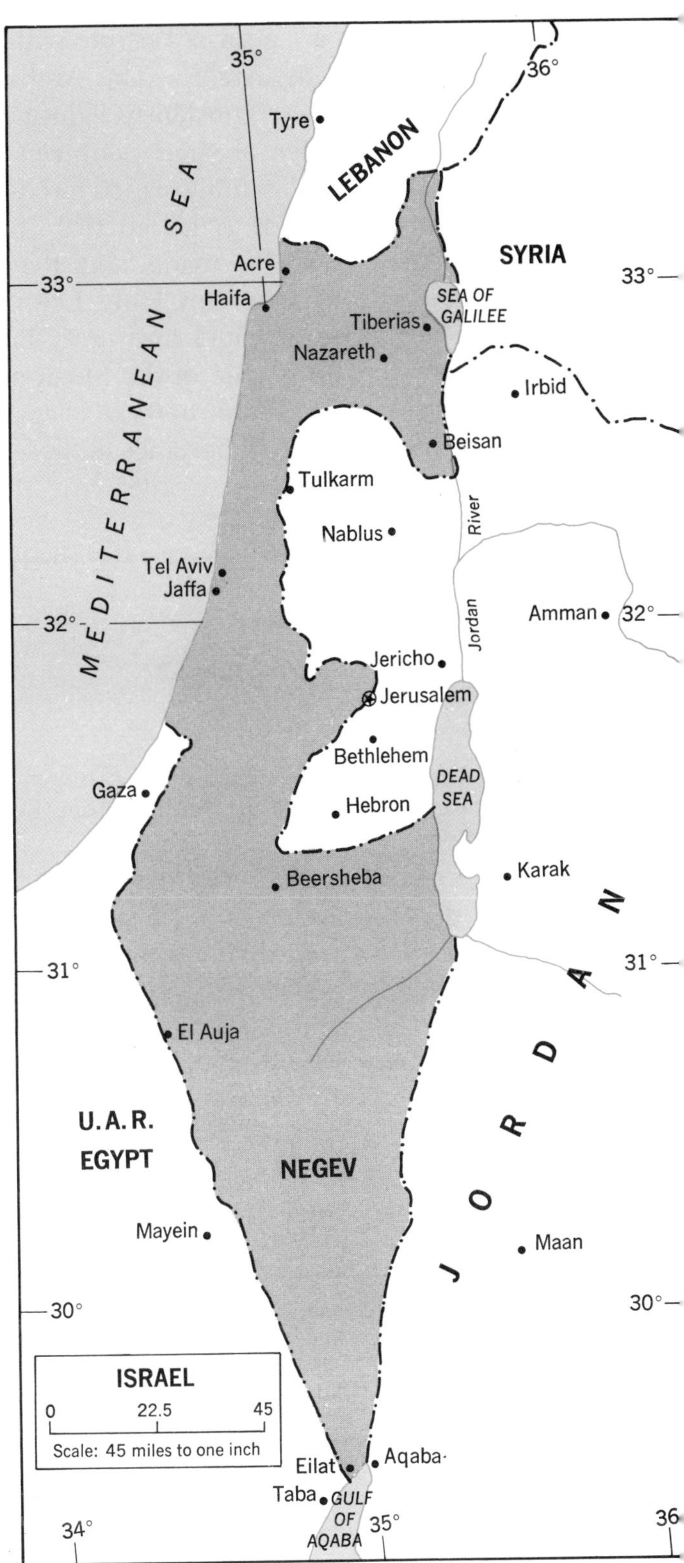

River is also a matter of dispute with the neighboring Arabs. The Arabs and the Jews are constantly fighting over the border of their countries. The costs of maintaining armed forces are increasing. It is hoped that an agreement will be made and that peace will reign in this Holy Land.

The people of Israel find unity in Judaism. The people of the Muslim countries find religious unity in Islam. The international importance of these countries cannot be overlooked in a world longing for peaceful cultural cooperation.

Today in the Dry World Region we see great progress. The people are learning ways to make the desert yield a better living for more and more people. As new resources are found in the desert and as better ways to use the old resources are developed, the people of this region will have a better life.

Do You Know?

1. What is the meaning of the word *sahra?* Name a desert that is within the Sahara region.

2. Which two cities of the Dry World Region have a population of one million? Where is each located?

3. Which areas of the Dry World Region are most favorable for settlement?

4. What is a one-animal economy? A multi-animal economy? Is the Dry World Region a one-animal or multi-animal economy?

5. What religions began in the Dry World Culture Region?

6. What are two cultural features which help to unite the people of the Dry World Region?

7. What are two regionalizing features of this region?

8. What parts of what continents are considered the Dry World Region?

9. What are trade winds?

10. What are the major rivers which supply water to the Dry World Region? Where is each river located?

11. What type of plants are able to live in the desert? Give an example.

12. What are two kinds of camels? How do they differ?

Learn By Doing

1. What Israel has done, all Dry Region countries can do. Use this statement for a debate.

2. Place the items listed below under the proper heading. Give a brief explanation of each. Can you add other words or expressions?

Land	Animals	People	Clothing

reg — nocturnal
sheik — felt
prophet — addax
erg — nomads
fennec — sahra

3. Select the correct words to complete each of the sentences below:

prophet Ramadan hegira
pillars Medina Allah
Koran mosque
alms minaret

a. A man through whom God speaks is called a ______.

b. ______ means "City of the Prophet."

c. The five rules that govern each Muslim are called the ______ of Islam.

d. During the month of ______ the Muslim must fast.

e. When one gives ______, he is generous to the poor.

f. The flight of Mohammed from Mecca to Yathrib is called the ______.

g. ______ is the Muslim name for God.

h. The ______ is the sacred book of the Muslims in which Mohammed revealed the teachings of God.

i. A ______ is the Muslim house of worship.

j. A call to prayer is sounded from a small tower called a ______.

4. Below are four areas where people of the Dry World Region might live. Select one area and answer the questions in the next column.

an oasis
the land of the nomads
a river valley
a Mediterranean City

a. How do the climate and landforms affect the lives of the people?

b. How are the people affected by the presence or lack of water? Think of all ways in which water is used.

c. Where are foods obtained? Is special clothing worn in the area? How do the people shelter themselves?

d. What role do animals play in the lives of the people?

e. What work must people do?

f. How large are the landholdings of each family? Are they carefully marked off?

g. How are the children educated? Will they attend schools or be taught by their parents?

Test Your Knowledge

1. How do the Northeast trade winds affect the Sahara?

2. What features of the camel make the animal well suited for life on the desert?

3. How does the construction of the water jug show the cleverness of the nomad?

4. How does shopping at a bazaar differ from shopping in your community? Are there any similarities?

5. Notice the uses of wood in your community. What might the people of the Dry World Region use in place of wood for these objects?

6. How have some of the ways of living of the people in this region been changed by the discovery of oil?

7. How does the Sahara differ from the Southwest Asian deserts?

8. How does the dry climate affect the vegetation on the desert?

9. Do the titles "Dry World Region" and "Muslim World Region" name the same area? Explain.

CHAPTER 10

AFRICA SOUTH OF THE SAHARA

Stretching south of the Dry World Region of Africa is a vast area with a great variety of climate and terrain. There are areas of thick rainforests near the equator where such African animals as monkeys, gorillas, and crocodiles may be found. There are also regions of hot, dry summers and cool, damp winters where the plants must be able to live through the summers with little moisture.

In this vast region south of the Sahara man lives in many different ways. He uses the great variety of climate and plant life to suit his needs. In this chapter you will see how the climate and terrain have influenced man's ways of living in this culture region.

A CONTINENT CHANGES

The area south of the Dry World Region of Africa is called the Tropical and Subtropical Culture Region. People in other parts of the world have known about the Dry Muslim World since the time of early conquerors. They have known about the region of South Africa since the time of the early explorers. However, little was known about the inland region of Africa south of the Sahara.

After centuries of neglect, explorers penetrated the land and made it possible for Europeans to colonize it. These people developed many of the resources of the Tropical and Subtropical Culture Region. In doing this, they changed the ways of living of many of the native people of the region.

In recent years most of the countries of Africa have become independent nations. Before World War II there were only four nations in Africa that were independent: Liberia, Ethiopia, Egypt (the United Arab Republic), and South Africa. The rest of the lands of Africa were under the control of Western European nations. Since World War II most of the countries of Africa have become independent. The territorial maps on page 184 show that Africa has changed from a continent largely controlled by European countries to one that is filled with newly established nations.

Exploring the Unknown

There are several reasons why the region of Africa south of the Sahara was relatively unknown to Europeans and even to Africans on other parts of the continent. First, exploration and trade with the interior of Africa were difficult. There are few natural harbors along the smooth coastline of Africa. Shifting sandbars at the entrances of great rivers made entry difficult. Endless desert coastlines and swampy shores looked uninviting to explorers.

The second barrier to exploration lay in the typical landforms of the continent of Africa. Most of the interior of this region of Africa is a series of great plateaus or rolling uplands. These plateaus, several hundred feet above sea level, have a comfortable climate. The temperatures on the plateaus are lower than on the narrow rims of plains which border the coast.

These plateaus, however, made explorations from sailing ships difficult. Usually explorers have tried to penetrate, or enter, continents by following the rivers. After entering the river mouth, they would proceed upstream by boat, if possible, or on foot along the riverbanks. When this was tried in Africa, it did not work. Not far from the mouths of the great Afri-

The landforms of Africa made it very difficult for explorers to reach the interior of the continent. Although European exploration of the coast of Sub-Saharan Africa started in the 15th century, little was known about the interior until the late 18th and early 19th centuries.

can rivers, the explorers were stopped by rapids. The rapids were at the points where rivers from the interior fell over the edges of plateaus onto the lowlands near the ocean. On some rivers there were very narrow gorges in which water roared and tumbled over scattered rocks and cliffs. Can you find these rivers on the map of Africa? Find the Niger, the Congo, and the Zambezi. Each of these rivers has been difficult to use as a highway.

The Climate of Africa

We have seen that the Europeans met with many difficulties in trying to explore this region of Africa. Once they had explored the land, a major obstacle which made them unwilling to settle there was the hot, humid climate. This extremely hot and humid land was the breeding ground for several fatal tropical diseases. These conditions prevented the development of large European settlements in the tropical region of Africa south of the Sahara.

Let us look at this region of Africa on a globe. Find the **equator,** the zero degree of latitude. It cuts across the middle of the African continent. Now look at the east-west **lines of latitude** that are $23\frac{1}{2}^\circ$ north of the equator and $23\frac{1}{2}^\circ$ south of the equator. Each of these latitude lines circles the globe, and each is parallel to the equator. When you read about Egypt, you met the northern one, the Tropic of Cancer. The southern line of latitude is called the **Tropic of Capricorn.** The region on the globe lying between these two lines is often called the **Tropics.**

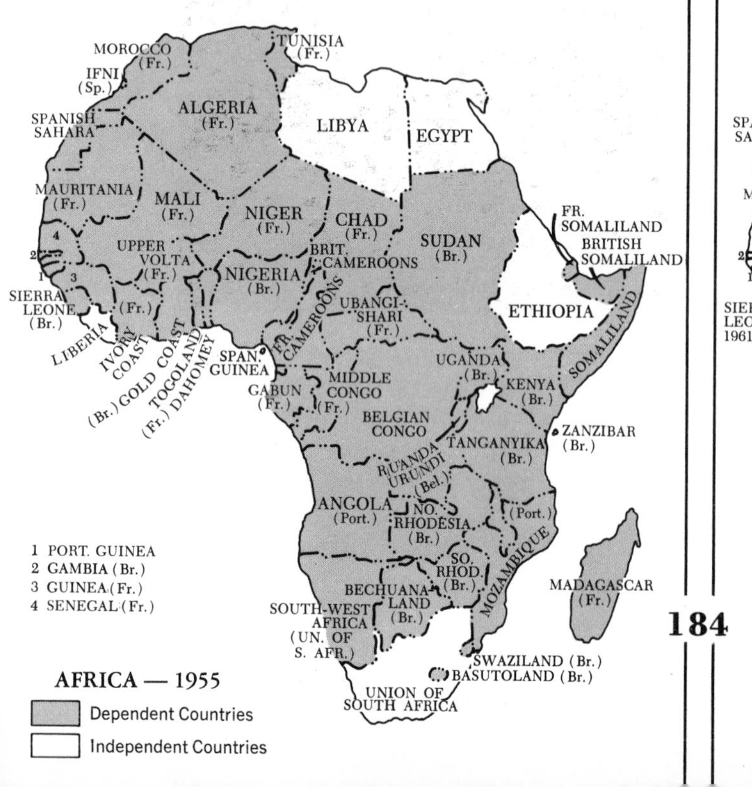

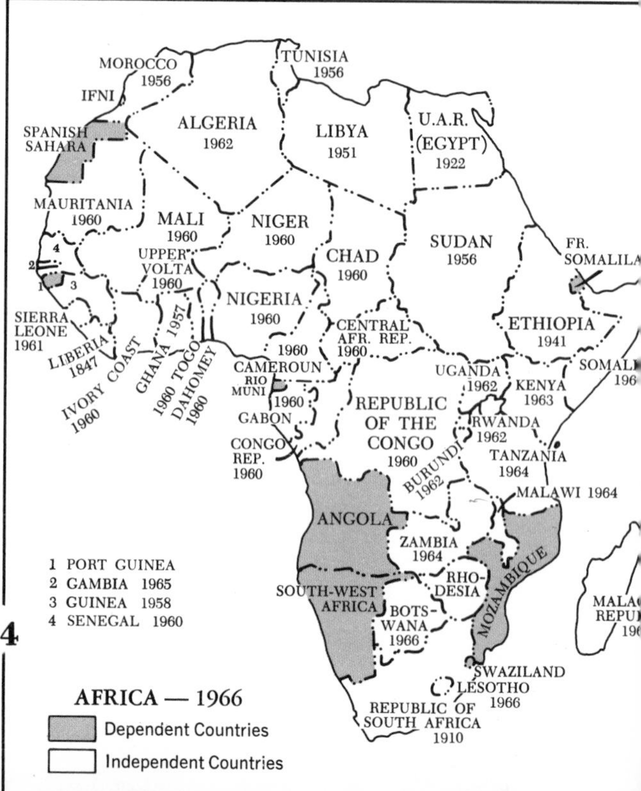

As you remember from Chapter 4, the Tropic of Cancer is the northernmost point at which the sun's rays shine directly upon the Earth. The rays of the sun shine directly on the Tropic of Cancer on June 21st. What would be the southernmost point at which the sun's rays shine directly upon the Earth? The rays of the sun shine directly on the Tropic of Capricorn six months later on December 21st. The region between these two lines, the Tropics, is the region of the Earth on which the sun's rays shine most directly.

You have learned that direct rays of the sun have a greater capacity to heat the surface of the Earth than slanted rays. On December 21st, the direct rays of the sun are at the farthest point away from the Northern Hemisphere. When it is summer in the Southern Hemisphere, it is winter in the Northern Hemisphere. Can you see why?

The direct rays of the sun reach the Tropic of Cancer once a year. The same is true for the Tropic of Capricorn. Notice .that the direct rays of the sun pass over the equator twice during the year. The Tropics are warm the year round. The difference in temperature between the coolest month and the warmest month is very small. What about the word *subtropic?* It means "nearly tropic." It refers to the lands near the Tropics.

Natural Climate Regions

You read in the last chapter that air flowing towards the equator warms and rises. It continues to rise up, up, and up, until it cools. When it cools off, the water vapor in the air begins

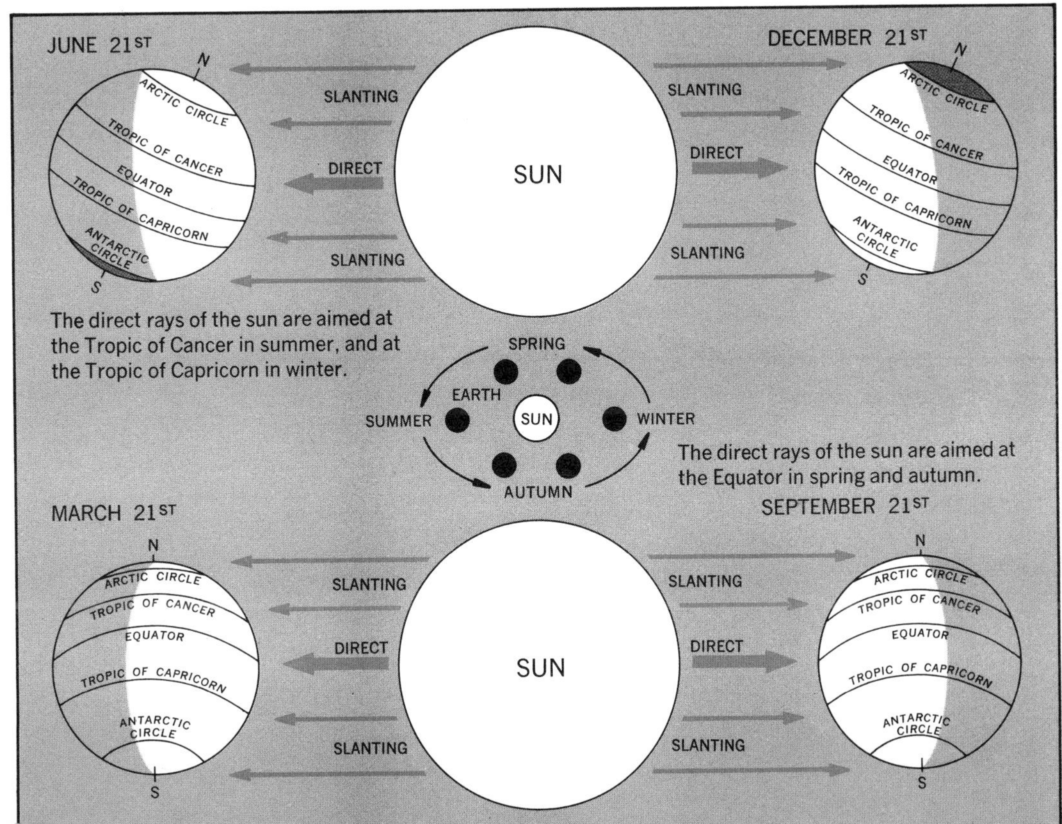

The direct rays of the sun are aimed at the Tropic of Cancer in summer, and at the Tropic of Capricorn in winter.

The direct rays of the sun are aimed at the Equator in spring and autumn.

Three kinds of African vegetation are the tropical rainforest (top), the mixed plant life typical of areas where elephants are found (center) and the tall grass (bottom). Mount Kilimanjaro, the highest in Africa, can be seen in the background.

to appear as clouds. As cooling continues, these clouds become rain clouds which empty upon the land below. Year-round high temperatures and frequent rains join in producing a heavy forest in the area nearest the equator, the Tropic Region of Africa. This region has no cool season during which plants rest. Nor is there a dry season when growth stops and plants turn brown. Plants remain green throughout the year. Plants grow rapidly and thickly. This region is a **tropical rainforest.**

Both north and south of the equator, in the lands between the 5° and the 15° lines of latitude, there is less heat and less rain. The climate is drier and the plant life not as tall and heavy. These lands have wet and dry seasons. They have fewer trees and more grass. They are called the tall grass regions, or savanna. As one nears the $23\frac{1}{2}$° lines of latitude north and south of the equator, one comes to regions of short grass and small trees.

A JOURNEY THROUGH AFRICA

Let us pretend we are in a low-flying plane traveling the length of Africa. As we travel, we shall describe the climate and vegetation of the continent of Africa. We travel first over the Mediterranean coastline, a region of little rainfall. The next stretch of land we view is the dry Sahara.

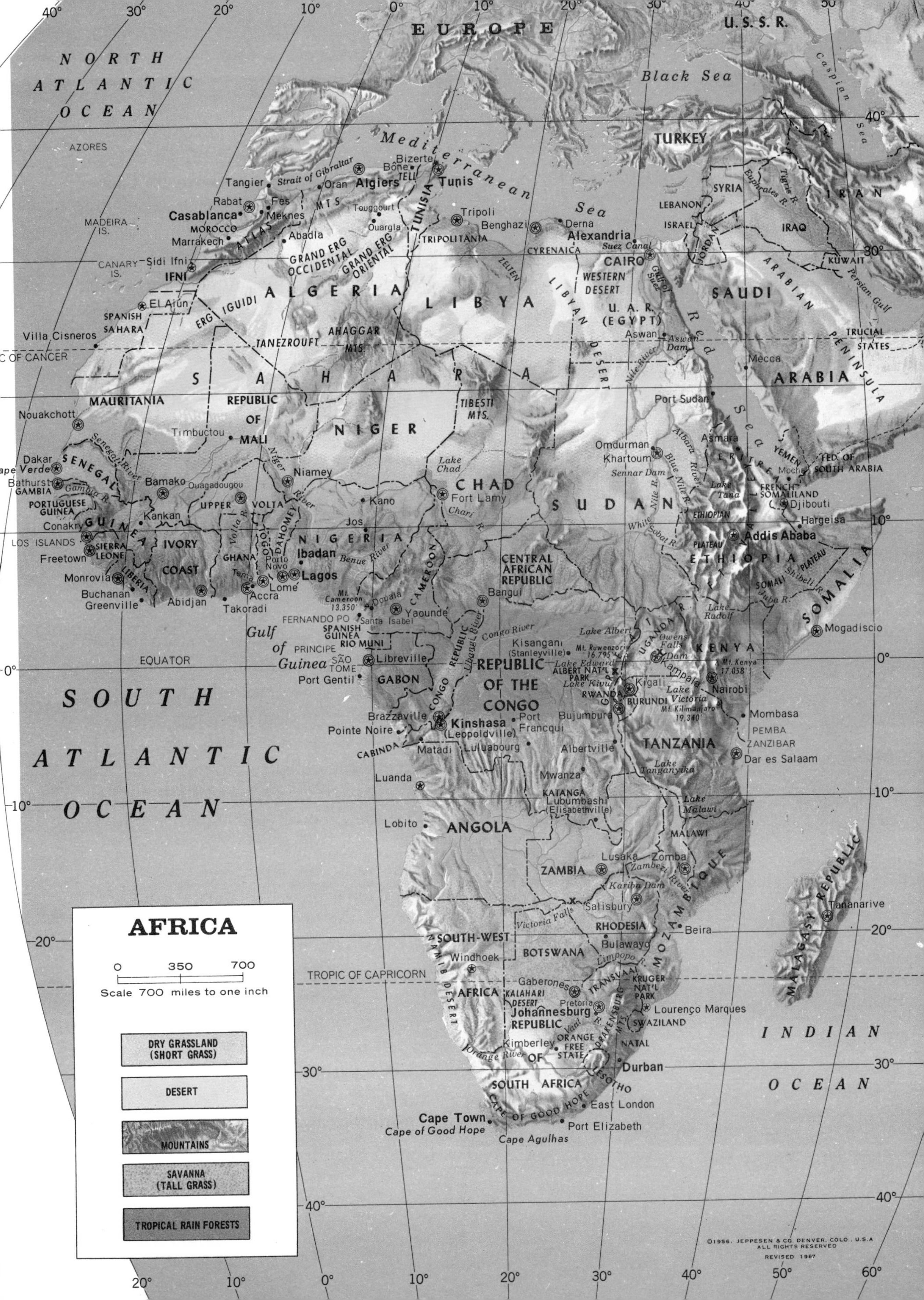

EUROPE
U. S. S. R.
NORTH ATLANTIC OCEAN
Black Sea
Caspian Sea
AZORES
TURKEY
Mediterranean Sea
Bizerte
Bône
Tangier
Strait of Gibraltar
Oran
Algiers
TELL
Tunis
Rabat
Fes
Casablanca
Meknes
ATLAS MTS
Touggourt
Tripoli
Benghazi
Derna
Alexandria
MADEIRA IS.
MOROCCO
Marrakech
Abadla
Ouargla
TUNISIA
TRIPOLITANIA
CYRENAICA
Suez Canal
CAIRO
SYRIA
LEBANON
ISRAEL
JORDAN
IRAQ
IRAN
Euphrates R.
Tigris R.
KUWAIT
Persian Gulf
CANARY IS.
Sidi Ifni
IFNI
GRAND ERG OCCIDENTAL
GRAND ERG ORIENTAL
ZELTEN
LIBYAN DESERT
WESTERN DESERT
Gulf of Suez
U. A. R. (EGYPT)
ARABIAN PENINSULA
SAUDI ARABIA
El Aiun
ERG IGUIDI
ALGERIA
LIBYA
SPANISH SAHARA
AHAGGAR MTS.
Aswan
Aswan Dam
Red Sea
TRUCIAL STATES
Villa Cisneros
TANEZROUFT
TROPIC OF CANCER
SAHARA
Nile River
Mecca
MAURITANIA
REPUBLIC OF MALI
TIBESTI MTS.
Port Sudan
Nouakchott
NIGER
Timbuctou
Senegal River
Niger River
Omdurman
Khartoum
Atbara River
Asmara
ERITREA
YEMEN
FED. OF SOUTH ARABIA
Dakar
Cape Verde
SENEGAL
Lake Chad
Niamey
Sennar Dam
Blue Nile R.
Mocha
Bathurst
GAMBIA
Gambia R.
Bamako
Ouagadougou
CHAD
Fort Lamy
SUDAN
Nile R.
Lake Tana
FRENCH SOMALILAND
Djibouti
PORTUGUESE GUINEA
UPPER VOLTA
Kano
Chari R.
Conakry
GUINEA
Kankan
Jos
Hargeisa
LOS ISLANDS
Volta R.
DAHOMEY
NIGERIA
White Nile R.
Sobat R.
ETHIOPIAN PLATEAU
Addis Ababa
ETHIOPIA
SOMALI PLATEAU
SIERRA LEONE
Freetown
IVORY COAST
GHANA
TOGO
Ibadan
Benue River
CENTRAL AFRICAN REPUBLIC
SOMALIA
Monrovia
LIBERIA
Tema
Porto Novo
Lagos
CAMEROON
Shibeli R.
Buchanan
Greenville
Abidjan
Accra
Lome
Mt. Cameroon 13,350'
Douala
Bangui
Lake Rudolf
Juba R.
Takoradi
FERNANDO PO
Santa Isabel
Yaounde
Ubangi River
Gulf of Guinea
SPANISH GUINEA
RIO MUNI
Congo River
Kisangani (Stanleyville)
Lake Albert
Mt. Ruwenzori 16,795'
UGANDA
Owens Falls Dam
KENYA
Mogadiscio
PRINCIPE
EQUATOR
SÃO TOME
Libreville
REPUBLIC OF THE CONGO
Lake Edward
ALBERT NAT'L PARK
Kampala
Mt. Kenya 17,058'
Port Gentil
GABON
Lake Kivu
Kigali
RWANDA
BURUNDI
Lake Victoria
Nairobi
Mt. Kilimanjaro 19,340'
SOUTH ATLANTIC OCEAN
Brazzaville
Kinshasa (Leopoldville)
Port Francqui
Bujumbura
Mombasa
Pointe Noire
PEMBA
CABINDA
Matadi
Luluabourg
Albertville
TANZANIA
ZANZIBAR
Dar es Salaam
Lake Tanganyika
Luanda
Mwanza
KATANGA
Lubumbashi (Elisabethville)
Lake Malawi
Lobito
ANGOLA
MALAWI
Lusaka
Zomba
ZAMBIA
Zambezi River
Kariba Dam
MOZAMBIQUE
MALAGASY REPUBLIC
Salisbury
Tananarive
Victoria Falls
RHODESIA
Beira
SOUTH-WEST AFRICA
NAMIB DESERT
Bulawayo
Windhoek
BOTSWANA
Limpopo R.
TROPIC OF CAPRICORN
Gaberones
TRANSVAAL
KRUGER NAT'L PARK
KALAHARI DESERT
Pretoria
Johannesburg
Lourenço Marques
DRAKENSBURG MTS.
Vaal R.
SWAZILAND
REPUBLIC OF SOUTH AFRICA
ORANGE FREE STATE
INDIAN OCEAN
Kimberley
NATAL
Orange River
LESOTHO
Durban
East London
CAPE OF GOOD HOPE
Cape Town
Cape of Good Hope
Port Elizabeth
Cape Agulhas
AFRICA
0 350 700
Scale 700 miles to one inch
DRY GRASSLAND (SHORT GRASS)
DESERT
MOUNTAINS
SAVANNA (TALL GRASS)
TROPICAL RAIN FORESTS
©1956, JEPPESEN & CO. DENVER, COLO., U.S.A
ALL RIGHTS RESERVED
REVISED 1967

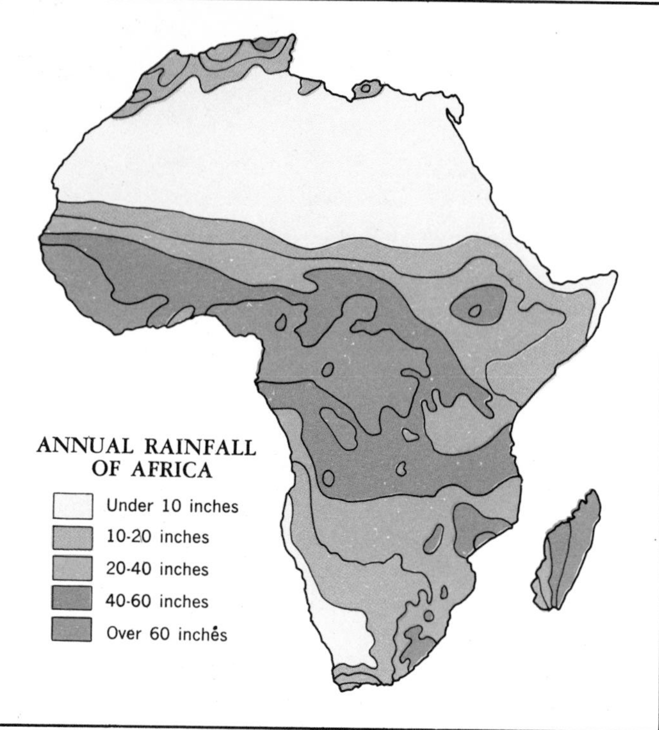

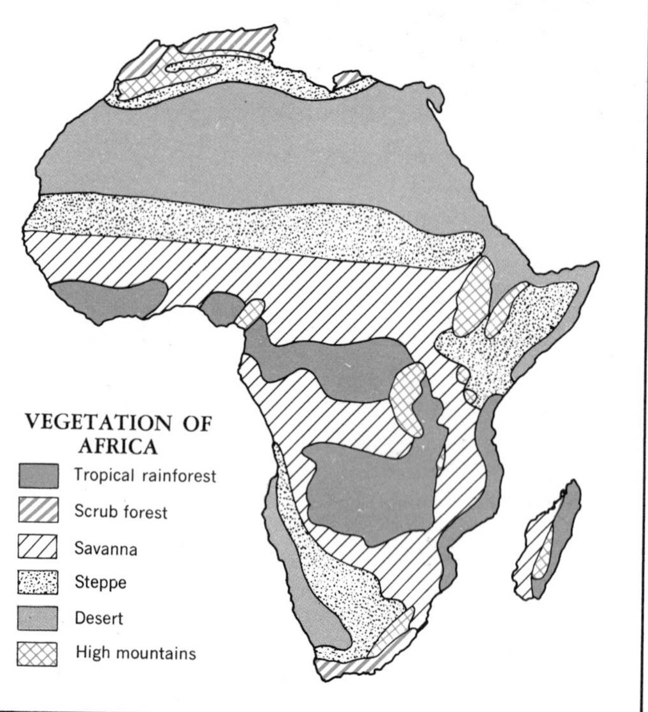

South of the Sahara near the Tropic of Cancer, we fly over the short grass region, or steppe. As we fly farther south, we see the short grass region merge into the region of taller grasses. In this region we might see from the air some of the animals for which Africa is famous: lions, antelopes, zebras, and giraffes.

Still farther south, we come to a zone or region where the grasslands merge into the rainforest. Here we see a mixed plant life—shrubs, short trees, grasses, and occasional tall trees. In this transition zone, we might see a herd of elephants or hippopotamuses.

The next natural zone over which we fly is the true tropical rainforest. This region is nearest the equator. The thick, green vegetation below hides the rich animal life beneath the treetops. The monkeys, gorillas, crocodiles, and snakes that live here cannot be seen from the air. Evergreen trees tower 125 feet in the air. Smaller trees form a thick undergrowth. Travel through the undergrowth is difficult.

Suppose we land at an airport in a small clearing of the tropical rainforest region and walk a little way along a path into the forest. The climate here is always humid and hot. Trees are huge. The forest floor is shaded from the sun by large branches and leaves of tall trees. Vines twist around tree trunks as they climb upward to reach sunlight.

Shortly after noontime, the forest becomes quiet. Birds and monkeys cease their chatter. The air feels hot and sticky. The humidity and heat are almost unbearable. Suddenly there is a roaring sound. Rain pours from the sky. It is as though the skies had opened. The noise caused by the rain is frightening. In a half hour it is all over. Sunlight begins to filter through the trees, and steam begins to rise from the damp vegetation.

If we return to the airport and continue our flight south, we will find an interesting pattern. We will pass over the natural climate regions in reverse order. After the tropical rainforest we will, in turn, pass over natural regions of tall grass, short grass, and desert. As we near the southern part of the African continent, we will come to a region with a climate like that of the coastlands of North Africa nearest the Mediterranean. This last climate region has hot, dry summers and cool, damp winters. Plants in this region must be able to live through the long, dry summer. The leaves of the plants that hold moisture often look waxed or leathery.

The description of Africa thus far has been a general one. There are exceptions to this general picture. For a look at one of these, we turn to East Africa.

East African Landforms

From the 10° North Latitude to the 15° South Latitude in East Africa, there is a great crack in the Earth. This deep "rift," as it is called, is a series of valleys filled at several places with water. If you locate Lakes Malawi, Tanganyika, and Albert on the map on page 187, you will have located the Great Rift of Africa. These lakes form a chain within the rift. By looking at their shapes, you can tell in which direction the rift runs.

East Africa is marked not only by the Great Rift, but also by spectacular mountains. Some have snow-covered peaks. A few are volcanoes. These high mountains are found around Lake Victoria. Lake Victoria is the largest lake in Africa and the third largest inland body of water in the world. The Caspian Sea and Lake Superior rank first and second in size.

Mt. Kilimanjaro and the Ruwenzori Mountain Range, near Lake Victoria, have a cool climate region of their own. It contrasts sharply from the hot, steaming rainforest and tall grass country of lower elevations. Because both mountains lie in the Tropic Region, their lowest slopes have the true tropical rainforest. As one continues to climb the mountains, however, one passes through different climate zones with different types of vegetation. Eventually one comes to the snow-capped mountain peaks.

Mt. Kilimanjaro is world famous for its height. Its highest peak rises to an elevation of 19,340 feet. It is possible to climb the mountain but one must climb it in short stages in order to become used to the thin air of the high altitude.

Africa's wild animals, for instance the massive rhinoceros, have attracted big game hunters for centuries. More important to Africa's economy, however, is agriculture. Coffee, shown being gathered here, is a valuable export.

Animals of Africa

To many people, the word *Africa* brings to mind a continent that is the home of a great number of different and interesting animals. A land that has such animals as the elephant, gorilla, giraffe, hippopotamus, rhinoceros, zebra, leopard, hyena, vulture, and ostrich is rich indeed.

The number of the larger, wild animals has dropped in recent years. Some species, such as the white rhinoceros, are in danger of becoming extinct. Farmers have turned the land upon which these animals once lived into cropland or grazing land for domestic animals. Uncontrolled hunting in the past also caused a decline in the number of some of the larger animals. Although laws have been passed to protect the animals, they are often hard to enforce. Poachers shoot elephants for the valuable ivory in their tusks. Natives, who do not realize the value and interest to the world of a rare animal, may kill it for much needed meat. One solution is to establish national parks for the protection of wildlife. The Kruger National Park has been established in South Africa.

A LAND OF TWO ECONOMIES

At present there are two ways of living in the Tropical and Subtropical Culture Region. One, the **export economy,** is the way of life which has been brought in by the Europeans. The other, the **native economy,** is the way of life which has existed for hundreds of years. During the nineteenth century, most of Africa was divided among the British, French, Belgian, Portuguese, and German nations. These nations saw the African lands as a source of raw materials lacking in their own countries. In their development of the natural resources of Africa, the Europeans introduced many modern ideas, methods, and tools to the people of Africa. This European economy is directed toward the export of industrial goods and raw materials.

Modern European Methods

Europeans who have settled in Kenya in East Africa number less than one per cent of the total population of Kenya. On the nation's plateau, they have introduced the use of farm machinery. They have brought with them the idea of fertilizing the soil. The Europeans have introduced coffee, tea, and cotton plantations. They have experimented with different varieties of corn, wheat, rice, and fruit trees.

Nigeria and her neighboring republics in Central Africa have welcomed outside help and suggestions. Swamps have been drained, and people have learned how to grow **"wet" rice.** This is rice raised in water on low, swampy land. Before, they had known only how to grow dry upland rice. Dams have been built to check floods and to provide electricity.

In Ghana, a nation west of Nigeria, dams have been built to hold back water. The lake that forms above the dam often fills in what used to be rough country. Once the lake has been formed, it becomes a water "highway." People who once grew only rice can now easily meet people who grow yams or root crops. They can exchange information about growing different kinds of crops.

In Central Africa railroads have been built to link peanut, cacao, and banana plantations with the coast. Other lines have been built to gold, diamond, and magnesium mines. These railroad lines carry people and new ideas into areas that have been unchanged for centuries. They carry out products that are extremely useful in the modern world.

New and improved methods have helped to increase agricultural yield.

The Export Economy

Nigeria exports both agricultural products and minerals. It lies in the tropical rainforest region of Central Africa. It exports great amounts of palm oil, cacao, and peanuts which grow well in the rainforest region. Nigeria is the third largest cacao supplier in the world. The United States imports one-sixth of all the cacao that Nigerians produce. Close to 200,000 farmers tend cacao trees planted on one million acres of ground.

The United States also imports from Nigeria an important mineral, called columbite. This mineral is mixed with steel. The result is a stronger metal which can be used in jet engines and gas turbines. It will not melt or change shape under great heat.

The Belgians once controlled the Congo which contains one of the world's richest mining regions. The mines in the Katanga Province of the Congo produce great amounts of copper as well as cobalt, zinc, lead, and uranium. Ninety-five per cent of the world's industrial diamonds come from the Congo region of Central Africa. Industrial diamonds are used in drilling oil wells. Diamonds are so hard that they are placed on the cutting edge of a drill to help the drill cut through solid rock. The minerals of these mines in the Congo are important to the world's economy. Railroads to the coast have been built to aid in speeding up the process of exporting these resources.

Before the discovery of these resources and the European development of them, many of the areas of Central Africa were thinly populated. With the new farming methods and industrial processes, these areas now support a much larger population. Nigeria is one of the most highly populated nations of Africa.

The Native Economy

In contrast to the export economy and industry of Africa is the native economy. Ways of making a living which existed before the Europeans came are still used in much of Central Africa.

The native economy has scarcely been touched by modern techniques. Africa's population is chiefly rural. Although cities are rapidly growing larger, most of the people still live in small, scattered groups or tribes. The population map on page 193 shows that people are thinly sprinkled over a vast area. The great grasslands encourage cattle raising. Dense tropical forests force people to hunt and gather food from the forests. Permanent, well-built homes and fixed garden plots are rare.

For the people of the grasslands, cattle is an important symbol of wealth and a means of trade. The number of cattle a man owns may be more important to him than how fat they are or how much milk they can give. A young man may have to buy his bride by paying cattle to his future father-in-law. In times of stress, periods of little food and very low water supplies, herdsmen have been known to "stick their cattle" and drink the blood. They do this by jabbing a very small, sharply pointed spear or dart into the neck of the animal. The animal feels no more pain than we do when a doctor gives us a "flu" shot. The natives do not waste any of the life-giving blood. It serves as food and drink.

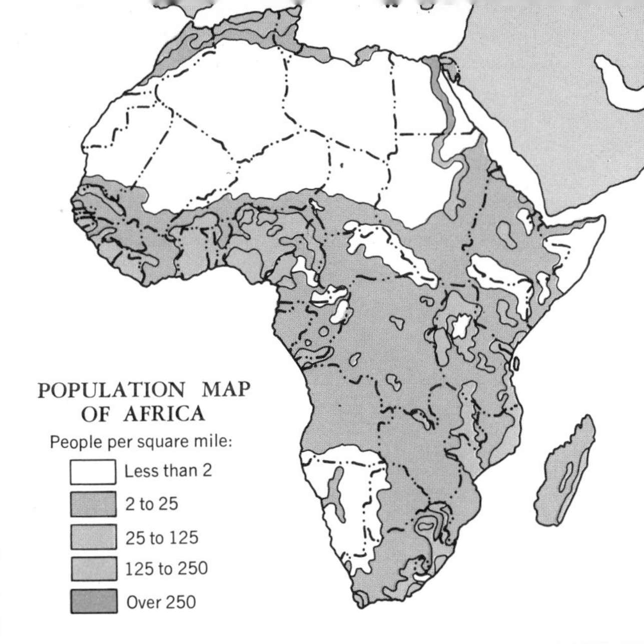

Subsistence Agriculture

In the hot, wet region of Africa, the natives live solely on what they can raise. This is called **subsistence agriculture.** Crop yields are low. With no surplus, trade is not possible. It is a region where a sharp, pointed, wooden stick, the digging stick, is the main type of farming tool. It is a region of shifting agriculture where tribes move regularly. After two or three years of farming in one spot, a tribe will move to another and clear the new land for farming. The method of clearing and preparing land for subsistence agriculture has given a label to this culture region.

"Slash-and-Burn" Culture Regions

In tropical Africa, as in tropical lands throughout the world, the **"slash-and-burn"** method is used to clear forest land. By this method, forest areas are cleared by cutting trees. The trees that are cut are left on the land to dry. Often branches from trees in the surrounding forest are brought to the clearing and stacked on the cut trees already there to dry. Sometimes the pile of wood on a clearing rises to a height of 10 feet. When dry, the wood is set on fire. The use of fire to prepare land for farming or to improve it for grazing is an ancient practice. Its beginning in time is unknown.

Why do these people clear forest land rather than farm on nearby grasslands or on land that has already been farmed? There are many reasons. The soil of freshly cleared and burned forest land is easier to work. It crumbles easily. Seed holes may be punched with a pointed stick. Ashes from the burned trees and branches fertilize the soil by supplying needed minerals. Also, newly burned land is free of weeds.

With only wooden tools, grassland is almost impossible to use for farming. Grassland has a deep layer of **sod**—that is, a layer of soil filled with roots of grasses. Roots are so interwoven and tough that they can be cleared or turned only by the hardest work or by mechanical tools. Even if fire is used to clear the surface, it does not destroy the roots. After the rains, the grasses quickly grow again.

Fertile Soil Is Needed

In uncleared forests, trees and soil live in a state of balance. Leaves, branches, and trees that fall to the forest floor become **humus**—that is, decayed or rotted vegetable matter. In this way, organic matter that has been taken from the soil is returned to it. Growing plants draw upon the minerals in the humus for food. Thus, plant life that falls to the forest floor supports further plant life. Lands that have been cleared of trees may have difficulty in returning to forest lands. When the layer of humus is thin, it is easily eroded or washed away. The soil loses its fertility.

When the protective covering of trees is removed, the sun's rays strike the soil and the humus directly. The direct rays make the ground warmer than when it was protected from the sun by a leafy cover. The rate at which the humus is destroyed by micro-organisms increases with the rise in soil temperature. This hap-

More careful use of the soil, together with controlled irrigation, has replaced the wasteful "slash and burn" system in some parts of Africa.

pens because the number of micro-organisms in the soil increases with the rise in temperature in humid areas. The removal of the layer of humus not only makes the soil poorer, but also helps to erode, or wear away, the soil. Water, that was once absorbed by the layer of humus, now seeps through the soil and removes valuable minerals. The process of removing minerals from the soil by water seepage is called **leaching.** Leaching takes place in this way. Heavy, daily rains pour down on the open soil. The warmer and more acid the water, the greater its power to dissolve certain minerals and wash them from the soil.

If the protective tree covering is gone and the layer of humus has been destroyed, minerals, such as calcium and phosphate, disappear quickly from the soil. Nitrate deposits dissolve almost immediately. In tropical rainforests the soil is usually protected from this leaching, or washing action, by a heavy layer of humus which can absorb the water. The leaves of the forest trees also protect the soil from being washed away by rainwater.

The "Slash-and-Burn" System

A cleared space may be farmed from one to three years before the humus is destroyed and the minerals lost through leaching. When this happens, the farmers are forced to find new farmland. Grasslands and cleared lands must be avoided. When an uncleared forest area is decided upon, the farming cycle begins again. The tribesmen "slash-and-burn" the area. There is little danger in fire spreading to the nearby living forest.

The farmer pokes holes in the soil with the fire-hardened point of a stick. He then drops seeds into the hole and pushes dirt over the hole with his foot. Several types of seeds and tubers will be planted in the same clearing. One clearing may have yams, corn, peppers, beans, and peanuts. Remember that weeding is not necessary in such a farming system. There were few weeds in the forests. Whatever seeds or weeds were there were probably burned.

In a "slash-and-burn" culture region, crops need protection from forest animals. Fences give some protection from small, plant-eating animals. Elephants, however, are a serious problem in some areas. Elephants enjoy the tender growing plants and can easily push down fences. The crops must also be protected from birds. Platforms for bird watchers are sometimes built. The watcher frightens away swarms of birds either by making noise or by throwing stones.

In tropical regions, the period of time during which "slash-and-burn" land should remain unfarmed is between 25 and 30 years. It takes that much time for the forest to grow again and for enough humus to be laid upon the soil.

The population density of "slash-and-burn" regions is usually not high. Large areas of land must remain unfarmed for a long time. The soil of cleared land is quickly exhausted. For these reasons, one can see why these regions are not able to support large numbers of people.

Health of the Natives

The people who live by "slash-and-burn" farming may have a poor diet. They have few animals, so that their diet is often lacking in meat. They sometimes add to their meat supply by trading grain and vegetables to the "hunters of the forest," the Pygmies, for meat. Crops grown on soils that have been leached of essential minerals will lack these minerals. The health of the farmers will suffer from the lack of a proper diet.

Poor diet and diseases sap the strength of many Central Africans. Many insects carry diseases. We know that mosquitoes spread malaria. By wiping out their breeding places and by spraying mosquitoes, malaria is being reduced. We also know that in Africa, sleeping sickness is spread by the tsetse fly. Scientists are finding ways to destroy these flies which live in many parts of Africa.

Very large parts of tropical Africa are infected by the blood-sucking tsetse fly. Wild animals are not subject to sleeping sickness, although they may carry the micro-organism that causes it. However, it will kill domestic animals, such as horses, cattle, and dogs. The tsetse fly carries a parasite which lodges under the skin of a person or an animal bitten by the fly. The person with sleeping sickness stays asleep. His body wastes away slowly. Death finally comes.

Africa is plagued by diseases that sap the strength and energy of its people. The prevention of these diseases is one of the major problems faced by the people. A start has been made, but many more doctors and nurses are needed.

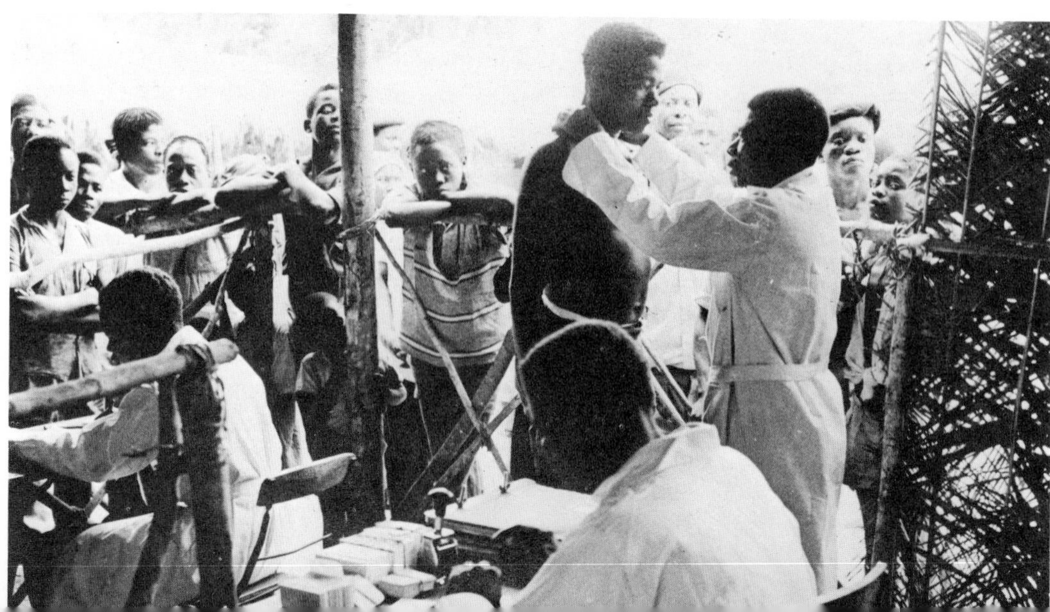

Until recently, sleeping sickness was a killing disease. Now, if treatment is begun during its early stages, patients will recover. People can be injected with modern drugs that will protect them against the disease. Far greater numbers of medical persons are needed to help reduce these diseases.

THE NATIVES OF AFRICA

Many of the native Africans still live in tribes. Most African tribes are made up of several families. The people feel a strong loyalty to their tribal leaders. One family is usually the ruling family. The chief of the tribe comes from this family. He may be the oldest member of the family. African families are very large. They include not only father, mother, and children, but also grandparents, aunts, uncles, and cousins. Some families believe the dead can control the living. Many families continue to consider the dead as members of their families. Family members own land in common. They remain very close together. One member of a family helps another when aid is needed.

The Pygmies

Two groups of Africans, small in number but very interesting in their characteristics, are the Pygmies and the Bushmen. On the average the Pygmies are about four and one-half feet tall. They have yellow-brown skin and sometimes downy hair on their bodies. At one time they may have lived throughout the region of the tropical rainforest. Today there are only about 30,000 to 40,000 of them. They live in small scattered groups in the dense rainforest. They live by hunting antelope, birds, and monkeys. They also gather wild fruit and vegetables. They hunt with bow and arrow and with blowguns. They sometimes trade surplus meat to their Bantu neighbors for yams and beans.

The Bushmen

The Bushmen may once have lived throughout South Africa. As Bantu tribes from the north pushed southward into South Africa, they killed or drove the Bushmen back. The few remaining Bushmen today live mostly in the Kalahari Desert area of southwest Africa. Bushmen average about five feet in height and have a wrinkled, yellowish skin. They live by hunting and by digging roots.

Some tribes accept Western ways very quickly. They change their ways of dress and tribal customs easily. Other tribes hold on to their old ways of living and resist change. These tribes still practice their old religious customs. The witch doctor continues to be an important part of the tribe. He is called to treat the sick, and to advise the members of the tribe on other matters.

Western clothes, a wristwatch, and shoes mark this man as a city worker.

INDUSTRY BRINGS INDEPENDENCE

Many Africans have moved to the cities in search of jobs and a better life. Many of them cannot read and write. They usually have low-paying jobs. They live in very poor shacks in slum sections of the cities. Most Africans regularly return to the bush to visit their families. Many still hold positions in their tribes. Few cut themselves off from their families when they move to the city.

Most African cities are in the coastal areas. For example, among the large cities of West Central Africa we find Dakar in Senegal, Monrovia in Liberia, Accra in Ghana, Lagos in Nigeria, and Kinshasa in the Republic of the Congo. In East Africa, Nairobi in Kenya, and Kampala in Uganda are important cities. Many of these large cities were built by Europeans as centers of export for African products. The Africans still depend upon the Europeans for the export of raw materials, but a great change is going on in these countries. The Africans, themselves, are beginning to process the raw materials within their own countries. With improved transportation, more cities have been built in the interior and many of the small cities are growing.

The parts of Africa that have been rapidly becoming industrialized have given rise to the descriptive phrase, "Africa in transition." The people are building plywood factories, cement plants, weaving mills, and even soft drink bottling plants. Soap, margarine, tile, furniture, and cigarettes now come off African manufacturing lines in steady streams. Goods such as these formerly had to be imported. Now the Africans import machinery, tools, fuel, and lubricating oils in order to process raw materials in their own lands.

Educated Africans hold many kinds of jobs in the cities, including important positions in government. One of the serious problems which the new governments face is the uniting of all the tribes. Tribal leaders, to whom the people have a strong loyalty, must be educated in the new way of life. The people will then follow their leaders' acceptance of the new government. Since World War II, the new political leaders have brought most of the countries of Africa to independence. Today, people throughout the world are watching the ways in which the new nations are solving the problems that come with independence. There are problems of self-government, of establishing new trade patterns, and of introducing modern ways of living among great numbers of people.

THE REGION OF SOUTH AFRICA

European explorers approached the southern area of Africa and the island which is now called the Malagasy Republic from the seaward side. Early settlements began along the coastline when ships on their way to India stopped for supplies. Gradually, the people in these coastal settlements penetrated inland.

The region of South Africa where these early settlements were made has very few coastal lowland sections. These coastal lands have tropical climate conditions. There is no continuous band of coastal settlements. There are, however, a few important harbors and ports. A **harbor** usually means a sheltered place, safe enough to anchor. A **port** has a large harbor, with many docks, larger settlements, and a larger hinterland (land in back). Locate on the map on this page these large ports: Cape Town, Port Elizabeth, East London, Durban, Lourenço Marques, and Beira.

Inland from the narrow coastal lands of southern Africa are high plateaus and mountains. As the settlers moved to the interior, they had to climb the Drakensberg Mountains and the High Veld plateau. They found that the edges of these high places had a subtropical climate. In this climate the natural vegetation was better for farming and grazing.

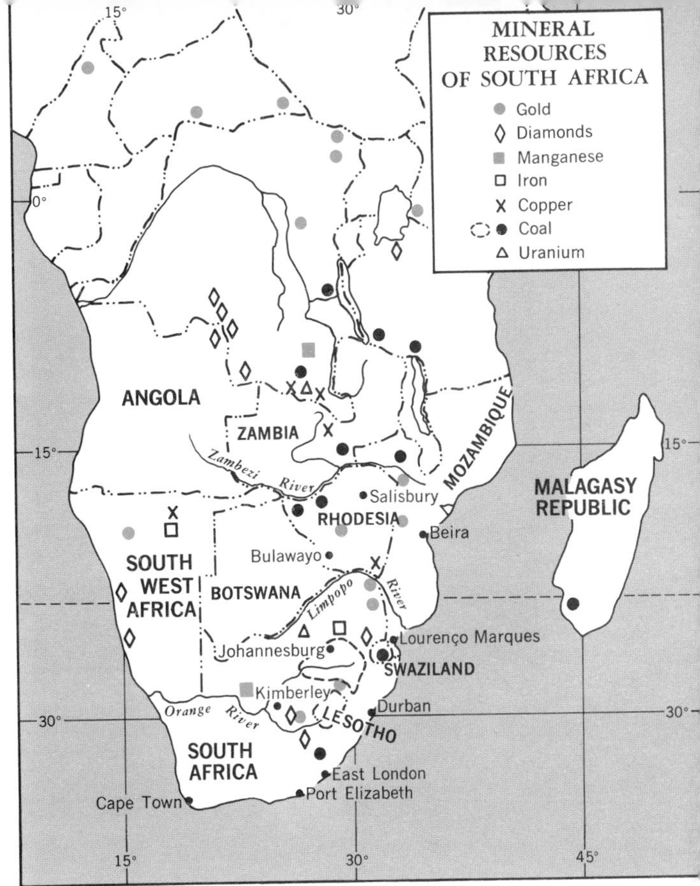

Cape Town, near the southern tip of Africa, is South Africa's chief port and one of its two capitals.

The "Big Hole," an abandoned diamond mine, is a symbol of 19th century South Africa, just as the Kariba Dam in Rhodesia, with its enormous generating capacity, is a symbol of today.

The temperature was lower, and the rainfall was moderate. The natural vegetation was a grass, excellent for cattle raising.

Settlements grew in size and number. Many became commercial centers for cattlemen and wheat growers. Others grew in the areas of diamond and gold mines. Kimberley is an important diamond center. Johannesburg and Pretoria are important gold settlements. In recent years other valuable minerals, such as manganese, have been discovered. Asbestos, used for making insulating materials, comes from Gaberones.

Farther north, in Rhodesia, commercial and industrial development took place on a central strip. This strip extends from Bulawayo on the southwest to Salisbury on the northeast. Minerals—gold, chromium, silver, as well as asbestos and iron—are taken from this strip of territory. The rest of the state is devoted to grazing and the gathering of forest products.

Still farther north, extending into the Subtropical Region, a great business enterprise sprang up. It was the mining of copper from one of the richest copper ore districts in the world, the Katanga. It is located in the southern part of the Congo. From 1927, when the "copper boom" began, until 1931, immigrants entered by thousands. They came from the lands of Africa and from other countries. Other mining enterprises for lead and zinc were started. Today 90 per cent of the exports of Zambia are copper, lead, and zinc. Most of these exports go to the outside world through the port of Beira.

One of the most remarkable achievements in this region of Africa is the Kariba Dam. It lies on the Zambia-Rhodesia frontier. Locate it on the map on page 187. Built at a cost of 200 million dollars, this great source of electricity from water power now stands as a symbol of the future. The unlimited supply of water comes from the huge Zambezi, the fourth largest river in Africa. Electricity is now directed to the copper mining districts, to the factories and food processing plants, and to homes which previously had no source of light. Great progress can now be foreseen in this region of South Africa.

While many Europeans have come to Africa, the Negro population is still much greater than the white. For example, the Negro population is dominant in the "bush-and-forest" parts of Zambia. Even in the industrial areas, the Negro population outnumbers the European population by at least five to one. In the Republic of South Africa three million white settlers rule nearly ten million Negroes, Bushmen, Hottentots, and Indians. The ruling whites favor the policy of **apartheid**—that is, the separation of black and white people. They are unwilling to give non-whites power and property because they are afraid they will be out-voted by the greater number of non-whites. The problem of race relations in parts of Africa is very serious. It is hoped that the problem will be solved by the people themselves in the near future.

Africa's future depends on education. These students are studying at the Royal College of Nairobi, in Kenya.

AN ENCOURAGING FUTURE

For years Africa has been looked upon as a source of raw materials for European and American industry. The basic economy was an export economy. This is changing today. There is a growing number of industries in Africa. Many manufactured goods which were imported in the past are being made in Africa today. In East Africa new farming methods have been introduced. Farm machinery and fertilizer are used to improve farming.

While progress is being made, many Africans hold on to old ways of living and working. Families and tribes are important to the Africans. They frequently are more loyal to their tribe than to their new governments. In many parts of Africa the natives still use a "slash-and-burn" system of agriculture.

The culture region south of the Sahara has great promise. New nations are developing. Old economies are giving way to new ways of making a living. As the people of Africa learn to use what the continent offers, they will be able to have a better life.

In trying to regionalize this part of the African continent, we meet several problems. We can use the political divisions but since we are more interested in the people and what they do, we need to find a different way to divide the land. We may decide to regionalize by what people do and by how they live. We will find places where there is a "slash-and-burn" system of agriculture. Other ways of life and living include mining, plantation crop-growing, and grain and cattle farming. We may try to understand these ways of living. But each way of dividing Africa does not coincide with the location of groups of people. In Africa there are Negroes, the native Africans, and non-Negroes, mostly Europeans. In some areas the two groups of people live close together and in other areas they are quite separated. We finally come to the conclusion that there is no "best" way to regionalize every area. The people, the ways of living, and sometimes the political divisions change too rapidly in this region of remarkable progress.

Do You Know?

1. What are the two reasons why the lands of Africa were difficult to settle?

2. How often do the rays of the sun shine directly upon the Tropic of Cancer? The Tropic of Capricorn? The Equator?

3. What do we call the region of the Earth on which the sun's rays shine most directly? Where is it located?

4. What mineral is used by industry for drilling hard substances? Where is it found?

5. What are some of the outstanding physical features of East Africa?

6. What two economies are found in Africa south of the Sahara?

7. What two elements of the climate produce a heavy forest near the equator?

8. What are two products that the United States imports from Nigeria?

9. How does the addition of the mineral columbite affect steel?

10. Why are cattle important to the native Africans?

11. What is subsistence agriculture? What do we call the regions where it exists?

Learn By Doing

1. Match column **B** with column **A.**

A	B
1. Nigeria	gold
2. Lake Malawi	Mt. Kilimanjaro
3. Beira	cacao
4. Kimberley	port
5. Pretoria	rainforest
6. Katanga	diamonds
7. Kariba Dam	part of Great Rift
8. Tanganyika	largest lake
9. Lake Victoria	copper
10. Congo	electricity

2. Pretend you are moving to Africa south of the Sahara. Select the country in which you would like to live. Plan your trip. Briefly describe the following features: climate, landforms, and natural resources. Then carefully answer the following questions:

a. Is the country noted for industry or agriculture? From what kinds of work could your father choose? Select a job for your father.

b. Describe the area in which you would live (city, plantation, mining area, rural area).

c. Describe what your new home might be like.

d. Could your present clothing be worn in the new land? What new types of clothing would you see when you reached Africa?

e. What new foods would you have to learn to like?

f. How would your government change?

g. How would your education change?

h. What means of transportation would your family use?

3. Compare the journey of the early European explorers with a modern safari expedition.

a. How would the group get to Africa?

b. What supplies would be brought?

c. Who would be present?

d. What dangers would be met?

e. How would the group protect itself?

f. What would the accomplishments of this group be?

4. On a blank sheet of paper briefly sketch the continent of Africa. Think before you start. What is the longest part of Africa? The widest? Where are the major indentations?

Test Your Knowledge

1. Give three reasons why it is difficult to explore Africa.

2. How has the European economy changed the population in many areas of Central Africa?

3. Name some customs which are meaningful and important to the people of African tribes. Do you feel that some customs should be preserved as European ways of living are adopted? Explain your answer.

4. Many natives use the "slash-and-burn" system of farming. Explain briefly how they have developed the best method of farming in their region by using the following: a digging stick, newly cleared forest land, and the shifting agriculture of the three-year cycle.

5. Why is cleared forest land used for farming in Africa rather than the grasslands? Show how sod and leaching present problems. How does humus help the farmer?

6. Use a dictionary to find the differences in meaning of cacao, cocoa, coca, and chocolate.

7. Does preservation of animals mean that none will be killed? For what reasons might man kill an animal?

8. Why is disease a serious problem in Africa? Discuss the importance of preventing disease in Africa. What progress has been made?

9. In what ways has the European economy helped develop the cities of Africa?

10. Has the European influence helped or hindered the native African gain his independence? What changes has it brought to his way of life?

REVIEWING PART 3

Do You Remember?

1. What is a harbor? What is a port?

2. What are the three major rivers of Africa?

3. What is the third largest inland body of water in the world?

4. What is the highest point in Africa?

5. What are some of the chief exports of Africa?

6. Why do you think the desert lands of Southwest Asia developed more rapidly than the desert lands of North Africa?

7. Who are the nomads? What is their chief means of support? How can we say that this way of life is a form of subsistence?

8. What religion is dominant in the Dry World Region? What is the major language?

9. What do we mean when we say that the people of the Dry World Region irrigate their land?

10. What problems do the educated African leaders of the new governments face?

11. What is meant by the phrase "Africa in transition" when it is applied to Africa south of the Sahara?

12. What is the Great Rift? What three lakes are found within it? Where is it located?

13. Do you think the expression "Africa in transition" can be used to describe the Dry World Region? Explain your answer.

Projects and Reports

1. Compare the populations of the northern coast, the southern coast, the desert, the central cities, and the "slash-and-burn" region. Draw a map showing your findings.

2. Write a report on the development of Kuwait.

3. Select and read about an animal of Africa. Then draw a picture of your animal showing its use or its importance to man.

4. Pretend you are a cacao bean on a plantation in Nigeria. Explain all the steps you would go through to become a cup of cocoa in Chicago.

5. Using an encyclopedia or reference books, prepare a report on one or more of the following topics:

Albert Schweitzer	The Bantu
Livingston and Stanley	The Watusi
Egyptian Art	The Pygmies
Cecil Rhodes	The Boers
The Aswan Dam	Cheops

6. Plan a north-south journey through Africa. Use the map on page 187.

a. What meridians of longitude could you use? Select one.

b. Through what countries would you pass?

c. What natural climate regions would you see?

d. What native people might you meet as you traveled?

e. What large cities would you be near?

f. What interesting landform features of Africa would you see?

g. Which section would be the hottest? The wettest?

h. What animals would you see?

Using Maps and Globes

1. Name the bodies of water that lie at each of the following locations:

a. north of the Dry World Region

b. west of the continent of Africa

c. east of southern Africa

d. east of the Sahara

2. What is the largest nation that is totally in the Dry World Region?

3. What is the largest nation of North Africa?

4. What nations of Africa and Southwest Asia border on the Mediterranean Sea?

5. Through what bodies of water could you travel if you went from Kuwait to Israel?

6. What two continents does the Strait of Gibraltar divide? What two bodies of water does it connect?

7. How many deserts can you locate in the Dry World Region? In Africa south of the Sahara?

8. Compare the size of the Sahara with the size of the United States.

9. Find the Congo River. Where is its source? Where is its mouth?

10. What is the most southern nation of Africa?

11. Locate each of the following on the map on page 187. Carefully describe the location of each. Is it toward the north, south, northwest, southeast, or central part?

0° Latitude	Cape Town
0° Longitude	a large island
Tropic of Cancer	Canary Islands
Tropic of Capricorn	Gulf of Guinea

12. Through how many time zones would you pass if you traveled from the most western to the most eastern part of the African continent? Study the map on page 463.

13. About how many miles would you travel if you flew from Tunis, Tunisia to Cape Town, South Africa?

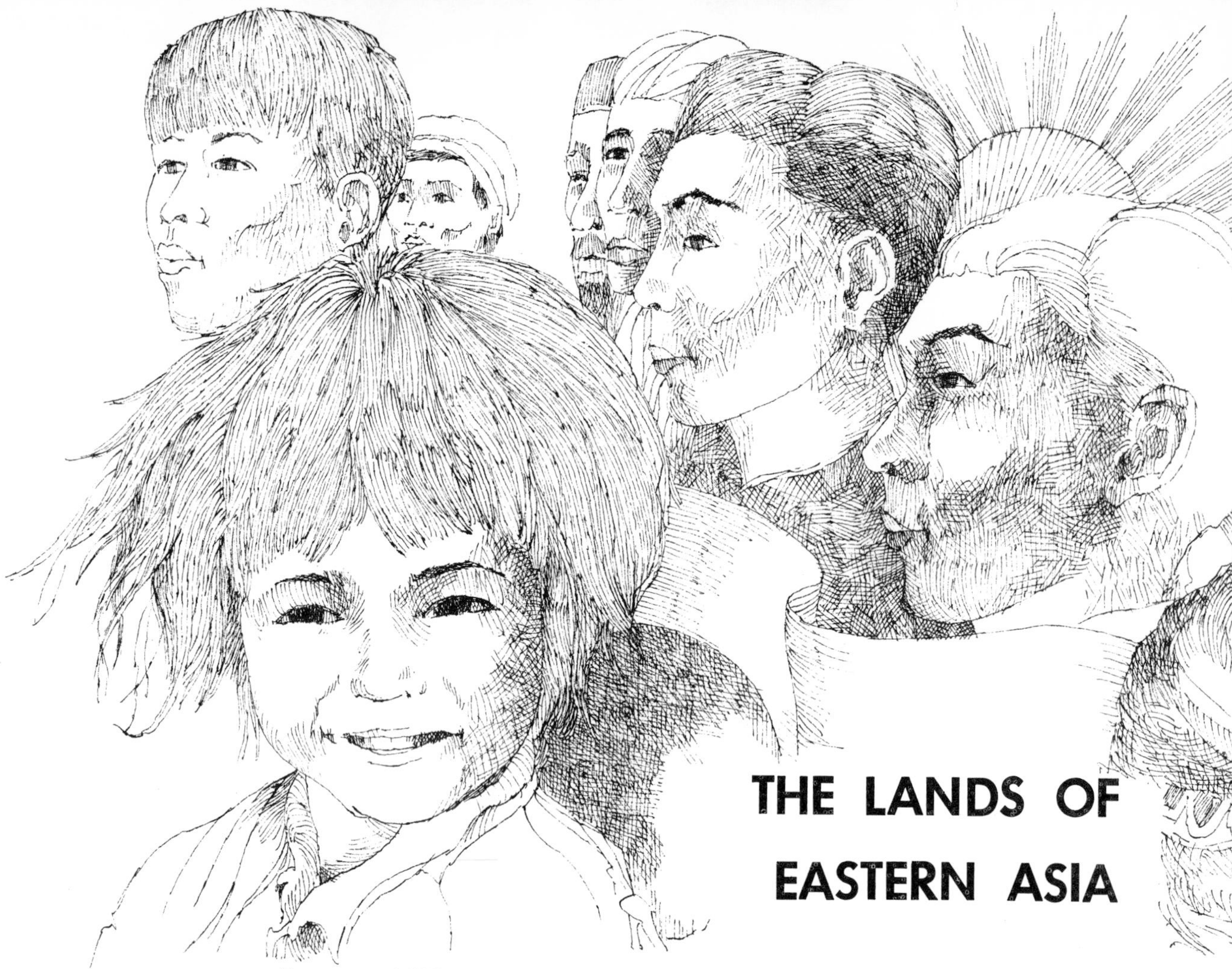

THE LANDS OF EASTERN ASIA

PART 4

Millions of people live in Eastern Asia. Many of their cultural ideas are changing greatly and rapidly. These changes affect family life, religion, industry, farming, and forms of government. In this part, you will read about the many changes in the culture regions of Japan, China, the Indian Sub-continent, and Southeast Asia.

There is one regionalizing feature common to all of these regions. This feature is the growing of rice as a staple crop and its use as an important item in the diet of the people. Rice requires a warm, moist climate to grow well. This climate requirement is met throughout many parts of these regions.

Japan is a small island country with a very large population. Agricultural land is scarce on the mountainous islands of Japan. All of the usable land is carefully tended to grow as much food as possible for the many people of Japan. Although lacking native minerals, Japan has become one of the leading industrial countries in the world.

The Chinese civilization is very ancient. As you remember, the valley of the Hwang Ho was one of the four ancient culture homes

of civilization. Today there are two Chinese governments. The Republic of China controls the island of Taiwan. The other, the People's Republic of China, controls mainland China. It is a communist dictatorship.

The third Asian region, the Indian Sub-continent, is the site of another ancient culture home of civilization, the Mohenjo-Daro and Harappa culture near the Indus River. Today, there are three major countries in this region, India, Pakistan, and Ceylon. All of these countries were formerly controlled by the United Kingdom. They gained their independence after World War II. Today, most of the people of the Indian Sub-continent make their living by farming.

A fourth Asian region is Southeast Asia. It is a region of many kinds of people, of many languages, of many different religions, and of a wide variety of products. It is a region of mountains, valleys, rivers, and many islands, large and small. One of the regionalizing features of this area is its tropical climate. It is a region of much rain and warm, humid, growing conditions where rainforests thrive.

CHAPTER 11

JAPAN'S SUN IS RISING AGAIN

Japan is a beautiful island country off the mainland of eastern Asia. Through hard work the Japanese have done remarkable things with the resources of their islands. Japanese farmers raise most of the food needed by the overcrowded population. They use all available farming land carefully and well. Japanese fishermen reap a rich harvest of fish from the seas that surround their country.

The forests of Japan are an important resource for building and industry. The Japanese people turn out products ranging from tiny radios to huge locomotives in their many factories. These products are sold in all parts of the world.

JAPAN AND CHINA— THE FAR EAST

Look at a globe and locate the place where you live on the North American continent. Next find Japan and China in eastern Asia. These two countries are far away from us in what is called the **Far East.** Why is this region of the world called the Far East? Surely if you travel far to the west, you could also reach these nations. The term *Far East* goes back several centuries, back before the discovery of America. It goes back to a time when Europeans knew of only one way to reach China; they had to travel east.

Look at the globe again and find the Mediterranean. Centuries ago, when Western Europeans wanted to travel to lands at the eastern end of the Mediterranean, they sailed east. Because they had to travel east to reach them, Western Europeans called these lands the **Near East.** They knew that if they continued to travel in the same direction, east, they would eventually reach far distant China. These early adventurers and traders called the lands bordering on the great eastern ocean the Far East. The terms *Near East* and *Far East* were simply useful words to describe the Eastern lands that were near and far away from Europe.

Today, you would not have to follow in the footsteps of those early European traders to get to the Far East. You can fly directly to the Far East over northern Polar routes or cross the Pacific Ocean by traveling westward. Although we travel westward, the term *Far East* remains as a reminder of a time when travel and trade from Europe to China went east.

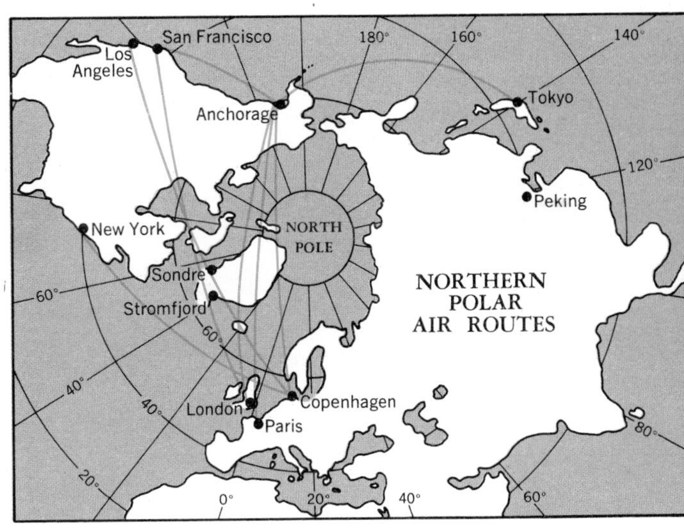

Today, planes fly a northern route to reach the Far East.

Japan and China Are Alike in Many Ways

Both China and Japan have cultures that are very old. China's civilization existed long before Japan's. The Japanese did not copy the Chinese, but they did borrow some of the cultural ideas and customs to build their own civilization. China's influence on Japan can be seen in the similarities of the religion, the dress, and the homes of the people.

Both China and Japan have a **monsoon climate.** This means that warm, moist air flows in from the sea during the summer months and drenches the lowland fields with rain. These summer rains water the trees on the high mountain slopes. These rains that accompany the monsoon wind cause some varieties of young bamboo sprouts to grow more than a foot in height in one day. In the winter, the winds reverse and blow off the Asian continent toward the oceans. Winters in the Far East are long and dry.

For most of the people of the Far East rice is the staple, or principal, food in the diet. Rice is a plant that thrives best in a tropical or subtropical climate. Rice is grown in all but the most northern provinces of China and Japan. Here wheat is the staple crop and dietary food. Most of the people of China and Japan, however, have never eaten wheat bread as we know it. Rice fills the starch role in their diet that potatoes and bread do in ours. Rice lacks the sticky substance that holds wheat dough together. Instead of being ground into flour and made into bread, the grain is steamed or boiled and eaten plain with beans and peas. Sometimes it is flavored with a little meat or fish.

Look at the map on page 237. Nearly one-fourth of the world's

Fish and rice are two of the main foods of Japan. While fish are caught off the shore of all the islands, rice only grows in the warmer southern part of the country.

population lives in the Far East. China and Japan have in common their very dense populations. They are faced with the problem of supplying enough food for the present population. As the population continues to grow, these two nations are finding it difficult to supply even a minimum amount of food for every person.

THE SMALL COUNTRY OF JAPAN

Japan is an island country made up of four large islands and more than 3,000 smaller ones. It lies along the eastern coast of Asia in the Pacific Ocean. The four largest islands, Kyushu, Shikoku, Honshu, and Hokkaido, are about equal in total land area to the state of California. These mountainous islands extend about 1,400 miles from north to south. They are part of a sunken mountain range that extends along the western shores of the North Pacific Ocean. Although the land area is about the size of California, Japan has a population equal to about half of the population of the entire United States. Approximately 98 million people live in this small country. They average about 686 persons per square mile.

Climate of Japan

No part of Japan is farther than 90 miles from the sea. The climate of Japan is milder than that of the mainland. It is influenced by two great ocean currents which flow past the Japanese coast. One of them, the Japan Current, is a fast moving stream of warm water that flows northward from the Philippines. As this warm current flows past the southern and eastern coasts of Japan, air blows across and makes southern Japan warmer than places on the mainland of Asia in the same latitude. The other great current, the Kurile Current, flows south from the Sea of Okhotsk and the Bering Sea. The colder waters of this current meet the Japan Current east of Japan, as you can see on the map on this page. This cold current and the cool air above it make the northernmost islands and the seas surrounding them foggy, stormy, and colder than places on the mainland in the same latitude.

As you might expect with a country that extends 1,400 miles from north to south, there are differences in Japan's climate from north to south. Winters in Hokkaido, Japan's northernmost main island, are long and cold. In Kyushu, the southernmost large island, winters are much warmer with temperatures very rarely below freezing. There are also differences in the amount of precipitation that falls. The cold northern part of Japan receives an average of 40 to 60 inches each year, mostly in snow. Many areas in the warmer south receive about 80 to 100 inches of rain each year. Ten inches of snow equal one inch of rain. Imagine the snowfall on the island of Hokkaido.

Land Features of Japan

Four-fifths of Japan's surface is hilly and mountainous. The mountains are not only high, but are frequently steep sided. Japan's highest mountain, Mount Fujiyama, is 12,389 feet above sea level. Many ranges of mountains in Japan have snow-covered peaks that are almost as high.

From whatever point one views this perfect cone, Mount Fujiyama, one sees some of the most beautiful scenery in the world. Fuji's mirror image can be seen in the waters of the five lakes near its base. In addition to its physical beauty, Mount Fuji means something more to each Japanese. It is a symbol of Japan

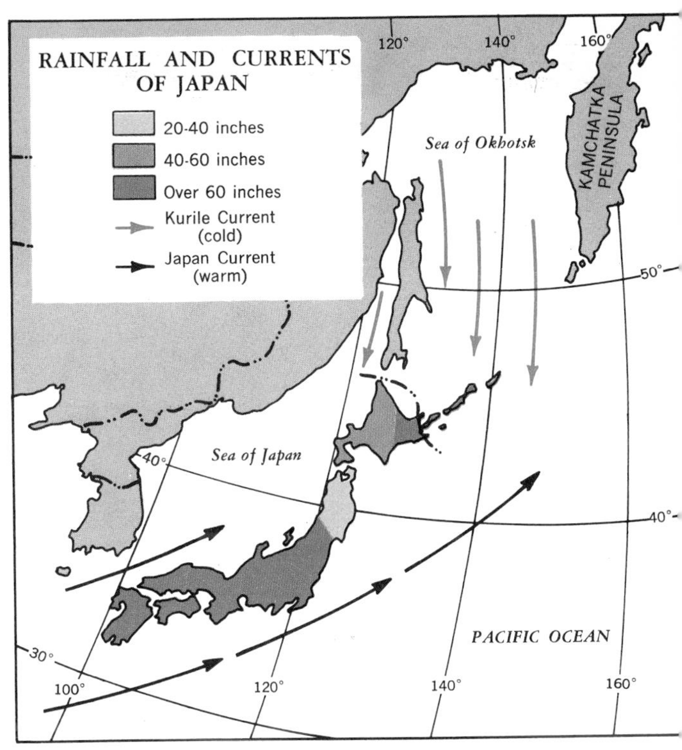

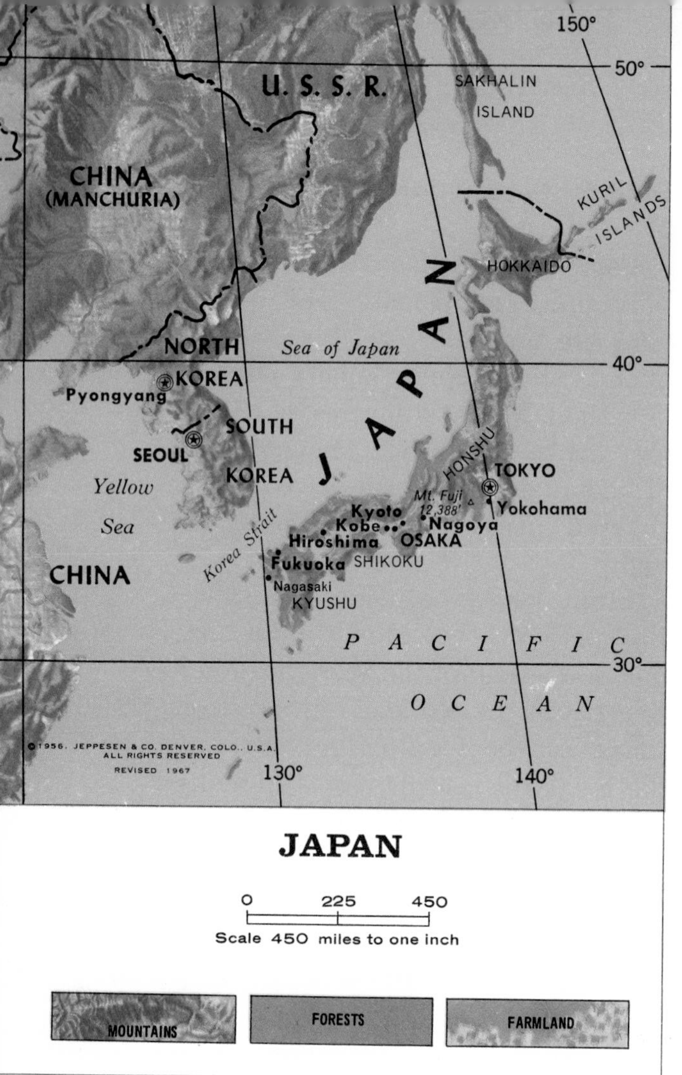

itself and her history of more than two thousand years. It is a place where heaven and earth meet. The Japanese have long considered Fuji a sacred mountain. During the summer thousands of white-clad pilgrims climb to the top of this national shrine.

Although it has not erupted since 1707, Mount Fuji is a live but inactive volcano from which occasional wisps of steam arise. Among Japan's numerous mountains, there are seven volcanic systems which are active ones. Sometimes they are the cause of the earthquakes which occur in Japan. Faint tremors occur almost daily. Occasionally quakes cause great damage. Usually, these quakes are due to breaks in the Earth's crust. The rocks which make up the outer crust of the Earth are continually being stretched and squeezed by forces from within the Earth. When the rocks break, they cause shock waves to move through the Earth. These breaks are called **faults.** Faults are more common to "young" mountain systems, such as those found in Japan.

The islands of Japan are young—that is, they have risen from the sea in recent geological times. Unlike old mountain ranges that have been worn into smooth, rounded forms by the forces of erosion, the mountains of Japan rise sharply and suddenly. In many places along the coast, the mountains slope almost vertically into the sea. Many of the islands that dot the coast are very steep and high, so high that they appear to be the tops of undersea mountains which, in fact, they are.

On the larger islands, there are fairly level areas in the valleys between mountains. Over a period of many years, rain, wind, and streams have carried soil from the mountains and left **alluvial deposits** that have filled in the valleys. *Alluvial* means "to wash" or "to flow." Alluvial deposits refer to the soils which have been left by the floods. Rivers carrying silt from the mountains have formed deltas that reach farther and farther from the mainland. However,

Mount Fuji, the sacred mountain of Japan, overlooks valuable forest land and many small farms.

even with the forces of erosion that have been wearing down Japan's mountainous land for centuries, only about 15 per cent of Japan's land surface is suitable for farming. Many of the steep-sided mountains are too abrupt for terracing. This leaves the Japanese farmer with very little land that lends itself to raising the needed crops.

FARMING IN JAPAN

With so few acres of arable land, how are the Japanese farmers able to feed so many people? How do they provide about 80 per cent of the food consumed in this densely populated country?

The Japanese farmers are very efficient. By following carefully laid out plans, their yield per acre is two to three times that gathered by the farmers of most other countries. Two crops are frequently planted in the same field. Rice is grown on all the islands during summer months. Where climate conditions permit in the south, three rice crops are planted and harvested each year. Wheat and barley are grown on the more northern islands in the winter months.

Fertilizers are especially important to the Japanese farmers because the same crops are planted year after year in the same fields. The farmers make use of all available waste materials. Decayed roots, leaves, straw, and other organic wastes are accumulated into large piles and left to decompose. These decomposed materials become valuable fertilizers. Also, in recent years, the average farmer has increased his use of chemical fertilizers.

Most farms are small, averaging only about two and one-half acres. Almost everything the Japanese farmer grows is farmed with his own hands. Rice is planted by hand, weeded and tilled by hand, and harvested by hand. Every plant is treated with care. Soil is kept moist, loose, and free of weeds. Insects are frequently removed by hand.

Every available square inch of soil is so carefully put to some use by Japanese farmers that every valley looks like one large garden. Wherever possible, land has been leveled or terraced for the growing of rice. For this reason, a forested mountain will often rise at the edge of a valley or rice paddy.

Terraces are built on mountainsides that are not too steep. They are held in place with large rocks. These rocks, however, are not fitted together perfectly. Spaces are left between the rocks. Plants whose roots will work their way back into the soil are placed in these gaps. Strawberries and other vinelike berry plants hang from the face of the rock. Even the banks of water ditches, used for irrigating fields, are planted. They are lined with shrubs and with bamboo.

Crops are planted and harvested carefully. Young plants are set in between rows of older plants in the field. As the older plants ripen and are harvested, the younger ones are spread or transplanted to give them more growing space. During the season of heavy rains, June and early July, when the rice paddies are flooded, fish are brought in and "raised" along with the rice seedlings.

All parts of the rice plant are used. Even the straw from the rice plant is saved and sold. When the rice is cut, the bundles are hung from wooden rails to dry. This keeps the straw from being damaged by touching the wet earth. When the rice grains are removed, the straw is sold to factories which make it into useful articles. The main use is to make mats called **tatamis.** These mats are used in most Japanese homes to cover the entire floor.

The Land of Many Uses

Rice is the main crop. Other important crops include wheat, barley, and soybeans. Farmers also grow some potatoes and a variety of vegetables. Tea is a very important crop in Japan. Very little land is given to the growing of tea plants. Only about one-half acre out of every 100 acres is used for tea growing. On this small acreage the Japanese grow enough tea to supply their own needs and to export to other countries. Tea export is a very important part of Japanese trade.

Tea plants, carefully set out on this hillside, are characteristic of Japan's systematic and intensive use of its land.

Tea grows well on the hillsides in southern Japan. The Japanese make use of some of the steeper hillsides for this crop. It is a familiar sight to see a hillside, planted in tea, rising out of a flat rice paddy. In the autumn when the rice is a golden yellow, the green tea plants on the slopes above present a beautiful picture.

Tea plants grow very close together. The Japanese keep the bushes well pruned, so they will remain small and produce many branches. The more branches produced, the more leaves each bush will produce. It is the tender young leaves near the end of the branches which make the best tea. The leaves are picked from two to four times a year.

Many Japanese farmers raise silkworms as an extra means of earning money. A few mulberry trees will produce enough leaves to feed a large number of silkworms. When the silkworms have made their cocoons, the farmers sell the cocoons to the silk mills. At the mills the strands of silk made by the worms are unwound from the cocoons and spun into thread for use in weaving cloth.

Land is so scarce that Japanese farmers for many years have raised very little livestock. Most farmers will have a few chickens, and some

A hydroponic vegetable "factory."

will have hogs. In some parts of Japan, farmers are beginning to raise dairy and beef cattle. The herds are small, but the dairy products and the meat are of very high quality. Kobe beef is considered among the best beef in the world. This is obtained from cattle raised in the section around the city of Kobe, on the island of Honshu. The cattle are fed on rice grain and given very special care so the beef will bring a good price.

More Food Is Still Needed

To get the most from their land, the Japanese farmers must be hard and industrious workers. They work their land from dawn to dusk. During the busy times of the year, especially during the planting or harvesting season, men, women, and children work in the fields.

In spite of their hard work, many Japanese farmers find it difficult to make a living from farming. During the winter thousands of farmers seek jobs in industry. Wages from such work help these farmers earn a living.

In an effort to increase the food supply, some Japanese have learned to use a method of growing plants called **hydroponic** farming. With this method, instead of using regular soil in outdoor conditions, plants are grown in greenhouses in water to which chemical plant foods are added. Japanese farmers have made other improvements. The use of more effective fertilizers and an increased use of farm machinery have helped the Japanese increase their food supply to some extent. They have produced enough to keep pace with the increase in population, so that food imports have risen only 20 per cent in recent years.

THE DEVELOPMENT OF JAPAN

Matching the efforts of the diligent and hard-working farmers to supply their overcrowded nation with food are the many fishermen of Japan. The Japanese look to the sea for the supply of proteins that are needed in their diet to maintain health. The average person in Japan consumes only 5 pounds of meat from animals each year, but eats 65 pounds of fish. To furnish 98 million people with fish, there are over 660,000 full-time fishermen in Japan. An added one-half million people combine fishing with farming.

Thousands of fishing villages dot the broken coastline of this island nation. The coastline of Japan is generously sprinkled with deep and sheltered bays, steep coves, and navigable inlets. The coastline of Japan is so broken and jagged that it is over twice as long as that of continental United States! Thus, there are many places from which the Japanese fishermen can set sail to reap the harvest of the sea. More than 1,400 harbors provide a haven for the 400,000 vessels that make up the fishing fleet. Most of these are small craft that work the more shallow waters near the islands. Other fishing ships are large vessels that are capable of staying at sea for days and weeks at a time.

A wholesale tuna market in Tokyo.

The Efficiency of Fishermen

As you have learned, the farmer of Japan leaves nothing undone in his efforts to make full use of his land. The inhabitants of the fishing villages also see that nothing is wasted. An illustration of this is a procedure followed by many people who live in seaside towns along the coast of Japan. During ebb tide as the water recedes from the shore, men, women, and children gather on the shore with sticks and containers. They comb the tidal shore, poking for signs of life. They collect shellfish, crabs, and pieces of seaweed.

Some of the larger boats for the fishing fleet are equipped with refrigeration to keep fish fresh. Some even have canning factories on board. Large quantities of mackerel, halibut, cod, and herring are frozen, canned, or dried for export. Canned tuna and crabmeat are also important export items. No part of the fish is wasted. Even the **entrails,** or insides, are useful as fertilizer. Fish scraps are an important source of fertilizer for the Japanese.

Japan ranks as one of the major nations in the whaling industry. Ships from Japan sail as far as the Antarctic in search of these valuable animals. Factory vessels, accompanied by powerful "catcher boats" equipped with harpoon guns, make up the whaling expedition of today. On board the factory ship is machinery to process whale meat and fat into oil and other products. The most valuable product of the whale is the oil derived from its blubber. This oil, when processed, is used in the making of margarine, soap, varnishes, glue, glycerine, and other products.

Japan is ideally situated to be the leading commercial fishing nation in the world. She is rich in fishing grounds, numerous harbors, and many miles of coastline. With a fishing fleet that numbers nearly half a million craft, she leads the world in pounds of fish caught each year.

The Pearl Culture

Pearls are made by oysters and other shellfish. When a foreign substance, such as a grain of sand, gets into the shell of the oyster, it causes the oyster to form a pearl. Oysters and other shellfish make a special substance called **nacre.** This substance forms a smooth lining so that the soft body of the oyster is comfortable in its shell. When a rough grain of sand gets into the shell, the oyster covers it with the smooth nacre. As the foreign substance continues to irritate, the oyster covers it layer upon layer with the nacre. This gradual process forms a **natural pearl.**

Men have known about pearls for many centuries. People have always considered them very valuable. A string of natural pearls can be very expensive. The oysters which produce valuable pearls are found in tropical

The oysters in wire cages have had seed pearls placed in them. When the pearl is large enough, it is removed from the oyster.

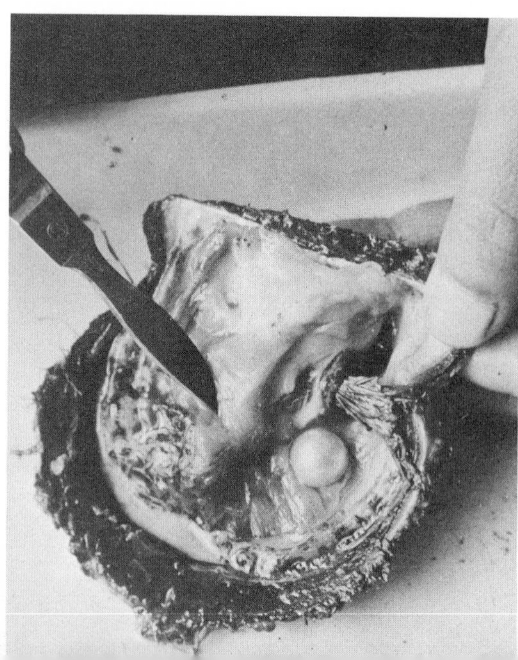

seas. Sometimes it is necessary to open hundreds of oysters before finding a pearl which has any value.

In the early 1900's, Kokichi Mikimoto of Japan developed a way to help the pearl oyster make pearls. This meant that man could control the number and size of pearls produced by oysters. In the process developed by Mikimoto, young pearl oysters are brought up from the bottom of the ocean by women divers. These young oysters are taken to a laboratory where a small seed pearl is placed in each oyster. These seed pearls are made from ground up mussel shells found in the Mississippi Valley of the United States.

After the seed pearl is placed in the shell, the oyster is put in a wire cage with other oysters. These cages are then hung in the ocean water under floating rafts. They are left in the water from three to five years. During this time each oyster covers the seed pearl with nacre to protect itself from the foreign substance in its shell. When the oysters are removed from the water and opened, there is a **cultured pearl** in each one.

Japan is the leading producer of cultured pearls in the world. This is a very important source of income for the Japanese people. About 70 per cent of the cultured pearls are sold in the United States.

Buyers at a pearl market examine samples and make their bids.

Extensive Forests

As you have learned, four-fifths of Japan is hilly and mountainous. A great many of these mountains have steep sides. In a land of moderate to heavy rainfall, loss of soil on lower slopes by the action of running water could be great, if unchecked. Hilly or mountainous land that has been stripped of its cover of trees or natural vegetation will quickly lose its topsoil. Tons of soil can be lost through the action of moving water and wind. Fortunately, more than one-half of the land in Japan is covered with forests. The roots and leaves of the trees help to stop a rapid run-off. One of the best ways to prevent damaging river floods is to protect the natural groundcover in the headwaters of the river.

The forests of Japan not only help to protect topsoil, but also serve as an important part of the Japanese economy. They supply Japan with lumber, wood pulp, and fuel. Wood is

Japan's shipyards are among the most productive in the world.

the main building material in Japan. The reason for the extensive use of wood in building is not difficult to understand. Small earthquakes occur almost daily in Japan, and large, severe ones are not uncommon. Houses built of wood sway and give a little during a quake. Walls built of more rigid materials, such as brick or stone, might crack and fall in an earthquake that would leave a wooden house unharmed. Since builders are learning to use steel and concrete in a way that withstands earthquakes, these materials will be used in more and more buildings and homes.

The greatest danger during an earthquake comes not from the quake itself, but from the possibility of fire. In 1923 more than half of the city of Tokyo was ruined by an earthquake which struck at noon when hundreds of thousands of cooking fires were lighted. About 60,000 people died from the fire that spread throughout the city. This is a good reason for using materials other than wood for buildings in the large cities.

We might say, however, that the people of Japan live in a **wood economy.** Wood is used in thousands of ways. Chopsticks are made from wood. Ships, houses, furniture, and buckets are made from wood. Temples, umbrellas, lanterns, windows, handkerchiefs, books, and even clothes are made from wood. The Japanese make every possible use of one of their great natural resources, the forests.

Few Mineral Resources

Although Japan has a variety of mineral resources, they are small in quantity. Few minerals are found in large enough amounts to meet the demands of Japan's industries. For example, petroleum is found in a few places in Japan. However, the year's production from these oil fields is no more than is produced in one day in the United States. Thus, Japan imports 98 per cent of its petroleum.

Japan has fairly large deposits of coal, but most of it is of low quality. It is not suitable for the production of high-quality coke, a necessary fuel in the manufacture of iron and steel. Only 20 per cent of the iron ore needed by the iron and steel industry comes from mines in Japan; the rest must be imported.

Growing Industries

In spite of the lack of basic minerals to keep its factories supplied, Japan is the most highly industrialized nation in Asia. It may surprise you when you look at a camera, a sewing machine, or a transistor radio and see "made in Japan" stamped on it. Did you realize that Japan is the world's foremost producer of these articles? Japan is the leading exporter of ships, rayon goods, cement, toys, pottery, and porcelain dishes and vases.

The amazing thing about Japan's industrialization is that it has been done in so short a time. During World War II, four-fifths of Japan's ships were lost and one-third of her factories were destroyed. Within six years after the war, Japan had recovered from these losses. She now ranks among the first ten nations in world trade. Through her industrialization and world trade, Japan and her people enjoy the highest living standards of any country in Asia. How could a country with little agricultural land and almost no minerals become one of the leading industrial nations of the world?

Reasons for Industrialization

Japan has several advantages which have helped her become industrialized. First, until little more than a hundred years ago Japan had shut herself off from the rest of the world.

Long a leader in silk production, Japan now also spins much cotton.

When the Japanese opened their doors to Western trade and ideas in 1853, they were immediately able to bring in inventions that had taken Western nations hundreds of years to develop. Second, lacking coal and oil, the Japanese made full use of the swift rushing rivers that flow from the steep mountains. These provided an excellent source for electric power for use in their industries.

Third, no part of Japan is far from the sea. Thus, raw materials brought to Japan by ship do not have to be carried far inland to interior factories. Fourth, Japan is well located for trade with both the nations of Asia and the nations of North and South America. Fifth, the Japanese were willing to borrow ideas and inventions that they thought were good from Western nations. Yet, they kept many of their own ways of living and of working.

These two photographs reveal much about Japan's history. Her own traditions, centuries old, exist side-by-side with a bustling, Westernized culture.

JAPAN HAS A LONG HISTORY

About 3,000 years ago the ancestors of the present-day Japanese settled in southern Japan. The exact date and the details of the settlement have been lost in time. People may have come by way of Korea or from the South Pacific. As these Japanese settlers gained control of the islands, they drove an earlier people, the Ainu, northward. Today, the Ainu live on the northern islands of Hokkaido and the Soviet islands of Sakhalin and the Kurils. They number only a few thousand and speak a language unlike any other.

According to Japanese legend the first emperor of Japan, Jimmu, came to the throne in 660 B.C. The present emperor traces his ancestry back to Jimmu. Jimmu was believed to have been a descendant of the sun goddess.

During the sixth and seventh centuries A.D., Japanese scholars were sent to China to study. They returned with the Chinese idea of a central government. The emperor became the head of a centralized government. The Chinese system of writing was introduced into Japan. Until that time, the Japanese had no way of keeping written records.

In the thirteenth century, the emperor of China, Kublai Khan, sent a great fleet of ships to conquer Japan. These ships were destroyed by a typhoon. Believing that the gods had sent this wind to protect them, the Japanese called it **kamikaze** which means "divine wind."

Japan's Middle Ages

During the thirteenth century the controlling rule of Japan passed from the hands of the emperor to the hands of great lords called **shoguns.** This was a period of feudalism in Japan. It resembled the feudal period in Europe. The shoguns surrounded themselves with warriors called **samurai.** They, like the knights of Europe, fought for the feudal lords, the shoguns. At times, one shogun ruled the whole country. At other times, different shoguns controlled different parts of the country.

Ainu culture differs greatly from that of other Japanese. Here the Ainu celebrate an age-old festival.

Trade with Other Countries Stops

In the middle of the sixteenth century the Portuguese reached Japan, and both Portugal and Spain began to trade with Japan. The Europeans brought Christianity with them. By the early seventeenth century about 700,000 Japanese had become Christians. Fearful that Christianity might weaken their power, Japanese lords issued an order banning Christianity. The government also ordered that trade with Western nations be stopped. Not only was Japan closed to other nations, but the people of Japan were forbidden to leave to visit other countries.

Only one tie was kept with the outside world by which the government could gain knowledge of what was going on elsewhere. The Dutch were given a small island in the port of Nagasaki. Dutch ships were allowed to land at this island once a year. For the following two hundred years, Japan remained closed to the outside world.

A Trade Treaty

In 1853 four American men-of-war appeared in Tokyo Bay. They had been sent by the American government to make a treaty with Japan. Commodore Perry, commander of the ships, was sent to ask three things of the Japanese. One was fair treatment of American sailors who landed in Japan because of shipwreck. Another was a request that American ships that traded with China might stop in Japanese ports for food, water, and fuel. The third was a request that American ships be allowed to enter Japanese ports to carry on trade. The shogun told Commodore Perry to return in a year for an answer.

Perry returned in 1854 with some American products. Included were agricultural tools, clocks, sewing machines, and even a miniature train and a telegraph set. The Japanese saw that other countries had made advances that they could use. Perry concluded a treaty of friendship between the United States and Japan. Other nations quickly followed the example of the United States.

Japan Copies the West

The shoguns ruled Japan until 1868 when the last shogun was overthrown along with serfdom. Ruling power was passed back to an emperor. The new leaders modernized the country and the government. You remember that the Japanese sent scholars to China to study Chinese ways of living in the sixth and seventh centuries A.D. After the opening of Japan in the nineteenth century, the Japanese again sent scholars to study other peoples. The Japanese people began to drop some of their old customs and to introduce new ones from Europe and the United States. They patterned their government after that of the Germans. They modeled their school system after those of the French.

Japanese visitors to the United States saw, to their surprise, horses pulling carriages. They brought the idea of a horse-drawn carriage back with them to Japan. However, in Japan, manpower was cheaper than horse-power. The Japanese adapted the idea of the horse-drawn carriage to the idea of the jinrikisha pulled by a man. The jinrikisha became popular in Japan and its use soon spread to China. Recently, the ricksha has been outlawed because the idea of "human horses" is degrading to the dignity of man.

Japan Expands Her Territories

The Japanese noted that European powers were seeking colonial lands. They saw that Great Britain, Germany, France, and Belgium were dividing Asia and Africa among themselves. Seeing the need to be strong in the same way, the Japanese set out to build their own empire.

In 1894 Japan entered into fighting with China over the control of Korea. The Japanese won and gained its control from the Chinese. They also gained possession of the island of Formosa, or Taiwan. In 1904 Japan went to war with Russia. They fought over which country was to control Korea and North China. Japan amazed the world with her crushing defeat of the Russian Far Eastern Fleet in naval battle. As a result of the war, Korea and the South Manchuria Railway in China came under the protection of Japan. In 1910, Japan formally annexed Korea.

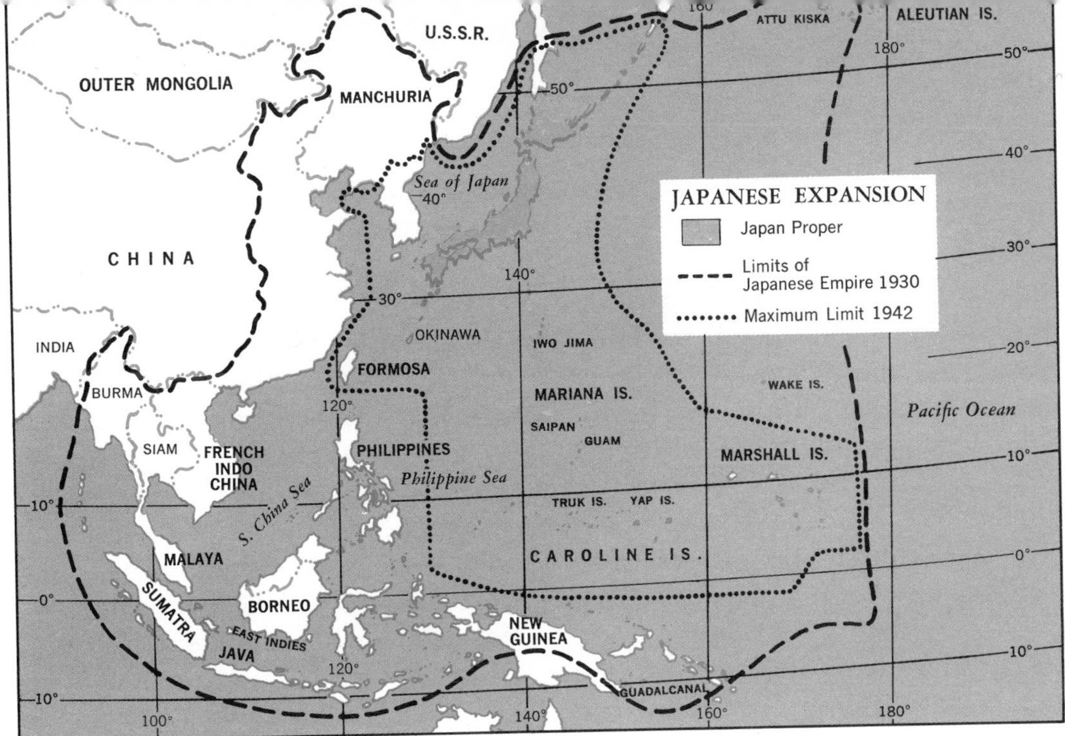

During World War I Japan fought on the side of the Allies. She seized German territory in the Pacific north of the equator. Later, the League of Nations gave these islands to Japan to hold in trust. Japan was one of the original members of the League of Nations. Japan signed many peace treaties agreeing to reduce the size of her navy and to leave China alone.

In the early 1930's the situation changed. Japan, afraid of China's growing power in Manchuria, created an excuse to wage war on China. The Japanese exploded a bomb near their South Manchuria Railway and blamed the Chinese. By 1937, Japan had seized Manchuria and overrun large parts of China. The League of Nations investigated Japan's actions and condemned them. Many people feel that these invasions by the Japanese into China were the start of World War II.

In 1940 Japan occupied French Indochina. This aggression angered the United States. They cut off all trade with Japan. Japan joined with Germany and Italy as the Axis powers.

In 1941 Japan attacked Hawaii, the Philippines, and Thailand, causing the United States to declare war on Japan and the Axis powers. In the early part of the war, Japan quickly overran Guam, the Philippines, Hong Kong, Thailand, the East Indies, Malaya, Burma, and many of the Pacific islands. From late 1942 on, Japan was on the losing side of the war. By early 1945 the Americans had won control of the islands just south of Japan. Using these islands as bases, American airplanes dropped incendiary bombs on Japanese cities. These exploding bombs ignited the homes which were made largely of wood. Whole cities became huge bonfires. Almost all of the major cities of Japan were destroyed by American bombing.

On August 6, 1945 the Americans dropped an atomic bomb on Hiroshima, and three days later another one on Nagasaki. These two bombs killed great numbers of people in the two cities. Japan saw that it was hopeless to continue the war and signed an unconditional surrender. The territories which she had taken, over a period of 70 years, were taken from her. Japan faced the task of rebuilding her cities and industries, and providing food for her people. American occupation forces aided in Japan's swift recovery.

The bride wears traditional dress for her Shinto wedding ceremony.

WAYS OF LIVING IN MODERN JAPAN

In recent years architects in the United States have become interested in Japanese buildings and gardens and have begun to copy some of their ideas. Japanese decoration lies in the structure of the house itself and in the carefully chosen woods of which it is built. Care is taken to add to the beauty of the house by careful placement in a natural setting. Very little paint is used on the private homes. The Japanese see beauty in the plain surface of natural wood and paper.

Western houses have solid outer walls and fixed inner walls that separate one room from another. The typical Japanese house can be made into one large room. It has sliding partitions in place of fixed walls. The sliding paper screens can be drawn to separate an area from the rest of the house. Since the weight of the roof rests upon pillars instead of the walls, the outer walls can consist of sliding doors. On a sunny day, the sliding doors along one side of the house can be drawn back so that the interior of the house merges into the garden.

Furnishings are in as simple and as good taste as the house itself. The floor is covered with soft tatami mats made of woven straw. At night, pillows and padded quilts are taken from closets and placed on the floor for sleeping. In order to protect the floor from dirt, the Japanese exchange their shoes for slippers when they enter a house.

Japanese Fashions

The Japanese wear two types of clothing, Western and Japanese. Western-style clothing is often worn at work, and Japanese-style clothing at home. The **kimono** is worn by men, women, and children. A kimono is a long, loose robe of cotton or silk, tied with a sash called an **obi.** Differences between men's and women's kimonos lie in the colors and patterns of the kimono. Red is worn only by women or girls. Japanese prefer to wear padded kimonos at home during the winter. Japanese houses are difficult to heat. Padded kimonos keep the wearer warmer and more comfortable than Western dress.

The Japanese often wear shoes like ours. However, two types of Japanese footwear have continued to be popular. The first is the **geta,** a wooden sandal. The second is the **zori,** also a sandal, but made of rice straw. Today zoris made of rubber or felt are popular in the United States. Called thongs, they have straps that fit between the toes. Many people use them at the beach.

Although Japanese houses are often crowded together, the interiors are starkly simple and give a feeling of spaciousness.

The Japanese custom of greeting another person with a bow is still used. The handshake, a European custom, is used only by people who know each other very well. The use of the handshake has not become widespread. The bow of respect may be made either sitting or standing. One sits on a tatami mat by folding his legs under him. From this position, one bows from the waist when greeting someone. If the person one is greeting is very, very important or if one is bowing to the gods, his head almost touches the tatami mat as he bows.

Each year, on the third of March, family dolls are displayed at the Hina Matsuri or Doll Festival.

Holidays and Festivals

The Japanese celebrate many special events with festivals and holidays. For example, Setsubun, the bean throwing ceremony, is celebrated on the eve of the first day of spring. Roasted beans are thrown at doorways and into the rooms of the home. The throwers shout as they scatter the beans, "Away with the devil. Welcome, good luck." The ages of 25 and 42 for men and 19 and 33 for women are considered to be the years of bad luck. People who happen to be one of these ages may get rid of the bad luck during Setsubun by eating as many beans as the number of years in their age.

Another festival is that of the Hina Matsuri, the Dolls Festival. In ancient times, this day was one in which evil was driven away. Sorcerers transferred evil to paper dolls which were placed on the river to float away. During the rule of the shoguns, this festival was a time when all Japanese lords paid homage to the shogun. Today, the Hina Matsuri is a festival mainly for girls. On this day, the dolls that belong to the family are placed on shelves as shown in the picture on the left. A complete set of dolls includes an Emperor and Empress, ladies-in-waiting, ministers, musicians, a laughing man, a weeping man, and an angry man. Sweet rice cakes are offered to the dolls. Peach blossoms are used for decoration on Hina Matsuri.

On May 5, Tango-no-Sekku, or Boys' Festival, is celebrated. Some of the customs associated with this day go back over 1,200 years. The iris flower is thought to drive away evil spirits and bad luck. Therefore, on Tango-no-Sekku, baths are scented with iris. Iris leaves are placed on the roof. Huge paper fish, as many as there are sons in the family, are flown from poles outside the house. Dolls of warriors are shown on this day.

Japanese skiers head for the slopes at Tengudaira, a favorite spot for skiing 200 miles north of Tokyo.

Popular Sports

The Japanese enjoy many kinds of sports. Modern sports that have become popular in Japan during this century are soccer, table tennis, volleyball, basketball, baseball, swimming, and skiing. There are also some traditional Japanese sports that have been popular from ancient times.

Perhaps the two most popular sports are baseball and **sumō.** Sumō is a form of wrestling. During the period of the shogun, sumō was practiced by warriors as preparation for hand-to-hand fights in battle. Sumō wrestlers are very large men. They may weigh as much as 300 pounds. Before the wrestling begins, each man shows that he has no weapons hidden in folds of fat. Each wrestler purifies himself with water. He purifies the arena by sprinkling it with salt.

A sumō wrestler can win in two ways. He can force his opponent out of the sand arena. Or, he can win by making his opponent touch any part of his body except the soles of his feet to the ground. The most highly regarded sumō wrestlers are those that hold the rank of **yokozuna,** or grand champion.

Another popular traditional sport is **kendō,** a Japanese style of fencing. The weapon is a bamboo stave, or sword. Each dueler is protected by bamboo armor, thick padding, a mask, and heavy gloves. The kendō fencer who makes two points in the match is the winner. A fencer may make a point by striking his opponent on the head, throat, hand, or body.

This torii marks a shrine at Hakone on the island of Honshu.

Japanese Religions

Several religions have influenced Japanese life. The oldest religion is that of Shintō. Shintōism began in Japan before Confucianism, Buddhism, or Christianity came to the islands. It still plays a major role in Japanese life. It may best be described as a system of nature and ancestor worship. It includes a deep respect for such forces of nature as the wind, the sea, and the sun. It grew to include ancestor worship. It considered the Emperor as divine.

The most famous Shintō shrines in Japan are at Ise. Ise has two sacred shrines, one belonging to the goddess of rich harvests and the other to the sun goddess. Like many Shintō shrines, the two at Ise are hidden in an ancient forest. As you walk through the woods along gently winding paths to the shrine, you pass through three gateways. These **torii,** or gateways, are found near the entrances to Shintō shrines throughout Japan. Just as a bell tower marks a Christian church or a minaret a Muslim mosque, the torii marks the presence of a Shintō shrine. It is a symbol of the shrine. The torii is an example of simplicity in Japanese architecture. It is made by placing two pillars in the ground and connecting them at the top with a wooden rail.

The shrine of the sun goddess at Ise is thought to be the oldest wooden building in the world. Records show that it was in existence in A.D. 685. The simple, unpainted, cypress wood shrine, covered with thatch, is built today exactly as it was in ancient times. It is an example of pure Japanese architecture, unchanged for hundreds of years. How then, in a land of earthquakes, has it lasted? It is completely taken apart and rebuilt every twenty years. This rebuilding keeps it strong enough to withstand the earthquakes.

The most important religion in Japan is Buddhism. The Buddhists believe that suffering is caused by the desire for material pleasures. These desires must be destroyed in order to find peace of mind. A knowledge of one's self is most important. Only by insight can one gain spiritual freedom. The practice of love and unselfishness and goodness are added to the desire for truth. Many Japanese have practiced both Shintōism and Buddhism. They considered Buddhism a religion and Shintōism a form of patriotism.

Buddhism came to Japan from Korea and China as early as A.D. 552. There are more than 100,000 Buddhist temples and shrines in Japan. There is a famous giant statue of Buddha in the shrine at Kamakura. It is 44 feet high. It was built in 1252 and has withstood earthquakes, storms, and tidal waves.

Confucianism came to Japan from China. It has never become a strong religion, but it has had an important influence on moral teaching in Japan. This religion is based on the teachings of Confucius, a Chinese philosopher. Confucius taught that men could realize heavenly harmony and justice if they observed the duties and responsibilities of five basic relationships. He taught that the five basic relationships were ruler and subject, father and son, husband and wife, elder and younger brother, and friend and friend. Each relationship involved specific duties and manners which were taught to all followers of the religion. In Japan these teachings were often included in the education of people who were not followers of Confucianism.

Tokyo is the world's most populous city. Founded in the 12th century as the city of Yedo, it took its present name when it became the imperial capital in 1868. Destroyed by an earthquake in 1923 and by World War II, it has been rebuilt as Japan's center of finance, industry, and culture.

JAPANESE CITIES

Over 60 per cent of Japan's people live in cities and towns. Many of these people live on farms located near the large cities. This means that in areas where there are many large cities, there are more farm people than in areas of fewer cities.

Nagoya, about 100 miles from Tokyo, is a leading industrial city.

The map shows you that the most heavily populated area extends across southern Japan. Beginning in the area of Tokyo, the section of heavy population extends across the southern part of the Honshu Island into northern Kyushu. Here Japan's largest cities and many of its smaller ones will be found. This is also the area where most of Japan's industry is found.

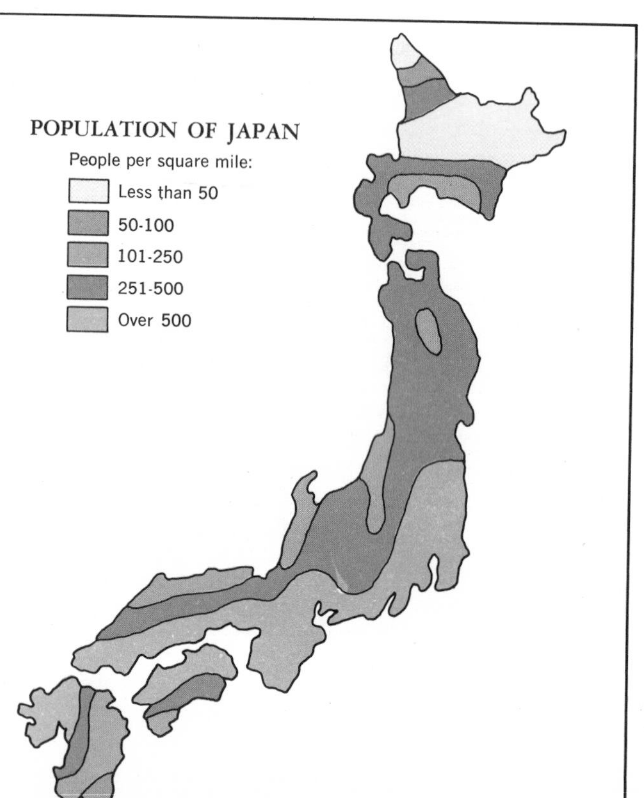

Tokyo, the capital of Japan, is the largest city in the world. It has fine modern office buildings and stores, wide streets, and beautiful parks. The city has been rebuilt twice in the past fifty years. In 1923 a great earthquake followed by a fire destroyed large parts of the city. During World War II much of the city was destroyed by air raids. Each time the Japanese rebuilt the city, they made improvements. Today there are many buildings that are as much as ten stories high. This is possible because the Japanese have learned how to construct tall buildings that will withstand violent earthquakes.

Tokyo still has many of the Japanese traditional characteristics. Many people continue to build their homes of wood in the characteristic Japanese style. Throughout the city there are simple wooden Shintō shrines and elaborate Buddhist temples. Many people wear the traditional kimono and wooden sandals.

Toyko is a busy city. There are more than 50,000 factories that manufacture about a fifth of Japan's total industrial products. The streets are crowded with automobiles, taxis, buses, and streetcars. Thousands of commuters travel each day on subways and railroad trains to their jobs in the city. Large numbers of tourists visit the city each year to see the many landmarks and historical sites.

Osaka is Japan's second largest city. It is often called the "Chicago" of Japan. Osaka and its port city of

Kobe are the leading centers for heavy industry. Locomotives and other iron and steel products are manufactured here. Kobe is a leading shipbuilding center. Cotton spinning and pottery manufacturing are also important industries in Osaka.

Nagoya is an industrial center with a variety of industries. It is an important textile center. It also manufactures many types of machines. It is noted for its manufacture of porcelain and pottery. The Noritake factory is located in Nagoya. This is the leading manufacturer of porcelain dishes in Japan.

Yokohama, Japan's fourth largest city, is one of the country's largest ports. It is about eighteen miles south of Tokyo. Shipping and the import-export trade are Yokohama's leading industries. Shipbuilding is also an important industry.

Yokohama was just a tiny fishing village in 1854. You have read that about this time Commodore Perry of the United States Navy signed a treaty with the Japanese that opened Japan to trade with the United States. In a few years foreign traders opened offices in Yokohama. The city grew rapidly after that.

Kyoto is located thirty miles inland from Osaka. Kyoto was the capital of Japan from 794 until 1868 when the capital was moved to Tokyo. Kyoto is an important religious center. There are many temples and shrines and many valuable works of religious art. The city is famous for

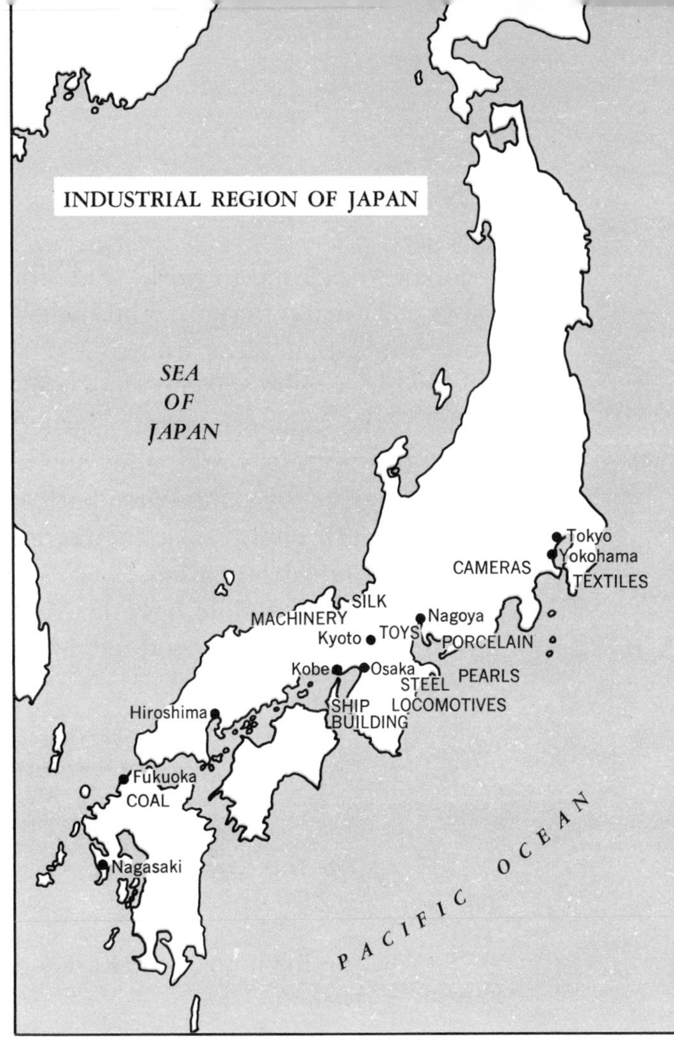

its festivals. Thousands of tourists visit the city each year.

Kyoto is a leading city for the manufacture of silk fabrics. It also manufactures light electrical equipment, aircraft parts, and chemicals. It is a center of the art industries of Japan. Fine embroidery, porcelain ware, and lacquer ware are made here.

Fukuoka, one of Japan's largest cities, is the industrial center for the island of Kyushu. It is a center for the manufacture of paper, pottery, dolls, and textiles. It is located near important coal fields.

A Resourceful People

Japan was closed to world trade for over 300 years because the rulers were afraid that ideas from the outside world would weaken their control. As the Japanese people learned about the outside world, they made rapid progress. By the early part of the twentieth century Japan was an important industrial nation.

The Japanese people have learned how to make their land produce much of what they need. They have learned how to produce the goods that other people want. In this way, they can earn the money to buy what their land does not produce. Their careful use of resources might well serve as a model to other Far East nations which need to improve the lives of their people. Japan's flag shows a rising sun. As it flies over the nation, it symbolizes the peace and prosperity that continue to rise.

Do You Know?

1. What do the terms Near East and Far East describe?

2. What are the cultural similarities between Japan and China?

3. What are the major islands of Japan? About how many smaller islands are there?

4. What two major currents affect the climate of Japan? In what direction does each flow?

5. How do the currents affect the climate of northern Japan? Of southern Japan?

6. What are two of the causes of earthquakes in Japan? What is the greatest danger during an earthquake?

7. Why has Mount Fujiyama been reguarded as a sacred mountain?

8. What are two types of pearls? For which type is Japan noted? Who developed this process?

9. What is one of Japan's greatest natural resources? What resources does she lack?

10. Who were the first dwellers of Japan? In what area of Japan do their descendants live today?

11. What are three items of clothing which are part of the native dress of the Japanese? Describe them.

12. What are two popular traditional sports in Japan? Explain briefly.

13. What is the oldest religion of Japan? The most important?

Learn By Doing

1. For one week list all things you see or hear about which are marked "Made in Japan."

2. Select one of the following titles and write a report: The Tea Plants of Japan, Holidays and Festivals, Japanese Sports, or Japanese Religions.

3. Draw or make a model of a Japanese house and garden. Be sure to include pillars, sliding doors, and screens. Furnish the home and add models of Japanese people. Include kimonos, tatami, getas, and zori.

4. Locate your home on a globe. Follow the parallel of latitude on which your home is located around the world. Does it pass through Japan? Would it be shorter to travel over the pole or east-west if you went from your home to Tokyo?

5. Below are listed seven important facts about Japan. Select the correct item to complete each sentence.

a. No part of Japan is farther than (60, 90, 120) miles from the sea.

b. One inch of rain is equal to (3, 6, 10, 15) inches of snow.

c. In Japan (2/3, 4/5, 7/8) of the land's surface is mountainous.

d. In Japan (10, 15, 25, 40) per cent of the land can be farmed.

e. Although the population of Japan has risen greatly, the amount of food imported has only increased (10, 20, 30, 40) per cent.

f. The coastline of Japan is (2, 3, 4) times as long as the coastline of continental United States.

g. More than (1/8, 1/3, 1/2) of the land in Japan is forested.

h. Japan is one of the top (3, 5, 10, 15) nations in world trade.

Test Your Knowledge

1. How have the Japanese learned to adjust to the difficulty of frequent earthquakes?

2. What do we mean when we say that Japan is a young land? What effect does this have on the mountains and on the valleys of the country?

3. Describe several ways in which the Japanese farmers show that they are efficient.

4. Describe the formation of natural and cultured pearls.

5. What physical features have helped Japan become the leading commercial fishing nation in the world? What man-made developments have helped the fishermen of the nation?

6. Why are the forests a valuable resource for the Japanese? What is a "wood economy"?

7. Give several reasons why Japan was able to develop her industries so quickly after hundreds of years of isolation from the world.

8. Each of the following items played an important part in Japanese history. Place them in order giving dates and explain briefly.

European ideas	Jimmu
Nagasaki port	Ainu
Commodore Perry	shoguns
Japanese expansion	Chinese ideas

9. What are the basic beliefs of the Shintō religion? How is the way of life of the Japanese influenced by this religion?

10. Give a brief definition of the following terms. Explain the relationship between each term and Japan.

fault	alluvial deposits
nacre	jinrikisha
tatamis	entrails
samurai	kamikaze
torii	yokozuna

hydroponic farming

CHAPTER 12

RIVER AND MOUNTAIN PEOPLES: CHINA

Well over half of the world's people live in the region of Eastern Asia. China and India, two of the world's largest countries, occupy most of the mainland region. The Far East includes several smaller mainland countries and also several island countries.

No one knows exactly how old the Chinese civilization is. Nor do they know exactly how many people live there today. But it is believed that China has one of the oldest civilizations and one of the largest populations in the world. Many changes are taking place in this country. The government is developing its resources and changing the ways of living of the people.

THE LANDS OF EASTERN ASIA

In the Dry World Culture Region, you found that there were few people except in the settlements of the Nile and the Tigris-Euphrates River Valleys. From this, you learned that one of the simplest ways to locate the people of a region is to find the well-watered river valleys. The eastern part of the mainland of Asia is a region of many major rivers. It also has many of the highest mountains in the world. Millions of people live in the well-watered, river valleys of Eastern Asia. The people of China, India, and Southeast Asia have a riverine culture.

Great Rivers

As the great rivers of Eastern Asia are mentioned, locate them on the map on page 239. Notice that many of these rivers start in the mountains of the interior. Trace these rivers from their sources as they flow outward to the China Sea and the Indian Ocean.

The first of these great rivers is found in mainland China. It is called

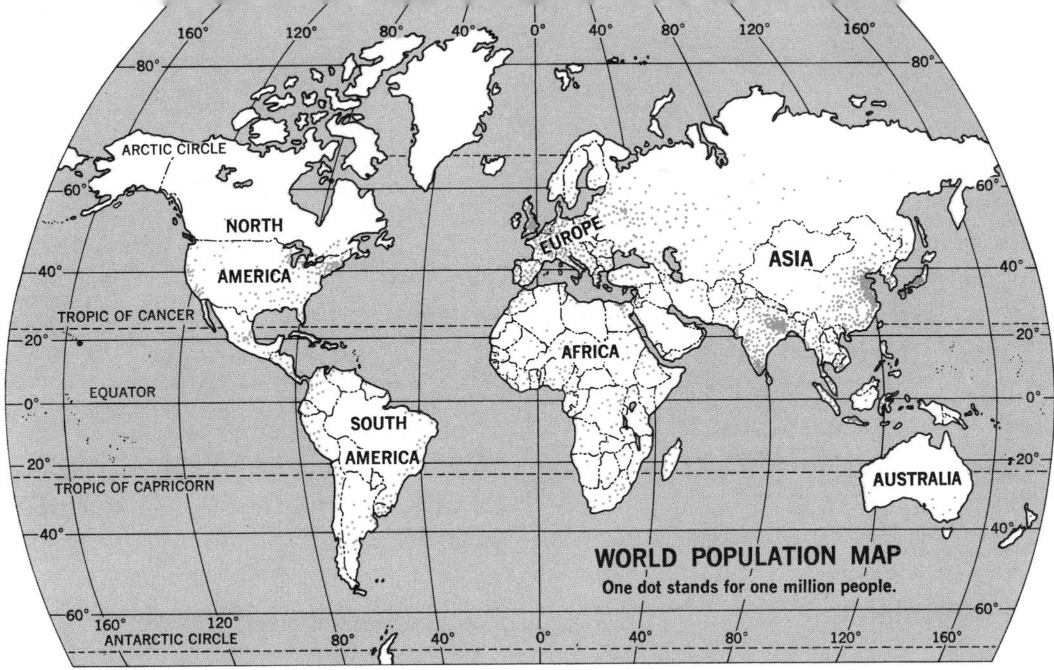

the Hwang Ho, or Yellow River. In clockwise order after the Hwang Ho, locate the Yangtze and the Si Rivers. The Yangtze empties into the East China Sea, the Si into the South China Sea. Next locate the Red River which flows through North Vietnam. The Mekong River serves as part of the western boundary for the state of Laos. Farther downstream it serves as the great waterway of Cambodia. Thailand's famous river is the Menam. Burma's river highway is the Irrawaddy. The Brahmaputra, which starts in the Himalaya Mountains, flows southward through East Pakistan. The mighty Ganges is in eastern India. West of India, the Indus River flows through West Pakistan.

The length of these great rivers may be hard to imagine. Two of them, the Hwang Ho and the Yangtze, are longer than the distance across the United States from east to west. A third river, the Mekong, is almost as long as the United States is wide. It is 2,600 miles long. Can you imagine these rivers filled to overflowing? In the summer, floods are a constant danger to the people. Yet these river valleys and their side stream areas provide the best places for living. The people are able to produce the highest yields per acre in these places.

Large Cities

Most of the large and well-known cities of Eastern Asia are located in the great river valleys. They are on sites that are relatively level and in areas where the climate is relatively mild. These large cities may be located easily by following the same clockwise direction that was used to find the major rivers. Starting in China, locate the following cities: Peking, Nanking, Shanghai, Canton, and Hong Kong.

Continuing in the same direction, find Hanoi in North Vietnam and Saigon in South Vietnam. The largest city of Cambodia is Phnom Penh; in Thailand, the largest city is Bangkok. Rangoon is well known as Burma's leading city. Farther west lie Calcutta in India and Karachi in West Pakistan.

High Mountains

The mountain ranges of Eastern Asia from which the great rivers come are among the highest in the world. Snow and ice on the high mountains serve as water reservoirs that feed the rivers throughout the year. For this reason most of the rivers in Eastern Asia are never empty.

Mountains of Eastern Asia and Their Height Above Sea Level

Mt. Everest	29,028 ft.
Godwin-Austen	28,250 ft.
Kanchenjunga	28,146 ft.
Makalu	27,827 ft.
Dhaulagiri	26,795 ft.

Among the mountain ranges are the five highest peaks in the world. The height of these peaks is hard to imagine. Each of them is a mile higher than North America's highest mountain, Mt. McKinley in Alaska. This mountain is 20,300 feet high. The peak of Mount Everest, at 29,028 feet, is the highest point in the world. The top of Mount Everest was first reached in 1953 by Tensing Norkay of India and Sir Edmund Hillary of New Zealand.

Throughout history mountains have acted as a barrier to the movement of people. In Eastern Asia the Himalaya Mountain Range and other natural barriers, such as deserts and high, cold plateaus, have checked the westward movement of large numbers of people in the great river valleys of China.

THE CHINESE CIVILIZATION

The Chinese civilization is more than three thousand years old. The civilizations of the Sumerians and the Babylonians began earlier, but these did not last. The Chinese reached a high stage of civilization very early in history. As early as 444 B.C., Chinese astronomers realized that the year has 365¼ days. An irrigation system that was built about 333 B.C. is still in use. The Chinese observed sunspots 1,600 years before Galileo discovered and wrote about them in A.D. 1613.

Since the beginning of the Chinese Empire in the third century B.C., China's boundaries have changed many times. They have shrunk and grown time and again, but China's history has been continuous. To protect the Chinese Empire from nomad invaders from the north and north-

ICE AND SNOW
FORESTS
SEMIARID GRASSLAND AND FOREST
TUNDRA
GRASSLAND
DESERT
EVERGREEN FORESTS
DRY GRASSLAND
SAVANNA
TROPICAL RAIN FORESTS
MOUNTAINS
NEW SIBERIAN IS.
East Siberian Sea
Verkhoyansk
VERKHOYANSK MTS.
CIALIST REPUBLICS
Bering Sea
Sea of Okhotsk
KAMCHATKA PENIN.
SAKHALIN
KURIL I.
ATTU I.
KUZNETS BASIN
Novosibirsk
Novokuznetsk
Ob River
Lake Baikal
SAYAN MTS.
ALTAI MTS.
Amur River
Ulan Bator
PEOPLE'S REPUBLIC OF MONGOLIA
THE GOBI
INNER MONGOLIA
MANCHURIA
Lake Balkhash
Alma Ata
Urumchi
SINKIANG
TIEN SHAN
Vladivostok
HOKKAIDO
JAPAN
Sea of Japan
Huhehot
SHENYANG
NORTH KOREA
Hwang Ho (Yellow R.)
PEKING
TIENTSIN
Port Arthur
Pyongyang
SEOUL
SOUTH KOREA
HONSHU
TOKYO
Yokohama
Yellow Sea
SHIKOKU
KYUSHU
PAMIR
HINDU KUSH
KASHMIR
KHYBER PASS
Rawalpindi
WEST
Lahore
PEOPLE'S REPUBLIC OF CHINA
ASIA
KANSU
PLATEAU OF TIBET
TIBET
Hwang Ho (Yellow) R.
Mekong R.
Salween R.
Yangtze River
Lhasa
SHANGHAI
Hangchow
Chungking
East China Sea
HIMALAYAS
NEPAL
BHUTAN
Delhi
NEW DELHI
Indus R.
Hyderabad
Karachi
Darjeeling
Ganges R.
Brahmaputra R.
Tungting Lake
Formosa Strait
Taipeh
TAIWAN
E. PAK.
Dacca
Chittagong
CALCUTTA
Mandalay
BURMA
Canton
Si River
Macau
HONG KONG
NORTH VIET-NAM
Hanoi
PACIFIC OCEAN
Kiungshan
HAINAN I.
BOMBAY
INDIA
Bay of Bengal
Irrawaddy R.
Salween R.
Vientiane
LAOS
Mekong R.
Rangoon
Gulf of Martaban
THAILAND
BANGKOK
LUZON
REPUBLIC OF THE PHILIPPINES
Quezon City
Manila
MINDORO
South China Sea
SOUTH VIET-NAM
CAMBODIA
Saigon
Phnom Penh
Gulf of Siam
LACCADIVE IS.
ANDAMAN IS.
PANAY
NEGROS
CEBU
MINDANAO
NICOBAR IS.
CEYLON
Colombo
MALDIVE IS.
Jesselton
BRUNEI
SABAH
Celebes Sea
MALAYA
Kuala Lumpur
FED. OF MALAYSIA
SARAWAK
Kuching
BORNEO
SUMATRA
SINGAPORE
KALIMANTAN
SULAWESI (CELEBES)
INDIAN OCEAN
EQUATOR
80°
70°
60°
50°
40°
30°
20°
10°
0°
90°
100°
110°
120°

west, early rulers of China built a great wall. This wall was built more than two thousand years ago. It is over 1,500 miles long.

The Great Wall was first built by the Chou Dynasty, probably sometime in the third century B.C. It has been strengthened and repaired many times over the centuries. Most of the Great Wall as we know it today dates from the time of the Ming Dynasty (A.D. 1368 to A.D. 1644). It follows mountain ridges where possible. The height of the Great Wall varies from 15 feet to 30 feet. The top of the wall was used as a roadway to send troops quickly to trouble spots. Bonfires were lit on the tops of square watchtowers to signal danger.

Family Life

Chinese history is often organized by **dynasties.** A dynasty is a series of rulers belonging to the same family. One of the early great dynasties was the Chou Dynasty which lasted from about 1027 B.C. to 256 B.C. Some Chinese ways of living have continued from Chou Dynasty times to the present day. Family ties were strong during the early days. Family elders were held in great respect by sons, daughters-in-law, and grandchildren. When a son married, he brought his wife to his ancestral home. Here they lived with his parents.

A Chinese New Year's custom shows the pattern of respect for one's elders that was taught. You recall that on New Year's Day the youngest child in a family stands in front of the oldest member of the family. The child bows low and says aloud, "A Happy and Prosperous New Year." He then goes to the next oldest member of the family and repeats the phrase. He does this to each member of the family that is older than he. Other members of the family also bow and wish their elders a "long life" and "good fortune."

Family graves were cared for and offerings were made to the spirits of the ancestors. Homes had small shrines where wooden tablets were kept. On each tablet were written the name and the dates of birth and death of an ancestor. Candles were lit before these wooden tablets and incense was burned.

A son was responsible for his father while the father was alive and after he was dead. The spirits of the dead were believed to have the same powers as the living. The spirits of a man's ancestors were thought to know what was going on in the world. They could help keep a family well and wealthy. It would be unwise to risk the displeasure of the ancestral spirits by neglecting to perform traditional ceremonies of worship.

Village Life

For centuries in old China, life in a village meant poverty and hard work. In early spring the farmer began hoeing his fields of winter wheat. If water was lacking, he sometimes carried it in buckets from wells to the fields. In late spring the farmer planted his summer crop of millet or cotton. The farmer and his whole family then harvested the winter wheat crop.

The threshing and winnowing of wheat were done carefully by hand. Each member of the family took care that no wheat grain or stalk was lost. Although the soil could be enriched with organic material by turning wheat stalks back into the soil, this was not done. Wheat straw was too badly needed as fuel for cooking and for warmth. Other ways of enriching the soil were used. Animal manure was carefully collected and spread on the fields. Sun-dried bricks, made with straw which was worn or broken, were pounded to pieces and scattered on the fields.

If crops were not ruined by drought or flood and the harvest was good, the farmer had plenty to eat. During the winter the farmer repaired his tools and the roofs of his sheds and house. Straw was woven into mats, and cotton into cloth. Even shoes were made from cloth.

Village life was not entirely hard work. It was varied by holiday festivals, wedding ceremonies, and religious feasts. Traveling storytellers made their rounds from village to village. Wealthy farmers made pilgrimages to famous shrines. The New Year's holiday was the main winter festival. Another time of relaxation was the spring festival. At this time all members of the family visited the family graveyard. They burned yellow paper money for the use of the dead and also cleaned and repaired the graveyard. The ceremonial offerings to the ancestors were followed by a feast.

At the Temple of Heaven, the Hall of Prayer (left) and the Temple of the Universe (right) lead to the Altar of Heaven where the emperor came each year to offer a sacrifice.

Peking, A Cultural Landmark

The city of Peking is one of the world's great cultural landmarks. The site on which Peking stands has been inhabited for over 4,000 years. The first known city on this site was called Chi during the Chou Dynasty. When Marco Polo visited this city in the thirteenth century, it was called Cambaluc and was the capital of the Mongol Empire. Marco Polo was deeply impressed by what he saw. He stated, "Everything that is most valuable and rare in all parts of the world finds its way to Peking." Peking has been the capital city of China from 1421 to 1928 and from 1949 to the present.

Peking is really five cities in one—all within a wall. These five cities are the Purple or Forbidden City, the Imperial, the Tartar, the Legation Quarter, and the Chinese City. The innermost city, the Forbidden City, is surrounded by two and one-fourth miles of high walls. The name, Purple City, came from the purple-colored plaster which was used on the walls. In the days of the emperors, only a few privileged Chinese were allowed within the walls of the Forbidden City. It held the palaces and courts of the emperor and his high officials. The emperor's palace contained countless open buildings, flowering courtyards, and long halls and works of art.

Architecture of Ancient China

One of the most striking features of early Chinese architecture is the massive roofs. The roofs of important buildings were covered with richly colored tiles. The palaces of the Forbidden City are magnificent with their double roofs covered with yellow glazed tile. Curved eaves are a familiar feature of Chinese buildings. Just why the eaves are curved is not known. Perhaps they were designed to give relief from the straight lines of the building, the platforms upon which they were built, and the heavy roof.

Peking has temples with marble altars and golden ornaments. Scenes of the land and the past history of China are woven into silken drapes. In the Chinese City is the Temple of Heaven, built by the great Emperor Yong Lo. This compound was completed in 1420. It consists of the Hall of Prayer, the Temple of the Universe, and the Altar of Heaven. Each section of the compound contains circular terraces which represent the heavens. Enclosed by a walled square which represents the earth, the three circular terraces of the Altar of Heaven lead to a round, white marble altar. The Chinese believed this to be the center of the Universe.

Another type of Chinese architecture which has become well known to the Western World is the **pagoda.** It is a tower-like shrine. Very few pagodas have been built during this century. However, hundreds of pagodas built in preceding centuries have survived. These pagodas, or shrines, were thought to bring good fortune. In China the pagoda is often octagonal, or eight-sided, in shape. The number of stories in a pagoda varies widely, but the number is always uneven.

This modern pagoda in Hong Kong, although not a shrine, is similar to the older religious pagodas.

Chinese Art

In the Peking region are found some of the earliest writings and paintings done by man. Writing and painting were thought to be closely related arts. The names of famous **calligraphers,** or handwriters, are as important in Chinese history as

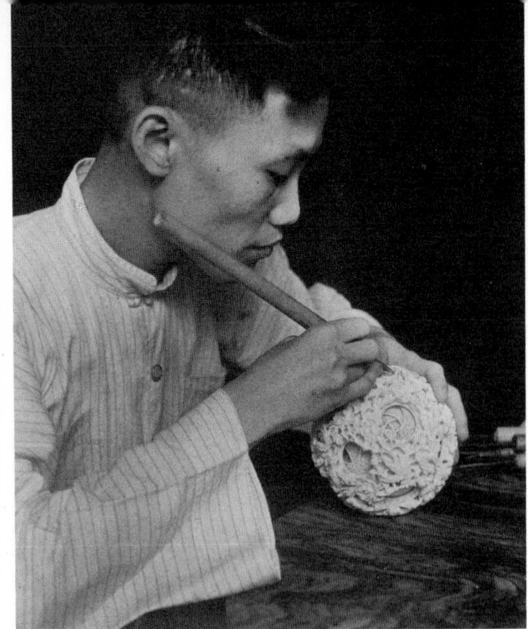

Hand-woven panels of pure silk and intricate carvings of ivory and jade are part of China's long heritage of art and beauty.

the names of famous painters. The early Chinese had no ink pens. They used brushes. To be an expert in either painting or writing, it was necessary to be skilled in the use of the brush pen. By the use of brushes, instead of sharp pens or pencils, in writing Chinese characters, or letter symbols, the Chinese created a very special kind of art work. Throughout the world, these scrolls of skilled handwriting are highly prized.

The use of brushes also gave Chinese art the special quality of softness. Many of their designs show this softness and gentleness, while others reveal boldness, strength, force, and even fear. This kind of painting was achieved by using harsh lines and contrasting colors. There is a merging of reality with imagination in this art. Early Chinese brush paintings are art treasures of great value.

The First Paper

Did you know that the Chinese were the first to use paper? They used it as early as A.D. 105. The way the early Chinese made paper is interesting. First, the stringy, inner bark of the mulberry tree was soaked. Then, it was pounded so that the fibers separated. A soupy substance made from the outer bark was poured into the spaces between the fibers. When this soft, matty material dried, it was a crude sheet of "paper."

In other types of paper, the pores between the fibers were filled with wet clay. The clay turned white when it was dry. On this type of paper, brushes moved smoothly.

Chinese paper, although fragile, has been long lasting. Specimens have survived from the Han Dynasty (202 B.C. to A.D. 220), and the Sung Dynasty (A.D. 960 to A.D. 1279).

Silk, A Gift of Nature

It is interesting to note that the mulberry tree played another role in the Chinese culture. Its leaves were used to feed the silk worms. Many Chinese homes were small "silk factories." There were several shelves in the home set aside for the purpose of raising silk worms. On the shelves were many trays covered with silk worms greedily eating mulberry leaves. The worms would spin fine threads to make their cocoon. These fine, silky threads of the cocoon were unwound and woven into silk cloth.

The secret of how silk was made was kept by the Chinese for many centuries. This enabled the Chinese merchants to become very rich trading the beautiful silk goods to other countries. Pure silk is very expensive even today.

The Chinese Gave Us Porcelain

The Chinese turned to deposits of clay to make some of the finest pottery known to man. We do not know when they invented **porcelain,** a fine, very hard, white, and semi-transparent pottery. Chinese porcelain is made of a white paste coated with a glassy substance called **glaze.** The glazed porcelain is then fired in a kiln, a furnace made of brick or stone. Often, a coloring or decoration is painted on the dried paste before the glaze is added. In this way the decoration is permanently fixed by the baking.

In the Sung dynasty some very fine porcelain ware was made. The lotus bowl is a masterpiece from that time. The cracked glaze was purposely produced by the potter. Porcelain of this type is known as **crackle ware.** When it was introduced into Europe, porcelain became very popular and was named after the country of its origin, Chinaware or China.

Porcelain is both useful and decorative. Because it does not absorb liquids, it is very useful in the form of plates, teapots, cups, bowls, and drinking fountains. Porcelain is used also as an insulator in the high voltage wires that carry electricity.

Scientific Contributions

The early Chinese explored the far and the near. **Astronomy,** the study of the stars, was a challenge to the early Chinese. They made accurate observations of eclipses and movements of the planets nearly twenty-five hundred years ago. They built observatories that contained precision instruments.

Two thousand years ago most Chinese thought that an eclipse of the moon or sun was a warning that heaven was displeased. A scientist of that time, Wang Ch'ung, said that this was not so. He wrote that eclipses are natural events that occur regularly and have nothing to do with the way people behave.

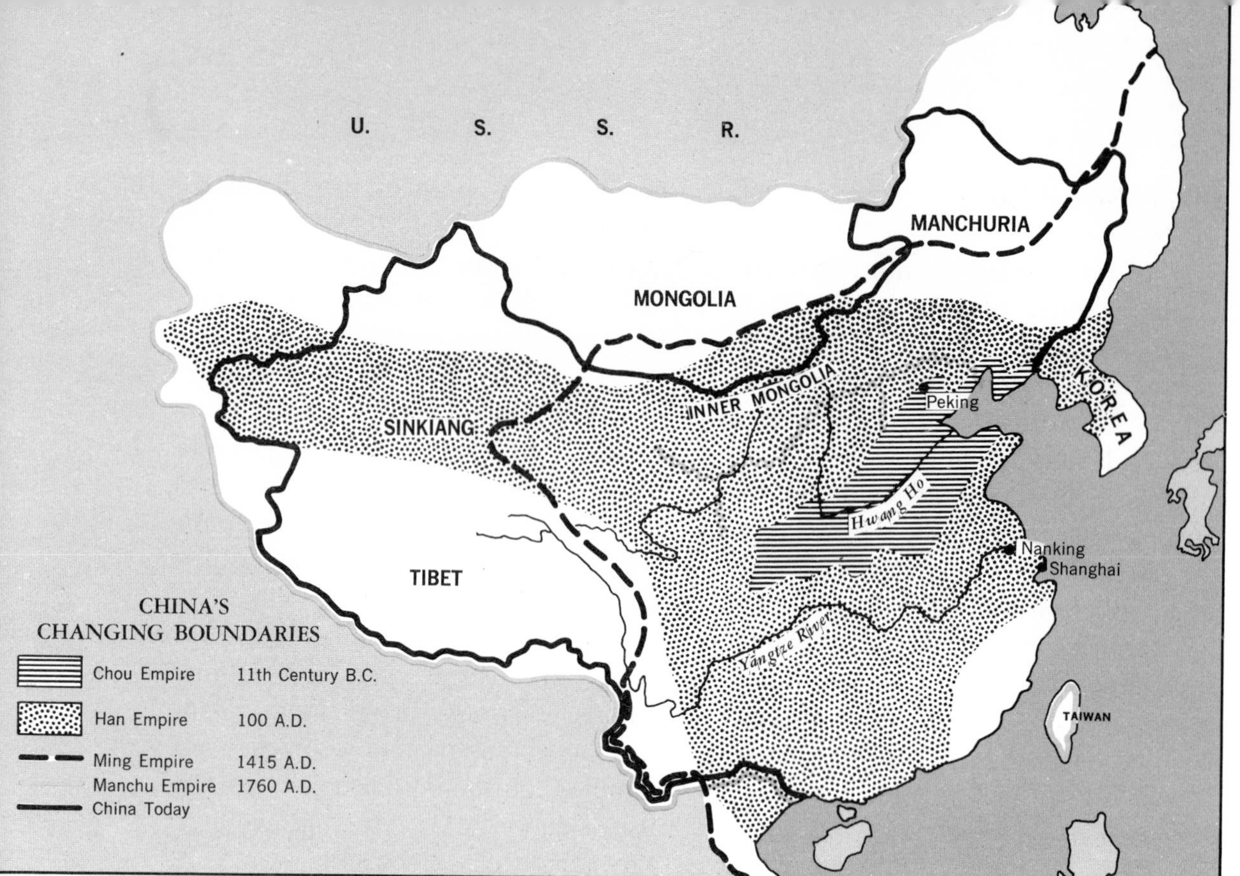

IMPORTANT CHANGES IN CHINA

On the map on this page, find the ancient Chinese Empire. It included the lands south of the Great Wall and east of the Plateau of Tibet. Today this land is called China Proper. It is divided into North China and South China by a natural boundary, the Tsinling Mountains. They lie between the Hwang Ho and Yangtze River. This land of China Proper has been invaded many times by many different peoples.

In the thirteenth century China was conquered by the Mongolians. After they had been driven out, the Manchus, another group of people from the North, invaded. The Manchurians ruled China for several centuries. During this time, very little progress was made.

During the nineteenth century China's ports were opened to Western trade. New ideas and modern advances became known to the people. Dissatisfied with the Manchurian rule, the Chinese people revolted. Under the leadership of Sun Yat-sen, the Republic of China was started in 1912. War lords governed many of the provinces of China. A lack of unity and poor government caused confusion.

In 1928 Chiang Kai-shek became the leader of the Republic of China. He tried to unite China Proper and Manchuria under one central government, but the Japanese had other ideas. They invaded Manchuria.

The dispute between China and Japan over Manchuria became a major part of World War II. The Japanese were driven out, and Manchuria became part of the Republic of China.

The Chinese Are Divided

Shortly after World War II, a **civil war** broke out in China. A civil war is a fight between two parties or sections for the control of one government. The government of Chiang Kai-shek, called the Nationalist government, fought against the invading government of Mao Tse-tung, or the Communist government. In 1949, after years of bitter fighting, the Communists seized control of the central government of China. The defeated government retreated to the island of Taiwan off the coast of the mainland. Since then the Chinese have been a divided people. Both the Communist government and the Nationalist government claim to be the rulers of all the Chinese people.

Mainland China is known as the People's Republic of China. Under the leadership of Mao Tse-tung, the Communist government now controls not only mainland China, but also the sub-regions of Inner Mongolia, Sinkiang, and Tibet. The government has its capital at Peking. The ruling men of this dictatorship are placed in power by the Communist Party. They tightly control all the elections in the country.

Taiwan, often called Formosa, and the other nearby islands have been possessions of China for many centuries. Today they are known as the Republic of China. The government of these islands is the government which was defeated by the Communists in 1949. Chiang Kai-shek is still the leader of this free government. The Nationalist government has its capital at Taipeh. The people elect a national assembly which in turn elects the president and vice-president.

Victory parades and celebrations are often dominated by photographs and slogans of Mao Tse-Tung, founder of the Chinese Communist Party.

Taiwan, the seat of government of the Republic of China, must emphasize agriculture to feed its large refugee population. Available land is intensively farmed.

Taiwan

Many Chinese people have fled from mainland China to the island of Taiwan. There are approximately 12 million people living on this very small island. There is an average of about 850 people per square mile on Taiwan. With such a large population, the Nationalist government faces a serious problem of feeding the people and maintaining public health.

Agriculture is an important means of earning a living on Taiwan. More than half of the people work as farmers. Farms are small. The average farm only has about three acres. Much fertilizer must be used to make the land produce. Farmers work intensively on their farms. Two crops are produced each year. Sometimes two crops are grown together. For example, sweet potatoes will be planted between rows of sugar cane.

Sugar and tea are the main export crops. Rice, sweet potatoes, and peanuts are the chief food crops. Other crops include bananas, jute, oranges, pineapples, tobacco, and watermelons.

Irrigation is necessary since most of the island has a warm climate with long summers and short winters. The southern part has a drier, hotter climate than the northern part.

Fishing is very important. Fish are the main source of protein in the diet of the people. Many cities have farms where fish are raised. The flooded rice paddies are also used to raise fish. But the most important source for fish is the ocean.

Taiwan's chemical plants supply fertilizer for agriculture.

Taiwan has a number of industries. There are a few large factories but most are small. Factories produce enough cloth for the people of the island. There is a chemical plant near Taipeh which supplies enough fertilizer for farming needs. Other plants produce aluminum, cement, flour, bricks, and ironwork. There are also pineapple canneries, sugar refineries, and tea factories on the island.

MAINLAND CHINA

Most of the Chinese people live in the river valleys of mainland China. China is the largest country in Eastern Asia. Its area is slightly larger than the area of the United States. More people live in China than in any other country of the world. The population is over 700 million. This is almost four times as many people as live in the United States. There is an average of 198 people per square mile.

The present government is stronger than any other government in China's recent history. This government has set out to change China from an agricultural country to an industrial one very quickly. The government plans to develop the great resources of China as rapidly as possible. The people must work very hard and for long hours.

The present government feels ancestor worship is old-fashioned. Customs, such as worshiping at the tablets of one's ancestors, are being discontinued. The idea of the family as a group that includes the dead and the unborn is changing. Whether the old Chinese patterns of close family life and ancestor worship will continue or die out is yet to be seen.

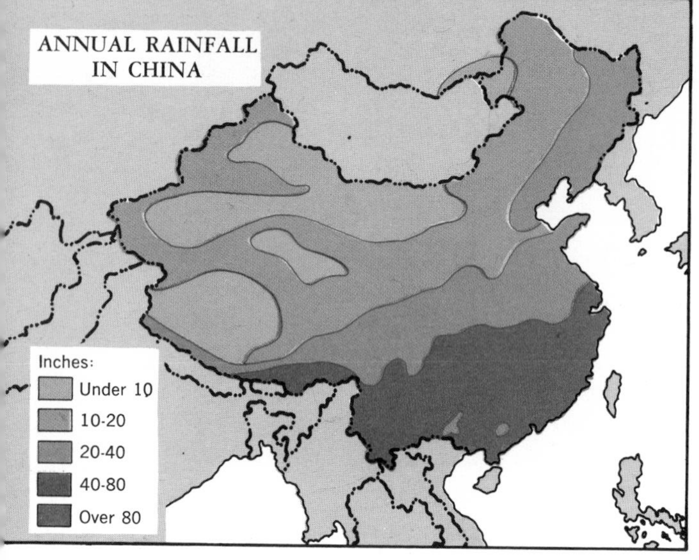

Climate

You have learned that land areas heat and cool more rapidly than water areas. The larger the land area, the warmer or cooler it becomes. Asia is the largest land mass in the world. Thus, there are large areas where extremes of temperature can be found. This type of climate is called a **continental climate.**

Much of northern and western China has very hot summers and cold winters. The amount of rain that falls in these areas differs widely from year to year. Snow falls in large amounts in the most northern areas.

Along the seacoasts and most of southern China the climate is mild. Winds off the large bodies of water help to keep the temperature fairly even. However, during the summer the monsoons bring heavy rains to these areas.

Natural Resources

China has great mineral resources, many of which have not been touched. Large deposits of iron ore and coal can be found in many parts of China. There are also deposits of tungsten, antimony, tin, lead, zinc, copper, manganese, and mercury. **Kaolin,** a clay from which fine porcelain is made, is found in great quantities in China.

At the present time mainland China has few forest areas. At one time the forests of China were important resources. Through the years the forests have been cut for firewood and the land cultivated for crops. A few forests remain in northeastern China. Some new forests have grown in southern China. Here the warm climate and the heavy rainfall make it possible for trees to grow rapidly. The Communist government has begun a project to plant new forests.

An important resource to the Chinese people is the bamboo plant which grows wild in many parts of China. This plant serves many purposes for the Chinese. The people eat the young bamboo sprouts. They make furniture and build houses and boats out of the full-grown plants. They weave sandals, hats, and many other items from strips of bamboo. Pulp, which is rolled into paper, is made from the bamboo stalk.

China's greatest resource for centuries has been the earth. Every square foot of soil that can be worked has been farmed throughout China's

For more than 35 centuries, the rich soil of the Chinese deltas (left) has been used to grow rice. Near some rivers, fish farms (right) are found in flooded fields.

history. There are many kinds of soil in China. The richest soil is found in the valley of the Yangtze River in southern China. Good soil is also found in the Hwang Ho Valley and in Manchuria. The rich farmlands of Manchuria would produce more if the rainfall in this region were more regular, and if the winters were not so long and cold. Soil in China's mountain areas is thin and rocky, and usually not fit for farming.

Farming Regions of China

Southern China is, for the most part, a hilly region. There is heavy rainfall and rich soil, but farming is done mostly on terraced land. Fruit trees, nut trees, tea, and some rice are grown. The Red Basin and the valleys of the Yangtze and the Si Rivers are exceptions. The Red Basin got its name from the rich, red soils found in the region. Grain crops, such as rice, are the chief products of these areas. Winter crops of beans, wheat, and cotton may be grown in the ricefields. In the valley of the Si River, two crops of rice may be grown in a year. Shallow ponds are used for raising fish and growing lotus roots and water chestnuts.

In northern China a rich, fine, yellow soil covers large areas. This yellow soil is found in the Loess Highlands and on the delta of the Hwang Ho, or Yellow River. **Loess** is a kind of yellowish-brown soil carried by the wind from deserts and other areas and deposited on the places where it is now found. In the Loess Highlands of China, there are places where the loess soil is over 300 feet deep. This soil is good for growing crops such as millet and wheat, but farming is difficult because there is not enough rain. One year out of three is usually not a good agricultural year. Since northern China has a larger population than can be supported by its crops during a good year, bad years bring near starvation to millions.

Saving the Precious Soil

Soil erosion and floods are a problem in many parts of China. For several centuries, China's population has been rapidly increasing. Providing food is constantly a problem.

Terraced farmland helps Chinese farmers to conserve the precious soil.

In some areas, peasants have carved farms out of hillsides and cut trees and bushes for fuel and livestock feed. Hillsides that have been stripped of their protective covering are easily eroded. Silt, or loose soil, washed from hillside farms is carried downstream by rivers, such as the Hwang Ho. The silt covers crops on nearby flatland farms. Over the centuries the riverbed of the Hwang Ho has been built up by deposits of silt. The deposits of silt have made the Hwang Ho shallow. At floodtime the Hwang Ho easily overflows its banks. The crops on millions of acres of land are destroyed.

For thousands of years, Chinese farmers near the Hwang Ho have tried to protect their farms from flooding by building dikes along the riverbanks. As the riverbed gets higher and higher, the dikes are raised. At floodtime the river surface in some places is 17 to 25 feet above the surrounding countryside. Can you imagine the destruction that occurs when a dike breaks and waters pour out onto the farmlands?

Where the Hwang Ho empties into the Yellow Sea, there are many channels. The power of the river is so great that a flood may change the course of these channels. When this happens, some farmers may find that their farms, which were once right near the river, are now a hundred miles away from it. Other farmers may find that the new river channel cuts right through the middle of their farms.

Today the Chinese government is working to prevent disastrous floods and to bring more land into cultivation. The Chinese are building many great dams, such as the Ming Tombs Dam outside of Peking. These dams serve three purposes. They check flooding, provide electric power, and store water for irrigation. The Chinese are also planting millions of trees. In a short time these trees should decrease flooding by preventing the rapid run-off of rain water from hillsides. They will also serve as a source of fuel.

The major cities of China, such as Chunking on the Yangtze River, are seaports or centers of the important river trade.

Improving the Food Supply

The Chinese government is also seeking to increase and to improve the food supply by introducing many new methods of farming. They are looking for plant strains that will resist disease and will give high crop yields. They are using new machinery to aid the farmer in planting and in harvesting. They are creating new markets for some of the products.

They are building a system of dams and irrigation ditches to provide water for crops. In this way they can cultivate land that has not been farmed because of scant rainfall. They will also increase the use of chemical and mineral fertilizers. These things, along with the use of better seeds, should help provide more food for the people.

Through these means, the danger of periods of starvation will be lessened. The need for bringing more land under cultivation and increasing crop yields is pressing. The population of China is expected to reach 1,000,000,000 before the end of this century. One wonders if the rate of increase in crop production will keep up with the increase in population.

Most Chinese live largely on a vegetarian diet. Although China has a long coastline and a rapidly growing fishing industry, most of China lies far inland away from the ocean. The inland people will not be able to benefit from ocean fishing until better means of transportation and of refrigeration are built.

To develop the coal industry of the Honan Province of central China, both industrial and residential buildings have been built.

Animal proteins are also scarce. In China, there is little room or feed for large numbers of animals. Land is too scarce and too precious to be used to raise livestock. As you know, many acres of land are required to support large amounts of livestock. Large work animals, such as oxen, donkeys, and water buffaloes, are used for plowing and for moving freight.

In the drier, cooler parts of northern and western China, yaks, camels, sheep, and goats provide milk and meat. In southern China, hogs and chickens are the principal sources of meat. These animals feed on kitchen scraps. Aside from some chickens and pigs, few animals are seen on small farms. In places where water buffalo are used for plowing, the old animal is eaten when a young bull takes its place.

The Development of Industry

Farming is the means by which most Chinese make a living. Before World War II there was very little industry in China. Since 1953 the Communists have been developing industry at a rapid rate. In 1953, the first **Five Year Plan** was started. This plan was designed by the Communist government to develop heavy industry. They wanted to develop industries that would build heavy equipment, such as locomotives, tractors, and power generators. In the Five Year Plans that have followed, heavy industry has been considered very important.

There are valuable deposits of iron ore in the northern and central provinces of China. These raw materials do not have to be carried long distances. Fortunately, these deposits of iron ore are near the deposits of coal. This makes it possible to develop the iron and steel industry.

Manchuria is the center of the largest iron and steel plants. For many years before World War II Manchuria was governed by Japan. The Japanese had developed the iron and steel industry in Manchuria. When the Chinese government gained control of Manchuria after World War II, they gained valuable industrial plants.

The Development of Transportation

As industry develops, China will need to improve transportation in the country so that manufactured products can be carried to markets more easily. Before World War II, China had less than 10,000 miles of railroad. Many rail lines were put out of order during the war, but since then great progress has been made in rebuilding them. The Communists are trying to build 1,000 miles of new rail lines each year.

There have never been many miles of good roads. The plans of the Communists call for the development of new highways. Air transportation is very important, and efforts are being made to build airfields and increase the number of airplanes.

In spite of their efforts to improve transportation rapidly, most of China's transportation is still by manpower. In North China, transportation is limited by the hilly country and the lack of water. The roads here are mostly narrow dirt tracks. Heavy loads are pulled on carts by mules, oxen, or men. Men carry great loads by means of shoulder poles, balancing them as they struggle up steep mountain roads. Men push wheelbarrows piled high with heavy loads. In some places men continue to pull rickshas in which one or two passengers ride.

In South China much of the traveling is done by water. Where there are no streams, the Chinese have built canals. Thousands of small boats, including junks, sampans, and barges, crowd the waterways. Boats are rowed or poled upstream. The canal boats are pulled by rows of men struggling against heavy leather thongs.

This river family appears more prosperous than most of China's large floating population.

The "boat people" are a special group of Chinese. These people own junks and sampans which they use as a means of earning a living by hauling freight from place to place. The boats are moved by oars or by a single sail. The entire family with chickens and a few other animals live on these houseboats. There are floating churches, schools, and hospitals for use by the boat people. Many people spend their lifetime on boats going ashore only to buy goods they need for living.

WESTERN SUB–REGIONS

West of the densely populated region of mainland China are three sub-regions. Inner Mongolia, Sinkiang, and Tibet are part of the People's Republic of China. They are controlled by the Communist government. They are high, dry lands which are sparsely populated. Vast territory in this part of the world is too rugged or too dry for farming. The few people who live here grow some crops that are suited to dry areas, and raise animals that can supply food, transportation, and materials for clothing.

Inner Mongolia

Inner Mongolia is the smallest of the three sub-regions of China. The long Hwang Ho passes through the southern grasslands. The northern section is part of the Gobi Desert. Most of the people are Mongols. They live a nomadic life and care for their herds. Some resources have recently been discovered and are being developed by the Chinese Communist government.

Sinkiang

Sinkiang is the driest of the three sub-regions of China. However, it does receive water from melting snow. The snowfields are in the Tien Shan and Kun Lun Mountains which surround it. In this sub-region are two of the world's driest, high basins. The Tarim and the Dzungarian Basins are quite hot in the summer and very cold in the winter. High mountains surround the Tarim Basin and block rain-bearing winds. One arm of the Tarim Basin, the Turfan Depression, sinks to 928 feet below sea level. Most of the Tarim Basin, however, is between 2,000 and 6,000 feet above sea level. The Takla Makan Desert, which makes up the Tarim Basin, is one of the driest regions in the world. The only water comes from springs around the edge of the desert. Few men in modern times have crossed this desert.

Most of the population of Sinkiang is Muslim and non-Chinese. The new Chinese government has been sending hundreds of thousands of Chinese workers into Sinkiang. An attempt is being made to use the water that flows from the high mountains into the desert basins for irrigation. Roads and airbases are being built.

Throughout this region, however, there is a feeling of "emptiness." Even though there is a chain of settlements along the oases near the mountains, life seems almost still. A little "hustle and bustle" takes place once in a while at the oases. In the past, these oases were part of the overland silk caravan routes from the west to the Far East. Today they have become centers for irrigation farming. Some important products are cotton, silk, and grain.

Communist influence reaches Inner Mongolia's people in the form of political posters and traveling propagandist groups.

Tibet

The third sub-region of China is Tibet. As you recall from Chapter 2, it lies north of one of the highest mountain ranges of the world, the Himalayas. These high ranges rise to a height of 28,000 feet and are snow swept in winter. One person has said that even in summer it is like a "graying paradise." This appearance is due to the snowfields which do not melt completely in the summer.

There are cities and farms in the lower parts of the Tibetan Plateau. Lhasa, the capital city, is 12,000 feet above sea level. Although Lhasa is in one of the lower parts of Tibet, it is more than twice as high in elevation as our mile-high city of Denver. Around Lhasa, a few hardy crops, such as barley, can be grown in the brief summer.

Elsewhere most of the people of Tibet are nomads. Their way of living is closely related to the climate and the landforms. They adapt to the cold climate of the very high plateaus and even higher mountains. They live in a one-animal economy.

Although the Tibetans raise sheep and goats, the most important animal is the yak. This animal is not found below 5,000 feet. It is well adapted to the scanty feed and the cold climate of the Tibetan Plateau. It serves as a source of meat, wool, and butter for the people. It is used to carry goods and to pull carts. Tibet is truly a yak region.

Before the seventh century A.D. the chief religion in Tibet was Bon-Po, a mixture of devil worship and magic. Buddhism was introduced into Tibet in the seventh century A.D. After a long struggle, the native religion of Bon-Po was replaced by Buddhism. During the struggle each religion took on some of the practices and beliefs of the other. Buddhism, when combined with some of the magic rites of Bon-Po, took a form of religion called Lamaism. For nearly a thousand years, Lamaism has been the chief religion in Tibet. It is a complex religion that is not easy to explain. One feature of Lamaism is the belief in the rebirth of the human soul in many different forms during many different lives.

The exiled Dalai Lama of Tibet.

The Dalai Lama

The major religious leader of Lamaism, the Dalai Lama, is believed to be a living god. When one Dalai Lama dies, it is believed his soul is reborn shortly afterwards in an infant. Several years pass before a chosen group of men go forth to seek the new Dalai Lama. This delay allows the reborn Lama to reach boyhood.

How do the Tibetans know where to find the new Dalai Lama and how to identify him? First of all, they believe the former Dalai Lama may have left clues as to where he would be reborn. The last Dalai Lama had often said that he would like to visit China. He died facing China. His successor was sought in the east and was found in China.

Sometimes it is hard to decide which of several young children might be the reborn living god.

The remote and forbidden capital city of Lamaism, Lhasa, is guarded by an immense Palace of the Dalai Lama.

Candidates are examined for physical features like those of former Dalai Lamas. To test which child is the true Dalai Lama, each is shown articles which actually belonged to earlier Dalai Lamas and some which did not. If a child recognizes the right articles or even claims them as his own, he has given further proof that he is the chosen one. This satisfies the men who are seeking the new Dalai Lama. They take the young boy to Lhasa where he governs as the chosen one.

Until very recently, one in five Tibetan males became monks, or lamas. The lamas live in monasteries. Most of the monasteries own their own crop fields and orchards. The most striking palace-monastery is the Potala, a many-storied, red and white building towering over Lhasa. It was the residence of the Dalai Lama.

For the past several centuries, political power in Tibet rested in the hands of the Dalai Lama. In 1959, the Tibetans revolted against the rule of Communist China. The revolt failed, and the Dalai Lama fled to India. The second leading Lama, the Panchen Lama, had returned to Tibet from China in 1952. He was chosen by the Chinese Communists to head a committee to organize Tibet as a self-governing part of China. In recent years, Tibet has been closed to outsiders. Chinese military forces have entered and re-entered the region to patrol the border in a dispute with India.

MONGOLIA

North of the People's Republic of China and south of the Union of Soviet Socialist Republics lies an independent country. It is called the People's Republic of Mongolia. It is in a crucial spot between two Communist countries. Although it is thought to be influenced by the Soviet Union, it struggles to remain neutral and independent.

From their earliest days, the Mongolians have been famous warriors. Mongol warriors have surged out of this region time after time. Once they even invaded Europe. In the thirteenth century the Mongol Empire stretched from China to Eastern Europe. The size of the area they controlled was one of the largest and greatest ever ruled over by so few people. The Great Wall of China to the east of Mongolia is a reminder of the past. It is a symbol of the fear the people of the eastern, fertile river plains had at one time of the Mongols.

A large number of people of the Mongolian People's Republic are nomads. Until recently the way of life of the Mongols was little different from that of the time of the great Mongol Emperor, Genghis Khan. Many Mongolians still live in the light, wooden, felt-covered tent or yurt. They move their herds back and forth from summer to winter grazing lands. This reminds us of the time when Mongol warriors rode forth to conquer the world.

The territory in which they live is well suited for raising sheep and goats. Some watered areas are grass-covered. For the most part it is too dry to raise cattle.

The simple exteriors of the Mongolian yurts are deceiving in comparison to the colorful and sometimes elaborate interiors.

The Liberation Day parade, on October 1st, before Peking's Gate of Heavenly Peace, is one way to demonstrate support of the government of Red China.

Today in Mongolia, many of the nomadic tents are being replaced by farmsteads. The farmsteads are clustered on Mongolia's few waterways. This vast, dry area has settlement patterns like those of our own early west. Roads are being built for modern trucks. Cities, schools, and hospitals are increasing in number. A few airfields have been built. These changes have been gradual.

CHINA, THE RE-AWAKENING GIANT

For many decades China was called the "Sleeping Giant." The word "Giant" could be used to refer to her great size. However, it has been used mainly to call attention to her huge population. The word "Sleeping" in the title referred to the lack of change that outsiders noticed in the ways of living in China. Until this century China seemed content with just looking at her long past. The Chinese saw little need to improve the present or plan for the future.

The situation is very different today. In the last twenty years the Chinese have made much progress. They have built roads, railroads, and dams. They have improved their farming methods. They have developed their heavy industries. But China must expand her economy much further in order to meet the needs of her growing population. She needs industrial aid, technical help, more trade and education for all.

Some people are concerned about the present government's efforts to build collective farms, to strengthen loyalty to the Communist government, and to weaken family unity. They feel that this means a loss not only to the Chinese, but also to the rest of the world. Some wonder whether the Chinese, in the long run, will lose their freedom or gain it. As the Chinese people build better ways of living, other nations hope that China will become a peaceful nation.

Do You Know?

1. What is meant by the statement, "The people of Eastern Asia have a riverine culture?"

2. Where are most of the major cities of Eastern Asia located?

3. What natural features act as boundaries for the lands of Eastern Asia? What man-made boundary protects parts of China?

4. Why are the snow-capped mountains important to the people of the valleys?

5. What is a dynasty? What was the first great dynasty in China? What important Chinese way of life has continued from that time?

6. What are some of the features of Chinese architecture?

7. How has the mulberry tree been used by the people of China?

8. What important observations were made by early Chinese astronomers?

9. Which part of the Chinese way of life has been affected the most by the present government?

10. What is kaolin? For what is it used?

11. In what valuable ways is the bamboo plant used?

12. What are the three sub-regions of western China? Why are these lands sparsely populated? What is the main way of life of the people?

Learn By Doing

1. Select one of the following topics and make an oral or written report. Use the encyclopedia or books from the library.

Communism in China
Sir Edmund Hillary
China's Boat People
Lamaism
The "Sleeping Giant" Awakens

2. Dates and numbers play an important part in the study of history. Can you find the answers to the questions

a. What does B.C. mean? What does A.D. mean?

b. How long ago was 444 B.C.? Why is this date important?

c. What did the Chinese build in the third century B.C. which still exists today?

d. About how many years did the Chou Dynasty last? How old is our country?

e. What would be the B.C. date if the Chinese Civilization were exactly 3000 years old?

f. How much older is Peking than your hometown?

g. If the great Chinese Wall were placed in the United States, it would extend from New York as far west as what city? How many miles are there between the two cities?

h. What rivers of China are about as long as the United States is wide? What is their approximate length?

i. How much higher is Mount Everest than Mount McKinley, North America's highest mountain?

3. Tell whether northern or southern China is being described.

a. The climate is mild throughout the year.

b. Summers are hot; winters are long and cold.

c. The rich, yellow soil is often 300 feet deep.

d. Grains are the chief crops grown in the rich, red soils.

e. Rice is the chief crop of the valleys.

f. Sheep and goats are the principal animals.

4. Select one of the following titles for a report. In addition to an encyclopedia and reference books, you may find important information in newspapers and magazines.

Singapore: Going It Alone
Hong Kong: Far East Listening Post
Kashmir: A Garden Spot In Trouble

Test Your Knowledge

1. What heritages of the past are important in the Chinese way of life?

2. Describe the important features of village life in old China.

3. What is the capital city of China? Why is this city an historical landmark? Why is it a cultural landmark?

4. What is a calligrapher? A character? Show how Chinese writing is similar to painting.

5. What is a civil war? Who fought in China's civil war? What was the result?

6. What is the greatest advantage of living in Taiwan? What are the problems faced by the government?

7. Why is the Hwang Ho a danger to the people? What is the government doing to control the river? How will these projects help?

8. What steps has the Chinese government taken to increase the food supply?

9. What is the Five Year Plan? How has the Five Year Plan helped to develop China from an agricultural to an industrial nation? Do you feel the plan has helped the people?

10. What is China's greatest resource? For what is the Red Basin noted? The Loess Highlands?

11. What is the important animal in Tibet's one-animal economy? Describe the environment in which this animal must live. What products do the people obtain from the animal?

12. What is the chief religion in Tibet? What name is given to the head of this religion? Explain how he is chosen.

13. How has the political power in Tibet changed in recent years?

14. Why is Mongolia in a crucial spot? How have the ways of living changed in this area?

15. What landform features are found in Sinkiang?

CHAPTER 13

SOUTH OF THE GREAT HIMALAYAS

South of the great Himalaya Mountains lies a very large, triangular land mass called the Indian Sub-continent. If it is part of the continent of Asia, why is it called a sub-continent? There are two reasons. First, the huge land mass is just under or below the size of a continent. And second, the Indian land mass is bordered by physical features that set it apart from the rest of the Asian continent. These natural features are the mountain ranges of the towering Himalayas, the desert-plateaus of Tibet, and the tropical rainforest of Southeast Asia.

THE INDIAN SUB-CONTINENT

The Indian Sub-continent is one of the world's large physical geographic regions. It is made up of three countries, India, Pakistan, and Ceylon. Locate these nations on the map on page 268. India is the sixth largest country in the world. It divides Pakistan into East Pakistan and West Pakistan. The island country of Ceylon is treated as a part of the Indian Sub-continent because it is separated from the Indian land mass by only a shallow strait.

As you can see, the Indian land mass forms a great rough triangle. On two sides of this peninsula are water, the Arabian Sea on the west and the Bay of Bengal on the east. South of the Indian land mass lies the Indian Ocean. On the northern side of the triangle lie the towering Himalaya Mountains.

The Himalayas form the highest mountain range in the world. The western end of this range, the Pamir Knot, appears on a relief map as a jumbled mass of rock. In the west, the Sulaiman and Kirthar Mountain Ranges extend southwestward from the Himalayas to the Arabian Sea. From the eastern end of the high, snowcapped Himalayas, the Baral, the Arakan Yoma, and other ranges branch out. These ranges extend southward and southeastward to the Bay of Bengal. Together, all these mountain ranges form a huge mountain wall. This mountain wall separates the Indian Sub-continent from the rest of the Asian continent.

Other physical features help to seal off the Indian land mass from the Asian continent. Hundreds of miles of high, cold desert-plateau lie north of the Himalayas. As you read earlier, the average height of the Tibetan Plateau is 15,000 feet. Great deserts lie beyond the mountain ranges to the west. A barrier just as effective as a desert lies to the east, the tropical rainforest in Southeast Asia.

The people of this region have not been as isolated as this description would lead one to think. For thousands of years people and ideas have entered and left the Indian Sub-continent. Invaders and traders have used easy passes or entrances in the northwest. One of the most famous entries into India is the Khyber Pass. Another easy entrance to the Indian Sub-continent is the narrow strip of land in West Pakistan between the Arabian Sea and the southern end of the mountain range that reaches to the Himalayas.

Three large sub-regions stand out on the Indian Sub-continent. You have already read about the first of these, the towering Himalaya Mountains in the north. The other two sub-regions are the flat riverlands just south of the Himalayas and the Deccan Plateau of the Indian Peninsula.

The land of India falls from the mighty peaks of the Himalayas to the fertile valleys along the Ganges River.

The Flat Riverlands

The huge snowfields of the Himalaya Mountains feed three giant rivers. The western river, the Indus, starts in the region known as Kashmir. It begins in these wet lands and flows southward through the dry lands of West Pakistan to the Arabian Sea. Like the Nile and the Tigris and Euphrates, the Indus River is a lifegiving stream. The people of West Pakistan depend on its water for irrigation.

A second great river, the Brahmaputra, also rises in the Himalayas. It flows eastward in Tibet between high ranges. Finally it breaks through the mountains in a deep gorge and then flows south through India. It joins the Ganges, the third huge river of the Sub-continent, in East Pakistan. For centuries the waters of these two mammoth systems have carried much mud and silt. A large **delta,** an alluvial deposit at the mouth of a river, has formed where the waters of these two rivers empty into the Bay of Bengal. The river channels in the delta have changed often as have those of Hwang Ho in China. This large delta region of the Ganges and Brahmaputra rivers is densely populated.

The Deccan Plateau

The third major sub-region of the Indian Sub-continent is the Deccan Plateau. This is a tableland that covers most of central and southern India. It is a somewhat irregular and sloping tableland that is higher in the west than in the east. The Deccan is not as well watered as the river valleys of the Ganges and the Brahmaputra. The climate of the Deccan Plateau is more arid. The Western Ghats, the mountain range which borders the plateau, causes the summer monsoon winds to rise. As they do so, they are cooled. Their ability to hold moisture is reduced. Rain falls on the western side of the Ghats. As the winds continue to blow over the ranges and across the Deccan, they get hotter. As they move down the sloping eastern side, they are more able to hold the moisture which comes from the warm surface. In this way, very little rain falls on the lands.

Part of the northern Deccan Plateau has an unusual but important type of soil. A long time ago, **lava,** or melted rock, poured out in great sheets over layers of rock. The entrance of hot lava took place along weak places between the layers of rock. When the hardened lava material is exposed to the sun, wind, and rain and to high and low temperatures, it breaks down into fine particles. The soil which results from the breaking down of the lava is very rich. When water is added, this fertile soil becomes highly productive. In western India there are great expanses of these lava-base soils. The wheat yields per acre are among the world's highest.

THE CLIMATE

Another highly important physical factor to be considered in the life of people of this region is the climate. Because the Sub-continent has many different types of landforms, the climate can be expected to vary. The highlands that edge the Himalayas have cool winters. The great flat river plains of the northern Indus and Ganges rivers have cool winters and very hot summers. However, the most important regional climate feature is the monsoon, a steady, seasonal wind.

In winter the monsoon blows from the heart of Asia toward the sea. It begins in the very dry lands of central Asia. The winter monsoon is dry and brings little or no rain.

The summer monsoon blows in the opposite direction. During the summer, warm air over the heated land mass rises. Cool moist air from the ocean flows in to take its place. The moist sea air blows from the sea across the land. If it meets a mountain barrier and rises, it becomes cooler and heavy rains pour down. Rains also result when a warm air mass slides over a cold air mass.

Agriculture Depends on the Monsoons

The pattern of agriculture on the Indian Sub-continent is tied closely to the monsoon. The growing season begins with the rains that accompany the summer monsoon. Some crops, such as wheat, are planted near the end of the rainy period. They mature during the cool dry season that follows the summer rains. Such crops often need to be irrigated in order to grow. From October on, winter crops are watered by irrigation.

The winter monsoon brings cooler, drier weather to the Sub-continent. Beginning in March the weather becomes warmer. Temperatures rise above 100 degrees. Plants stop growing, leaves fall from trees, and the grass becomes brown. The temperature rises higher and higher. Day after day the sun glares down upon the land from a cloudless sky. The heat seems unbearable. Hot winds raise the dust and cause duststorms. Nature seems to go to sleep. If only the rains would come!

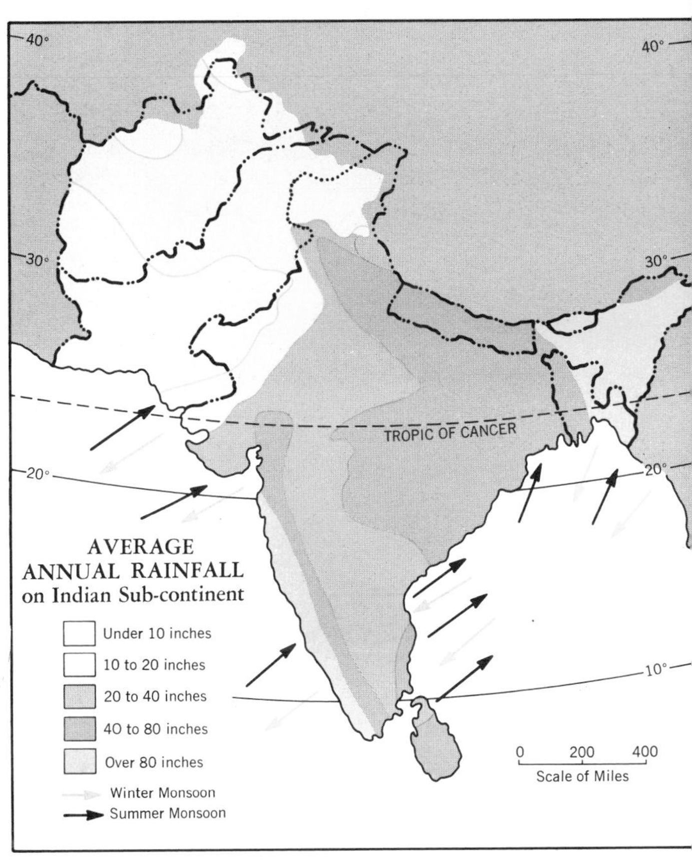

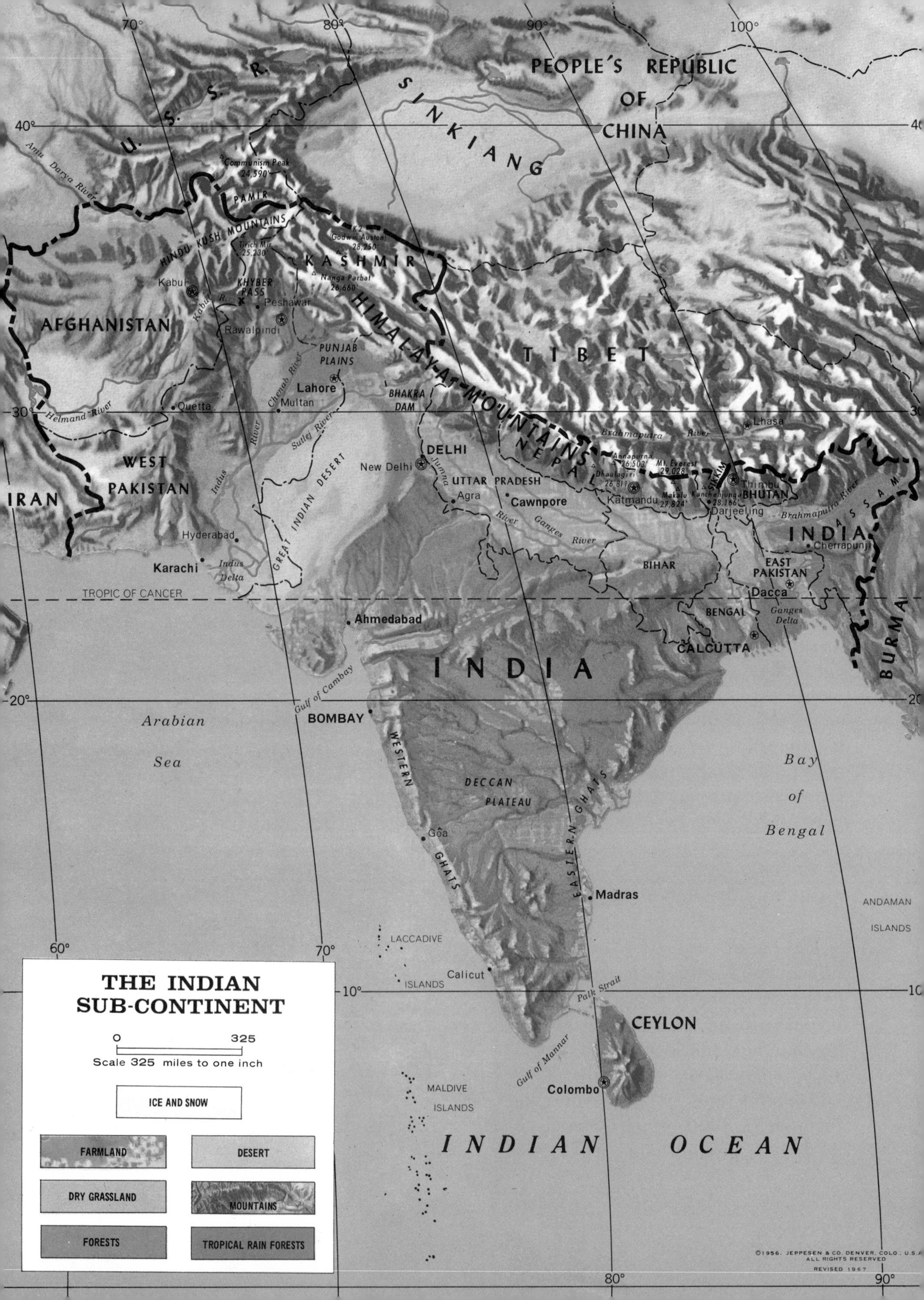
THE INDIAN SUB-CONTINENT
Scale 325 miles to one inch
ICE AND SNOW
FARMLAND
DESERT
DRY GRASSLAND
MOUNTAINS
FORESTS
TROPICAL RAIN FORESTS
PEOPLE'S REPUBLIC OF CHINA
SINKIANG
U. S. S. R.
TIBET
AFGHANISTAN
WEST PAKISTAN
IRAN
INDIA
KASHMIR
NEPAL
SIKKIM
BHUTAN
EAST PAKISTAN
BURMA
ASSAM
CEYLON
HIMALAYA MOUNTAINS
HINDU KUSH MOUNTAINS
PAMIR
KHYBER PASS
PUNJAB PLAINS
GREAT INDIAN DESERT
DECCAN PLATEAU
WESTERN GHATS
EASTERN GHATS
BHAKRA DAM
UTTAR PRADESH
BIHAR
BENGAL
Communism Peak 24,590'
K2 (Godwin Austen) 28,250'
Tirich Mir 25,230'
Nanga Parbat 26,660'
Annapurna 26,503'
Mt. Everest 29,028'
Dhaulagiri 26,811'
Makalu 27,824'
Kanchenjunga 28,166'
Kabul
Peshawar
Rawalpindi
Lahore
Multan
Quetta
Hyderabad
Karachi
DELHI
New Delhi
Agra
Cawnpore
Katmandu
Darjeeling
Thimbu
Lhasa
Cherrapunji
Dacca
CALCUTTA
Ahmedabad
BOMBAY
Gôa
Madras
Calicut
Colombo
Amu Darya River
Helmand River
Kabul R.
Indus River
Chenab River
Sutlej River
Jumna
Ganges River
Brahmaputra River
Indus Delta
Ganges Delta
TROPIC OF CANCER
Arabian Sea
Gulf of Cambay
Bay of Bengal
Palk Strait
Gulf of Mannar
LACCADIVE ISLANDS
MALDIVE ISLANDS
ANDAMAN ISLANDS
INDIAN OCEAN
©1956. JEPPESEN & CO. DENVER, COLO., U.S.A. ALL RIGHTS RESERVED
REVISED 1967

Food markets always draw large crowds in India; yet the threat of famine remains India's most critical problem.

The summer monsoon arrives sometime in June. Great banks of black clouds build up. The rains break so suddenly and come with such force that it seems as though the sky has cracked. In a few days, the world begins to turn green again. The monsoon rains bring cooler temperatures. The wet season has begun. During the rainy season the moisture in the air is so great that it is difficult to dry clothes. Clothing, books, and leather goods mildew easily.

Millions of farmers have to depend on the monsoon for water to feed their crops. The success or failure of their crops depends on the time of arrival of the summer monsoon. Many people may starve if the rains come too early or too late. When the rains of the summer monsoon come on time, these farmers feel that a new lifegiving season is beginning.

A few lucky farmers do not have to depend entirely upon the monsoon rains. In the northern river valley plains of the Indus and the Ganges rivers, there is no shortage of water. The melting snows of the Himalayas feed the rivers and streams in these areas throughout the year. A great system of irrigation canals is turning many acres of desert into rich cotton and wheat farms.

THE PEOPLE ON THE LAND

Over 600 million people live on the Indian Sub-continent. About three times as many people live in this region as live in the United States. Yet the two countries of India and Pakistan are only a little larger than half the size of our country. If the people of the Indian Sub-continent were evenly distributed, each square mile would still have over 250 persons. But as yet, each square mile is not productive enough to feed or support 250 persons. Thus, most of the people live in valleys of the Brahmaputra and Ganges rivers. Few places in the world are as crowded as the Indian states of Bengal, Bihar, and Uttar Pradesh. Some square miles in these states along the Ganges River have 2,250 people crowded together.

The Farming Village

The economies of the countries of the Indian Sub-continent are largely based on agriculture. Most of the people live in the several hundred thousand villages that dot the countryside. Most of the people in these villages are farmers who work the nearby land. The scattered farming villages often can be reached only by paths which lead through the fields that surround each village.

Villagers use materials at hand to build their houses. In moist tropical regions walls of huts are often made from bamboo. These bamboo walls have openings through which air can move. The movement of the humid air keeps the hut from becoming unbearably hot. In drier regions where little rain falls during the year, other than during the summer monsoon, walls of houses may be made of sun-dried mud. The houses may be roofed with straw.

The Village Family

Large families live in the villages. The large family is called a **joint family.** This is really a joining of many family groups under the same roof. The joint family consists of grandparents, aunts and uncles, and cousins. The oldest male member of the family is the head of the household. The joint family has several advantages. If one member of the family falls ill, he is cared for by the others. Someone is always available to take care of the children. The children have their cousins as well as their brothers and sisters to play with. The chores of the farm are shared by many people. In the cities, however, the joint family pattern is rapidly disappearing.

The members of a village family rise early. The farmer may begin plowing while it is still dark so that he does not have to work during the hottest part of the day. The women cook, make clothing, grind corn, churn buttermilk, and care for the babies. The older children work in the fields. Village people eat only two meals a day.

Farming Methods Are Poor

By Western standards, village farming is inefficient. A farmer owns one or two acres of land but the land is divided into small strips located in different places. He wastes much of his time walking from one strip of land to another. His farming tools are often poor. His plow may be little more than a stick with an iron point. A hand sickle is used to reap wheat and rice. The grain is threshed, or separated from the stalk, by the feet of cattle. After threshing, the grain is **winnowed**—that is, the good grain is separated from the chaff. Grain is winnowed by tossing it in the air. The wind blows the lighter chaff away from the grain. The grain falls onto the threshing floor.

Cattle Are Underfed

Half the world's cattle live on the Indian land mass. Hindus believe cattle are sacred animals. Their respect for life will not allow them to kill cattle or other animals. Thus, millions of sacred cattle are allowed to roam freely. The Indian farmer's respect for animal life is so great that he will only try to shoo away a herd of deer or group of monkeys eating his crops. Even in times of famine, the village farmer will not kill stray cattle for food.

In a land where feed is scarce, the huge cattle population can not be well fed. The sacred cattle compete with domestic work cattle for feed. The farmer's cattle that are used to turn wheels and pull plows are often weak and underfed.

Many Indian farmers use traditional methods for threshing wheat.

India's sacred cattle sometimes present problems. Other breeds are essential help to the farmers.

Water Is Scarce in Some Areas

Lack of water leaves much of the land a near desert most of the year. Often the village well is the chief source of water for the villagers. The people of the village draw their drinking water and cooking water from the well. They lower different sized jars into the well by ropes attached to the jars. Children carry the smaller jars from the well to their home.

Other wells supply irrigation water for crops. Water is drawn from these wells in several different ways. Sometimes a man or boy stands on a cross-pole. By walking or by shifting weight on one end of the pole, he causes the other end of the pole to lift a container of water. Another person spills the water from the container into a ditch which leads to the fields.

Cattle are sometimes harnessed to a wheel at the edge of a well. As the cattle walk down a ramp away from the well, water is raised from the well and tipped out into an irrigation ditch. For this method of lifting water, an animal skin is used as a water container. The skin holds a large amount of water and can be easily emptied into the ditch.

The Persian water wheel is another means of supplying water to a field. A draft animal, such as a cow or camel, walks endlessly around in a circle. This turns a wheel which operates a chain of buckets or clay jars. These containers dip into the water and spill it into an irrigation ditch. See the picture on this page.

Along with the village well, the village reservoir is a familiar feature of the Indian landscape. Water reservoirs store rainwater and stream water. In some villages these reservoirs serve as the people's only water supply. Besides being used for irrigation, clothes may be washed in the reservoir and cattle may drink from it. When the reservoir serves many purposes, it is often a source of disease.

Major Crops

The climate of the Indian Sub-continent is varied enough to support many kinds of crops. We have already mentioned that wheat is a major crop of the drier regions of the northwestern part of the Deccan Plateau in India. Other major crops are rice and jute. These are grown in the wetter regions of the Indian Sub-continent. Some other crops grown are tea, peanuts, sugar cane, grain sorghums, and cotton.

Some of these crops are grown not only for use at home but also for money to buy food for the people. These money-making crops are called "cash" crops. They are cotton, jute, and sugar. The staple crops, wheat and rice, are used as food for the people of India.

On the wet parts of the delta formed by the Ganges and Brahmaputra rivers, the two major crops grown are rice and jute. Jute fibers are used in making rope, burlap, matting, and gunny sacks. It is the "cash" crop for East Pakistan. In the fall, floodwaters cover wide areas of the delta where jute is grown. Because of the floods, the people must wade in water to harvest the jute. Harvesters have to bend and cut the stalks under three or four feet of water. Because of the floodwater, the stalks are loaded into boats rather than wheeled carts.

Rice is the chief crop in the areas of the Ganges region where rainfall is above 80 inches a year. In regions of less rainfall, such as southern India, rice is still an important crop. However, wherever rainfall is under 40 inches a year, rice may be grown only by means of irrigation. Although rice is India's largest crop, she does not grow enough to meet her own needs. To avoid famine, rice must be imported from Burma and Thailand.

Jute is an important source of income on the Sub-continent.

Crop Yields Are Low

In general, crop yields on the Indian land mass are low in comparison with crop production in other parts of the world. The land has been farmed for centuries. The fertility of the soil has long been exhausted by the lack of fertilizer and the leaching of vital minerals by heavy monsoon rains. Animal dung in other parts of the world is often saved to spread on the fields. In parts of India where wood is scarce, the animal dung is dried in cakes and used as fuel. Thus, one valuable source

Improved farming methods can ease the danger of famine.

of fertilizer for the land is lost. Great numbers of farmers are too poor to buy chemical fertilizer.

Life Expectancy Is Short

Life for the village farmer is a big question mark. The crop yields per acre are lower than is needed. There are occasional disasters, such as floods and drought. Most villagers do not have a proper diet. Disease is widespread. For these reasons, it is unusual to find many old people on the Sub-continent. The average life expectancy is about thirty years. Under normal conditions, an American can expect to live until he reaches the upper sixties. Improvements are being made so that the life expectancy of the people on the Indian land mass is gradually increasing.

Improvements in Food Production

To meet the food needs of the peoples, the Indian and the Pakistan governments are working hard to help the village farmer increase his crop yields. Experiments have shown that crop yields can be increased greatly by using better seeds and a little fertilizer. These governments are trying to introduce better seed. Fertilizer is being applied to worn out soils.

The governments are also bringing new farmland into crop production. Irrigation systems are being built to bring water to dry but fertile land. Great dams are being built to supply water to fields which at present have to depend upon an uncertain monsoon, which often has too little rainfall.

The increase in population still runs far ahead of the increase in food. With the checking of diseases, such as malaria, millions of people live who once would have died. With improvement of sanitary conditions and health, more children live to be adults. Better diets enable adults to live longer. But the task of feeding the millions of people on the Indian land mass remains very difficult.

AN OLD CIVILIZATION

Archaeologists believe that the Indian civilization dates back 5,000 years. In recent years archaeologists have uncovered the remains of ancient cultures that existed 3,000 years before the birth of Christ. These diggings have begun to tell us much about where and how these ancient people lived.

In the Indus River Valley, mentioned in Chapter 4, two sites of these ancient people have been uncovered. One, called Harappa, is near the Ravi branch of the Indus. The other lies south of Harappa and is called Mohenjo-Daro. These two cities were about 400 miles apart. But the similarity in building materials, houses, street plans, and drainage systems makes us believe these cities may have been under a central government.

Mohenjo-Daro ruins reveal traces of an advanced civilization.

We know that each city was built by people who were closely related by trade, language, and even by blood. The people of one city lived just like the people of the other. Building bricks were the same size and shape in both of these cities and throughout this early riverine culture region. These early people knew how to plan cities. Both Harappa and Mohenjo-Daro had straight streets and city blocks. Each house had a bath. Drains led from the bathroom to sewers under the streets.

Both cities used the same weights and measures in carrying on trade. They made pottery, cut stone, made fine jewelry, wove cotton cloth, went to market, and worshiped at temples. They had a writing system which we have not as yet been able to decipher. They combed their hair with ivory combs and shaved with copper razors. Many children's toys have been found. Some were toy animals with heads that moved. Toy monkeys slid up and down a string. Whistles shaped like birds have also been found.

Exactly what happened to these early civilizations is unknown. They may have been destroyed by invaders. The people may have been wiped out by a shift in the course of the river.

Early Invaders

About 1500 B.C. a group of people called the Dravidians lived on the Indian Sub-continent. It is thought that pastoral and warrior people called Aryans invaded from the northwest. The Dravidians were conquered or driven south. Some people believe that the dark-skinned people of southern India are descendants of these ancient Dravidians.

The Aryans settled on the lands near the Indus River which they called the Hindustan. The people became known as **Hindus.** They had brought with them the idea of grouping people by classes according to occupation. This practice became part of Hinduism, the oldest religion in India. The first and highest order, or class, contained the Brahmins, the priests. Next came the Kshatriyas, the warrior class. Third came the Vaisyas, the merchants and farmers. The invading Aryans gave the name of Sudras, or serfs, to the native people they conquered. The Sudras formed the lowest order, the laboring class.

Other invaders followed the Aryans. From Greece came Alexander the Great. Alexander established the Indus River as the eastern boundary of his empire. The influence of the Greek culture upon the Indian people is thought to have been very little. The most important result was the establishment of trade routes over land and sea between the East and the West.

Asoka Rules the Sub-continent

Following Alexander's death in 323 B.C., Maurya overthrew Greek rule in India. His empire was widened by his grandson, Asoka, the first of the great rulers of the Indian Sub-continent. Asoka's empire covered all but the southern tip of the Indian Peninsula. In the wars that built his empire, thousands of people were killed. When Asoka converted from Hinduism to Buddhism, he regretted his bloody conquests. He stopped short of conquering the entire peninsula. He had rock carvings made which told of his sadness over having caused so much suffering and death.

Asoka is remembered as a great king who led his people to righteousness and correct moral behavior. Asoka taught religious toleration and respect. He built hospitals. He spread the idea that neither animals nor men should be harmed. In one of his rock carvings he told of having reduced the number of animals killed daily in his kitchens. He played a strong role in making vegetarianism popular in India.

Asoka helped **Buddhism** spread in India. This religion was started in India by a man named Gautama. He was given the title *Buddha* which means the "Enlightened One." His followers came to be called Buddhists and his religion Buddhism. The Buddhists do not worship the Buddha but honor him as a great teacher. Whenever possible, they obtain some-

Many of the Sub-continent's Buddha temples are neglected and decaying.

Indus River
Delhi
Kausambi
Pataliputra
Ganges River

GUPTA AND MONGOL EMPIRES
Mogul Empire - 1690
Gupta Empire - 400 A.D.
Present Boundary

thing that belonged to the Buddha and preserve this as a relic of the great man.

One of the characteristic buildings of Buddhism is the **stupa.** It is a circular mound with a chamber in the center. The chamber contains a relic of the Buddha. The square on top of the mound represents the heaven of the gods that rule the earth. The umbrella above the square stands for the heaven of the gods of the invisible world. The stupa is surrounded by a platform. One act of worship consists of walking in clockwise direction around the stupa on the platform.

Asoka encouraged the building of stupas throughout his empire. The great stupa at Sanchi in central India was one of eight built there by Asoka. Today three of the eight remain. The Sanchi Stupa is 106 feet in diameter and 42 feet high. Four beautifully carved gateways date from the first century B.C. Each gateway consists of two columns, topped by three crossbars that curve upward in the middle. The gateways were carved from yellow stone brought from nearby hills. The carvings show many scenes from the life of Buddha and legends about him.

Buddhism remained a strong, although not the most important, religion in India until about A.D. 600. After that time, it declined in the land of its birth. It had almost disappeared 600 years later. But before it died out in India, Buddhism had spread to Burma, Ceylon, Indonesia, and China. It was later brought to Japan from Korea and China.

Parts of the 2,250 year-old Sanchi Stupa (left) are almost perfectly preserved. The huge Hindu temple, Kailasa (right) is 107 feet high and more than 1,100 years old.

The Golden Age in India

From about A.D. 320 to A.D. 544 members of the Gupta family ruled. Their empire spread across northern India. Two Chinese Buddhist monks, traveling two centuries apart, left accounts of their travels and stay in India during the Gupta Period. From their accounts we read that the Gupta Empire was peaceful and rich. A traveler could travel throughout the Gupta Empire without harm.

The Gupta Period was rich in painting and sculpture. Most of the surface buildings of that time have been destroyed over the centuries. However, some great cave-temples carved out of solid rock have survived. The village of Ajanta has 27 caves with splendid sculpture and paintings. The village of Ellora has 34 cave-temples hewn, or cut, out of rock.

The greatest of the rock-hewn temples is the Kailasa temple at Ellora. The Kailasa temple took 100 years to carve out of the mountainside. It differs from its neighboring caves in that it has no roof. The builders started at the top of the cliff and dug down. They left a huge block of stone in the center of the pit when they dug. This block of stone was carved into a temple to the Hindu God, Siva. This ornate and finely sculptured cave-temple is one of the wonders of India.

The Muslims Conquer India

For many centuries after the Golden Age of India, the Hindu people ruled the land and defeated any new invading tribes. Then in the early thirteenth century, the whole Indus-

Ganges Valley fell to Turkish invaders from the northwest. These Turkish invaders who ruled India for several centuries were Muslims. They brought with them their religion, Islam. Many Hindus became followers of Islam. The Muslims also brought with them many cultural gifts. They introduced their customs, art, and science to the Hindu people.

But the power of the Turks was threatened by invaders from the north. Early in the sixteenth century, their rule was overthrown by Mongol invaders. In India these invaders were called **Moguls,** a word that refers to a ruler or conqueror. The Moguls were also Muslims. They built a Muslim Empire in India which lasted into the eighteenth century. The outstanding Mogul emperor was Akbar. Akbar sought cooperation between Hindus and Muslims.

The foremost contribution of the Moguls to the world was their lovely buildings. One of their outstanding buildings is the Taj Mahal, a white marble tomb. It was built by the Shah Jehan, a grandson of Akbar. Shah Jehan built the Taj Mahal as a memorial and tomb for his beloved wife, Mustaz Mahal. This perfectly proportioned building, inlaid with semi-precious stones, was built over a period of 17 years. The **minarets,** or slender towers, at each corner of the platform on which the Taj Mahal stands are each 130 feet tall. Inside the Taj Mahal a lacy, marble screen surrounds the tombs of Shah Jehan and Mumtaz Mahal.

The Taj Mahal, one of the world's most beautiful buildings, is an example of late Muslim architecture.

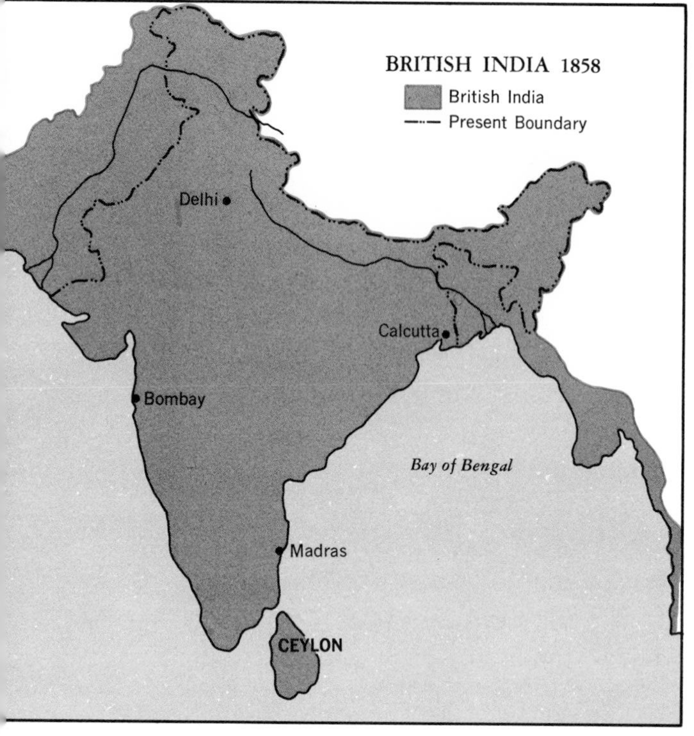

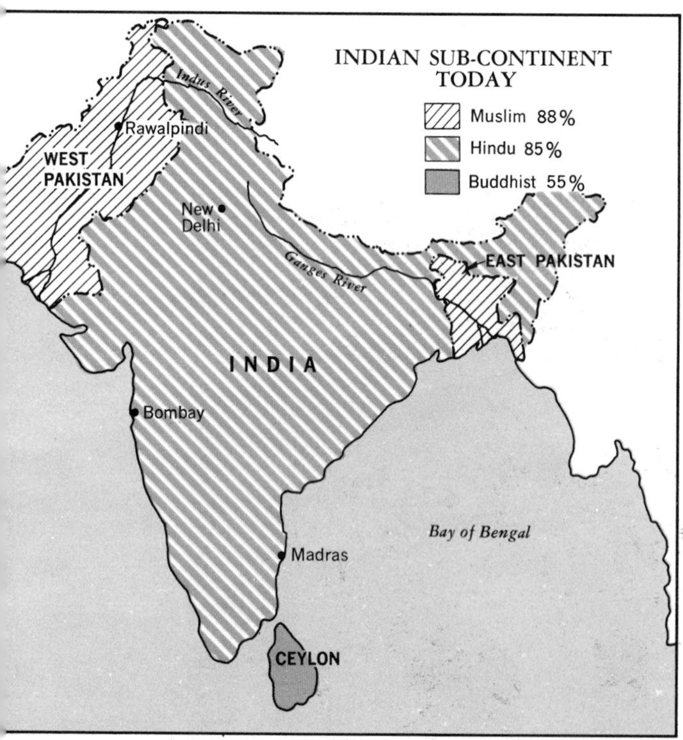

British Control of the Sub-continent

Direct Western European trade with the Indian people began with the discovery by Vasco da Gama of a sea route to India. By the nineteenth century, the British East India Company held control over most of the Indian Sub-continent. In the middle of the nineteenth century, the natives revolted against the company's rule. India became a possession of the British Crown. A **viceroy,** or governor, was appointed to rule. During the time the British controlled the Indian Sub-continent they made several lasting contributions. They built a good system of roads and railroads. They established a competent central government.

After World War I, the people of the Indian Sub-continent began to make strong demands for independence. A leader in this movement to freedom was Mohandas Gandhi. In the struggle for freedom, Gandhi urged his countrymen to use nonviolent resistance as their main weapon against the British. The Indians disregarded the titles and honors granted them by the British. They refused to attend the government controlled schools. They stopped importing British goods. Although some rioting did occur, Gandhi's plan was successful. In 1947, after 90 years of British rule, the Indian people were given their independence.

Gandhi hoped that British India would become one country when

The Parliament Building in New Delhi is the seat of India's government. Indira Gandhi, elected Prime Minister in 1966, is the first woman in modern times to lead a major nation.

freedom came. However, religious differences between the Muslims and the Hindus were too strong. British India was divided into two nations, India and Pakistan. The Republic of Pakistan is divided into an Eastern section and a Western section. These are the areas of the Indian Sub-continent where the majority of the Muslims live. The Republic of India is mainly made up of Hindu people.

The struggle which preceded the division of India was a bitter one. Muslims and Hindus could not agree on terms of the government. Mohammed Ali Jinnah, the leader of the Muslims, demanded the separate nation. Feelings ran high, and there was much bloodshed. Gandhi, a Hindu, was shot in 1948 by a member of his own religious sect because he was tolerant toward the Muslims.

After the division of the country, a representative assembly drew up a constitution for India. Jawaharal Nehru, a close associate of Gandhi, became Prime Minister. He served in this post until his death in 1964. Under his government the country made great progress. Industry was expanded and agriculture was improved. School enrollment was almost doubled. Malaria was almost wiped out. Large landowners voluntarily gave part of their farmlands to the poor. Nehru's successors have continued to work to improve living conditions.

A modern steel mill rises in a land where farmers still winnow wheat in the wind and one well of water serves an entire village.

LIFE ON THE SUB-CONTINENT TODAY

There are many different religions on the Indian Sub-continent. In Pakistan about four-fifths of the people are Muslims. The same proportion of Hindus live in India. The island of Ceylon is chiefly Buddhist. Other peoples on the Sub-continent follow Sikhism, Jainism, Zoroastrianism, and Christianity.

The leading religion of India, Hinduism, has at its center a belief in a Supreme Being. However, the powers of this Supreme Being have been assigned to three major gods; Brahma, Vishnu, and Siva. Their powers in turn have been assigned to many other minor gods. To the Westerner, Hinduism seems to show a confusion of thousands of gods in thousands of different shapes and forms.

Brahma, the god of wisdom, has four heads. Each head rules a quarter of the universe. Siva is the god who influences floods, death, and war. He is lord of the dance and lord of snakes. Thus he is often shown dancing with snakes about his arms and neck. He wears a necklace of skulls.

Vishnu, the "Preserver of the Universe," is often shown with four arms. One of his upper arms holds a conch, the other a discus. Vishnu has worked for the welfare of the universe. To do this, he has taken ten different forms at different times. Two of the most popular forms, or incarnations, of Vishnu are Rama and

Krishna. Rama is a hero who saved the world from the demon Ravana. Rama is usually shown carrying a bow and arrow. He is thought of as an ideal husband and brave leader. Krishna, often shown playing a flute, is the center of many interesting legends as a lover and hero. He is usually colored blue.

The Hindu believer need not worship all of the gods. After all, each is a part of the Supreme Being. Thus some worship Siva; others worship Vishnu. Still other Hindus worship both. Some choose to worship a minor god who controls an aspect of life in which they are interested.

The Ellora Caves are centered by a huge statue of the Hindu god, Siva.

The Caste System

One of the unique cultural features of the Indian region is the **caste system.** A caste is a division of the people of a society into different groups or classes. A man is born into a caste and cannot move out of it. The people of one caste or class may marry only people belonging to their caste. They eat only with members of their caste. A member of a higher caste may not eat food prepared by a member of a lower caste.

Just how the caste system began is not known. We know that it has existed in India for 2,500 years. Perhaps the Aryans brought the seeds of the caste system with them when they entered the Sub-continent. Although the early Aryans did not follow caste practices, they did have four orders of classes of people. In time, another large group of people were considered so lowly that they were classless. They were outside of caste and called "untouchables." So many different castes developed over the centuries that there were between 2,000 and 3,000 castes.

Today the caste system is outlawed. The government of India is trying to break down the class barriers of caste. This is very difficult to do because the origin of the four main castes is thought to have come from the Hindu gods. The present Indian constitution has abolished untouchability and ignores caste differences. The many ways of behaving that mark a member of one caste from a member of a different caste are beginning to weaken. Nonetheless, caste customs continue to be strong in rural India. It is still a powerful force and way of life for many of the Indian people.

Progress on the Sub-continent

Signs of progress on the Indian Sub-continent are many. Today, in modern India and Pakistan dams are being built to check terrible floods. The lakes behind them will provide pure drinking water during dry seasons. The dams will also provide waterpower all through the year. Electrical power, coupled with iron and steel products, will help build industry in these nations.

India has large stores of good-quality iron ore that are just beginning to be used. Coal and iron come from mines west of Calcutta. Today, cotton from the dry uplands and plateaus of India goes into Indian textile mills rather than to Great Britain.

Although new and large industrial plants are being built, the Indian government has continued to encourage home industry. Lace, fine cloth, and beautiful rugs of cotton and wool are made by skilled workers. Ivory, brass, silver, gold and wood carvings, and ornaments are turned out by thousands of skilled hands in hundreds of Indian villages.

City Life

Although most of the people on the Sub-continent live in small villages, there are many large and thriving cities. Business and political life are found in the large cities. Most cities have prosperous sections where businessmen and their families live. These sections often have beautiful modern buildings. Other parts of a city are usually crowded. These are the older sections built before modern transportation developed. The streets are narrow and winding. Here many people live crowded into little space.

Bombay, Calcutta, and Delhi are the leading cities in India. Bombay and Calcutta, the largest cities, are located at ports of entry into the country. They serve as important gate-

Shrimp caught near Karachi will be quickly frozen and exported. They are not likely to reach the market streets of Bombay.

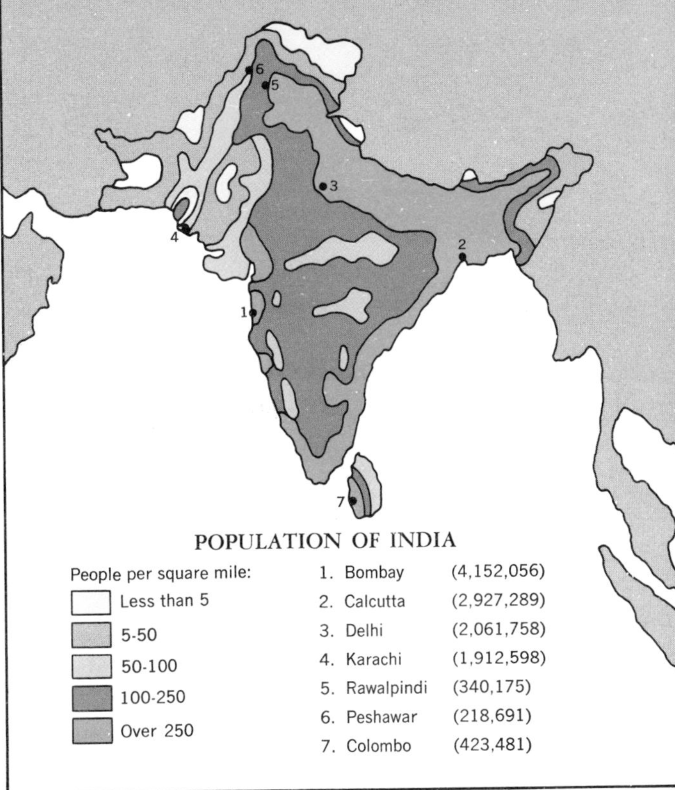

ways for trade by water, land, and air. New Delhi, a section of Delhi, is a new city built as the center of the government. The wide streets and the fine new buildings rival those found anywhere in the world.

In Pakistan, Karachi is the leading city. It is an important port for trade with all parts of the country. Rawalpindi, located in northern Pakistan, is the capital. Peshawar, a town near Pakistan's northwest border, is a thriving trading center. It is located at the Pakistan end of the Khyber Pass. For centuries, traders from many parts of Europe and Asia have exchanged goods in Peshawar's crowded open-air markets, or bazaars.

Ceylon has several important seaports. Colombo is the capital of the country and also the largest city. Ceylon is a land rich in many resources. The climate along the coast is excellent for growing rice and coconuts. Higher in the hills, rubber and tea plants thrive. The forests of the island supply fine hardwoods. The mountains have rich deposits of gold and gem stones. Tea and rubber are exported.

A Great Cultural Heritage

The great land mass which we have called the Indian Sub-continent is the home of nearly one-fifth of all the world's people. The countries of this region have recently gained their freedom from Great Britain. The new governments of India, Pakistan, and Ceylon are establishing new industries and programs to tackle old problems. These problems are severe. They include famine, a high death rate, and a rapidly growing population.

This Sub-continent has contributed much to the cultural heritage of the world. It has given the world rice, cotton, and sugar cane. It has also given us the game of chess and the decimal system. It was the birth place of Buddhism.

Many different religious groups live side by side in India. The world has long admired the ability of the Indian people of different religious beliefs to live together in peace. The compassion of the Hindus for all forms of life and their search for ways of living a moral life are lessons for the rest of the world.

Do You Know?

1. What are the three major countries of the Indian Sub-continent?

2. Why is the Indian land mass called the Indian Sub-continent?

3. What are some of the natural physical features which separate the Indian Sub-continent from other parts of Asia?

4. What are the major landform subregions of the Indian Sub-continent?

5. What kind of economy do the countries of the Indian Sub-continent have?

6. What are the three most heavily populated states of India? Where are they located?

7. What are the staple crops of India? What are the cash crops of India?

8. What two cities formed an early civilization on the Indian Sub-continent? On what river was this ancient culture home located?

9. What is the oldest religion on the Indian Sub-continent? In what country is it the major religion today?

10. What group of people was placed in each of the four classes of the early Hindus? What was the basis of the division into classes?

11. What is generally considered the most beautiful building in India?

12. Who led the Indian people in their fight for independence? In what year did the Indian people gain their freedom?

13. What was the major reason for dividing British India into two countries? What is the reason for the division of Pakistan?

Learn By Doing

1. The evidence of many historical events can be observed on the Indian Sub-continent. Number the sentences below so that the historical events which are indicated appear in the correct order. Then tell which person or group of people were responsible.

Mohandas Gandhi
Jawaharal Nehru
Turkish Muslims
Moguls (Akbar)
Gupta family
Great Britain
Asoka
Dravidians
Aryans

a. The dark-skinned people of southern India may be descendants of these ancient dwellers of the Indian Sub-continent.

b. A lasting system of roads and railroads was constructed and a central government was established during its time of control.

c. The widespread vegetarianism and the many Buddhist stupas throughout India are the results of this leader's influence.

d. The idea of the class system in India was introduced by this early group of people, known as the Hindus.

e. The people of the Indian Sub-continent gained their freedom through his efforts.

f. These invaders from the north-west brought with them their religion, Islam, and introduced some customs, art, and science.

g. Several Hindu cave-temples remain from this early empire. They are noted for their splendid sculpture and artistic paintings.

h. These northern invaders were responsible for the construction of many outstanding buildings, such as the Taj Mahal.

i. Industry was expanded, agriculture was improved, school enrollment almost doubled, and malaria was almost wiped out, when this leader was in office.

2. Can you identify each item listed below? Make three columns. Select for each a major religion, the nation in which the religion is the strongest, the time when the religion was brought into the area, a religious building, and the symbol of the religion.

a. Hinduism, Buddhism, Islam

b. Pakistan, India, Ceylon

c. oldest in India, began in India, brought by invaders

d. Sanchi stupa, Taj Mahal mosque, Kailasa temple

e. gateways, caves, minarets

3. Write a report on one of the recent leaders of India. In addition to reference books, you may use newspapers and magazines as sources of information.

4. Use the map on page 268 to answer these questions:

a. What are the capitals of India, Pakistan, and Ceylon?

b. What is the name of the government center in East Pakistan? In West Pakistan?

c. What is a leading port on the west coast of India? On the east coast?

d. What is the leading port of West Pakistan? On what sea is it located?

e. What is a trading center near the Khyber Pass?

Test Your Knowledge

1. In what ways is the Himalayan region important to the river valley regions?

2. Describe the climate and the soil of the Deccan Plateau.

3. How do the summer monsoons affect the agriculture of India?

4. Why are there so many cattle in India?

5. In what ways is water drawn from wells for irrigation?

6. How could better seeds and fertilizer, and more dams benefit the Indian farms? How might farmers obtain these?

7. What are some reasons for a short life expectancy on the Indian Sub-continent?

8. What findings of the archaeologists lead us to believe that the Indus River culture home had an advanced civilization?

9. Describe the Hindu belief in a Supreme Being.

10. What is a caste? What is the basis of the caste system? Who were the "untouchables"? What has happened recently to the caste system in India?

11. How will dams and hydroelectric power help the development of industry in India?

12. The Indian government encourages home industry. How does this show that the people of India still do manufacture many of their products? What are some of these handmade products?

CHAPTER 14

A REGION OF MERGING CULTURES

The region of Southeast Asia is an interesting one. It is a region of many kinds of people, of many languages, of many different religions, and of a wide variety of products. It is a region of mountains, valleys, rivers, and many islands, both large and small. Many of the peoples are descendants of people from Japan, China, and the Indian Sub-continent. They have ways of living that are similar to, as well as different from, those of the people in the neighboring culture regions.

SOUTHEAST ASIA

Locate the Southeast Asia Region on the map on page 290. It lies south of China and east of India. It includes both mainland countries and island countries. Four of the mainland countries make up the Indochina Peninsula. They are North Vietnam, South Vietnam, Laos, and Cambodia. Thailand, once called Siam, and Burma are the other mainland countries.

The many islands to the south and east of the mainland make up three countries. They are the Federation of Malaysia, the Republic of Indonesia, and the Republic of the Philippines. These islands are sometimes called the East Indies. Do you know where the West Indies are located? Can you guess why they are both called "the Indies"?

Physical Geography

Notice on the map that the mainland countries of Southeast Asia lie between the 25° North and the 10° North parallels of latitude. Also notice that there are mountain ranges which extend like fingers from the eastern end of the Himalayas south to the countries of Burma and Thailand. Notice the many rivers throughout this mainland region.

As you can see, the island countries of Southeast Asia lie between 20° North Latitude and 10° South Latitude. There is an easy way to remember the physical geography of these countries. Locate Malaya on the peninsula. Although it is on the mainland, Malaya is part of the Federation of Malaysia. This also includes the island areas of Sarawak and

Sabah. Starting with Malaya sweep your eyes east and north. You will find that the Federation of Malaysia and the Republic of the Philippines form a semi-circle around the South China Sea. The Republic of Indonesia includes all the islands which stretch east from Sumatra to West Irian on the island of New Guinea. The major islands are Sumatra, Kalimantan, Sulawesi, and the southern island of Java.

Throughout the islands of this region, mountains and volcanoes are common. This physical feature was also true of Japan. Perhaps the best known volcano in this region is Krakatau, today a small island between the two large islands of Sumatra and Java. During an eruption in 1883, Krakatau exploded. The cone of the volcano was blown off. Tidal waves caused by the explosion drowned 36,000 people on neighboring islands. The noise of the explosion was heard in far off places. Dust from the exploded volcano was carried around the world by winds at high altitudes. This caused unusually brilliant sunsets.

The Pattern of Living

Over 226,000,000 people live on the land of the Southeast Asia Region. One of the regional features of this area is the pattern of living. It is land where people are crowded together on small areas of rich farmland. It is a land where large stretches of land are scantily populated. There are several reasons for this pattern of population. In many areas, the people cannot make a living from the land. There are steep, rocky mountain ranges which stretch across the land. A tropical rainforest that covers much of the region is difficult to clear and quick to grow. Also, because of the warm climate and the heavy rains, many of the soils are leached. They are not as fertile as soils in cooler climates with less rainfall.

Most of the people of the Southeast Asia Region live in the lowland areas of permanent farming. These areas are located in the river valleys and on the lower slopes of the mountains. These lowland areas have better soils for farming. Crops can be grown in the fertile soil.

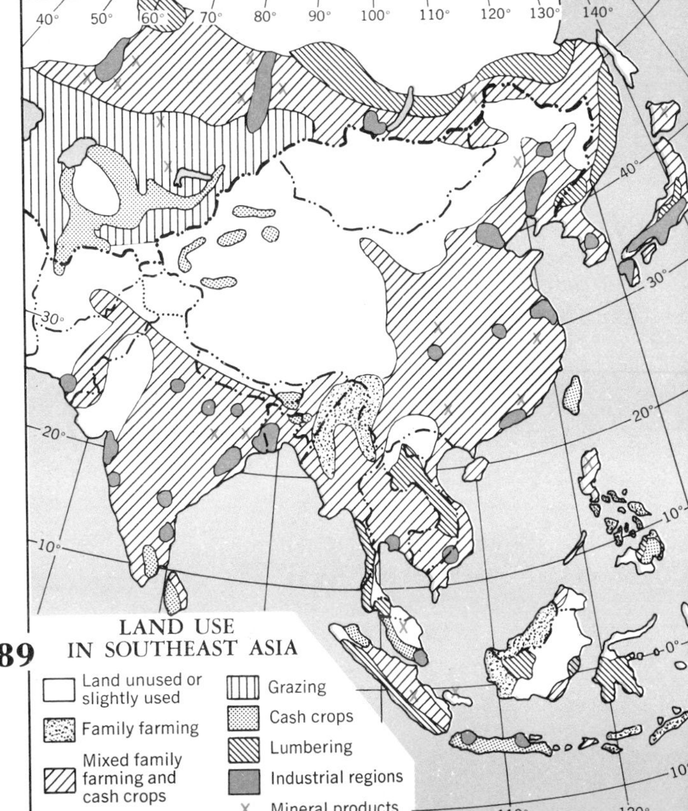

The Southeast Asia Region has many great rivers throughout its lands. These rivers and their system of canals are used for transportation, power for electricity, and for irrigation. Many large cities are situated on the banks of these rivers. Locate Vientiane, Hanoi, Bangkok, and Rangoon on the map below. These cities are seaports or capitals of countries.

On the hills, plateaus, and mountains, some shifting agriculture is carried on by the native peoples. These people plant unirrigated rice, corn, beans, and yams. They supplement their diet by hunting and by gathering food from wild plants. The

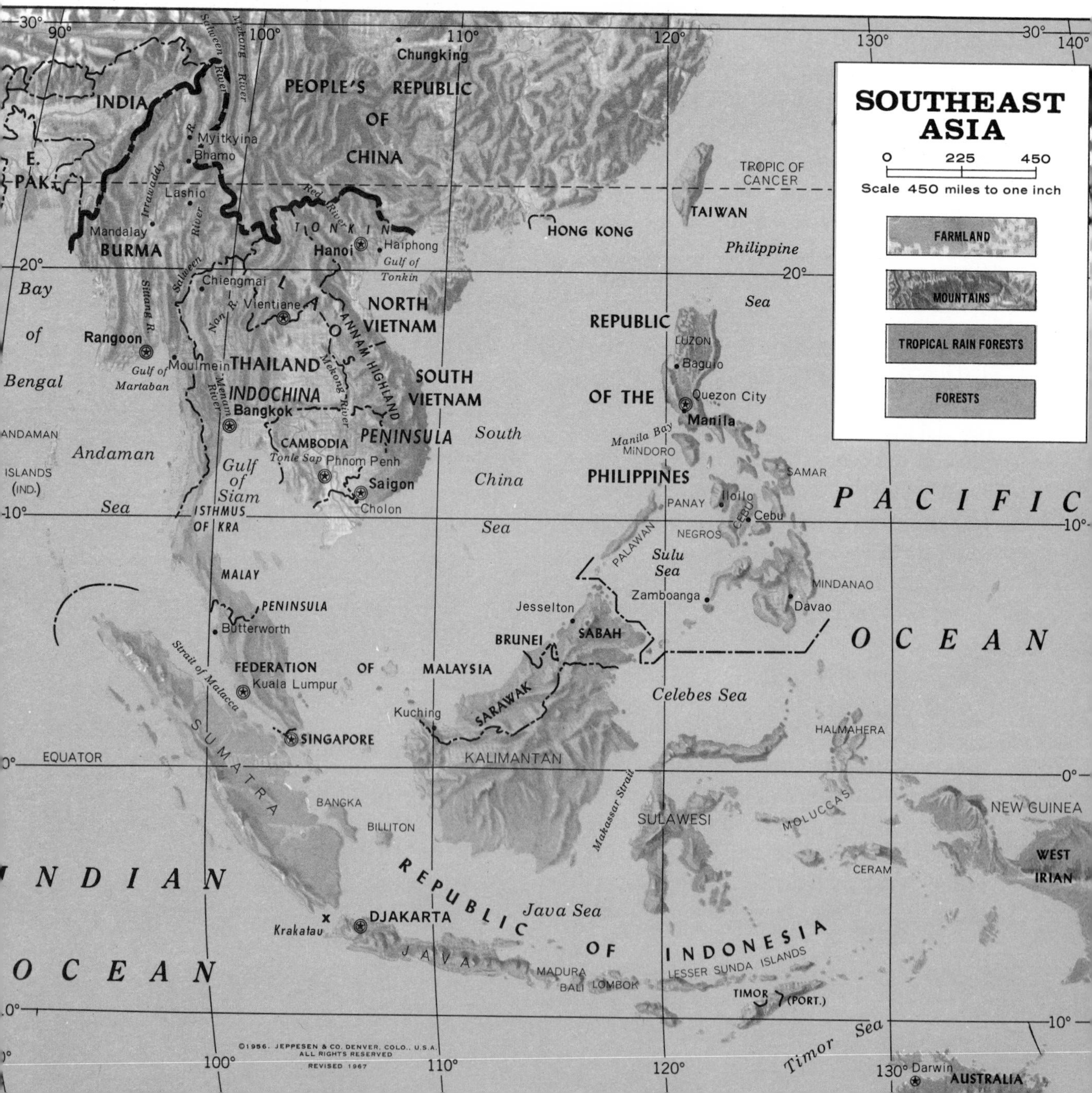

mountain or hill people are often descendants of early peoples who lived along the river valleys and were driven back into the hills by invaders.

One hundred and fifty years ago, only about 10,000,000 people lived in this region. Diseases, such as malaria, were widespread. They strongly affected the size of the population. Modern medicine, improved methods of food production, and hygiene have helped the population increase greatly. Some parts of this region may be nearing the limits which their present agriculture can support. Other areas may be capable of supporting larger populations if forests are cleared, irrigation systems are built, and diseases are further checked.

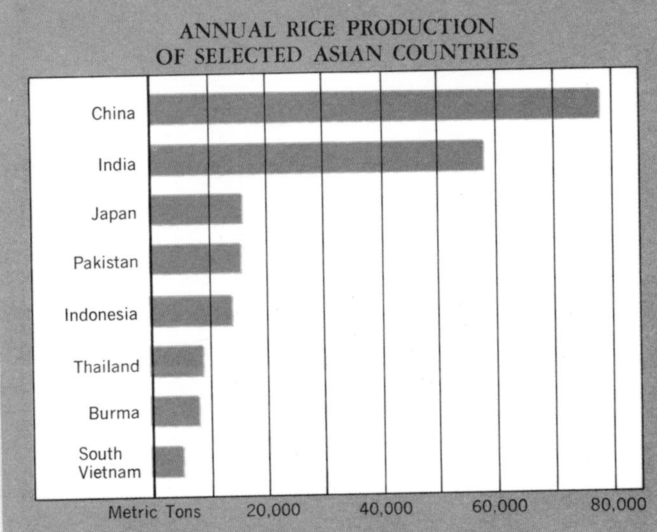

A Basket of Rice

Like Japan, southern China, and parts of India, rice is the main food crop of this region. Rice is grown on four-fifths of all the farming land in Thailand. In North Vietnam there is a region in the delta lands of the Red River called the "basket of rice." In this region, the areas of dense population and the areas where rice is grown are almost the same. Rice is the only crop that can support such a large number of people.

Although not all parts of each country are suited to rice production, each of the countries of this region grows rice. Where rice is grown, the scene is the same throughout Southeast Asia. One sees mile after mile of flooded rice paddies on the lowlands and rice terraces rising up the hillsides. One sees water buffaloes plowing rice paddies, and green, rice shoots rising above the water. These scenes are one of the typical features of this region. They are also scenes that are shared with parts of India, China, and Japan.

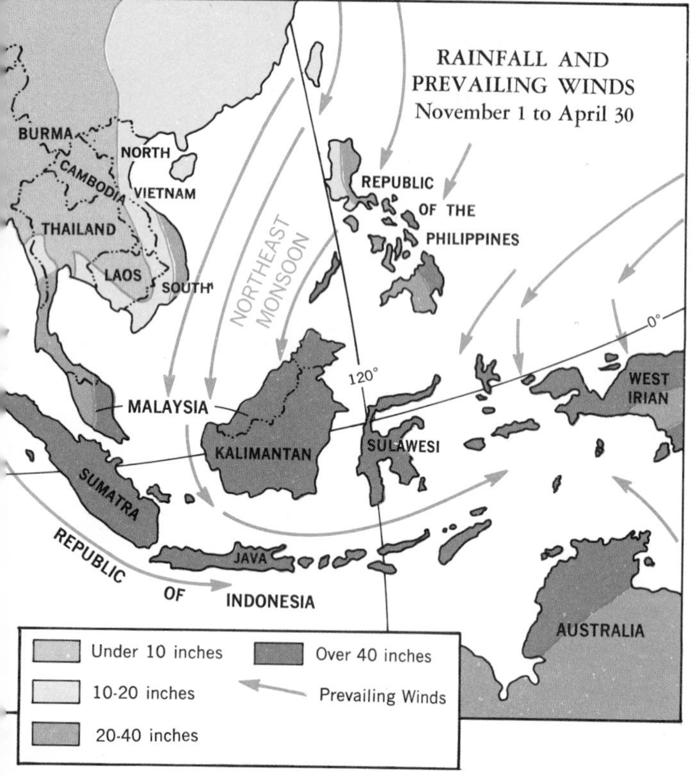

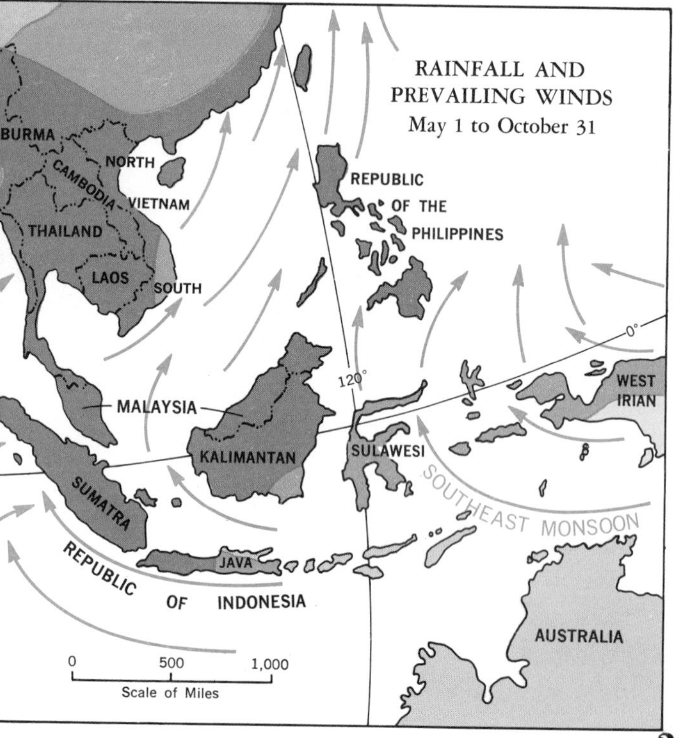

The Climate

Throughout this region there are two types of climate, **tropical monsoon** and **equatorial monsoon.** The mainland of Southeast Asia and the northern parts of the Philippine Islands have a tropical monsoon climate. In lands where the tropical monsoon exists, there is a wet season and a dry season. The islands of Indonesia and of Malaysia and the southern parts of Malaya and the Philippine Islands have an equatorial monsoon climate. In the equatorial monsoon area rain falls throughout the year.

The difference between the rainfall of the tropical monsoon countries and the equatorial monsoon countries can be understood by looking at the maps on this page. You will see that the summer monsoon winds blow from the ocean onto the Asian continent. They bring moisture from the oceans to the land. The winter monsoon winds blow from the land to the ocean. They drop very little moisture as they pass over the mainland. They continue over the oceans where they pick up moisture and drop it as they pass over the equatorial islands and peninsulas in Southeast Asia.

All of Southeast Asia is a region of abundant rain. Rangoon, the capital of Burma, has an average yearly rainfall of 99.0 inches. Singapore has an average annual rainfall of 95.1 inches. Manila, the capital of the Philippines, has an average annual rainfall of 79.6 inches.

An active volcano on West Java.

River traffic in Thailand.

Djakarta, capital of Indonesia.

A market scene in Laos.

Shrimp fisherman in the Philippines.

WOOD PRODUCTS OF THE TROPICAL RAINFOREST

The tropical rainforest is a feature typical of this region. With so much rainfall, it is easy to see why much of Southeast Asia is covered by a tropical rainforest. The forest is very important for the fuel, lumber, and valuable woods it supplies. Few people live in its dense growth.

Bamboo, a treelike grass, is widely distributed throughout the rainforest. It is one of the leading forest products of the Southeast Asia Region. It has many uses. Paper may be made from bamboo pulp. Young, tender bamboo shoots may be eaten. Bamboo is light, yet hard and long lasting. When the inside partitions are removed, the hollow stems may be used to pipe water. Large whole tubes of bamboo are used to support houses and bridges. When split, bamboo is used for roofing and for walls. Many useful articles are made from bamboo. They range from bows and arrows to chopsticks and fishing poles. A large section of bamboo can become a bucket if the partition is left at one end.

Weaving mats from rattan is a profitable skill for many Asians.

Rattan is a climbing vine which is widely used. This strong and flexible material is woven into sidings for buildings, mats, curtains, chair webbing, nets, and fans. Furniture is often made from bamboo and rattan.

The most valuable rainforest tree is **teak.** The teak tree is large. If allowed to grow to its full size, it may be 20 to 25 feet around. A red dye may be made from the leaves. The commercial importance of teak, however, lies in its wood. Teak is a heavy, dense wood. It takes a good polish. It resists fire, rot, and the attack of white ants. It lasts for several hundred years. For these reasons, it is highly valued as a building material and for furniture.

Harvesting Teakwood

Valuable as teak and other tropical hardwood trees are to the market, they are difficult to harvest. Tropical forest trees are not found concentrated in groves but are scattered throughout the forest. The dense undergrowth of the tropical forest

"Jungle bulldozers" remove teak from the rainforest; then huge rafts of logs float down river for processing.

makes it difficult to locate hardwood trees suitable for lumber. Even when found, the thick underbrush may make it difficult to get to a tree and to bring it out of the jungle.

A further problem in harvesting teak is the number of years that it takes for one log to get from the forest to the market. Three or four years may pass from the time a teak tree is selected for lumber until it reaches the market. Part of this delay lies in the fact that a green teak log is too heavy to float. The logs must be dried in order to be light enough to float downstream out of the forest to a market port.

If green teak were cut and allowed to dry on the earth, it might dry unevenly. For this reason teak is dried standing. First, the tree is **girdled**—that is, a ring of bark is cut from the tree. Sap is prevented from rising above the girdle. As a result, the tree dies.

The girdled teak tree is left standing two or three years. At the end of this time it has dried evenly. It is then cut down during the dry season. Elephants are sometimes used to move the heavy logs from the forest to nearby dry riverbeds. In many places today tractors are used instead of elephants to move the logs. When the rainy season arrives, the riverbeds fill with water and the logs are floated to a port. Sometimes the larger teak logs are tied to logs of lighter wood to keep them from sinking during their voyage down the river.

OTHER IMPORTANT PRODUCTS

In addition to valuable wood products from the rapidly growing rainforests, Southeast Asia produces other important crops. Shellac, spices, quinine, copra, and rubber are produced in this region.

A valuable product of this region is **shellac,** a varnish that comes from an insect. The insects feed on the sap of trees. The female insect secretes a dark red substance called **lac** on tree twigs and branches as she feeds. Branches that have been covered with this deposit are gathered. The twigs and branches are crushed, and hot water is poured over the material to wash off the coloring. In the next step the remaining material is melted and strained through heavy cloth. Through this process lac is separated from the wood and purified. Shellac is useful as a varnish, in wax fruits, and in fireproofing. Lac is used in considerable quantities by the phonograph record industry.

Pepper vines are trained to grow on long poles, much like grapes.

Spices

Spices grow best in a warm humid climate with plenty of rainfall. Several areas of this region have such a climate. Before World War II, Indonesia was the major grower and exporter of pepper. Today the Malabar Coast of India grows more of the pepper shrub than Indonesia. It is now the leading exporter.

Another valuable spice, nutmeg, first came from the Moluccas, a group of islands in the East Indies. At one time they were called the "Spice Islands." Nutmeg is the seed of a tropical evergreen tree. The nutmeg tree has been introduced into Brazil and the West Indies.

Cinchona for Quinine

The **cinchona tree** is a native of South America. From the bark of the cinchona tree we obtain **quinine,** a drug used to prevent malaria. At one time South America produced all the cinchona bark. The British and Dutch started cinchona plantations in Indonesia during the last century. These plantations produced a better product than that gathered from trees in the tropical forests of South America. For this reason, Indonesia has become the leading producer of quinine. The need for this natural cure for malaria has dropped sharply since World War II. At that time synthetic drugs, such as atabrine, were developed to control malaria.

Cash Crops

Two major money-making products are copra and rubber. Both of these products are plantation crops. **Copra** is the dried meat of coconuts. The vegetable oil that is pressed from copra is used in making soap, margarine, and shortening. The fiber that remains after the pressing makes excellent cattle feed. The southern Philippines produce the largest amount of copra. Indonesia, Ceylon, and Malaysia rank next, in that order, in the commercial production of copra.

Workers husk coconuts for copra.

Rubber Production

Although rubber can be obtained from many different trees, vines, and smaller plants, the most favored plant is *Hevea Brasiliensis.* As its name suggests, it is a native of Brazil. This tree requires a temperature range between 70° and 90° Fahrenheit and a high annual rainfall. Both of these conditions for growth are present in Southeast Asia. Today 40 per cent of the world's natural rubber comes from Indonesia.

There are several reasons why Brazil, the home of the rubber tree and the first large producer of rubber, lost its market to Indonesia and Malaysia. Rubber in Brazil was gathered from scattered trees in the rainforest of the Amazon basin. Laborers who would gather rubber in this dense region were scarce. Also this region was far from the ocean. The rubber had to be floated or carried by ship great distances to ports.

The British and Dutch did not have these problems of rubber production on their rubber plantations in Malaysia and Indonesia. Labor was available or could be brought in from nearby centers of population. The rubber plantations they started were near easy means of transportation, by sea and by railway. The planting of rubber trees in groves meant that the liquid from which rubber is extracted could be gathered more easily.

Rubber comes from **latex,** a milky fluid which is obtained from the rubber tree by tapping or cutting the bark. Tappings must be made at just the right depth so that only the latex flows from the tree and the layer that provides the lifegiving sap for the tree is unharmed. The tappings are made on a slant so that the latex will flow into a cup placed at the bottom of the cut.

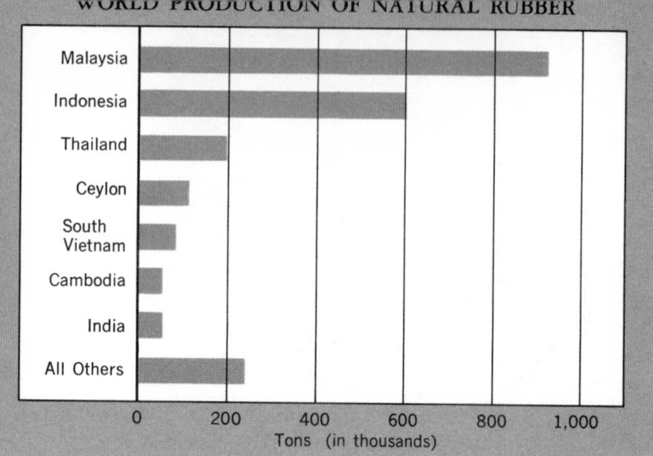

The liquid latex tapped from the rubber tree is processed into sheets, and inspected before being exported to world markets.

The latex that flows from the tree is about 30 per cent rubber. The latex is collected from each cup and placed in larger containers. The large containers of latex are then taken to a factory. There a weak acid is added to the latex. When the acid is added, the rubber quickly separates from the rest of the liquid. The acid helps small globules of rubber to come together, or **coagulate,** into a soft mass. This thickened mass is passed through rollers to remove excess water. It forms into thin sheets that can be dried and shipped.

Rubber Production Changes

About 92 per cent of the world's natural rubber is produced in the Southeast Asia Region. The United States imports one-fifth of the world's natural rubber. It is one of the most useful and widespread products in our country. It is hard to imagine how we could get along without it. We use rubber in tires, hoses, mats, belts, shoe heels and soles, jar rings, rubber bands, and electric cords.

During World War II, the Japanese seized control of Southeast Asia and its supply of natural rubber. The United States, with only a small supply of raw rubber on hand, quickly began to make synthetic rubber. Since the War, the production of synthetic rubber has increased greatly. Synthetic rubber is replacing natural rubber in many products. If this continues, the economies of these rubber-producing countries in Southeast Asia will be in serious trouble.

Tin, An Important Mineral

There are certain minerals which are located in only a few areas of the world. These scarce minerals are found in sizable amounts in these few spots. One of these minerals is tin. Tin is not rare but neither is it abundant. Southeast Asia is one of the world's great tin-producing areas. Twenty per cent of the world's tin is mined on the Indonesian islands of Bangka and Billiton. Can you locate these islands on the map on page 290? They lie east of Sumatra and west of Kalimantan. Great reserves of tin are also found in Burma and on the Malay Peninsula.

Tin is a very soft metal. It is easily worked. It can be spun, drawn, and rolled out into very thin sheets of foil. The common tin can has very little tin in it. The tin can is made from **tin plate,** which is a sheet of steel covered by a very thin layer of tin. This tin layer keeps the steel from rusting.

Tin ore occurs in veins in solid rock or in surface deposits of gravel. Most of the tin ore from Southeast Asia comes from surface deposits. The surface deposits are easy to mine. One of the simplest ways to mine these deposits is by dredging. A floating mining dredge sucks up sand and gravel that contains tin ore. The heavy tin ore is separated from the lighter sand and gravel. The dredge leaves the sand and gravel behind. Such a dredge makes its own pond as it moves through tin-bearing deposits.

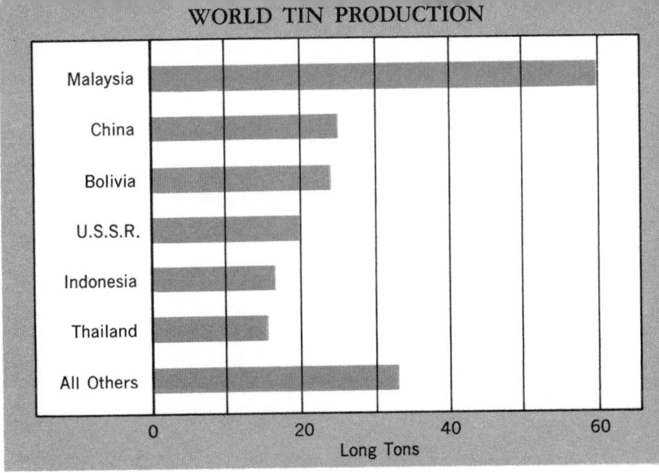

Rows of heavy tin ingots are ready for shipment at Penang, Malaysia.

LIFE IN A CAMBODIAN VILLAGE

The Southeast Asia Region has rubber plantations, coconut plantations, and mines in which men work as laborers. Most of the people of the culture region of Southeast Asia live in villages. These villages are concentrated in the rice-growing areas of the river valleys and of the lower slopes of the hills. Throughout this region, the peasant who lives in a village and who grows rice is the most common human cultural feature. Let us look at how a peasant farmer lives in a small Cambodian village. As you read about Ekavit, remember that his way of life is that of millions like him throughout the countries of this region. Remember also that important differences, such as language and religion, are present. As one goes from one part of a country to another or from one country to another, he will see these differences.

Homes of the Village People

In his Cambodian village Ekavit owns his rice paddy, his garden, and his house. His house stands on poles of mangrove wood driven into the earth. It was built on the poles so that it would be above the floodwaters of the nearby river. The one room house is about ten feet above the ground. Behind the house is a small shed, which is also built on stilts. This shed is used only for cooking.

Both the house and the cooking shed are made entirely of wood. Ekavit's ancestors were wise to separate the kitchen from the rest of the house. Can you explain why?

The Working Day

During the day, Ekavit works in his rice paddies. To help him plow the earth in the paddies and prepare it for growing rice, he uses a water buffalo. As you remember, the water buffalo is well suited to pulling a plow in a muddy, slick field. Ekavit also raises bananas, mangoes, citrus fruits, and coconuts. These, along with fish and some corn, green beans, and peanuts, add to his staple diet of rice.

The peasant's wife, Fuang, takes care of the house. She cooks, sews, and cares for the young children. She also helps her husband in the garden and in the rice fields with the planting, weeding, and harvesting.

Both parents know that one of their important duties is to prepare their son, Aree, for the time when he will live in a temple and study Buddhism. All young men in the Buddhist religion must serve for a period of time as a monk. At the end of his study, Aree will decide whether to remain a monk or to return to the village and become a farmer.

Perhaps the busiest time of the year for the farmer and his family is the time when the rice is harvested. At that time, the entire family becomes very busy cutting, husking, and

A small Cambodian village on the Mekong River is surrounded by flooded rice fields.

cleaning the rice. After the rice harvest, Ekavit drains the paddies of most of their water and plants them with a dry season crop, such as corn.

Life in the Home

Usually, Ekavit and his family eat two meals a day, one in mid-morning and the other in the evening. If the farmer has been working hard in the fields, he will take a bath before eating. The usual meal for the farmer consists of rice and dried fish. The food is placed in bowls on mats on the floor. The family sits on the floor around the bowls for the meal. Between meals, Ekavit and his wife drink tea. When a visitor comes, their first gesture of politeness is to offer the visitor a cup of tea.

At one time or another, Ekavit may fall ill with malaria or dysentery. These two diseases are widespread. The mosquitoes that carry malaria breed in the nearby swamps and rice paddies. They gather under the house where the farmer keeps his animals. He does not have insect poisons to kill the mosquitoes. His house is open so he does not have protection from the mosquitoes.

Ekavit's life is not as hard as the life of some peasants in other parts of the world. He has plenty of rice and fish. In keeping with his Buddhist religion, his wants and possessions are simple. The nearby temple is a center for worship and festivals.

A special day in Ekavit's life is the day of a wedding in the village. Then Ekavit may watch a troupe of traveling dancers entertain. The dancers spend many years learning the movements of the dance. Some of the dances are done in silence. The faces of some of the dancers are masked. Different dancers play the parts of good and bad characters. Pantomine gestures with hands and body are slow and meaningful. The village

Cambodia, like many Asian nations, has seen few changes. Old customs prevail in the countryside; the Royal Palace, too, is a fine example of existing traditions.

people enjoy the dancing and watch with great interest.

There is always entertainment in the village. Ekavit and his son have joined other villagers and formed an orchestra. On some evenings they play for pleasure. At other times they play at festivals. Cambodian music is different from our music. The Cambodian scale has five tones whereas our scale has eight. Melodies are simple and are not written down. If drums are not available, the simple steady beat of the music is carried by handclapping.

Clothing

Both Ekavit and his wife wear a sleeveless shirt and a **panung,** a loose-fitting garment which looks like a long skirt. The panung is made of cloth and is tucked at the waist. For ordinary wear, Ekavit and his wife wear panungs made from cheap imported cotton cloth. But for special occasions they wear cloth that has been handwoven in the village. Fuang's favorite panung has been made in a special way. The heavy silk threads that form the **warp,** or lengthwise threads, are one color. The heavy silk threads that form the **woof,** or cross threads, are another color. When woven together they form a shimmering, solid color. A panung that takes a long time to weave is called the **hol.** The threads of the hol are dyed with different colors before being woven into cloth.

THE MERGING OF MANY CULTURES

Many different peoples have come into the region of Southeast Asia over the centuries. For example, the early inhabitants of Thailand once lived in southern China. They came to live in Southeast Asia after their defeat by Kublai Khan in the thirteenth century. They brought with them the customs and ways of living of the early Chinese people.

Much of the eastern part of the Indochina Peninsula was ruled by the Chinese for nearly a thousand years. The Chinese influence lasted from about the second century B.C. to about the tenth century A.D.

Other peoples came to Southeast Asia bringing their cultures with them. People from Ceylon and India came before the eleventh century bringing their belief in Buddhism. These people were followed by the Muslims, the believers in Islam, who had a great influence on the culture of Southeast Asia. The white people from Europe and the Americas came much later than people from other parts of the world. The influences of peoples from Africa, Australia, Europe, and the Americas can be found throughout this region.

Many races are seen and many languages are heard on the streets of the large cities. There is a mixture of the old and the new in the buildings of these cities. There are new government, education, and trade buildings. There are old mosques, palaces, and merchant shops.

Elaborately decorated temples and sidewalk markets show two extremes of the culture of Southeast Asia.

Religions of Southeast Asia

All the major religions of the world are found in Southeast Asia today. Traces of one early religion, **Animism,** still exist in many parts of this region. Animism is a belief that all objects in the world—trees, rocks, rivers, mountains, and volcanoes—have souls or spirits. Some of these spirits are powerful and bring a man good or evil fortune. Some spirits must be offered rice or incense so that they will look with favor upon the person making the offering.

Some villagers believe in a village spirit that inhabits a tree, a swamp, or a rice paddy. This village spirit may be a kindly one or it may be a fierce one whom no person would dare offend. One must always give it a sign of respect as one passes the tree or the rice paddy where the spirit lives. Even villagers who believe in Islam, in Buddhism, or in Christianity may be careful to seek the favor of the village spirit. After centuries of the influence of other religions, the belief in village spirits has not lost its hold on the villagers in many parts of Southeast Asia. Although traces of Animism linger on in country villages, other religions have become more powerful in the last two thousand years.

Buddhism

Buddhism in various forms is the major religion of most of the mainland countries of the Southeast Asia Region. Buddhism was brought to Southeast Asia by Indian traders and priests.

Buddhist monks or priests play an important part in the life of each villager in Buddhist countries. Each village has a temple which is the religious center of the community. The temple compound, or yard, is called a **wat** in Thailand. Within the wat are shrines, temples, and a school. The wat and the monks who live within it are supported by the people of the village. Festivals are often celebrated within the grounds of the wat. The priests pray at weddings, funerals, and festivals. Sometimes they are the teachers of the young.

Islam

The Islam religion came to Southeast Asia about the thirteenth century. It was spread mainly by Indian traders who were Muslims. Islam became widespread throughout Malaysia, Indonesia, and the southern Philippines. Muslim architecture in Indonesia took on a different form than that found in the Dry World Region. In Southeast Asia, mosques usually lack the dome that is the feature of mosques throughout the rest of the Muslim World.

Christianity

When the Spanish conquered the Philippines, they brought with them Christianity. Over the years missionaries have worked hard to spread the Christian religion. Today, most Filippinos are Christians. The Republic of the Philippines is the only country of Eastern Asia in which the majority of people are Christian. Minority groups of Christians in other countries are slowly growing.

ARCHITECTURAL TREASURES

In Burma, near Mandalay Hill, there are great ancient shrines and beautiful temples. In and around the Buddhist temples, massive statues of stone still stand. The Shwe Dagon is found in Rangoon, the capital of Burma. This famous temple, whose main tower is plated with gold leaf, is often called the "Golden Pagoda." It is over two thousand years old. Buddhists from all over Asia come to worship at this temple.

Farther east, in Cambodia, we find the ancient city of Angkor Thom and the nearby temple of Angkor Wat. Angkor Thom was the capital city of an early civilization which lasted from the ninth to the fifteenth century. Angkor Thom was surrounded by 30 foot walls that enclosed a city of five square miles. Here, more than a million people lived. Many of the stone monuments, statues, and carvings still stand within the city walls.

The great temple of Angkor Wat rivals the pyramids of Egypt in magnificence. This great massive temple is in the form of a terraced pyramid topped by five towers. It is over two hundred feet high. It is faced with blocks of sandstone that are covered with carvings. Scenes from myths, daily life, and wars are captured in stone. Figures of gods, humans, kings on elephants, chariots, archers, lions, and monkeys are carved out of sandstone in endless number. Angkor Thom and Angkor Wat form one of the wonders of the world.

Two of the wonders of Asia's ancient religions are the Buddhist temple of Shwe Dagon and the Hindu Wat and its statues in Angkor Thom.

The City That Was Lost and Found

Angkor Thom was lost to history for centuries. The story of its disappearance and rediscovery is a fascinating one. Angkor Thom was abandoned in the mid-fifteenth century when it was conquered by enemy people. In the tropical climate of Southeast Asia, nature quickly covered the abandoned city and its great temples. Trees and vines began to cover the courtyards. They grew in cracks in the walls of buildings and between the blocks of carved sandstone. In a short time, the temple and the city had been swallowed up by the rainforest.

About a hundred years ago, a French botanist discovered the ruins. As he made his way through the jungle, he noticed an oddly shaped clump of trees. Pushing aside the leaves, he saw that the roots and trunks of the trees were growing around great carved stones. French archaeologists began to uncover the ruins in 1907. They have cleared the dense growth that covered the ruins and have restored many of the buildings. Today, the buildings at Angkor Thom and Angkor Wat are national treasures of Cambodia and are pictured on the stamps of that country.

Another architectural treasure from the past is the stupa of Borobudur in central Java. This great Buddhist temple was built during the eighth century. About 400 carved Buddhas and miles of carvings decorate this temple-mountain. The quality of its carvings matches that of Angkor Wat.

Borobudur, on Java, is outstanding because of the high quality of its carvings of Buddhist texts.

GOVERNMENT IN SOUTHEAST ASIA

With the exception of Thailand, all the countries of Southeast Asia have at one time been under the rule of Western powers. It was the Western powers that laid the beginnings of roads and railways. They helped to establish commercial crops, such as copra and rubber. They began the development of mineral resources, such as oil, silver, tungsten, tin, and lead. In some parts of the region they laid the foundations for school systems. When the countries of Southeast Asia demanded freedom at the end of World War II, they faced the task of governing themselves and solving their own problems. Only the Philippines had a background in self-government. All the other new countries faced great problems.

A large harbor is important to the independent island of Singapore.

Problems of Self-Government

Some of these countries have the problem of supplying enough food for rapidly growing populations. Other countries grow more than enough food for their own needs, but could grow more through the use of improved agricultural practices. For example, thousands of small dams and lakes have been used for centuries. However, they were used mainly for irrigation, as "fish farms," and to check erosion. Only recently have large dams been planned. These large dams will serve many purposes. The flow of the waters of the great rivers will be made more even. The danger of disastrous flooding will be lessened. Electrical power will be manufactured. With this inexpensive power source, factories and industry will develop.

To build dams and industries and to check disease, the people of these countries need capital, or money. What can they sell to get the necessary capital? These countries have many products needed by the rest of the world. They are rich in tin, tungsten, titanium, and manganese. Copper, silver, and gold may be exported as well as used at home. Rich deposits of oil underlie parts of Burma and the islands of Indonesia. Petroleum is in demand throughout the world. The tropical lands of Southeast Asia can grow several money-making crops. These are rubber, rice, tea, copra, tobacco, sugar, and spices. Special products are made in

Minerals from Malaysia, and bananas and salt from the Philippines are some of the important exports from the islands of Asia.

this region from teakwood, bamboo, and rattan. Articles made from these woods, as well as from ivory, brass, and bronze, can be marketed.

Money is not the only answer to the problems faced by the people of this region. Education and peace are necessary to the progress of Southeast Asia. The new countries face the responsibility of providing education for all children. New schools and more teachers are needed. Teachers are needed to prepare scientists, technicians, and additional teachers.

Communism in Southeast Asia

Today the people of Southeast Asia are in the center of changes and problems. Some problems arise because of "outsiders." Chinese, Russians, Americans, Indians, and some Europeans are placing pressures upon these countries to follow certain views.

Communist China has supported the growth of Communist groups within many of the countries of Southeast Asia. These groups have tried to overthrow the governments of a number of the countries and set up Communist governments. North Vietnam has a Communist government. Other countries, such as Cambodia, Laos, and Indonesia, claim a neutral attitude—that is, they favor neither the Chinese Communists nor the Western powers. It is believed, however, that in these countries there are strong Communist movements.

Fragments from a Communist grenade broke the photographer's camera as he took this picture of an American helicopter landing in a Vietnamese village.

South Vietnam, which is supported by the United States, has had great difficulty in preventing the Communists from taking over its government. In 1963 the Federation of Malaysia was formed from many smaller territories. The newest nation in this region, it is strongly pro-Western in its government. Its formation was strongly opposed by Indonesia's President Sukarno. When Sukarno was stripped of most of his powers, Indonesia's attitude changed and it ceased its opposition to Malaysia.

It will take many years to know whether the countries become Commusist or not. The answer will depend in part on how well the non-Communist governments can guide the economic development of these countries. If they can help the people produce more food and other goods needed for better living, the people will have less desire to turn to Communism.

The Future of Southeast Asia

This region of the world has an important role to play in the affairs of the world family of nations. Its history is rich in art and architecture. Its people have deep inner values of family life and religion. Its physical land base can supply the world with products that cannot be obtained elsewhere in such large quantities.

Now that these areas are no longer colonies, the peoples of this region want the respect of people in the remainder of the world. They are anxious to progress. They are anxious to be independent and to be accepted as developing countries making progress in their own right.

Do You Know?

1. What are the two peninsulas which make up the mainland region of Southeast Asia?

2. What name is given to the island countries of Southeast Asia?

3. What physical feature found in Japan, and able to destroy many lives, is also found on the islands of Southeast Asia? Which island is the most well known?

4. What are the three island countries? What is the mainland area which is part of an island country?

5. Why do most of the people of this region live in the river valleys or on the lower slopes of the mountains?

6. What is the major crop of the populated areas of Southeast Asia? What are the two major money-making products?

7. Because of the abundant rainfall, what important vegetation region exists in Southeast Asia? What is the most valuable tree of this region?

8. What important product is obtained from the cinchona tree? For what is this product used?

9. What two nations produce the largest amount of rubber? Which nation produces the most tin?

10. What has caused economic trouble for the rubber-producing countries?

11. What is the oldest religion in Southeast Asia? Which religion is probably the youngest?

12. What is the major religion found on the mainland countries? On the islands?

13. What is the name of the ancient capital of Cambodia which was lost for centuries?

14. Which country was never under the rule of a Western power? Which country had some experience in self-government when it gained its freedom?

Learn By Doing

1. Select the correct words to complete each sentence. Be sure to read each sentence carefully.

a. The Southeast Asia Region includes both ________ and ________ countries.

b. The majority of the population live in the ________ valleys and on the lower ________ slopes.

c. Two types of climate are the ________ monsoon and the ________ monsoon.

d. Two spices which come from the tropical areas of Asia are ________ and ________.

e. Two major cash crops of Southeast Asia are ________ and ________.

f. Two kinds of rubber are ________ and ________.

g. Two diseases which are widespread in this tropical area are ________ and ________.

h. The ________ and the ________ are the chief rivers of Vietnam.

i. The ________ and the ________ are two famous temples in this region.

j. ________ archaeologists have searched and found ancient treasures in Southeast Asia.

2. Select the product from group **B** which will most likely be made from each raw material listed in group **A.**

A

copra oil	tin
cinchona	lac
shellac	teak
rubber	copra
bamboo	latex
coconuts	rattan

B

house roofing	rubber
furniture	chairs
quinine	tires
varnish	cans
soap	oil
shellac	copra

3. Using the map on page 290, locate the countries of North Vietnam, South Vietnam, Laos, Cambodia, Thailand, and Burma. For each country name the capital and the river on which it is located. Explain why the location of these cities is important.

4. Study the newspapers and magazines to find mention of the countries of Southeast Asia. Tell whether the countries are free, under communist control, under the control of a Western power, aided by a Western power, aided by a Communist power, or a combination of the above.

5. Describe the food, clothing, and shelter for a village farmer in Southeast Asia. Include his customs, his values, and a description of his way of life. Add drawings and photographs.

6. Write a report or prepare an oral report beginning with one of these sentences. In preparing your report think about special places, important uses, and the value of the products.

a. Bamboo, one of Southeast Asia's most useful products, is ____

b. Rattan, a climbing vine, is ____

c. Teak, though difficult to obtain, is ______

d. Tin, a very soft metal, is ____

Test Your Knowledge

1. What are the major reasons for the pattern of living of the people of this region?

2. What are the major reasons for the "population explosion" in Southeast Asia? What needs to be done to help these many people?

3. Study the maps on page 292. Describe the difference between the equatorial monsoon and the tropical monsoon.

4. Explain why it is difficult to harvest teak.

5. Is the tin can really made of tin? Explain.

6. Explain why the rubber market has moved from Brazil to Southeast Asia.

7. Why was the region of Southeast Asia called Indochina?

8. Describe Angkor Thom and Angkor Wat.

9. From what areas did the early settlers of these lands come? What groups of people later settled in these lands? Explain the statement, "Southeast Asia is a region of various cultures."

10. What improvements did the Western powers make on the lands and economy of Southeast Asia?

11. What problems are faced by the governments of the recently established nations of Southeast Asia?

REVIEWING PART 4

Do You Remember?

1. What is a monsoon? How much of Eastern Asia is affected by the monsoons?

2. What is a delta? Which rivers have large deltas in Eastern Asia?

3. What is a staple crop? What are the two staple foods of Eastern Asia?

4. What is a cash crop? What are some of the cash crops of Eastern Asia?

5. Who is the Dalai Lama? How has the power of the Dalai Lama changed in recent years?

6. What is the major way of life of the people of China's sub-regions? On what animals do they depend? How do the people adapt their living to the dry, rugged land?

7. Where is the Khyber Pass? By whom has the pass been used?

8. What is a continental climate? In what area of Eastern Asia would it most likely be found?

9. What is meant by a riverine culture? In what areas of Eastern Asia would it be found?

10. What is a civil war? What were the results of the civil wars in China and India?

11. Which nation or region of Eastern Asia is being described below?

has the largest population?
has a large fishing industry?
contains the highest mountains in the world?
has many populated river-valley cities?
has a very high standard of living?
is noted for its rainforest products?
needs rapid improvements in agriculture?
was once a possession of the United States?
is changing from agriculture to industry?
is the second largest in the world?
is very highly industrialized?
has most people living in or near cities?
has many people living on boats?
hopes to be able to remain neutral?
was once a possession of Great Britain?

Projects and Reports

1. Write a short story pretending you live in a monsoon climate region. Describe some of the differences between the winter monsoon and the summer monsoon. Give a description of the area in which you are located, the types of crops you grow, and the effects of the rains on the growing season.

2. Select your favorite nation of the Far East. Find information about the people of this nation. Carefully report on each of the following topics: housing, clothing, education, religion, and government.

3. Can you find out the name of a leader who was important in the development of these nations?

Nationalist Taiwan	North Vietnam
Mainland China	Indonesia
Pakistan	India

4. The past, and especially the ancient religions, play an important role in the lives of the people of Eastern Asia. Describe how the values and the customs of the people are influenced by the past. How have the ruling powers tried to weaken the importance of the past?

5. Give the location of each item listed below and tell why it is important.

Mount Everest	Mount Fujiyama
The Red Basin	Tropical Rainforest
Taj Mahal	Loess Highlands
The Great Wall	Angkor Thom

6. Use the Appendix to answer the following questions about Asia.

a. Which island country is the largest?

b. Which mainland country of Southeast Asia has the largest population?

c. Which city in Southeast Asia has the largest population?

d. What are the two largest countries in the world?

e. Which two countries have the largest populations?

f. Would India, China, or Japan be more crowded?

g. What are three countries with a population of approximately 100 million?

h. What is the smallest country?

i. What country has the largest population per square mile?

j. Which city is the most heavily populated?

k. Is Japan or the Philippines larger?

Using Maps and Globes

1. What is the approximate distance from the most northern to the most southern part of Japan?

2. What is the difference in height between Mount Everest and Mount Fujiyama?

3. What two mainland countries lie on a peninsula west of Japan?

4. What desert exists in Mongolia?

5. What major rivers have their deltas at Peking, at Shanghai, and at Canton?

6. What range of mountains is on the Tibet-Nepal border?

7. What is the major landform feature of Tibet?

8. What are the water boundaries of the Indian peninsula?

9. What are the three major rivers of the Indian Sub-continent?

10. Approximately how far apart are East and West Pakistan? Bombay and Calcutta?

11. Where are Nepal, Sikkim, and Bhutan located?

12. What are the four major seas to the east of China?

13. Which island country is within the same lines of latitude as most of the mainland countries of Eastern Asia?

14. Name a line of latitude which passes through most of Indonesia.

15. What parallel of latitude separates North Vietnam from South Vietnam?

16. What continent lies south of the islands of Southeast Asia?

17. Tell the direction you would go when traveling from Singapore to Hong Kong. From Manila to Tokyo. From New Delhi to Rangoon.

18. One can travel from Hanoi to Saigon by sea or by land. Through what bodies of water or through what countries would one travel on the shortest route?

19. Locate Indonesia. Describe the yearly rainfall periods.

EUROPE AND THE UNION OF SOVIET SOCIALISTIC REPUBLICS

PART 5

The Union of Soviet Socialist Republics is the largest country in the world. It is also one of the most powerful. The U.S.S.R. stretches from the region of Eastern Europe to the Pacific. It lies partially on the continent of Europe and covers the northern half of Asia.

The U.S.S.R. or the Soviet Union, as it is often called, is a land of many different peoples and languages. The regionalizing characteristic of the U.S.S.R. is the Communist Party which controls the government of the country. The Communist Party directs and controls the lives of the millions of people that live in the vast territory of the Soviet Union.

One of the regionalizing characteristics of Europe is its diversity. It is a region of many languages and countries. It is a region of heavy manufacturing and intensive agriculture.

The people of Western Europe inhabit a fortunate "standing place." It is a region with a mild marine climate and a variety of soils. It is a region that lends itself readily to many types of agriculture. It is a region with many different minerals in the soil.

The people of Europe have made the most of their natural resources. Even the inhabitants of the less favored "standing places" have taken advantage of their physical environment. People of regions that lack coal and gas have turned to mountain streams for hydroelectric power. The Dutch have reclaimed land from the sea by an extensive system of dikes, and are turning it into valuable farming land.

If we used types of government as a basis for regionalizing Europe, we would find two major divisions. One region would be composed of the non-communist countries of Western Europe. The other would be the Communist countries of Eastern Europe. This division is a sharp one. It is symbolized by the wall that divides East Berlin from West Berlin.

Western Europe is important to the people of the United States as the cradle of our Western culture. Our language and the foundations of our arts, laws, religion, and government were transmitted from Europe. Europe is the culture home of North and South America.

CHAPTER 15

THE SOVIET UNION

A large nation stretches from Eastern Europe to the Pacific Ocean. For many centuries this region was known as Russia. The eastern section was often called Siberia. On this vast stretch of land were masses of peasant people ruled by a few rich nobility.

About fifty years ago the region became known as the Union of Soviet Socialist Republics, or the Soviet Union. A red flag with a hammer and sickle flies over this country which is ruled by a Communist government. Great advances have been made in industry but the people have gained few personal liberties in the process. The progress of the Soviet Union depends upon the development of its resources and the ways in which they are used.

THE WORLD'S LARGEST NATION

The culture region of the Union of Soviet Socialist Republics is the largest country in the world. In order to grasp the size of this region, study a globe or a world map. Look at all the land which rises out of the water. The U.S.S.R. makes up one-sixth of all the land on the Earth. The nation stretches from the Arctic Ocean in the north to the Black and Caspian Seas and China in the south. It extends from the Baltic Sea in the west to the Pacific Ocean in the east.

The U.S.S.R. is equal in size to Canada, the United States, and Mexico combined. The distance from the city of Riga near the Baltic Sea in the west to Cape Dezhnev near the Bering Strait in the east is about 7,000 miles. The distance across this nation is more than twice the distance across continental United States.

Another way to grasp the size of the Union of Soviet Socialist Republics is to look at the differences in time between Riga and Cape Dezhnev. When it is seven o'clock in the morning at Riga, it is about six o'clock in the evening at Cape Dezhnev. In the United States there is only a three-hour difference between the west and the east coasts.

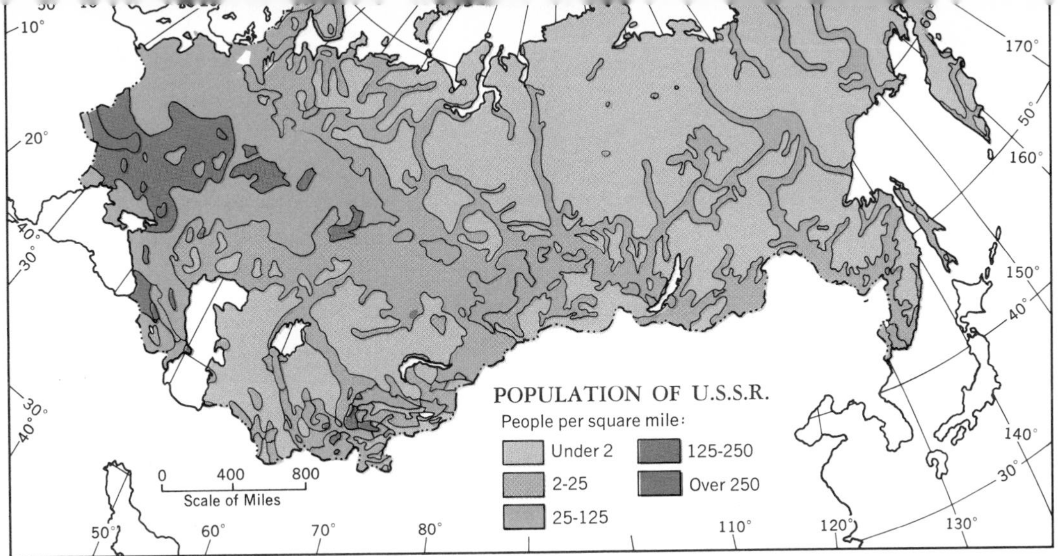

A Land of Many Peoples

The U.S.S.R. is one of the richest countries in the world. It has great reserves of petroleum, iron ore, precious minerals, coal, timber, agricultural land, and people. Over 234,000,000 people live on this vast expanse of territory. This nation places third in the world in size of population. Only China and India rank above it. Most of the people in the Soviet Union live west of the Ural Mountains. This low range of mountains is often used to separate the continent of Europe from the continent of Asia.

There are many different groups of people living in the U.S.S.R. The term "Russians" refers to one group of people who speak the Russian language and have similar customs and habits. Such a group of people is called an **ethnic group.** There are fifteen different major ethnic groups in the Soviet Union. Russians, Ukrainians, Tartars, Armenians, Germans, and many others make up the population. They have many different customs, habits, and languages. The fifteen republics of the Union of Soviet Socialist Republics are named for the fifteen major ethnic groups that live within them.

The Union of Soviet Socialist Republics had its beginning in the area called Russia. For this reason, the terms *Russia* and *Russians* are sometimes used to mean the U.S.S.R. and all its citizens. In their correct use, they mean a certain part of this nation and a certain ethnic group of people.

THE DEVELOPMENT OF RUSSIA

We do not know the exact time or place which marks the beginning of the Russian people. Most scholars believe that the earliest men and women of Russia were Slavs, the largest group of people in the U.S.S.R. today. They are believed to have settled in the marshy forest sections of what is now Western Russia. This is the area where the Great Russians, White Russians, and Ukrainians, all descendants of the Slavs, live today. Locate this area on the map on pages 326–327.

The early Slavic people were mainly hunters. They moved continually about the country. Such movement was easy because much of Western Russia is a level or gently rolling plain with many rivers. Two of the great rivers in this early Slavic land were the Dnieper and the Dvina.

Just as this vast plain was easy for the early Russians to cross and recross, so it was easy for other groups to enter Russia. They came from several directions. Nomadic invaders came from the lowlands east of the Caspian Sea and also from the northwest. The first invading tribesmen from the east, the Finns, held some control over Southern Russia for a while. However, the invaders from the northwest, the Northmen, or Vikings, made the greatest imprint upon Russia.

The First Russian State

The Vikings were interested in trading with the rich cities of Baghdad and Constantinople in the Byzantine Empire. The easiest and most direct routes to these cities for the Vikings lay through the lands of the Eastern Slavs. Roving bands of Vikings, called the Varangians, traveled along the rivers from the Baltic Sea to the Black Sea. In the land of the Eastern Slavs, the Vikings gathered furs and honey and wax. Sometimes they captured the Slavs and made them slaves. They traded these slaves for the money and fine goods

Vikings used the Dnieper as a route to Constantinople, where they marveled at the magnificent Church of Hagia Sophia.

of Baghdad and Constantinople. In time, the Vikings gained control of the country of the Slavs. The Viking leader, Rurik, established a kingdom here. When he died, his kinsman, Oleg, became ruler. He set up his capital at Kiev. The first Russian state grew from this settlement at Kiev, about half way between the Baltic and the Black Seas.

The Vikings affected the Slavs in two ways. First, they organized the Slavic territory into a fairly tight unit by seizing control of the towns. This nation was called Kievan Russia after its leading trading city, Kiev. Second, they encouraged trade between the land of the Slavs and the outside world. New goods and ideas came into Kievan Russia. The main trade routes through Kievan Russia ran north and south along the rivers that emptied into the Baltic Sea and into the Black Sea.

Some Viking warriors from Kievan Russia entered into the armies of the Byzantine emperor at Constantinople. These warriors from the swamps and forests of Kievan Russia marveled at what they saw in Constantinople, the capital of the Byzantine Empire. They could not help but compare this city of one million people with the small villages of their homeland. Their forest huts seemed crude compared with the splendor of the magnificent marble palaces and the great **hippodrome** of Constantinople. The hippodrome was an oval building for horseracing and chariot races.

The greatest wonder of Constantinople was the Church of Hagia Sophia. Its main dome was 102 feet in diameter. Its interior was covered with marble and gold mosaic. As the Viking warriors attended the church services at Hagia Sophia, they were greatly impressed by the building, the singing, the incense, and the solemnity and majesty of the service. Many of the Viking warriors and traders returned to Russia as Christians.

The Byzantine Influence

Late in the tenth century, the leading Russian prince, Vladimir, sent 6,000 warriors to aid the Byzantine emperor. In return, the emperor promised Vladimir the hand of his sister Anna in marriage. Vladimir was baptized a Christian and was married to Anna. When he returned to Kiev, Vladimir brought with him Anna and some Christian priests. Vladimir ordered all people subject to his rule to be baptized as Christians.

Some of the influences from Constantinople that Vladimir and other Russians brought back with them can be seen in Russia today. The Russians adopted the religion of the Eastern Orthodox Church and modeled their churches after those in the Eastern Roman Empire. Christian missionaries devised an alphabet for the Russians that was based on the Greek alphabet. Portions of the Bible were translated into the Slavic language and written in the new alphabet.

But the period of Kievan Russia was a time of unrest. Russian princes fought with one another and against the enemies that surrounded them. They fought against Finns in the north, Lithuanians on the Baltic, and Muslims to the south.

The Mongols Conquer Russia

Early in the thirteenth century a new influence came from the east. The Tartars, Asiatic horsemen under the rule of the Mongols, swept out of central Asia into Russia. The Russians were not prepared to meet the fierce invaders. The Tartars struck during the winter when the rivers were frozen. At this time of the year, the Tartars could cross the rivers as easily as they could cross the endless plains. The invaders from the east rolled westward in one wave after another. In a short time most of Western Asia and part of Europe were overrun by the Mongol armies. They conquered Russia, Poland, and Hungary. Cities that refused to submit to the Tartars were wiped out. By 1240, all Russian lands were either conquered or forced to pay tribute.

The Tartar armies became known as the Golden Horde. This name may have come from the splendor of the tent or camp of the Mongol leader, Batu Khan. Batu Khan was a grandson of Genghis Khan, the Mongol conqueror of China.

Russia remained under Mongol rule for 250 years. But Tartars did not colonize Russia. They lived as nomads, leaving many Russian princes as rulers. The Russian princes paid taxes and gave homage to the Tartars. The Tartars were pagans who ruled over Buddhist, Muslim, and Christian subjects. The Tartars allowed their subjects to follow the religion of their choice.

The Growth of Moscow

During the time that Russia was ruled by the Golden Horde, the city of Moscow grew in importance. It became an important center of the fur trade and began to widen its control over surrounding territory.

By the time Ivan the Great became the Grand Duke of Moscow (1462–1505), the Empire of the Golden Horde had broken into **khanates,** separate kingdoms each ruled by a khan. Ivan continued the policy of widening Moscow's territory. He conquered the rich city of Novgorod. He freed Moscow from the Tartars by refusing to pay tribute.

Ivan the Terrible ruled the Russian people with an iron fist.

Ivan the Terrible

The grandson of Ivan the Great became the Grand Duke of Moscow in 1533 and had himself crowned as tsar in 1547. **Tsar** is the title given to a Russian emperor or king. Ivan the Terrible, as he is called in history, seized the territory of Kazan, east of Moscow in 1552, and the territory of Astrakhan, southeast of Moscow in 1556. In seizing these territories from the Tartars, Ivan began an expansion of Russia to the east which did not stop until the Russians reached the Pacific.

The expansion of Russia into eastern Asia probably came from the wish to control the northern Asian lands, which were a rich source of furs. Fur traders took the lead in pushing eastward in search of game. During the nineteenth century, the Russians even established forts in Alaska and California that served as fur-gathering centers.

Ivan the Terrible increased the power of the tsar over the nobles. He did this in a very unusual way. In 1564, Ivan left Moscow and went to live at Alexandrovsk. He took with him his treasure, his bodyguard, and his army. Ivan sent a message to the nobles and priests in Moscow. He accused them of working against him. For this reason, he said, he was leaving his throne. He sent another message to be read aloud to the common people. In this message he said that he had no quarrel with them. He was only sad at the treason of his nobles

and priests. By the second message, Ivan made sure that the common people were on his side.

The nobles and priests in Moscow had no choice. They knew Ivan had taken an army with him. They did what Ivan expected. They sent a delegation to Ivan to beg him to return to the throne. Ivan said that he would return to the throne if he were given the right to execute or ban people he thought were traitors. He was also to be given the lands of anyone judged a traitor. Ivan became absolute master of Russia.

Ivan earned his title, the Terrible, by his very cruel treatment of the Russian people. During his rule the system of serfdom grew. Living conditions for the poor people, or serfs, were among the worst anywhere in the world. Serfdom in Russia lasted well into the nineteenth century. You remember that serfdom ended in most of Western Europe during the thirteenth and fourteenth centuries.

When Ivan the Terrible died, he was succeeded by his weak-minded son, Fyodor. This was the beginning of many years of unrest for the Russian people. Fyodor left no heirs to the throne. When he died, the national assembly elected his brother-in-law, Boris Godunov, as tsar. During his reign, there were threats of revolution from within the country and invasions from without the country. It was not until the late 1600's that the life of the Russian people began to improve. At this time, a new royal family took over. Peter the Great was a member of this royal family, known as the Romanovs.

Peter the Great, Catherine the Great

Peter became tsar in 1682 at the age of ten, although his sister Sophia ruled for him until he came into power in 1698. Eight years later, the young tsar decided to visit Western

Europe. He became the first Russian tsar to do so. During his travels through Western Europe, Peter visited Holland and England. He looked at factories, mills, and museums. While in England, Peter studied English shipbuilding, went to the theater, and even visited the House of Peers.

Peter returned to Russia convinced that his country should be modernized in several ways. He ordered the establishment of a permanent army. He ordered the construction of canals, roads, and ships. He ordered the members of his court to wear Western dress. He commanded the men of his court to shave off their beards. He reformed the calendar and the alphabet and made himself head of the church. Peter the Great fought and won a war with the Swedes. Through this war Russia gained land bordering on the Baltic Sea.

Peter thought that the capital should be closer to Western Europe. He hired Italian and French architects to plan a new city. This new city, St. Petersburg, was built in the marshes near the Baltic Sea. The classical buildings designed by Peter's architects make St. Petersburg one of the world's most beautiful cities. Peter made the new city the capital of Russia. Except for a brief time after his death, St. Petersburg remained the capital until 1918 when Moscow again became the capital. In 1914 St. Petersburg was renamed Petrograd. In 1924, the name was changed to Leningrad.

The many reforms of Peter the Great changed life in Russia greatly.

Peter was an unusual man in person and in the things he did. Peter was nearly seven feet tall. He was a skilled bootmaker. A pair of large boots that he made for himself are on display in the Moscow Museum. Peter had little formal schooling. He did not fully understand all the things he saw in Western Europe. He established some factories and ordered serfs to work in them. He ordered a tax to be placed upon each serf. Each peasant landlord was ordered to collect the tax. In this way Peter made the practice of serfdom even stronger. The peasants became even more closely bound to the land and the landlord.

Under Peter, the tsar became even more powerful. Tsar, government, and state became one. In the years following the reign of Peter, there were many attempts to overthrow the powerful tsars. These attempts were not successful. The **autocracy,** or the unlimited control, of the tsars continued with little change until 1917. Some of these Russian rulers continued the reforms begun by Peter. Catherine the Great came to the throne in 1762. She continued the attempts of Peter to westernize Russia. She introduced French culture and improved the education of the nobility. She also drew up a constitution for the country. This would have given many freedoms to the people but she never put the constitution into effect. This was due to a number of events, the most important of which was an uprising of the serfs in the area of the lower Volga River. Catherine put down this revolt but she feared another one. She decided not to extend freedom to the people.

Winter Palace, home of the tsars, was built in Leningrad by Peter the Great.

Catherine enlarged the territory of Russia. She gained new lands in the south and west. In wars with Turkey, Russia gained valuable lands on the Black Sea. Catherine joined with the Austrian and German rulers in wars against Poland. This led to the division of Poland. Russia gained the largest share of Poland at the end of these wars.

Years of Unrest

During the hundred years following the reign of Catherine, Russia experienced many difficulties. Napoleon's army invaded Russia in 1812 and Moscow fell to the French. Russian patriots burned the city, and Napoleon was forced to abandon it. In his winter retreat from Moscow, Napoleon lost many men and supplies. It was not until 1815 that a coalition between Russia, Austria, Germany, and Great Britain was able to defeat Napoleon.

In 1825, a group of discontented nobles and guardsmen revolted against the government. This revolt was put down. Tsar Nicholas I came to the throne at this time. He was a very cruel ruler. He executed the leaders of the revolt and exiled the other rebels to Siberia. Nicholas persecuted students, stopped publication of newspapers, forbade foreign travel, and tried to rid the country of all progressive thinking.

Alexander II succeeded his father, Nicholas I, to the throne in 1855. In contrast to his father, he was a reformer. In 1861, he freed the serfs and provided land for them which could be paid for over a period of 49 years. He established legislatures to carry on a representative government at the local level.

There were other reforms, but they were not enough to satisfy the discontented people. Secret revolutionary societies were formed to spread ideas opposed to the government. In 1881 Alexander II was killed, but the people were not successful in their revolt. Once again the people were persecuted. It was not until 1917 that the rule of the tsars was successfully overthrown.

The Revolution of 1917

Unrest in the Russian lands came at a crucial time in world history. Russia had entered World War I in 1914. Russia fought on the side of Great Britain and France against Germany and Austria-Hungary. She entered with a large army but suffered defeat after defeat. Poor leadership, lack of ammunition, and shortages of food and clothing were causes for the Russian difficulties.

By 1917 the Russian people were completely dissatisfied with conditions. A revolution broke out in Petrograd (Leningrad) on March 8,

The 1917 uprising brought about the arrest of many tsarist officials.

1917. The revolt began innocently enough in a bread line. Women and boys were standing in long lines waiting for bread. Upon being told that there was no bread, the people raised a cry demanding bread. In the next few days, several riots broke out. Factory workers went on strike.

The experienced soldiers were in the front lines of the War. The soldiers called upon to restore order in Leningrad were "green" and inexperienced. Many refused to fire at the mobs. The government of Nicholas II, unable to control the rioting, collapsed. A temporary or provisional government stepped in, but failed in its attempt to keep order. Unrest continued. The people were more interested in social reforms than in continuing in the war. Workers and soldiers organized into groups, or councils, called **soviets.**

Russian Soviet Federal Socialist Republic	**6,593,391 sq. mi.**
Estonian S.S.R.	**17,413 sq. mi.**
Latvian S.S.R.	**24,695 sq. mi.**
Lithuanian S.S.R.	**26,173 sq. mi.**
Byelorussian S.S.R.	**80,154 sq. mi.**
Ukrainian S.S.R.	**232,046 sq. mi.**
Moldavian S.S.R.	**13,012 sq. mi.**
Georgian S.S.R.	**26,911 sq. mi.**
Azerbaidzhan S.S.R.	**33,436 sq. mi.**
Armenian S.S.R.	**11,306 sq. mi.**
Kazakh S.S.R.	**1,064,092 sq. mi.**
Uzbek S.S.R..	**158,069 sq. mi.**
Turkmen S.S.R.	**188,417 sq. mi.**
Tadzhik S.S.R.	**54,019 sq. mi.**
Kirghiz S.S.R.	**76,642 sq. mi.**

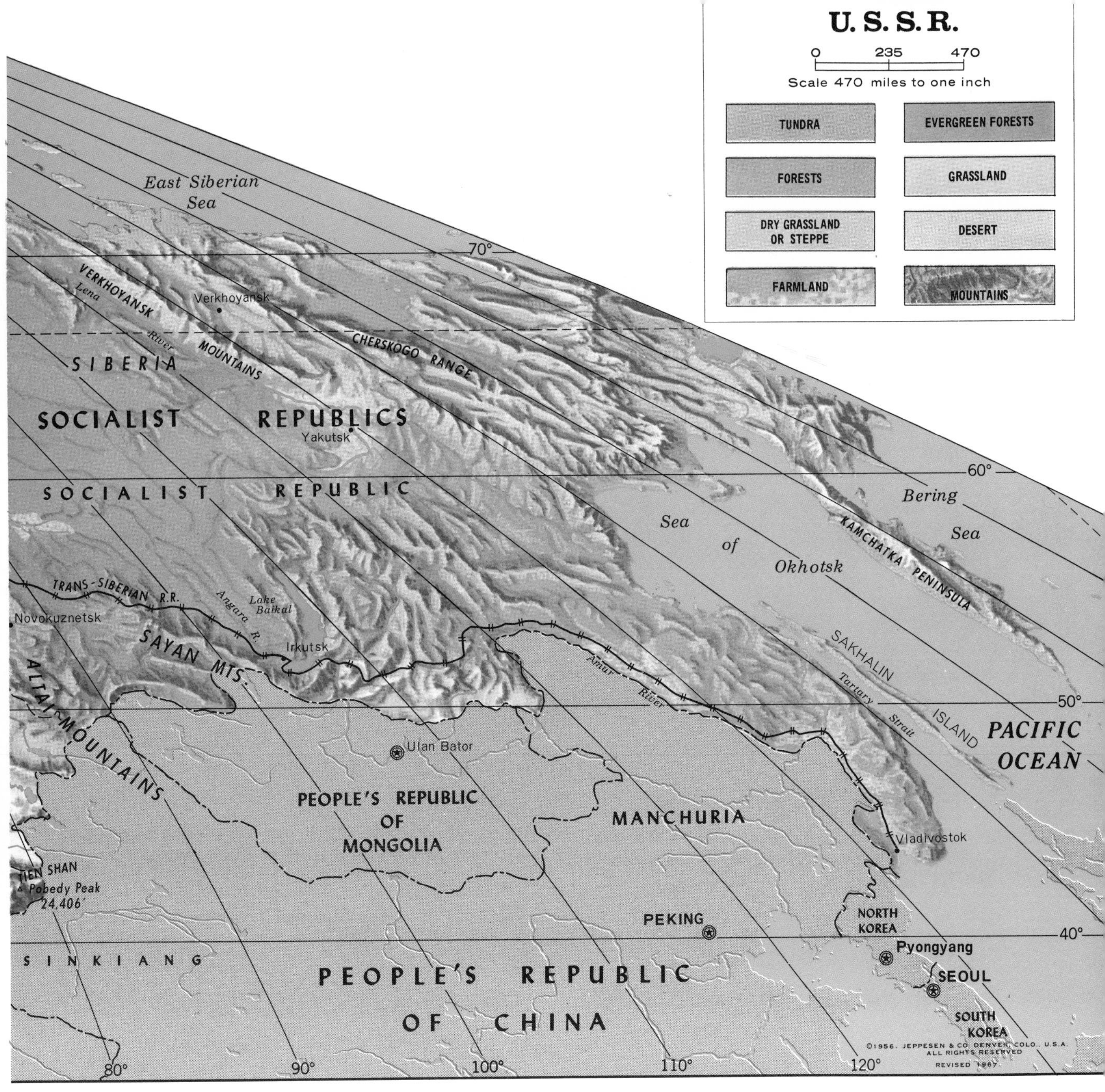

The Union of Soviet Socialist Republics was established in 1922 with four republics: the R.S.F.S.R., Ukrainia, Byelorussia, and Transcaucasia. In the 1920's three republics (Tadzhik, Uzbek, and Turkmen) were established in central Asia. In 1936 Transcaucasia was divided into the Azerbaidzhan, Armenian, and Georgian Republics. The Soviet Union also gained the Kazakh and Kirhiz Republics. In 1940, during World War II, the nation spread to the west. Four republics (Estonia, Latvia, Lithuania, and Moldavia) were added and Byelorussia and Ukrainia were enlarged.

The Supreme Soviet meets in the Grand Kremlin Palace in Moscow.

THE COMMUNIST PARTY AND THE U.S.S.R.

A group of people calling themselves **Bolsheviks** took over the leadership of the important soviets. By seizing control of the soviets, the Bolsheviks seized control of the country. The Bolshevik party, led by Nicolai Lenin, later changed its name to the Communist Party. The Communist Party, which seized control of the government in 1917, continues to rule the Soviet Union today.

The Government of the U.S.S.R.

The people of the Soviet Union are governed by two organizations, the Communist Party and the government. The Communist Party is the only political party in Russia. It has great power. The Party determines the policies of the country. The government puts the policies of the Party into action. The Party supervises and controls all the activities of the government. The leader of the Communist Party, or Party Chairman, is the leader of the Soviet Union.

The Council of Ministers forms the executive branch of the government. This is the real government of Russia. The Council consists of the premier, the deputy premiers, 25 to 50 ministers, and the premiers of the 15 republics. The Communist Party selects the members of the Council. Often the leader of the Communist Party is also the premier and dictator of the government of the Soviet Union.

The Supreme Soviet is the legislative branch of the government. It is made up of 1500 representatives elected by the people once every four years. The Supreme Soviet is composed of two chambers. One is the Soviet of Nationalities. The different republics and the principal subdivisions are represented by the members of this chamber. The other chamber is the Soviet of the Union. It is made up of representatives elected on the basis of one representative for every 300,000 people.

Only one candidate runs for office in each election district. He must be approved by the Communist Party. The Party encourages every voter to vote unless he is ill. Even though there is no choice but to vote for the candidate selected by the Party, nearly all of the voters go to the polls and vote for this official candidate. By this action they show their approval.

The Supreme Soviet meets in the Kremlin, the ancient fortified section of Moscow, once or twice a year. Sessions last only three or four days. During this time, the Supreme Soviet hears speeches on the budget and other government matters. It automatically approves any decisions and laws made by the Council of Ministers and the Communist Party.

The Supreme Soviet elects a Presidium to take care of legislative matters between sessions. The Presidium consists of a president, secretary, 15 vice-presidents, and 16 other members. It makes laws when told to do so by the Council of Ministers. Although the president of the Presidium is considered the chief of state, he has little or no power. Real power resides in the Communist Party chairman who usually serves as premier.

Governing the Republics

The Communist Party controls the local government in each of the fifteen republics. Each one of the republics has a Supreme Soviet much like the one elected for the nation. The Supreme Soviet in each republic appoints a Presidium and a council of ministers to manage the government of the republic. Like the national Union government, the local Supreme Soviets are a governing body in name only.

For many years, the secret police played an important role in enforcing the power of the Communist Party. It kept down political opposition by its very harsh treatment of anyone who opposed Party policies. People who opposed the Party were often sentenced to death or to exile in Siberia, without the benefit of an open trial. After 1953 the secret police began to lose their power. In 1955, the government declared that no citizen should be sentenced without a trial in open court. This was an important step forward. By 1960 the secret police was abolished. However, the Russian people still do not have the freedom that we in the United States consider our basic right.

The Communists did away with all other political parties and brought all of Russia under their control. The leaders of the Communist Party believe that they know best what is good for the country. They believe that the good of the state comes before the good of the individual. They have maintained their control of the Soviet Union even though only about one-fifth of the people are members of the Communist Party.

Five-Year Plans Improve the Country

When the Communist rulers came into power, they were determined to make sharp changes in the ways of living of the Russian peoples. The leaders of the Communist Party were determined to make the U.S.S.R. the most powerful country in the world. They knew that the Soviet Union would have to become an industrial nation if it were to become powerful. They passed laws putting all factories, lands, and mines under government ownership. Private ownership was abolished.

The new government established a series of Five Year Plans to change the nation. These plans called for careful planning in every part of economic life. They set forth the roads to be built, the canals to be dug, and the railways to be laid. They called for the development of the iron and steel industry. The Five Year Plans set quotas for factories as to the amount and type of goods to be produced. Farmers were told what and how much to plant.

Collective Farms

The farmers were reluctant to turn over their lands, crops, and animals to the government. The government tried hard to force all farmers to join **collectives.** A farming collective is a group or community of farmers whose land, animals, and crops are shared in common and are not owned by individuals. Many peasants killed their animals and burned their crops rather than turn them over to the government or share them in collectives. By 1940, however, almost all of the farmers of the Soviet Union had joined collectives.

The Kolkhoz and the Sovkhoz

Today in the U.S.S.R. there are two types of farms. One type of farm is the **kolkhoz,** or collective farm. The farmers or workers who belong to the kolkhoz work the land together. The land is owned by the government. Under the kolkhoz system of farming, the government buys the crops produced by the kolkhoz.

From the age of seventeen, each member of a family belonging to a kolkhoz is required to work a certain number of days each year. Each worker is paid according to the number of days he has worked and the type of labor he has done. Skilled workers receive higher pay than unskilled workers. The chairman of the kolkhoz, a government official and a member of the Communist Party, is the highest paid worker.

Until recent years, heavy farm machinery, such as tractors and harvesters, was owned by the government. The kolkhoz had to pay cash or crops for the use of these machines. In 1958 this practice was ended. Each kolkhoz can now own and operate its own machinery.

Another type of farm is the **sovkhoz,** or state farm. The sovkhoz is owned and run by the government. It is used as an experimental farm to test new methods and new fertilizers for farming. Laborers who work on the sovkhoz are paid wages just as factory workers are. The government receives all the crops raised on the farm.

Workers on both the sovkhoz and the kolkhoz live in villages. They are allowed to have a plot of ground behind their houses for their own use. On the private garden plot, each farmer may raise garden vegetables and keep a fixed number of farm animals. There is no limit to the number of fowl or rabbits that each farmer may keep.

Government Owned Industries

In the Soviet Union the government controls all industries. It owns nearly all the industries, but allows a few to be owned by **cooperatives.** A cooperative is an organization in which all the members share the profits or losses. The government decides what should be produced, how much of each item should be produced, and which types of industries should be built. Each factory, however, is organized much like those in the United States. People who work in the factories have many different jobs, such as salesman, office worker, plant manager, foreman, and laborer.

Women play important roles in the Soviet plan of collective farming, both as advisors at the professional level, and as workers in the field.

Providing adequate housing and improved medical care for her people are problems that the Soviet Union shares with other countries.

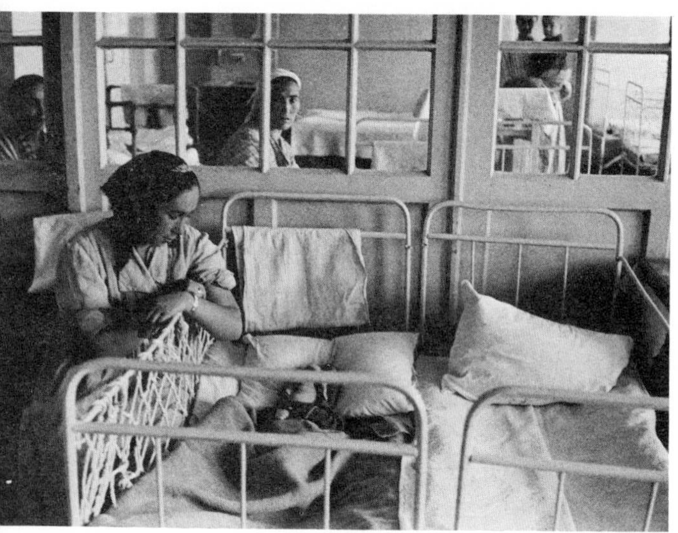

Perhaps the best way to describe the Soviet economy is the word *planned.* It is planned in detail in all areas controlled by the government, such as housing, banking, farming, industry, and foreign trade.

Medical Care

The government provides each citizen with free medical care. The Ministry of Health is in charge of medical research and the preparation of doctors and nurses. It controls the manufacture of drugs, the manufacture of medical supplies and equipment, and the building and running of hospitals.

The U.S.S.R. is divided into medical districts. In rural areas, there is one medical district for every six thousand people. In the city, there is one medical district for every four thousand people. Each district has a chief medical officer who is in charge of the health of the people in his district. Clinics have been established in most of the villages.

Housing

The government controls all the land and owns most of the housing. Some land is leased to individuals for building private houses. There has been a housing shortage in the Soviet Union. There are two reasons for the shortage. During World War II, in the areas overrun by the Germans, almost half of the housing was destroyed. Also, since the Russian Revolution, there has been a great expansion of industry which has caused a population shift to the cities. Housing has not kept up with the rapid expansion of industries and the growth of cities in some areas.

In the cities, three families may live together in an apartment. Where families live together, each family has one room to itself. Each family shares the kitchen and bathroom with the members of the other two families. The more important a citizen is, the greater the likelihood he will be assigned his own apartment.

Future power and progress lie in advanced research, encouraged and controlled by the Soviet government.

Progress of the Communists

Many of the ways of thinking of the Soviet people and their leaders came to them from ancestors different from ours. Very few Western European cultural developments, such as language, religion, family life, art, architecture, and education, were adopted by the Russians. Even farming methods were Russian methods. The southern, eastern, and some northern peoples of the world contributed to Russia's fund of knowledge.

Only in more recent years have ideas of industry, science, commerce, and transportation come from the so-called "Western World." They have been developed rapidly in the Union of Soviet Socialist Republics. The Soviet Union still has a long way to go to achieve conveniences and luxuries for all her people. Her engineers and scientists are trying their best to develop the Soviet's powers and resources very fast. All the world hopes that it can be done without conflict with the other countries nearby and throughout the world.

NATURAL REGIONS OF THE U.S.S.R.

The U.S.S.R. is much too large to study as one geographic region. We will look first at the different natural regions of the country. We will see that these regions are based on the climates, landforms, and vegetation of the region. We will then study the most important region of the U.S.S.R., the area of greatest manufacturing, farming, power, and population.

A Continental Climate

The Union of Soviet Socialist Republics is located in the far Northern Hemisphere. It has, for the most part, a **continental climate.** That is, it has a wide range of temperature because the large land area is not influenced by nearby oceans. Most regions of the U.S.S.R. experience long, cold winters and short, warm summers. Let us see why.

Find the U.S.S.R. and the United States on a map or globe. Notice that the main northern boundary of the United States is the 49° parallel of latitude. Where does the major part of the Soviet Union lie in relation to the same parallel of latitude? You will note that Canada and the U.S.S.R. lie north of the same degree of latitude. You can expect to find similarities in climate, natural vegetation, crops, and animals between the U.S.S.R. and Canada.

Although the Soviet Union has a wide range of climates, the general feature of the climate is its low temperatures. The eastern part of the U.S.S.R. has some of the lowest, monthly average temperatures ever recorded outside of Antarctica. Verkhoyansk is one of the coldest towns in the world. In January the average temperature there is 59 degrees below zero. In February, 1892 the temperature plunged to 90 degrees below zero. Three hundred miles to the south at Yakutsk, July temperatures average 66 degrees above zero, but January temperatures average 46 degrees below. How do the people plan their wardrobes when the temperature changes a total of 112 degrees? What can be planted and expected to grow in such a climate? Is this likely to be a manufacturing or an agricultural area? Do you think many people live in this area?

Causes of the Climate

As you recall, water does not lose or gain heat as rapidly as land. The ocean tends to keep islands or lands near the coasts less warm in the summer and less cool in the winter than lands far from the ocean. The continental climate of the Soviet Union results from the fact that moisture from nearby oceans does not reach much of the large land area. Most of the Soviet Union has a rainfall of less than twenty inches a year.

The Indian Ocean is far to the south of the U.S.S.R. Its moderating effect is reduced by the chain of high mountains and plateaus that are near the southern boundaries of the Soviet Union. In the east, highlands also act as a modifier of warm winds from the Pacific Ocean. Warm winds from the Atlantic Ocean and the Mediterranean Sea have the greatest influence on the southwestern sections of the vast plains. They have less and less influence on the temperature the farther away from the Atlantic one goes. East of the Ural Mountains, the effect of warm winds from the west is slight.

The low, flat plains of the Soviet Union stretch to the Arctic Ocean. There is no land barrier to masses of air from the Arctic in the north. But during the winter, the interior of the U.S.S.R. is an area of high atmospheric pressure. That is, it has a heavy cold air mass above it. Winds tend to flow out of this region rather than into it.

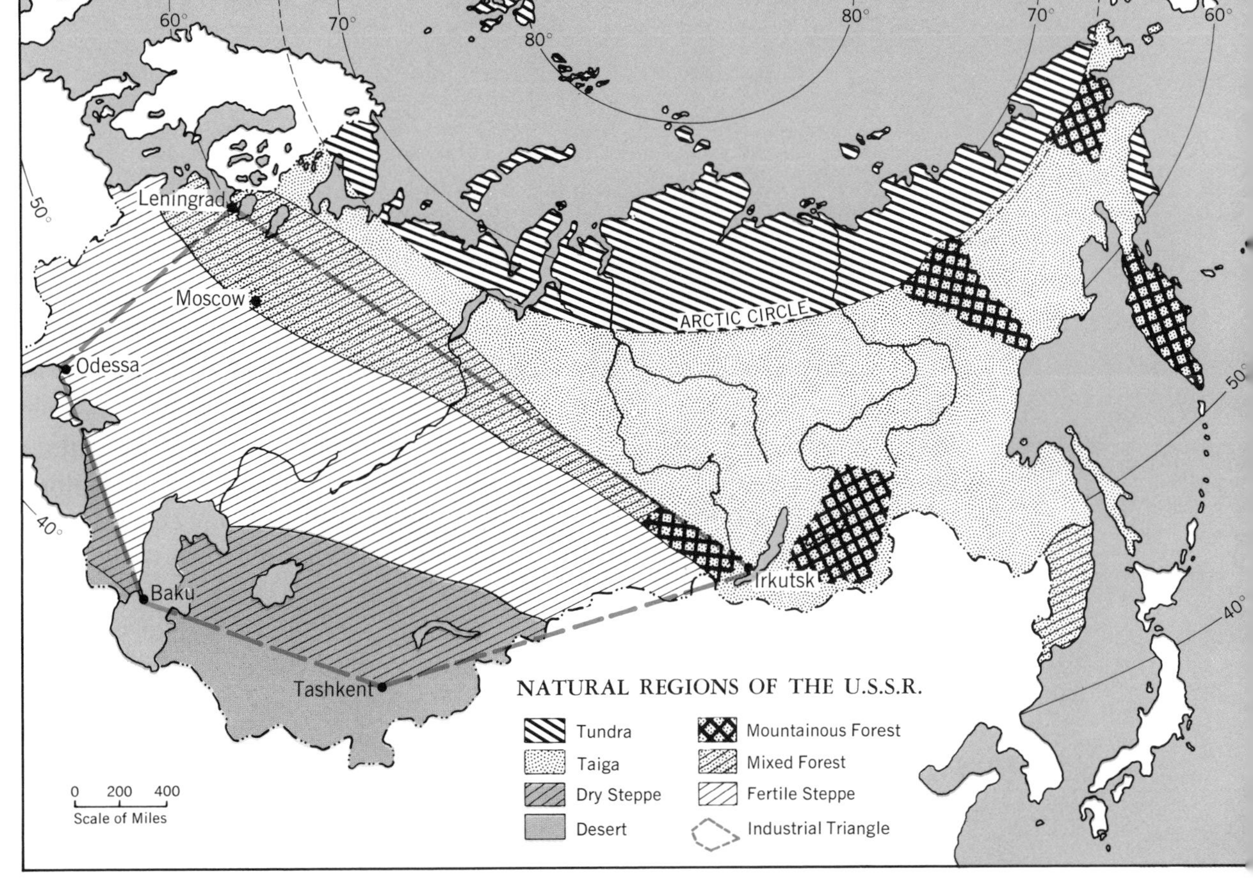

Warmer climate and good soils make the area outlined on the map a productive and heavily populated region.

The Arctic is not an important source of moisture for the Soviet Union. Most of the Arctic Ocean is frozen. Thus, the cold winds in the region contain very little moisture. Even in Central Siberia the major source of rain is the Atlantic Ocean, not the Arctic Ocean.

Both rainfall and temperature have a definite effect upon the type of vegetation that grows in an area. By looking at the vegetation of a region, a scientist can often tell much about the type of weather in the region. You have seen in earlier chapters how high year-round temperatures and heavy rainfall combined to produce the tropical rainforest. You have also seen how the intensity of the sun's rays affects the warming of the Earth. The U.S.S.R. is too far north of the Tropic of Cancer, the northernmost point at which the sun's rays strike the Earth vertically, to be affected by it.

The U.S.S.R. has five major climate zones or belts, particularly in the western part of the country. These natural zones run west to east. Locate them on the map above. As you cross them north to south, you meet in turn the tundra zone, the taiga zone, the mixed forest zone, the steppe zone, and the desert zone.

Huskies and reindeer are among the few animals hardy enough to survive in the harsh climates of the tundra and taiga regions.

The Tundra

The **tundra** is a narrow belt of treeless land bordering the Arctic Ocean. It is a zone of scanty vegetation, a land of mosses, lichens, and scrubby bushes, such as birch and willow. The sub-soil remains frozen throughout the year. This frozen sub-soil is called **permafrost.** In the summer, the frozen sub-soil prevents the drainage of water from the surface. The swampy surface of the tundra serves as a breeding ground for swarms of mosquitoes.

The yearly average temperature of the tundra zone is below 50 degrees. Even in the summer the land suffers the danger of frost. The summer growing season is from two to two-and-one-half months. Although the growing period is short, summer days are long. The long days of sunlight make up somewhat for the shortness of the growing season.

Animals found in the tundra zone are the reindeer, the lemming, and the arctic hare. The lemming is a mouselike rodent. The arctic hare is an animal with longer hind legs and longer ears than the rabbit. Two valuable fur animals, the arctic fox and the ermine, also live in the tundra zone. Ermine are members of the weasel family that take on a coat of pure-white fur during the winter. Only the tip of the tail remains black.

The tundra region is sparsely settled. Many of the people in the region earn their living from developing the natural resources of the area. Murmansk, the only ice-free port along the northern border, is an export center for fish, fur, lumber, and mineral products.

The Taiga

The **taiga** is a swampy forest area in which **conifers** are the principal trees. A conifer is a cone-bearing evergreen tree. Included among the coniferous trees are pines, larch, spruce, fir, and cedar. Some broad-leaf trees, birch and aspen, also grow well in this region. In the northern part of the taiga, the forest trees are too stunted and twisted to be used as lumber. Trees are taller and larger in the southern part of the taiga. The southern part of the taiga zone is one of the world's great lumber sources. Archangel, the largest city in the taiga zone, is the main lumber center in the Soviet Union.

The climate of the taiga belt differs from that of the tundra only in that the summer growing season of the taiga is slightly longer and warmer. One to four months of the year have an average temperature above 50 degrees. But there is still little farming in the taiga because the summers are short and the soils are poor. The main animals are elk, reindeer, bear, rabbit, and fox.

Great rivers, such as the Lena, the Yenisei, and the Ob, flow northward through the taiga and the tundra to the Arctic Ocean. These rivers are frozen for many months during each year. The ice and snow in the upper regions of these rivers melt before the northern or lower regions of the rivers thaw. Great floods result.

The Mixed Forest

The third great climate or vegetation zone of the U.S.S.R. is the **mixed forest zone.** Together the taiga and the forest regions form the largest continuous forest area in the world. The forest zone contains both the evergreens of the taiga and **deciduous** trees, trees that shed their leaves. The deciduous trees in this zone are oak, walnut, elm, maple, and beech. The mixed forest zone has a milder climate than the taiga. Its soils are more fertile, and its rainfall is slightly higher. Lumbering and farming are important industries. Moscow, the capital of the Soviet Union, is located in the mixed forest region.

Mixed forests, the source of valuable lumber, are scenes of natural beauty.

The Steppe

The **steppe** is a region of level plains used for farming and grazing. This vegetation belt has warmer summers, a longer frost-free season, and less rainfall than the mixed forest zone. For the most part the steppe region is treeless and covered with grasses.

The Ukraine is an important food-producing area of the steppe region.

The black, fertile earth in this region has a special Russian name, **chernozem.** It means "black earth." Similar soils in other parts of the world are also called chernozem soils. This rich black earth is one of the world's best crop growing soils because the grasses and their roots decompose into a rich humus. The rainfall in this region is not heavy enough to leach or drain away the plant food from the soil, but it is enough to grow crops. The steppe region is used for growing wheat, sugar beets, barley, rye, potatoes, sunflowers, and food for animals. Rainfall varies yearly so that harvests are often unpredictable.

For thousands of years, the steppe region was the home of nomads. Pastoral peoples moved about the grasslands with their flocks and herds. Rainfall in the steppe region, often too little to support trees, is enough to grow grasses. The grasses are used as feed for grazing animals, and these in turn are used as food for the nomads. The U.S.S.R. government has preferred to turn over the steppe soils to farming rather than keep them entirely in grazing. It has urged the nomadic people to work on the collective farms that have been created.

The Desert

The **desert** region has scanty vegetation. During the spring, short-lived grasses and flowers grow. The typical vegetation is scattered shrubs with wide-spreading roots. Sage and wormwood are the common shrubs. Winters are short, but very cold. Summers are very dry and hot.

The five major climate zones merge one into the other. Fingers of the taiga reach into the tundra. Pockets of the tundra may be found in the taiga. The mixed forest zone gradually becomes less wooded as one approaches the steppe. Streams that rise in snow-clad mountains provide irrigation waters for the desert.

The Mountains

Most of the people of the Soviet Union live in the west. Two reasons for this are the nearness of these lands to the European nations and the fairly level surface of the land. A close study of the map on page 327 will show you that the lands to the east have a more broken surface. About one-third of the entire nation is made up of high, rugged terrain. How many mountain ranges can you locate? The rivers that flow through many of these mountain ranges do not form valleys that can easily be settled. Many rivers are surrounded by high rock walls. This is especially true of the upper parts of the rivers.

While the eastern mountains are like a jumbled mass of hard rock, there is a single chain of mountains in the south. The Caucasus Mountains extend from the Black Sea to the Caspian Sea. The people must travel close to the sea along the edges of the mountains. Passage over the mountains can only be made with difficulty. The mountains form a strong political boundary for the Soviet Union. There is only one north-south pass that cuts through the center of this range of mountains. An all-weather road has been constructed 7,800 feet high.

Another chain of mountains, the Urals, have been used to divide the Soviet Union into east and west regions. These mountains extend north-south along the 60° East longitude line. The land east of the Urals is often called Siberia.

Each of these mountain areas has both created problems and provided benefits for the people of the Soviet Union. Transportation and the spread of people, objects, and ideas have been prevented. But where people have ventured forth into these more distant lands, minerals and farmlands have been found. Coal and iron ore have been obtained from the eastern mountains and the Urals. The snowfields and rivers of the Caucasus Mountains provide water for great irrigation farming projects.

Few people live in the lonely desert region or on the dry plains at the foot of the Caucasus Mountains.

THE INDUSTRIAL TRIANGLE

The most important region of the U.S.S.R. is the Industrial Triangle. Using the map on page 335, locate the borders of this important region. Place your finger on the city of Irkutsk near Lake Baikal in Siberia. Follow the line northwest to the city of Leningrad on the Baltic Sea. From Leningrad trace the line south to Odessa on the Black Sea. The third imaginary line is not exactly straight. In connecting Odessa with Irkutsk, trace the line southeast to Baku on the Caspian Sea, east to Tashkent, and then northeast back to Irkutsk.

Within this region live three-fourths of the people of the U.S.S.R. This is the nation's "heartland," the pulse of its population, industry, and agriculture.

Farming in the Industrial Triangle

There are three farming belts within this rough triangle. See the map on page 335. The first begins in the west near the cities of Kiev and Odessa. It extends east towards Irkutsk nearly 3,000 miles. This is the region of the chernozem, the rich black earth. This region supplies the U.S.S.R. with wheat, rye, oats, and meat from farm animals. It is also a major source of supply for the great industrial centers of the area.

The second farming belt lies to the north of the first one. Tallin and Minsk are its western cities. The belt extends east through Leningrad and Moscow, Gorki and Sverdlovsk to Irkutsk. This belt lies within the mixed forest zone. This farming belt supplies the U.S.S.R. with flax for linen, linseed oil and seedcakes, dairy products, potatoes, cabbages, onions, and turnips.

The third farming belt of the great Industrial Triangle lies south of the chernozem zone. Here irrigation is necessary because of little rainfall and high summer temperatures. Cotton, sugar, and grapes are produced in this desert region. Most of this farming region has an animal economy. Sheep, some goats, horses, dogs, and camels are seen in fairly large numbers in this region. The U.S.S.R. is supplied with textiles, meat, and fruit.

Industrial Sections

Within this great triangle are cities and their nearby villages which one geographer has said are all "linked together with an industrial chain." Leningrad has three-and-a-half million people. Moscow, one of the ten largest cities in the world, has six-and-a-half million people. The Leningrad-Moscow area lacks natural resources. Moscow, however, is a transportation center. Industries were established in these two cities during the time of pre-revolutionary Russia. It was the factory workers in these cities who began the Russian

An expanding iron industry prompted the construction of a powerful blast furnace in the Ukraine.

Revolution. This industrial region has chemical industries, paper processing, and food packaging.

The Soviet Union's major centers of trade and communication are located in the Leningrad-Moscow industrial area. Here also are the world-famous museums, art theaters, ballet, and opera houses. In Moscow is located Red Square where the people meet for important ceremonies and celebrations.

North of the Black Sea, in the southern part of the great triangle lies the Ukraine, the great grain producing area of the U.S.S.R. The Ukraine is also the center of iron and steel production. Iron ore comes from the Krivoi Rog mines, northeast of Odessa. Coal is essential in the blast furnaces that produce pig iron. Coal comes from the Donets Basin in the Eastern Ukraine. Manganese, an important alloy metal that makes steel strong and flexible, is found and mined near the Krivoi Rog iron deposits. The nearness of these three raw materials enables the Ukraine to be one of the world leaders in heavy industry—basic iron and steel. From these two products come automobiles, railroad cars, steel girders, rails, bridges, armaments, electrical goods, and chemical by-products. These two sections of the Industrial Triangle, the Ukraine and Moscow-Leningrad, are the leading manufacturing regions of the Soviet Union.

One of the first modern requirements for building iron and steel plants is available coking coal. Through exploration, some 170 coal basins have been discovered throughout the U.S.S.R. Some of the de-

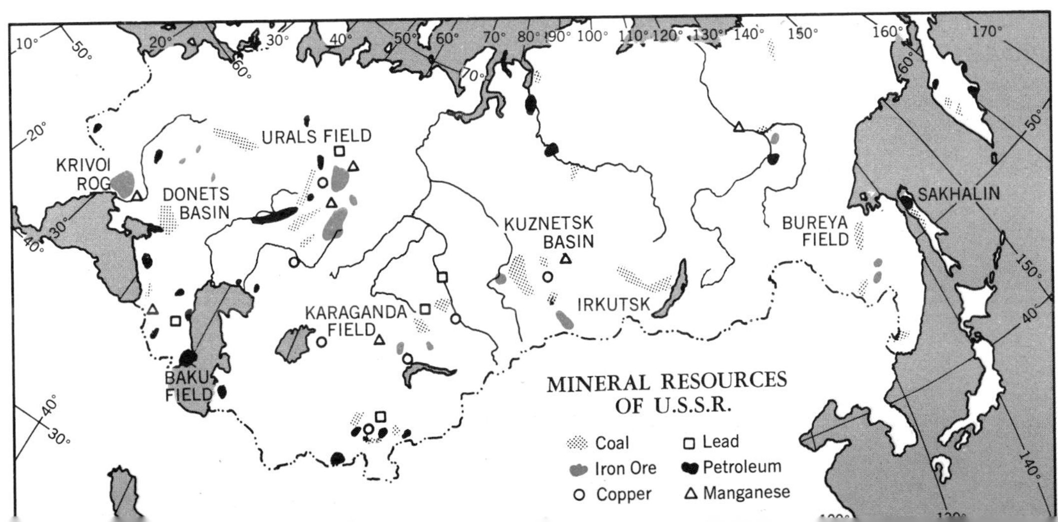

Progress is seen in many places in the Soviet Union today. A modern department store attracts many customers; a new oil community rises on pilings in the Caspian Sea.

posits are more easily mined than others. Ease of mining depends upon the depth and the thickness of the layers, or seams, of coal. Usefulness of coal for coking depends upon the quality of the coal, that is, the amount of ash left when the coal burns.

Three big coal fields are in western U.S.S.R. They are the Donets, Dnieper, and Moscow Basins. A second concentration of coal fields is in the Ural Mountains. The largest of the nation's coal reserves are in Siberia in two huge basins, the Lena and the Tungus. The U.S.S.R. leads the world in the mining of coal and in the production of iron ore.

Manufactured Goods

In America we think of certain manufactured products as "consumer goods." Clothing, automobiles, television sets, radios, refrigerators, vacuums, electric washers, and dryers are examples of consumer goods. "Luxury items," such as tooth paste, perfumes, soaps, electric razors, hair dryers, and even curlers, are also important in the United States. In the U.S.S.R. the emphasis is not on consumer goods and luxury items purchased by families. The range of selection of clothing and household goods is narrow. Luxury goods are scarce and high priced.

At present, the Communist Party and the government are placing more emphasis on heavy industry. Many tractors, railroad cars and engines, structural steel, and weapons of war are being produced. As the supply of these basic items increases, more and more consumer goods are being produced in the Soviet Union. Some luxury items are gradually being introduced.

A PROGRESSIVE POWER

Attempts to raise the standard of living and of production are being made under the absolute control of the Communist government. The importance of education has been stressed, and schooling is free for all. The best students are given the opportunity to continue their education with higher studies. They are urged to choose a field which will further the development of the nation. The highly intelligent are trained for the top positions in all fields: science, medicine, industry, law, and government. Other nations recognize the great advances which have been made by the Soviet Union in such a short time. They hope that she will use her power and her knowledge peacefully. The future progress of many nations depends on this. Only time will tell.

Do You Know?

1. Which mountains divide Europe and Asia? What is the area east of these mountains called?

2. Who were the earliest people to settle in Russia? Which group of Vikings invaded the Russian lands?

3. From which direction did the Mongols come? Which group of Mongols invaded Russian lands? Which city became important during their rule? Why?

4. What is a khanate? What is the tsar? What is an autocracy?

5. What is a soviet? Who were the Bolsheviks? Who was their leader?

6. What name is given to the ancient fortified section of Moscow? For what is it used?

7. What country in the Western Hemisphere is similar in climate and vegetation to the Soviet Union in the Eastern Hemisphere?

8. What type of climate does most of the Soviet Union have?

9. What is the most important agricultural soil of the U.S.S.R.?

10. Which natural region occupies most of the Soviet Union?

11. What name is given to the most important region of the U.S.S.R.? What features make this a leading region?

12. What are the two leading manufacturing regions of the Soviet Union?

13. What three raw materials make the Ukraine a leading industrial center? In what area is each mined?

Learn By Doing

1. Select the correct number to complete each of the following sentences:

a. The Soviet Union places (first, second, third) in the world in size.

b. The Soviet Union occupies (1/3, 1/4, 1/6, 1/8) of the world's land.

c. The Soviet Union places (first, second, third, fourth) in the world in the size of its population.

d. (1/5, 1/4, 1/2, 3/4) of the Soviet population lives within the Industrial Triangle.

e. (All, half, 1/3, 1/5) of the citizens of the Soviet Union are members of the Communist party.

2. Briefly explain why each of the following people are important:

Oleg	Catherine the Great
Batu Khan	Nicholas I
Ivan the Great	Alexander II
Ivan the Terrible	Nicholas II

3. Tell whether each of the following statements is true or false. Correct each of the false statements.

a. The Communist Party is the only political party in Russia.

b. The Communist Party determines the policies of the government and controls its activities.

c. The Communist government puts the policies of the party into action.

d. The Party Chairman is the leader of the Soviet Union.

e. The Supreme Soviet forms the executive branch of the government of the U.S.S.R.

f. The Council of Ministers is the legislative branch of the government.

g. The Soviet of Nationalities and the Soviet of the Union are two chambers of the Supreme Soviet.

h. At the time of election, there are only two official candidates for each office.

i. The leader of the Communist Party may <u>not</u> be the president of the Presidium.

j. The good of the people is placed before the good of the state.

4. Write a detailed report on one of the major cities of the Soviet Union, one which has also been important in the past. Give the location of the city. Tell why the city was important in the past. Describe some of the famous buildings. Tell why the city is important today.

5. Compare the organization of the Communist government with the government of the United States.

a. Which branch is similar to the President? To the cabinet? To Congress (both the Senate and House of Representatives)?

b. What additional branch of government does the Soviet Union have? Why is this branch necessary?

c. What is the major difference in the choice of candidates by the people?

Test Your Knowledge

1. What is an ethnic group? How many are there in the Soviet Union? What is the connection between the ethnic groups and the republics of the U.S.S.R.?

2. What is the correct use of the term Russian? Of the term Russia?

3. Why did the Vikings travel through the lands of the Slavs? What route did they use?

4. What was Vladimir's greatest influence on the Russian people? How can this be seen in the Russian lands today?

5. What were the two major effects of the Vikings on the Russian lands?

6. Who were the Romanovs? Describe the reign of Peter the Great. Include the westernization, the expansion, and the effect of his rule on the people.

7. What were the causes of the Revolution of 1917? Why did it succeed?

8. What is a Five-Year Plan? Do you think this has been more successful in farming or in industry? Why?

9. What is a farming collective? What is an industrial cooperative?

10. How does a Kolkhoz farm differ from a Sovkhoz farm?

11. Name the five natural regions of the Soviet Union. Give one important feature of each.

12. Why is the climate of the west milder than that of the east? What makes the northern regions so cold? Why does most of the U.S.S.R. have a short growing season and little rain?

13. Find some information about the contributions of Tolstoi, Tschaikovsky, Pavlov, Nijinsky, Marx, Pasternak, and Gagarin to the culture of the U.S.S.R.

14. How do the Soviet Union and the United States compare in the production of consumer goods, luxury items, and heavy items? Give an example of each.

Using Maps and Globes

1. Using a globe, locate Washington D.C. and Moscow. Which would be the shortest trip between the two cities: to fly "around the world" from west to east, to fly from east to west, or to fly over the "top of the world?"

2. On what parallel of latitude is Moscow located? What city of Fennoscandia is located on about the same latitude line? Through what part of the United States does this latitude line pass?

3. What are the important rivers in southern U.S.S.R. which could be used for irrigating the dry lands?

4. Which sea, to the west of the Soviet Union, would be used as a passageway to the Atlantic Ocean? What is the major port on this sea?

5. Using the legend for the map of the U.S.S.R. answer each of the following questions:

a. What is the natural region in the most northern lands?

b. Which natural region covers most of the Soviet Union?

c. Which landform is found in the eastern part of the nation?

d. What natural region is located west of the Ural Mountains?

e. In what part of the Soviet Union is the largest area of desert land?

f. Where is the grazing land found? What is this region called?

g. Where is the best farming land of the Soviet Union?

6. What body of water separates the continents of Asia and North America?

7. What is the name of the major railway of the Soviet Union? Where does it begin and end?

8. Can you locate the fifteen republics of the U.S.S.R.? Answer these questions:

a. Which republic is located mostly in the taiga region?

b. Which republic is located near the steppe region?

c. In which republic is Kiev located?

d. In which republic is Riga located?

e. What is the government center of Uzbek Soviet Socialist Republic?

f. What is the capital of the Russian Soviet Federated Socialist Republic?

9. What two seas form part of the southern border of the Soviet Union? What mountains are found on the strip of land between these two seats?

CHAPTER 16

THE EUROPEAN WORLD

The story of Europe and her people can be told by using three words beginning with the letter "D"—Dispersal, Diversity, and Development. These three words tell much about Europe. They are three regional characteristics of Europe. They suggest the activities and contributions of the Europeans which have been important to people all over the world.

THREE REGIONAL CHARACTERISTICS

Dispersal, diversity, and **development** are three regional characteristics of Europe. An understanding of these three words will help you in your study of Europe and her people. Study each word carefully. Think of these words as you read the chapters on Europe. You will come to understand the meaning of these words and their importance in describing Europe.

The first word, *dispersal,* comes from a Latin word which means "to scatter, to spread, to separate, or to go into different parts." Many of you are descendants of people who have dispersed from Europe. Dispersal means far more than the spread of people to other parts of the world. In addition to people, ideas and ways of living have been dispersed. Our language, and many of our customs and our foods came from Europe with our ancestors.

The word *diversity* came into our language from the Latin word *diversus* which means "various." When we add the letters "ity" to the first part of the Latin word *divers,* we make a word which means "variety, difference, or unlikeness." As you read about the many countries of Europe and its different regions, you will understand why diversity is a good word to describe Europe.

The third of the three words, *development,* should be more familiar to you. You have heard it used in several ways throughout your life. For instance, your mind, body, and ideas have been developing. If you look back to the time you were in the first grade, you can see how much your body has grown since then.

How have your ideas changed or expanded? We will now look at some of the ways in which the people of Europe have developed themselves and their resources through the centuries.

Both our government and much of our architecture reflect the heritage of Greece and Rome.

DISPERSAL

In Chapters 5 and 6 you read about the early Greek and Roman cultural developments. Rome and Athens, the centers of these two great cultures, can be located on a map of Europe. The map, however, does not show how the ideas and inventions of the Greeks and Romans have been dispersed throughout Europe and the world.

Dispersal of Ideas

Today we can see many signs of the dispersal or flow of ideas from the Greeks and the Romans. When you see classic buildings, hear or speak words that were once Greek or Roman, or look at engravings on coins, you see the heritage of Greek and Roman ideas that have been dispersed throughout Europe and America.

One of the most important ideas that we have inherited from the ancient Greeks is the idea of democracy. Demos, a city in early Greece, was a place where people became concerned about their own government. The Greek words *demos,* which means "people," and *kratos,* which means "rule," form the basis of our word *democracy.* The democratic right to assemble in order to discuss problems and decide how to solve them is treasured by free people throughout the world.

As you know, the Romans expanded their Empire far to the North. They carried the Roman language and Roman law with them. Even today, British laws and our laws are based on many of the Roman laws. The holding together of such a large empire required well-trained soldiers and good roads. The organization of the Roman armed forces was admired by later peoples. It has been copied by many modern nations. Roman roads were built so well that they lasted for centuries as travel highways and routes of trade.

EUROPEAN WORLD
0 150 300
Scale 300 miles to one inch
ICE AND SNOW
TUNDRA
EVERGREEN FORESTS
FORESTS
FARMLAND
MOUNTAINS
ICELAND
Reykjavík
ARCTIC CIRCLE
NORWAY
SWEDEN
FINLAND
SCANDINAVIAN PENINSULA
Oslo
Stockholm
Helsinki
SCOTLAND
NORTHERN IRELAND
Edinburgh
Belfast
IRELAND
Dublin
UNITED KINGDOM
WALES
ENGLAND
LONDON
North Sea
Baltic Sea
DENMARK
Copenhagen
Amsterdam
The Hague
THE NETHERLANDS
English Channel
Brussels
BELGIUM
LUXEMBOURG
WEST GERMANY
Bonn
EAST GERMANY
BERLIN
NORTH EUROPEAN PLAIN
POLAND
Warsaw
U. S. S. R.
Prague
CZECHOSLOVAKIA
GERMANY
Rhine River
Danube River
Vienna
LIECHTENSTEIN
AUSTRIA
Budapest
HUNGARY
RUMANIA
Bern
SWITZERLAND
ALPS
Po River
PARIS
FRANCE
Bay of Biscay
Rhone R.
ATLANTIC OCEAN
PORTUGAL
SPAIN
Lisbon
MADRID
SPANISH MESETA
PYRENEES
ANDORRA
MONACO
Bologna
SAN MARINO
APENNINES
ITALY
ROME
Adriatic Sea
CORSICA
SARDINIA
SICILY
MALTA
YUGOSLAVIA
Belgrade
Bucharest
Danube River
BALKAN PENINSULA
Sofia
BULGARIA
Tirana
ALBANIA
GREECE
Athens
Aegean Sea
CRETE
Strait of Gibraltar
Rabat
MOROCCO
ATLAS MOUNTAINS
Algiers
TELL
ALGERIA
Tunis
TUNISIA
AFRICA
Mediterranean Sea
70°
60°
50°
40°
30°
20°
10°
0°
©1958, JEPPESEN & CO. DENVER, COLO., U.S.A.
ALL RIGHTS RESERVED
REVISED 1967

So far we have talked about the dispersal of Greek and Roman ideas. Ideas and people have dispersed from other parts of Europe as well. People from every country in Europe have settled in the Americas. The Industrial Revolution, that began in England, has touched every part of the globe. Communism and Democracy are ideas about two ways of life that began in Europe and have dispersed throughout the world. Europe is truly a region of dispersal.

Dispersal of Languages

An easy way to look at Europe as a center from which ideas and peoples have dispersed is to look at the languages of the world. Most of the languages of Europe belong to a group of languages known as **Indo-European.** The origin of languages of the Indo-European family can be traced back to a common ancestor. The people who spoke the original Indo-European language probably lived somewhere in Eastern Europe. The descendants of these people scattered eastward into Asia and westward into Europe.

Modern languages of Europe and parts of Asia developed from the common ancestral language. For instance, Icelandic, the language of Iceland, and Eastern Hindi, one of the many languages of India, are related. They both come from a common ancient language. They are living reminders of an ancient dis-

Many French settled in Quebec, many Spaniards in Venezuela, and many Dutch and English in South Africa. Each of these areas today reflects the culture of its European settlers.

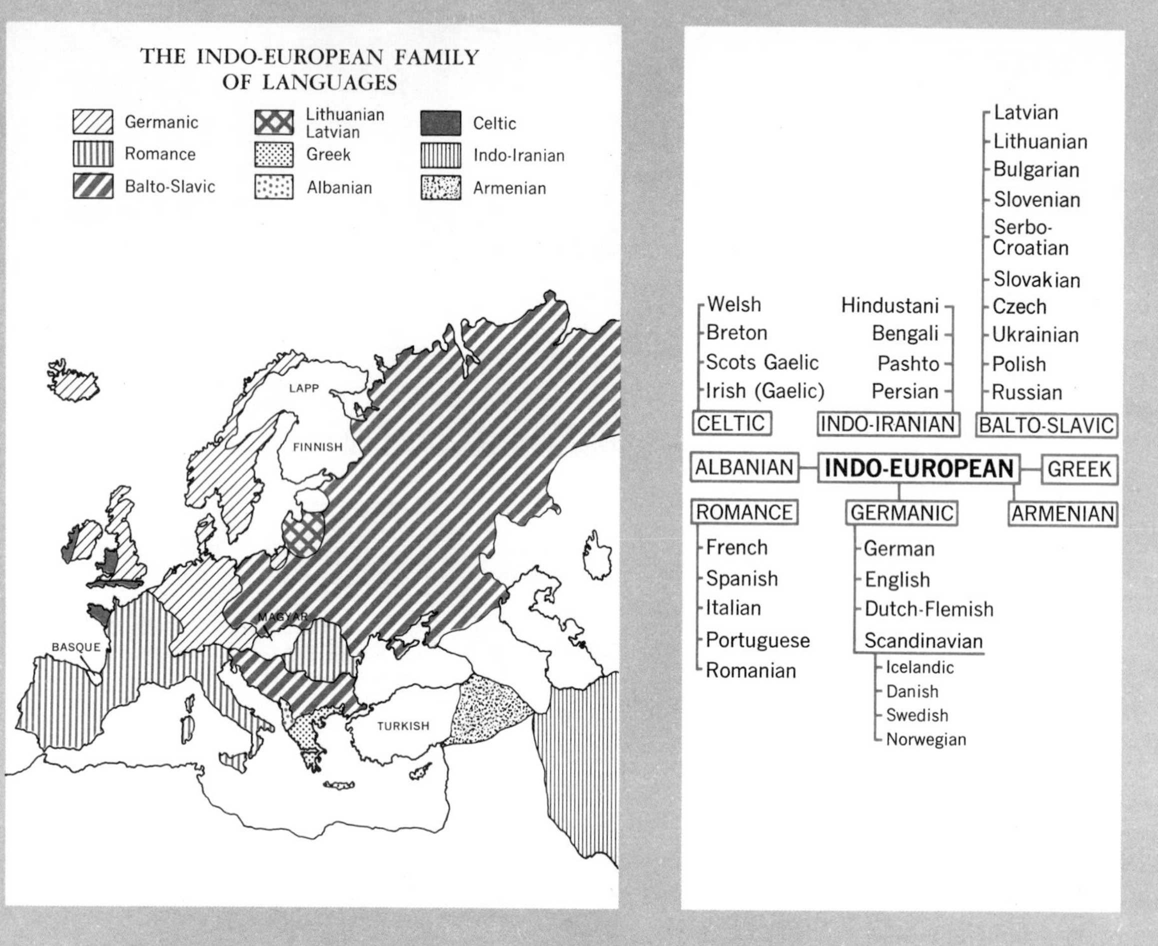

persal. The chart on this page shows the major divisions and subdivisions of the Indo-European languages.

The language map shows us where the major divisions are spoken in Europe. Can you explain where the names *Slavic* and *Romance* came from? To what major division are the Scandinavian languages related? Why has Finland been left blank?

Modern members of the Indo-European language family have been dispersed to all corners of the world. Each language serves as a symbol of the ideas that the people who spoke that language brought with them. Wherever you find a European language spoken, you can be sure to find many customs and ideas like those in the country from which the language came. The Australian people, for instance, have many customs and ideas like the people in the mother country, England. English is the **official language.** This means that government records are kept in English and that the language is taught to children in school. English is also the official language of the United States and Canada. Ways of living in Central and South America are much like those of Spain, the country which sent its people and its language to this part of the world.

REASONS FOR DISPERSAL

Over the last few centuries millions of Europeans have left Europe. In the years between 1815 and 1914 alone, approximately 60 million Europeans emigrated to other parts of the world. Of these 60 million, more than half came to the United States. Why did people disperse from Europe? What were the reasons that led them to go to other countries to live?

Riches Were Sought

One reason for dispersal was the desire to become rich. Greed for gold led Pizarro in 1531 to invade the Inca Kingdom of South America, capture the Inca ruler, and ransom him for gold and silver. In 1848, gold was discovered at Sutter's Mill in California. This discovery brought thousands of men from Europe who wanted to become rich. Gold discoveries in Australia, little more than a century ago, brought thousands of immigrants to that country.

Better Ways of Living Were Desired

Another reason for emigration lay in the living conditions of many people. Many parts of Europe were overpopulated. A lack of farmland, jobs, and the opportunity to improve their way of living led millions of people to leave Europe. They sought a new country where land was free and spacious, where jobs were available, and where all men were equal. Perhaps the greatest number of Europeans to emigrate to other countries did so for these reasons. They wanted to find a better way of living and to move to a land that offered more opportunities.

Famine Drove People from Europe

Famine sometimes drove people to leave Europe. Famine means that there is very little food to eat. Many go hungry, and some actually starve to death. An example of how famine drove people out of Europe can be found in Ireland. For the five years preceeding 1851, the potato crop of Ireland failed. As a result, Ireland suffered from famine. About 1,000,000 Irish died during the famine. Over a million Irish left Ireland to live in other countries. Most of them migrated to the United States.

People Wanted Religious Freedom

Another important reason for emigration was the desire to escape religious persecution. In 1685, the French king took away the religious and political rights of the Huguenots, a group of French Protestants. Thousands of the Huguenots fled to other countries. Many took refuge in England. Some came to America.

Large groups of Puritans, dissatisfied with life in England, sought religious freedom in Massachusetts. Another group, the Quakers, was persecuted in England. Under the leadership of William Penn, they established a colony in North America named Pennsylvania. English Catholics sought religious freedom through the establishment of the colony of Maryland.

People Were Sent to Colonies

Some dispersals of people from Europe were planned by the governments. During the eighteenth century, the English often sent convicts to their colonies. Many convicts were shipped to the North American colonies to work on plantations. The landowners paid the British government for the labor rights of the convicts. In this way, they bought near-slave labor.

The American Revolution brought a halt to the practice of shipping convicts across the waters to North America. The new government of the United States passed a law against importation of convict labor. The British government sought a new place to send convicts. Botany Bay, present-day Sydney, in Australia was selected. In this colony, the prisoners could raise their own food. Once the colony was established, the prisoners were able to support themselves. They were no longer a financial burden on the government. This prison colony was the first settlement in Australia.

Freedom and new opportunities greeted Hungarian immigrants in 1956.

A Need for a Different Government

One major reason for dispersal exists today as strongly as it did in the past. This is the desire of people to change one political system for another. In 1652, the Dutch dispersed from Holland to Cape Town, South Africa. In the early nineteenth century, when the British captured South Africa, they made a second dispersal. Many of the Dutch settlers who resented British rule settled to the north. These settlers formed new republics in which they could govern themselves.

A more recent example of people who left one country for others occurred in 1956. The people in Hungary, dissatisfied with Communist rule, started a revolution. The revolution was crushed with the help of the Russian troops. When the revolution failed, more than 200,000 Hungarians fled their country. They now live in parts of free Europe, the Americas, and Australia.

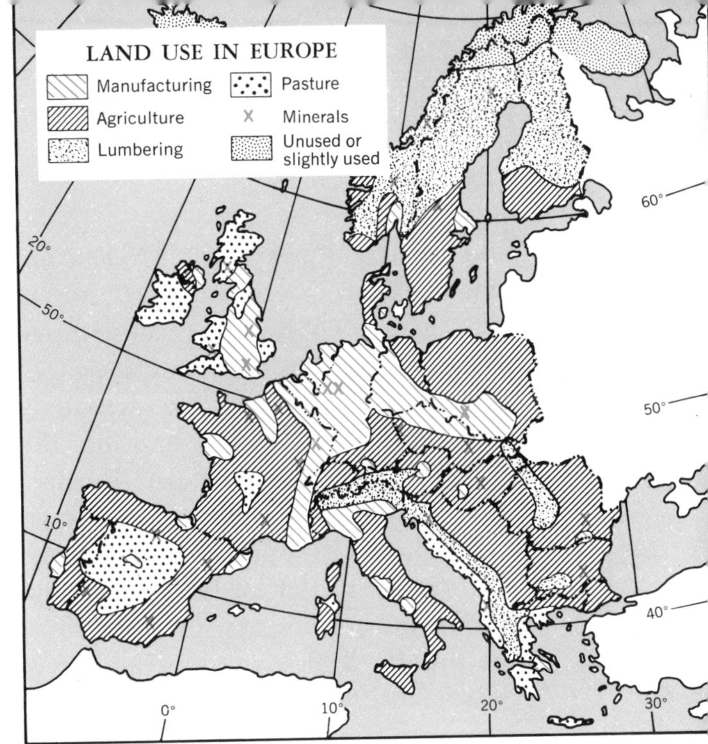

DIVERSITY

Diversity is another regional characteristic of Europe. Diversity is represented in Europe in many different ways. You have read of the diversity of languages in Europe. This region also has diversity in its landforms, climates, and crops. There is a great variety in the peoples, the ways of making a living, the cultures, and the countries of Europe.

Diversity in Landforms

There are many different landforms in Europe. As they are mentioned, locate them on the physical map on page 355. Much of Spain is a plateau, or **tableland.** Mountain ranges run the length of the Italian, Balkan, and Scandinavian peninsulas. Sicily and Sardinia, two Mediterranean islands, are mostly mountainous. The island of Ireland has a large central plain with surrounding low-lying mountains. Switzerland is mountainous. Her high, rugged mountain scenery is one of Europe's major tourist attractions. The great North European Plain that crosses northern Europe, west to east, contrasts with the hilly, rugged, choppy landscape of southern Europe.

Diversity of Climate

The diversity of landforms naturally helps create a diversity of climate. However, there are other causes for the variety. Among them is the length of the European continent. The northern areas of Europe have a Marine climate, while southern Europe has a Mediterranean climate.

Another cause is the shape of Europe. No nation is far from the ocean. Warm ocean currents flow northward and bring warm air to all parts of western Europe.

Diversity of Crops

The diversity of climates in Europe means different crops can be grown. The diversity of European agriculture is shown in the different types of cereal grains grown. Rye is widely grown in the U.S.S.R. and on the sandy plains of northern Europe. Barley, oats, and wheat are grown throughout Europe. France, Italy, and Spain, in that order, lead in the production of wheat. Rice is grown in the Po Valley of Italy and to a lesser extent in other countries of southern Europe.

Other major European crops are apples, citrus fruits, grapes, sugar beets, olives, and lumber. Pigs, cattle, and sheep are raised in each major region of Europe. Europe is a region of diverse vegetation.

Diversity of Occupation

The diversity of the European regions is represented in the variety of ways of making a living. There are the lumber industry of Fennoscandia, the manufacturing economy of the United Kingdom, and the dairy industry and the mining and manufacturing industries of Western Europe. There are the corn and wheat plains of Eastern Europe, and the citrus groves, olive orchards, and fields of grapevines of the Mediterranean Lands.

Europe is a region of busy people. The population of Europe is estimated to be about 443 million. To support this heavy population, every inch of the rich soil must be made to produce food. The factories must produce a great variety of products to supply the demands of so many people. To do this, every available resource must be used.

The many and diverse occupations of the Europeans are enriching the lives of people throughout the world. European workmen have become noted for their special skills and abilities. Danish craftsmen are known throughout the world for their fine porcelain, home furnishings, and silverware. The Portuguese are skilled fishermen. They contribute large catches of cod, sardines, and tuna to the markets of the world. The Dutch and the Swiss are famous for their many dairy products. Swiss watchmakers are well known for the very fine watches they produce. Many Europeans are skilled mechanics. French, German, Swedish, and English cars are shipped to many parts of the world.

Diversity of People

The different peoples of Europe present a picture of diversity. The mainland of Europe is a region that has suffered invasions many times by people from the east and from the north. Wave after wave of invading nomads came into Europe from the plains of Asia. One of the groups of Asiatic nomads, the Magyars, settled

Natural Regions of Europe
North Cape
Barents Sea
Norwegian Sea
Salt Fiord
SCANDINAVIAN PENINSULA
SCANDINAVIAN HIGHLANDS
Gulf of Bothnia
LAKE REGION
Sogne Fiord
ATLANTIC OCEAN
SCOTTISH HIGHLANDS
CENTRAL PLAIN
Irish Sea
PENNINES
North Sea
Skagerrak
Kattegat
JUTLAND PENINSULA
SKANE
Baltic Sea
PLAIN
FENLAND
Lake Ijssel
Elbe River
EUROPEAN
Vistula River
English Channel
FLANDERS
NORTH
Rhine River
Oder River
ARDENNES HIGHLAND
SUDETEN MTS.
Saxon Gate
MORAVIAN CORRIDOR
PLATEAU OF BRITTANY
Seine R.
PARIS BASIN
BOHEMIAN FOREST
BOHEMIAN PLATEAU
CARPATHIAN MTS.
Loire River
BLACK FOREST
Danube River
Bay of Biscay
JURAS
ALPINE FORELAND
Danube R.
HUNGARIAN PLAIN
Garonne R.
CENTRAL PLATEAU
ALPS
Rhône R.
Po River
DINARIC ALPS
Sava River
TRANSYLVANIAN ALPS
CANTABRIAN MTS.
PYRENEES
Iron Gate
Black Sea
Douro River
IBERIAN
RHÔNE DELTA
APENNINES
Adriatic Sea
Danube River
FORELAND
MESETA
Tagus River
BALKAN
BALKAN MTS.
PENINSULA
PENINSULA
Bosporus
SIERRA MORENA
Guadalquivir River
Strait of Otranto
Sea of Marmara
Tyrrhenian Sea
PINDUS
Dardanelles
SIERRA NEVADA
Strait of Gibraltar
Mediterranean Sea
Ionian Sea
Aegean Sea
ISTHMUS OF CORINTH
Strait of Messina
© 1960 JEPPESEN & CO., DENVER, COLO., U.S.A. ALL RIGHTS RESERVED

in Hungary. Many barbaric tribes from the region of present-day Germany pressed southward and westward. The Lombards moved into northern Italy. The Franks gradually migrated into what is now France. The Goths and Vandals migrated southwestward, going as far as Spain and the Straits of Gibraltar. The Angles, Saxons, Danes, and Normans invaded England.

During the Middle Ages, Vikings from Scandinavia raided England and the coasts of mainland Europe. In the east they descended the Dnieper River to Constantinople. In the country of the Slavs, the Vikings settled and laid the beginnings of Kievan Russia. Thus, the cultural diversity of Europe developed from the many groups of people who invaded and settled in the different parts of Europe.

Reindeer are important to Laplanders.

A Continent of Many Nations

The diversity of peoples in Europe is reflected in the great number of nations. Although Europe is a small continent, it has a great many independent nations. This great diversity can easily be seen on the map on page 348.

In northern Europe locate Iceland, Norway, Sweden, Finland, and Denmark. Starting from Ireland in northwestern Europe and proceeding east, locate Northern Ireland, Scotland, England, and Wales. The last four make up the United Kingdom. Continuing eastward find France, Belgium, and Czechoslovakia. The nations of Belgium, Netherlands, and Luxembourg are called the "Benelux" countries. Can you figure out how this name was selected?

In central Europe locate Switzerland, Austria, Hungary, and Rumania. And finally to the south, starting at the Atlantic Ocean, locate Portugal, Spain, Italy, Yugoslavia, Albania, Greece, and Bulgaria.

If you look closely at the map, you will also find some very tiny, independent states. Can you locate Andorra in the Pyrenees Mountains and Monaco on the southern edge of France? Can you locate Liechtenstein just east of Switzerland? And, do you know that the Vatican City, where the head of the Roman Catholic Church lives, is an independent political unit? It is located within the city of Rome. As you can see, the continent of Europe is really made up of many nations.

Diversity of Cultures

National boundary lines, however, do not show the complete picture of the diverse nature of the peoples of Europe. Many cultural differences can be seen within the nations. For example, there is a small group of people in southwestern France and northern Spain called the Basques. The Basque language is unlike any known language. Apparently, the Basques once lived in a wider area. They were pushed into their present region by invading tribes. Some scientists suggest that they are descendants of the Cro Magnons, a race of prehistoric man.

In the far north of Finland live another interesting group of people called the Lapps. They are quite unlike the rest of the people of Scandinavia who are generally tall and blond. The Lapps are, in fact, the shortest people in Europe. They have black hair. Some of the Lapps are nomads who follow their herds of reindeer and live year round in tents.

Many European countries have two or more nationality groups. Many have two or more languages spoken within their national boundaries. For example, Yugoslavia has five

Three brilliantly colored scenes reflect European culture. A Swedish woman weaves on a loom; guardsmen parade in London on Queen Elizabeth's Birthday; and the Spanish dance at the Seville Fiesta.

nationality groups. Three languages are spoken, and two alphabets are used. The Croats, Montenegrins, Serbs, Slovenes, and Macedonians make up the population of Yugoslavia. Each group has its distinct culture. The people look different and have very different customs and ways of living.

The Serbs are dark-skinned, with dark hair and dark eyes. The Croats are usually fairly short people and blond. The Slovenes are much like their neighbors, the Austrians. Most of them are short and have light hair and blue eyes. The Montenegrins are among the tallest and heaviest people of Europe. The Macedonians resemble their neighbors, the Greeks and Bulgarians.

The three different languages that are spoken in Yugoslavia are Serbo-Croatian, Slovenian, and a mixture of Serbian and Bulgarian which is spoken by the Macedonians. These three languages are similar to each other, but each language has its own unique qualities. The Croats write their language with the Roman alphabet, which is the alphabet we use. The Serbs and the Montenegrins write their language with a very different alphabet called the Cyrillic alphabet. These patterns of cultural differences are repeated throughout Europe. They add charm and interest to life in Europe. These differences have great appeal to people from other continents. They help to explain the great flow of tourists to Europe each year.

CONFLICT AMONG NATIONS

With so many different nations and peoples living within the small continent of Europe, it is not surprising that they sometimes have difficulties. They have not always completely understood each other. They have not always lived in peace. It would be very difficult indeed to cover all the conflicts and wars which have occurred in Europe.

Nevertheless, we will look at a few of the wars that have occurred in the last 500 years. As we do so, you will learn the major reasons, such as greed for power and territory, that led nations to go to war. However, do not forget that there were many other reasons that supported the main cause of each war.

The Thirty Years' War (1618–1648)

Some wars in Europe were caused by differences of religion. For example, the Thirty Years' War of the seventeenth century was caused by a conflict between Protestant powers and Catholic powers. It began in Bohemia, now a part of Czechoslovakia. Matthias, the Holy Roman Emperor, attempted to force the people to re-elect one of his Catholic relatives to the Bohemian throne. The Czech people resented this act and rose against the Bohemian king, Ferdinand. They chose Frederick, the Protestant Elector of Palatine, to be their king.

Other Protestant rulers in Europe joined Frederick in the war against Ferdinand. Before the end of the Thirty Years' War most of the nations of Western Europe had become involved. Some of them joined because it was an opportunity to seize territory. Others wanted to fight for religious reasons. The war, which had begun as a quarrel over the throne of Bohemia, turned into a war of religion and greed. The war was one of the most terrible in history. Whole sections of Germany and Bohemia were laid waste, or destroyed. Soldiers, famine, and disease killed one-third of the inhabitants of Germany and Bohemia.

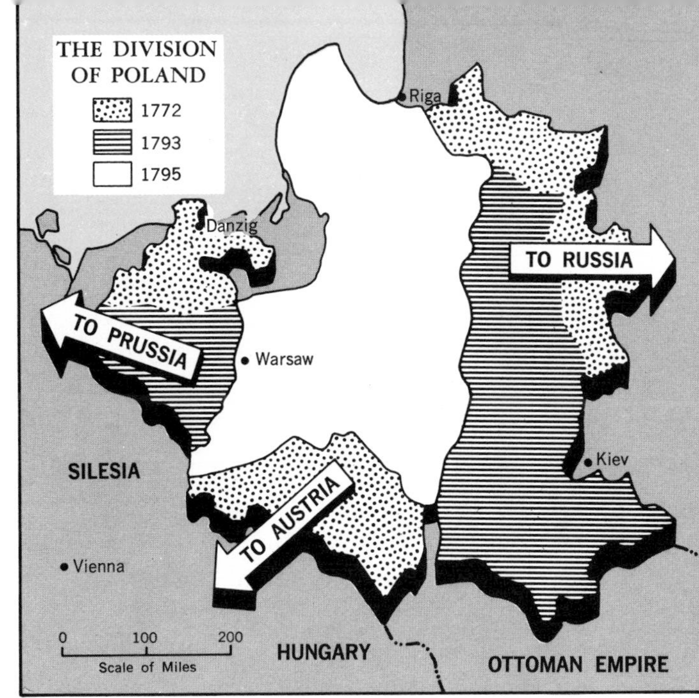

The Invasion and Division of Poland

Greed for territory was a major cause of the wars which have occurred in Poland. In the late-eighteenth century, greedy, land-hungry neighbors erased the large nation of Poland from the map. Before 1772 Poland had grown into a large and powerful nation extending from the Baltic Sea almost to the Black Sea. Unrest and disagreements among the ruling nobles within the country weakened Polish power and gave her neighbors an opportunity to seize her territory. In 1772 Russia seized some of the eastern provinces, Austria took a southern province, and Prussia took a western portion. Poland lost about one-third of its territory and about one-half of its population.

Poland, then, began a program of internal reform. The government was strengthened, and a constitution was adopted. This progress within the country alarmed the powers which had divided Poland. They did not want a strong Polish government because of the threat it posed to their power. In 1793, the three countries took additional Polish territory.

In the two years that followed, a Polish leader, Thaddeus Kosciusko, lead a movement opposing the breaking up of Poland. His forces were defeated. In 1795 a third division of Poland occurred, and Poland ceased to exist as an independent nation. It was not until the end of World War I in 1918 that Polish territory was reunited under an independent government. The boundary lines of the new Polish nation were much as they were before 1772. But Poland did not remain a free nation long, as we shall see later.

The Napoleonic Wars

A power-hungry dictator might be said to be the cause of the series of wars which occurred in Europe between 1796 and 1814. In 1796 a young French soldier, Napoleon Bonaparte, was ordered to assume command of the French Army in Italy and drive the Austrians from Italy. So successful was his campaign in Italy that he returned to France a national hero. In 1799 Napoleon seized power and set up a new government of three members called the Consulate. He became the First Consul and ruled France as a dictator.

Napoleon was not only a fine general of the army, he was also a good statesman. He set out to improve the government of France. He established a code of laws called the Code Napoleon which continues to be the basis for all French laws. He established the Bank of France which greatly strengthened the French money system, and he made other reforms needed in the French government.

Napoleon ruled France well, but he found it very difficult to settle down to a peacetime government. He wanted new conquests. Austria continued to control parts of northern Italy. Napoleon succeeded in driving Austria from Italy in 1801.

Napoleon was not satisfied with his position in France. He began to assume control of all powers of government. By 1804, he was able to have himself declared Emperor of France. On December 2, the coronation ceremonies took place in Notre Dame Cathedral. As the Pope prepared to place the crown on his head, Napoleon snatched the crown and placed it on his own head. By this act, he was showing that he did not acknowledge the power of the Church to bestow the crown nor to take it away.

Napoleon Bonaparte leads his army.

Conquests and Defeat

In 1805, Napoleon smashed the German and Austrian armies in eastern Europe. He planned to invade Great Britain, his major enemy, but abandoned his plan in order to continue fighting on the continent. Believing that the victor in war had the right to occupy the conquered territory, Napoleon began to change the map of Europe. He made his brother, Joseph, king of Naples and another brother, Louis, king of Holland. He carved territories he had conquered in Germany and Italy into dukedoms and awarded them to his favorite generals and marshals.

Napoleon went on to conquer Prussia and Russia. He occupied Portugal because the Portuguese refused to stop trade with Great Britain. He issued decrees banning all British goods in Europe. In 1809, after Napoleon had seized Spain, Great Britain attacked his armies on the Spanish peninsula. This campaign lasted for five years.

Great Britain, Prussia, Russia, Spain, and Sweden allied themselves against Napoleon. Although he raised another army, Napoleon was not able to defeat this alliance of his enemies. In 1814, he gave up the throne of France and was exiled to the island of Elba off the coast of Italy. A year later he escaped and landed in France. With a small group of followers, Napoleon began marching to Paris. Troops, sent by King Louis XVIII to arrest him, joined him in his march on the city. He was hailed as emperor, and King Louis fled Paris.

The allies again sent armies against Napoleon. In the hundred days that followed, battles raged north of Paris. Finally on June 18, 1815, he was defeated by the allied armies under the command of the British general, Lord Wellington. He spent the rest of his days as a prisoner of the British on the island of Saint Helena off the west coast of Africa.

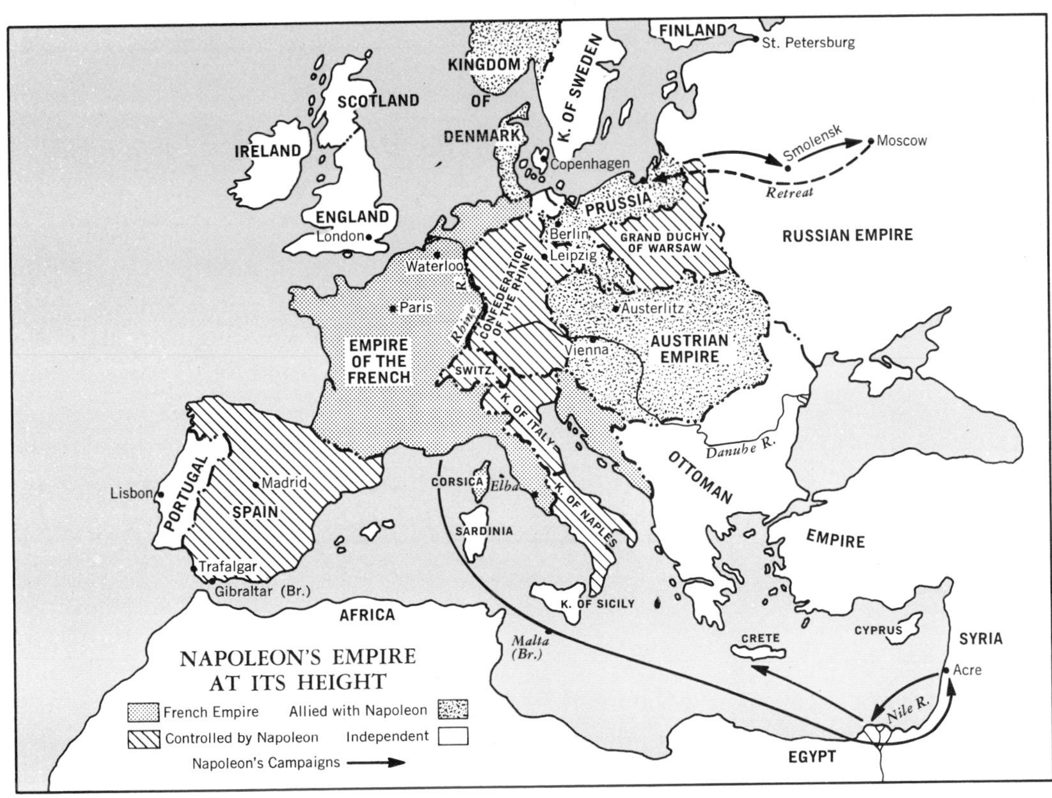

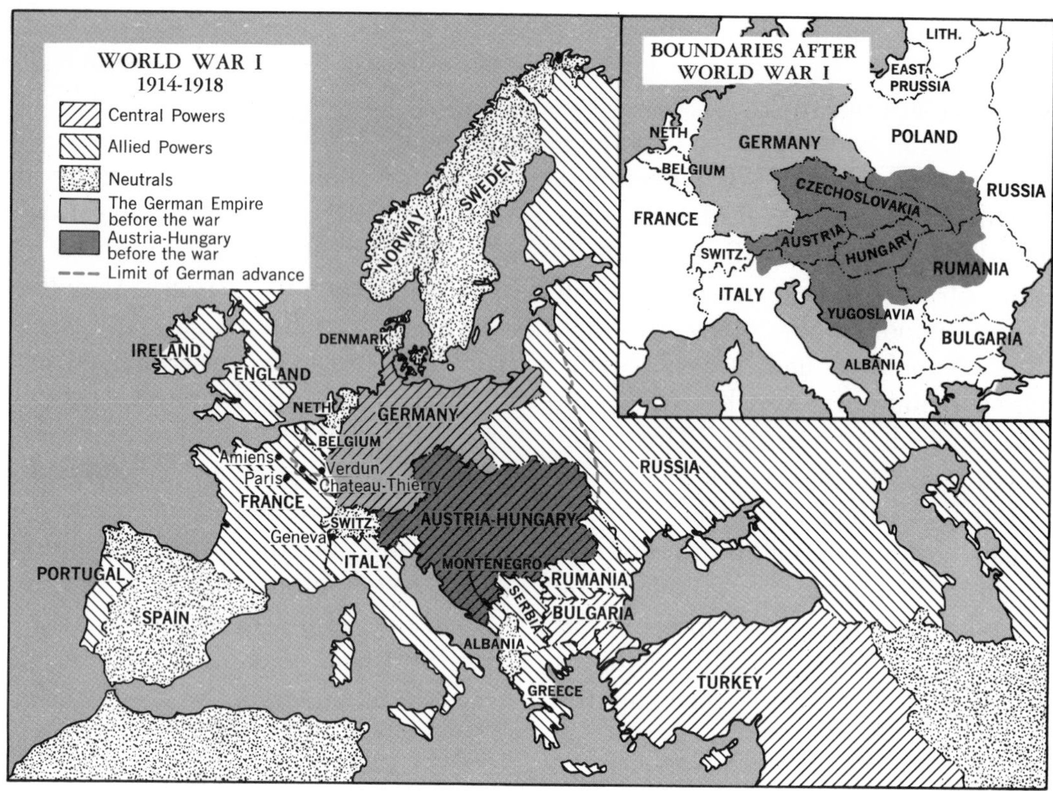

Conflicts of Our Century

In the first half of the twentieth century, two wars raged in Europe that involved many of the countries of the world. There were many causes for these wars. The struggles between European countries for territory and colonies was a major cause. The struggle for power was another cause. In many ways these wars were a continuation of the earlier struggles between European powers. These struggles have grown from the closeness of many national groups on the European continent and the need for more living-space for the many people of Europe.

World War I

Three pistol shots marked the beginning of World War I. On Sunday morning June 28, 1914, crowds gathered in Sarajevo, the capital of the Austrian province of Bosnia. They had come to see Archduke Francis Ferdinand, heir to the throne of Austria-Hungary, and his wife, Sophie. As the couple drove through the streets, a man jumped on the running board of their open car and fired three shots. Two bullets hit Ferdinand and one hit Sophie. Both died instantly. The man responsible was Gavrilo Princip, a young Bosnian student who had lived in Serbia.

The Austrian government suspected that Serbia had planned the assassination of Ferdinand and declared war on Serbia on July 14, 1914. By October, Austria-Hungary, Germany, and the Turkish Empire were at war with the Allies, Belgium, France, Great Britain, Russia, and Serbia. Other countries later joined the fighting. The United States entered the war on April 6, 1917.

The three shots that killed Ferdinand and his wife marked the outbreak of the war, but this was not the cause of the war. At the beginning of the war, Austria-Hungary and Germany planned to conquer new territories and colonies. They won early victories. But in September, 1914 at the First Battle of the Marne, the Allies stopped the German advances. This ended Germany's chances for a quick victory.

The war was fought mainly in trenches in central Europe. The largest armies ever seen up to that time were assembled. New weapons were used to kill the enemy. Tanks, trucks, and automobiles were introduced into land warfare. Airplanes were used for the first time dropping bombs. Submarines destroyed troop and supply ships without warning.

The war ended on November 11, 1918. The peace treaty changed the map of the world. New governments were established in Austria, Czechoslovakia, Estonia, Finland, Germany, Hungary, Latvia, Lithuania, Poland, Russia, Yugoslavia, and many countries of western Asia. However, the problems of Europe were not solved by this war.

The League of Nations

After the war the nations of the world made an attempt to prevent war by organizing the League of Nations. Most of the European nations belonged to the League. The United States did not join even though our President, Woodrow Wilson, was responsible for the founding of the organization. The League of Nations was dissolved in 1946, when the United Nations took its place. The League had few successes during its 26 years of existence.

The palace of the League of Nations symbolized European hope in unity.

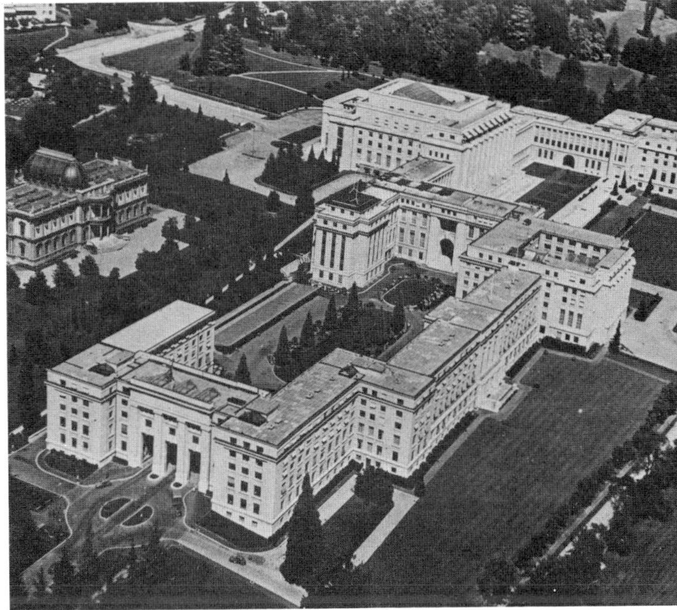

The Second World War

The Second World War was largely the result of the ambitions of a German dictator, Adolf Hitler, to control more territory. He was joined in this ambition by the Italian dictator, Benito Mussolini and by the War Lords of Japan. Each of these rulers had seized extensive territories without becoming involved in major wars. The Japanese had seized Manchuria and parts of China. Mussolini's troops had marched into Ethiopia, seizing that country with little difficulty. These nations justified their invasions by claiming that they needed more "living-room."

Hitler began his march to power by building a large army and navy even though the treaty signed at the end of World War I forbade this. He then seized territory taken from Germany by the treaty. Other European powers, fearing war, dared not stop Hitler's expansion. He seized Austria and demanded a section of Czechoslovakia. He promised that this demand would be his last one. Prime Minister Chamberlain of Great Britain and Premier Daladier of France conferred with Hitler and Mussolini in Munich, Germany. They agreed that Germany might occupy the section of Czechoslovakia that Hitler demanded. They believed that Hitler was satisfied and that peace was achieved.

But Hitler broke his promise and demanded a section of Poland. In

March 1939, his armies occupied the remainder of Czechoslovakia. Next he seized a portion of Lithuania. In April, the armed forces of Italy occupied Albania.

Hitler's broken promises finally convinced Great Britain and France that he intended to conquer all Europe. Giving in to his demands had not stopped his desire for territory. When he again demanded the section of Poland, Chamberlain announced that Great Britain would support Poland if it resisted a German attack.

On September 1, 1939, Hitler's troops invaded Poland. Britain and France ordered Hitler to withdraw his troops. Hitler paid no attention. On September 3, Britain and France declared war on Germany. Great Britain, France, Russia, and the many other countries siding with them were called the **Allies.** Germany, Italy, Japan and a few other countries were known as the **Axis.** The United States entered the war on December 7, 1941 when Japan attacked Pearl Harbor. This war became a truly world war with battles being fought in Europe, Asia, and Africa, as well as in the Atlantic and Pacific Oceans.

War ended in Europe in May, 1945 and in the Pacific in September, 1945. This war had taken the lives of more people than any other war in history. It was also the most expensive war in history. Many nations continue to pay for the war as they repay loans and care for wounded veterans of the war.

National flags fly to symbolize membership in the United Nations.

The United Nations

In October, 1945, just after the fighting was ended, the United Nations was founded. This organization was to replace the League of Nations. Its purpose is to unite the nations of the world in keeping the peace. It recognizes that to preserve peace all people must be helped to live together in harmony. The United Nations works to settle disputes where ever they occur. It also works to help people live better by improving health and agriculture throughout the world.

DEVELOPMENT

The world is indebted to Europe for many of the developments in travel, communication, industry, art, literature, and music which have contributed to man's progress. The rapid progress of man today had its beginning in many of the developments which began during the Renaissance in Europe. You may recall that the period of rebirth after the Middle Ages was a time when new ideas about the Earth and its place in the universe were developed. Men began to study nature and to try to satisfy their curiosity about the world, other planets, and the sun. It was a time when new inventions were made that had a great effect upon our ways of living. Ways of printing books were invented. Men studied ways to harness the forces in nature, such as steam and falling water. The Renaissance was a time when new lands were discovered. Men moved out of Europe, to the east and to the west, in search of new trade routes to India and the Orient.

Progress began slowly during the Renaissance. Most of the people of Europe were uneducated and unable to understand the changes that were taking place around them. Some of the thinkers and scholars, who were developing these new ideas, were not always understood by the people and were imprisoned for their ideas. It took a brave man to teach new ideas or to propose new inventions. Nevertheless, progress was made.

Since 1960, Europeans have achieved the highest standards of living in their entire history. Industry in Europe is booming. European products flow out of Europe to markets all over the world. People earn more today than ever before in history. While many Europeans still live in poverty, more and more are gaining opportunities for an education and good jobs. Let us look at some of the developments in Europe which have made this progress possible.

The Development of Education

During the Middle Ages few people could read and write. Books were found only in the monasteries where they had been copied by hand. The invention of printing during the Renaissance increased the supply of books. As education was offered to more and more people, there began to develop a class of scholars and educated people. As more and more people became educated, a middle-class group began to grow. Today, the growing middle class has taken over social and political power from the old **aristocracy,** or upper class.

Most Europeans today can read and write. Countries of Central, Northern, and Western Europe take great pride in their excellent educational systems. Denmark and Sweden have the highest literacy rate in Europe and probably in the world. About 99 per cent of their people

Though architecture has changed, the search for knowledge continues at an ancient Spanish and a new Swedish university.

can read and write. In 1960, it was estimated that the literacy rate in the United States was 98 per cent, or 1 per cent below that of Denmark and Sweden. The people of the poorer countries of Eastern and Southern Europe are not so well educated. In Spain, only about 75 per cent of the people can read and write.

One of Europe's most valuable contributions to the world has been the university. Most universities in the world have been patterned on them. European universities grew out of the cathedral or monastery schools. The universities were established to permit students to advance their education. By 1500, Europe had nearly 80 universities. The oldest is believed to have been established in Bologna, Italy during the eleventh century. The University of Paris was established in the twelfth century.

Today, most European cities support a university. Since World War II, many countries help pay the expenses of students studying at universities. In Russia the government pays all the expenses of students accepted for study at universities. More and more Europeans are seeking a university education as they recognize its importance to the development of their countries.

The Development of the Arts

All of the **arts,** music, painting, sculpture, architecture, and literature, have been an important part of the people's lives in Europe. The great artists of the Renaissance awakened the people to the beauty of expression. You recall that Michelangelo and Da Vinci were engaged to decorate the churches with their beautiful paintings and sculpture. The names of other European artists are well known. Cézanne, El Greco, Picasso, Rembrandt, Renoir, and Van Gogh have created many of the world's finest paintings.

Europe has made a great contribution to the music of the world. The symphony, the ballet, and the opera began in Europe. Musicians, such as Bach, Beethoven, Haydn, Mozart, and Tchaikovsky, have written great music which is known all over the world.

Today, music is an important part of life in Europe. Many towns and cities support fine symphony orchestras. Many of the smaller towns have concerts in the parks during the summer months. These concerts are free to all who wish to hear them.

Opera and ballet are popular with the people of Europe. Most major cities have opera companies which present opera throughout the year. There are many well-known troupes of ballet dancers in Europe. Some of these, such as the Bolshoi Theater Ballet of Moscow and the Royal Ballet of Great Britain, have performed in the United States.

The Louvre, constructed as a fortress-palace in 1204, is today a national museum in Paris, France.

The lives of people throughout the world are also enriched by European literature. Since the days of the ancient Greeks, literature and drama have thrived in Europe. The ancient Greek writers have made contributions which we continue to enjoy today. You may know the hero of one of Homer's poems, the *Odyssey*. In this poem, Homer tells of the wanderings of the hero, Ulysses. Other great writers of Europe include Dante, Goethe, Shakespeare, Shaw, and Tolstoi.

Today, artists, musicians, and writers in all parts of the world are making their contribution to man's living. We can recognize the debt they owe to Europe for the early development of these arts. Europeans have contributed much to the development of beauty.

The Industrial Revolution

Europe was the place that saw the development of the Industrial Revolution, a revolution that changed the ways of living for thousands of the world's people. You read about the Industrial Revolution in Chapter 8. Let us take another look at it and see how and why it developed.

In Northern Europe the climate was, and still is, very cool most of the year. The cold temperatures, especially in the winter, made people look for ways of keeping warm. Wool clothing, solidly built houses, and huge log fireplaces did the job of providing warmth quite well. However, the forests of Europe were rapidly being cut for timber and fuel. But then a hard, black substance which would burn for a long time was discovered in Northern Europe. The long veins of coal, found under the Earth's surface, began to be mined when the long, steady heating qualities of coal were recognized.

The Invention of the Steam Engine

Soon it was discovered that a kettle or pot of water could be heated by the coal. The water would get so hot that steam would be formed. The inventor who improved the steam engine so that it could be harnessed to turn machinery was James Watt. You have read about his discovery and about the way steam was harnessed to turn wheels.

The steam engine was only a beginning. A steady stream of improvements and new inventions followed. The progress of the world we see today had its start when coal was harnessed to water. One might say that man's great enemies, fire and water, then became his friends and helpers.

With the invention of the steam engine, a new era of power was ushered in. Large industrial cities began to develop near the source of raw materials. Resources under the ground, such as coal and iron, became as important as those above the ground, the soil, vegetation, and animals. Power-driven machinery took the place of hand-driven devices. European cities began to grow as people came to work in the factories. The cities changed in appearance and in the problems they faced. The selling of large quantities of better goods led to wider and greater business interest.

The Industrial Revolution began in Europe, but many of the ideas that were developed were carried to other lands. These developments, which began slowly, have continued at an ever-increasing speed right into the 1960's. Since the discovery of steam, scientists have developed other sources of power. The discovery of electrical power and the development of the gasoline engine have hastened man's progress. Today, the discovery of atomic power opens up more wonderful possibilities for development and progress.

Europe has rich resources of minerals. The great deposits of coal, iron ore, and bauxite (aluminum ore) have contributed to the development of tremendous manufacturing centers on the continent. Much of the continent also has rich soil that produces large crops. As a result of these resources, only a few areas remain undeveloped.

Learning to Work Together

European countries are trying to develop ways to work together to bring about even greater prosperity. Statesmen have felt for many years that progress in Europe has been slowed down by the separation which has existed among the many different countries. They have urged Europeans to work to bring about a greater unity among the nations. In the 1950's and 1960's much progress has been made toward cooperation and unity.

One of the problems which has existed is the lack of free movement of goods, workers, services, and capital among European nations. No one nation of Europe produces all the goods and services it requires. Goods and services need to flow freely from one country to another. This has not been possible because of the restrictions placed on trade by the governments of the separate countries. High **tariffs,** or taxes, were placed on goods coming into a country to protect its own industries. Workers were not able to move from country to country. Money, available in one country and needed as capital to develop the business and industry of another country, could not be moved because of government restrictions.

In 1957, six nations set up an organization called the **European Economic Community,** also known as the Common Market. These nations were Belgium, France, Luxembourg, Italy, the Netherlands, and West Germany. The organization works to bring about true cooperation between the six member nations in matters of trade and economic development. The Common Market has agreed to gradually remove all re-

France's President Charles de Gaulle has exerted important influence on the policies of the European Economic Community, or Common Market.

strictions in the free movement of goods, services, and capital among the nations involved.

The Common Market has achieved a degree of success. It has abolished limits on quantities of goods which may move from country to country. It has lowered tariffs on goods traded between countries and has moved toward a single tariff on goods from nations outside the Common Market.

In 1959, seven nations which do not belong to the Common Market formed an economic union known as the **European Free Trade Association.** These nations, sometimes known as the Outer Seven, are Austria, Denmark, Great Britain, Norway, Portugal, Sweden, and Switzerland. Finland became a member in 1961. This group, like the Common Market, plans to eliminate tariffs and encourage free trade.

In 1961, the members of the European Free Trade Association applied for membership in the Common Market. The efforts failed in 1963 when France refused to vote for the admission of Great Britain. French President Charles de Gaulle feared Great Britain's economic ties with the nations of the British Commonwealth. He believed these ties would interfere with the operation of the Common Market.

These trade organizations and defense alliances such as NATO mark real progress in the unification of Europe. Even though there have been difficulties between France and Great Britain, there is hope that their differences will be settled before many years. When they are, Europe will have the opportunity to move toward greater cooperation, greater development, and greater progress.

Do You Know?

1. From whom did we inherit the idea of democracy? What is the meaning of this word?

2. What two cultural developments of the Romans have been dispersed? Which is more important to us?

3. Which reason for dispersal of people exists today in many countries?

4. What are three reasons for the diversity of climate in Europe?

5. What are the major ways of living in the five regions of Europe?

6. What four tiny independent states are located in Europe? What are the "Benelux" countries?

7. Why is Yugoslavia a good example of a nation with cultural diversity?

8. What was the cause of World War I? What was the outbreak of World War I?

9. When did World War I begin and end? Name some of the nations involved and tell the side on which they fought.

10. What is the origin of many European universities? Where is the oldest? Why are they important for the people of the world?

11. What are the "arts?" In what fields of music have the Europeans made great contributions?

12. What organization of nations was founded at the end of World War I? What replaced it at the end of World War II? Give the chief purpose of each.

13. What discovery and what invention aided in the development of the Industrial Revolution?

14. What discovery and what invention, made more recently, have hastened man's progress in industry?

Learn By Doing

1. Select the correct words and dates to complete the following sentences.

a. The __________ were fought in Europe between 1796 and 1814.

b. A major cause of these wars was a dictator who was hungry for __________.

c. After a successful campaign in __________ Napoleon Bonaparte returned to __________ as a national hero.

d. When he became First Consul, he established the __________ and the __________.

e. In __________ he declared himself __________ of France.

f. Napoleon wished to gain control over the continent of __________.

g. __________ was occupied because she refused to stop trade with __________, the most powerful enemy of Napoleon.

h. An alliance of European nations defeated Napoleon in __________ and exiled him to the island of __________.

i. But Napoleon escaped and returned to the city of __________ where he again became __________.

j. Finally in __________ he was defeated by __________ and exiled to the island of __________.

2. List the six major reasons for the dispersal of European peoples throughout the world. Give examples for each reason. Tell why people were *driven* from Europe and why they were *attracted* to other lands.

3. Using a blank piece of paper draw a large outline to represent continental Europe. Use the map on page 348 as a reference. Draw a small square to represent the British Isles and a rectangle to represent Northern Europe. Show where the early peoples settled by writing their names in the approximate location. Pages 355–356 will help you.

4. Select an artist, a musician, and a writer from those mentioned in the text. What was their nationality and their dates of birth and death? Briefly describe their lives. Give the title of one of their major works.

5. Using the language chart on page 350, answer the following questions:

a. From what ancestral language family did the languages of Europe come?

b. What eight major language groups came from this language family?

c. What three major language groups do not have minor languages related to them?

d. From which major language group did the Scandinavian languages come?

e. From which major language group did most of the languages spoken on the British Isles come?

f. From what language group did the languages of southern Europe come?

g. Which language of the British Isles is Germanic?

h. Are the German and French languages directly related?

6. Gather information about European ancestors from members of your family and from neighbors. With your class, make a chart using these headings:

a. Nations and Languages
b. When Our Ancestors Came
c. Methods of Travel Used
d. Reasons for Emigration
e. Favorite Recipes
f. Special Celebrations

Test Your Knowledge

1. What is meant by the official language of a country? Can you find out the official languages of Belgium?

2. How does the diversity of climate affect the diversity of crops in Europe?

3. What was the major cause of the Thirty Years War? Between what two powers did the conflict occur? Which two rulers fought for the Bohemian throne?

4. Answer the following questions about World War II:

a. When did the war begin and end?

b. What caused the outbreak of the war?

c. Which three countries were responsible for the war? Why?

d. Who were the leaders of each nation responsible for the war?

e. Which nations were the Allies?

f. Why did the United States enter the war?

5. What discoveries, during the Middle Ages and the Renaissance, aided in the development of Europe?

6. What are the six member nations of the Common Market? What is the goal of the organization?

7. Name the nations which belong to the European Free Trade Association. Explain the purpose of the organization.

CHAPTER 17

REGIONS OF EUROPE

The diversity of Europe, the well-developed continent, can be seen in the various regions of the continent. Europe may be divided into five regions: Fennoscandia in the north, the British Isles to the west, the Western European mainland countries, the Eastern European mainland states, and the lands surrounding the Mediterranean Sea. There are great areal likenesses as well as differences between these regions and between the nations of this continent. The continent of Europe has been of major importance for many centuries. From the nations of this region have come some of the most famous scientists, educators, authors, political leaders, musicians, and artists.

TYPES OF REGIONS

Geographers regionalize the world in order to help us understand the people, places, and ways of living in the world. You have read about many of the ways of **regionalizing**—that is, dividing the world into regions. You have seen that one way is to figure out temperature averages and rainfall totals of selected areas of the Earth's surface. It is possible to regionalize the entire surface of the Earth by temperature and rainfall. The regionalizer uses the facts of climate, temperature, and rainfall to draw climate regions.

Yet another way to regionalize a country, or the world, is to use the height of the land or the roughness of the earth to draw landform regions. Still another way to draw a region is to use soil color or texture. In this way the different kinds of soils are used as features that distinguish one soil region from another.

In Chapter 15 you read about several natural regions. You saw how vegetation may be used as the basis for forming regions. There you found types of vegetation, such as desert plants, grasses, and forest trees, closely related to the climate of the area. They were so closely related that the climate regions and the vegetation regions had the same boundary lines. The word, *tundra,* described a region of vegetation having small Arctic plants, lichens, and mosses. It also described an area where the temperature did not rise above 50 degrees in the summer.

All of the regions just mentioned are **physical regions.** They are formed on the basis of facts about the natural physical environment in which we live, facts about climate, landforms, soils, or plants.

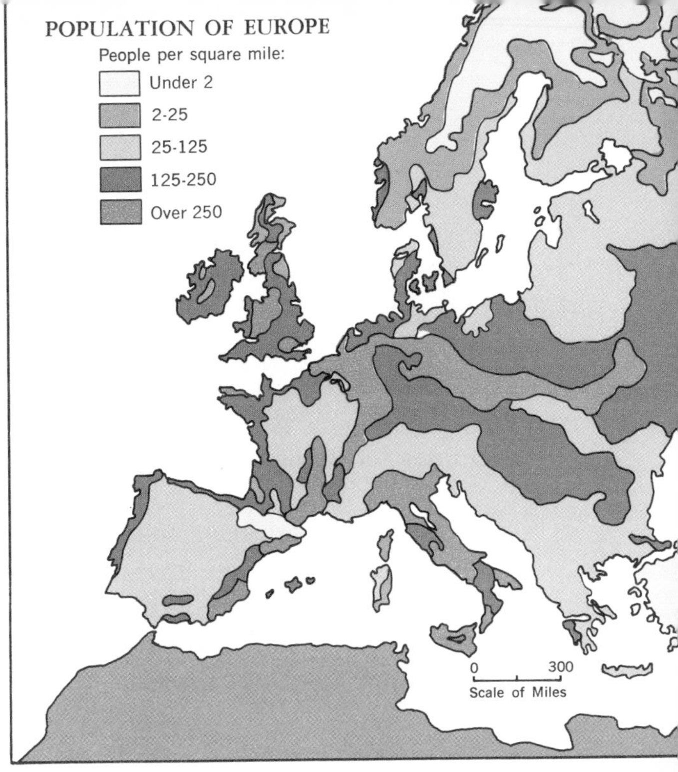

Could regions be drawn on the basis of population? What might the heavily populated areas have in common? Why is the population low in some areas?

Drawing Culture Regions

More difficult to draw, but often much more meaningful, are the regions where man has altered the Earth's surface. A **culture region** is formed on the basis of what man has done with the natural physical environment in an area. The rice growing regions of Eastern Asia are culture regions. There, hillsides have been terraced into rice paddies. Fertile river valleys have been so intensively farmed that little of the original natural vegetation remains. We call these areas rice culture regions.

This type of culture region is one which shows farming areas or types of farming. In place of the word "farming," we might use the word *agriculture.* This word comes from the Greek word *agros* meaning "field," and the Latin word *cultura* meaning "cultivation." A map of the agriculture regions of the world would show man's use of the surface of the Earth to secure food. It would show the different major crops that are grown and the different types of animals that are raised throughout the world.

Other types of culture regions may be shown on maps. Regions may be drawn on the basis of facts about manufacturing, transportation, languages, and religions.

A map of a **political region** is drawn on the basis of the form of government. It is the type of regional map with which you may be most familiar. The easiest part of such a map to understand is the lines that are drawn around the regions. These lines show the limits of certain governments. The hardest part to understand is that there is much more to each region than its boundary lines.

Inside the lines are a great number of physical and cultural features. To truly understand a political region, one needs to know these "inside" facts in geography.

Guides for Regionalizing

From what you have read thus far, you realize that regionalizing can be hard work. It also can be fun. When drawing regions, three important guides must be kept in mind.

Many farms are needed to form a farm region, an area where people are united by their closeness to land.

First, the area selected should not be too small. Let us see what would happen if the basis for drawing a region was too small. Suppose that each farm in Europe was used as a region. If a regional map showing each of these farms was drawn, it would be so cluttered that it could not be read. However, if lines were drawn around areas where most of the people lived by farming, the regional map would be much easier to draw as well as much easier to read.

Second, in each region there should be some unity. This means that there should be some fact or feature about the region which exists throughout. There should be a sameness of land surface, or of language, or of occupation. There were many unifying facts or features in the region called the Dry Muslim World. These were: little rainfall, sparse vegetation, animal and plant life adapted to dry areas, nomadism as a way of life, and the Muslim religion. These features are areal likenesses.

Third, there should be areal distinctions. Each region should be different from the regions around it. These differences should be important; they should stand out. An example of this can be seen in the two regions you studied in Chapter 15, the tundra and the taiga. In these two regions, the winters are much the same. They are very cold. The short summers, however, have important differences. Summer months in the tundra are too cold for coniferous trees to grow. Summer months

Both the beauty and the hardships of mountain life face the villagers of Bavaria, Germany (left) and Austria (right).

in taiga regions are warmer. They are warm enough for conifers to grow. The taiga in the U.S.S.R. is a great region of coniferous forests.

The regional distinctions, or differences, between the tundra region and the taiga region involve summer temperatures and vegetation. These are, of course, not the only differences between these two regions. Summer temperature and plant life were just two of several important differences. These two were selected to illustrate the point that a region should be different from surrounding regions.

Five Major Regions

In this book we have used the three guides to divide Europe into five large regions. Each region will be described in terms of areal likenesses. You will read about the facts or features that give each region unity. As you read about first one region and then another, you will also be meeting regional differences. That is, you will be reading about the features that distinguish one region from another.

The five major regions are Fennoscandia, the British Isles, Western European Mainland Countries, Eastern European Mainland States, and the Mediterranean Lands. Each of these major regions is made up of countries or parts of countries. You will need to learn the names of the countries so that you can understand the various parts of the major regions. Each of the major regions is divided into **sub-regions.** A sub-region also has to meet the three-point test for regionalizing. Let us turn first to the northernmost of the European regions, Fennoscandia.

FENNOSCANDIA

The region of Fennoscandia is made up of four countries: Norway, Sweden, Denmark, and Finland. Locate these countries and their capitals on page 380. Fennoscandia has several important features that are characteristic of the region.

The Importance of the Sea

Most of Europe's people benefit from the shape of the land. The oceans, their seas, and the currents interfinger with the peninsulas and islands. The entire region of Fennoscandia is almost surrounded by water. These waters abound in fish and are navigable. The shaded areas on the map on this page represent fishing regions. Lofoten Islands, Viking, Great, and Dogger Banks are among the world's greatest fishing sites. The inland seas serve as water highways. The Skagerrak and Kattegat Straits, south of Sweden, are major waterways which link the people of this region.

The women who sell fish in Copenhagen, Denmark are among the many who understand the importance of the sea to Fennoscandia.

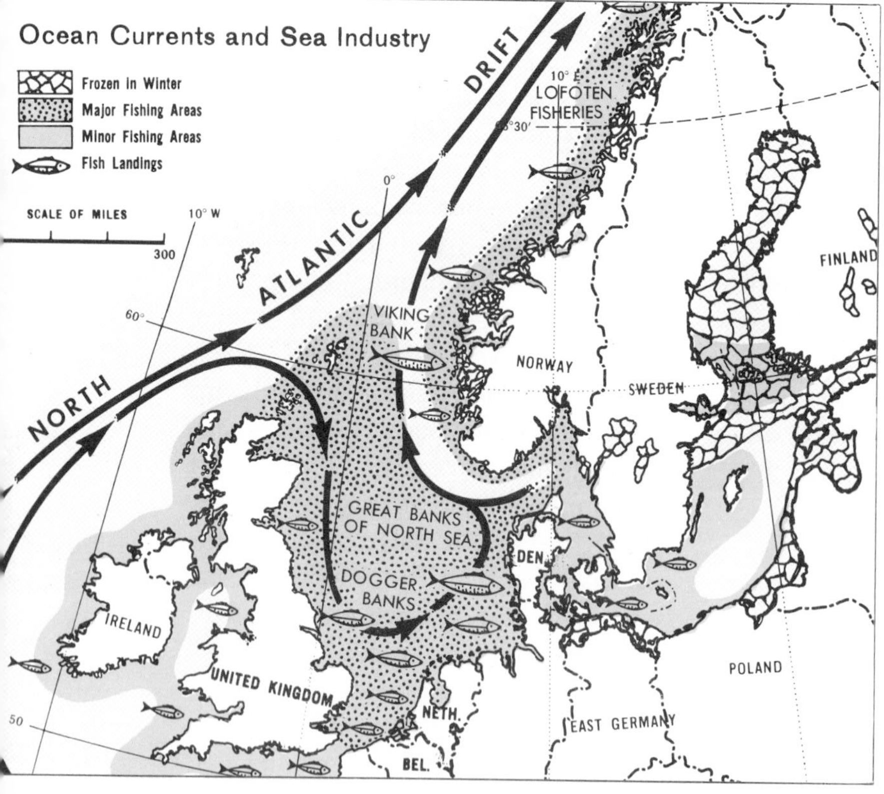

Along the coast of the entire Fennoscandian region fishing and shipping are of major importance. Norway has the third largest merchant fleet in the world. She is the leading fishing nation of Europe. Fish is an important item in the diet of the Norwegians. The fishermen catch cod and herring. They also maintain a large whaling fleet in the Antarctic. Many years ago, when the amount of whales found in the Arctic and North Atlantic Seas began to decrease, the Fennoscandian fishermen searched for them in the vast expanse of water around the Antarctic continent. In Norway the whale flesh is used for meat. The oil taken from the whale blubber is used in making soap and margarine.

There is an ocean current flowing northward in the North Atlantic Ocean which is warmer than the land it passes. This current is called the North Atlantic Drift. It comes from the Gulf Stream. When winter winds blow across the warm Drift, they bring higher temperatures and considerable moisture to the shore. The North Atlantic Drift has a **tempering** effect upon Fennoscandia. This means that the winters are warmer and the summers are cooler than those of other lands in the same latitude. The moisture helps trees to grow faster. The mild temperatures mean that crops can be grown quite far north.

The North Atlantic Drift also causes some inconveniences for the people. Thick masses of low clouds and fogs are frequent, especially in winter. Shipping is dangerous. At times, it comes to a standstill. Woolen clothing, slickers, boots, and umbrellas are seen everywhere. Rain pours on the slanted roofs, filling deep gutters.

Farmlands and Forests

Because of Fennoscandia's northern location and its short growing season, the farmers plant quick-growing root crops. Among these are potatoes, turnips, rutabagas, and parsnips. Some celery and cabbages are also grown. The summers are too cool and too damp to dry hay on the ground. After it is cut, it is placed on racks or poles for drying. Hay is carefully stored to be used as feed for animals in the winter. Some crops and many flowers bloom in greenhouses.

In each country there are trees of the coniferous, or cone-bearing, type. These are the pine, fir, larch, and juniper. Most of these conifers have needle-like leaves. They stay green throughout the year. Since conifers grow straight and have soft wood, they are excellent for saw logs, paper pulp, and building. Skilled carpenters and woodworkers live in this northern region.

The Fennoscandian countries have no coal, and only a little peat. Thus, the forest provides a major source of fuel for cooking and heating. **Naval stores,** such as pitch, tar, and turpentine, are also obtained from the forests. *Naval stores* is a term that

FENNOSCANDIA
0
125
Scale 125 miles to one inch
ICE AND SNOW
EVERGREEN FORESTS
TUNDRA
FORESTS
MOUNTAINS
FARMLAND
ARCTIC OCEAN
North Cape
Hammerfest
Barents Sea
LAPLAND
LOFOTEN ISLANDS
Narvik
Kiruna
Bodö
Salt Fiord
Lönsdal
Gallivare
Porjus
Kelloseilka
ARCTIC CIRCLE
ATLANTIC OCEAN
Norwegian Sea
NORWAY
KJÖLEN MOUNTAINS
NORRLAND HIGHLANDS
SWEDEN PENINSULA
SCANDINAVIAN PENINSULA
Lulea
Gulf of Bothnia
FINLAND
Umeå
Trondheim
Sogne Fiord
Bergen
Tampere
Turku
ALAND IS.
Helsinki
Haugesund
Stavanger
Oslo
Oslo Fiord
Stockholm
Gulf of Finland
Lake Vener
Skagerrak
Göteborg
Kattegat
SKANE
GOTLAND
ÖLAND
North Sea
Viborg
DENMARK
Copenhagen
Malmö
ZEALAND
JUTLAND
Baltic Sea
BORNHOLM
U.S.S.R.
W. GERMANY
E. GERMANY
POLAND
©1958, JEPPESEN & CO. DENVER, COLO., U.S.A.
ALL RIGHTS RESERVED
REVISED 1967

comes from the days when tar and pitch were used in building, waterproofing, and repairing wooden ships.

The forests are important for another reason. They provide homes for fur-bearing animals. These animals are hunted and trapped. Animal pelts, when sold, add a considerable amount to the family income.

Minerals in Fennoscandia

This entire region has been searched for minerals. In the hard-rock mountain areas, granite and marble of great beauty and durability are quarried. Stockholm, Oslo, and many mainland cities have beautiful columns of marble in their large government buildings and churches.

Other mines yield iron ore of very high quality. Much of this ore is exported to other countries. The Fennoscandian countries lack the coal necessary to manufacture steel in competition with other countries. They do refine some of their iron ore into steel through an electric-furnace process. This process costs far more than the process of making steel with coal. This steel is of a very high quality and is used in making fine steel products.

We have looked at some of the areal likenesses of the region of Fennoscandia. There are, however, areal differences within the region. We can see these differences by looking at the five sub-regions of Fennoscandia.

The Lowland Sub-Region

The first sub-region is located in the southern part of Fennoscandia. On the map on page 380, find this lowland section which includes Denmark, a small area in southeastern Norway, and the southern part of Sweden. It also includes a narrow strip of land in southern Finland. These lowlands of Fennoscandia are tied by water transportation to each other and to the other nations of Europe and the world.

The Lowland Sub-region has the greatest concentration of people in Fennoscandia. Factories, business houses, insurance companies, paper companies, and shipping headquarters are located in the modern cities of the lowlands. A railroad connects

Helsinki is one of four capitals located on the coast in Fennoscandia.

Stockholm, Sweden, is an important port (above). Farms of dairy cattle are found throughout Denmark (below).

the three important Swedish cities of Stockholm, the capital, Goteborg, and Malmo. Malmo lies just across a narrow strait from Copenhagen, the capital of Denmark. The areas around the capitals of Norway and Finland are included in this sub-region. Oslo in Norway and Helsinki in Finland are very busy coastal ports.

The country of Denmark is entirely within the Lowland Sub-region of Fennoscandia. It was once a wet, stony, marshland country. Today, it is a real agricultural "showpiece." The stones have been placed in stone walls, and the marshlands have been made productive. The Danes have worked hard to change their lands into fertile farmland. At one time, the chief occupation of Danish farmers was wheat growing. In the 1880's, wheat from countries which could raise it more cheaply threatened to put Danish farmers out of business. The Danish farmers began to produce other farm products. Today, they are among the best farmers in the world. Agricultural yields per acre rank among the highest in the world.

Many Danish farmers have organized cooperative groups. These cooperatives have made it possible for the farmers to use the most scientific machinery and farming methods. No one farmer could afford to buy all the machinery needed for a modern scientific farm. By joining with other farmers in buying and using the machinery, he can have what he needs. The farm and dairy cooperatives set their own high standards for products. They require each farmer to keep a careful record of his production. They also set the price that each member can ask for his farm products.

Hogs and dairy cattle are the most important products of the Danish farms. Large crops of beets, potatoes, oats, barley, and rye are also produced. Large amounts of these crops are used as food for the hogs and dairy cattle.

The resourceful Danish farmers produce great surpluses of bacon, eggs, potatoes, butter, cheese, pork, veal, and pastries. These surplus products are packaged attractively and sent to densely populated areas of Europe. Danish bacon is so excellent that it is in demand all over the world. Large quantities are shipped to the United States.

The clay soils of Denmark have been used not only for agriculture, but also in making world-famous pottery and porcelain articles. Royal Danish porcelain is well known for its fine quality and for the beautiful blue color which is used to decorate many of the pieces. Fine silverware, produced in workshops in Copenhagen and elsewhere, is prized throughout the world. Fine furniture is also made in Denmark and shipped to markets outside the country.

Ships enter Norway's major shipping center, Bergen (above). Codfish are drying in a northern village (below).

The Fiorded Coast Sub-Region

The map on page 380 shows Norway as a region of deep valleys and irregular coastline. When the ice cap which once covered the highlands of the Scandinavian Peninsula got larger, it moved outward. Heavy, thick ice, imbedded with stones, gouged huge U-shaped valleys into the western coastline of Norway. These valleys are now little arms of the sea called **fiords.** They have steepsided walls on either side. Water tumbles in many falls to the bottoms of these fiords. The fiords are often very deep and have smooth rock bottoms. These many inlets of the sea, or fiords, make the coastline of Norway very irregular indeed.

The fiords make excellent harbors. Most Norwegian towns are at the heads of fiords. For this reason, almost all towns in the Fiorded Coast Sub-region are ports. Lumber, fish,

Norwegian fiords range from narrow rivers to deep lakes, passing through fertile farmlands and mountains.

and some minerals flow through the ports of Norway to the rest of the world.

The fiords are part of Norway's beautiful scenery. Thousands of tourists come to see them. They visit such towns as Trondheim, Narvik, and North Cape. The fishing villages, lumber mills, beautiful forests, and iron ore docks are also very scenic. Tourists who visit Norway and the rest of Fennoscandia are impressed by the friendly, vigorous, healthy-looking, hardworking people who live there.

At North Cape, summer tourists can see a sight of matchless beauty—the sun at midnight! But to see the sun the tourists would have to look north, not east or west. By using a globe you, too, can imagine you are

As the sun moved from left to right, it was photographed at thirty minute intervals. Notice that at the lowest point (the third shot) the sun is still above the horizon. There has been light throughout the night.

looking at the sun at midnight. Hold the globe between you and a light. Find the northern tip of Norway on the globe. Imagine that it is midnight on June 21. You are on the opposite side of the Earth where the sun is shining. The Earth's axis on June 21 is tipped toward the sun. Tip the globe toward the light so that the North Pole goes away from you toward the light. The sun's rays are like the light's rays. As they come over the pole, you can see them. While it is noontime on the other side of the pole, it is midnight where you stand. But you can see the sunlight!

The model town of Kiruna, Sweden, was built in 1900 to house the workers of a newly opened iron mine.

Northern Lights

Another beautiful sight often seen in this northern region is the **Aurora Borealis,** or Northern Lights. These are a display of great brilliance and interesting colors caused by electrical charges from the sun. The Earth's magnetic field directs the charges toward the magnetic poles. As they move, they collide with particles in the atmosphere and change their electrical charge. As they do this, they glow and shine much like a fluorescent light. The movement of particles in the Earth's atmosphere causes the change of colors which seem to move as if they were in a breeze. The Aurora Borealis have been seen as far south as Mexico, but are most brilliant in the far northern regions of the Earth.

The Mineralized Zone

Located in the north, a third sub-region of Fennoscandia extends across both Sweden and Norway. This small area is sometimes called the Mineralized Zone or Corridor. Some of the highest-grade iron ore in the world is mined in this sub-region. High-grade steel articles, such as surgical instruments, knives, forks, and cutlery of all kinds, are produced from the steel that comes from this iron ore.

Because this Zone lacks coal deposits, the Scandinavians long ago learned to use charcoal in smelting iron ore. They made charcoal from their trees. The steel that they made was turned into spears, swords, daggers, armor, and shields. Today, you can see some of these early-day pieces of steel in museums. Swedish steel is famous for its high quality.

The four major towns in the Mineralized Corridor are Narvik, Kiruna, Gallivare, and Lulea. Narvik in Norway is the western export harbor for the iron ore mined in the Corridor. Kiruna and Gallivare are mining centers within the Corridor, and Lulea is the eastern export center on the Gulf of Bothnia. Most of the iron ore is exported to the great steel-manufacturing centers of England, France, Germany, Belgium, and even the United States.

An Area of Darkness

One interesting thing about living in the Mineralized Corridor Sub-region is that several months of darkness occur during the winter. The people go about their work with electric lights burning all the time. Can you explain the period of darkness in Narvik and North Cape?

You will need your globe again to help you. You remember how the globe was used to help you "see" the sun at midnight. The date then was June 21. Now imagine you are living in North Cape and the date is December 21. The time is noon, not midnight. This time hold the globe so that both you and the light are on the same side. Tip the globe as you did before, away from you, until the direct ray from the light is shining on the Tropic of Capricorn. Is any light shining on North Cape? Remember it is noontime; no light reaches North Cape.

Turn the globe. Does North Cape get any light as the Earth spins? No, it does not. The explanation for the period of darkness in winter here is that the Earth's axis is tipped away from the sun's direct rays. It is tipped enough ($23\frac{1}{2}°$) so that long periods of darkness occur in winter inside the Arctic Circle.

The Forested Sub-Region

The fourth sub-region is called the Forested Area. It is divided into two parts by the Mineralized Zone. It covers parts of Norway and Sweden and northern Finland. The coniferous tree is the unifying feature of this highland sub-region. Snow remains on the highlands for several months. It melts slowly so that the water runs off gradually. On the edges of this sub-region, great dams have been built to supply water for hydroelectric power. Hydroelectricity has now replaced charcoal and wood in smelting iron and in heating homes. This power can be sent long distances by wire.

The Forested Sub-region has a sparse population. It is a region where the whine of a saw or the bite of an axe cutting into a tree can be heard for many miles. This region is one of the great lumber resource areas of the world. The lumber is obtained from **"pure stands."** This means that the trees are nearly all

Chain-bound logs are brought through one of Finland's 60,000 lakes to a paper mill. Many small factories are spread throughout the forest-covered land.

of one kind and not mixed with other species. The tall, straight conifers grow quite close together. This forested region is important because it is not far from large centers of population in other parts of Europe. Its heavy lumber products have nearby markets.

The Forest and Lake Country

The fifth sub-region is the Forest and Lake Country of Finland. When the great continental ice-sheets melted, they left this southern part of Finland with a rough, pocketed surface. Evergreen trees now stand on land between the pockets or depressions. The depressions are filled with water. These lakes and ponds freeze during the winter. The Lake and Forest Sub-region supplies the Finnish people with fur, fish, timber, and winter recreation. The Finns are known for their skill in the arts and crafts, and for the major industries based on their forests.

THE BRITISH ISLES

The second major region of Europe consists of two large islands off the northwest coast of Europe and separated from the continent by the English Channel. They are Great Britain and Ireland. Together they make up the British Isles. They differ from the Fennoscandia Region in language and in the character of the land formation. In each of the four countries of the Fennoscandia Region, a different language is spoken. In contrast, English is the major language of this region. While Fennoscandia is a region of peninsulas, the British Isles is an island region. One is never very far from the sea. The sea has played a very important part in the development of the British Isles.

Sub-Regions of the British Isles

One way to regionalize the British Isles is by political boundaries. There are two nations in this region. One is the Republic of Ireland, which covers most of the island of Ireland. The other nation is the United Kingdom. The United Kingdom is composed of England, Wales, Scotland, and Northern Ireland. See the map on page 389. At one time, each of these subdivisions of the United Kingdom was a separate country. England conquered Wales and Northern Ireland. James the First of England inherited the crowns of both England and Scotland in 1603, but the governments of the two countries were not united until 1707.

A different way to regionalize the British Isles would be by languages. The Republic of Ireland has two official languages, English and Irish (Gaelic). Although Welsh, Scottish, and Irish are spoken, English is the official language of the United Kingdom. Mail is addressed and government records are kept in English. However, throughout the British Isles there are differences in ways of speaking English. These different dialects of English could be used as a basis for drawing regions.

Manufacturing Resources

The United Kingdom is one of the leading manufacturing centers in the world. Manufacturing is possible in this region because great seams of "coking" coal are found in the range of low mountains called the Pennines. This scenic range of mountains is referred to as the "backbone of England." Most of the leading manufacturing cities are found in this industrial region.

You may wonder what is meant by the term "coking coal." You will first have to learn how coal is ranked and graded. **Coal** is decayed vegetation. It is classified from soft to hard as peat, lignite, bituminous, or anthracite. **Peat** is coal in an early state of decayed vegetation. When dried, it can be burned. It has the lowest amount of carbon. **Lignite** is the next

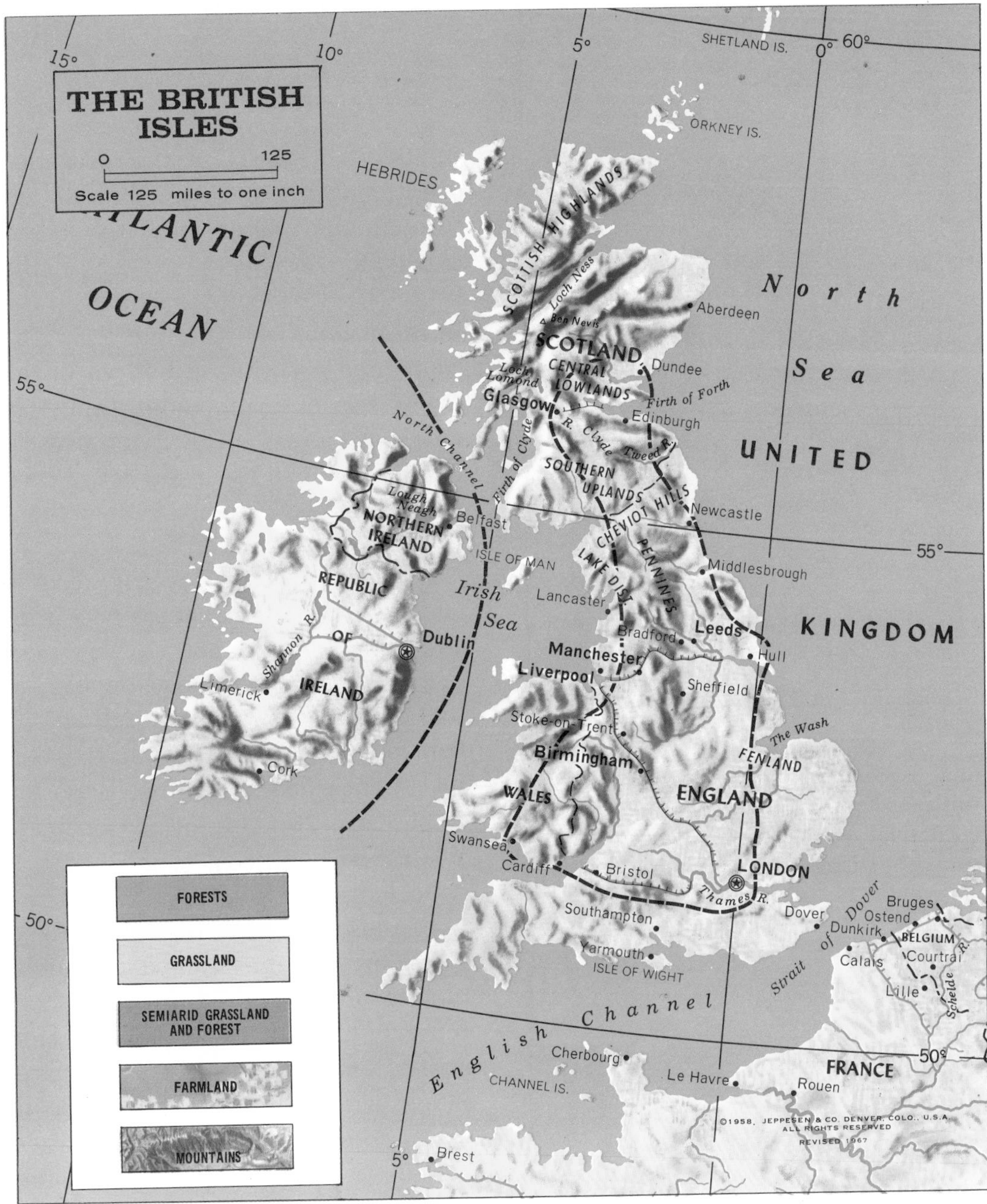

lowest in amount of carbon. It burns with a smoky flame and gives less heat than older, more compressed coal. **Bituminous** coal, or soft coal, has considerable gas which is released when the coal is heated. Its flames are extremely hot. Gases from bituminous coal are used in other industries. **Anthracite,** or hard coal, has the least amount of gases and the greatest amount of carbon. When burned, it is a clean, smokeless fuel. It leaves little ash, or "clinkers."

The word *coking* applies to some types of bituminous coal. Bituminous coal is changed to coke when it is burned in an air-tight oven. In the great heat of the oven, the coal

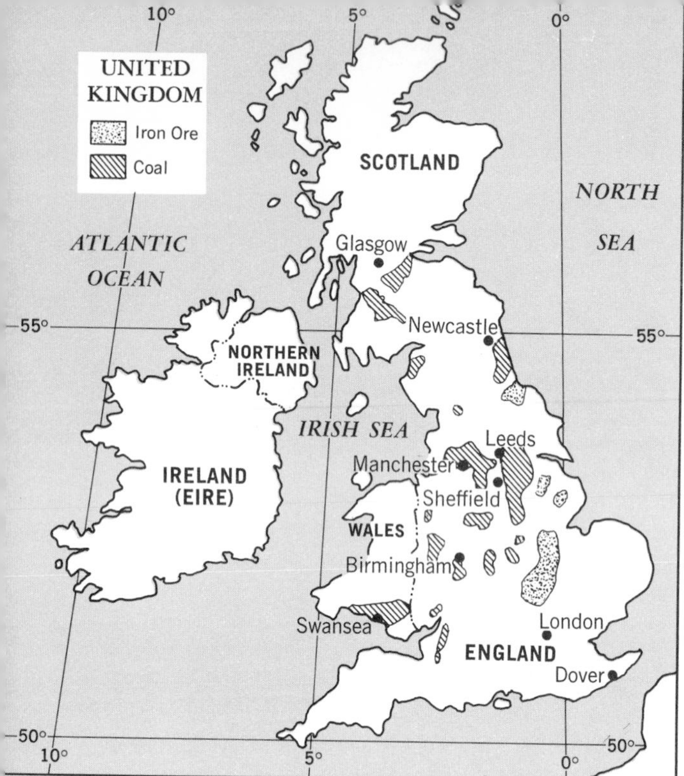

Coal is washed and sorted before it is shipped from southern Wales to the industrial cities of the British Isles and other European nations.

melts. The parts of the coal that change easily to vapor bubble up through the melted coal and collect at the top of the oven. These by-products of coal are drawn off in the form of ammonia, gas, and tar. The remaining coal, in the bottom of the oven, hardens into solid lumps of **coke,** or carbon. This is the process by which coke is made from coal. Coke produces intense heat without smoke when it burns.

A large supply of "coking" coal is needed by nations that produce iron and steel. In Chapter 15 you read that the Ukraine had large deposits of coal and iron ore near each other. Iron and steel industries have been set up near both types of deposits. Trains carry iron ore to the coal fields and return with coal to the iron ore deposits.

You also read that the Mineralized Corridor of Fennoscandia has high-quality iron ore deposits. Unfortunately, these iron ore regions lack nearby coal deposits. Therefore, much of their iron ore is shipped to other countries, such as the United Kingdom, where there are greater supplies of coal. Study the map on this page.

Anthracite is used mainly for heating homes. It is more expensive than other types of coal because it is difficult to mine. Often the seams in which it is found are twisted and curved at deep levels below the surface of the earth. In order to mine it, shafts have to be sunk deep into the earth. Bituminous coal is easier to mine than anthracite, because it is found in seams close to the surface. Layers of earth covering the coal seams, or veins, are stripped off, and the coal is mined in open pits.

Products of British Manufacturing

The United Kingdom led the world in the development of modern industries. One reason may have been the presence of supplies of iron ore and coal. Another reason may have been her lead in the early invention and manufacturing of machines made from iron and steel. Another factor was the invention of the steam engine which supplied power to machinery. Today, however, England, Wales, and Scotland import iron ore from foreign sources, such as Fennoscandia. Basic iron and steel rods, sheets, and "pigs" (chunks) are made in vast quantities from the imported ore.

The **secondary processes,** through which basic iron and steel are put, are more important to the economy of the United Kingdom than the basic industry. What do we mean by "secondary processes"? A secondary process is the reheating and reshaping of chunks of iron and steel. When raw iron is changed into a fender for an automobile, it has gone through a secondary process. The same is true when slabs of steel or rods of iron are transformed into steel girders for buildings, or into nails. The girders and nails are the result of a secondary process in manufacturing. This process increases the value of the products.

The industrial centers of the United Kingdom produce machinery for farms and homes, for knitting and weaving, and for ships, autos, planes, and rockets. Today, the United Kingdom sends these products along with many others, such as clothing, shoes, and metalware, all over the world. Many of her exports, however, go to former British colonies and to members of the Commonwealth of Nations.

Manufacturing Cities

Some of the great manufacturing cities of the United Kingdom are Leeds, Manchester, Sheffield, Birmingham, Bristol, Swansea, and Cardiff. Glasgow and Dundee are great

Glasgow is the largest city and the most important seaport of Scotland.

London, on the Thames River, is both a center of government and a leading industrial city.

shipbuilding cities. Ports through which manufactured products flow to other countries are London, Liverpool, and Hull.

Special notice should be taken of London, the capital of the United Kingdom. Although London is not located near coal and iron fields, she is a leading manufacturing city. She produces electrical equipment, clothing, automobiles, aircarft engines, and processed foods.

London is the major port of the United Kingdom. She exports not only her own products, but also those of the other industrial centers. At one time, sailing ships and early steam-driven vessels docked right at London. Today, with so many large ships, the docking space is spreading downstream. The ships dock at an outer port called the Port of London.

London has been an important trading center since Roman times. Its position has had much to do with its importance in trade. It lies close to the European continent and is near the open Atlantic. Trade and manufacturing have helped make London one of the world's greatest cities. Still another factor contributing to London's importance is her position as the government center of the Commonwealth of Nations.

Agriculture in the British Isles

Around the central manufacturing region of the United Kingdom lie productive farmlands. The climate and soils of the United Kingdom are favorable for the growing of grass. The grasslands support the sheep and beef cattle that are raised. Meat and dairy products are the two leading agricultural products of the United Kingdom. In addition, wheat, oats, and barley are grown.

Agricultural Ireland is a striking contrast to the largely industrial United Kingdom. The Republic of Ireland lacks industrial centers since resources, such as coal and iron ore, are not found in the earth. The entire landscape, however, is well watered. Moisture-laden winds from the Atlantic drop 30 to 100 inches of rain yearly. Ireland's climate is so heavily influenced by the ocean that it is called a **marine climate.** The temperature range from summer to winter is small compared to temperature ranges of other countries in the same latitude. Midsummer temperatures average about 60 degrees; winter temperatures, in January, are about 40 degrees.

Ireland has often been called the "Emerald Isle." Nearly one-half of the Republic of Ireland is used as permanent pasture and meadow land. Cattle and potatoes are the major exports. Based on agriculture, the industry of Ireland is largely connected with the preparation of food products, such as flour, bacon, and jam.

Farms are spread throughout the rolling, green fields of Ireland.

Cities on Ireland

Dublin is the capital and the largest city of the Republic of Ireland. It lies on the east coast and is a major seaport. The city has many broad streets and beautiful parklike squares. O'Connell Street, which is 150 feet wide, is one of the widest streets in Europe. Monuments of famous men in Irish history stand in the center of the street.

Most of the products of Ireland pass through Dublin on their way to other countries. Most of Ireland's trade is with Northern Ireland, the United States, and the United Kingdom. The

Dublin's O'Connell Street is one of the world's great avenues. Notice that, as in England, traffic keeps to the left.

United Kingdom, the largest customer, buys about 75 per cent of the products of Ireland.

Belfast is the capital of Northern Ireland. It is a world center for shipbuilding and linen manufacturing. In Northern Ireland, one-third of the world's flax is spun into beautiful white linen. Despite the fact that farms occupy about nine-tenths of the land of the country, the majority of people make their living in the manufacturing industries.

The United Kingdom as a Sea Power

Throughout its history, the United Kingdom has been important as a sea power. As the British Isles became industrialized and their population and products grew larger in number, the British turned seaward to other lands. They built a worldwide commercial empire. They established colonies in Australia, Canada, New Zealand, South Africa, and in many other areas in Africa, Asia, and the Americas. They imported raw materials from and exported manufactured articles to these colonies.

In the last century, many of Great Britain's former colonies have become independent. For a long period, the leaders of the colonies had felt that their nations should have equal rights and status with the United Kingdom. In 1931, the Parliament of Great Britain passed a law giving the Dominions the equal rights they wished. The British Empire became the Commonwealth of Nations. Each colony became an independent governing unit. These nations work together for the common good of all.

Many areas of land which are important in world trade are still British possessions. They are Bermuda, Bahama Islands, Barbados, Falkland

Islands, Pitcairn Island, Fiji, Hong Kong, Brunei, Ascension Island, and Gibraltar. Using a world map or globe, locate these British territories. You will find that you have circled the globe. Although the United Kingdom retains some of her worldwide empire, it is gradually shrinking.

The Structure of the Government

The United Kingdom of Great Britain is a **constitutional monarchy.** This means that the country has a reigning monarch, but is actually ruled by the **Parliament.** This legislative assembly consists of the monarch, the House of Commons, and the House of Lords. The Houses of Parliament really govern Great Britain. They act on legislation which the monarch must approve.

Queen Elizabeth II is the reigning monarch. Her husband is Prince Philip. In England, the husband of the Queen is never designated a king, and he does not inherit the throne. If the reigning monarch is a king, his wife does not inherit the throne. The throne passes from the reigning monarch to the oldest son. If there are no sons, the eldest daughter inherits the throne.

The power of the reigning monarch is called the **Crown.** The Crown has many responsibilities. The Crown approves the acts of Parliament before they can become laws. The Crown is head of the Church of England. All public officials work "On Her Majesty's Services." This is often abbreviated as O.H.M.S. The armed forces are called Royal, and naval vessels bear the initials H.M.S. for "Her (or His) Majesty's Ship." Coins and stamps bear a portrait of the monarch. Most important of all, the Crown is a symbol which holds all the peoples of the Commonwealth together.

The House of Commons is the real authority in the British government. Its members are elected by the people for a term of five years. If the Prime Minister calls for a special election, the term of the members may not last five years. All laws for the country are passed in the House of Commons.

The House of Lords has less power in the British government. The House of Lords must pass all bills for raising or spending money approved by the House of Commons. Other bills can become laws after a year's time, even if the House of Lords does not approve them. This house is made up of members of the nobility in the United Kingdom. Each member serves for life.

The Prime Minister is the actual head of the government. He is usually the leader of the party which has a majority of members in the House of Commons. He chooses a cabinet of ministers to help him run the government. The monarch approves the list of ministers. The Prime Minister and the Cabinet, with the cooperation of Parliament, govern the country.

WESTERN EUROPEAN MAINLAND COUNTRIES

The third major region of Europe is probably the most diverse and the most developed. Western Germany, the Netherlands, Belgium, Luxembourg, Austria, Switzerland, most of France, a large part of Spain, and all of Portugal are included in this region. Both areal likenesses and areal differences can be seen in this region.

What are the common features that make this area a region? First, this region has a **marine west coast climate.** This means it is strongly affected by the nearby ocean. Rainfall is abundant throughout the year. Winters receive the greatest moisture totals, often in the form of snow.

Harvests from Holland's farms begin their journey to market in open canal boats.

Second, this region has a mixed vegetation. There are many types of deciduous trees, trees that lose their leaves in cold seasons. There is a great variety of fruit trees, such as cherries, peaches, pears, and apples. Many acres are covered with grapevines. Different grains are seen in field after field. These grains include barley, rye, oats, and wheat.

Third, this region is characterized by farms, industrial towns, and mining centers. Almost all areas of the countries have been developed. It is a region where a house and garden on the outskirts of a great city are almost next door to a small farm. It is both a great manufacturing region and a great agricultural region. The countries of this region try to maintain a balance between agriculture and manufacturing.

This third major region of Europe is also a region of many languages. German, Dutch, Flemish, Breton, French, Spanish, and Portuguese are some of the languages spoken in this region. Many people of this region understand two languages. Others speak and understand four or five.

In Western Europe there are excellent systems of transportation. The many airports, railroads, highways, and waterways help unite the people. They are used for transportation and for trade. The map on page 398 shows that nearly all parts of Europe have railways. The most densly concentrated systems are near

London and Paris. Notice that even in the mountainous sections there are railroad lines. Passenger cars and freight cars run on regular, frequent schedules.

Sub-Regions of Western Europe

There are two ways, among many, which can be used to subdivide this region of Western Europe. One way is to use a landform map as a guide to drawing the sub-regions. When we do this, we divide the region into the northern lowlands and the southern highlands. A second way to regionalize this major region of Europe is on the basis of economies, that is, on the basis of ways of making a living. In the pages which follow, these ways will be combined.

The titles of the sub-regions will help you to understand why ways of living and landforms are both used. The first region is called "The Northern Lowland Sub-region of Manufacturing and Agriculture." The second is called "The Southern Highland and Valley Sub-region of Agriculture and Manufacturing." In these two titles landforms are mentioned. The land in the north is mostly lowland. In the south there are highlands and valleys. Manufacturing and agriculture are important in both regions. However, notice the order of the ways of living in each title. As you read about the activities of the people in both regions, keep the order in mind.

The Northern Lowland Sub-Region of Manufacturing and Agriculture

The northern section of Western Europe is mainly a lowland or plain. The land is rich in coal fields and iron ore deposits. These valuable resources make mining important in this part of Europe. The network of canals and rivers in this sub-region allows coal and iron to be transported

Railroads transport goods to and from industrial cities such as Dusseldorf.

at low cost to iron-and-steel-making centers. The Minette district of Belgium and Luxembourg, the Saar region between France and West Germany, and the Ruhr Valley of West Germany are major iron-and-steel-manufacturing centers of the world. European cities such as Essen, Dusseldorf, and Dortmund in West Germany, Metz and Mulhouse in eastern France, and Liége in Belgium resemble the United States cities of Pittsburgh and Birmingham.

This sub-region of heavy manufacturing is also a sub-region of intensive farming. Over the centuries the people have become excellent farmers. They farm the land with great care and use scientific methods and modern machinery in most areas. They grow a wide variety of grains, root crops, and fruits. They also raise a wide variety of animals: cattle, hogs, sheep, and goats. Wheat, dairy products, and livestock are important to the farm economy of this sub-region.

Millions of people live in this Northern Lowland Sub-region. Therefore, there is a demand for an enormous supply of food. This demand is met by a high production of crops per acre.

Transportation on the Rhine helps Duisberg and other cities expand.

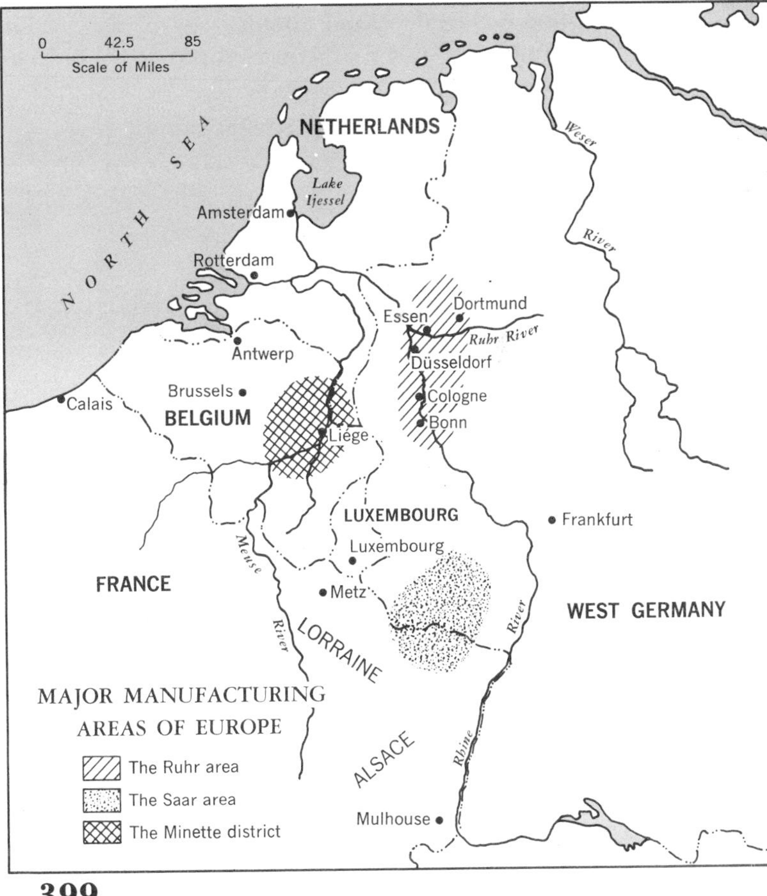

Glass-covered canal boats serve as sightseeing buses in Amsterdam.

Farmland is developed by irrigation canals, and sometimes by windmills.

Grazing land lies beside a road and bicycle lane on the twenty-mile dike that has created Lake Ijssel.

The construction of dams in the south will make it possible to control the river currents of the delta.

The Netherlands Waterway System

A regional feature of this lowland area is its highly developed systems of transportation. Railways, highways, and waterways connect all parts of the region. They are used for transportation and for trade.

The waterway system is the most extensive within the Northern Lowland Sub-region. The many rivers are connected by canals. Thus, there are no "breaks" in water transportation. Notice on the map on page 397 the direction in which the following rivers flow: the Loire, the Seine, the Somme, the Rhine, the Ruhr, the Weser, and the Elbe.

Let us take a closer look at a section of one of the great northward-flowing rivers, the Rhine. The part we shall study is the delta of the Rhine. Here the river divides and distributes its water through several branches to the North Sea. The low, level land between these distributaries makes up a greatly admired country. It is the Netherlands.

Reclaimed Lands

Over the past seven centuries, the people of the Netherlands, the Dutch, have reclaimed land from the swamps and shallow seas near the North Sea. They have done this by building dikes and by draining water from the land enclosed by the dikes. A piece of land that has been surrounded by a dike and drained of water is called a

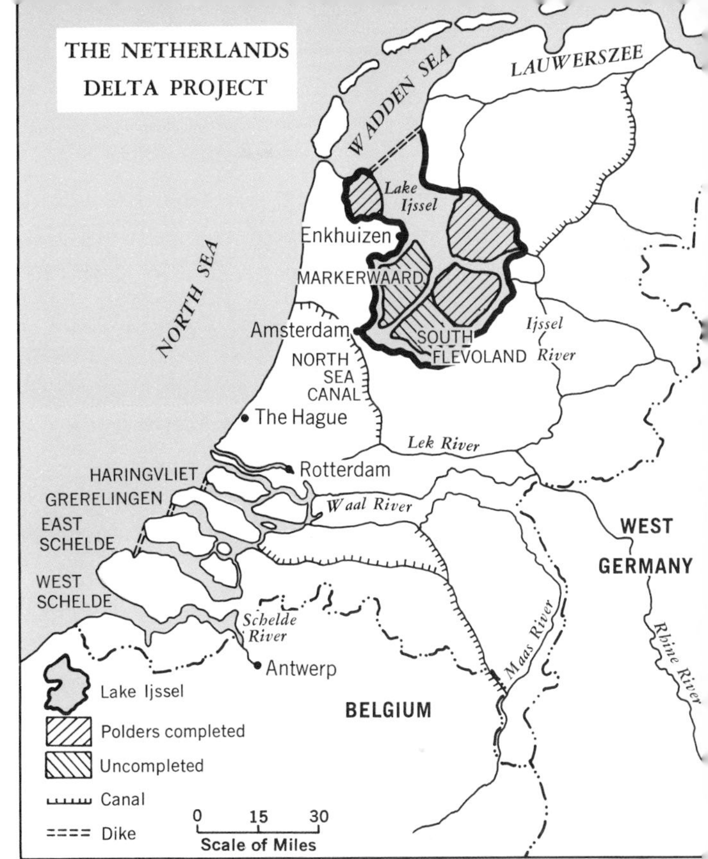

polder. To remain dry, a polder must be continuously drained by pumping.

At one time, the windmills which dot the polder landscape were used to pump water from the polders into drainage canals. Today, motor-driven pumps do the work of the windmills. The canals serve not only as drainage ditches, but also as highways. They are used to carry farm produce from the polders to the central market places.

Polders form 40 per cent of the Netherlands agricultural land. Crop yields from the fertile soils are high. Farmers harvest carrots, beets, and flowers. The tulips of the Netherlands are world famous and important to the economy of the country. Tulip bulbs from Holland can be found in markets in many parts of the world. The rich grasses of the polders also support a highly profitable dairy industry.

New Lands Are Being Made

The Netherlands government is working on an important project called the Netherlands "Delta Plan." It is considered to be one of the five future wonders of the world. This plan was begun in 1952 when engineers drew plans for the building of new dikes to claim new land.

In 1953, the worst storm in 500 years broke dikes, flooded farmland, drowned 1,800 people, and damaged over 45,000 homes, farms, and schools. The Dutch became more determined than ever to protect their land. The result was that the "Delta Plan" was enlarged to include plans to prevent storm damage as well as plans to claim new land. Work began in 1955 and will continue through 1978.

The target is the southwestern part of the Netherlands where five arms of the sea extend into the land. Locate this area on the diagram on page 401. Through these inlets roll heavy seas and powerful tides. The Dutch plan to close four of these sea arms by building heavy dams near the sea mouths. There will be other dams farther inland to strengthen the control over floods. One sea arm and one canal will be left open to allow ships to reach the ports of Rotterdam in the Netherlands and Antwerp in Belgium.

One dam, which is called the Schelde Dike, is nearly two miles long. It was completed in 1961. It is located where a sea arm joins the North Sea. At this point, the sea pushes 20 billion gallons of water into the arm. This was difficult to build. What the engineers learned by working in this area will help them in their other projects. At one point a five-mile-long dam, or dike, will be built to hold back 290 billion gallons of sea water.

This great project will provide protection from flooding by stormy seas. It will also open up much new land for agriculture. It is a good example of how man can change his environment when he uses his knowledge and the resources he finds around him.

A Center of Transportation and Trade

Paris, France, is an example of a city which owes its importance to the transportation facilities it has built. It is located in the heart of the Paris-basin area of France. From the earliest days, Paris could easily be approached from all sides. The main roads of the country meet in Paris. The city is served by five railroads.

The main branches of the Seine River flow together near Paris. Great wharves along the river serve the numerous barges and steamboats which carry both goods and people. Paris is also a great air center. Most of the international airlines of the world fly

The great Orly Airport today links Paris with the outside world, but the Seine continues to be an important outlet to the Atlantic Ocean.

into the two airports which serve the city of Paris.

Paris is the trade center for France. Goods from all over the world flow through Paris. Most of the large factories of Paris are in the suburbs. Automobiles, machinery, railroad supplies, chemicals, soaps, dyes, and leather goods are manufactured in these towns.

Paris has long been famous as a center for fashions and luxury items. Well-known designers of women's clothes have their workshops there. Perfumes, jewelry, and fine artificial flowers are made in the many small plants scattered over the city.

Tourists from all parts of the world come to Paris. They are attracted by the fine examples of art and architecture which may be seen there. For hundreds of years, each new French government has worked to make Paris larger and more beautiful. Its wide streets, its beautiful squares, its fine buildings, and its monuments make it one of the world's most beautiful cities.

People are drawn to the Swiss Alps by the scenery and the invigorating air. Farther west, in parts of the Central Massif of France, farming is productive and profitable.

Agriculture and Manufacturing in the Southern Highlands and Valleys

The southern part of Western Europe is called the Highland and Valley Sub-region. Starting in Austria and moving westward on the map on page 355, you see the Austrian Alps, the Swiss Alps, the Central Swiss Plateau, the Jura Mountains, the Rhone River Valley, the Central Massif, the Garonne River Valley, and the Pyrenees Mountains. The Pyrenees separate France from Spain. Farther south you find the plateau of Spain, known as the Spanish Meseta. These land features make this a very different region from the Northern Lowland Sub-region.

Agriculture and manufacturing can be found throughout this sub-region. Agriculture is placed first because most of the land in this sub-region is used for it. Farming is the way of life in the lower, wider parts of the river valleys. It is also the way of life on the upper slopes and even in the more mountainous areas.

Manufacturing is found in a few parts of this high-level region. See the map on page 399. Water tumbling down from the melting snowfields on the high Alps has been converted into power for electricity. This is especially true in Switzerland and in Austria.

Two of the industrial cities in Austria are Vienna and Graz. Vienna, the capital, is located on the Danube River and is the largest manufacturing center in the nation. Graz is noted for its metal products. These are made from the nearby iron ore deposits.

The products which are made in the cities of Switzerland are of very high value. For example, Geneva, Switzerland, is noted for the manufacturing of engineering tools, watches, clocks, and chemicals. Another Swiss city, Lausanne, like Geneva, is in the upper drainage basin of the Rhone River. This beautiful city started as a cathedral town. It has changed now to become a residential, tourist, and industrial community. This city still has its early charm. Its workshops turn out high-grade paper, printing sets, and woodworks.

Important Farm Products

Where the Rhone River and its branches widen out into valleys, agriculture takes over. The Garonne River, which empties into the Atlantic Ocean, has industrial cities on her banks. She also has fertile, highly productive farms reaching from her banks upward to the surrounding hills. Nearly all of the basin of the Garonne River is favorable for fruit growing. Among the trees are groves of sweet chestnuts, walnuts, and pears.

Grapevines are plentiful in the southern region. Most grapes are brought to wineries to be crushed and made into wine. The rest are sold as table grapes. The farms also produce sheep and goats. Meat from sheep and lambs, and butter and cheese are distributed all over Western Europe. The market towns to which the agricultural products go are Bordeaux, Toulouse, and Marseilles. The processing and canning of foods occupy many hands in the seaport cities. Some of the dairy products find their way to the United States.

Separated but Similar

As you can see from the map on page 397, Spain and Portugal appear cut off from the rest of Europe by the Pyrenees Mountains. Sometimes these two countries are treated as a separate region. They have been included in the third major region of Europe on the basis of their location in Western Europe and on the basis of their marine west coast climate.

They deserve a place in the Southern Highland and Valley Sub-region of Agriculture and Manufacturing because they fit the tests of landforms and ways of living. The two nations have broken plateaus, mountain

Ships, large and small, have sailed from Portugal for many centuries.

ranges, and rounded hills. They also emphasize agriculture more than manufacturing. From the broad valleys of the Ebro, Tagus, and Guadalquiver rivers, one can see the rimming mountains. On a map these mountains look like cords laid around a depression. High mountains such as these, elongated and slightly curving, have been named **cordilleras.**

Madrid, the capital and largest city of Spain, has a growing industrial section. However, the most important work of the people of Madrid is their employment in running the government of the country. Madrid is the most important city in Spain for banking, insurance, and finance. It is the airline and railroad center for the country. The city is located on a high plateau in central Spain. The Spanish people call this area the "Heart of Spain."

Between France and Spain is the small independent state of Andorra.

Bordering on the Atlantic Ocean, Portugal and western Spain have the marine west coast climate, which is a common feature of Western Europe. Much of the interior of Spain is dry or semi-dry. Portugal, turning to the sea, leads the world in sardine fishing. Spain's interior has large land holdings upon which cattle and sheep are raised. Much of the Spanish Meseta is badly eroded from overgrazing.

Lisbon is the capital and leading city of Portugal. Located where the Tagus River enters the Atlantic Ocean, it has one of the world's finest harbors. It is the main point of export for Portugal's salt, canned sardines, tuna, olive oil, and wine. Shipbuilding is an important occupation of the people. Lisbon also serves as a terminal for airlines flying the Atlantic Ocean.

Spain and Portugal were, at one time, great naval powers. Their explorers opened up large sections of the Western Hemisphere. Latin Americans today trace much of their backgrounds to these two nations of Europe.

Different Forms of Government

These two countries differ from other countries in Western Europe in the form of government which they have. Each one is ruled by one man. Such a form of government is often

Tourists visiting Spain will see the modern city of Madrid, the many ancient towns, and the large areas of farmland.

called a **dictatorship.** The opposite of a "one-man rule" form of government is one in which the majority of the people rule. The latter type, at its best, is found in a truly effective democracy. If the former has an honest, fair person as the dictator, or one-man ruler, the country may prosper. The people may be happy. But if this benevolent dictator dies, there is no real assurance that he will be followed by another benevolent one-man ruler.

In most other Western European Mainland Countries, there is a democratic form of government. When the elected leader dies, retires, or is replaced by another elected leader, the form of government stays much the same. It is as good as the majority of the people want it to be and try to make it. In the Western Mainland Countries people are well educated and well informed. In some cases, they are very outspoken about their countries and world affairs.

In the next great region of Europe, the Eastern European Mainland Countries, you will read about a different form of government. Each of these countries is ruled by a group of men. The group, however, is not elected in the same manner as that used by the Western European democratic countries. The citizens of the Eastern European Countries are not encouraged to speak freely about affairs of government. Regular elections are not permitted or are very rare.

Do You Know?

1. What are the three major guides by which the regions of Europe were drawn?

2. What four countries make up Fennoscandia? What are some of the areal likenesses of the region?

3. What are three effects of the lack of coal in Fennoscandia?

4. What is a fiord? Where are they located? For what are they noted?

5. What two islands make up the British Isles? What are the four parts of the United Kingdom? What other nation is located on the British Isles?

6. What are the Pennines? Where are they located? What are they noted for?

7. What are four reasons why London is the major city of the United Kingdom?

8. What is a constitutional monarchy? What is Parliament? What is meant by the Crown?

9. What are three major iron-and-steel-manufacturing centers in the Northern Lowland Sub-region? Where is each located?

10. What two valuable resources are found in the Northern Lowland area? By what systems are they transported to manufacturing cities?

11. What are some characteristics of a marine west coast climate?

12. What is the major landform of northern Western Europe? What are the major landforms of southern Western Europe? In which sub-region is agriculture the most important?

13. What is a polder? How are they used by the Dutch?

14. What source of power is used for manufacturing in the Highland and Valley Sub-region? What is the source of this power?

15. Along the banks of what river are major manufacturing cities of this region located? Name three and give an important product of each.

16. What agricultural products are grown in the basin of the Garonne River? To what market towns are they brought?

17. Why are the Pyrenees Mountains sometimes called a cordillera?

18. What is a dictatorship? Which countries of Western Europe have this form of government?

Learn By Doing

1. Various types of maps have been included in this book. Sketch and label several different types of maps. For example, you might sketch a landform map, a political map, a population map, or a rainfall map of a region of Europe.

2. Prepare a report on one of the following features of Norway. Make up a title for your report.

Fishing (whaling)
Mining (iron ore)
North Cape (unusual sights)

3. Name the sub-region of Fennoscandia which contains each of the following items:

a. many cities, people, and industries

b. a large portion of Finland

c. coniferous trees and lumber products

d. many harbors and picturesque scenery

e. many lakes and picturesque scenery

f. deep valleys and an irregular coastline

g. many iron ore deposits

h. furs, fish, and timbers

i. all of Denmark

j. famous steel products; export cities

4. Compare the structure of the government of Great Britain with the structure of the government of the United States. It might help to draw a chart to show which branches are similar.

5. Sketch a map of the British Isles. Study the map on page 389 first. Think of the size of each land area. Locate the major water inlets and islands.

a. Label the two nations and the four sub-divisions of the United Kingdom.

b. Locate and label the cities of Dublin, Belfast, London, Leeds, Manchester, Liverpool, Swansea, and Glasgow.

c. Label the Pennine Mts.

d. Label the English Channel, the Irish Sea, the Atlantic Ocean, the North Sea, and the Irish Sea.

e. Draw and label the Shannon River, the Thames River, Lough Neagh, and Loch Ness.

6. Prepare a report on the delta region of the Rhine. Be sure to include these terms: Netherlands, Dutch, polder, windmill, dike, canals, agriculture, Delta Plan, floods, and "new lands."

7. Make a booklet on the ways of living in Spain and in Portugal. Collect pictures and write captions for each. Be sure to include information on the bullfights, the architecture, the major cities, and the importance of the sea.

Test Your Knowledge

1. What is the North Atlantic Drift? What effect does this have on the climate of Fennoscandia?

2. How do the Danish farmers benefit from the farm and dairy cooperatives? What are the major products produced?

3. What is coal? How is it ranked? What is coke? How is it obtained?

4. Give several reasons why the United Kingdom led the world in industrial development?

5. What are the characteristics of a marine climate? What effects does this type of climate have on the way of life in Ireland?

6. Where are the cities of Dublin and Belfast located? Explain why each city is important.

7. Explain the statement, "The British Empire became the Commonwealth of Nations."

8. Name five common features of the Western European Region.

9. What are two reasons for including Spain and Portugal in the region of Western Europe?

CHAPTER 18

EASTERN EUROPE AND THE MEDITERRANEAN

The Eastern European Mainland States will be studied by sub-regions based on political boundaries. The nations of this major region of Europe have both common features, such as a Communist form of government, and unique differences, such as languages and nationalities.

The region around the Mediterranean Sea was at one time the center of the known world. This region still plays an important role in world culture and in world trade. The type of climate, called Mediterranean, is a common feature of the entire region. Because of this climate and the types of crops grown in each of the countries, this region will be studied as a whole.

EASTERN EUROPEAN MAINLAND STATES

The fourth major region of Europe, the Eastern European Mainland States, lies between the U.S.S.R. and the Western European countries. Locate on the map on page 411 the countries included in this region. From north to south, they are East Germany, Poland, Czechoslovakia, Hungary, Rumania, Yugoslavia, Bulgaria, and Albania. The contrasts and unique features of these countries make the region easy to divide into sub-regions. The sub-regions will be based on the political boundaries of the nations.

A major reason for dividing this large part of Europe into political regions is the language. As one crosses any border between two nations, he meets people using different sounds and words. Border policemen, customs officers, clerks in stores, and the people on the streets all reveal a distinct difference when they speak. Languages unite people, but they also divide people, especially when people cannot understand each other.

There is one major language selected as the official language in each

EASTERN EUROPE
0 125
Scale 125 miles to one inch
EVERGREEN FORESTS
FORESTS
GRASSLAND
FARMLAND
MOUNTAINS
Baltic Sea
EUROPEAN PLAIN
POLAND
EAST
NORTH
GERMANY
WEST
GERMANY
CZECHOSLOVAKIA
AUSTRIA
HUNGARY
RUMANIA
U. S. S. R.
YUGOSLAVIA
BULGARIA
ALBANIA
GREECE
TURKEY
ITALY
SAN MARINO
BALKAN PENINSULA
Rostock
Gdansk
Szezcin
Furstenburg
Elbe
Oder
BERLIN
Magdeburg
River
Poznan
Vistula
River
Warsaw
River
Lodz
Lublin
Dresden
SUDETEN MTS.
Wroclaw
SAXON GATE
Plauen
UPPER SILESIA
Prague
Krakow
BOHEMIA
Plzen
PLATEAU
Brno
MORAVIAN CORRIDOR
CARPATHIAN MTS.
Danube
River
Vienna
Bratislava
Miskolc
River
Debreczen
Budapest
Tisza
Lake Balaton
Cluj
Szeged
Ljubljana
Zagreb
TRANSYLVANIAN ALPS
Galati
Braila
Ploesti
Sava
River
DINARIC ALPS
IRON GATE
Belgrade
Bucharest
Constanta
Zenica
Vares
Sarajevo
Morava
River
Danube
River
BALKAN FORELAND
Varna
Black Sea
BALKAN MTS.
Sofia
Burgas
Maritsa River
Plovdiv
RHODOPE MTS.
Istanbul
Adriatic Sea
ROME
Tirana
Aegean Sea
Athens
10°
15°
20°
25°
30°
55°
50°
45°
40°

of the eight countries. However, within some of the countries themselves there are sub-languages, or dialects. Probably the best example is in Yugoslavia. *Yugoslavia* means "South Slavs." You read in Chapter 16 that the languages of Serbo-Croatian, Slovenian, and Macedonian are used. Each is sub-divided into a number of dialects.

The languages of the other nations are each different with many dialects. Just think of the diversity of tongues! In addition to those already mentioned are Slovakian, Czech, Polish, German, Hungarian, and Bulgarian. Mixtures of Russian, Italian, and Greek are spoken in the border countries. But let us look at each political division more closely.

Can the German people, united by language, be divided by a wall?

THE GERMAN DEMOCRATIC REPUBLIC

At the close of World War II, Germany was divided into four zones. Each of the Allied powers, Great Britain, France, the United States, and the Soviet Union, occupied and governed a division. The three Western powers helped the Germans in their sectors to set up a Democratic government. The Russians established a Communist government in the eastern part of the country, which they controlled. Germany has remained divided since then. East Germany is now called the German Democratic Republic, although it is neither democratic nor a republic.

A Divided City

Berlin, the largest city in Germany, is divided between Communist East Germany and Democratic West Germany. Just as the country was divided into four sectors after World War II, so was the city of Berlin. The three sectors controlled by American, French, and British troops became known as West Berlin. The Russian sector is East Berlin. All of Berlin is located in East Germany. Locate this city on the map on page 411. It is 110 miles from the West German border.

Shortly after the War, West Berlin became a stronghold for freedom and democracy. Each year thousands of refugees from East Germany fled to

During World War II the industrial cities of Germany were heavily bombed. Then, at the end of the war, the nation was divided. Both the East and the West faced industrial problems. There has been progress in the East, though perhaps we are more aware of the progress in the West. For example, since World War II, the production of Volkswagens at Wolfsburg has become one of West Germany's leading industries.

the western sector to escape Communist rule. Between 1945 and 1961 over three million persons escaped by way of West Berlin. The Communists sealed off this escape route in August, 1961. They built a 26-mile concrete and barbed-wire wall across the heart of the city. They boarded up windows and doors in buildings that faced the western sector.

A few refugees still manage to escape, but for most East Germans the door to freedom and democracy has been shut tight. Green-uniformed East German police guard the wall to make sure no one escapes. They have orders to shoot anyone who tries to go over or under the wall and the barbed wire.

The people of West Berlin are allowed to bring supplies from West Germany through a narrow corridor controlled by East Germany. This has been a problem for West Berliners. On occasions, East Germany has closed the road making it necessary to fly supplies into West Berlin.

Most of West Berlin has been rebuilt since World War II, but the Communists have been slower to rebuild East Berlin. Some bombed out buildings and great open spaces still remain. Before the wall was built, many East Germans worked in West Berlin. After 1961 employment dropped sharply. East Berlin produces only about one-half the amount of manufactured goods produced in West Berlin. Consumer goods, such as automobiles, refrigerators, and other household equipment, are scarce in East Berlin.

Industrial Problems

The separation of Germany caused several problems for the leaders and the people of East Germany. They found that they were cut off from the two greatest industrial zones of Germany, the Ruhr and Silesia. The latter is a large industrial zone located on the upper Oder River. Excellent coking coal is mined nearby. When this region came under Polish rule, the East Germans lost access to it. The former, the Ruhr, is in the valley of the Ruhr River, a tributary of the great Rhine River. The iron and steel production of this manufacturing area went to West Germany. The result was a shortage of iron and steel products in East Germany.

Famous Dresden china is made in Meissen, now a part of East Germany.

A search for industrial sites was made. Now, near Magdeburg, huge blast furnaces using lignite coal make this region a leading iron producer. Eisenhuttenstadt, located near Fürstenburg, is one of the world's most recent and most modern iron-and-steel-producing centers. The government has encouraged the growth by importing coal from Poland and iron ore from Sweden and the U.S.S.R. Basic iron and steel made at these two centers are used to manufacture a wide variety of items. Among them are the bulk products of rails, structural steel, tools, and utensils.

Other industries have flourished nearby. These include toys, musical instruments, and optical instruments such as telescopes, microscopes, and spectacles. The power generated through electricity aids in the making of gloves, shoes, furniture, and paper. Glass and china articles also are made, especially in Dresden. Leipzig is the main fur market for all of Europe. Several minerals found in the soil have been basic to the development of the chemical industry. Cotton and woolen goods are made and colored in Plauen. Rostock is a shipbuilding center along the Baltic Sea.

The Use of the Land

About four out of every ten persons in East Germany work in industries in cities. The rest are scattered throughout the country in other occupations. Forests cover about one-fourth of the land. Many people work in lumbering, wood cutting, and pulp mills. The area remaining, which is arable, is used for growing cereals and root crops. Potatoes and rye are widespread in the northern part. Hops, used in beermaking, makes a good cash crop. Apple and plum orchards are abundant on the slopes in central and southern parts. Large areas of land, however, are still devoted to forage and to pasture.

The government has broken up many large estates. Land holdings, which were once over 250 acres, have been cut to plots ranging from 12 to 50 acres. These new plots are called "state lands" or "national properties." The process by which groups under a governmental head are forced to co-operate in the use of the land is called **socialization of agriculture.** It has increased rapidly in East Germany since 1960. It has been estimated that the standard of living in East Germany is lower than in West Germany. The cost of living, however, is higher. Can you explain the difference between a standard of living and a cost of living?

POLAND

Along with the language difference, one would note another feature on entering Poland from East Germany. Most of the surface of Poland is one immense **plain.** While there are low, rounded hills, the land is mostly level. The soils for the most part are clayey.

Until World War II, Leipzig was the center of German books and music.

In the northern part, they are sandy. The sands permit water to go through quickly. Because the drainage is poor, the clay soil sometimes holds water too long. The land, then, is swampy and boggy.

Streams and rivers wind from side to side on the flat surface. Such a pattern is called **meandering.** The great Vistula River has many meanders, or turns, in its lower and middle parts. In such areas the development of water power is difficult. Travel by boat is very slow. Cross traffic calls for many bridges and the filling in of bogs. The peat formed in the bogs does provide a fuel for heating homes and for cooking. However, peat is not a profitable industrial fuel, like the lignite or bituminous coals.

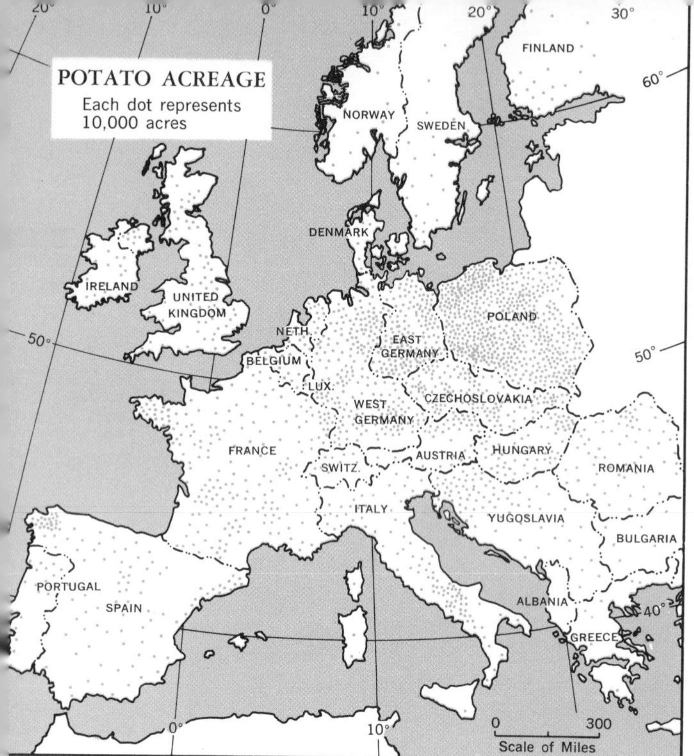

Which two European nations have the best farmland for producing potatoes?

Many Polish ships have been built since World War II. Trade with the nations of the West is increasing.

Productive Southern Soils

Over the surface of the original rock layers, especially in the south, there is a very fertile soil called chernozem. It is often called "black earth." In many places, it is covered with wind-blown dust and fine silt. When the soil is cultivated, it yields big returns of wheat, rye, and especially root crops, such as sugar beets, turnips, and potatoes. The production of root crops is so high and the actual pasture lands so small that the animals are fattened on the root crops. Flax and hemp, which grow very well in the wet lowlands, are basic to the linen, fiber, cordage, and rope businesses. Experiments are now being carried on to produce new plant fibers and special kinds of tobacco. The tobacco, judged on the basis of flavor, taste, and especially aroma, is sold throughout Europe.

The Soviets have tried to organize the farms into those which specialize in cereals, in industrial or money crops, or in stock-breeding. Attempts have been made to increase the use of fertilizer on poor soils and to train people in the use of machinery. Progress has been slow. Some say it may be traced to the fact that the farmer does not really own his own land.

Developing Natural Resources

The recent developments in industry and transportation in Poland are quite remarkable. The growth of in-

The rebuilt city gates of Warsaw are reminders of Poland's past; military parades roll by modern buildings of today.

dustry is based on the fact that coal is found in great abundance in southern Poland. It is used in the growing chemical and metal industries. Using Polish coal and German technicians, many factories are producing excellent products. Trade is gradually expanding.

The second development is represented by the vast improvement in two ports, Gdansk and Szczecin, located along the Baltic shores. These ports are noted for shipping and for shipbuilding. The enlargement has allowed Poland to develop an important fishing industry.

Many of Poland's cities were badly damaged in World War II. Some have been rebuilt and are among the most modern cities of the world. Warsaw, the capital, was rebuilt carefully. Photographs of the old Warsaw were used. Fine features were restored. New artistic structures were added. There is a "new look" to the city.

As we have seen, Poland does possess two features which a modern nation needs in order to grow. They are coal and a fine agricultural base. Her problem lies in uniting these two features. If she succeeds, the cities will grow. There will be such centers as Poznan and Lodz in the central part. Krakow and Lublin will prosper in the south and east. Along with Warsaw, the northern port cities will expand. The cities will provide markets for farm products and minerals. In time, Poland may have surpluses to send out through her new ports. The incoming money may then help raise the present standard of living and make the country grow.

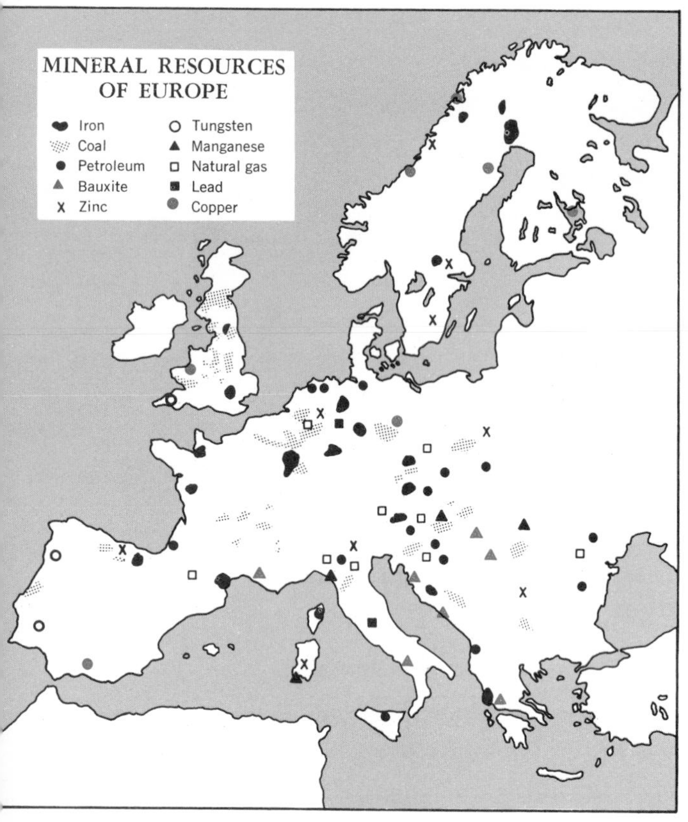

CZECHOSLOVAKIA

South of East Germany and Poland lies the **land-locked** country of Czechoslovakia. Halfway between the Baltic Sea and the Mediterranean, it is about 200 miles from the nearest seacoast. Earlier you read that East Germany was "born" after World War II. Czechoslovakia was "born" after World War I. It was formed from part of the Austria-Hungary Empire. Three western districts, Bohemia, Moravia, and Silesia, were joined with an eastern district named Slovakia. The people in the western lands are called Czechs. Thus, the new nation was named Czechoslovakia.

Since then, much of the planning has been to give growth and balance to agriculture. Wheat, the largest crop, is grown on about one-third of the cultivated land. Other crops are rye, barley, and some potatoes and sugar beets. Many root crops are used to feed the animals. Many of the animals are slaughtered for their hides as well as their meat. The famous Bata shoe, sold all over the world, is made in this country. In 1960, over 76 million pairs of boots and shoes were made. The manufacture of gloves is also increasing in importance.

One can subdivide this nation into three parts. In the western part, Prague and Pilsen (Plzen) are the major cities. Prague, the capital and largest city, has about one million people. This western part has landscapes and ways of life which are similar to those in Western Europe. One is reminded of the way of life in Switzerland and southern Germany.

The eastern part is the really mountainous section of Czechoslovakia. The Carpathian Mountains contain enclosed but fertile valleys. Because entrance from the south is easier, these valleys reflect very little of Western Europe's influence. While agriculture dominates, there is considerable mining and some manufacturing. Copper, gold, lead, iron, manganese, antimony, and tungsten are taken from the earth. The last three are very necessary as **alloys** in steelmaking. They give toughness and **resiliency,** the power of coming back when struck, to high-priced steel.

The Moravian Gate

Between the western and eastern parts of Czechoslovakia lies one of the most important land transportation routes in all of Europe. It is called the Moravian Gate. Morava is the name of a river in the valley which makes up part of the passageway. The Moravian Gate links the plains of southern Poland to the valley of the Danube River. The map on page 411 shows you that the great Danube flows southeastward to the Black Sea. In Czechoslovakia the Morava waters enter the Danube near Bratislava. The Danube then crosses Hungary and Rumania, breaking through the Carpathian Mountains to do so.

This central part of the nation, often called Moravia, has always been important as a transit zone. The area is basically agricultural, but its importance in industry is growing. Now many textile towns dot the route from northwest to southeast. The largest is Brno, located in about the center of the country. Besides textile goods, Brno manufactures iron and steel, and engineering tools and equipment.

Hydroelectric power is being generated on tributaries north of the southern city of Bratislava. A few wells are pumping petroleum in this region. The refining of it, the making of chemicals, precision instruments for drawing and surgical use, and the creation of glass articles give fame to the Moravia region. Valuable glass articles called Jablonec ware are known all over the world. Today, Czechoslovakian window glass, glasses, bottles, and glass for laboratory experiments are ordered from all continents. Truly, this land-locked nation is of major importance to all its surrounding neighbors.

The Charles Bridge at Prague, used since the 14th century, spans the wide Vltava (Moldau) River.

The Danube connects Budapest with the rest of Europe and provides rich farmland along its rolling plains.

HUNGARY

This country has several very interesting features. Though a small country it had, before World War II, some of the greatest estates in all of Europe. A third of all the cultivated land was in estates of more than 1,200 acres. One family owned more than 320,000 acres. On these acres were 164 villages. Naturally, then, about three-fourths of the peasant families owned no land at all. Today, fortunately, there has been a change in this situation.

Hungary's leading industry is still agriculture. Many improvements have been made in the quality and quantity of food for people and feed for cattle. Wheat and maize harvests are larger. Sugar beets and ground nuts, or peanuts, are being sold for cash. Jute, grown for its fibers, is an added crop.

Two million of Hungary's ten million people earn their living through agriculture. Several million consider themselves city folk, but they still cling to rural centers and their relatives, rural folk. The industries in the rural towns, or "peasant" towns as they are called, are connected to agriculture. They include flour-milling, canning, spinning, weaving, the making of tobacco products, and even starchmaking.

The Standard of Living

The Communist government of Hungary claims that the standard of living in that country is on the rise. The large urban centers are Budapest in the north, Miskolc and Debreczen in the east, and Szeged in the south. Budapest, with over one-sixth of the total population of the country, is the capital and the largest city. It is an important manufacturing and transportation center. Budapest straddles the great Danube River. Buda is the old historic part on one side of the river; Pest is the modern, bustling, business-like section across the river. The majestic Danube flows along under several graceful bridges which link the two sections of Budapest. One interesting fact is that the city which ranks second to Budapest in the number of Hungarians is Cleveland, Ohio, in our own United States! More than 1,500,000 Hungarians live in the United States today.

In Hungary's southwestern part, oil and oil refineries will provide more fuel and power. More foodstuffs will move from the improving farmsteads owned now by individuals or collectives. The increased wealth will enable Hungary to develop her drier lands to the east. These lands should be good for grazing. Hungary's trade with the West is increasing. Along with this trade in goods will be an exchange of ideas. Peace must prevail in order for this to continue.

RUMANIA

When you look at a landform map to try to determine the population distribution, you expect to find most of the people living on the plains or lowlands. In Europe you found several exceptions – Switzerland, Scotland, and parts of Norway and Czechoslovakia. Rumania ranks second to Switzerland as a country where the majority of the people live in the mountains. The people live in the Carpathian Mountains, which you can locate and follow on the map on page 411. Swinging eastward from Czechoslovakia, they extend along the southeastern border of Poland and loop in a north-south direction through central Rumania.

These colorful dresses are traditional with Rumanian women.

Rumania has been called "A Carpathian Land." Its history, its geography, its folklore and legends, plus its distinctive charm lie in that part of the Carpathians called the Transylvanian Alps. The word *transylvania* is made up of the word *sylva* meaning "forest" and the word *trans* meaning "across." It is across this wide area of forests and meadows that Rumanian life reaches its highest levels.

There are cuts into the mountain mass and several easily traversed passes. The numerous small basins and open corridors, the forested slopes, and the mineral wealth attracted and held the earliest settlers. The "heartland" is now known as **Transylvania.** This central part was held by the Romans until A.D. 270. The original Latin state has expanded somewhat, but most of the 19 million Rumanians cluster in the thickly settled hill country of south central Rumania. The high, rugged mountains and the flatter plains are thinly populated. The upper parts of the Prut, Siret, and Danube rivers provide navigable waterways. The Danube emerges into the Black Sea through many distributaries. Only two large towns are found in low, swampy land along its lower course. They are Galati, specializing in shipbuilding, and Braila, noted for metallurgy. Constanta is an important port on the Black Sea.

The villages and hamlets of Transylvania are picturesque sights. Many homes are built in places which have an excellent view. Gardens and orchards surround some clusters of houses. Nearly every home has a balcony with a flower box running along the railing. The balcony, which is sheltered, takes the place of an extra bedroom when guests arrive.

Industry is growing, but most Rumanians remain farmers. Corn, a major product, grows well in the climate.

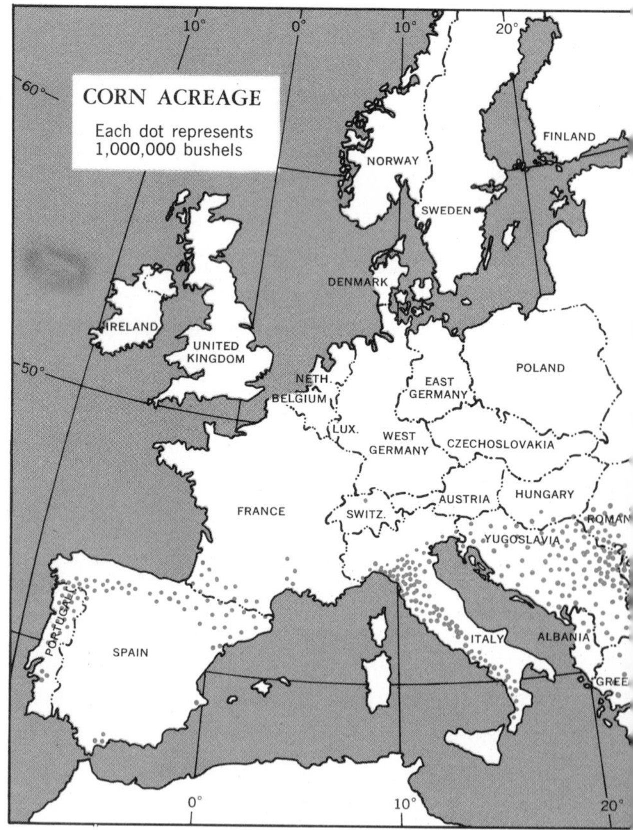

Modernizing a Scenic Land

In the newly developing towns a definite plan can be seen. The towns are patterned after those in Western Europe. A central square may have streets radiating from it as spokes in a wheel. Or, it may be a crossroad with streets at right angles to each other. New apartment blocks, especially in Bucharest, the capital, even have supermarkets on the ground floors.

The new developments in technology and trade are largely in the hands of the Soviets. This is especially true of the oil and natural gas industries. Some of the largest oil-pools in Europe are in Rumania at Ploesti, just north of Bucharest.

The food supply and diets have remained unchanged for centuries. Rumania is a fine producer of maize, or corn. There are long, hot summer days with humid nights, similar to conditions in the United States corn belt. Note the heavy production of corn as shown on the map on page 422. In addition to rye, oats, and barley, the farmers grow sorghum and buckwheat. Fruits and wines are exported. Forage crops are now being given greater attention, because the farmers want to improve the quality of meat. Rumania's brown soils, which show their forest origin in the top layer, along with the black earths give her a very fine agricultural base.

The Communists face one great problem in their planned develop-

The oil fields at Pitesti and the newly built streets of Bucharest are signs of modern Rumania.

ment of this gracious land. The Rumanians are an agricultural people who love their land. Each one cherishes the plot he owns. This way of life has been unchanged for over 1500 years. The Communists know that to disrupt this pattern quickly would be disastrous. They must find a way to use their methods and ideas to gradually change the way of life and the traditions of these people.

BULGARIA

Bulgaria occupies an important position between Europe and the Near East countries. It is one of the major crossroads of Eastern Europe. The

Varna, Bulgaria, a port on the Black Sea, has become a popular resort.

Danube River, along the northern sides of the Balkans, links Bulgaria with the U.S.S.R. on the east. It also connects her with Rumania, Hungary, Austria, and Czechoslovakia. Its location on the Black Sea has helped increase trade with the Soviet Union.

The Turks conquered this area in the fourteenth century. Other nations have invaded the country and brought with them their ideas. Since 1944, Bulgaria has been controlled by the Communist Party. It is one of the Soviet satellite countries.

While most Bulgarians are Orthodox Christians, there is a Jewish population and a group called Tziganes. The Tziganes, about 82,000 in number, are gypsies. The Jewish population, which came originally from Spain, has been greatly reduced in recent years. A large percentage have migrated to Israel.

The Balkan Mountains to the north and the Rhodope Mountains to the south provide many sheltered pockets and valleys. Through the years, the people who live here have changed their ways of living only slightly. In the villages the houses are made of wood. Strong fences are built around the one-room dwellings. Thatched-roofed cottages cluster around the urban centers in the Maritsa River Valley. Though few in number, these centers are quite modern.

Sofia, the capital, and Plovdiv are on the railroad route which stretches from Calais in France to Istanbul in Turkey. Plovdiv is a tobacco center on the Maritsa River. The Maritsa is the main drainage stream of the east-west central lowland. From Plovdiv, railroads extend to Varna and Burgas on the Black Sea. Burgas is a copper metalworks and textile center. Varna is a small seaport and fishing center.

Bulgaria has two features which are of great interest. The apples, table grapes, and prunes from Bulgarian orchards and vineyards are considered the best in all Europe. But the most unique feature is found in the Vale of Roses. There 16,000 acres of land are covered with rose bushes. **Attar of roses,** used as a base in perfume, is the product of this area. Unfortunately, the making of synthetic perfumes from oil and chemical combinations is gradually hurting this Bulgarian enterprise.

This town, originally settled by the Turks, is typical of those that line Yugoslavia's rivers.

YUGOSLAVIA

One characteristic common to all parts of Yugoslavia is the broken, rugged, and jumbled relief. There is a narrow coastal plain along the Adriatic called Dalmatia. Getting in and out of the rugged interior of Yugoslavia is difficult. In winter, there is a harshness in the climate. Rainfall is not regular nor even in amounts. The climate plus the rugged terrain have been real problems for the people.

In this country where high mountains are cut by deep, narrow valleys, crop farming is limited. Hence, we find that pastoral life is widespread. Sheep graze in large numbers on high pastures in summer and on sheltered lowlands in winter. Notice the great number of sheep in this area as shown on the map on page 426. In the much grazed areas, there is often a bare appearance.

In the parts of the country where crops are grown, the farming methods are primitive. Lack of machinery and modern fertilizers, and poverty have hindered the progress of these people. They have kept their primitive methods longer than people in any other European country.

Yugoslavia is one of the nations of southeastern Europe in which sheep are plentiful. The sheep are found in the drier areas of each nation.

Poor transportation, poor means of communication, and a lack of power have slowed industrial development. Equipment is old. Craftsmen, though skilled, do not produce large quantities. Their products are too expensive. Some progress is slowly being made by the government of Yugoslavia.

Signs of Change

The population, now totaling over 18 million, is still growing. Large numbers of young people are moving to towns. Their jobs are in new factories. Their problems are social and economic. How can the hill people learn new skills quickly? How can they learn how to get along in the large, more densely populated cities? Belgrade, the capital, has over a half-million people. Second in size is Zagreb in the north. These two are by far the closest to great metropolitan centers as we know them in the United States.

Hydroelectric power will be the great source in the future. Note the hydroelectric areas as shown on the map on page 427. At the present time, it furnishes about half of all the current used. More dams are being built along the many water courses. "Mushroom" towns, those towns which seem to spring up overnight, are seen near these dams. Examples of these towns, to which former shepherds and peasants migrate, are many. There is Ljubljana with

Industry in a "mushroom" town.

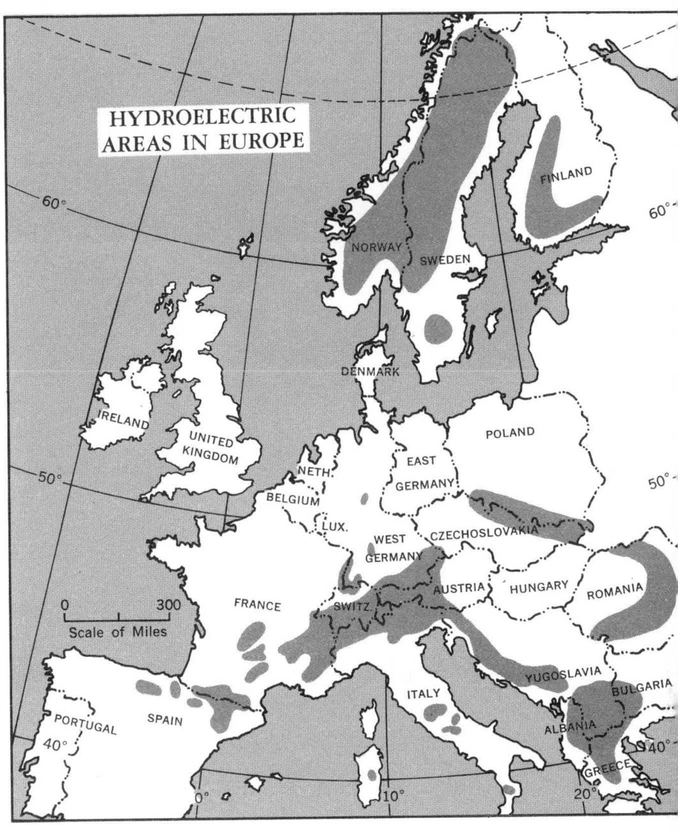

its new suburban factory turning out electrical equipment. Around Sarajevo in the center of Yugoslavia, new towns, such as Zenica and Vares, are making products from the nearby iron sources. **Bauxite,** a source of aluminum, is being used more and more. Two new "industrial twins," other than coal and iron, may be seen here. They are water power and aluminum.

The tourist industry is booming. The scenery in Yugoslavia is not surpassed by many other European nations. There are mineral springs, mammoth caves, lakes for cruises, and Mediterranean-like sandy beaches to attract the tourists. Castles built into the mountains, coupled with the friendliness of the people, make this an ideal land for tourists.

While Yugoslav world trade is increasing, it is not doing so rapidly. Perhaps the form of government, communistic but close to a one-man authority, causes nations to be slow to trade. Yugoslavia is trying to steer a middle course between the Soviet influence on the east and the European influence on the west. Her rugged isolation is helping her to do this. But she cannot remain too isolated. She needs the "know-how" of progress of both her East and West neighbors.

A narrow street in an Albanian town.

ALBANIA

The smallest of the Eastern European Mainland States, Albania stands out in many ways. Its language is of Asian origin, and its predominant religion is Muslim. The people have worked hard to maintain their independence and resist the overpowering of neighboring nations. This has its drawbacks. Progress has been slow. Her ways of life and living still revolve around rural activities and market towns. There are few large cities such as the capital, Tirana. For a long time she had no railroads at all. Roads are widened trails.

Most of her land is above 3,000 feet in elevation and is quite broken. Mountain people live in clans called "fis" or "stripes." Such groups cling fast to their traditions. Only recently were women released from what was almost a condition of slavery.

On the hills are oaks, pines, and hickory trees. Domesticated trees include peaches, apricots, and figs. In the southern part of Albania citrus fruits, such as oranges, lemons, and limes, are grown. The most widely cultivated tree of all, however, is the olive. Cattle and sheep are found in the villages and on surrounding hills.

Nearness to the sea and the hard life on the land seemed to urge Albanians to migrate. Hundreds of thousands are now living in the neighboring lands of Greece, Italy, and Sicily. Most of the emigrants are in the United States. They have contributed their hard work and strong character to our nation. The United States, in turn, has tried to assist with loans to the Albanian government.

The Dispersal of Culture

The contributions of the people of the Eastern European Mainland States are brought out by noting the numbers who came to the United States. From 1620 to 1963, records show that close to four-and-one-half million emigrants from this large region came to the United States.

These people brought great diversity in customs, habits, skills, and hopes. Their dress, music, arts, ideas, and willingness to work contributed to the great store of differences in which Americans take pride. In the classrooms of your school today there may be several descendants of Eastern European peoples.

THE MEDITERRANEAN REGION

Terra means "lands," and *medi* means "middle." Thus, the word *Mediterranean* refers to the body of water which is between or in the middle of the land masses of Europe and Africa. The fifth major region includes parts of all the countries which border on the Mediterranean Sea. Can you locate some of the countries of this region on the map on page 437? You have read about some of these countries in the earlier chapters.

A Unique Region

In the regions of Europe already studied, it was quite easy to draw sub-regions. In the Mediterranean, it is probably a mistake to do so. Of course, we could take the parts of each country which are included and deal separately with each part. If we did this, we would lose the most important point to remember about the Mediterranean. The Mediterranean Region is more than an orderly collection of crops, animals, trees, industries, and people. It is a region of great diversity held together by a common feature, its climate. Let us see how this is evident.

Suppose we start in Mediterranean Spain and follow along the coast. You might want to trace this route on a map. From Spain we would travel through southern France, never far from the sea. Then we would fol-

Tile-roofed houses cling to terraced hills above the blue Mediterranean. The climate and beauty of Beausoleil in France, Amalfi in Italy, and other villages of the Riviera make this a sought-after resort area.

low the west coast of Italy, crossing Italy in the south. Along the shores of the Adriatic Sea, our route would continue. Then we would cross Greece and move southward in Turkey along the eastern end of the Mediterranean Sea. On our swing westward again, we would touch parts of the northern coast of Africa.

On our trip we would find rocky coasts, small valleys, river deltas, offshore islands, and peninsulas. We would see a great variety of life and ways of living on land and sea. The many different crops, fruits, and nut trees would impress us. The animal life and the fish would remind us of great displays of meat and fish in supermarkets. All the above would be destroyed if we attempted to "sub-regionalize" the great Mediterranean Region. We should remember it not for its many differences, but for its uniqueness in possessing practically everything.

A Mediterranean Climate

The Mediterranean Region is one which does not experience extremes of climate. It rarely experiences the cold, snowy, very wet, winter storms of northern Europe. Neither does it experience regularly the hot, dry blasts of warm air from the desert region of North Africa. Only once in a while does it have the violent summer thunderstorms that are common in Eastern Europe. Instead, this fifth major region of Europe has what is called a **Mediterranean climate.** This type of climate has sunny, dry summers and cool, rainy winters. Higher areas have cooler temperatures than areas close to sea level. This feature binds these lands of great variety into a well-defined region.

The Mediterranean type of climate is found in other parts of the world. Mediterranean regions are located between the latitudes of 30 and 40 degrees in both the Northern and Southern Hemispheres. All Mediterranean climate regions are located on the western sides of continents. Can you find some countries that have this type of climate? None of them, however, have the same characteristic variety of the true Mediterranean Region.

Mediterranean Landforms

Most of the landscape of the Mediterranean, unlike the climate, is rough and uneven. One finds small basins in the highlands and numerous valleys with openings to the sea along the eastern coast of Spain, in southern France, and in southern Greece.

Several famous Spanish cities are located on or near the sea-exits of the rivers that flow into the Mediterranean Sea. There is Malaga, noted for grapes and wine; Cartagena, a major source of olives; Murcia, producer of delicious dates; Valencia, whose name is used in other countries to mean excellent oranges; and Barcelona, famous for citrus fruits.

Marseilles, on France's southern coast, is one of the Mediterranean's greatest ports and tourist attractions.

The great Mediterranean seaport of Marseilles is located in southern France. East of this city lies the French Riviera. The Riviera is a winter playground for Western Europeans, just as Southern California and Florida are winter resorts for citizens of the United States. Monaco is a small state existing mainly on money spent by tourists.

In Italy and Greece, valleys are small. Mountains are close to the sea. Some rise quite steeply from the water's edge. Sunlight streams down on southward facing slopes and cliffs. In Italy, people have created garden spots wherever there is a shelf or a ledge of earth. Tourists who travel the narrow Amalfi Drive from Naples to Salerno see flowers, vegetables, small trees, and cleverly built homes in niches on the rocky hillsides.

The Atlas Foothills

In North Africa the land along the Mediterranean is hilly except in Egypt where the Nile delta region is low and flat. In Algeria the Mediterranean coastal area is also called the **Tell.** The Arabic word *tell* means "hill." The Algerian hills are foothills of the Atlas Mountains which lie back of the coastal area. In Libya, Tunisia, Algeria, and Morocco, most of the people live in the hilly Mediterranean coastal region. Fertile soils and moisture from the sea make this the area where most of the crops are produced and where most of the limited industry is located. Tunis, Algiers, and Tangier are major ports for the trade. You will recall that south of the coastal areas in North Africa lies a great desert region.

Non-irrigated farmland in Italy.

WAYS OF LIVING

In this region of varied elevations and of numerous large and small lowland pockets or valleys, many different ways of living may be found. The ways of making a living from agriculture may be grouped under two headings, irrigated and non-irrigated. Let us study the types of agriculture under the latter—the non-irrigated. One of these types is pastoral; the other is crop farming. Each is adapted to the normal Mediterranean climate of winter rain and summer drought. Each has been adjusted to the landforms.

Where there are open, fairly flat expanses of land, wheat and barley are grown. The golden fields of ripened wheat ripple and wave in the brilliant sunlight. Where the land is uneven, animals, especially sheep and goats, graze. They follow the ripening green grass patches up and down the slopes. They move up in the dry season, down in the wet season.

In the lands around the eastern end of the Mediterranean and in North Africa, a unique feature of the animal economy is the fat-tailed sheep. This sheep has been raised for many generations by the nomadic peoples of these countries. The nomads use the coarse, low-grade wool for clothing, the meat for food, and the tail for cooking fat. The tail of the fat-tailed sheep is almost entirely fat, and may weigh as much as 35 or 40 pounds. It has been the major source of fat for these people. They do not eat the meat or fat from hogs because of religious beliefs. As fats made from vegetable oils become available to people in this part of the world, there will be less need for the tail fat of this sheep. Enlightened farmers today are turning to other breeds of sheep which produce more and better wool and meat of a higher quality.

Irrigated Farming

The irrigated types of agriculture include tree crops and horticulture. **Horticulture** is the art or science of cultivating gardens and orchards.

The growing season is made to be year-long in the horticulture section. During the rainy period in the winter, vegetables and flowers of all kinds are grown. As soon as the rains cease, crops are harvested by hand. They are sent northward. The land is retilled, and more crops are planted. But water needs to be added from the mountain streams and reservoirs. Spring, summer, and early fall are rainless. The sun is warm, however, and the soil is fertile. When the water is added, production is high.

The second type of irrigated farming is not as exact as the former. It is not as regular, either. But the people know that trees, especially citrus, olive, and date trees, do better if they are not thirsty. While the tree-crop specialists hope they will not have to use water, they are ready to do so.

The map below shows the production of grapes, olives, and citrus fruit in the rim of lands around the Mediterranean Sea. Note how close the citrus fruit-growing areas are to the Mediterranean. Olive production extends farther from the Sea. This is due to the ability of the olive tree to grow in higher, cooler elevations and to produce fruit with less moisture. While grape production is heavy in the Mediterranean Region, notice that there are other areas of heavy production in Europe.

Grapevines in southern France.

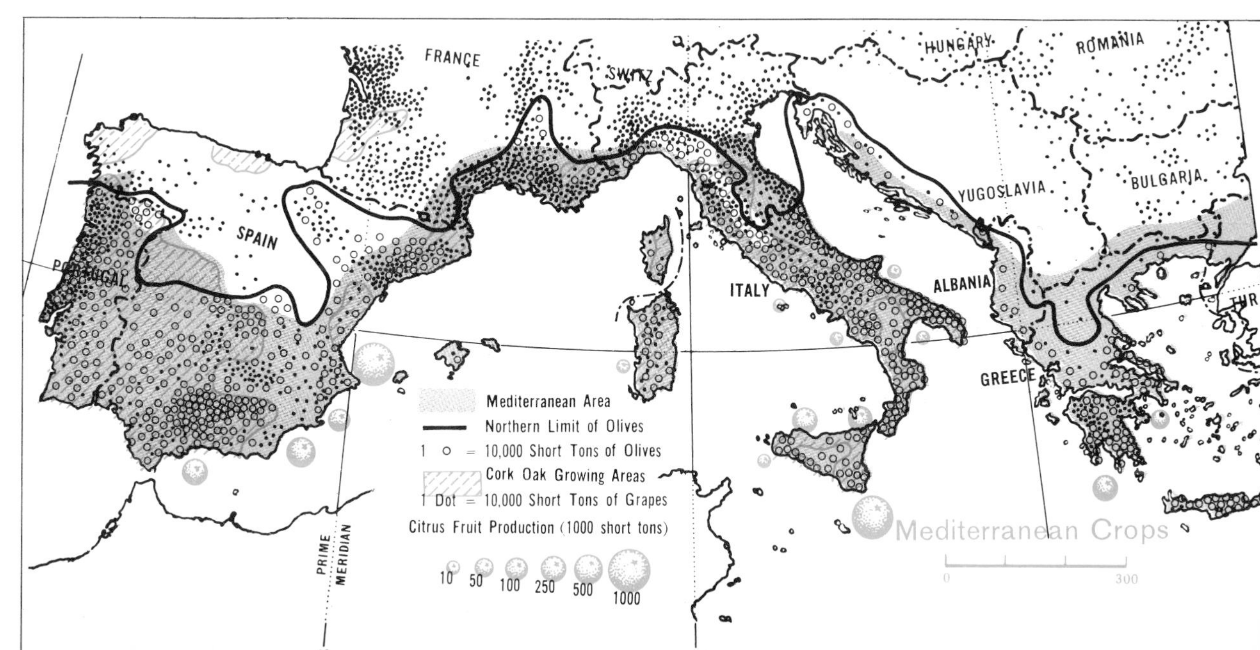

With skilled speed, Turkish women weave rugs at home. Men display the rugs on the streets and bargain over their sale.

Leading Industries

Manufacturing is also an important way of life in the Mediterranean Region. Textile, chemical, and leather goods come from the northern Italian manufacturing cities of Milan and Turin. The Po River Valley is the industrial heartland of Italy. Water power comes from the mountain slopes surrounding this valley in northern Italy.

While Italy represents the most highly developed industrial area in the Mediterranean Region, there is industrial growth in other areas. In southern Spain, where silk worms are raised, silk weaving is an important occupation. Olive oil is processed in the province of Andalusia. There are glassmaking factories, sugar refineries, wineries, and some aluminum-and-steel-manufacturing plants. Seville is an important center for cork products.

There is little industry in the North African countries. Algeria has shown some development, but only about three-tenths of Algeria's income comes from industry. Leading industries include food processing, and the manufacture of chemicals for use in paints and in fertilizers. There are also wool and cork manufacturing plants in northern Algeria.

Turkey has made great strides in developing industry. Although Turkey is still mainly an agricultural country where four out of five people earn their living by farming, the government is encouraging industrial development. An iron and steel plant has been built at Karabuk near coal fields. Cotton textile mills have been built in several areas. Other factories produce chemicals, paper, cement, shoes, and glass. Turkey has small handicraft shops that produce valuable rugs, inlaid wood, and metalwork.

Mining a Beautiful Stone

Another way of making a living in this region of Europe is mining. Building stones of great beauty and durability are quarried from the Apennines, the mountain backbone of Italy. At Carrara, a fine white marble is quarried. Carrara marble has a fine, smooth texture like "cream of wheat." It is cut carefully from the mountainside so that it will not split, crack, or be marred. Carrara marble is used in sculpture.

The greatest handicap to the wide sale of marble is its weight. This causes a high cost of transportation. Its use is also curtailed by another building material. This competitor is concrete, "the rock that is poured."

Men prepare to cut marble from the polished side of a mountain peak.

CENTERS OF EARLY CULTURE

The Mediterranean Region saw the rise of two great ancient civilizations, the Greek and the Roman. From these two civilizations came invaluable parts of our cultural heritage. Signs of the ancient civilizations may still be seen in many parts of the Mediterranean Region. Athens in Greece and Rome in Italy are among the world's greatest historic cities. Throughout these cities may be seen the most remarkable displays of ancient architecture in the world.

Modern Athens spreads in a great half circle around the flat-topped hill called the Acropolis, which was the site of the ancient city. The remains

A reconstructed market building, now a museum, stands on the site of the ancient market place in Athens.

The Castel St. Angelo and Victor Emmanuel Bridge are Roman "treasures."

of the great architecture and sculpture of the early period have been carefully preserved by the Greeks. Much work is being done to restore some of the most famous of the early buildings. The new city of Athens serves as the government center for Greece. It includes beautiful modern buildings and wide avenues leading from a central square. The National Museum houses the finest collections of ancient relics of any museum in the world.

Modern Rome, the capital of Italy, was built on the site of the ancient city. The Palatine Hill was the home of most of the wealthy Romans. The Capitoline Hill is the center of government today, as it was in ancient days. Rome is more important as the center of Italian government, education, and religion than it is as an industrial or trading center. There are a few small factories, but they are not an important part of life in Rome.

Ancient Ruins Remain

Visitors to Rome can view ruins of many of the famous Roman buildings. The best known and most impressive of the ancient buildings is the huge Colosseum. It stands today as a well-preserved ruin. It was a four-storied oval building, which seated from 50,000 to 80,000 spectators. Nearby are the ruins of the famous Roman Forum, the center of Roman life in ancient days. One of the best-preserved buildings in Rome is the Pantheon, a huge circular building. Once a temple to all the Roman gods, today it houses a Christian church.

Within the city of Rome is the Vatican City. This independent state is the home of the head of the Roman Catholic Church. It is built on the west bank of the Tiber River, across from the largest part of Rome which is east of the river.

Rome, like many other cities in the Mediterranean Region, is a great tourist attraction. Money from tourism is an important source of income to many areas of this region. The beautiful scenery, the great variety of people and ways of living, and the mild comfortable climate attract many thousands of tourists to this region each year.

THE MEDITERRANEAN REGION

0 135 270

Scale 270 miles to one inch

EVERGREEN FORESTS

FORESTS

DRY GRASSLAND

SEMIARID GRASSLAND AND FOREST

FARMLAND

MOUNTAINS

An Important Waterway

The Mediterranean Sea has played an important role in the development of the lands along its shores since ancient times. It is still a very important waterway to many people in Europe, Asia, and Africa. Europe owes much of its development not only to the Mediterranean Sea, but also to its closeness to the seas on all sides. As you study the next section of this book, you will again see how closeness to the sea can affect man's ways of living and his development through the years. Life in the Pacific World also shows the powerful influence the sea can have on man.

Do You Know

1. On what are the sub-regions of Eastern Europe based? What is the main reason for this division?

2. What name is given to the farm plots of East Germany? What is "socialization of agriculture?"

3. What is the major physical feature of Poland? What is a meandering stream or river? Which river in Poland has many meanders?

4. What type of soil is found in northern Poland? In southern Poland? What crops, grown in the south, are used to fatten animals?

5. What is the valuable resource of southern Poland? For what industries is it used? What industries have the ports of Poland helped develop?

6. Which country of Eastern Europe was born after World War I? After World War II?

7. How are manganese, antimony, and tungsten used? Why are they important minerals?

8. What is the largest city of Hungary? What river divides the city? For what is the city noted?

9. What is a "mushroom" town? What caused the towns of Yugoslavia to "mushroom"?

10. Why is the location of Bulgaria important? On what body of water is it located?

11. What two resources, found in Yugoslavia, might be called the new industrial twins? What resources have they replaced?

12. What two types of non-irrigated agriculture are found in the Mediterranean region? How are they adapted to climate and landform?

13. What stone of great value is quarried in the Apennine Mountains? What are its qualities?

Learn By Doing

1. Match each capital, listed in column **B,** with the proper nation, listed in column **A.**

A	B
1 East Germany	Budapest
2 Poland	Tirana
3 Czechoslovakia	Prague
4 Hungary	East Berlin
5 Rumania	Sofia
6 Bulgaria	Belgrade
7 Yugoslavia	Warsaw
8 Albania	Bucharest

2. Take a journey down the Danube River. Give the location of its source and mouth. Describe the landforms you would see and name some of the cities through which you would travel. Explain what the Iron Gate is.

3. Match a raw material from column **A** with a finished product from column **B.**

A	B
1 hops	burlap
2 flax	linen
3 jute	perfume
4 attar of roses	leather shoes
5 animal hides	beer
6 hemp	rope

4. Write a letter describing a trip you plan to take around the Mediterranean Sea. Name the countries and the islands you would like to visit. Describe some of the important physical features. Name at least three rivers. Choose four cities you would like to visit and tell why.

5. Select one of the following titles for a report:

The Vineyard
A Garden of Olives
A Family of Fruits
A Stone of Lasting Beauty

Test Your Knowledge

1. What is the Berlin Wall? When and why was it built?

2. What problem has the division of Germany created for the people of West Berlin? How has this been solved?

3. What was the major industrial problem of East Germany? How was the problem solved?

4. Give the meaning of the terms "standard of living" and "cost of living." Name a country of Eastern Europe which has recently improved its standard of living.

5. Where is the Moravian Corridor? Why is this area important? How has this area changed in recent years?

6. Why is Rumania compared to Switzerland? What is the major way of life in this nation? What problem have the Communists faced in this nation?

7. Give the meaning of "transylvania." Describe the location and the importance of this area.

8. To what does the word Mediterranean refer? What areas are included in this region? What is the common feature of the region?

9. What are the four major characteristics of a Mediterranean climate? Where are Mediterranean climate regions located?

10. What animal is important to the nomads of the eastern and southern Mediterranean? Explain.

11. Prove that Italy is the most developed industrial area in the Mediterranean region: name the heartland area; name two manufacturing cities; and give the source of water power.

12. What progress has Turkey made in industry? What is its form of government?

13. Why has the Mediterranean Region always been important to the people of Europe and the world?

REVIEWING PART 5

Do You Remember?

1. What three words are used to describe the regional characteristics of Europe? What is the meaning of each word?

2. What type of climate does northern Europe have? Southern Europe?

3. Where do the Basques live? The Lapps? What does each group of people have in common?

4. What are three major reasons why nations are led to war?

5. What is meant by a literate person? Which two countries of Europe have the highest literacy rate?

6. How have nations of Europe tried to work together?

7. Why do geographers regionalize the world?

8. What is the major landform feature of Fennoscandia? Of the British Isles? Of the Mediterranean Region?

9. What are the three chief occupations of the Fennoscandian people? What are the two chief occupations of the people on the British Isles?

10. Why is the Netherlands Delta Plan a good example of man's ability to change his environment to suit his needs?

11. What are the five major regions of Europe?

12. What systems of transportation have been developed to help unify the people of Europe?

13. Why are Spain and Portugal "separated but similar"?

14. What are the Eastern European Mainland States?

15. What four nations occupied and governed a division of Germany at the close of World War II?

16. Why were people willing to settle in the Transylvanian Alps?

17. What are the major tree crops of the Mediterranean Region? What products are obtained from each?

18. Why are Athens and Rome important cities today?

19. What is hydroelectric power? Which regions of Europe depend upon this source of power? Why?

Projects and Reports

1. Use the Appendix on pages 528–530 to answer the questions listed below.

a. Of all the European countries, which three are the largest in area?

b. Which three countries are the most populated?

c. Which two capitals have the largest population?

d. Which two countries have the largest population per square mile?

2. Write a brief definition of each of the following words:

tableland	strip mining
famine	naval stores
aristocracy	pure stands
shaft mining	land-locked
secondary process	

3. Select a major industrial city of Europe. Write a report including as many of the following topics as you can:

a. location and physical features
b. important nearby raw materials
c. manufactured products
d. methods of transportation
e. important tourist attractions

4. Many emigrants from Europe were responsible for the rapid progress which was made in the development of our country. Write a brief biography of one of the following men:

Andrew Carnegie
Alexander Graham Bell
Albert Einstein
John Ericsson
Joseph Pulitzer

5. Name the nation of which each city, listed below, is a capital. Give at least one important feature of each city.

Dublin	Vienna	Copenhagen
London	Athens	Stockholm
Lisbon	Amsterdam	Helsinki
Madrid	Luxembourg	Brussels

Bonn Oslo Rome Bern Paris

6. Use a world map or globe to help you name areas of the world to which each of these languages have dispersed: English, French, Dutch, Spanish, Portuguese.

Using Maps and Globes

1. What name is given to the part of Denmark which is a peninsula of the mainland? Do the islands of Denmark lie mainly to the east or the west of the peninsula?

2. What body of water lies to the west of Europe? What are the two major seas to the north? Which sea lies to the south? Which seas border the Soviet Union in the north and south? What body of water lies north of Spain and west of France?

3. Briefly describe the location of each of the following mountain ranges: Alps, Carpathian, Transylvanian, Balkan, and Pyrenees.

4. From north to south, follow the 10° East Longitude on the map on page 348.

a. What countries and bodies of water do you cross?

b. Through what mountains and valleys would you travel?

c. On your trip, how would you expect the climate to change?

5. Briefly describe the location of each of the rivers listed below. One good way to do this would be to list the major countries through which they flow.

Rhine	Danube	Po
Seine	Douro	Vistula
Loire	Rhone	Tiber
Garonne	Elbe	Ebro

6. Fly west on the 40° parallel of latitude from Ankara, Turkey, to the Atlantic Ocean. Use the map on page 437.

a. What peninsulas would you cross?

b. What large islands would you cross?

c. Over what seas would you travel?

THE PACIFIC WORLD

PART 6

There is no one Pacific World; there are many. Honolulu, capital of Hawaii, is as bustling and modern as any city in the world. Yet there are islands in the Pacific barely touched by modern life. People of the Pacific World vary in their ways of living from the most primitive to the most advanced.

There are towering volcanic islands. There are low-lying coral atolls that rise only a few feet above the surface of the ocean. In Hawaii there are white coral sand beaches, but there are also beaches of black volcanic sand. The latter type of beach may surprise you, but it has its own beauty. The Pacific World will fulfill many of your expectations.

The Pacific World is a region of water. It is the region of the world's greatest ocean. Man's "standing places" in the Pacific Region are the thousands of small islands scattered throughout the vast waters. Australia and New Zealand are exceptions to this. They offer larger "standing places."

New Zealand and Australia are included as part of the Pacific World in this book because of their location and because they are islands. Another reason is that the native people of New Zealand, the Maoris, are closely related to the Polynesians. The Polynesians are the people who live on the Hawaiian Islands and nearby islands.

New Zealand and Australia have several features that make them very different from the rest of the islands of the Pacific World. First of all, much of Australia and all of New Zealand lie south of the Tropic of Capricorn. Second, Australia and New Zealand have been settled by people from Great Britain, mainly within the last one hundred and fifty years. There are close cultural ties between these two countries and Great Britain. Third, the island of Australia is so large that it is a continent. It is about the size of the United States. Most of the population of Australia live on the rim of the island. Its mountains, its great interior desert, and its mixed industrial and agricultural economy make it very different from the small tropical islands to the east.

Before the coming of European settlers, both Australia and New Zealand had been isolated for thousands of years. Because of their isolation from other islands and the Asian land mass, animal and plant life developed and survived on these islands that are found nowhere else in the world. For example, Australia is the home of the eucalyptus, a genus of trees that has great numbers of species. They range in size from small shrubs to mighty timber trees. In the chapter on these two countries, you will read about the unique animals such as the platypus and the kiwi that exist on these islands.

CHAPTER 19

MELANESIA, MICRONESIA, AND POLYNESIA

What wonderful ideas of adventure come to our minds when we hear the words, "We're off to the South Seas." We have visions of sunny, sandy beaches where the blue waters of the Pacific lap lazily against the shore. We see native peoples in light, brightly colored garments with flowers in their hair. We thrill to the daring of surf-board riders. We marvel at the skill of paddlers in small outrigger canoes or larger war canoes.

THE VAST PACIFIC WORLD

On your globe locate the Fiji Islands. They lie on the 180° meridian of Longitude and near the 20° South parallel of Latitude. Tip the globe so that you are looking directly at them. These islands are at the center of a large circle. Far to the upper right you can see the western mountains of North America. To the lower right lie the Andes Mountains of South America. To the upper left you can see the Japanese volcanic mountain range. To the lower left, inside the large circle, you can see Australia and New Zealand. Far to the bottom of the circle you can see the edges of Antarctica.

These mountains that border the Pacific Ocean are often called the "circle" or "rim of fire." Some of the volcanoes in this "rim of fire" are dormant, or sleeping. Others are active. You may be familiar with some of these volcanoes. Mount Lassen and Mount Shasta are in California. Crater Lake and Mount Hood are in Oregon. Mount Fujiyama in Japan and Mount Krakatau near Java were mentioned in earlier chapters. The "rim of fire" is the region of the world where volcanoes erupt and earthquakes occur most often. Within these great earth-movement sections of the world lies the vast Pacific Ocean.

Again tip the globe so that the Fiji Islands are in the center of the imaginary "rim of fire." You might say that the half of the Earth at which you are looking is a "water half."

The Pacific World is in the "water hemisphere." The Pacific Ocean is the largest in the world. It covers more of the Earth's surface than all the land put together. You can get a good idea of how large the Pacific Ocean is if you know that half the distance around the Earth is 12,000 miles. At the equator, the Pacific Ocean is 11,000 miles wide. From north to south, the Pacific Ocean is 9,000 miles long.

The Pacific Ocean is also the deepest ocean in the world. Its average depth is 14,000 feet. But scientists have found some great "deeps," or trenches, in the ocean floor that are more than twice as deep. On the map on page 453, find the Marianas Islands in the western part of the

Pacific Ocean. The Marianas Trench is east of these islands. It is 35,800 feet deep. If Mount Everest were dropped into this trench, its peak would be more than a mile below the surface of the sea. There are other great trenches in the Pacific Ocean. The awesome Tonga-Kermadec Trench, one of the deep cracks in the ocean's floor, is over 1,600 miles long.

LANDS OF THE PACIFIC WORLD

By the Pacific World we mean the lands and the peoples within the region of the Pacific Ocean. It includes the island continent of Australia. It also includes thousands of islands sprinkled throughout this vast ocean. The northeast Pacific has few islands. Most of the islands lie between the Tropic of Cancer and the Tropic of Capricorn. One important group of islands, New Zealand, lies south of the Tropic of Capricorn. Throughout history, the climate and landforms have influenced the ways of living of both the natives and the settlers of this region.

A volcano dominates the desolate island of Tanna, New Hebrides.

Volcanic Islands of the Pacific

There are many types of islands in the Pacific World. Some are primarily volcanic. Mount Fujiyama in Japan is called **strato-volcanic.** This type of volcano tends to erupt explosively, or with force. It gives off alternating layers of lava and layers of cinders that build a **cone**—that is, a steepsided mountain. Mount Fuji is a perfectly formed strato-volcano.

Another type of volcano, the **shield volcano,** has a very different form. Its slope rises gently. Lava from the shield volcano is very hot and can flow for many miles. Repeated outpourings of sheets of lava form **domes** instead of cones. The Hawaiian Islands have been formed from shield volcanoes.

Not all volcanic mountains rise above the sea. Some are hidden below the surface of the ocean. These "hidden" islands are called **guyots,** or **seamounts.** They are really flat-topped, submarine volcanic cones.

Recently, many seamounts have been discovered and mapped. Some of the seamounts along the western shores of the United States have been named. They are called the

Erben, Jasper, Henderson, and Crest Guyots. One guyot is called the California Seamount. Sometimes submarines use the tops of the guyots as resting places while underwater tests are being made.

Natives of the fertile island of Tahiti carve out large tree trunks for their outrigger canoes.

Coral Islands of the Pacific

Many of the volcanic islands of the Pacific World have **coral reefs** attached to their coasts. Coral reefs are submerged formations of hard skeletons of **coral polyps.** Coral polyps are small animals with jelly-like bodies. The skeleton which surrounds and protects the soft body of the polyp has come to be called **coral.** Coral polyps grow in clean, warm seas. They thrive when the water temperature is above 68°F. They grow from about 200 feet below the surface of the sea to sea level. Since coral polyps grow only in the warm waters near the surface of the ocean, they must have some land or rock to which they can attach themselves. They attach themselves to the sides of underwater mountains.

The polyps live in clusters. As old polyps die, new ones build their skeletons on the skeletons of dead polyps. The young coral polyps are also free to float away from one submerged mountain to another. They may attach themselves to a rock, grow a protective skeleton, and begin a new coral formation. Colonies of coral polyps grow in many different forms. Because coral polyps grow best in clean water stirred by waves or currents and do not grow in muddy water, the mouth of an island river may lack a coral formation. However, a nearby headland that is washed by clean ocean waters may have a thriving one.

There are three types of coral reefs. A coral reef that is connected to an island is called a **fringing reef.** It extends into the sea on the fringe, or edge, of the island. A coral reef that is separated from an island by a shallow body of water is called a **barrier reef.** It follows along the shoreline

Living coral and marine life.

A fringing reef, French Oceania.

Part of the Great Barrier Reef.

Coral reefs surrounding a lagoon.

of the island. It may be one long reef or a series of reefs. The barrier reef may lie close to the island or several miles off the shore of the island.

A third type of coral reef is the **coral atoll.** Coral atolls are islands made of coral formations. Scientists are not fully certain how coral atolls are formed. One theory suggests that the coral islands began as fringing reefs or barrier reefs around a mountain that rose above sea level. As the mountain sank into the ocean or the level of the sea rose, the coral polyps continued to grow upward fast enough to keep the reef near the surface of the ocean. The original mountain may have eroded or sunk far under the sea, but the coral reef remained. Its outline resembles the shape of the top of a small volcano.

The skeletons of the coral polyps build up into a circular reef or series of reefs. Waves and winds sometimes combine pieces of dead coral and sea shells into small islands that rise above the reef. When they emerge from the sea, a **lagoon** is formed. The lagoon is the body of water surrounded by the emerged reefs. Several channels may lead from the lagoon to the open sea. The coral atoll that surrounds the lagoon is usually quite flat. It is seldom more than a few feet above sea level. It may be covered with a thin layer of soil on which tropical plants can grow.

The small young atolls lack organic matter and minerals other than the calcium carbonate that formed the polyp skeletons. Even on older, larger atolls pockets of soil may be thin and small. People who live on such islands, unless they have outside sources of food, may have to depend upon the meat and milk of the coconut and upon the sea life of the lagoon.

One reason why coconut palms are so widespread throughout the Pacific World is that the nuts of the palm drift in the ocean. They wash up on a coral atoll and take root. The coconut palm grows well on a coral atoll, whereas other types of trees cannot. The atoll is so little above sea level that the water which feeds the roots of a tree is likely to be salty. The coconut palm is not bothered by such water.

Since the surface of an atoll is too small to collect much rain water, a steady supply of drinking water is a problem. People on atolls try to collect water when it rains, and then store it and use it carefully.

Tiny coral atolls dot the Pacific.

Tsunamis and Typhoons

The greatest dangers to life on an atoll in the Pacific come from tidal waves and from violent storms. A **tsunami,** or tidal wave, may be caused by a violent earthquake in the ocean floor. A tsunami may also be caused by a volcanic explosion, such as the one that occurred at Krakatau in Indonesia, mentioned in Chapter 14. Tsunamis do no harm at sea but when nearing the shore of an island, they reach great heights and may rush far inland or completely over an atoll.

The "rim of fire" that borders the Pacific is one of the world's great earthquake regions. **Seismologists,** men who record and study the shocks and motions of earthquakes, keep careful watch over them. If they think an earthquake near Alaska is likely to cause a tsunami, they send warnings to the areas that might be struck. These warnings give the people some time to prepare.

Some of the world's most violent storms occur in the Pacific Region. In the North Pacific Ocean there are fearful storms, especially in winter. Great low pressure centers of whirling air hum across the ocean north of the Hawaiian Islands. The storms of the North Pacific are beyond the tropics and are called **extra-tropical cyclones.** When these cyclonic storms strike the northwestern coast of North America, the rain comes in torrents. The wind sometimes reaches speeds over 60 miles an hour.

Swirling black clouds are warning signs of an approaching typhoon.

In the Atlantic Ocean the tropical cyclone is called a **hurricane.** In the Pacific Ocean, the tropical cyclone is called a **typhoon.** The winds of a typhoon blow in a spiral fashion at great speeds. The **eye** of the typhoon, or the center of the storm, may be five to ten miles across. In the eye of the storm, the skies are usually clear and the winds light. The circumference of the typhoon, where the winds reach their highest speed, may be anywhere from 100 to 200 miles. The high winds are accompanied by heavy driving rains.

The typhoon, unlike the tidal wave, is dangerous to people at sea as well as on land. Winds whip up giant, raging waves. These waves may pound and even cover an atoll. They smash and wash away docks, boats, palm trees, houses, gardens, soil, and men, women, and children.

Weathering a Typhoon

Gina lives on an atoll in the typhoon region of the Pacific. She and her family have been warned that a typhoon is expected to hit their island. Gina's mother has told her to come home when she sees unusual streaks across the sky. These are caused by very high altitude clouds called **cirrus clouds.** They announce the coming of the typhoon. As the typhoon nears the island, Gina races home. The winds become stronger and stronger. Gina notices the needle on the barometer swing far to the left. She knows that this means the atmospheric pressure is falling. From her house, Gina sees a black bank of clouds move closer and closer to the island. These **cirro-stratus clouds** bring heavy rains. High waves pound the island shores.

Gina's father decides that the family should leave the house and move to higher ground. Walking against the tremendous gusts of wind is so difficult and dangerous that the whole family joins hands. They know that they could easily be swept apart by the strong winds. Gina's father points out that the people of their island are fortunate that the highest point of land is 12 feet above sea level. He reminds Gina that in 1958 the island of Jaluit in the Marshall Islands was under three and four feet of water during a typhoon.

When Gina's family reaches their destination, they huddle together behind sandbags that have been placed in a protective ring. They are thankful that the wall has been built for the high winds are snapping coconuts from the palms and sending them, like deadly bullets, through the air. The rain tastes salty. Gina's father explains that the ocean spray is being driven over the island by the winds. The storm goes on and on for hours.

Suddenly the winds die down. Gina notices that the sky has become lighter. Some of the people begin to move, but Gina's father tells the family to stay where they are. He says that the typhoon is not over. The calm is only the eye of the storm passing over the atoll. The raging storm will begin again shortly.

Soon, the winds and rain are as fierce as before the calm. This time the force of the storm is coming from the opposite direction. Once again, the island suffers from the typhoon. It lasts through the night.

Gina wakes the next morning to lighter skies and winds that become calmer during the day. The people of the island begin to check the damage. It could have been worse. Several palm trees were blown down. The small patches of sweet potatoes and taro were flattened, but the soil remains and has not been damaged too greatly by salt water. A few homes were destroyed. The people decide to place a temporary thatch roof on the store to replace the tin roof that the typhoon winds have blown away. But best of all, no one has been hurt or lost.

Tahitian dancers and a Fiji native drying copra follow ancestral customs, but modern industry, like this cannery on Samoa, is growing in the islands.

ISLAND REGIONS OF THE PACIFIC

The Pacific World has been divided into three regions: Melanesia, Micronesia, and Polynesia. The names of these regions are based on their location and on their people. *Nesia* comes from the Greek word *nesos,* which means "island." *Melanesia* means "black islands," *Micronesia* means "small islands," and *Polynesia* means "many islands."

One way to remember the location of these three regions is to locate them on a map. As you can see from the map on page 453, most of the islands of Melanesia lie south of the equator, while those of Micronesia lie north of the equator. Except for New Zealand, the islands of Polynesia lie east of the 180° Longitude line.

Melanesia

The major island groups of Melanesia are New Guinea, the Solomon Islands, and the Fiji Islands. Many of the islands of these groups are volcanic islands. The region is inhabited by dark-skinned, thick-bearded people. The Melanesians are believed to have originally settled in New Guinea. Over the years, the people have spread throughout the smaller islands.

In this tropical region of the Pacific, the homes do not have to be solidly built. The people need only temporary shelter from the warmest hours of the day and from the storms. The fast-growing, thick jungle around the village looks as though it intends to swallow up the village. The Melanesian men are skilled in carving and inlaying wood with shells. When at work in small groups, they squat rather than sit on the ground.

Micronesia

Although some of the islands of Micronesia are volcanic, most of the islands of this region are atolls. The main island groups of Micronesia are the Marianas, Carolines, Marshalls, and Gilberts. Guam, an American military base, is in the Marianas.

The people of these "small islands" are believed to have come from the Philippines and the East Indies. The Micronesians have copper-colored skin and short, straight, black hair. Since they are, for the most part, atoll dwellers, they have turned to the sea for much of their food. Their swift, outrigger canoes are ingenious craft of well-balanced design. The outriggers are used for fishing and sport. Besides fish, the diet of the Micronesians includes fruit, coconuts, and root crops, such as taro. Often a pig barbecue highlights a feast.

Polynesia

The last large region of the Pacific World forms a triangle. On the map on page 453 a triangle is shown with Hawaii at the northern point,

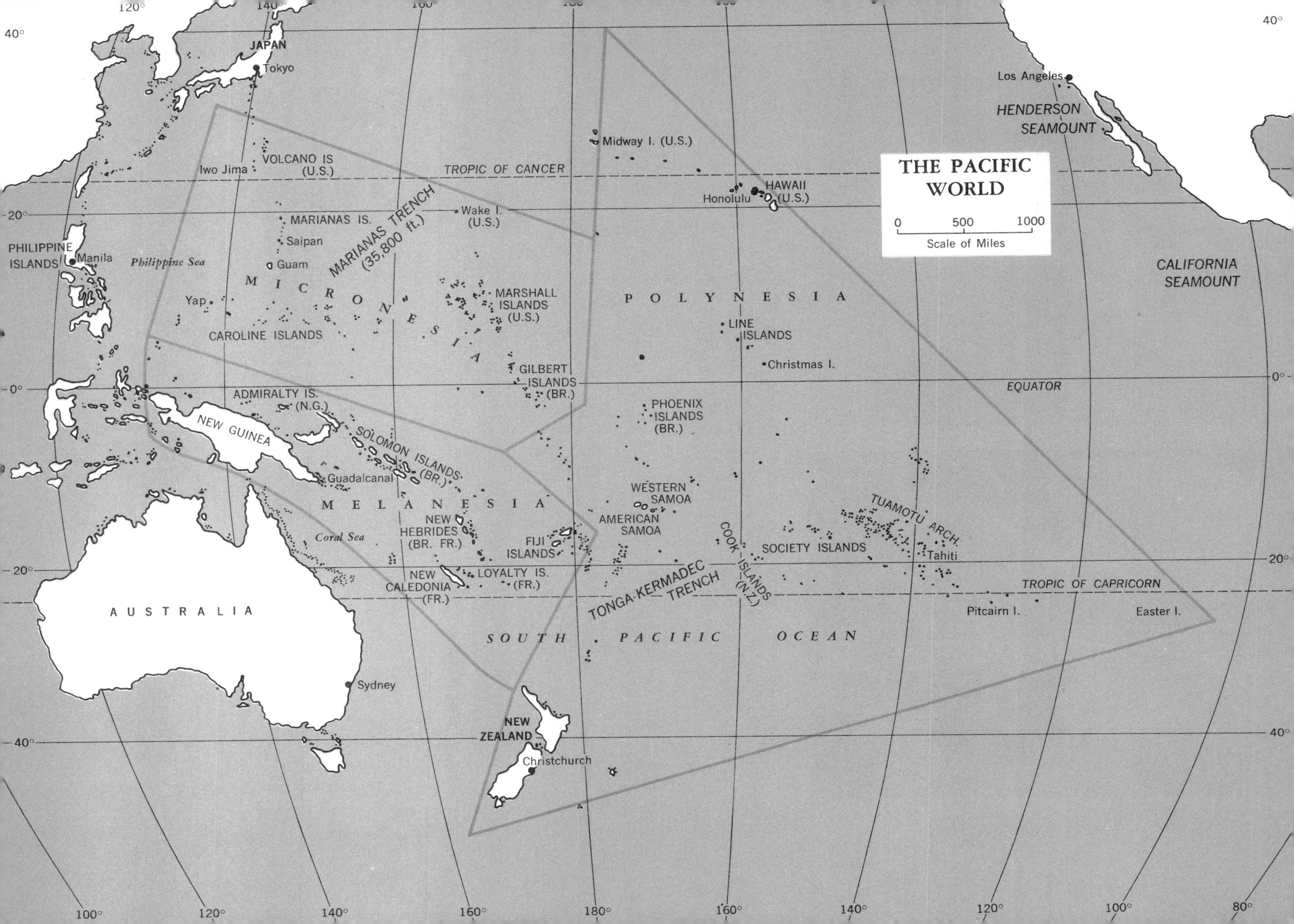
THE PACIFIC WORLD
0 500 1000
Scale of Miles
JAPAN
Tokyo
Los Angeles
HENDERSON SEAMOUNT
CALIFORNIA SEAMOUNT
Midway I. (U.S.)
Iwo Jima
VOLCANO IS (U.S.)
TROPIC OF CANCER
HAWAII (U.S.)
Honolulu
MARIANAS IS.
Saipan
Guam
MARIANAS TRENCH (35,800 ft.)
Wake I. (U.S.)
PHILIPPINE ISLANDS
Manila
Philippine Sea
M I C R O N E S I A
Yap
CAROLINE ISLANDS
MARSHALL ISLANDS (U.S.)
P O L Y N E S I A
LINE ISLANDS
Christmas I.
GILBERT ISLANDS (BR.)
EQUATOR
ADMIRALTY IS. (N.G.)
NEW GUINEA
PHOENIX ISLANDS (BR.)
SOLOMON ISLANDS (BR.)
Guadalcanal
M E L A N E S I A
WESTERN SAMOA
AMERICAN SAMOA
TUAMOTU ARCH.
NEW HEBRIDES (BR. FR.)
Coral Sea
FIJI ISLANDS
COOK ISLANDS (N.Z.)
SOCIETY ISLANDS
Tahiti
NEW CALEDONIA (FR.)
LOYALTY IS. (FR.)
TONGA-KERMADEC TRENCH
TROPIC OF CAPRICORN
Pitcairn I.
Easter I.
AUSTRALIA
S O U T H P A C I F I C O C E A N
Sydney
NEW ZEALAND
Christchurch
40°
20°
0°
20°
40°
100°
120°
140°
160°
180°
160°
140°
120°
100°
80°

Fiji Islanders show their skill at wood carving; Bora Bora natives, like all Polynesians, are expert fishermen.

Easter Island at the eastern point, and New Zealand at the southern point. Within this large triangle are the thousands of islands that make up Polynesia. Some major groups of small islands are the Society Islands, the largest of which is Tahiti, and the Samoan Islands, which are divided into Eastern Samoa and Western Samoa. Eastern Samoa is also called American Samoa.

The Polynesians are tall, large people with light brown skins, straight or wavy hair, and black eyes. The Polynesians and Micronesians have often been described as "the greatest ocean pathfinders in history." Long before Magellan sailed into the Pacific Ocean, the Polynesians crossed and re-crossed thousands of miles of ocean in their frail canoes.

For long voyages, the Polynesians used double canoes. They secured poles across two canoes and built a platform on the poles. Each canoe acted as an outrigger and made the whole craft very stable. Sometimes a small hut was built on the platform.

How did the Polynesians find their way across such wide stretches of ocean? They plotted their courses by the stars, by the way the ocean currents moved, and by the flight of certain birds. They even watched for the greenish reflection of coral atoll lagoons on the undersides of clouds. Imagine setting sail in a 40 foot outrigger from your own tiny island to another tiny island 200 to 300 miles away. Imagine doing this with no compass, no radio, no radar, and no carefully drawn map. Today, some "civilized" people get lost on super-highways with detailed road-maps on their laps!

The Micronesians and Polynesians sometimes used a crude chart as a memory aid in navigation. The frame was made of the inner strips of palm leaves. Small shells indicated the location of atolls. Other palm strips represented the direction of ocean waves and the presence of reefs.

THE PEOPLE OF THE PACIFIC

The earliest settlements in the Pacific World are believed to have been made by people from Southeast Asia. About two thousand years ago is the best guess historians have made about the time of earliest settlement. It is thought that waves of different peoples came from the East Indies and Southeast Asia to the islands of the Pacific World. Recently, the idea was presented that settlement could have been made from South America. There may have been some exchange of ideas between the people of South America and those of the South Pacific. However, most scientists agree that the culture, languages, and people of the Pacific came from Southeast Asia.

Early European Explorers

Marco Polo in his travels to and from China probably had seen the

Outrigger canoes are sturdy, sea-going craft, and are widely used for both fishing and transportation.

Pacific Ocean. But the first man to bring word of the great Pacific World to Europe was the Portuguese navigator, Antonio d'Abreau. This navigator approached the Pacific from the west. He probably touched on New Guinea in 1511.

In 1513 Vasco Núñez de Balboa, a Spanish soldier of fortune, approached the Pacific from the east. He crossed from the Atlantic to the Pacific at the Isthmus of Panama. The Isthmus of Panama extends in an east-west direction. After crossing the Isthmus, Balboa looked south upon a great ocean and named it *Mar del Sur*, or "Sea of the South."

Magellan's Voyage

In the years 1520 and 1521, Ferdinand Magellan became the first to circumnavigate the world. Magellan sailed across the Atlantic and entered the great ocean through the straits at the tip of South America now bearing his name. During the thirty-eight-day passage through the Straits of Magellan, the ships met with gales and rough seas. They welcomed the calm ocean at the end of the strait. Although troubled by scurvy, a lack of water, and a lack of proper food, they met few storms as they crossed the great ocean. The ocean seemed so peaceful to Magellan that he called it the Pacific. People who have experienced a typhoon, however, know that the ocean can be far from *pacific*, which means "peaceful."

Sir Francis Drake's Exploration

The first Englishman to cross the Pacific was Sir Francis Drake. He entered the Pacific through the Straits of Magellan and plundered Spanish cities and ships along the west coasts of South America and Middle America. Drake knew the Spanish were eagerly waiting for him to try to return to Europe by the southern passage. Instead, he sailed northward along the Pacific Coast of North America. He sailed as far north as Canada's Vancouver Island in his search for a passage eastward to Europe. Cold weather forced him to turn south again. Finally, he decided to sail westward across the Pacific. In order to prepare for the long journey, he landed at a small bay north of San Francisco. There his men overhauled the ship so as to make her seaworthy for the long voyage. Drake called the land *Nova Albion* and claimed it for Queen Elizabeth I of England.

Drake placed a brass plate on a post. The plate bore this message:

BEE IT KNOWN UNTO ALL MEN BY THESE PRESENTS

JUNE 17 1579

BY THE GRACE OF GOD AND IN THE NAME OF HERR MAIESTY QUEEN ELIZABETH OF ENGLAND AND HERR SUCCESSORS FOREVER I TAKE POSSESSION OF THIS KINGDOME WHOSE KING AND PEOPLE FREELY RESIGNE THEIR RIGHT AND TITLE IN THE WHOLE LAND UNTO HERR MAIESTIES KEEPING NOW NAMED BY ME AN TO BEE KNOWNE UNTO ALL MEN AS NOVA ALBION

FRANCIS DRAKE

Oddly enough, the plate was found by a motorist near San Francisco Bay in 1936. The man had stopped to repair a tire puncture and noticed the plate lying near the road. He took the plate to the University of California at Berkeley. There, experts declared that the plate the man had found was the same brass plate Drake had posted in Nova Albion. The plate is on view today in the library of the University of California at Berkeley.

Drake returned to England by way of the Pacific Ocean, the Indian Ocean, and the Atlantic Ocean. He returned laden with Spanish treasure and was knighted by Queen Elizabeth. He was the first Englishman to circumnavigate the globe.

Explorers from Many Countries

During the next three centuries, explorers from Spain, England, Holland, and France located most of the islands of the Pacific World. They were searching for the rich continent that was thought to be in the South Pacific. The great Dutch explorer, Abel Janszoon Tasman, discovered Tasmania and New Zealand.

Captain James Cook, an Englishman, made three voyages into the Pacific. He thoroughly explored the South Pacific Ocean and proved that the rich continent for which many were searching did not exist. On his third voyage, Cook sailed from Tahiti to the northwest coast of North America in search of a passage eastward from the Pacific to the Atlantic.

Sir Francis Drake

On his way to the northwest coast, he found the Hawaiian Islands which he named the Sandwich Islands. Unable to find the passage to the Atlantic, Cook later returned to these islands. On February 14, 1779, he was killed in a skirmish with Hawaiians at Kealakekua Bay.

PROGRESS IN THE PACIFIC WORLD

During World War II, a Dutch pilot flew his one-seater combat plane over the western interior of the island of New Guinea. He was flying low looking for some land marks. He was startled when he saw some dark-skinned people in a small clearing throwing rocks and clubs at his plane. They were trying to frighten it away. They must have thought the airplane was a mysterious bird coming to destroy them.

New Guinea remains one of the most primitive lands in the world today.

Upon his return to his base in northern Australia, he looked for information on the people he had just seen. As he read more and more about New Guinea, he realized that he had seen a group of people the modern world had passed by. They were just one step beyond Stone Age people. They hunted with clubs, spears, and crude bows and arrows. The smelting of ores and the manufacturing of clothes and agricultural tools were unknown to them.

Work of the United Nations

When the United Nations became a reality after World War II, the members realized that many of the island peoples needed help. Feeling a strong responsibility towards these peoples of the Pacific World, the United Nations set up two very important councils. One was the Social and Economic Council. The second was the Trusteeship Council, which was given the job of supervising the administration of territories under the United Nations.

On some of the islands that had belonged to Japan, there was no longer any government. On other islands the war had created hardships and much destruction. Still other islands were without supplies. The Trusteeship Council gave to some of the members of the United Nations the responsibility of looking after these distressed island groups. The United States was made responsible for some Pacific islands. Other trustee nations in the Pacific were the United Kingdom, France, Australia, and New Zealand.

In July of 1947, the United States Pacific Trust Territory included the Marianas Islands, the Marshall Islands, and the Caroline Islands. These islands are in the Micronesian region of the Pacific World. There are 2,140 islands that have been counted in the United States Territory. They are scattered over three million square miles of water. The total area, land and water, is equal in size to the United States mainland. But in the 3 million square miles, there are only 687 square miles of land. About 76,000 people live on these islands.

The United States and the other trustee nations in the Pacific agreed to help the inhabitants advance to a goal of self-government and independence. They would give assistance and guidance in helping the islands become economically self-sufficient. They would improve the social conditions, but only according to the desires of the people themselves. And finally, they would provide more and better education.

In order to accomplish these aims, the United States set up headquarters on key islands. The main headquarters are on Saipan in the Marianas. Other headquarters are on the islands of Yap, Truk, and Ponape in the Carolinas. Guam, the largest island in the Marianas, is an important American military base. On other islands, fully-equipped "tracking" stations have been set up. These stations track the space vehicles which today orbit the Earth.

Attempts have been made to help the island peoples in the Trusteeship Territory feel more unified. This is not an easy job. One problem is the wide area over which these islands are spread. Another is the fact that two different groups of people have settled these islands. Still another problem is the large number of languages spoken in the region. Many different dialects are spoken. Many of these languages are unrelated to the major languages of the world. They are, therefore, difficult to learn. Some natives had learned Japanese during World War II when the islands were controlled by that country. Now the people are encouraged to learn English.

The islands of Fiji and Tahiti draw tourists from all over the world.

Life on Tahiti

Let us look closely at a Pacific island where progress is being made. Life on Tahiti in the Society Islands is typical of life on many of the smaller islands in the vast Pacific.

Parking is a problem on the streets of Papeete, the capital of Tahiti.

The island of Tahiti is volcanic in origin. Its high, green-clad mountains soar to over 7,000 feet. Coral reefs, broken by inlets, circle the island. On the northwest side of the island is Papeete, the capital of the Society Islands. Papeete is a crowded city with a population of about 20,000.

The native Tahitians have the reputation of being among the world's happiest people. They recover quickly after every trouble, big or little. When they speak, the listener is pleasantly surprised. They have no harsh sound in their language. The sound of their words, like their laughter, seems to express a steady, easy-going life.

Although many of the old Tahitian ways of life still remain, many modern changes have come to Tahiti. People travel by trucks and buses. The bus may be crowded not only with people but also with boxes and bicycles. These may be piled high on top of a bus. Fish may hang out of the windows.

If a bus driver sees a palm frond on the road ahead, he stops the bus and blows the horn. The man who had signaled the bus driver by the palm leaf rises from his nap and enters the bus.

Some of the passengers, men and women, are wearing **pareus.** These are gaily colored squares of cloth used as a kind of shirt. They may be sitting beside other men and women wearing white linen suits. Almost every young girl wears flowers in her hair.

A **luaus,** a Tahitian feast, is tempting. Cooked and uncooked fish of many kinds are served. Some of the uncooked fish have been steeped in lime juice. Others have been flavored with coconut milk. Coffee and coconut milk are drunk at the feast. A pig has been prepared by filling its insides with hot stones. The pig is then placed in a pit, the bottom of which has been covered with hot stones. The pig is covered with mats and layers of leaves and earth and left to bake for several hours. Breadfruit, fish, and sweet potatoes may also be placed in the pit to be cooked with the pig. Fruits of many kinds are offered: mangoes, guavas, pineapples, papaya, and bananas. Tiny red and golden-yellow are two of the many kinds of bananas.

Growing Industries of the Pacific

Eastern, or American, Somoa in the Polynesian region has been controlled by the United States since 1900. Fine progress has been made in establishing new industries here. A fish cannery, a textile mill, and a coconut processing plant are now in operation in Samoa. Copra has long been the major cash crop of the Pacific World. Copra is coconut meat which has been dried to keep it from spoiling. Oil obtained from copra is used in the making of soap, margarine, and candles. Although copra from this region forms only a small portion of the world's production, the income from this export crop is important to the people.

Tourism is beginning to bring much new revenue into the islands. There is a new modern hotel at Pago-Pago in Samoa. The island's harbor serves both steamship and aircraft passengers. A 7,000 foot long runway for jets is near completion.

Good transportation means that people can leave the islands as well as visit them more easily. The younger Samoans are leaving for other islands and mainland countries. They hear of "far away places" just as you do. "Off to the South Seas" has been changed by many islanders to "off to the Pacific Rimlands."

Island villages often resemble one another, even though they are miles apart. The village on the left is on the island of Guadalcanal; the other is a part of Western Samoa.

THE INTERNATIONAL DATE LINE

On a globe the Pacific Ocean has a very important "line" drawn through it from north to south. Look again at the globe so that the half you see is mostly water. Look at the central spot of this "water hemisphere." Do you see the two north-south lines of longitude near the center of the Pacific Ocean, one marked 170° East Longitude and the other 170° West Longitude? Find the line between them. It is marked 180° Longitude. Can you explain why it does not have "East" or "West" written beside it?

The 180° Longitude line was used as the guiding line for drawing the International Date Line. This Line marks the place where each day begins. To find out how this works, let us learn more about the grid lines on a globe.

Ships sailing west from Pago Pago harbor in Samoa soon cross the International Date Line.

We know the Earth rotates from west to east, 360° every 24 hours. How many degrees will it move in one hour? The correct answer is 15°. This is why the Earth is divided into 24 time zones each covering a span of 15° of the Earth. There are lines on your globe which are drawn every 15° beginning with the 0° Longitude line or prime meridian. These lines are called central meridians. Each of these meridians on the globe is the center of a time zone. The time zones extend $7\frac{1}{2}$° east and $7\frac{1}{2}$° west of each of these longitude lines. In the zone to the east the time is one hour later, while in the zone to the west the time is one hour earlier.

If you were traveling by plane west from Hawaii to New Guinea, you would cross the International Date Line. You would leave Hawaii on Monday and arrive in New Guinea on Tuesday, even though the flight may have taken only a short time. There is a difference of one second and yet a difference in the name of a day every time you cross the International Date Line.

To understand how this Line works, have someone shine a light right on the prime meridian, the 0° Longitude line on the opposite side of the globe from the International Date Line. If the light represents the sun, it is noon at the 0° Longitude line. It is midnight at the 180° Longitude line. This shows that when it is 12:01 A.M. on Thursday at the International Date Line, the rest of the world is on Wednesday. Doesn't it make more sense to start a new day or date during the dark period than during the light?

Hold the light, which represents the sun, in the same place. Rotate the globe slowly, until the "sun" is shining on the 90° West Longitude. Now it is noon at 90° West Longitude and midnight at 90° East Longitude. That means, that when it is 12:01 A.M. at 90° East Longitude, it will be Thursday in the area between the International Date Line (180°) and the 90° East Longitude. The rest of the world will still be on Wednesday. Can you tell what time of what day it would be in Sydney, Australia if it is 7:00 P.M. Tuesday in New York?

The time zone lines are not always straight. Notice on the map how the International Date Line in some places is many degrees and many miles away from the 180° meridian of Longitude. The leaders of the nations of the world set up the zones this way so that the people living in the same city, in the same country, or in the same group of islands, such as the Fijis, would be on the same time of the same day. It would be very difficult to schedule an event,

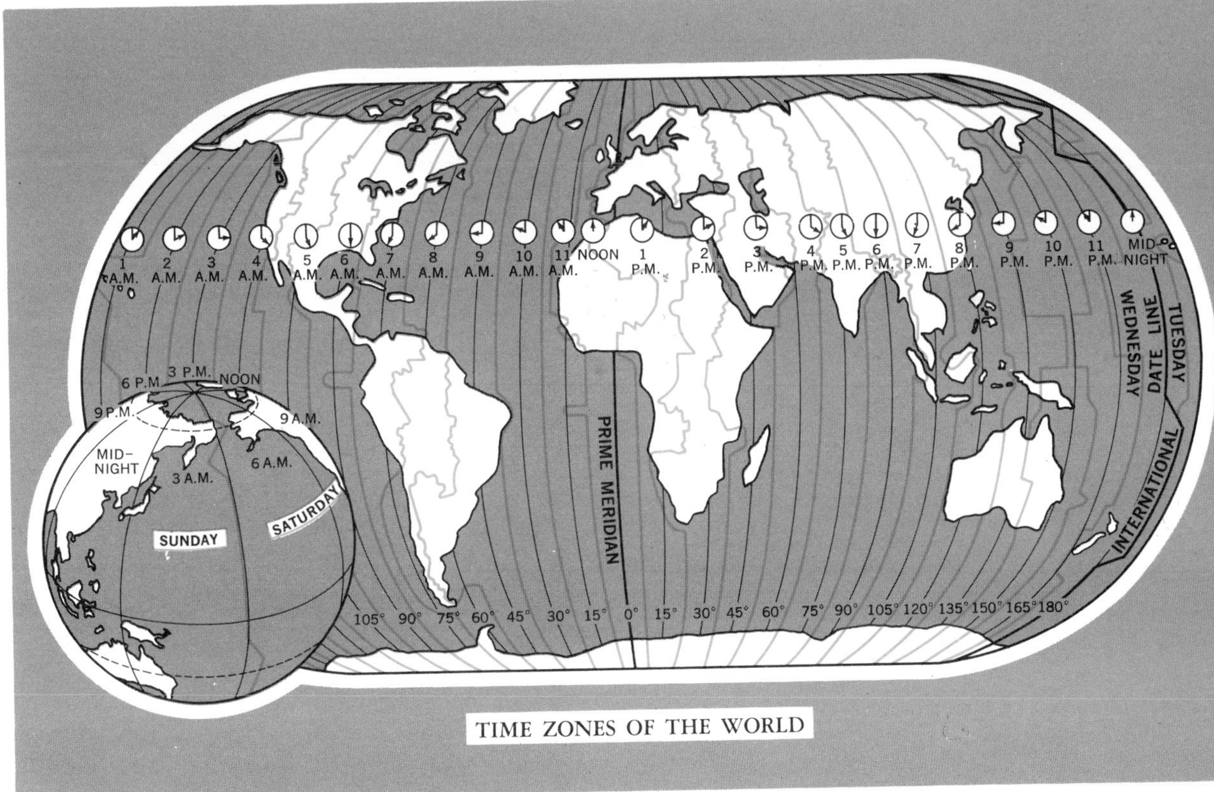

TIME ZONES OF THE WORLD

such as a baseball game, if the people in the same city or on the same island had two different times, one hour apart or one day apart.

If you follow the International Date Line from the north to the south, you might keep these facts in mind. First, the Line is close to, but not always exactly on, the 180° meridian. Second, when it is Sunday to the east of the Line, it is Monday to the west of the Line. Third, wherever possible the Line has been drawn around land bodies rather than through them.

A GREAT FRONTIER

Today, the Pacific, the largest of all oceans, is being crossed faster and more easily than ever before. In many parts of the sea, there are regions of peaceful islands and easy-going communities that change very slowly. In other parts of the Pacific World the way of life is like that of modern America. Bustling cities and new industries are growing rapidly. The way of life for many people is changing rapidly.

The Pacific World still remains one of the great frontiers. This is particularly true of the part of the Pacific World below the surface of the ocean. As we learn how to profitably extract minerals from sea water, new sources of wealth will open for people of the Pacific lands. As we learn how to use the resources of the seas for food production, the Pacific World will have a more important place in the world's economy.

Do You Know?

1. What are two staple foods in the diet of atoll dwellers?

2. What are the two greatest dangers to life on an atoll?

3. What are the three island regions of the Pacific? What do the words mean?

4. Between what two latitude lines do most Pacific islands lie? Which island region lies south of the equator?

5. What did the Polynesians use to tell the direction in which they were sailing?

6. When did the first people come to the islands of the Pacific? From which continent did they come?

7. How far do you travel if you circumnavigate the world? Who were two early explorers who made this trip?

8. What two councils of the United Nations were set up to help the people of the Pacific World?

9. What are the major island groups of Micronesia?

10. Why isn't the International Date Line perfectly straight?

Learn By Doing

1. Select the correct definition from column **B** for each word in column **A.**

A	B
1. Marianas	a deep trench
2. Mt. Fujiyama	hidden islands
3. coral	shield volcanoes
4. guyots	the polyp skeleton
5. Hawaiian Islands	a strato-volcano

2. Select the correct answer to complete each sentence.

a. The International Date Line is drawn from (north to south, east to west).

b. The (0, 90, 180) degree Longitude Line was used as a guiding line to draw the International Date Line.

c. The Earth rotates from (north to south, east to west, west to east).

d. The Earth rotates (90, 180, 360) degrees every twenty-four hours.

e. There are (12, 24, 36, 60) time zones on the Earth.

f. Each hour the Earth rotates (15, 10, 30, 60) degrees.

g. The prime meridian is the (0 degree, 90 degree, 180 degree) Longitude line.

h. Each time zone extends about (5, $7\frac{1}{2}$, 10, 15) degrees east and west of a central meridian.

i. If it is Monday to the east of the International Date Line, it is (Monday, Sunday, Tuesday) to the west of the Line.

j. The International Date Line is drawn (around, through) important bodies of land.

3. Draw an outrigger canoe. Label each part of the canoe and tell why it is helpful. Write a short story describing a day's journey in the canoe.

4. Sketch a fringing reef, a barrier reef, and a coral atoll. Shade the water blue. Label the land.

5. Copy the "face" of an aneroid barometer. Show where the indicator would be before a hurricane, during the eye of a storm, and after a hurricane.

6. Make a booklet of pictures of the native people living in the three Pacific regions. Briefly describe each picture. Magazines and newspapers will be good sources. Pictures may be copied from encyclopedias and books. Groups within the class may select different regions.

Test Your Knowledge

1. What is the meaning of the phrase "Rim of Fire"? What lands are described by these words?

2. What is an oceanographer? What are some of their findings in the Pacific?

3. What is the difference between a shield volcano and a strato-volcano?

4. What is a coral reef? What are the three types of coral reefs?

5. Describe some of the problems of living on an atoll.

6. What is a barometer? How can a barometer be helpful?

7. Why did the United Nations set up the Trustee Council? Is this council still being used today?

8. What is another name for the white meat of the coconut? Why is it important to the island peoples?

9. Explain the terms "water hemisphere" and "land hemisphere."

CHAPTER 20

AUSTRALIA AND NEW ZEALAND

Do you know what a boomerang is? Have you heard about such things as the kangaroo, the dingo, and the kiwi? They are found on the islands of Australia, Tasmania, and New Zealand. These islands are often called the "Land Down Under" because they lie entirely south of the equator.

These lands are unique in many ways. Here can be found people who live much like the men of the Stone Age. Alongside these primitive people will be found people living in very advanced ways. There are great ranches where fine herds of sheep and cattle are raised. There are modern cities with growing manufacturing industries.

THE PACIFIC'S LARGEST ISLANDS

Australia and New Zealand are the largest islands in the Pacific World. Australia is the largest island in the world. It is often called the "Island Continent." Australia, with its neighboring island of Tasmania, and New Zealand are members of the British Commonwealth of Nations. They are English-speaking nations. The climate in some sections is similar to that found in some sections of our country, and the people wear the same type of clothing as we wear. There are many modern cities located on these large island nations.

But not all of the land nor all of the people have benefited from modern progress. Because these lands are surrounded by water, the native peoples developed their own ways of living. They did not have neighbors from whom they could borrow ideas and trade goods. As a result their primitive ways remained unchanged.

UNIQUE ANIMAL LIFE

One of the regionalizing features of Australia and New Zealand is the unique animal life. This uniqueness is a result of the isolation of these islands from the Asian land mass. The isolation of New Zealand preserved the kiwi, moa, and tuatara until the coming of man. European settlers

The kangaroo

Koalas (top) A tuatara (bottom)

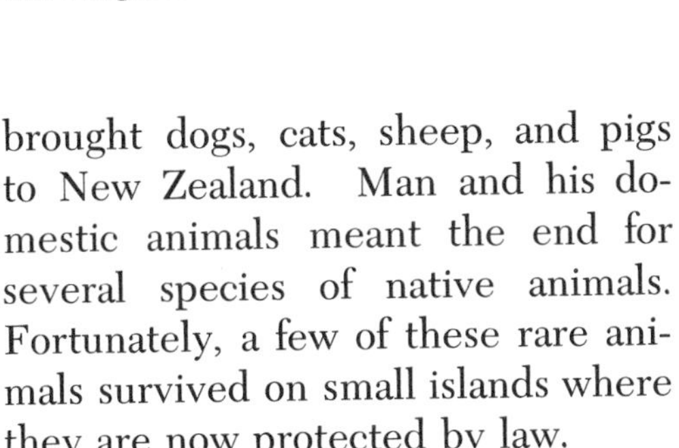

brought dogs, cats, sheep, and pigs to New Zealand. Man and his domestic animals meant the end for several species of native animals. Fortunately, a few of these rare animals survived on small islands where they are now protected by law.

Marsupials of "Down Under"

Marsupials are pouched animals. The young are born alive. But they are so undeveloped when born, that they must live in a pouch on the mother's body, feeding on milk until able to care for themselves. The marsupials of Australia developed into an amazing variety of forms.

One of the best known Australian marsupials is the kangaroo. The chief features of the kangaroo are its strong, large hind legs, its small, short front legs, and its powerful tail. Different types of kangaroos vary in size from large, man-sized to tiny, rat-sized animals. Australians call the larger kangaroo a wallaroo. The smaller one is called a wallaby.

Another marsupial, the koala, is related to the kangaroo. Furry and tailless, it looks like a teddy bear. The koala is found today in the forests of eastern Australia. It feeds only on the leaves of certain types of eucalyptus trees. It prefers to feed at night and sleep during the day.

Another marsupial native to Australia and Tasmania is the wombat. The wombat is about three feet long and has short, sturdy legs, and no tail. It has two incisor teeth in each jaw. These incisors keep growing throughout the life of the wombat. The wombat nests at the end of a burrow that may be 15 to 100 feet long.

Two other marsupials are the Tasmanian devil and the Tasmanian wolf.

These two animals exist only in Tasmania, Australia's island state. Both of these animals carry their immature young in pouches until such time as they can be left alone in nests. The Tasmanian devil lives on small animals such as rats, mice, and frogs. The Tasmanian wolf, about the size of a large dog, is the largest meat-eating animal found in this region. It hunts in the evening and feeds on kangaroos and smaller animals. European settlers waged war on the Tasmanian wolf because it killed their sheep. So many wolves have been killed that they are now almost extinct.

Other Australian Animals

The dingo is a wild dog. Scientists believe that the dingo may have been brought to the Australian continent by prehistoric man. If captured when very young, it makes a good pet. The wild dingo hunts at night. Its chief food is the wallaby. But because it also kills sheep, the Australian government has spent large sums of money in an effort to exterminate, or destroy, this wild dog.

Perhaps the most unusual Australian animal is the platypus. The platypus is a furry mammal that lays eggs and nurses its young on milk. It has a duck-shaped bill and webbed feet. The male platypus has a spur on each hind foot. Each spur is connected to poisonous glands. The platypus poisons its enemies by scratching them with the spur.

The platypus probes in the mud with its bill in search of worms, insects, larvae, and shellfish. It builds its nest in the riverbank with an underwater entrance. When the platypus was first described to Europeans, they thought the duck-like bill had been made up or fastened on by man.

People who have tried to raise the platypus report some astonishing facts. One is that it has an enormous appetite. Two of these animals have been known to eat over 1,200 earthworms and 50 crayfish in a twenty-four-hour period. During the same day they also ate a few appetizers, such as beetles and small tadpoles.

A dingo.

The Animals of New Zealand

The kiwi is a flightless bird found only in New Zealand. At about four pounds, it is approximately the size of a chicken. It lays an egg much larger than a chicken's egg. The kiwi egg weighs about one pound. After the female kiwi lays the egg, the male bird sits on the egg for 75 days. The

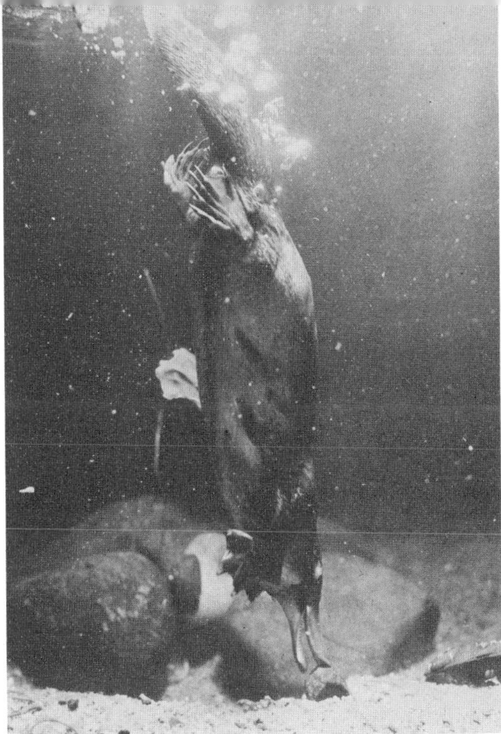

A platypus

A kiwi (top) A wombat (bottom)

kiwi has hair-like feathers. It also has a long beak. Unlike other birds, it has nostrils near the end instead of at the base of the beak. The kiwi finds its food by its keen senses of smell and hearing. It eats berries, worms, snails, insects, and larvae. It hunts for food at night. At one time the kiwi was in danger of becoming extinct. It is now protected by the New Zealand government.

A giant cousin of the kiwi, the moa, is now extinct. The moa was an enormous bird that weighed as much as 500 pounds. It stood about 12 feet high. The native people of New Zealand, the **Maoris,** hunted the moa to extinction. Until the coming of man to New Zealand, the moa and the kiwi had had no animal to fear. The only mammal on the islands was the bat.

In the animal kingdom there are many species of reptiles. You have probably seen or read about snakes and lizards, crocodiles and alligators, and turtles. One species, the tuatara, may have a longer history than the others. Its ancestors date back about 200 million years to a time before the Age of the Dinosaurs. The tuatara survives only in New Zealand on small rocky islands. It has been called a "living fossil." A **fossil** is an animal or plant, or any trace or impression of an animal or plant, of prehistoric times imbedded or preserved in a rock. Why is the term "living fossil" fitting for the tuatara?

The tuatara is an olive-green, lizard-like animal with three eyes, one of which is on the top of its head. Scientists believe that at one time this third eye actually functioned to help the tuatara see. Today, the third eye is covered with skin. However, it is possible that even today it is sensitive to light.

Hobart is the capital and chief port of the island state of Tasmania.

HISTORY OF THE REGION

Australia, Tasmania, and New Zealand have been separated from the Asian land mass since very ancient times. Among the many, early explorers who ventured into this isolated region, there are two of particular interest. The first was a Dutchman, Abel Tasman. The second was an Englishman, James Cook.

The Explorations of Tasman

Eager for gold and silver, the directors of the Dutch East India company sent Abel Tasman on his first expedition in 1642. He was sent to discover a "Great Southland" that was thought to lie in the Southern Hemisphere. The Company instructed Tasman to sail west from Java to Mauritius, an island in the Indian Ocean off the coast of Africa. Locate these places on the map on page 471. At Mauritius, he was to take on water, food, and firewood. From that island he was to sail to the 54° South Latitude. If by that time he had not discovered the Great Southland, Tasman was to sail east to the longitude of New Guinea exploring any lands or islands that he discovered on the way. Tasman was instructed to be very careful in dealing with the natives he met. He was told:

> *In landing with small craft extreme caution will everywhere be used, seeing that it is well-known that the southern regions are peopled by fierce savages, for which reason you will always have to be well armed and to use every prudent precaution, since experience has taught in all parts of the world that barbarian men are nowise to be trusted, because they commonly think that the foreigners who so unexpectedly appear before them, have come only to seize their land, which (owing to heedlessness and overconfidence) in the discovery of America occasioned many instances of treacherous slaughter. On which account, you will treat with amity and kindness such barbarian men as you shall meet and come to parley with, and connive at small affronts, thefts and the like which they should put upon or commit against our men, lest punishments inflicted should give them a grudge against us; and by shows of kindness gain them over to us, that you may the more readily from them obtain information touching themselves, their country, and their circumstances, thus learning whether there is anything profitable to be got or effected.*

The final line of the above quotation states that the purpose of the voyage was to find riches. The Company promised to reward Tasman and his men if they discovered rich lands. Tasman was told that if he met civilized people who possessed gold or silver, he was to pretend to value these two metals less than copper or lead. Why do you think he was told to do this?

In command of two ships, Tasman sailed south from Mauritius to about 49° South Latitude. He then turned eastward, taking advantage, as he had been instructed, of the westerly winds in these latitudes. Some idea of how fast the westerly winds blow between the 35° South Latitude and the 45° South Latitude is obtained when you look at the distance between Mauritius and Tasmania. After just seven weeks of moving swiftly along with sails full, Tasman's crew sighted land on November 24, 1642. Tasman called the newly discovered land Van Dieman's Land in honor of the head of the Dutch East India Company. The land was later named Tasmania after its discoverer.

From Tasmania, Tasman sailed eastward until he and his crew sighted a second new land. Tasman thought that this land might be a part of the Great Southland he had been sent to find. It was, of course, the southern island of the two large islands that make up New Zealand. He began to sail along the coast, mapping it and searching for a good harbor.

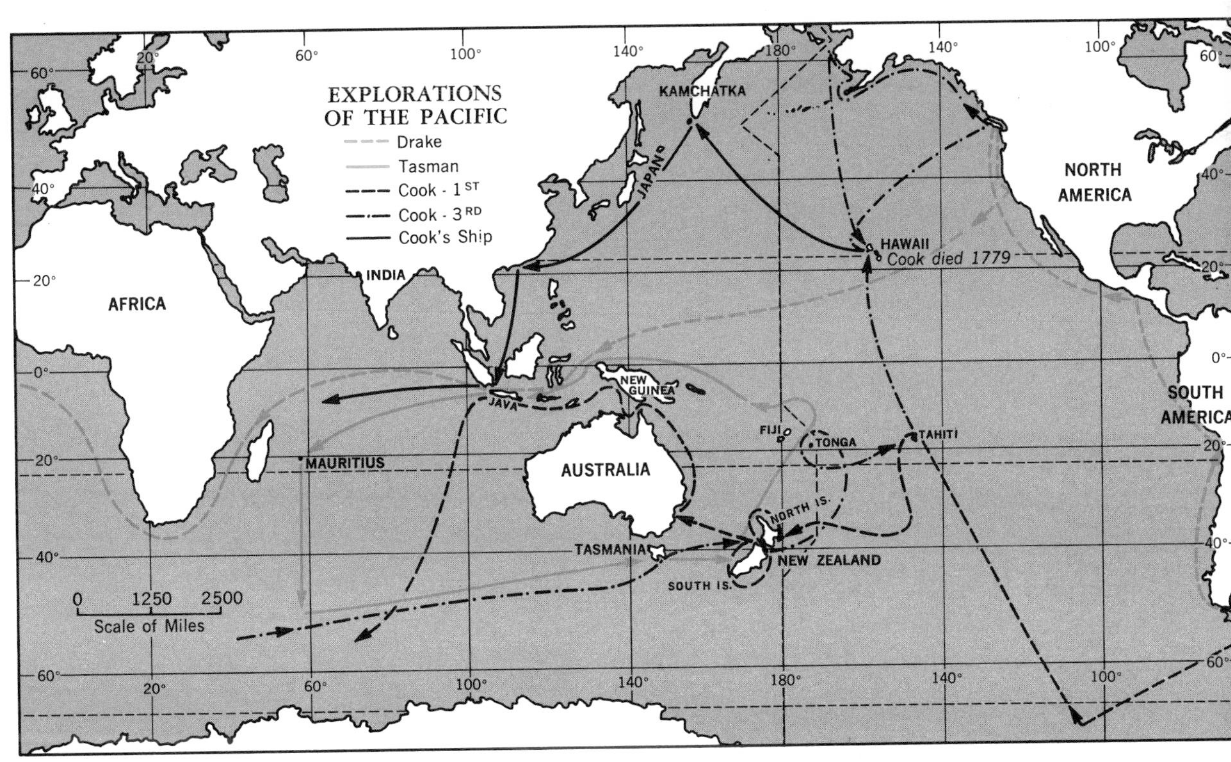

Tasman Meets the Maoris

Tasman anchored in a calm bay and sent out two small boats to look for a place to take on fresh water. The two boats returned at nightfall followed by two boats with natives. The men on ship and the natives called out to one another, but neither party was able to understand the other. Early the next morning, a boat with 13 natives approached the ship. Tasman described the natives and their boat. In so doing, he gave the first European account of the Maoris, the inhabitants of New Zealand.

As far as we could observe, these people were of ordinary height; they had rough voices and strong bones, the colour of their skin being between brown and yellow; they wore tufts of black hair right upon the top of their heads, tied fast in the manner of the Japanese at the back of their heads, but somewhat longer and thicker, and surmounted by a large, thick white feather. Their boats consisted of two long narrow prows side by side, over which a number of planks or other seats were placed in such a way that those above can look through the water underneath the vessel . . . For clothing, as it seemed to us, some of them wore mats, others cotton stuffs; almost all of them were naked from the shoulders to the waist. We repeatedly made signs for them to come on board of us, showing them white linens and knives that formed part of our cargo. They did not come nearer, however, but at last paddled back to shore.

The Maoris returned later in the day with more men and more boats. The Dutchmen sent a small boat to meet them. At a signal, the Maoris in one boat began paddling very fast and rammed the ship's boat. They knocked one Dutchman overboard and killed three others with short clubs. Three of the Dutch sailors swam to the safety of another small boat which had been sent to help them. Tasman, remembering his instructions to treat the natives with kindness and not to overpower them, decided to sail away. His men named the bay *Moordenaersbay,* or Murderers' Bay.

From New Zealand, Tasman sailed north. He discovered some of the Tonga Islands, sighted the Fijis, and returned to Java by way of the north coast of New Guinea. Tasman had not found the Great Southland with its gold and silver, but he had found fame as an explorer. He left his name on the sea passage between Australia and New Zealand and on Australia's island state of Tasmania.

Explorations of Captain James Cook

A century later Captain James Cook made a long and admirable record of Pacific World discoveries. In Chapter 19, you learned about his discoveries of the Hawaiian Islands and the Polynesian people. Between the years 1769 and 1779, Cook made three long voyages of exploration in the Pacific. He thoroughly explored the South Pacific Ocean. He sailed as far as the 71° 10′ South Latitude at the 106° 54′ West Longitude. His travels cast doubt on the existence of the "Great Southland" rich in gold and silver for which the Europeans were searching. Today, we know that there are two continents in the southern Pacific World, Australia and Antarctica. Much gold has been found in Australia.

Cook also explored and mapped the coast of New Zealand. He proved that New Zealand and Australia were not connected. He claimed New Zealand and the east coast of Australia for Britain. Cook found that New Zealand was composed chiefly of two large islands. These were later named North Island and South Island. The journal of his voyage described the great forests with their tall trees suitable for shipbuilding and for masts. Cook and his men noted that the soil of the North Island was well suited for agriculture and for settlement by Englishmen.

The journal also described the Maoris, their war dances, and their great carved war canoes. It told of their agriculture which consisted mainly of growing yams, sweet potatoes, and gourds. The journal noted that the Maoris dressed like the natives of the Polynesian Islands to the northeast. Cook also noted a similarity in the boats and in the language of both peoples. He believed that the peoples of New Zealand and of the other islands of the Pacific had a common ancestor.

The Arawa tribal and architectural traditions have been retained, but most of North Island is now a productive agricultural region.

Polynesian customs still influence the lives of today's Maoris.

Wellington has few tall buildings due to the threat of earthquakes.

The Maoris Came from Polynesia

Cook's theory was right. The Maoris had come to New Zealand from Polynesia. Legend tells us of a Polynesian man named Toi reaching the island in 1150. But the main wave of Polynesians came to New Zealand in 1350. Most Maoris today are descendants of this group of immigrants. Eight of the fleet of large double canoes that brought the Maoris are known by name. To this day, a Maori can say that he belongs to the Aoetea canoe or to the Arawa canoe, or to one of the other canoes that survived the long and difficult trip to New Zealand. Just how many people set out on the trip is not known. Some did not reach New Zealand. Those who did went through a trip of much hardship and starvation.

White Settlers Come to New Zealand

Early in the nineteenth century, whalers and missionaries visited the islands of New Zealand. They were followed by white settlers from Great Britain. The settlement of New Zealand by the British began in 1840 when a company was formed in England to send colonists to the new continent. The first settlement was in the area of the modern city of Wellington. The Company that sent these colonists was formed to help the poor of the large industrial cities of England get a start on a better life. Many of these settlers became farmers. They grew crops and raised sheep.

As usually happened when native peoples of the Pacific came into contact with the Europeans, the Maoris suffered greatly from diseases to which they were not immune. Their numbers dropped sharply. However, this trend has been overcome by modern medicine. Today the Maori population of New Zealand increases. About 175,000 Maoris live in New Zealand today, most of them on North Island.

The white settlers and the Maoris have been at peace since 1869. Although the descendants of the white settlers outnumber the Maoris, both groups have equal social and political rights.

The boomerang is an effective weapon for the Australian aborigines.

The Tasmanians

Least advanced of the groups of native peoples living in this South Pacific Region before the white settlers came were the natives of Tasmania. They had black, curly hair, heavy eyebrows, and dark skin. Their noses were short and wide. Their teeth and lips were very large. They worshiped many gods but had no common religion. Measurements on unearthed skulls show that they had small brain cavities.

The Tasmanian **aborigines,** or native people, ate anything which could be swallowed: fruit, roots, shellfish, animals, and beetles. They wore little or no clothing. They sometimes placed an animal skin over their backs for protection against the rain. They had only crude, sharpened sticks or clubs to use as weapons and tools. They did not have the boomerang. They were able to build fires and windbreaks.

The number of original Tasmanians was never large. After the coming of the white man, their number dropped sharply. They were also unable to withstand the diseases brought by the white man. There may have been as many as five to ten thousand on the island at the time of Tasman's landing. By 1835 there were only a few hundred. The last pure-blooded Tasmanian died in 1879.

Natives of Australia

The story of the Australian natives is somewhat more pleasant than that of the Tasmanian natives. These people were dark-skinned, had black, wavy hair, and were often quite tall.

They lived a "gathering" life. Natives of the dry, empty interior of Australia lived in a region of scarcity. They lacked surplus foods. Even if a surplus of food had been available, they lacked the means to keep it fresh.

The day began with the members of the tribe scattering throughout the countryside in search of food. They became highly skilled in tracking animals and in searching the desert for edible, vegetable materials. The women searched the land for edible roots, bulbs, and seeds. The men used the **boomerang,** spear, and club to hunt wild animals. They also used snares and poison to take wild animals. The most effective weapon was the boomerang. This is a curved club which, when thrown, returns to the thrower if it does not strike its target.

When food was plentiful, the natives ate well. They stopped hunting because they knew that a recently killed kangaroo would not last long. Also, until the animal was eaten, there was no reason to hunt for other meat. The early settlers thought that the natives were lazy and unable to plan ahead. They did not realize that the natives were living wisely in their region of scarcity.

Most of the population of the original natives lived on the coastal lands. Life there was easier than in the interior. Unfortunately for the native Australians, these were the first lands to be settled by Europeans. The native Australians suffered the same blow that struck the Tasmanians and the Maoris. They were not immune to the diseases brought by the Europeans. They were hit by measles, smallpox, tuberculosis, very bad colds, influenza, and dysentery. Hundreds of the natives soon died. Today, with the help of modern medicine, the natives have built a partial resistance to disease. There are, however, only about one quarter of the original number of Australian aborigines left. It has been estimated that before the coming of the white man about 300,000 natives lived on the island.

Today, the aborigines seem to face a bleak future. Most of them live in the northern region where there is little rain and few rivers. They are isolated by a large desert south of them. They live under hard, subsistence conditions. Some live as nomads. Others live on the reservations set aside for the natives by the settlers. This is similar to the treatment given to the Indians in our country. The European settlers of Australia have moved further and further ahead of the aborigines in farming and industry. Some natives now work as laborers on cattle and sheep **stations,** or ranches. But most of the aborigines still live in the primitive ways they had lived before the settlers arrived.

Colonization of Australia

One of the regionalizing features of New Zealand and Australia is that

Port Arthur, Tasmania, was originally settled by the British as a penal colony in the 19th century.

most of the people of these countries today are descendants of settlers from the British Isles. The cultural heritage of the people in this region comes from the British Isles. The settlement of Australia by Great Britain occurred before the settlement of New Zealand. The colonization of Australia was unusual. It began during the period of great colonization when it was a common practice to establish **penal colonies.** A penal colony is composed largely of prisoners and their guards. For many years it was impolite to ask a citizen of Australia about his ancestors because they might have been prisoners.

In Great Britain, people who had been arrested for various reasons were required to pay fines or be subjected to punishment. The long list of crimes ranged from petty thievery to murder. Prisoners who could not pay the fine were often sent to a new land to work out their punishments. Those who were too outspoken about the government were also sent to penal colonies. These people were sentenced because of their political activities.

At one time, these prisoners were sent to the American colonies. After the American Revolution, new lands were sought. One of the early penal colonies in Australia was at Sydney. Close to a thousand persons made up this colony. This number included both prisoners and soldiers. In the year 1803, a convict colony was started on Tasmania near present-day Hobart. In 1824 another colony was founded north of Sydney at Brisbane, Australia.

England's practice of forming convict colonies came to an end late in the nineteenth century. Such colonies were expensive to establish and to support. The colonies seldom became self-supporting as quickly as the English government wished. Furthermore, free citizens in the colonies and Englishmen at home complained about the practice.

Other Colonies "Down Under"

It would be incorrect and quite unjust to say that all settlements of Australia began as convict colonies. As time passed, more free settlers and fewer convicts came to live in the newly developing lands. Some of the first free settlers in Australia came to raise sheep. Often convicts, who promised to remain in Australia after their sentence was up, were allowed to live and work on the sheep ranches.

Australia got its greatest boost in population not from soldiers, convicts, and sheepmen, but from another source. Gold strikes in the 1850's brought thousands of people to the continent. The population of Australia tripled in the 1850's because of the gold rush. Many of the miners remained in Australia and became farmers.

News of the great grass expanses in Australia and New Zealand, suitable for raising sheep and cattle and for growing grain, brought a steady stream of settlers from the British Isles to both countries. This region is one in which more than 40 per cent of the land is used for meadows and pasture land. New Zealand has more favorable land than Australia because all of New Zealand receives an adequate amount of rainfall. In general, the number of acres needed to raise sheep or cattle in New Zealand is smaller than in Australia. Both New Zealand and Australia are heavy producers of wool, meat, and dairy products, such as milk, butter, and cheese.

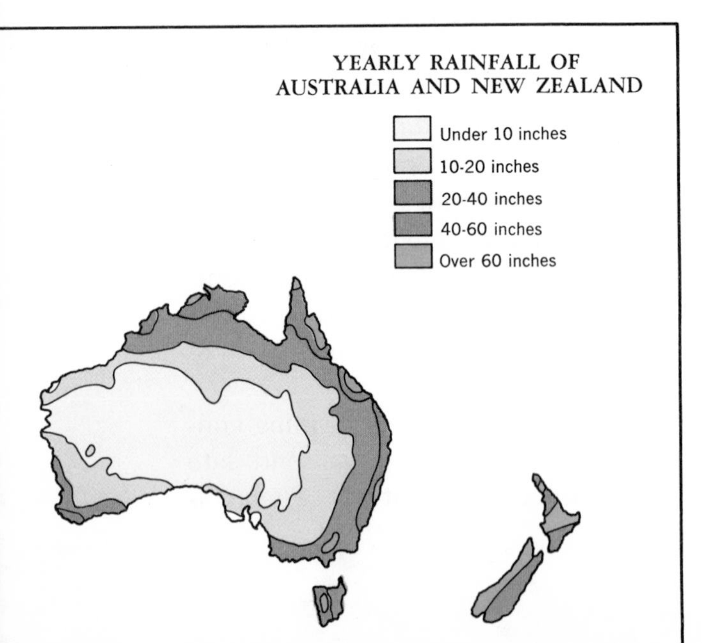

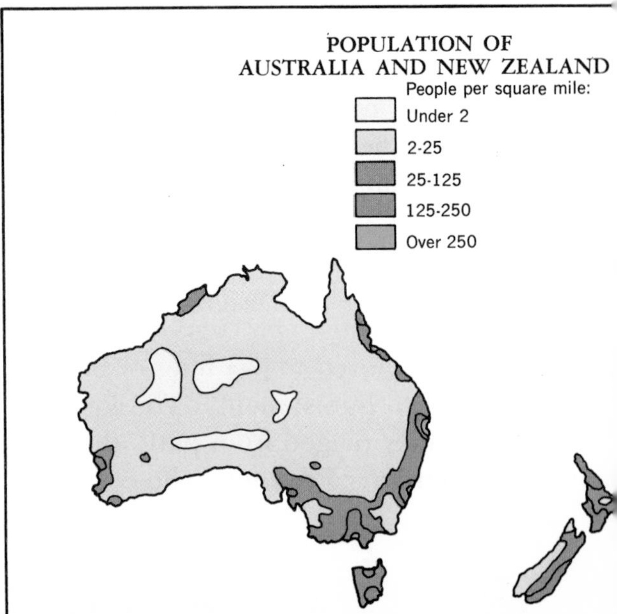

NATURAL FEATURES OF AUSTRALIA

Australia is as large as our own mainland United States. However, rainfall in the interior of Australia is scanty and inadequate. Although the **hinterland,** the land in back, near each of Australia's great cities is productive, the early settlers found that this productive area was limited.

It mattered little what direction the early settlers sought to penetrate the interior of Australia. They found that the farther inland they went, the drier the land became. The tall grass areas changed to thorny desert plant areas. Finally, no vegetation at all was seen. From east, west, south, and north, the "hollowness" of Australia was soon apparent.

The Desert of Australia

In the south central part of the continent the interior desert region reaches to the coast. Here a flat, featureless plain extends along the coast for three to four hundred miles. It is so flat that the railroad tracks which connect the well-watered settlements to the east and west run as straight as a yardstick. The name of the plain gives you a clue to the rainfall. It is called the Nullarbor Plain. *Null* means "having no existence; equal to nothing." *Arbor* means "a shelter or roof formed by trees or vines." Yes, *Nullarbor* is a fitting term for this region of Australia.

Australia's vast lands differ sharply from region to region. Compare the desolate Nullarbor Plain and Finke River to the fertile Yarramalong Valley on the east coast.

The Merino's thick coat of wool is sheared in one piece called a clip.

One person said that Australia was like an "empty egg." This is not exactly true. For even though the "egg" may be empty, the "eggshell" is one of the most important areas of the world. The emptiness of the interior has caused Australia to have an unusual pattern of population. It is called a **peripheral pattern,** that is, most of the settlements are located around the edges of the continent.

Around the edges of Australia, "the eggshell," British settlers and their descendants have helped the country to become a leading area of scientific herding. Many types of sheep are raised for wool and meat. Merino sheep are raised for their high-grade wool. Cattle for beef and dairy products are of the best breeds. Grapes, grain, apples, and pears are grown on the hillsides in Australia's southwestern and southeastern sections. Check the latitude and you will find these sections are exposed to moist winds from the west. The climate is like that of the Mediterranean Region.

Outback Country

Australians call the vast arid and semi-arid region of the interior the **outback country.** Cattle and sheep stations are sprinkled throughout this huge region. The size of each station or ranch is tremendous. In some parts of this arid region, an average of 30 acres is necessary to support just *one* sheep. Imagine how big a station with 5,000 sheep would have to be. Beef cattle need even more acres per animal than sheep. In some places 70 acres are used. In much of the arid grazing region, cattlemen and sheepherders on horseback must be constantly on the move with herds and flocks. But they are not cut off from the modern world. Airplanes, two-way radios, and television sets keep them informed and up-to-date.

Outback stations are so far apart that many children do not go to school on foot or by bus. They remain at home, and the school comes to them. Teachers reach their pupils by way of the television screen and over two-way radios. Regular lessons are assigned and discussed over the air.

The people of the outback stations are more aware of their neighbors than some people who live next door to each other. Neighbors who are 100 miles apart call each other by first names. Medical aid, needed supplies, books, and even machinery are transported quickly in planes.

The establishment of sheep and cattle stations far from local and world markets has been possible only through modern inventions. Refrigerated ships keep meat from spoiling. About 150,000 tons of beef go to world markets from Australia each year.

There are about 150,000,000 sheep in Australia. About four-fifths of all Australia's income comes from the sheep. The greater number of Australian sheep are Merinos, a breed noted for its wool. The Australians brought this fine animal from Spain because it thrived on a dry climate.

The Merino has a long-staple fleece. Woolen goods made from woolen yarn from Merino fleece bring high prices. During shearing time, expert shearers move from station to station doing their job well and swiftly. The "clip," the coat of wool, is often sold at auctions and sent overseas.

The introduction of the rabbit into Australia in the last century has caused real problems. One rabbit can live on very little grass. But fifty rabbits will eat the grass that could support one sheep. In a region where rainfall is scant and grass is thin, rabbits are a menace to the livelihood of cattlemen and sheepmen. Once introduced into Australia, the rabbits multiplied rapidly. They met few natural enemies except for the wild dingo.

Australia's economy depends greatly on the many by-products of both sheep and cattle.

Attempts have been made to control the spread of rabbits by trapping, fencing, and poisoning. Attempts have also been made to export rabbit meat and skins. Rabbit meat is used in some dog foods. Perhaps the rabbit fur can be used in the making of clothing more than it is today.

Wheat Production

With a small population and with vast areas that are excellent for wheat growing, Australia is able to produce great surpluses of wheat. Australian wheat is shipped mainly to Great Britain and other northwestern European countries. Wheat farms lie on the semi-arid lands where from 10 to 20 inches of rain falls. In southeast Australia, inland from the coast, wheat is a cash crop from Brisbane to Adelaide. The Murray River Basin is one of the world's great producers of this number-one grain in world trade. In the interior just back of Perth in southwestern Australia, there are also vast wheat ranches. The Perth area has only about five per cent of the population of Australia. Most of the people in this area grow wheat. One will frequently hear them discussing its price on the world market.

Mining

The gold strikes in 1851 encouraged Australians to prospect for other minerals. Each "boom" in gold, lead, zinc, tin, silver, or bauxite brought more immigrants to Australia. The search for and discovery of valuable minerals lured more people to the interior of the continent. Gold strikes, such as the one at Kalgoorlie, and the opal mines at Coober Pedy have attracted mining experts to Australia.

The summer can be very hot in the interior of Australia. Some miners live with their families in underground homes. These homes have been dug into the solid rock. Many of the miners' homes, though small, are equipped with modern appliances. Oil, gasoline, and in some cases coal supply the energy converted to electricity. Very high wages are paid to these miners. They are only two to three hours away, by

MINERAL RESOURCES OF AUSTRALIA

Iron	Lead
Coal	Bauxite
Petroleum	Tin
Zinc	Gold
Copper	Silver
Tungsten	Uranium

The deep open pit mine at Mt. Morgan yields much gold and copper.

plane, from Australia's large urban centers. But in some cases, the miners do not have to fly into the cities to shop. The uranium boomtown, Broken Hill, has many modern shops. The supply of uranium ore at Broken Hill seems inexhaustible.

The huge eucalyptus log will be used for lumber. Pulp mills manufacture paper products from other kinds of trees.

MODERN AUSTRALIA

In the northwestern part of Australia one of the greatest river basin developments ever attempted is under way. The river involved in the project is the Ord River. It is in the Kimberley District of the Western Plateau. Attempts are being made to regulate the flow of the Ord River. At times, water rushes downstream in flood stage. At other times it is bone dry. A ten-million-dollar dam will hold back some of the waters of the Ord. Over three times that amount of money will be spent before the Ord River Project is finished.

Cities and Towns

Australia's cities and towns are among the world's most modern. Locate on the map on page 485 Canberra, the capital, Sydney, Melbourne, Perth, and Darwin. Apartment houses rival any in the world in their conveniences. New universities of ultra-modern design are very well equipped and fully attended. Investors from other countries have become interested in the Australian economy. Automobile firms from England and the United States have opened branches in Australia. Australia has many "two-and-three-car" families. Department stores display Australian-manufactured furniture, clothing, and all kinds of sporting goods. There are many kinds of recreation available in Australia. The range of sports includes skiing, fishing, hunting, swimming, horseracing, and sightseeing.

The seat of the government is in the capital, Canberra, but the port of Sydney is Australia's largest and busiest city.

Immigration to Australia

You have read that Australia began as a penal colony. Later, colonists came to found sheep and cattle ranches. The gold strikes of the 1850's brought thousands of people from Europe, America, and Asia to Australia. The European and American miners did not get along well with the Asian miners. Since Australia is so near Asia, many Australians thought that there was a danger of great numbers of Asians immigrating to Australia. They feared that the Asians would soon be a majority of the population. For these reasons, the leaders of Australia established what has been called a "White Australian Policy."

For many years, the Australian government carefully regulated the kinds of people who came to settle. Although the "white only" policy is not as strictly upheld, immigration remains carefully controlled by the government. Only the number of people who can find work can enter the country. Some Australians argue that the "White Australian Policy" eliminates race problems that are present in other countries. Others say that the abilities and willingness to work of "nonwhites" would be a great asset to Australia.

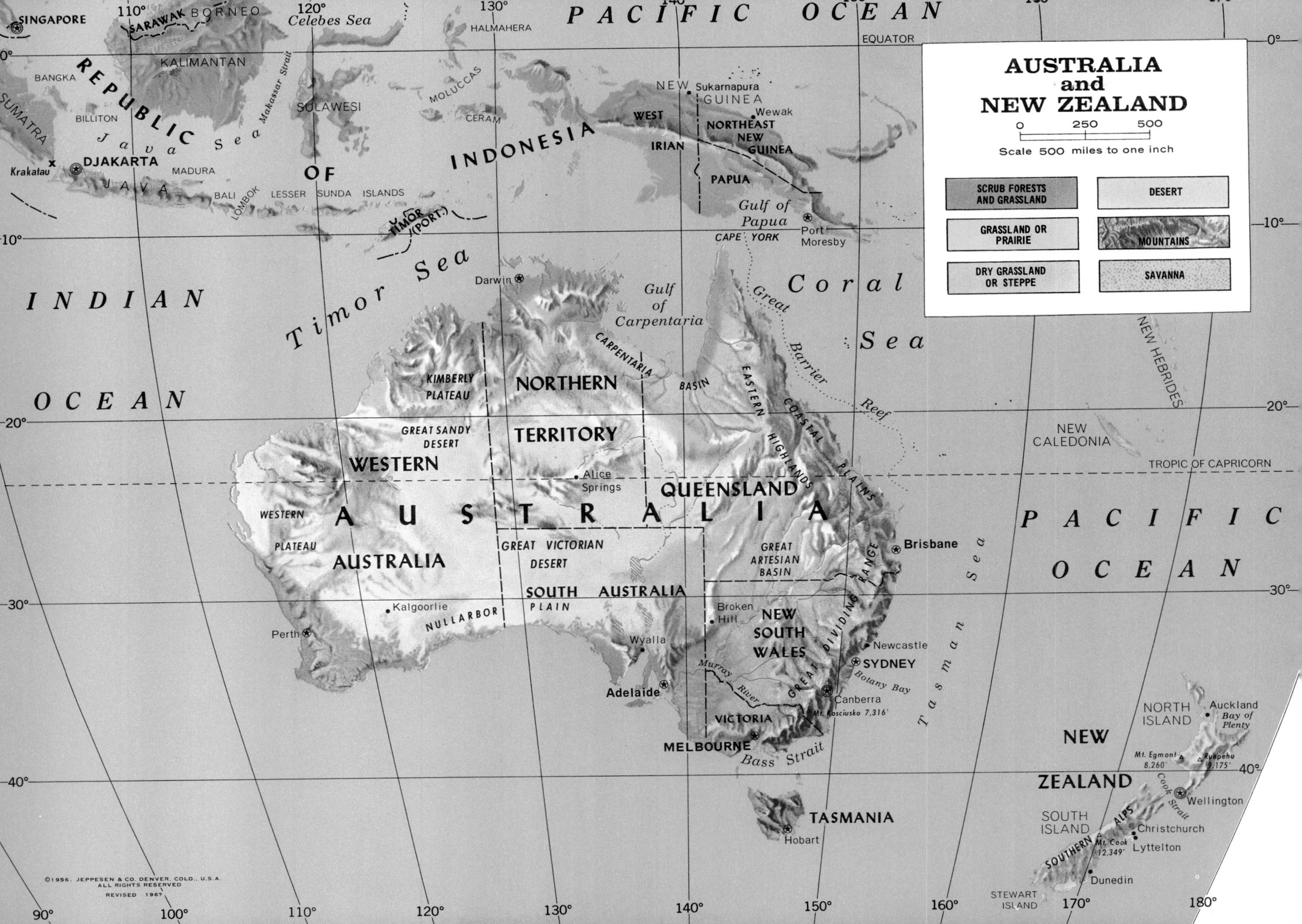
AUSTRALIA and NEW ZEALAND
0 250 500
Scale 500 miles to one inch
SCRUB FORESTS AND GRASSLAND
DESERT
GRASSLAND OR PRAIRIE
MOUNTAINS
DRY GRASSLAND OR STEPPE
SAVANNA
PACIFIC OCEAN
EQUATOR
SINGAPORE
SARAWAK
BORNEO
Celebes Sea
HALMAHERA
KALIMANTAN
BANGKA
SUMATRA
REPUBLIC OF INDONESIA
BILLITON
Java Sea
Makassar Strait
SULAWESI
MOLUCCAS
CERAM
Krakatau
DJAKARTA
JAVA
MADURA
BALI
LOMBOK
LESSER SUNDA ISLANDS
TIMOR (PORT.)
NEW GUINEA
Sukarnapura
Wewak
WEST IRIAN
NORTHEAST NEW GUINEA
PAPUA
Gulf of Papua
Port Moresby
CAPE YORK
Timor Sea
Darwin
INDIAN OCEAN
Gulf of Carpentaria
Coral Sea
Great Barrier Reef
CARPENTARIA BASIN
KIMBERLY PLATEAU
NORTHERN TERRITORY
EASTERN HIGHLANDS
COASTAL PLAINS
GREAT SANDY DESERT
WESTERN AUSTRALIA
TERRITORY
Alice Springs
QUEENSLAND
AUSTRALIA
WESTERN PLATEAU
GREAT VICTORIAN DESERT
GREAT ARTESIAN BASIN
Brisbane
SOUTH AUSTRALIA
NULLARBOR PLAIN
Kalgoorlie
Perth
Broken Hill
NEW SOUTH WALES
GREAT DIVIDING RANGE
Newcastle
SYDNEY
Botany Bay
Canberra
Mt. Kosciusko 7,316'
Wyalla
Adelaide
Murray River
VICTORIA
MELBOURNE
Bass Strait
TASMANIA
Hobart
Tasman Sea
NEW HEBRIDES
NEW CALEDONIA
TROPIC OF CAPRICORN
PACIFIC OCEAN
NEW ZEALAND
NORTH ISLAND
Auckland
Bay of Plenty
Mt. Egmont 8,260'
Ruapehu 9,175'
Cook Strait
Wellington
SOUTH ISLAND
SOUTHERN ALPS
Christchurch
Lyttelton
Mt. Cook 12,349'
Dunedin
STEWART ISLAND
0°
10°
20°
30°
40°
90°
100°
110°
120°
130°
140°
150°
160°
170°
180°

LIFE IN NEW ZEALAND

New Zealand, though settled by people of a common cultural heritage, only slightly resembles Australia. Some of the earliest settlements in New Zealand were sponsored by churches. Dunedin, settled in 1848, and Canterbury, settled in 1850, were church colonies. Today, they are important modern cities.

The early colonists in New Zealand found the climate to be very much like that of England. The climate was mild with plenty of rain. The land, however, was more rugged, higher, and more heavily forested than was England. The settlers found plenty of wood for building their houses. They also found that the level or gently rolling areas were excellent for such familiar English crops as wheat, oats, hay, and barley. Cattle and sheep thrived on the nutritious grass.

Cattle and Sheep Raising

So much of New Zealand is given over to cattle and sheep raising that the country is one of the world's best examples of a **dairying-pastoral economy.** On clearings throughout the islands of New Zealand, you will find improved pastures. In many of these pastures, fertilizers are added to the already well-cared-for grazing land by **dusting** — that is, dropping chemicals from planes. New Zealand sheepherders ride on horses which are well-bred, rugged, strong, and com-

Wool is king in New Zealand where sheep outnumber people more than twenty to one. Dunedin, on South Island, is a thriving port city noted for its many woolen mills.

fortable to ride. Saddles made from New Zealand leather rest on sturdy blankets made from New Zealand wool. The shepherd's clothes, his heavy, knitted sweater, felt hat, warm, woolen socks, and sturdy boots, are made from New Zealand-produced wool and leather.

Keen-eyed, strong, well-trained dogs obey their master's commands. The dogs are likely to be a combination of collie and shepherd. Often the dogs know their job so well that the shepherd need not speak to them. The dogs drive or circle the sheep by barking, by jostling, and by gently tugging. Fences are present, of course, but with such able dogs, many fences are not needed.

New Zealand dairy herds are among the world's best. New Zealanders are every bit as skilled as the Dutch of the Netherlands in making butter and cheese. They have learned that, since their markets are far away, butter and cheese need to be packaged well and attractively so as to be able to compete in the world market.

Industries

Although primarily a dairying-pastoral country with some wheat growing, New Zealand has some manufacturing cities. Some of the finest-looking, most well-planned houses and shopping centers in the world are in Auckland, Wellington, the capital, and Christchurch. With little coal available in New Zealand, the people have developed their water and steam power. Where hydroelectric power is available, manufacturing has been established. New Zealand's North Island is volcanic. The New Zealanders are tapping underground steam as a source of energy. Rubber manufacturing, shoemaking, textiles, and even automobile manufacturing are developing in many areas.

Geothermal power stations harness the energy of hot springs which lie beneath the surface of New Zealand.

SIMILAR PROBLEMS "DOWN UNDER"

The original inhabitants of Australia and New Zealand sometimes had difficulty remaining alive. It was not easy for man to control nature in this region. The white settlers brought with them inventions, skills, and tools that helped to produce surplus crops. They brought with them a different, more advanced culture. Much progress was made. But at the same time, part of the native culture was swept away. It is a problem for both Australia and New Zealand to try to retain their native culture and at the same time add modern ways of living.

Both nations are faced with other problems of greater importance. New Zealand is a major exporter of butter. Australia is a major exporter of wheat. Both countries face the disadvantage of being far from the wealthy markets of Europe and the United States. If you have to send products a long distance, how do you keep the prices down? Furthermore, both countries produce large surpluses of wool and meat. If too much is produced, what is to be done with the surplus? Should it be destroyed or should it be given away?

Both countries face a drift of population from farm to town. Because agriculture is becoming more and more scientific, fewer people can produce more farm products. The men who once farmed now must learn new jobs. The cities must plan for the added population of farmers and immigrants. New Zealand and Australia, like other countries of the world, are faced with the problem of providing an even better standard of living for all.

Do You Know?

1. What is a marsupial? What are some of the marsupials found in Australia?

2. What is a fossil? What animal has been labeled a "living fossil"?

3. What are two regionalizing features of New Zealand and Australia?

4. Who were the native peoples of New Zealand? From where did they come?

5. What is the capital of Australia? Of New Zealand?

6. What four groups of people settled in Australia? Which group gave the largest boost in population?

7. Why did the penal colonies come to an end?

8. Which country has the best physical features for settlement and development? What are they?

9. What are the major products exported from New Zealand and Australia?

10. Why did the rabbit present a problem when introduced into Australia? How have the Australians tried to solve the problem?

Learn By Doing

1. Select one animal native to Australia or New Zealand. Give a detailed description of the animal. On which island was it originally found? Does the animal exist today? What is the setting in which the animal lives?

2. Select one of the following titles and write a report. Use an encyclopedia or reference books from the library.

The United Nations Helps the People
Tourism, The Pacific's New Industry
The Great Barrier Reef
The Davis Cup
Progress in the Cities

3. Make an exhibit of ways of life found in Australia or New Zealand. Find pictures or objects which show life in a city, a sheep station, a cattle station, a mining area, and a wheat farm.

4. Tell briefly why the following men were important: Abel Janszoon Tasman, Captain James Cook, Vasco Núñez de Balboa, Sir Francis Drake, and Ferdinand Magellan. Select one explorer and write a detailed report answering as many of the following questions as possible.

a. When and where was the explorer born? What events of his early life led him to become an explorer?

b. For what country did he sail? Did he have difficulty finding someone to finance his trip?

c. What areas of the world were explored? What difficulties or interesting experiences did he have?

d. Were any lands or bodies of water named after the explorer? Were any lands claimed by the mother nation?

e. What were the major contributions of the explorer?

Test Your Knowledge

1. What effect did the coming of man have on the native animals of Australia and New Zealand?

2. Australia and New Zealand have two major problems, a great distance to markets and a surplus of products. Explain this statement. How might the problems be solved?

3. Although the "Great Southland" was never found, do you think this expression could be used to describe Australia? Why?

4. Who were the first to settle Australia and New Zealand? From where did they come? Why did they wish to settle in the new land?

5. Should Australia be labeled an "empty egg"? Explain your answer.

6. What is the outback country? How does life in the outback country differ because the homes are so far apart? How has the problem of education and distance between children been solved in Australia?

7. What problems did Tasman expect to face on his trip? What did he expect the natives to be like? Were his expectations accurate?

8. What is meant by a peripheral pattern of population? What has caused this to develop in Australia?

9. Name three things for which the "eggshell" is noted.

10. Australia, Tasmania, and New Zealand are members of the British Commonwealth of Nations. What does this mean? How does it affect the people and their government?

11. What is meant by the "White Australian Policy"? What effect does this have on the country?

12. What is the meaning of the word "aborigine"?

13. What are the major minerals found in Australia?

REVIEWING PART 6

Do You Remember?

1. Has the Pacific Ocean been properly named? Explain your answer.

2. Would it be possible to unite the islands of the Pacific? What problems would have to be met? Do you think this should be done?

3. What are some of the problems that the people of the Pacific face because they live on islands far from their neighbors and far from the populated centers of the world?

4. Are the natives of Polynesia related to the natives of New Zealand? How did this happen?

5. What caused the unique animal and plant life on Australia and New Zealand?

Projects and Reports

1. Select the correct words to complete each of the following sentences:

communication	platypus	largest
dairying-pastoral	volcanoes	sea
Great Southland	deepest	kiwi
New Zealand	typhoons	riches
transportation	Australia	copra
earthquakes	tourists	land

a. The Pacific Ocean is the ______ and the ______ ocean in the world.

b. The Rim of Fire is the region of the world where ______ erupt and ______ occur most often.

c. ______ is the largest island in the Pacific Ocean.

d. A tidal wave does more harm on ______ than at ______.

e. ______ are dangerous to people at sea as well as on land.

f. Modern advances in systems of ______ and ______ have helped the people of the outback country to solve the problems of distance.

g. Tasman was searching for the ______ where he hoped to find ______.

h. Samoa has made great progress in industry. She exports ______. Many ______ come to the land.

i. A ______ is a furry mammal with a bill. The ______ is a flightless bird found only in New Zealand.

j. New Zealand has a ______ ______ economy.

2. Select one of the following titles and write a report.

Seismologists and Seismographs
Seamounts and Submarines
The U.S. Pacific Trust Territory
Tropical and Extra-Tropical Storms

Using Maps and Globes

1. Locate each of the following groups of islands. Tell whether they are located in Micronesia, Melanesia, or Polynesia.

Easter Island	New Guinea
Hawaiian Islands	Guam
Caroline Islands	American Samoa
Chatham Islands	Solomon Islands

2. What islands are found in the center of the Pacific Ocean? What group of islands lie east of the 180° Longitude line? Hint: Where does the 180° Longitude line meet the 0° Latitude line?

3. On which island are each of the following cities located? Hobart, Dunedin, Perth, Auckland.

4. You have read about the International Date Line. Can you answer the following questions?

a. Study the Time Zone map of the world. When it is noon at the Prime Meridian, what time is it 15° to the east?

b. When it is 7 A.M. in New York City, what time is it in San Francisco, California?

c. If it is 3 P.M. at the Prime Meridian, what time is it in New York City?

d. A person listening to a short-wave radio at noon heard an announcer in Greenwhich, England (on the Prime Meridian) say, "It is now exactly 9 A.M. here." Can you tell on what meridian of longitude the listener was located?

A Special Map Project

1. Using the map on page 485 as a guide, draw on a blank piece of paper the important longitude and latitude lines that pass through Australia. The equator will be at the top of the page. Place an **"X"** at the following points:

a. 22° South Latitude, 115° East Longitude

b. 35° South Latitude, 115° East Longitude

c. 22° South Latitude, 150° East Longitude

d. 37° South Latitude, 150° East Longitude

Use these guide lines and points to sketch an outline of the continent of Australia.

2. Because Australia is south of the equator, you have used South Latitude lines and East Longitude lines for your map. On a new sheet of paper draw latitude and longitude lines with the same numbers but change the direction of the numbers. This time the equator will be at the bottom of the page and the 160° meridian of longitude will be on the left side of the paper. You will use the North Latitude lines and the West Longitude lines. Place an **"X"** at the following points:

a. 20° North Latitude, 115° West Longitude

b. 35° North Latitude, 115° West Longitude

c. 22° North Latitude, 150° West Longitude

d. 20° North Latitude, 150° West Longitude

Using the world map on pages 12 and 13, sketch land you find within or near this region. Label each body of land.

3. Study the maps you have drawn before you answer the following questions:

a. How much of the United States is within this region? What is this part of the United States like?

b. What body of land is located near the western part of this region? What is it like?

c. If Australia was located in the Northern Hemisphere, what would the climate be like?

d. Locate exactly Los Angeles and Honolulu. What places in Australia have a comparable location?

e. What parts of the United States lie a distance north of the equator equal to, or almost equal to, the distance Australia lies south of the equator?

f. How does the size of Australia compare with the size of the United States? Which is wider? Which is longer?

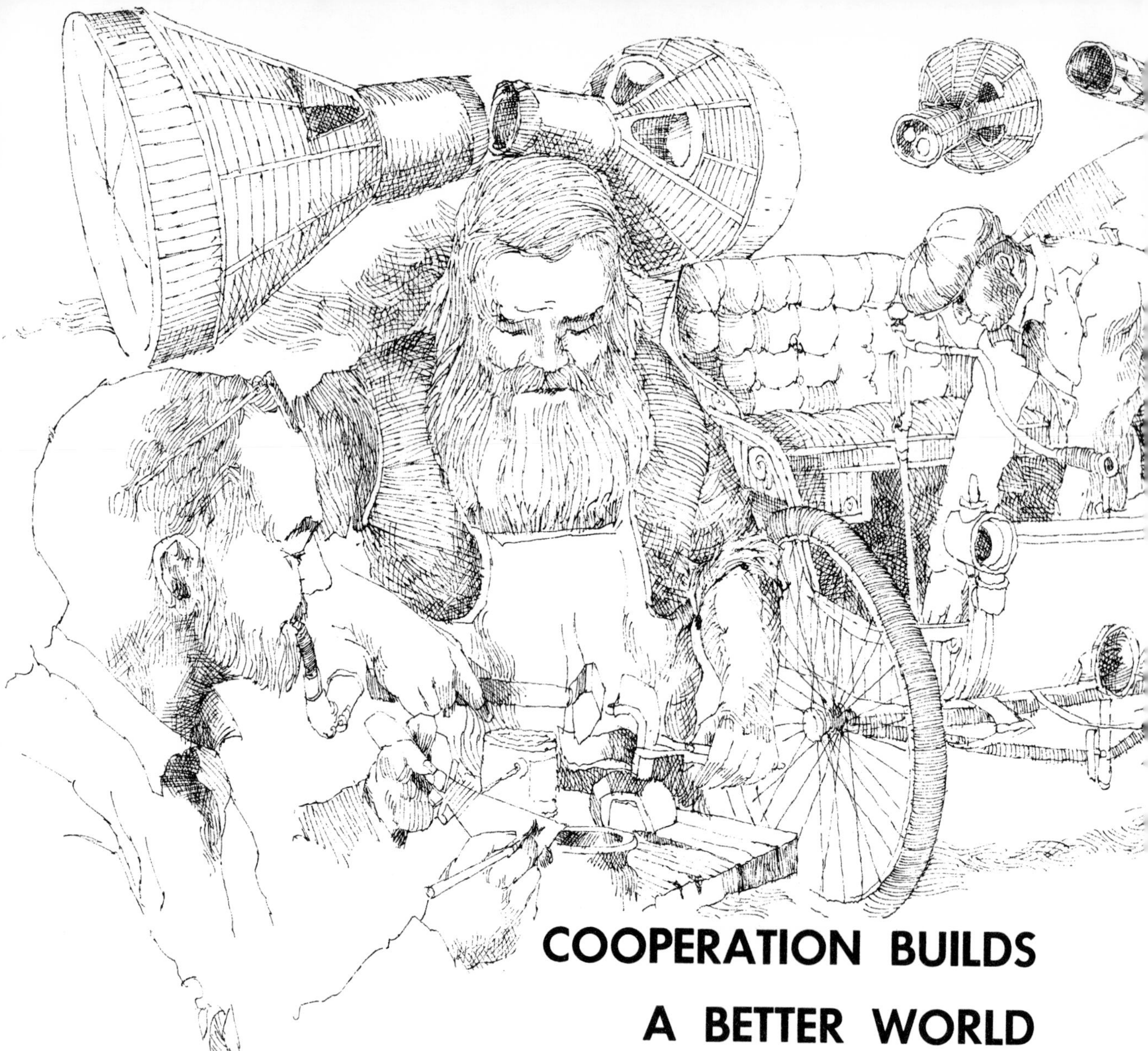

COOPERATION BUILDS A BETTER WORLD

PART 7

In this text the world has been divided into culture regions. This was done to make it easier for you to understand how man has used his natural and cultural resources to obtain his living from the earth. Actually, these culture regions are all sub-regions of a great World Culture Region.

For several centuries, men in many parts of the world lived in isolation from men in other parts. They managed to make a living from the earth. In some places this was difficult, and men had only the barest of necessities. In other places this was easier, and men lived well. Through the years, men have slowly learned ways to share the resources of the entire Earth. Trade has enabled men to sell what they have in great surplus and to buy what they

do not have. When traders began to travel over the Earth, they began to exchange ideas. These ideas have helped people make better use of their resources.

Today, great changes are taking place. The rapid advancement of means of transportation and communication helps people to exchange goods and knowledge. The development of science and technology makes it possible for more and more people to improve their ways of living. Nations of people, who until recent years lived in ignorance and poverty, are emerging into a twentieth century world of greatly improved living. As these changes take place, the closeness of people makes it possible to begin to think of the world as one great Culture Region.

CHAPTER 21

OUR CHANGING CULTURE REGIONS

The last half of the twentieth century has been a time of great change throughout the world. You have read in this book about many of these changes. Even as you have been studying this text, other changes have taken place. New governments have been established in many countries. And, men have found new and better ways to supply their basic needs. In this chapter, as you review the basic needs of people in the world's culture regions, you will see the different ways men meet these needs. You will see some of the changes which are being made in the world.

CULTURAL CHANGES

Throughout the text you have read certain basic words. Words such as *region, change,* and *environment* were repeated many times. These words were used as "windows" through which you could look into the "culture homes" of people. In the culture homes, or as we called them culture regions, you saw how people lived and worked. You saw how the culture regions changed, some more rapidly than others. For example, you read about the Dry World Culture Region which until very recently was changing very slowly. Today, rapid changes are being made. The development of oil resources and the building of dams are helping to improve conditions. Even so, not all parts of this region are changing in the same way or at the same rate of speed.

You saw how the islands of Australia and New Zealand, isolated from the Asian continent and from one another, were the culture homes of the Australian aborigine and the Maori. The natives of these islands lived in societies of little change. With the arrival of the European settlers, these two islands underwent striking cultural changes. The settlers from the British Isles brought their cultural heritage with them. The British cultural heritage of the people of Australia and New Zealand is one of the regionalizing characteristics of this part of the world.

The Effects of Physical Environment

You have seen that the physical environment often affects the way people live. In some regions of the world the physical environment offers the people within it a meager living. The coral atoll, though lovely to look at, cannot support a large population. The lagoon of an atoll might be 20 to 40 miles across, but the amount of surface land that makes up the islets of the atoll is usually very small. Furthermore, the supply of fertile soil is poor so that few crops can be grown.

The coconut tree is very important in the life of an islander. The coconut palm is able to grow with its roots in salty water. Fiber from the coconut husk can be made into rope. The leaves of the coconut tree can be woven into mats, containers, and material for roofing. The meat and milk of the coconut are important in the diet of the people on the atoll.

Nonetheless, the people must supplement the coconut and the root crops obtained from the small patches of soil. They have to turn to the sea for food which will provide protein to balance their diet.

In contrast, the physical environment of a volcanic island, such as Tahiti, yields far more with far less work on the part of the people. The fertile volcanic soil is well watered by streams and rains that owe their origin to the height of the island. Fruit and root crops grow well. The soil supports a wide variety of plant life. In the past, the people of some volcanic islands faced periods when overpopulation caused a lack in food supply. The people learned to store their surplus breadfruit and taro in pits. Thus, they had supplies of food which could be used in times of famine.

In Lapland reindeer provide meat, milk, clothing, and transportation.

Physical Resources Differ

The physical environment in other areas of the world is often rich so that far more is obtained with much less effort. In these regions people are able to make rapid advances because sources of power can be harnessed. In England the invention of the steam engine, coupled with supplies of coal and iron ore, enabled the people to make great changes in their ways of living. Power from the steam engine was harnessed to turn hundreds of machines in factories and do the work of thousands of hands.

Progress on the British Isles makes it necessary for many to move from farm villages to industrial cities.

However, the development of new sources of power brought problems as well as benefits. Great numbers of people came to work in the factories. They gave up their rural farming life for a life based on a salary earned at the factory. Problems in the manufacturing cities were quite different from those which the family faced on the farm. Food was purchased, not grown. To earn enough money, the father of the family had to either become skilled or work longer. If the amount of money earned was still too small, the women and children of the family had to go to work.

People found they had to make decisions about the problems that the changes in ways of living brought. For example, groups talked about the long hours of work, low wages, and poor working conditions. Laws were passed to improve these conditions.

THE NEEDS OF PEOPLE

Throughout this book we have stressed the regionalizing features that make one region different from another. However, when you take a closer look at the people of these culture regions, you see that they have much in common. Some of the similarities possessed by all peoples can be called **basic needs.** Of course, not all peoples meet these needs in the same way. In this chapter we will look back at some of the culture regions described in this book. We will see the variety of ways the people in different culture regions meet the same needs.

Three Essential Needs

All culture groups provide first for the essential body needs, food, clothing, and shelter. For example, you read that the Australian aborigines gathered food from the desert. They ate the meat of birds killed by the boomerang. They ate insect larvae, roots, bulbs, and seeds. They did not grow crops or save surplus foods for times of scarcity. They led a hand-to-mouth existence. They lived in a "gathering" economy.

A very different way of obtaining food was seen when you read about the people of the United Kingdom. The people in this part of Europe do not produce enough food to support their entire population. They must import large amounts of raw materials and processed foods. The people of the United Kingdom live in a "manufacturing" economy. Through the sale of their manufactured products to other countries, they obtain money to buy food. The Australian aborigines and the people of the United Kingdom face the common need of obtaining food in different ways.

The people of the United Kingdom live in a cool, wet climate. They often wear woolen clothing to protect themselves from the physical environment. They manufacture these clothes from raw materials. The aborigines meet this same need, the need for clothing, in a much more simple way. Their major article of clothing is an animal skin thrown over the shoulders for protection against rain. And this skin is not too comfortable for the people do not **tan** the leather. That is, they do not make it soft and workable.

You and a nomad of the Dry World Region have a common need for shelter. Both of you meet this need, but the way in which it is met is different. Contrast your shelter with his. Who is to say which is the best? The nomad certainly could not use the type of house or apartment in which you live. In his nomadic way of life he needs a different type of shelter. He needs a type of shelter that is light enough to be carried, and one that can easily be set up and taken down.

On several Pacific Islands, coconuts are a main source of food and income.

Although these essential needs are met in different ways, they are common to all peoples in all culture regions. Food, clothing, and shelter must be provided for all people in order to have a better world.

Power

Another basic need common to all people is the need for forces stronger than the muscle power of the body. The Australian aborigine found a source of power in his boomerang. He used it to kill small birds. He hunted kangaroos with spears and used a spear-thrower to give the spear even greater force and speed.

Some people have harnessed animals to provide this extra power. The term *horsepower* remains in our language as a reminder that horses were once a very common source of power in our culture. The invention of the steam engine gave the people of Europe a tremendous new source of power and sparked the Industrial Revolution.

The people of the Dry World Region have found a source of power in the oil beneath their land. They have used it to develop new industries. Man has also learned to harness water power and use it to produce electricity. Hydroelectric power is responsible for much of the progress made in Europe and the United States.

Goals

Also common to the peoples of all culture regions is the need for a set of goals. These goals might be customs, or habits, or laws through which the people seek order and purpose in their lives. You have seen that many ancient customs are still in practice. Every part of the festive celebrations has meaning and order.

All groups live and have lived by laws, either written or unwritten. This would be as true of the natives of Africa as it would be of a member of a Soviet collective farm. From time to time it was thought necessary to write some of the ways of behaving in the form of laws. You recall, for example, the Code of Hammurabi which drew upon the laws of the ancient Sumerians. Also, many of the laws of the United Kingdom and the United States are based on the laws of ancient Rome. All laws are based on the needs of the people at the time they are written.

Expression

All peoples seek ways to express important thoughts and feelings. Some of the great ideas about man were expressed in the plays of the ancient Greeks. The Maori war canoe was a work of art. The Egyptian tomb paintings tell us much about the daily life of the ancient Egyptians. They also symbolize the inner feelings of the painters about things which they saw at that time.

Today, we see around us many forms of expression. Some people express themselves in song and in dancing. Opera and ballet are the results of man's need to express his musical ability. Still others paint or write. The artists and writers reflect in their works not only their own ideas, but also the expressed ideas of other people. These talented people reveal both humorous and serious thoughts. Some means of expression are modern, but the de-

Though religious beliefs and the place of worship differ, the need for religious expression is found the world over.

sire, or the urge, to express oneself is as old as man.

People express their belief in a Supreme Being through religion. The religion of Islam is a force that unites much of the Dry Muslim World in a way that no other tie could. This unifying feature can be seen in the Muslim architecture which is unmistakable in form. It is one of the characteristic features of the Dry Muslim World.

Cooperation

The need for cooperation, for people to work together, is expressed in very different ways. There are groups of people who work together, but are only loosely tied together. There are other groups of people who work closely together and unite to face outsiders. We have noted in many chapters how people who have worked together have accomplished much. We began by talking about the Sumerians who, by working together, built a canal system that brought water to desert lands. In doing so, they developed a civilization that could produce surplus food. An abundance of food made possible the development of special occupations. Men had time to become weavers, stone workers, and priests.

The results of specialization and cooperation are right in front of you when you look at an automobile. You can see that a car is made up of many parts. However, it is more difficult to see the ideas behind the working together of the parts. It is even harder to picture the thousands of men and women who helped to produce the machine itself. However, cooperation—the working together of men, machines, and ideas—was necessary to accomplish the result. This need to cooperate not only applies to automobiles, but also to all we hope to accomplish.

As you glance back through the culture regions in today's world, these basic needs will be used as guides. Sometimes these needs may be hidden; at other times they will stand out clearly.

THE DRY WORLD REGION

In the Dry World Region water is basic to everything the people do. The centers of heavy population are the oases. These are the few "core" areas where the water supply is abundant enough and steady enough to support irrigation farming. Throughout the rest of the Dry World Region the population is scattered. Nomads live where there is enough grass to support grazing animals.

Irrigation will make dry land useful.

Much of the economy of this region is dependent upon animals. Animal power is still widely used. Camels and horses are used for transportation. Animals are used to pump water from wells.

The people of the Muslim World value highly their past greatness. This region is the home of three major religions of the world: Judaism, Christianity, and Islam. After Mohammed, Islam spread rapidly. In a very short time, the Islamic World stretched from the Atlantic Ocean eastward to the South Pacific.

Progress toward industrialization is being made in the Dry World Region. The great Aswan Dam on the Nile now supplies water for electricity and for irrigation. Thousands of acres of land are being made fertile. The Persian Gulf area has vast reservoirs of oil and is an important source of gas. These natural resources are sent to more industrialized regions where they serve as important sources of power. The people are developing new ways of living. The future will depend on how well they use their new-found resources.

AFRICA SOUTH OF THE SAHARA

The people of this tropical region number over 200 million. In parts of this region the societies are largely tribal. In this land of many countries and many languages, the people have many problems to face. Most of the countries have recently become in-

The discovery of oil has brought wealth to some desert lands.

Knowledge and cooperation are helping to improve farming in Africa.

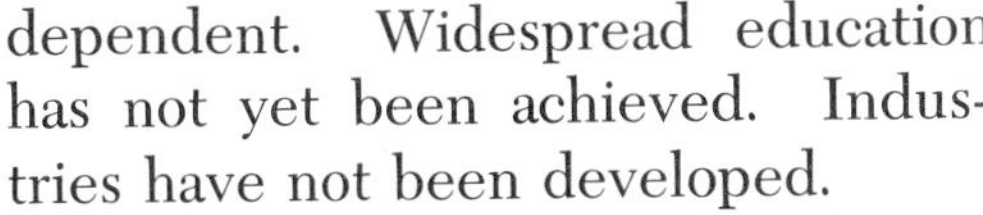

dependent. Widespread education has not yet been achieved. Industries have not been developed.

Presently, the feature that characterizes this region is change. There have been many changes from colonial governments to self-rule. In some places great effort is being made to bring education to larger numbers of people. However, in other places, education or schooling is still a far-off goal.

Some sub-regions, such as the Congo, have rich mineral resources. Other countries, such as the tiny nation of Gambia, have limited mineral resources. Gambia presently has a one-crop economy, peanuts. But changes are being made in the economies with the introduction of industrialization.

THE SUB–CONTINENT OF INDIA

On the great peninsula south of the Himalayas, the world's highest mountains, are three nations. Two of these nations, India and Pakistan, were formerly British colonial possessions. After World War II both India and Pakistan were granted their independence. Pakistan was founded as a Muslim nation. India was founded as a Hindu nation. These religious differences have made it difficult for the people of these nations to work together. The third country of this region, Ceylon, has a large Buddhist population. The great sub-continent, thus, is divided by religious beliefs.

In this region the people face the need to provide better living condi-

A center of commerce and education, Bombay is the largest city in India.

tions for over 600 million people. Their first goal is to provide enough food for the enormous population. The people are working to improve "exhausted" land that has been farmed for centuries. They are trying to do this by improving farming practices. Many farmers are now applying fertilizer and growing crops from better seed strains. The people of Pakistan and India are harnessing the force of great rivers to provide electric power and water for irrigation.

Customs, habits, and languages vary widely from one part of India to another. For example, the Tamil-speaking people of southern India strongly resist Hindi as a national language. The building of strong national unity has been difficult in India because of the local language differences.

THE FAR EAST

One part of the Far East has been called the Communist Far East. This title emphasizes the form of government under which the people of Communist China live. The 700 million people in this culture region are passing through a period of great change. The government of Communist China is attempting to weaken traditional family ties and to strengthen the individual person's ties to the government. Remnants of ancient Chinese customs still exist, but most people are turning away from the old customs and habits.

While standards of living are low, great advances are promised. Dams are being built to check erosion and floods. They will supply water for electric power and for irrigation. Better roads are being built. Industries are being developed. The government is attempting to increase the food supply by combining small, individually owned farms into huge collective farms. This is a section of the world which is being watched by the anxious eyes of its neighbors in the world.

SOUTHEAST ASIA

Close to 200 million people live in this culture area. The regionalizing factors of this part of the world are its rice economy, its tropical rainforest, and its plantation crops, such as rubber.

Rice and rubber are mainstays of Southeast Asia's economy. Most rice is consumed locally; most rubber is exported.

This is also a region of differences. All the major world religions are present in this region. It is a region of mainland countries and island countries. With the exception of Thailand, all the countries of this region were former colonial possessions of Western powers. The former colonial powers included France, the United Kingdom, the United States, and the Netherlands. At present, the native peoples are eagerly looking for, even fighting for, self-rule.

There are many kinds of government in this region. They range from democracies to governments with one-man control. Under the different kinds of government, several things are happening. In some countries the government officials and the people are unhappy with their living conditions. Each group blames the other. In other countries feelings of resentment, even anger, are held against the former colonial rulers. In still other countries, there is a desire to compete with neighboring lands for trade and for power.

Progress in industry has been slow in Southeast Asia. The colonial powers preferred to grow plantation crops which supplied raw materials to their industries. Since independence, the new countries face the problem of building local industries. At the same time, they are still heavily dependent for cash upon the export crops that the Europeans introduced into the region. A few valuable minerals, such as tin, and a few export crops, such as rubber, are important sources of surplus cash and credit. This region is in need of economic security and political justice.

A FAR EAST ISLAND REGION

The culture region east of mainland China is making great advances. Japan is a blend of West and East. Many phases of Western European and American culture can be seen mingled with those of the Far East. Japan is very heavily industrialized. Power from Japan's rivers and streams, in the form of electricity, is used to run many of her industries. Japan is a leading shipbuilding nation. She has been a leader in the development of fast, efficient railway transportation.

Western dress is worn by many in Japan. However, traditional dress and customs are still widespread. For example, tea is served to people kneeling or sitting on mats, parental regard is high, and bowing low before respected persons is common. Religious tokens and ceremonies play important parts in the lives of the people, both at home and in shrines.

Japan suffered greatly in World War II. Some of her cities were destroyed by bombings. Japan lost much of her empire in Southeast Asia and in the Pacific. Changes have occurred in other ways. Japanese values, particularly those that supported a military government before and during the war, have changed. Peaceful existence in the world is the watchword now.

AUSTRALIA AND NEW ZEALAND

In the southwestern Pacific lies a culture region resembling Western Europe and the United States. The language of the people of New Zealand and Australia is English. Like the original thirteen colonies of the United States, these two countries began as colonies of Great Britain. Unlike the United States, immigration into these two countries was almost entirely from the British Isles. The governments of these two countries are modeled after, yet not exactly like, that of the mother country, the United Kingdom.

Australia and New Zealand have many wonderful features. They have vegetation and animals which are unique to these islands. The customs

Australia is tied, through history, to the Western nations, but her location near the Far East must also be considered today.

and arts of the large Maori population are treasured and kept alive in New Zealand.

The people of this region have a high standard of living. Their income, largely from surplus wool, meat, dairy products, and wheat, provides for a comfortable living well beyond the levels merely needed for survival.

THE PACIFIC CULTURE REGION

The vast Pacific Ocean is sprinkled with thousands of islands. On some islands, disease has swept away whole populations. Other islands are thriving. The scattered islands, once far distant from one another and from the American and Asian continents, are today very close to the rest of the world. Distance is now measured in a few hours, not in thousands of miles. A few islands have been developed into very important landing spots for the planes which fly the trans-Pacific route from Los Angeles to Tokyo. Locate on the Pacific map on page 453, Los Angeles, Honolulu, Midway Island, Wake Island, Guam, Manila, and Tokyo. These landing places are often called "stepping stones" across the Pacific. Today, modern rapid transportation places the once far-off South Pacific at our doorstep.

Modern transportation and World War II have brought changes to the Pacific World. Trading vessels, whaling ships, missionaries, and cable lines began the process of change. World War II and the establishment of Trust Territories by the United Nations have hastened change. Old cultural traditions of the Polynesians and Micronesians are gradually being discarded.

In the Pacific World, copra and tourist attractions are the major means of income for the islanders. The amount of land for coconut palms is limited. Even so, the people depend so much upon copra, the white meat of the coconut, that a name is given to that kind of farming. The name is "a coconut civilization." Food and extra cash come from the coconut palm and the sale of its products.

The scenery of these islands today is also "on the market." Travel folders show the probable tourists the beauty which can be reached and enjoyed in only a few hours.

EASTERN EUROPE AND THE U.S.S.R.

In this region there are different types of people: Slavs, Bulgars, Poles, Tartars, Armenians, Russians, Ukranians, and many others. Even though the people of this part of the world have different backgrounds, the same form of government closely controls the lives of all the people. A communist form of government is in power in all of the nations occupied by the many different peoples listed above. The lands, factories, businesses, and apartment buildings are usually owned and controlled by the government.

Until recently, living conditions provided few luxuries for the people of this region. To improve the situation, great strides have been made

Natives of the Pacific travel over coral reefs towards a festival.

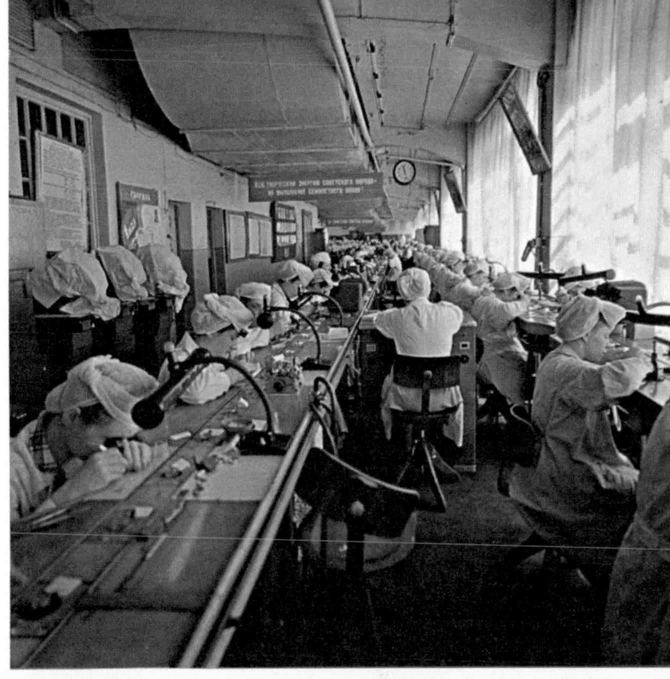

Government policies, industrial production, and agricultural yields are controlled in Communist countries.

in the development of industries. Heavy industry has been concentrated where mineral resources, especially coal and iron, are available. The governments of the Eastern European countries wish to make this region a leading industrial area. Nevertheless, farming is still the major occupation of the people of Eastern Europe.

The U.S.S.R. is not as favored as some of the other areas of the world in the amount of rich, productive agricultural land. The tundra, taiga, and mixed forest zones cover much of the U.S.S.R. However, the soil of the steppe is one of the best soils in the world. Unfortunately, crop yields are unpredictable because of light rainfall and occasional periods of drought.

The governments within this region want the people to follow closely the plans and ideas of the state. They wish this so much that even religious ideas and practices are tolerated to a very small degree. The local communities and their people are allowed to cling to their own dress, customs, habits, and ideas. Unfortunately, they cannot be outspoken about their ideas, especially their political ideas.

Some Western Europeans live in small towns that seem untouched by time; others live in great modern cities.

WESTERN EUROPE

The Greek and Roman civilizations are considered the "cradle" of Western culture. They gave us a heritage of greatness. They gave us invaluable ideas, art, architecture, literature, and laws. However, we have not inherited their cultures intact. For example, the Greeks preferred simplicity in their food, dress, and homes. They valued conversation, ideas, athletics, and the arts. Their literature and architecture have not often been equalled. Do we today have the same values? Do we have the same goals or aims?

The people of modern Western Europe have an excellent educational system. They have incomes which are above the average of most of the world's people. Life for the most part is comfortable. A high value is placed on music, painting, dance, literature, and drama. In fact, these arts have become a part of almost everyone's life, rich and poor alike.

The use of the land in Western Europe is intense. This means that effort, thought, time, and money are used to get the highest returns from the land. Both agriculture and industry are well developed in Western Europe. A great network of roads, railroads, canals, and airways provides excellent transportation in Western Europe. This vast network makes travel and the transportation of raw materials and finished products easy. The many seas that branch out from Western Europe to the rest of the world may also be thought of as extensions of the land network of transportation that criss-crosses Europe. Excellent transportation in Western Europe has promoted progress and spread ideas.

Western Europe has many different political units and many different languages. Differences in the past have often led to war. Even after wars have ceased and treaties have been signed, all the differences have not disappeared. While it is difficult to satisfy all, some signs of cooperation are seen. Trade agreements represent one favorable sign. Mutual assistance pacts—nations agreeing to help each other if trouble starts—are another.

Two of Western Europe's great resources since ancient times have been the sea and the fertile land.

PEOPLES' NEEDS ARE SIMILAR

Regions are different, but the people in the regions are alike in many ways. They work to supply basic needs which are much the same throughout the world. As rapid communication and travel draw the people of the world together, the similarities among people will increase. Today, men share their knowledge and skills. Better ways of producing food or providing for other needs discovered in certain parts of the world are quickly carried to other parts. Cooperation and sharing are moving us toward one great World Region where similarities and differences can be used to improve the ways of living of all.

What similarities and differences do these pictures show about India (left) and Hungary (right)?

Do You Know?

1. What are the basic needs common to all cultures of the world?

2. In which three culture regions has the basic need for expression been suppressed or controlled the most?

3. What source of power, recently discovered, will help the people of the Dry World Region progress? What major source of power does most of the region lack?

4. What are three major goals of the native people of Sub-Saharan Africa? Of India?

5. What are three major regionalizing features of Southeast Asia?

6. Which nation of Eastern Asia has been strongly affected by Western European and American culture in recent years?

7. What are two unique features of the Australia—New Zealand region?

8. What are four countries of the Eastern Hemisphere that are former British possessions?

9. Why are dams, such as the Aswan Dam on the Nile, being built in many parts of the world?

Learn By Doing

1. Give a reason for each of the following statements:

a. All culture regions change, though some change more rapidly than others.

b. The physical environment affects the way people live.

c. Changes in ways of living cause problems for the people.

d. Ways of living are based on the way people in different regions meet their common needs.

e. Cooperation is important in all culture regions if progress is to be made.

2. Follow the directions given below to prepare a booklet.

a. Sketch a map of the Eastern Hemisphere.

b. Find or draw pictures which show the characteristic features of each culture region.

c. Find or write an article about a change or a sign of progress in each region.

3. Compare some of the types of shelter found in the various culture regions. You may wish to draw or find pictures of the various homes of people.

4. Throughout history man has sought ways to express himself. Make a chart of the artistic contributions of the people in each culture region you have studied.

5. As a class project, prepare a bulletin board of magazine or newspaper articles which discuss the changes in government of the countries you have studied.

Test Your Knowledge

1. Explain why life on a volcanic island is easier than life on a coral atoll. Why is the coconut tree important to the people on an atoll?

2. Describe a "gathering" economy. A manufacturing economy.

3. Compare the different needs for shelter of the nomad, the aborigine, and the Norwegian. Do you think each has met his need in the best way? Explain your answer.

4. What are the important sources of power in the world?

5. Name several ways the living conditions in India are being improved.

6. Give several reasons why Southeast Asia is a land of differences.

7. In what ways has World War II affected the islands and the people of the Pacific?

8. Why is Western Europe one of the most well-developed areas of the world?

9. If the basic needs are common to all cultures, why are the culture regions of the world different?

10. Which basic need, discussed in this chapter, tends to separate people? Which basic need tends to unite people? Explain your answers.

Using Maps and Globes

1. Which continent of the Eastern Hemisphere is the largest? Which is the smallest?

2. Which continent lies entirely south of the equator?

3. On which continent is the civilization the most developed and the population per square mile the heaviest.

4. Which large nation is located in both Europe and Asia?

5. Name the ocean which lies to the west of Europe, to the east of Asia, and between Australia and Africa?

6. Which major sea lies between Europe and Africa?

7. Name some of the peninsulas that are part of the continent of Europe.

8. Locate the Tropic of Cancer and the Tropic of Capricorn. Name the continents through which they pass.

9. Along the banks of what four rivers did the early civilizations begin?

10. Name at least one area of the world where there is an abundance of ice and snow, mountains, desert, tropical rainforest, or tundra.

CHAPTER 22

OUR WORLD CULTURE REGION

You have read about the many differences in the culture regions of the Earth. These differences make our world more interesting. Today, there are many factors which are pushing men toward closer world cooperation. Cooperation will build a great World Culture Region in which men can share their knowledge and skills to make a better life for all.

OUR EARTH AS A STANDING PLACE

A globe represents our Earth. It is a model of the home of all men. In this book sections of the Earth were selected for careful study. Now you need to see how these pieces fit together.

About three-fourths of the globe shows a water covering. The waters of the Earth—oceans, seas, rivers, and streams—are one. They are interconnected. All the land parts, the continents and the islands, are also connected although not visibly on the surface. The land area, which juts above the surface of the seas, represents the homes, or "standing places," of people.

Today, we know much about our world. We have globes to help us study it. We draw maps to help us learn about the regions of the world. Maps are used to show the landform, the climate, the drainage, the soils, and many other items of a region. These are the nature-made physical features. Maps are also used to show many of the man-made items. Among them are cities, farms, roads, air routes, and the so-called cultural factors.

Study the wheel-like diagram on page 513. If you peeled the surface off a globe and pressed it flat, it could be made to look like the world map in the center of the diagram. Of course, you would have to be careful in cutting the "peeling," so that most cuts would be in the water parts. The land parts, where people live, would then stand out quite sharply. Compare this map with the Map of the World on pages 12–13. Are they alike? What name is given to this type of map?

Physical and Cultural Impactors

Study the "wheel." Look first at the spokes on the left side of the "wheel." You will see the words—minerals, weather and climate, landforms, vegetation, animals, and soils. These should be familiar to you. You have learned that these are the physical or natural forces that must be considered in studying life in a region. For example, you saw that the South Pacific coral atolls, often islands of great beauty, are small and infertile. You also read about the rich and productive soil of the steppes in the Soviet Union.

Now look at the words written between the spokes on the right hand side of the "wheel." These are the cultural forces that must be considered in studying life in a region. For example, you have read that the people of the Dry World speak the Arabic language and believe in the Muslim religion. You have also learned that the people of India speak many languages and practice Hinduism.

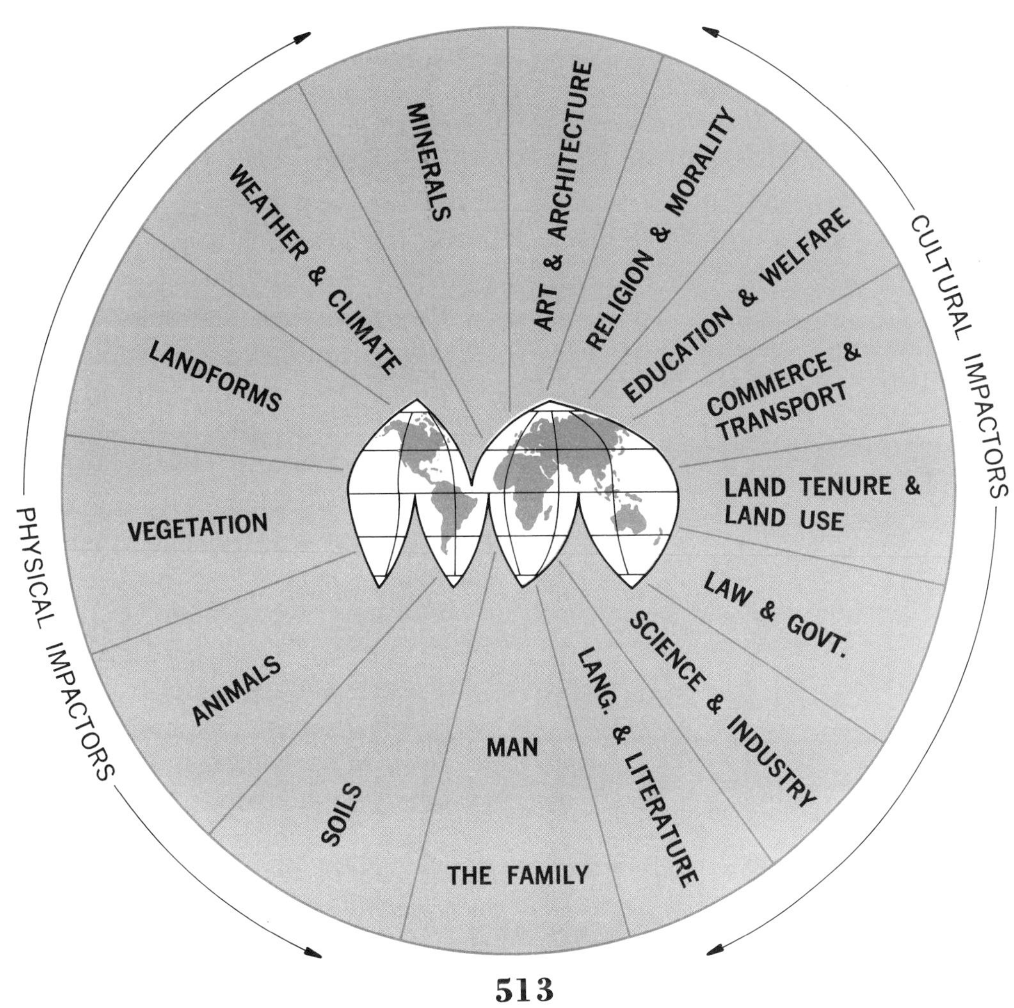

As you can see, the people of the world feel the force, or the impact, of the items written between the spokes of the "wheel." These items are called **impactors** because they exert force on the lives of people. But the people, too, make an impact on the physical and the cultural impactors. The three forces, man, nature, and culture, work together in the World Region. Each has a marked effect upon the others. The results of these forces differ from place to place. However, all are part of one Earth.

Changing Ways of Living

You have looked carefully at many large and small regions of our planet Earth. You have seen how the lack of water in the Dry World Region influences the way of life of people in that region. The nomads depend upon the animals they raise to supply many of their basic needs. Some people have turned to the sea for food because much of their land is not suitable for farming. You can see that nature, or the physical environment, has had a great impact on the ways of living of people in many of our culture regions.

Man builds huge dams to create new water supplies and electric power.

Gradually, man has learned many ways to use, control, and change his physical environment. He has developed the physical elements of soil, minerals, water, and climate to his advantage. He has used the vegetation and the animal life to support himself. He has created cultures, or ways of living, from working with the physical impactors in the world.

You have seen that some regions, Western Europe for example, have been favored in the physical elements. The people have been able to use the natural resources easily. They have developed regions of excellent manufacturing and productive farming.

In other places, man has had to plan well and work hard to accomplish the changes which are necessary for a better way of life. In Fennoscandia, you learned that the people have developed a modern and advanced way of living. They have made use of their abundant source of water by converting its power into electricity.

FACTORS IN A WORLD REGION

In the last chapter you read that the peoples of the world have common basic needs which must be satisfied. You learned that people use the resources of their regions to meet these needs. But the regions of the world are not all the same. Some have better resources than others. Some peoples have been able to make better use of their resources. What does this mean for people in every part of our Earth? What is man doing to make the Earth into a great region in which all men have what they need for living?

There are many ways modern man is trying to make the world a better place in which to live. Some of them are closely related to the basic differences which exist in the World Region. Let us see how these differences are gradually bringing the peoples and the regions closer together in a great World Culture Region.

Rural Afghanistan and urban Hong Kong show how population varies.

Populations Are Different

A basic difference in the regions of the world is that the people are not distributed evenly over the Earth's surface. In some areas of the world, there are so many people that not enough food can be produced to supply their essential needs. In other less crowded areas a surplus can be produced.

Not only are people distributed unevenly, but they differ among themselves in many ways. Their desires and values are different. They have different religions and languages. Some have had more education than others. People in some regions live longer, on the average, than those in others. Some people are physically stronger and healthier than others. These are just a few indications of the differences among people.

Natural Resources Are Different

Another basic difference among regions is that the natural resources are unevenly distributed on, over, and under the Earth's surface. Natural resources are found in both the land parts and the water parts of the world. The amount and kind of resources differ, however, from one part of the world to another. For example, some areas may be excellent sources of coal, gas, or electricity, while others may be excellent for growing wheat or cotton. Most of the world's tin is produced in Malaysia, Indonesia, and Bolivia. The Dry World Region has vast oil reserves.

Working with These Differences

As man works towards a better world, these differences of people and of resources present major problems. All peoples need certain basic resources to make a better life for themselves. To help meet the needs of the world's people, modern man is trying to share the great resources of the Earth. He is also sharing his knowledge and his skills.

The exchange and sharing of the vast resources of the world can be found among all regions. For example, several countries may obtain goods from the same excellent supply. Some people in the United States use electricity generated in Canada.

The economies of most countries in the Dry World Region depend on oil; modernization is needed in many places if the world demand for these precious oil deposits is to be met.

In England, a nuclear power station conducts experiments that will aid other nations as well; in Africa, students share in the discoveries of their teacher.

Many countries, which do not have supplies of their own, share the vast oil reserves of the Dry World Region and the great quantities of wheat grown in the United States. The peoples of the world are sharing these goods which are needed by all.

Cooperation among different peoples can also take other forms. In some regions of the world, man has used his resources to develop modern science. New knowledge and inventions have been introduced which have helped to provide better living conditions. People are learning that better foods and modern methods of sanitation will improve their health and prolong their lives. As a result, they are making great progress toward a better way of life.

Africa is one region which has benefited greatly from the progress made by people in more advanced regions. New machines and modern methods are being used by the people in both industry and farming. Faster, more efficient ways are helping the people produce better goods. More people are able to obtain the goods which they need to enjoy a better way of life. The sharing of knowledge and skills has made this possible. Only through cooperation can people have what they need.

The Development of Resources

Although the differences in distribution of peoples and of natural resources are of great importance, the development of resources is just as important. We have seen that the world's peoples differ greatly in the extent to which they have developed the resources available to them. In working towards a better world, all peoples need to develop their resources. They need to learn new ways to use their resources.

When people have developed their resources to a high degree, the level of living is usually high. The people have extra material, or a surplus, which they can trade. And with trade, ideas are exchanged. Through this cooperation in the exchange of goods and ideas, all regions may eventually be able to develop their economies. One good example of how this has been done is Japan.

Japan's ultra-modern express train is a striking example of progress.

When Japan opened its doors to trade in 1854, her people were interested in learning about new ways. Scholars went abroad to learn about new discoveries and the new methods. The economy of the nation began to expand. World War II temporarily put an end to this.

Through the help of the United States, Japan has, in a very short time, rebuilt herself into the most progressive and most industrialized nation in Eastern Asia. The Japanese have learned to use modern scientific methods in farming, in fishing, and in industry. They have learned how to make the most of their limited resources. As a result, Japan has a surplus of goods which can be traded with other countries. None of this would have been possible without the sharing of knowledge and resources of other peoples.

Developing Systems of Exchange

As resources are developed, better communication and transportation systems become necessary. Coal must be carried from the mine to the place where it is used. Messages must flow swiftly from one region to another.

The development of transportation and communication systems is another important difference among the regions of the world. This factor is a good indicator of the standard of living. It is also a contributor to improved stages of development.

Why do you think Heidelberg, Germany, has developed more rapidly than this remote Moroccan village?

Transportation and communication are a means by which the people of the world can learn about and trade with each other.

Some regions of the world have not developed these systems. For example, in parts of Central Africa the people travel mainly on foot. This limits the amount of contact they have with other peoples. News and ideas are exchanged mostly by word of mouth. Thus, the people do not learn new methods and do not develop modern ways of living. Their economy does not improve quickly.

In Western Europe, where the systems of transportation and communication are well developed, the people can learn about new changes, products, and technical advances almost immediately. They are able to exchange goods and ideas quickly. This makes it easier for them to improve their living conditions.

MOVING CLOSER TOGETHER

Today, through the development of new and better communication links as well as faster transportation systems, man is gradually bringing all peoples and all regions of the world closer together. People are learning about the needs of others more quickly. They are sharing their knowledge and their resources more easily. Technical assistance is being transported to the most isolated regions of the world.

People are traveling to the undeveloped areas of the world to help others develop their natural resources and improve their living conditions. They are learning to work together to provide for the needs of all peoples and to make our World a better place in which to live. Cooperation is bringing our World Region closer to what we want it to be.

Modern methods of communication link world regions; telephone cables joining the continents help newspapers report world events.

Communication Unites People

What are some of the ways the different peoples and the different regions are being brought closer together in a World Culture Region? Perhaps some of you who are reading this book sell newspapers. Did you ever stop to think that you are a part of the great communication network of the world? You are helping other people learn about local, state, national, and international affairs. The daily paper which you sell is one of the more than 1,800 newspapers published every day in the United States. The news it prints is written by men and women all over the world.

Reporters work together so that all people are informed about the important events that take place. International "wire services" now enable messages and photographs to be carried to all regions of the world. Today, even the most isolated people can learn about such events as the outbreak of war, the launching of satellites, and the discovery of new scientific methods in industry and in medicine. The telegraph, the telephone, radio, television, and the new communications satellites are used to send and receive information. These modern means of communication help unite the peoples of the world.

Another important means of communication are the conferences among heads of state. International pacts are made which affect ways of living and relationships among world peoples.

Transportation Unites People

Modern means of transportation also help people share knowledge and resources. Today, people and goods can be transported to all parts of the world by jet planes and swift ships. The development of refrigerated freight cars and trucks enables perishable products to be transported quickly from one area to another. Space ships may soon enable people to travel to the moon.

Modern developments make transportation more efficient than ever before. For example, goods can be loaded on truck trailers at the factory. The trailers are driven to a railroad yard and transferred, without unpacking, onto a train. At their destination, the "piggy-back" trailers are again attached to trucks and driven directly to the customer's plant or warehouse. Similar methods can be used to transport goods by ship. Because the goods are handled less often, the cost of transporting them is lowered. More people in more regions are able to buy more goods.

However, cooperation is necessary if all people are to obtain the goods and the ideas that they need to make progress. Trade agreements have been made among many nations. Airports are being built, and ports enlarged. New roads, bridges, and tunnels are being built to shorten land routes. The peoples in some regions have worked together to establish laws protecting the free flow of goods and the safety of the people who travel.

People and ideas are brought closer together by modern transportation; in 1961, Vice-President Johnson visited Germany and Konrad Adenauer, then the German Chancellor.

PROMOTING A BETTER WORLD

Through the use of modern transportation and communication systems, people are coming in contact with one another more often. They are learning about one another's values, customs, and cultures. An understanding of the differences in language, religion, and forms of government of the peoples of the world is becoming more important. People are working together on some of the problems that exist in the world. They are making our World Region a better place in which to live.

Peoples in all regions of the world want to have better food, better health, more education, freedom to live as they wish, and peace. People are trying to achieve some of these goals that they have in common. They are exchanging people, goods, and ideas on local, national, and world levels in the hope of accomplishing their aims.

World Organizations Cooperate

Many programs have been established to help all peoples achieve these goals. In the United States, for example, many programs are aimed at raising the standard of living of all people in the nation. People are being trained to use new methods and machines. In this way, people will be able to work for a salary, which they can use to buy better food, clothing, and shelter.

Other organizations are working at the international level. UNICEF is designed to help needy children. It is supported by the governments of many countries in the world. In order for a country to receive help it must spend an amount equal to that given by UNICEF. Supplies are sent to regions which lack proper food or which have suffered from an emergency. Trained workers are sent to provide for the needs and improve the living conditions of the children.

"Head Start" helps deprived children in the United States.

The World Health Organization, an agency of the United Nations, and the Red Cross are working to improve the health of all peoples. Doctors, nurses, new medicines, better sanitation, and social and mental hygiene are some of the services provided. Workers are trying to make each individual healthier and happier. Through education, they hope all peoples will learn to care for themselves. People are slowly learning that cleanliness will help prevent many diseases and prolong life.

An example of the way in which one nation can help others is the Peace Corps developed by the United States. Volunteers travel to other countries to work on many different projects. Some try to help the people improve their agriculture. They have introduced better tools and methods, high-grade seeds, new fertilizers, and better ways of storing crops. Others teach children and adults how to read and write. They plan educational programs and build educational facilities.

UNESCO, an agency of the United Nations, also works on many programs. It aids in the fields of education, science, and culture. Teams are sent to many areas to train teachers, write textbooks, and build schools. Others help the people explore and develop the natural resources. These workers help to expand the transportation and communication facilities in the regions. Many improvements have been made through the efforts of this worldwide organization.

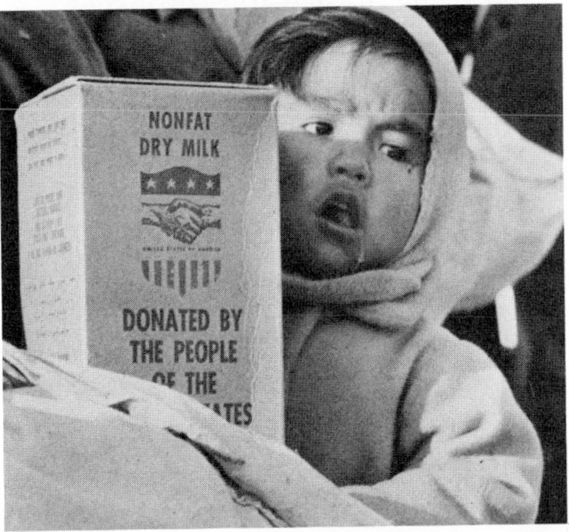

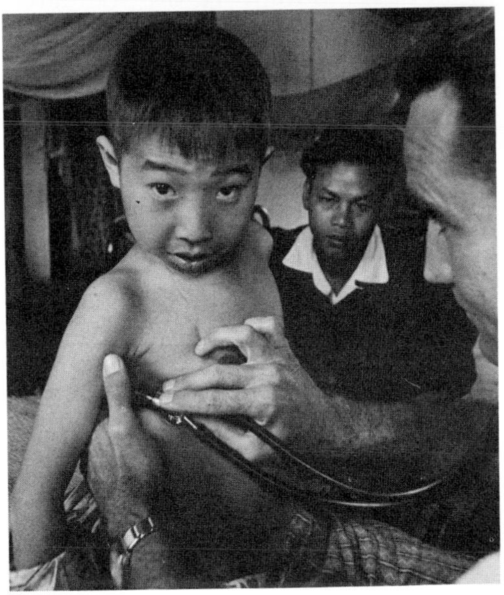

Help for the world's needy takes many forms; it means a new school in Ghana, food in Chile, and medical care in Vietnam.

Peace, A Worldwide Need

In order for the work of these organizations to continue and to be effective, worldwide peace is necessary. Peace is a human need in our World Culture Region. It does not come from the natural resources. It comes from our human resources. Man has the knowledge and the understanding necessary to attain peace for all. He must learn to use his human resources to recognize the differences among people and respect their right to be different.

The United Nations is the major organization working to maintain peace in the world. The majority of the nations in the world are members of the U.N. The members cooperate in an effort to improve the standards of living and to insure the freedom of all peoples in the world. They work together through their agencies to meet the needs of all, to prevent war, and to maintain peace.

You have seen small family groups, communities, nations, and groups of nations trying to make progress for all. Look again at the classroom globe. The world has great differences. People follow different customs, speak different languages, believe in different religions, and prefer different forms of government. Can not they continue to do this and yet work together for world peace, for enough food for all, for adequate shelter and clothing for all, and for better education for all? Can not the people of the world unite in working to meet the common needs shared by all peoples and yet maintain the differences that each value so highly? Can not diversity be maintained within unity? Here is our question and also our goal.
Will you help to attain it?

Do You Know?

1. What is a globe? What is a map? How do they differ?

2. What are the three major forces which work together within the World Region?

3. What are five ways of living which man has developed by working with the physical environment?

4. What are some of the cultural differences among the peoples of the world?

5. What are two basic differences common to all regions?

6. What are two major means of exchange?

7. What is the "piggy-back" method of transportation? Why is this method of transportation favored?

8. What are two ways modern man is trying to help meet the needs of the world's peoples?

9. How does trade help the people in regions that have poor natural resources?

10. What are five major goals of the peoples of the world?

Learn By Doing

1. Read each sentence. Decide on the word or words needed to complete each sentence. Then write the complete sentence on your paper. Circle the words which you have chosen.

a. About __ of the Earth's surface is covered with water.

b. The physical and cultural elements are called ______ because they exert force on the lives of people.

c. Man has created _____, or ways of living, from working with the physical environment.

d. Only through _______ can all peoples have what they need for a better way of life.

e. ___ is the exchange of goods and ideas.

f. _________ and _________ are the means by which people exchange goods and ideas.

g. Many organizations have been developed to help meet the three basic needs, ___, _____, and ____, of people.

h. ____ is a human need of all peoples in the World Region.

i. WHO and UNICEF are two agencies of the _________ which help the needy peoples of the world.

j. Man must learn to respect the right of others to be _____.

2. Study the wheel diagram on page 513. Select a culture region of the Eastern Hemisphere. Write a composition describing three physical impactors and three cultural impactors which are present in the region. Show how these impactors make this region different from other regions of the world.

3. Pretend that you are working for an advertising company that wishes to promote world peace. Plan and draw a billboard which would be used in many countries of the world. Perhaps the class could make a large mural promoting world peace.

4. Discuss with your class several reasons why Japan is a highly industrialized nation, while Africa still retains many primitive ways of living. Remember that Japan is a land of few natural resources, while southern Africa is a land rich in natural resources.

5. The United Nations is an organization which is working to make the world a better place in which to live. Find out the full names and the purpose of the following agencies of the United Nations: UNESCO, FAO, IFC, WHO, and ITU. Perhaps members of the class could write letters to agencies of the U.N. for information and pamphlets.

6. Select one of the following topics for an oral report to your class:

a. The wheel is the basis of many types of land transportation.

b. Water transportation is important in many parts of the world.

c. Air transportation is bringing the peoples of the world closer together.

Include information on the development of the system you have chosen. Find pictures of the different types used in the regions of the world. Explain how they are used by the different peoples.

Test Your Knowledge

1. Do you think the sea regions are as important as the land regions as a major source of food for people? Explain your answer.

2. How has man learned to control his physical environment?

3. What is the major problem in the overpopulated areas of the world?

4. Give three examples of how the people of the world share the Earth's great resources.

5. What is the most important means of communication? Make a list of as many means of communication as you can. (For example: books, radios, telegraph).

6. Give three examples of how modern transportation has united the peoples of the world.

7. The development of modern means of communication is important, but the understanding of peoples' ideas is more important. Explain this statement.

8. How will more and better education help the peoples in the underdeveloped regions of the world?

9. World organizations are examples of cooperation. Describe three ways the workers of these programs are helping people.

10. How will respecting the right of others to be different help achieve and maintain peace among the nations of the world?

REVIEWING YOUR KNOWLEDGE

Can You Remember?

1. Why do we know more about the ancient Egyptian civilization than the other ancient culture homes?

2. What are some physical differences among regions of the world?

3. Describe four ways in which all peoples are alike.

4. How have modern communication and transportation brought the peoples of the world closer together?

5. Why can some countries develop their resources more easily than others?

Projects And Reports

1. Below are brief clues to periods in history. Identify the people or the time that is described. Then write an additional fact, name, or cultural contribution for each.

a. irrigation systems, sun-dried bricks, cuneiform

b. Pharaohs, papyrus, mummies

c. city-states, acropolis, thinkers

d. consul, toga, Forum, atrium

e. emperor, roads, conquests

f. A.D. 476, barbarians, little trade, plagues

g. manors, nobles, serfs, feudalism

h. guilds, oversea trade, cities, cathedrals

i. printing press, art and architecture, explorers

j. scientific discoveries, new inventions, factory towns

2. Define the following terms using complete sentences. Then locate an important example of each that you have read about in this book.

fiord	delta	steppe
cape	plain	trench
tundra	oasis	volcano
erg	rift	desert
coral reef	loess	cataract

3. Food, clothing, and shelter are provided for in different ways in different regions. As a class project, draw a mural showing the different types found in the Eastern Hemisphere.

4. The phrases below describe physical or cultural features of regions in the Eastern Hemisphere. Select three of these phrases. Choose an area or nation that fits the phrase. Briefly describe the life of the people.

a. rice culture region
b. one-animal economy
c. coal mining area
d. monsoon climate region
e. dairying-pastoral economy
f. "slash-and-burn" culture region
g. rubber plantations
h. fishing region

5. Many of the unusual physical features of the world exist in the Eastern Hemisphere. Can you name and locate the following: the highest mountains, the longest river, the island continent, the largest desert, the great land rift, the largest continent, the country with the largest population, and the largest inland body of salt water?

6. Select two countries, each on a different continent, which you have learned are different in many ways. Compare their size, population, landforms, rainfall, vegetation, and major ways of living. You may want to show your information on a chart for the bulletin board. Also include the differences in religion, form of government, language, and customs.

Using Maps and Globes

1. What do we mean when we say that the regions which you have studied are in the Eastern Hemisphere?

2. What continents lie within the Southern Hemisphere?

3. In what latitude—low, middle, or high—do most people live? Why?

4. In what directions could you travel, if you were at the North Pole?

5. What sea is bordered by Asia, Africa, and Europe?

6. Are parallels used to show longitude or latitude?

7. What does a physical map show? What does a political map show?

8. Which map would show more detail—one which had a scale of 50 miles to the inch or one which had 500 miles to the inch?

9. Give the location of the following major rivers—the Nile, Hwang Ho, Ganges, Danube, Congo, and Rhine. In what direction does each river flow?

10. Give two reasons why large cities are found inland in Europe as well as on the coastline.

APPENDIX

NATION (CAPITAL)	AREA (sq. mi.)	POPULATION in 1,000's	per sq. mi.
AFRICA			
Algeria (Algiers)	919,593	10,975	12
Chad (Fort Lamy)	495,754	3,300	7
Congo, Dem. Rep. of (Kinshasa)	905,565	15,300	17
Congo, Rep. of (Brazzaville)	132,047	826	6
Ethiopia (Addis Ababa)	471,777	22,200	47
Ghana (Accra)	92,099	7,537	82
Kenya (Nairobi)	224,959	9,104	40
Liberia (Monrovia)	43,000	1,041	24
Libya (Tripoli)	679,360	1,559	2
Malagasy Rep. (Tananarive)	230,035	5,940	24
Mauritania (Nouakchott)	419,230	900	2
Morocco (Rabat)	171,834	12,959	75
Niger (Niamey)	489,190	3,250	7
Nigeria (Lagos)	356,668	56,400	158
Rep. of South Africa (Pretoria)	471,444	17,474	37
Somalia (Mogadiscio)	246,201	2,350	10
Sudan, Rep. of (Khartoum)	967,497	13,180	14
Tanzania (Dar es Salaam)	361,799	9,990	28
Uganda (Kampala)	91,134	7,367	81
United Arab Rep. (Cairo)	386,101	28,900	75
Zambia (Lusaka)	290,585	3,600	12
ASIA			
Afghanistan (Kabul)	249,999	15,227	61
Burma (Rangoon)	261,789	24,229	93
Cambodia (Phnom Penh)	69,898	6,230	89
Ceylon (Colombo)	25,332	10,965	433
China, People's Rep. of (Peking)	3,691,512	690,000	187
India (New Delhi)	1,197,153	471,624	401
Indonesia, Rep. of (Djakarta)	575,894	102,200	177
Iran (Tehran)	636,294	22,860	36
Iraq (Baghdad)	173,260	7,004	40
Israel (Jerusalem)	7,992	2,476	310
Japan (Tokyo)	142,726	96,906	679
Jordan (Amman)	37,738	1,898	50
Laos (Vientiane)	91,429	1,960	21
Malaysia, Fed. of (Kuala Lumpur)	50,700	7,810	154
Mongolia (Ulan Bator)	592,665	1,050	2

Nepal (Katmandu)	54,362	9,920	182
Pakistan (Rawalpindi)	365,528	100,762	276
Philippines, Rep. of (Quezon City)	115,830	31,270	270
Saudi Arabia (Riyadh)	870,001	6,630	8
Singapore (Singapore)	224	1,820	8,125
Syria (Damascus)	71,498	5,200	73
Taiwan (Taipeh)	13,883	12,070	869
Thailand (Bangkok)	198,456	29,700	150
Turkey (Ankara)	301,381	30,677	102
U.S.S.R. (Moscow)	8,649,512	227,687	26
North Vietnam (Hanoi)	63,344	15,917	251
South Vietnam (Saigon)	66,263	14,200	214
EUROPE			
Albania (Tirana)	11,100	1,814	163
Austria (Vienna)	32,374	7,215	223
Belgium (Brussels)	11,781	9,378	796
Bulgaria (Sofia)	42,729	8,144	191
Czechoslovakia (Prague)	49,370	14,058	285
Denmark (Copenhagen)	16,619	4,720	284
East Germany (East Berlin)	41,802	17,181	415
Finland (Helsinki)	130,120	4,580	35
France (Paris)	211,207	48,417	229
Greece (Athens)	50,944	8,510	167
Hungary (Budapest)	35,919	10,120	282
Italy (Rome)	116,303	51,090	439
Luxembourg (Luxembourg)	998	328	329
Netherlands (Amsterdam)	12,978	12,127	934
Norway (Oslo)	125,181	3,694	30
Poland (Warsaw)	120,664	31,161	258
Portugal (Lisbon)	35,510	9,106	256
Rep. of Ireland (Dublin)	27,135	2,849	105
Rumania (Bucharest)	91,699	18,927	206
Spain (Madrid)	194,884	31,339	161
Sweden (Stockholm)	173,666	7,661	44
Switzerland (Bern)	15,941	5,874	368
United Kingdom (London)	94,220	54,213	575
West Germany (Bonn)	95,743	56,097	586
Yugoslavia (Belgrade)	98,766	19,279	195
PACIFIC			
Australia (Canberra)	2,967,885	11,136	4
New Zealand (Wellington)	103,736	2,594	25

AREAS OF CONTINENTS AND MAJOR BODIES OF WATER

CONTINENT	SQUARE MILES
Asia	16,900,000
Africa	11,500,000
North America	9,300,000
South America	6,800,000
Antarctica	5,300,000
Europe	3,750,000
Australia	2,950,000

The continents include neighboring islands. All figures are estimates.

OCEAN OR SEA	SQUARE MILES
Pacific Ocean	63,801,668
Atlantic Ocean	31,839,306
Indian Ocean	28,356,276
Arctic Ocean	5,440,197
South China Sea	1,146,000
Mediterranean Sea	966,757
Bering Sea	875,753
East China Sea	482,317
Sea of Japan	389,074
North Sea	222,124

MAJOR CITIES OF THE EASTERN HEMISPHERE

CITY	POPULATION	CITY	POPULATION
Tokyo, Japan	11,021,579	Osaka, Japan	3,214,330
London, United Kingdom	7,986,100	Manila, Philippines	3,100,000
Shanghai, China	6,900,000	Calcutta, India	3,003,556
Paris, France	6,437,000	Djakarta, Indonesia	2,906,533
Moscow, U.S.S.R.	6,334,000	Madrid, Spain	2,599,330
Bombay, India	4,537,926	Rome, Italy	2,359,550
Peking, China	4,010,000	Sydney, Australia	2,349,590
Leningrad, U.S.S.R.	3,636,000	Bangkok, Thailand	2,318,000
Cairo, Egypt	3,518,200	Delhi, India	2,298,455
Berlin, Germany	3,257,200	Melbourne, Australia	2,121,900
Tientsin, China	3,220,000	Chungking, China	2,121,000

MAJOR RIVERS OF THE EASTERN HEMISPHERE

RIVER	LENGTH (miles)	RIVER	LENGTH (miles)
Nile, Africa	4,145	Murray-Darling, Australia	2,310
Ob, U.S.S.R.	3,900	Volga, Europe	2,290
Yangtze, China	3,400	Indus, Asia	1,900
Hwang-Ho, China	3,000	Bramaputra, Asia	1,800
Congo, Africa	2,718	Danube, Europe	1,770
Mekong, Asia	2,600	Euphrates, Asia	1,700
Niger, Africa	2,600	Rhine, Europe	820

A SHORT GLOSSARY

The meaning given for each word in the glossary is that of the word as it is used in this book. You will find other meanings in your dictionary.

The Thorndike-Barnhart Dictionary Program* is used as the reference for pronunciation. Its key is printed below:

a hat	ē see	k kind	oi oil	TH then	z zero
ā age	ėr term	l land	ou house	u cup	zh measure
ã care	f if	m me	p cup	u̇ full	ə represents:
ä far	g go	n in	r run	ü rule	a in about
b bad	h he	ng long	s say	ū use	e in taken
ch child	i it	o hot	sh she	v very	i in pencil
d red	ī ice	ō open	t it	w will	o in lemon
e let	j jam	ô order	th thin	y young	u in circus

Words of more than one syllable have accent marks. The mark ′ is placed after the syllable with the primary or strong accent; the mark ′ after a syllable shows a secondary or lighter accent.

aborigines (ab′ə rij′ə nēz): the earliest known inhabitants of a region or country.

alloy (al′oi): a metal made either by mixing other metals or by mixing a metal with other substances to produce certain desired characteristics; also one of the metals mixed with another.

ally (al′ī): a person or state joined with another for a common purpose.

anthropology (an′thrə-pol′ə ji): the scientific study of man's origin and culture.

arable (ar′ə bəl): suitable for plowing or cultivation.

archaeology (är ki ol′ə ji): the scientific study of materials, relics, and fossils that remain from ancient times.

atoll (at′ol): a ring-shaped coral island, or group of islands that encloses or partly encloses a lagoon.

autocracy (ô tok′rə si): government by a ruler with supreme power.

basin (bā′sən): land drained by a river and its tributaries.

canal (kə nal′): a man-made waterway. Some canals carry boats or ships; others are used for irrigation.

cape (kāp): a piece of land extending into the sea or other body of water.

cash crop (kash krop): a crop that is produced to be sold.

* By E. L. Thorndike and Clarence L. Barnhart. Copyright 1962 by Scott, Foresman and Company, Chicago.

cataract (kat′ə rakt): a large waterfall or series of falls; sometimes, rapids.

centralization (sen′trəl ə-zā′shən): bringing under central control; concentration of power in a central government.

channel (chan′əl): the deeper part of a river, strait, harbor, or other waterway.

circumference (sər kum′-fər əns): the boundary line or perimeter of a circle.

civilization (siv′ə lə zā′-shən): an advanced state of human society brought about by progress in arts, government, and science; also the total culture of a people, period, or region.

civil war (siv′əl wôr): war between groups of citizens within one nation.

clan (klan): a group of related families that are descended from a common ancestor.

climate (klī′mit): the average weather conditions of a place, including temperature, precipitation, and presence of winds and clouds.

collective (kə lək′tiv): an organization in which materials are shared in common and are not owned by individuals; the collective farm or factory may be partially or totally controlled by the government.

communism (kom′ū niz-əm): an economic system in which the right of individuals to hold property is limited or denied entirely by the government.

continent (kon′tə nənt): one of the larger, unbroken masses of land into which the surface of the earth is divided.

cooperative (kō op′ər ə-tiv): an organization in which the members share the profits and losses.

coral (kôr′əl): a substance formed from the skeletons of certain small sea animals called polyps.

culture (kul′chər): the total way of life of a particular group at a particular time.

custom (kus′təm): a particular and often traditional way of doing things that is followed by all or most of the members of a group.

delta (del′tə): deposits of earth and sand that collect at the mouth of a river, forming many channels or outlets to the sea.

democracy (di mok′rə si): government by the people; power is exercised directly or indirectly through representatives.

desert (dez′ərt): a dry, barren region without moisture for vegetation.

dictatorship (dik′tā tər-ship): government in which one man has total or absolute authority.

economy (i kon′ə mi): management of the affairs and resources of a community; also, a system of production, distribution, and consumption of wealth.

elevation (el ə vā′shən): raised place; the height above sea level.

environment (en vī′rən-mənt): all that surrounds man: the people, objects, and natural conditions.

erosion (i rō′zhən): the wearing away of the land surface by glaciers, running water, waves, or wind.

ethnic (eth′nik): pertaining to races of people with common characteristics and customs.

fiord (fyôrd): a narrow inlet of the sea between high banks or cliffs.

harbor (här′bər): protected inlet of a body of water, where boats can anchor and be sheltered.

heritage (her′ə tij): something that has been or may be handed down by ancestors, such as a culture or body of traditions.

horticulture (hôr′tə kul-chər): the art or science of cultivating plants, gardens, and orchards.

humid (hū′mid): damp, moist, containing much water vapor.

humus (hū′məs): a brown or black substance in the soil composed of decayed or rotted vegetable or animal matter that contains valuable plant foods.

monsoon (mon sün′): a seasonal wind of the Indian Ocean and Southeast Asia, blowing during summer months from the southwest and during winter months from the northeast.

mosque (mosk): a Muslim place of worship.

natural resources (nach′ə rəl ri sôrs′əs): minerals, waterpower, and other sources of wealth supplied by nature.

nomads (nō′madz): people who move from place to to place, usually to find pasture land.

oasis (ō ā′sis): an area within a desert made fertile by the presence of water.

pagoda (pə gō′də): a tower-like shrine in India, China, Japan, and southeast Asia.

physical (fiz′ə kəl): pertaining to the laws of nature; material, natural.

plain (plān): a large area of level land usually at a low altitude.

plateau (pla tō′): a raised area of land that is level or mostly level; tableland.

polder (pōl′dər): a piece of lowland reclaimed from the sea or another body of water by dikes, dams, etc.

political (pə lit′ə kəl): pertaining to a state or nation or to a government and its policies.

port (pôrt): a place where ships and boats can load and unload.

raw material (rô mə tēr′i əl): material in its natural state that can be manufactured or processed to make it more useful or increase its value.

reef (rēf): a narrow ridge of rocks or sand at or near the surface of the water.

region (rē′jən): a space or place; an area of the world in which a feature or a combination of features stands out.

republic (ri pub′lik): a state or nation in which representatives are elected to govern.

silt (silt): very fine earth, finer than sand, deposited by moving water.

sod (sod): a layer of soil filled with roots and grasses.

steppe (step): level, generally treeless plains, especially those in Asia and Europe.

stupa (stü′pə): a dome-shaped Buddhist monument or shrine.

sub-continent (sub kon′tə nənt): a large land area, smaller, however, than what is usually called a continent.

subsistence agriculture (səb sis′təns ag′rə kul-chər): farming that supplies the needs of the farming family but does not yield a surplus for sale.

tangible (tan′jə bəl): capable of being touched; real, definite.

tariff (tar′if): a tax paid on imported or exported goods.

tropical rainforest (trop′ə kəl rān fôr′ist): a hot, wet, evergreen forest in the area near the equator; rainfall is heavy, there is no cool or dry season.

tundra (tun′drə): a large, treeless plain in the arctic regions.

typhoon (tī fün′): a tropical cyclone; a violent storm occurring in the Pacific.

values (val′ūz): ways of acting, ideas, or goals considered to be especially good by a group.

winnow (win′ō): to separate the grain from the chaff.

INDEX

Page numbers that appear in this Index in boldface type (**76**) indicate where the word or term is defined. See page 531 for the Key to Pronunciation.*

Aborigines (ab ərij′ə nēz), **475**

Acropolis (ə krŏp′əlĭs), **76,** 82, 83, 435

Africa, 182–201; animals of, 188, 190; cities, 198, 199, 200; climate, 184–185, 199–200; economy, 190–193, 200; exploration, 183; farming, 193–197; landforms, 183–184, 189; *map*, 187; nations, 184, 192, 198; natural regions, 185–189

Agriculture, in Africa, 19–21, 69–70, 170, 191–196; Asia, 25–28, 42, 56; Australia, 482; China, 241, 250–254; diversified, **22;** Europe, 93–94, 113–115, 354, 382–383, 393, 401–402, 405, 416, 432–433; India, 266–269, 270–274; Japan, 213–216; socialization of, **415;** Southeast Asia, 290–291, 300; U.S.S.R., 330–331, 338, 340; Taiwan, 248

Ainu (ī′nü), 222

Akbar, 279

Albania, 428; *map*, 411

Allah (al′ə), 172, 173

Alluvial deposits, 212, 266

Alps, 90, 103, 104, 404

Andorra, 356, 406

Angkor Thom (ang′kôr-tom), 305–306

Animals, of Africa, 188, 190; Asia, 56, 254, 256, 258; Europe, 382, 405, 406, 425, 428, 432; on a manor, 114; nomads, 40–41, 164–168, 256–258, 260–261, 357; Pacific, 467–469, 480–481, 486–487; U.S.S.R., 336–337

Animism, 303–304

Apartheid (ä pärt′hāt), **201**

Apennine Mountains, 90–91, 102, 435

Aqueducts, 98

Arabic language, 156, 175

Arabs, 123, 172, 175, 180

Archangel, 337

Aristotle, 88, 131

Art and Architecture, Asian, 305–306; Chinese, 242–244; Egyptian, 65–67; European, 368–369, 435–436; Greek, 83–84; Indian, 277–279; Japanese, 226, 230; Middle Ages, 122, 126–127; Renaissance, 130, 133–135; Romans, 94, 98–100; Russian, 319, 323; Sumerians, 57, 59

Aryans, 276, 283

Asia, 10, 24–34; *maps*, 24, 163, 239. *See also* Eastern Asia, Southwest Asia

Asia Minor, 75, 80, 83, 86, 103, 105

Asoka (ə sō̧′kə), 276–277

Astronomy, Chinese, 238, 245; early, 67, 86, 136; Renaissance, 138–140

Aswan, 62, 64

Athens, 76, 78–82; Golden Age, 82–83, 91; modern, 435–436

Atlas Mountains, 431

Atrium, 94

Augustus, Caius Octavian, 105

Aurora Borealis (ô rō′rä-bō rēăl′ĭs), **385**

Australia, 446, 446–484, 504–505; animals of, 466–468; climate, 480; exploration of, 470–473; industry, 481–483; *map*, 485; natural regions of, 479–483; problems, 487–488; settlement of, 474–478, 484

Austria, 396, 404; *map*, 397

Autocracy, 324

Babylon, 61

Baghdad, 55, 318

Balboa, Vasco Nunez de, 456

Balkan Mountains, 424

Balkan Peninsula, 74

Bangkok, 25, 238

Barbarians, 90, **108,** 110, 111, 122

Basques (basks), 357

Batu Khan, 320

Bauxite (bôks′īt), 370, 427

Bazaars, 171

Belfast, 394

Belgium, 396, 402; *map*, 397

* By E. L. Thorndike and Clarence L. Barnhart. Copyright © 1962 by Scott, Foresman and Company, Chicago.

Belgrade, 426
Benelux countries, 356
Berlin, East and West, 412–413
Bohemia, 358–359
Bolsheviks (bọl′shə viks), **328**
Bombay, 284
Bon-Po, 258
Book of Kells, 132
Borobudur (bôr′ō bə dür′), 306
Boyle, Robert, 147
Brahmaputra River (brä-mə pü′trə), 33, 237, 266, 270, 273
British East India Company, 280
British Isles, 374, 388–395; countries of, 388; *map,* 389. *See also* United Kingdom
Bruno, Giordano, 137
Bucharest, 423
Budapest, 420–421
Buddha, 231, 276, 277; *See also* Gautama
Buddhism, 230, 231, 258, 276–277, 300, 304–306
Bulgaria (bul gãr′iə), 410, 424–425; *map,* 411
Burma, 24, 25, 237, 277, 288, 299, 305; *map,* 290
Byzantine Empire, (biz′-ən tēn), 319–320

Caesar, Caius Julius, 96, 105
Cairo, 62, 164
Calcutta, 284
Cambodia (kam bọ′di ə), 305; *map,* 290
Camel, 165–167, 500
Canals, of China, 255; of Ancient Egypt, 65, 69; of Netherlands, 401–402; of Southeast Asia, 290; of Sumerians, 56–57, 58
Canberra, 483, 484
Carpathian Mountains, 418–419, 421
Carrara, marble, 435
Carthage, 103
Cartwright, Edmund, 149
Caste system, 283
Cathedrals, 126–127, 138, 360
Catherine the Great, 324
Catholic Church, 121, 123, 137, 139, 436
Cattle, of Africa, 41, 192–193; of Australia, 480–481; of India, 271, 272; of Japan, 216; of New Zealand, 486–487
Caucasus Mountains (kô′kə səs), 339
Central Africa, 191–197
Ceylon (si lon′), 24, 264, 277, 282, 285, 297, 501; *map,* 268
Chernozem (chĭr nŭ-zyôm′), **338,** 416
Cherrapunji (chĕr ȧ pŏŏn′ jĭ), 30
Chiang Kai-shek (chyäng′ kī′shek′), 246–247
China, art and architecture, 242–244; climate, 250; customs, 37–39, 240–241; farming, 27–28, 251–254; gifts, 244–245; history, 141–142, 238–242, 246–247; and Japan, 209–210, 222, 225; *map,* 239; resources, 250–251, 254–255; sub-regions, 256–261
Christianity, 172, 179, 436; in Middle Ages, 100, 121–127; in Asia, 304; in Bulgaria, 424; in Japan, 223, 230; in Russia, 319–320
City-state, 61, 76–83
Climate, of Africa, 62–64, 160; Asia, 28–32, 55–56, 161–162, 184–186, 199–200; China, 250; Europe, 353, 379, 393, 396, 425, 430; India, 266–269; Japan, 209–211; Pacific, 449–451; Southeast Asia, 292; U.S.S.R., 333–335; continental, **250,** 333; humid, **25;** marine, 353, **393;** marine west coast, **396,** 405, 406; Mediterranean, 353, **430;** Monsoon, **30**–32, 55–56, 209
Clouds, types of, 63, 450
Coking coal, 388–391
Collectives, 330
Colombo, 285
Colosseum, 100, 436
Columbus, Christopher, 145
Common Market, 370–371; *map,* 371
Commonwealth of Nations, 280, 391, 392, 394
Communism, in China, 247, 249–261, 502; Eastern Europe, 353, 407, 412–415, 420, 423–424; Southeast Asia, 308–309; U.S.S.R., 328–333, 342
Confucianism (kən fū′-shən iz əm), 230–231
Congo, Republic of the, 18–22, 192, 200, 501
Congo River, 143–144, 184
Constantine, Emperor, 106
Constantinople, 106, 126, 131, 132, 173, 319
Constitutional monarchy, 395
Continents, 10
Cook, Captain James, 457, 470, 472–473, 474; *map,* 471

Cooperatives, 331, 382
Copenhagen, 382, 383
Copernican Revolution, 140
Copernicus, Nicolaus, (kə pėr′nə kəs), 137–138, 139, 140
Copra, 297, 461
Coral reefs, 447–448
Crusades, 53, 122–124, **123,** 128, 132; *map,* 123
Cultural environment, 14–18, 36–49
Culture regions, 22, ancient, 54, 61, 238, 275; Eastern Asia, 24–34; World, 494–509; types of, 22–24, 374–377
Cuneiform (kū nē′ə fôrm), **60**
Czechoslovakia (chek ə-slō vä′kiə), 358, 410, 418–419; *map,* 411

Dalai Lama (dä lī′ lä′mə), 258–259
Dalmatia, 425
Dams, 45, 65, 191, 274, 284, 307, 426, 502; Aswan, 64, 500; Kariba, 201; Ming Tombs, 253; Ord, 483. *See also* Dikes
Danube River, 404, 419, 420, 421, 422, 424
Darius, 80–81
Dark Ages, 109, 111
Deccan Plateau, 33–34, 226, 273
DeGaulle, Charles, 371
Deltas, 212, 251, 266, 273, 401–402
Democracy, 80, 88, 347, 349
Denmark, 367, 378–387; *map,* 380
Deserts, of Africa, 40, 64, 158–160, 197; of Asia, 33, 161–162, 256, 260; of Australia, 479–480; of U.S.S.R., 338
Development, 346; of Europe, 366–370
Dias, Bartholomew, 144
Dictatorship, 105, 407
Dikes, 252; Schelde, 401–402
Dispersal, 346; from Europe, 347–353
Diversity, 346; in Europe, 353–358
Dnieper River (nē′pər), 318, 319, 356
Drake, Sir Francis, 456–457
Dravidians, 276
Dry World Region, 158–180; animals of, 165–168; climate, 160–162; *map,* 163; population, 164; religions, 172–174; resources, 176–177
Dublin, 393–394
Dutch, in Africa, 352; in Asia, 297; in Japan, 223; in Pacific, 457, 470, 472

Earthquakes, 212, 220
East Africa, 189–191, 198
Eastern Asia, culture regions, 24–34; physical features, 236–238; *map,* 24, 239
Eastern Europe, 407, 410–428, 506–507; *map,* 411
East Germany, 412–415; *map,* 411
East Pakistan, 264, 266, 281; *map,* 268
Economy, 23; animal, 23, 41, 165, dairying-pastoral, 486; export, 190, 192; native, 190, 192; planned, 332; wood, 220
Egypt, 54, 159, 164, 182, 431; ancient, 64–71; climate of, 62–64; *map,* 63
Eisenhuttenstadt (ī′zən-hōōt ĕn shtät), 414
Elburz Mountains, 164
Elizabeth, Queen of England; I, 456–457; II, 395
Emperors, Byzantine, 320; Chinese, 242, 243, 261; early Roman, 100, 105, 106; Japanese, 222, 230
England, 92; colonies, in India, 280–281; in Pacific, 466, 474, 476–478; exploration, 145, 456–457, 472–473; Industrial Revolution, 149–151, 369–370; scientists, 140, 147–149. *See also* United Kingdom
English language, 44, 350
Environment, 10; and change, 48–49. *See also* Cultural environment, Physical environment
Erg, 159, 161
Ethiopia, 62, 182
Ethnic group, 317
Euphrates River (ū frā′-tēz), 52, 54–61, 156, 161, 164, 236; *map,* 57
Europe, 346–371, 374–407, 410–428; development, 366–370; diversity, 353–358; languages, 44, 349–350, 396; major regions, 377; *maps,* 348, 355; nations of, 356; wars, 182, 358–365
European Economic Community, 370–371
European Free Trade Association, 371
Explorers, in Africa, 182; English, 145, 456–457; French, 145; *maps,* 144, 471; in Pacific, 455–457, 470–473; Phoenecians, 74; Portuguese, 143–144, 145; Spanish, 145

Exports, 25; African, 191, 192, 200; Asian, 296; Japanese, 214, 219, 220; Pacific, 461

Far East, 131, 141–143, 173, **208**–210, 502–504; *map,* 239
Faults, 212
Fennoscandia, 374, 377, 378–387; cities, 382, 384, 386; countries of, 378; farming, 379, 382–383; fishing, 378–379; forests, 379–380, 386–387; *map,* 380; minerals, 385–386
Feudal system (fū′dəl), 111, **118,** 128, 130
Finland, 357, 378–387; forests, 386–387; *map,* 380
Fiords (fyôrdz), **383**
Fishing, in Fennoscandia, 378–379; in Greece, 75; in Japan, 217–219; in Pacific, 452, 461; in Portugal, 406
Five Year Plan, in China, 254; in U.S.S.R., 330
Forests, of Africa, 176, 186, 188–189, 193–196; China, 250; Fennoscandia, 379–380, 386–387; Japan, 219–220; New Zealand, 486; of Southeast Asia, 294–298; U.S.S.R., 336–337; coniferous, **336,** 377, 379, 387; deciduous, **337**
France, 44, 145, 396, 429; cities, 399, 431; Common Market, 370–371; history, 360–361; *map,* 397; Paris, 402–403
Frescoes, 134
Fulton, Robert, 148

Galilei, Galieo (gal ə lē′ō), 138–140
Gama, Vasco da, 144–145
Gandhi, Indira, 281
Gandhi, Mohandas, 280–281
Ganges River, 33, 237, 265–267, 270, 273
Garonne River, 405
Gautama, Siddhartha (gô′tə mə), 276
Genghis Khan (jeng′gis kän′), 260, 320
Geocentric theory, 137
Germany, history, 358–359, 364–365; **East,** 410, 412–415; *maps,* 397, 411; in Russia, 332; **West,** 396, 399
Gladiators, 100, 104
Gobi Desert, 256
Gods, of Egypt, 64, 70–71; Greek, 83–84, 101; of India, 278, 282–283; Roman, 92–93, 97, 101; Sumerian, 58–59; *chart,* 101
Government, 47; of Asia, 246–247, 249, 307–309; feudal, 53, 111, 121, 128; Roman, 102–103, 105–106, 109–110; Semitic, 61; Sumerian, 60; of U.S.S.R., 328–333; of Western Europe, 406–407
Gravitation, law of, **140**
Great Rift, 189
Great Wall, 240, 246, 260
Greece, ancient, 74–88, 103; *maps,* 91, 437; modern, 91, 430, 431, 435–436
Greek, architecture, 83, 134; drama, 83–84; games, 84–85; gods, 83–84, 101; manuscripts, 130–131; philosophers, 86–88; wars, 80–82
Guilds, 108, **124,** 125, 126
Gulf Stream, 379
Gutenberg, Johann, 132

Hagia Sophia, 319
Hammurabi, 61
Hannibal, 103
Hargreaves, James, 149
Hawaii, 442, 446, 449, 457
Hebrew language, 179
Hegira (hi jī′rə), 173, 174
Heliocentric theory, 137
Helsinki, 382
Henry the Navigator, 143–144
Hieroglyphics (hī ərə glif′-iks), **67**
Hillary, Sir Edmund, 238
Himalayas (him ə lā′əz), 33–34, 238, 257, 264–265, 266, 267, 288
Hinduism, 276, 278–279, 281, 282–283, 513
Hinterland, 199, **479**
Hippodrome, 319
Hiroshima (hir ə shē′mə), 226
Hitler, Adolf, 364–365
Hokkaido (ho′kī dō), 210, 211, 222
Holland, *see* Netherlands
Holy Land, 53, 123, 173, 180
Honshu, 210, 216, 232
Horticulture, 432
Hungary, 353, 410, 420–421; *map,* 411
Hwang Ho, 32, 54, 237, 246, 251–253, 256, 266
Hydroelectric power, in Europe, 386, 404, 419, 426
Hydroponics, 216

India, 264–285, 501–502; caste, 283; cities, 284–285; climate, 266–269; history, 276–281; landforms, 264–266; *map,* 268; population, 32, 270; religion, 282–283; states of, 270

Indonesia, Fed. of (in dō nē′zhə), 288, 293; climate, 292; government, 309; *map*, 290
Indus River (in′dəs), 54, 265–266, 267, 275, 276
Industrial Revolution, 149–151, 369–370
Industrial Triangle, 340–342
Industry, in Africa, 176–177, 198, 201; in China, 254; in Europe, 149–151, 391, 399, 404–405, 414, 426, 434–435; in India, 284–285; in Japan, 216–221, 232–233; in Pacific, 461, 486; in Southeast Asia, 294–299; in Taiwan, 248–249; in U.S.S.R., 331, 340–342
Inner Mongolia, 256, 257
International Date Line, 462–464
Inventions, of bricks, 57; DaVinci, 136; Galileo, 138; locomotive, 148; paper, 244; porcelain, 245; power loom, 149; printing press, 132–133; silk, 245; spinning jenny, 149; steamboat, 148; steam engine, 146–148, 369–370; writing, 60
Iran, 60, 161, 164, 176
Iraq, 54–56, 161; ancient, 56–61; *maps*, 57, 163
Ireland, Republic of, 132, 351, 388–394; agriculture, 393; Dublin, 393–394; *map*, 389
Irrawaddy River, 237
Islam, 23–24, 48, 123, 172–175, 278–279, 281, 303, 304, 499
Islands, Africa, 199; Greek, 74, 75; Italy, 90–91; Japan, 210; Pacific, 464, 466–488; Southeast Asia, 288–289; U.S.S.R., 222
Israel, 177–180, 424; *map*, 179
Italy, ancient, 92–106; modern, 90–92, 367, 429–438; history, 360, 364–365; *maps*, 91, 437
Ivan the Great, 321
Ivan the Terrible, 321–322

Japan, 26, 208–234, 504; and China, 209–210; cities, 231–233; climate, 210–211; fishing, 217–219; history, 222–226, 246–247, 364–365; landforms, 210–213; *map*, 212; religion, 230–231
Japan Current, 211
Jews, 178–180, 424
Jinnah, Mohammed Ali (jin′ə), 281
Johannesburg (jō hăn′ĭs-bėrg), 200
Jordan River, 179–180
Journeymen, 125
Judaism, 172, 179, 500

Kagera River, 62
Kailasa Temple, 278, 283
Kalahari Desert, 197
Karachi, 238, 285
Kariba Dam, 201
Katanga, 192, 200
Kenya, 191, 201
Kepler, Johannes, 137–138
Khyber Pass, 265, 285
Kiev, 319–320, 340
Kievan Russia, 319–320
Kimono, 227
Kobe, 216, 233
Knights, 108, 118–120
Kolkhoz (kol hôz′), **330**
Koran, 48, 172, 175
Korea, 224, 231, 277
Krakatau (krä kä tou′), 289, 444, 449
Kremlin, 329
Kruger National Park, 190
Kublai Khan, 142, 222, 303
Kurile Current (kür′əl), 211
Kyushu (kyü′shü), 210, 211, 232

Lakes, in Africa, 189; Baikal, 340; Chad, 40; in Europe, 387, 401; Victoria, 62, 64, 189
Lamaism, 258–259
Languages, 23, 44; ancient, 60, 67; Indo-European, 349–350; *map*, 350; modern, 317, 357–358, 388, 396, 410, 412, 502; official, 350. *See also* individual languages
Laos (lā′os), 288, 293, 308; *map*, 290
Lapps, 357
Latitude, lines of, 184; low, 28; Northern, 160, 189, 288; Southern, 160, 288, 444, 470
League of Nations, 225, 363
Lenin, Nicolai, 328
Leningrad, 323, 325, 340–341
Lhasa (lä′sä), 257, 259
Liechtenstein (liH′tən-shtīn), 356
Lippershey, Hans, 138
Lisbon, 406
Loess Highlands (lō′is) 251–252
London, 392, 397
Longitude, lines of, 462–463
Low pressure areas, 30, 31, 55

Luxembourg, 356, 396; *map*, 397

Madrid, 406, 407
Magellan, Ferdinand, 145, 454, 456
Malagasy Republic, 199; *map*, 187
Malaysia, Fed. of (mə lā′-zhə), 288; climate, 292; government, 309; *map*, 290; products, 297, 299; religion, 304
Manchuria, 225, 246–247, 254, 364; *map*, 239
Manor, 111–118
Manorial system, 110
Manuscript, 122, 131; illuminated, 132
Maoris (mä′rĭ), 442, 469, 473–475, 505
Mao Tse-tung (mou′ tse′-tüng), 247
Marianas Trench, 446
Maritsa River, 424–425
Marsupial (mär sü′pi əl), **467**
Mecca, 172–173
Mediterranean Lands, 429–438; agriculture, 432–433; cities, 430–431, 434; climate, 430; countries, 429–430; industry, 434–435; landforms, 430–431; *maps*, 91, 437
Melanesia, 452
Merino sheep, 480–481
Mesopotamia, *see* Iraq
Michelangelo, 134, 135
Micronesia, 452, 458
Middle Ages, 53, 108–128; Church in, 121–123, 126–127; discoveries in, 141–142; life of nobility, 116–120; life of serfs, 113–116; trade in, 123–126
Mikimoto, Kokichi, 219
Minarets, 174, 279
Minerals, of Africa, 177, 191–192, 200, 501; of Asia, 176, 284, 299, 307; of Australia, 482–483; of Europe, 381, 385–386, 388, 398, 414, 423, 427, 435; of Japan, 220; of U.S.S.R., 341–342
Moguls, 279
Mohammed, 172–174
Mohammedanism, *see* Islam
Mohenjo-Daro, 275
Monaco, 356, 431
Monasteries, 108, 121–122, 131, 132, 259
Mongolia, 260–261
Mongols, 142, 242, 246, 256, 260, 320
Monsoons, 30–32, 55–56, 209, 267–269, 292; *maps*, 30, 292
Morava River, 419
Moscow, 321–322, 324, 340–341, 342
Mosques (mosks), **174,** 279
Mounts, Etna, 91; Everest, 33, 238, 257, 446; Fujiyama, 211–232, 446; Kilimanjaro, 186, 189, McKinley, 238; Parnassus, 79; Taygetus, 78; Vesuvius, 91, 92
Mountains, of Africa, 159, 189, 199, 431; of Asia, 33–34, 164, 211–213, 238, 257, 264–265, 288; of Europe, 90–91, 103–104, 404–406, 418, 421, 424; of U.S.S.R., 317, 334, 338–339
Murmansk, 336
Muslims, 123, 143, 144, 172–174, 179–180, 256, 278–279, 281, 303, 428
Muslim World, 23, 172–174; *map*, 172
Mussolini, Benito, 364
Napoleon Bonaparte, 67, 324, 360–361
Nationalist Chinese Government, 247, 248
Natural resources, of Africa, 191; of China, 250–251; of Dry World, 176–177; of Europe, 336–338, 354, 370; of Japan, 220; of World Region, 516
Near East, 53, **208**
Needs, basic, 40, 496; for peace, 524
Nehru, Jawaharlal, 281
Netherlands, 396, 401–402
New Delhi, 284–285
New Guinea (gin′i), 452, 456, 457–458, 470
Newcomen, Thomas, 147
Newton, Sir Isaac, 140
New Zealand, 446, 466–475, 486–489, 504–505; animals, 466; cities, 486; history, 470–473; *map*, 485; settlement, 474–475; industry, 486–487
Niger River, 184
Nigeria, 191, 192
Nile River, 52, 54, 61–65, 70, 156, 159, 164; *map*, 63; sources, 62
Nomads, 40–42, 57, 164–175, 256–261, 354, 357
Norkay, Tensing, 238
Norsemen, 141, 318; *map*, 143
North Africa, 55, 156–160; animals, 165–168; climate, 160, 430; countries, 158, 434; landforms, 158–160, 431; *maps*, 163, 165; religion, 172–174; resources, 176–177, 432. *See also* Dry World Region
North Atlantic Drift, 379
North Vietnam, 237, 288, 309; *map*, 290

Northern Ireland, 388, 393; *map,* 389
Norway, 378–387; *map,* 380
Nullarbor Plain, 479

Oasis, 162, 170–171
Oder River, 414
Oil, in Eastern Europe, 423; in Dry World, 176–177; *map,* 176
Olives, 75, 93, 432–433
Olympic Games, 84–85
Oslo, 381

Pacific Ocean Region, 446, 442–488, 505–506; climate, 449–451; explorers, 455–457; geography, 444–449; *maps,* 445, 453; regions, 452–455; Samoa, 461; Tahiti, 459–460; U.N., 458–459. *See also* Australia, New Zealand
Pagoda, 243
Pago Pago, 461
Pakistan, 264–285, 501–502; cities, 285; dams, 284; division, 264, 281; food, 274; *map,* 268; religion, 281, 282; size, 270. *See also* East and West Pakistan
Palestine, 123, 178
Palladio, Andrea, 135
Pantheon (pan′thi on), 99, 134, 436
Papeete, 460
Papyrus (pə pi′rəs), 68
Parchment, 132
Paris, 397, 402–403
Parliament (pär′lə mənt), **395**
Parthenon, 83
Patricians, 102
Pearls, 218–219
Peking, 237, 242–243, 261
Penal colony, 477
Pennines Mountains, 388
Perry, Commodore Matthew C., 223, 224, 233
Persian Wars, 80–82; *map,* 81
Perth, 482
Peter the Great, 322–324
Petrarch, 131
Petrograd, 325. *See also* Leningrad
Philippines, Rep. of, 23, 145, 225, 288, 289, 292, 293, 304, 307, 452
Phoenecians (fə nish′əns), 74, 103
Physical environment, 11, 14, 18, 495
Picard, Jean, 140
Piraeus (pī rē′əs), 77
Pizarro, Francisco, 351
Plateaus, in Africa, 183–184, 199; in Australia, 483; in Eastern Asia, 33–34, 257, 265, 266, 273; in Europe, 404, 405–406; in Southwest Asia, 161
Plato, 87, 88, 131
Plebians, 102
Po River, 90, 91, 434
Poland, 410, 415–417; agriculture, 416; cities, 417; geography, 415; *map,* 411; resources, 416–417; wars in, 324, 359, 364–365, 410
Polder, 401
Polo, Marco, 141–143, 242, 455; *map,* 142
Polynesia, 444, 452–455, 461, 472, 474
Population, Africa, 192, 201; Australia, 476, 478, 480; China, 249; distribution, 515; Dry World Region, 164; Eastern Asia, 32, 209–210, 236; Europe, 381, 399, 420, 426; Indian Sub-continent, 270; Japan, 210, 231–232; New Zealand, 475; Pacific Region, 458; patterns of, 289, 421, 480; Taiwan, 248; Southeast Asia, 289, 291; U.S.S.R., 317, 340; *World map,* 237
Portugal, 143, 144, 396, 405–406; *map,* 397
Prague (präg), 418
Pretoria, 200
Printing press, 132–133
Pygmies, 196, 197
Pyramids, 64–68
Pyrenees Mountains, 356, 404, 405–406

Rainfall, in Africa, 62, 160, 186, 200; Asia, 25–26, 31, 161–162, 211, 251, 266–267, 292; Australia, 482; Europe, 393, 396, 425, 430; Pacific, 449–450; U.S.S.R., 334
Rainforests, tropical, 186; in Africa, 188–189; in Southeast Asia, 265, 289, 294–297
Rangoon, 25, 238, 290, 292, 305
Rawalpindi, 285
Reg, 159
Regions, 21; climate, 28–32; crop, 25–28; cultural, 22–24, 375; guides to, 374–377; landform, 32–34; physical, 374–375; political, 24, 375
Religions, *see* names of individual religions
Renaissance, The (ren ə-säns′), 130–152, 366, 368; art and architecture, 133–135; inventions, 146; discoveries, 141, 143–146; science, 136–140
Rhine River, 401, 414
Rhodesia, 200, 201

Rhodope Mountains, 424
Rhone River, 405
Rice, growing of, 25–27; paddy, 26; in Asia, 209, 213–214, 273, 300
Riverine culture, in Africa, 54, 61, 71, 164; in Asia, 33, 54, 236, 266
Rivers, of Africa, 61, 184, 201; Australia, 482, 483; China, 32, 251; Eastern Asia, 236–237, 290; Eastern Europe, 414, 415, 419, 421, 422, 424; Indian Sub-continent, 33, 54, 265–266; Iraq, 54, 161; U.S.S.R., 318, 337, 339; Western Europe, 90, 91, 401, 404, 406
Roman Catholic Church, 123, 137–139, 436
Roman Empire, 92, 93, 102–106, 110; **Eastern,** 106, 123, 131; government, 105; growth, 102–105; life in, 105–106; *maps,* 104, 105; **Western,** 106, 108, 110–111
Roman Republic, 93–103, 105; architecture, 98–100; customs, 93–98; games, 100; government, 102; religion, 101
Rome, ancient, 91–106; founding of, 91–93; modern, 436
Romulus, 92–93
Rosetta Stone, 67
Ruhr River (rür), 399, 414
Rumania, 410, 421–424; *map,* 411
Russia, *see* U.S.S.R.
Ruwenzori Mountains, 189

Saar Region (sär), 399
Sahara, 40–43, 157–160, 176–177, 186; climate, 160; landforms, 159; resources, 176–177; size, 158–159. *See also* Dry World Region
St. Peter's Church, 134–135
St. Petersburg, 323. *See also* Leningrad
Samoa, 454, 461
Sanchi Stupa, 277
Saudi Arabia, 161, 172, 175, 176; *map,* 163
Savanna, 186
Scientific discoveries, Chinese, 245; Egyptians, 65–67; Greek, 86; Renaissance, 136–140; modern, 146–149
Scotland, 388, 391
Seamounts, 446–447
Seine River (sān), 401, 402
Semites, 60–61; centralized government, 61
Sheep, in Australia, 480–481; in Europe, 393, 406, 425, 428; *map,* 426; in New Zealand, 486–487; in North Africa, 168, 432
Shintoism, 230
Shwe Dagon, 305
Si River, 237, 251
Siberia, 339, 340
Silesia, 414
Sinkiang (sin′kyäng′), 256
"Slash-and-Burn" method, 193–196
Slavs, 318–319, 412
Society Islands, 459–460
Socrates (sok′rətēz), 86–87
Sofia (sō̦ fē′ə), 424
Solon, 79–80
South Africa, Region of, 182, 197, 199–202; cities, 199, 200; climate, 200; landform, 199; *map,* 187, 199; resources, 200–201
South Africa, Rep. of, 182, 201; cities of, 200
Southeast Asia, 25–27, 236–238, 288–309, 502–503; architecture, 305–306; climate, 292; farming, 291, 300; geography, 288–289; government, 307–309; *map,* 290; products, 294–299, 307; religion, 303–304; village life, 300–302
South Vietnam, 238, 288, 309; *map,* 290
Southwest Asia, 158, 161–180; countries of, 161; landforms, 161; climate, 161–162; *map,* 163; religion of, 172–174, 178–180; resources, 176–177; *see* Dry World Region
Soviets, 325
Soviet Union, *see* U.S.S.R.
Sovkhoz (sō̦v′kôz), **331**
Spain, 99, 396, 405–407, 429–434; cities, 406, 430, 434; government, 406–407; *maps,* 397, 437; rivers, 406
Spanish language, 23
Spanish Meseta (mə sā′tə), **404,** 406
Sparta, 77–78, 80–82
Steam engines, 146–149, 369–370
Steppe, 188, 337–338
Stockholm, 381, 382
Streams, meandering, **415;** migrant, **55,** 62
Sub-Saharan Africa, *see* Africa, Central Africa, East Africa
Subsistence agriculture, 193
Sumerians, 56–61; canal system, 56–57; gods of, 58–59; *map,* 57; specialization, 58; writing, 60
Sun Yat-sen (sün′ yät′-sen′), 246

Sweden, 378–387; *map,* 380
Switzerland, 396, 404–405; *map,* 399
Sydney, 477, 483

Tahiti (tə hē′ti), 459–460
Taiga (tī′ga), **336**–337, 376–377
Taiwan (tī′wän′), 26, 224, 247, 248–249; *map,* 239
Taj Mahal, 279
Tartars, 320, 321, 506
Tasman, Abel J., 457, 470–472; *map,* 371
Tasmania, 466–488; aborigines, 475; animals, 467–468; exploration, 470–472; *map,* 485
Tatamis (tə tä′mē), **214**
Teakwood, 294–295
Tel Aviv, 178
Temples, China, 243; Egyptian, 64–67; Greek, 79, 83; India, 277, 278; Japan, 231; Roman, 99; Southeast Asia, 305–306; Sumerian, 59
Thailand (ti′land), 24–27, 42–43, 236–237, 288–309; cities, 236; farming, 24–27, 291; government, 307; *map,* 290
Thales, 86
Tiber River, 91, 92, 102
Tibet, 256–259; *maps,* 239, 268; Plateau of, 33, 257–258, 265
Tigris River, 52, 54–61, 156, 161, 164; *map,* 57
Time Zones, 316, 462–464
Tokyo, 220, 231, 232
Tombs, 65–67, 70–71, 98, 279
Transportation, 58, 59–70; in China, 255; in Western Europe, 401–402, 519, 521–522
Transylvania, 421–422
Tropic of Cancer, 62, 184–185, 188, 446
Tropic of Capricorn, 184–185, 446
Tsunami, 449
Tundra, 336, 374–377, 507
Turkey, 161, 279, 324, 434
Typhoon (tī fün′), 449–451

Ukraine (ū krān′), 341, 390
Union of Soviet Socialist Republics, 314–343, 506–507; climate, 333–335; government, 328–329; history, 318–325; Industrial Triangle, 340–342; *map,* 326–327; natural regions, 336–339; progress, 330–333, 343
United Arab Republic, 61, *See also* Egypt
United Kingdom, 23, 388–395; as a sea power, 394–395; cities, 391–392; countries, 388; resources, 388–390; government 395
United Nations, 178, 363, 365, 458–459, 522–523
United States, 43, 46, 192, 517; in Japan, 223–226, in Pacific, 458–459
U. S. Pacific Trust Territory, 458–459
Ural Mountains, 317, 334, 339, 342

Varangians, 318
Vatican City, 356, 436
Verkhoyansk (vůr kō-yãnsk′), 334
Vikings, 318–320, 356
Vinci, Leonardo da (vēn′-chē) 134, 136, 137, 368
Vistula River, 415
Volcanoes, 91, 212, 289; types of, 446
Volga River, 324
Wales, 388; *map,* 389
Warsaw, 417
Watt, James, 147–148, 369
Wellington, 474, 487
Western Europe, 396–407, 508–509, 519; climate, 396; common features, 396; countries, 396, 405; farming, 399; 401–402, 404, 405; government, 406–407; landforms, 397, 404, 405, 406; manufacturing, 398–399, 404–405; *map,* 397; rivers, 401, 402, 405, 406; wars in, 358–365
Western Ghats, 33–34
West Pakistan, 264–285; cities, 285; division, 281; landforms, 161, 162, 265–266; *map,* 268
Wheat, in China, 27–28; in Australia, 482; in Europe, 75, 93–94, 393, 399, 416, 418, 432; in India, 266, 271, 273; in Japan, 209, 213; in U.S.S.R., 338, 340, 341
Wind patterns, 29–32; diurnal, **30;** monsoon, **30**–32; trade, **160,** 161–162
World War I, 362–363; **II,** 182, 198, 207

Xerxes (zėrk′sēz), 81, 82

Yak, 258
Yangtze River (yang′ tsē), 32, 237, 251
Yugōslavia (ū′gō slä′vi ə), 410, 425–427; cities, 426–427; climate, 425; government, 427; *map,* 411; minerals, 427

Zambesi River, 184, 201
Ziggurat, 59

67 68 69 70 71 72 73 PP 9 8 7 6 5 4 3 2 1